The Textile Institute

Computers in the World of Textiles

Papers presented at the Annual World Conference September 26 – 29 1984 Hong Kong

The cover picture shows punched cards used in the system of handloom patterning control invented by J. M. Jacquard in Lyon, France, in the late eighteenth century. Punched-card systems, of which Jacquard's is regarded as the first commercial example, are widely considered to be the forerunners of computerized techniques. The textile industry's rôle in the origins of automation and computerization is therefore of considerable significance.

The Textile Institute,
International Headquarters,
10 Blackfriars Street,
Manchester,   M3 5DR,
England

ISBN 0 0900739 69 X

The papers in this book have been reproduced directly
from the authors' typescripts and have not been
subjected to the usual editorial processes of the
Textile Institute. The Institute accepts no
responsibility for any material contained in the papers.

CONTENTS

Printed in Hong Kong by New Champion Printing Co. Ltd.

FOREWORD

Dr. J. R. McPhee, C.Text., F.T.I.
(President of the Textile Institute)

The textile industry is well used to technological change and to taking full advantage rapidly of all relevant modern technology.

Advances in chemistry have resulted in new fibres, dyes, and finishes, and these have been rapidly incorporated into improved textile products. Advances in engineering have made possible faster and more consistent spinning, knitting, and weaving, and the industry has eagerly taken advantage of these. Advances in computers are potentially of even greater importance and will come upon us faster than any of the previous technological advances.

The reason for this is simple: the time, money, and talent being poured into research and development in the computer industry dwarf the investments in previous scientific areas that have affected the textile industry. The rate of advancement in computers is quite staggering: for example, the amount of computer power one can buy per dollar has increased at about 30% per annum for the past 25 years. The computer industry expects this rate to continue for as far ahead as it can see. The implications for the cost/benefit of various possible or potential computer applications is that what is much too expensive one year is indispensible a very few years later.

Computers have been used in the textile industry for a number of years, but despite this we are only on the threshold of a revolution. The spread of computerized methods in the immediate future will be rapid and extensive.

The use of computers in the past has been in certain, well-compartmentalized areas: fibre measurement, economic modelling, production planning, colour measurement and matching, machine control (especially knitting machines), and commercial (book-keeping, payroll). These areas have progressed, and some new ones are beginning to show: computer-aided design, computerized control, cutting-room lay-outs, etc. All these computer applications are becoming available to smaller and smaller companies as computer hardware and software become cheaper.

Looking ahead, the big advance is likely to come from integration of computer applications. Designs produced with the aid of a computer will automatically be turned into operating instructions for a knitting machine or loom. Introduction of orders will trigger automatic scheduling of machines and automatic calculation of raw-material requirements. It is not clear whether this integration will come from multi-purpose computers handling computer-aided design (CAD), computer-aided manufacturing (CAM), as well as the commercial business of the company, or from special-purpose, but communicating, machines "talking to each other". Nevertheless, integration will come, and it will make possible considerable gains in efficiency.

Despite the undisputed achievements and potential of computers in textiles, my attitude to each new advance is one of scepticism until I see it successfully integrated into industry and sensibly applied. The advance of computerization is fast because it is fuelled by huge investments in money and people, not because the people are infallible. Many so-called advances turn out to be irrelevant, inconsequential, or uneconomic, but the ones that succeed can bring a bonanza, so that all the knowledge and judgement that can be mustered should be applied to identify winners as early as possible. Never has there been a time in the history of the textile industry when it has been more important to make the right decision about available technology. The potential benefits are enormous, the penalties of being left behind are great, but the punishment for being wrong can be severe.

The 1984 Annual Conference of the Textile Institute, on computers in the world of textiles, could not be more timely. The collection of papers covers all aspects from research, to design, to manufacturing. The conference will provide a great opportunity for delegates to compare progress, to consider new ideas, and to institute development programmes that will have a strong influence on the success of their organizations during the next few years. Equally, the conference and papers will assist the computer industry in evaluating the needs of the textile and clothing industries so that it can more accurately assess the opportunities in these enormous industries.

International Wool Secretariat
Wool House
London S W 1
ENGLAND

COMPUTER-AIDED TEXTILE DESIGN: A LIBERATING PROSPECT

J.W.S.Hearle, A.Newton and P.J.Grigg

ABSTRACT

The paper starts by discussing advances in computer-aided aesthetic and engineering design since the Textile Institute conference in 1972. There is a summary of the range of available computer systems, and a short account of networks. The freedoms which the computer can provide to the textile designer are enumerated, and illustrated by examples of work at UMIST. The need for systematic engineering design of textiles and textile processes is considered and the QAS method, now known as TK problem-solver, is mentioned. Research at UMIST on applications of computing in fabric geometry and in machine and process modelling is discussed. The paper concludes with an account of the way in which a computer can usefully link the design, technical, and commercial operations of a company.

1. INTRODUCTION

1.1 Historical perspective

Twelve years ago two of us (J.W.S.Hearle and A.Newton), together with M.Konopasek, presented a paper at the Lucerne annual conference of the Textile Institute with the title "computer-aided textile design"(1). This paper analysed a variety of aspects of the problem, and gave a broad survey of possibilities which seemed to be right for commercial exploitation. If the economic and intellectual climate in a traditional industry like textiles had been more favourable since then, the present paper might have been sub-titled "a record of liberation". As it is, the analysis given at Lucerne remains valid, but its widespread practice remains in prospect, although individual companies have moved strongly in some particular applications.

Economically an inhibiting factor has been the emphasis in the decade after 1972 on short-term profitability. This has made it difficult to break out of the vicious circle that, on the one hand, insufficient resources are put into the expensive development of basic ideas into operating systems because systems are not being bought and used; and, on the other hand, that systems are not being used because what is needed is not on the market. At some time, and it is difficult to predict exactly when, there will be a rapid surge forward as the interaction of supply and demand turns into positive feedback.

There are several new favourable circumstances for computer-aided design (CAD) in the textile industry. Firstly, industry is now taking a longer view of R and D. Secondly, the cost of computers has fallen dramatically and their power has increased; and the younger generation are coming to accept - and expect - them as a naturally available tool. Thirdly, in academic work, basic research is not only continuing to advance engineering design, but is also slowly opening up the difficult problem of the inter-action between artistic designers and the computer. Fourthly and most significantly, in two other areas, the surge forward has taken place in the last 5 years: ITMA 1983 showed it in the

control of textile machines by microprocessors, which forms
part of the increasing industrial use of computer-aided
manufacturing (CAM); and offices show it in word-processing
and data-handling.

1.2 Aesthetic and engineering design

Textile products depend for their success in the market-place
on the right combination of aesthetic and engineering quality
with cost and meeting this need is the brief of the textile
designer or design engineer. As in the Lucerne paper, we use
the term 'textile designer' to refer to the person, typically
with an art-school training, whose interest is mainly in aesthetic design; 'design engineer' for the person, typically with a
training in textile technology, whose main concern is functional;
and 'designer' in a general sense to include both functions.
Following the Shorter Oxford English Dictionary we can define
the aesthetic character of a fabric as related to impressions
"received by the senses [and] pertaining to the appreciation of
the beautiful", although in commercial reality the second part
of the definition might be better phrased in sociological rather
than artistic terms as reinforcing selected cultural life-styles.
The modern view of the engineering function is not reflected in
the Shorter OED but is well enough understood.

Sometimes the two aspects of design are clearly separate: in
prints, aesthetic appeal to the visual sense is dominant; in
filter fabrics there is only practical value of collection
efficiency and useful life. But often they are mixed, with the
designer's brief being to combine functional performance with an
appeal to the senses. Furthermore, the aesthetic appeal may
depend on subtleties of texture which depend on the internal
engineering of the fibre, yarn, and fabric structure.

Not only are there two distinct needs, there are also distinct
differences in the approaches and methods used by aesthetic and
engineering designers, and it is necessary to understand these
in order to develop successful CAD facilities.

Aesthetic design starts with a creative idea, and then goes
through a period of detailed development of the total design using
a medium acceptable to the designer. There follows conversion to
the explicit features of the textile material, and so to the instructions for machine control and the production of samples.
Throughout this process, there must be consideration of functional performance and cost, of the market needs, and of the
equipment and expertise of the company concerned.

Engineering design in the textile industry may be regarded as of
three forms: (1) the rapid provision of numerical or graphical
information as an aid to the traditional qualitative trial-and-
error methods of fabric development; (2) detailed product design,
as practised in a mechanical engineering or architectural design
office; (3) large-scale modelling of product performance or
process operation.

1.3   Liberation or constraint

All too commonly in everyday life we come across statements that
something cannot be done because the computer will not allow it.
Rarely is it any limitation in the computer; the problems are in
the quality of the software, or, in financial terms, on the amount
spent on the skill and effort needed to plan good systems and
write good programs.

Dominance by the computer is neither necessary nor right in design.
The computer should provide more freedom and more power, in a form
with which a designer finds a constructive rapport. Particularly
for the aesthetic designer, this involves not only the quality of
the software, but also the physical characteristics of the input
and output devices of the hardware. Computer engineers can take
the view that a key-board and a joy-stick provide a complete
range of input operations, but it does not necessarily follow that
this would be a stimulating environment for designers, who for
success must be highly sensitive to sensual impressions.

It is in the area of dialogue between the artistic designer and
the systems engineer that there remains most need for research
and development. It is not enough to say that the designer needs
a system giving complete freedom. Firstly, there is the obvious
constraint of cost. But, secondly, total freedom can be as inhibiting as too much restriction of choice.

What is needed is continuing analysis of the way in which designers work - or could work given computer facilities - and innovative development to meet this need. This is not an easy research
area, because the scientifically oriented systems engineer and
the artistically oriented designer cannot easily conceptualise
in each other's terms in order to specify a CAD facility which
utilises what the engineer can do in ways which best suit the
designer.

The limitations which the designer can accept need to be explored.
For example, it is easy to say that we would like a perfect
visual representation of the appearance of a fabric. But that,
even insofar as it is possible with modern technology, would be
excessively expensive. But, also, that is not how artists work.
A sculptor will make preliminary sketches which enable him to
visualise what will form as the stone is carved away; a good
architect sees in his mind's eye the appearance of a building
on the basis of schematic plans. We need to know what, in the
context of computer facilities, the textile designer needs as an
aid to visualising the material and as a means of providing the
information for manufacturing.

2   COMPUTER PERFORMANCE AND PRICE

2.1   The change since 1972

There is at least one statement in the 1972 paper which has been
proved wrong. We wrote "[the cost of a computer] means that it
must be a communal and not an individual tool." In 1984
microcomputers have become a home commodity sold in the shopping
centres; and, in an inversion of what might have been expected,
industrial companies, research institutes, and progressive

3

universities are now following by making personal computers widely available to their staff. At the same time, there remains a market for the most powerful, and most expensive, computers which can only be justified in terms of the needs of a whole organisation or group of organisations.

It seems likely that the pattern may now be stabilising and that the cost of any particular *style* of computer will not reduce much more. What will happen is that, at each level, the available computing power will continue to increase. This is because a large proportion of the cost now comes from the hardest of hard costs, the mechanical performance and quality of such peripherals as the keyboard, the screen and the printer, and the softest of soft costs, the overheads of marketing and research, including at the top end of the market the design of systems for competitive tender to meet particular needs.

2.2   Characteristics of the range of computers

To-day the range of available computers is very wide, and, before going on to consider the detail of CAD for textiles, it is useful to characterise their features and relevance on the basis of a somewhat arbitrary categorisation in decades of price from under £10 to over £1m.*

UNDER £10 *Simplest hand calculators*. Four functions $(+,-,x,\div)$. Useful to designers for simple numerical information, e.g. cost of yarn in 1 m^2 of fabric.

£10 TO £100 *Powerful hand calculators*. Based on a dedicated mathematical chip. May also be programmable as embryonic computers. Useful for more elaborate costing or engineering calculations.

£100 TO £1000 *The "home computers"*. Based on a general purpose processor capable of handling a complexity of programmed interactions. Memory limited to cassettes or small floppy discs. May use home TV as monitor. Possibly a cheap printer. Applications software available in: computer games; word-processing; graphics; business, scientific and engineering programs. Powerful in creating and controlling fast sprites (moving shapes). Provides minimum essential facilities for graphic design and complex engineering analysis.

£1000 TO £10,000 *The "professional personal computer"*. A single-user microcomputer. Floppy discs (3", 5¼" or 8") with secondary storage up to 1 million characters per disc; or, at higher price end, hard disc units (Winchesters) with 500,000 characters in working memory and up to 40 million in secondary storage. Visual display unit (often only monochrome). Quality printer. Much available software. Widely used for small-business data processing (accounts etc.); production planning, monitoring and control. Provides a powerful individual facility for the design engineer, and, potentially, for the textile designer (with colour display, and improved software).

The prices in US dollars can be taken in this approximation as the same; the prices in Hong Kong dollars will be about 10 times larger.

£10,000 TO £100,000 *Small joint systems.* More powerful, faster, more memory. Linked to a number of terminals with simultaneous utilisation. Extensive range of peripherals and software. Enables larger problems to be handled, provided access is limited. An alternative way of providing the facilities needed by the designer.

£100,000 TO £1M *Large joint systems.* Very powerful systems, *either* with connection of a large number of terminals, *or* for very demanding computation. Can provide design facilities, along with services to other departments, within a large company or on a bureau basis.

OVER £1M *The most powerful computers.* Often used in a simple sequential batch mode to perform excessively large calculations. Could be used in R and D in textiles for large-scale process or product modelling.

The diversity of the textile and fibre industries results in all the above categories being used somewhere or other, and it is dangerous to generalise since requirements vary greatly even for companies operating in the same sector. What is important for a company is to choose computer facilities which meet current needs but can be expanded with development of the company.

With the greatly increased power and reduced price of individual computers, a choice has now to be made between a widespread provision of personal computers and the alternative of a larger central facility with multiple access.

In some instances, the requirements dictate the choice: for example, an airline booking system must bring all the information into a large central processor from terminals all over the world; but a single free-lance designer would be limited to a personal computer. Where there is a real choice, the cost-benefit must be worked out. A multi-user system gives benefit of inter-connection of operations and can be a lower-cost option, but, too often, an inadequate system with too many users results in delays in response which would be unacceptably frustrating to a working designer.

2.3 Networks and links.

The previous section has implicitly been limited to computer systems with a single central processor. But the reality is often otherwise, since computers can be linked to other computers through local cables, telephone, or radio. With more than two computers in a system, there is a network, which may be in many forms, such as ring or star arrangements. The individual computers in the network must be enhanced for inter-communication capability according to a common protocol. The computers connected directly to the main network are defined to be at nodes, and these nodal computers may themselves have a smaller local network or connections to a collection of terminals. The terminals may be 'dumb' and thus depend on their own host computer for all processing activities, or be "intelligent" with their own processing capability and a need to interact with the host only for heavy processing or access to a communal database.

A network offers a very flexible way of working for the textile designer or design engineer, who can use programs hosted at any other node in the network by transferring data over and getting results fed back, or get access to programs and have them transferred to local nodes. An interesting and important point here is that programs do not have to move between computer systems which overcomes the frequent problems of portability, adaptation of programs, and incompatability of systems. Furthermore in a network the computing resources have been distributed so that in the event of a failure only part of the system is disabled.

Although physical links between the collection of computer hardware work effectively in some places, and although, in principle, software should be mobile for transfer between computers, the practical reality today in many organisations is often far from satisfactory with a variety of difficulties inhibiting easy communication. However by the end of the century, one can anticipate a regional/national/international communication network where every telephone exchange is an access point into a public network to which computer systems are connected. In this situation, computing from the home could draw on the substantial resources of bigger computers on the network. The next decade could transform communications based on information technology and networks.

3. AESTHETIC DESIGN

3.1 The liberating role of the computer

Computer facilities offer a number of freedoms to the textile designer.

Firstly, there is freedom from chores. Operations such as putting a pattern into repeat, completing the multiple sectors of a symmetrical pattern, and carrying out the detail of conversion to machine instructions become automatic.

Secondly, there is freedom of visualisation. The computer can easily and rapidly display the design in a variety of scales and colourways, and could also display it in an environment such as the drape of a skirt.

Thirdly, there is the freedom of additional sources, since it becomes easy to introduce different inputs: geometrical shapes, letter and number typefaces, and so on can be available in the computer store; random number generators can provide irregular regions; scanners can incorporate photographic material; and so on.

Fourthly, there is the freedom of new design possibilities. There is no real limit to the size of a design, with computer control of machines. It would be possible for the Oxford University Press to carpet and curtain their offices with the text of the Oxford English Dictionary if they wished - more realistically a floral design, with an underlying regularity of form, could be modified by a random number generator so that no two elements were identical, just as no two flowers are identical. Creative designers will find other new opportunities.

Fifthly, there is freedom of ease and speed in sampling. The links from the design computer to a sample machine enable produc-

tion to be rapid. Cost and time can be saved in the dialogue
between designer and customer.

Sixthly, there is the freedom of information flow to and from
the rest of the organisation. Technical and market information
can be fed into the design office; and the information needed
for purchase of materials, for machine control, and production
planning can be fed out.

Seventhly, there is freedom of geography. The design studio can
be located where it is best suited - in a stimulating design
environment close to the market - and the information needed for
production can be sent by radio satellite to a manufacturing
operation on the other side of the world.

Finally, one can summarise the freedoms in the statement that
computer design is a dynamic operation. In traditional designing once a line has been put on paper it cannot be moved or
easily removed. If the designer wants to make a change, a new
start is needed. But the essence of a computer is to move and
manipulate information in its store, and the changes are reflected in the image on the screen.

Already the techniques of digital information processing make
possible sophisticated trick effects in television production.
Much simpler techniques will enable the designer to allow elements
to be introduced, and modified, developed or deleted in order to
achieve the final effect.

There can be no doubt that within 10 or 20 years, these freedoms
will be widely available and used. In the next two sections we
describe ways in which we have been opening up the possibilities
in research at UMIST.

3.2 A low-cost system

One development in CAD of textiles, which would have been considered remarkable in 1972, is the linking of computers to handlooms.
At that time the contrast between the price and physical size of
the computer and the hand loom was enormous, and their spheres of
influence were completely separate. But we had by then begun to
experiment with computer graphics to display the structure of
woven fabrics by programming the computer to draw plan and cross-
sectional views. The ultimate aim was to be able to produce on
the screen a picture which would resemble the appearance of a
woven fabric by inserting into the computer the parameters
required to produce that fabric, such as weave, draft plan of
the shafts, lifting plan, warping and wefting plans of the yarn
colour arrangements, yarn counts and setts, and so on. The first
package to achieve this to any degree of success had one important drawback, namely absence of colours. Now there is cheaper
availability of colour monitors, and also the possibility of
using an ordinary colour television set; and the problems,
inherent in the production of colour, of conflict between the
appearance of dyed yarns and its representation by a screen
image have turned out to be less serious that we once thought.

Another factor has been the discovery by designers and craft
weavers of the possibilities of the home computer, quite often

through the enthusiasm of schoolchildren known to them. There also appears to have been an increase in interest in crafts in the home, in addition to the increasing recognition of the importance of design in industry. As a result of these influences, the linking of computers to hand looms, both for the design and creation of fabrics, has been achieved.

Programs developed at UMIST have been adapted for the 32K BBC B Microcomputer, which is cheap and widely available in the UK, and used by Emmerich (Berlon) Ltd., to link with their electronically controlled hand-loom. There are then two systems which interconnect. One system is the hand-loom and controller, itself with some storage and manipulation facilities. The other is the BBC computer and associated monitor, which can be an ordinary TV or a VDU. In one mode of operation the designer creates colour and weave effects on the computer by entering and modifying parameters such as the lifting plan and draft, and sees a representation of the fabric on the screen, with instantaneous change of colourway. The design specification may be printed on paper, stored on a floppy disc in the disc drive for future use, or sent down to the hand-loom controller to enable a sample to be produced. The research effort on the programming side has been concentrated on developing a system which the designer finds sympathetic and easy to use with the minimum of training.

Another mode of operation, which emphasises the value of the links to a hand-loom, is that the system allows the designer the alternative of starting by developing a design on the hand-loom, and then transmitting this design back to the computer for storage and modification. Thus the designer has the possibility of creativity in the use of yarns, linked with the computer facilities of speed and size of storage capacity in a compact form.

This form of CAD system could be used by students, practising designers, or hand-loom weavers. It should be the beginning of a change in which the use of point paper as a medium for the creation and storage of woven fabric designs becomes obsoloete and is replaced by the computer.

3.3 A full design station and system

CAD systems for textiles emerged in the 1970's with Scitex at the 1971 ITMA and increasing numbers in later years, although 1983 saw a decrease as some manufacturers dropped out. The buoyant double-jersey knitting sector led the way but this spread, somewhat slowly, into other areas. The early systems were developed by textile machinery manufacturers in order to promote their machines, and were based around a minicomputer, sketch tablet, early colour display system and paper tape. In the middle 70's computer system manufacturers in the graphic arts saw parallel opportunities in the textile sector, and introduced systems, such as the HELL PATROSCAN, featuring automatic scanning based on a drum. Most of the systems available in the late 70's were of high capital cost, so that only the big companies or specialised design houses could afford them. The possibility of introducing CAD into the small studio environment was commercially out of the question. However the advent of the microcomputer in 1977 and related microelectronic developments transformed this prospect, and a grant from the Wolfson Foundation enabled us at

UMIST to develop a CAD system aimed specifically at the small operation.

Investigation of the nature of the systems available at that time identified certain characteristics: designers had to become computer operators using a keyboard for both design and system functions; there were ergonomic and communication difficulties; storage depended on paper tape; some of the input/output devices were clumsy; the automatic scanning attachments were expensive; and some peripherals were special proprietary devices.

Bearing these points in mind, the system implementation took two important decisions. Firstly, in order to contain cost, an off-the-shelf modular approach was adopted. This linked a standard microcomputer, colour display system and sketch tablet; and unique software was written to turn the assembly into a unified design system. Automatic scanning was discarded in favour of sketch-tablet input, both because of the lower cost and the future potential for direct sketching into the computer. Secondly, the system was designed around the needs of the designer for easy, friendly and consistent operation. This was achieved through the use of a MENU placed on the smaller tablet of a dual tablet system. This menu consists of a matrix of squares in which operations such as those listed in the Table are defined.

Table of Menu Operations

COPY	VIEW
MIRROR	PALLETTE
HALF DROP	STORE IN LIBRARY
REPEAT	RECALL FROM LIBRARY
SKETCH	REPLACE IN LIBRARY
ZOOM	DELETE FROM LIBRARY
FILL	Rotate
Punch Tape/CARD	Motif
Rescale	FACE BINDERS
	BACK BINDERS

Detailed Set of Menu Operations

Copy	Set Pallette
Copy & Mirror Across	Fix Colour
Copy & Mirror Down	Change Colour
Copy & Inverse	Add Colour
Mirror Across Even	Store in Library
Mirror Across Odd	Recall from Library
Mirror Down Even	Replace in Library
Mirror Down Odd	Delete from Library
Copy Motif	Punch Tape
Copy Motif & Mirror Across	Punch Card
Copy Motif & Morrir Down	Punch Card
Copy Motif & Inverse	

The designer has only to point to the necessary square with the same device (stylus) as for drawing the sketch. Thus the keyboard was avoided, Furthermore, all the terminology was in the designer's terms, and the computer was relegated to the background, allowing the designer to concentrate on the primary function of designing. This was psychologically important, and we found that designers could easily and quickly use the system because of the MENU technique.

When we started the development, the industry was wedded to point paper and was extremely wary of direct sketching. Hence the initial work was centred around the development and processing of designs on point paper. It is only in the last two years that a substantial shift in attitude has polarised around sketch input. Technology has also moved dramatically during the time of the development. From a designer's viewpoint the most significant is the improvement in the cost/performance of the colour displays. We started with 64 colours and a screen resolution of 512 x 256 picture elements costing £8000. Now, the commercial implementation of the system includes a display system having 1000 x 768 elements with 16.8 million (!) for a fraction of the original cost. Another important technological development is that of higher computer storage capacities, so that much larger designs can be handled. For certain applications, automatic scanning through a videcon type camera may be the best method for input. In summary, there are today systems available for at least half the cost of the 1970's, but with a vastly improved performance and more facilities which can easily be used by textile designers.

4. ENGINEERING DESIGN

4.1 The need and the practice

Traditionally textile materials have been designed by trial and error. Long experience enables a textile man to make a good guess at a likely specification and a sample can then be made and tested. If it fails, it is not a disaster (unlike building bridges or aeroplanes) and the construction can be revised and tried again. Consequently there is no background of calculation or draughtsmanship in the industry, except at a trivial level of costing; and there are no engineering design offices ready for CAD.

But the situation is changing for several reasons. Firstly, the range of choices has increased enormously. A rope manufacturer (2) estimates that, with the range of available fibres and range of new rope constructions, he has to choose from a million possibilities. The same situation exists throughout the textile industry. Optimisation is only possible with computational assistance. Secondly, there are now a number of demanding industrial and civil engineering end-uses for textiles where a large and expensive product has to operate effectively, possibly for many years, so that design calculations and an evaluation of performance are essential. Thirdly, there are social factors, such as mobility in employment, education, and computing in the home, that both make the old ways more difficult and the new ways expected.

Fortunately, the coincidence of the research into the structural mechanics of fibre assemblies since 1920, and particularly in mathematical analysis since 1945, with the development of computing power makes textile engineering CAD a realistic possibility.

4.2 QAS to TK problem solver

In the Lucerne paper (1), we described a computational Question-Answer system developed by Konopasek (3) to handle the inter-relations between the parameters of models of woven fabric geometry: for example, in a race-track geometry 38 parameters of interest depend on 9 independent variables and 29 equations. The number of possible combinations of independent variables is excessively large, and it would not be possible to write separate programs for each set. Instead Konopasek developed a flexible and powerful network system which automatically handled any choice of independent variables.

This QAS system also had many other useful facilities: variable names, e.g. fibre types, with associated numerical data on properties; numerical non-linear relations between quantities, e.g. fibre stress-strain curves; tabular and graphical output, optimisation routines; and so on. In its first form, it was limited to algebraic and numerical relations, but later Shanahan (4) developed a facility for handling partial differential equations in order to facilitate an energy method for analysing the mechanics of woven, knitted and other fabrics with a repetitive structure.

A number of QAS programs were developed at UMIST and elsewhere, and these were extremely instructive and useful, but, for a decade, the method was not widely adopted. Probably it was unsuited to the computer environment of the times.

Now, with the advent of personal microcomputers, the time is right, and the system has been marketed by Software Arts Inc. as TK Solver (5). The visible form has changed from the conversational mode of QAS to the spread sheet format pioneered in VisiCalc by the owners of Software Arts, but the essence of the method and the computational techniques remain the same. The general software package is being widely sold. The textile

community now needs to develop and document a range of particular applications packages.

4.3 Applications to textile geometry

Most of the work on the theory of mechanics of textile materials,
at UMIST and elsewhere, has followed the classical methods of
applied mechanics and used computation at the end to obtain
numerical results for comparison with experiment. This is appropriate for fundamental research, but most of the published work is
limited to plain weave and plain knit fabrics, and also stops a
long way short of providing convenient and useful working packages
for the design engineer. One exception is the work of Moghe (6)
who refers to methods used by Goodrich in the design of industrial fabrics.

We have progressed further in practical methods at UMIST with
programs related to the geometry of fabrics.

One approach has been to adopt a well-known simple geometry that
appears to simulate the situation known to occur in the range of
fabrics with which the designer is concerned. For instance, the
race-track modification of Peirce geometry can be used to model
woven fabrics, and the computer then predicts practically important geometrical features of fabrics with this assumed geometry.
The computer can also be used to analyse weaves so as to isolate
multilayer situations prior to applying geometries to the arrangement. The increasing power of computers and the development of
numerical methods have meant that this approach need not be
limited to geometries in which the threads take paths which can
be represented by simple sets of equations such as those formulated by Peirce, but the thread paths may be defined instead by
matrices of co-ordinates. More data is generated, but is easily
dealt with by computers.

Another approach is to design by extrapolating from previous
experience. This method was demonstrated in a QAS model developed
by Konopasek and Cooke (7) for double jersey fabrics. The simple
basic model made use of an extensive set of data consisting of
measurements on wool fabrics from which it is possible to predict
the dimensions on fabrics, similar to, but not identical to, those
measured. A similar exercise has been carried out by Panagio-
talidis (8) on plain-woven fabrics. The derivation of basic
equations relating dimensions and other factors such as cost was
found to be fairly simple. The main problem was the development
of a data base for woven fabrics which could be used as a basis
for design. This was found to have considerable difficulties,
mainly due to the large number of independently variable parameters. For instance, two very useful parameters on which to
base calculations are the warp and weft yarn crimp values.
However, the accurate evaluation of these on real fabrics was
found to be difficult to achieve. When this problem had been
solved, a number of relationships between yarn crimp and other
fabric parameters were developed, which then led to the creation
of a useable database.

4.4 <u>Machine and process modelling</u>

Traditionally textile machines have been designed either on the
basis of an empirical craft, as with a complex and poorly understood process like carding, or on a deterministic statement of
the response required in the material, as in the number of turns
to be positively inserted in ring-spinning or in pin-twisting, or
the fixed temperature to be maintained for a fixed time in a
thermal process. The design offices of the machinery makers
typically contained experts in the mechanical and electrical
engineering of the machines, who would make the usual engineering design calculations, but there was generally less detailed
attention to the material passing through. On the other side,
the mill managers adjusted machine settings on the basis of
empirical experience and judgement of the product emerging from
the machine.

Here again, the needs are changing. · The range of choices increases. The diverse new forms of textile processing carry no
background of experience. The increased speeds of machines and
of machine development, as well as the social factors mentioned
earlier, impose new demands. The possibilities of on-line
measurement by modern transducers and fast and specific response
by microprocessor control offer new opportunities. But apart
from these features, which are common to all industries, there
is the special feature that many of the newer textile operations
cannot be set positively and deterministically: the response is
a consequence of a dynamic interaction between the machine and
the material. This can be seen in twist insertion in rotor,
friction, or aerodynamic spinning; in friction-twisting or jet-
bulking in texturing; in the fluid jet entanglement of spun-
laced fabrics; in the fast movement of material through a hot
zone or a chemical concentration; and so on.

If we are to approach optimisation, we must develop the means of
computing the response to different machine configurations, and
the control information needed to produce the right product,
technically and economically, from raw material with specified
properties. This is the rationale for attempting to develop
computer modelling of textile processes as part of the broad
effort towards CAD in the textile industry.

The problems are formidable,firstly, because of the complexity of
the operations, with movements of up to 10^{12} fibre elements per
minute through fields of mechanical force, temperature, and
chemistry, and, secondly, because of the intense non-linearity
of the responses. We need more experimental and theoretical
research to generate understanding, and creative and imaginative
ways of reducing the complexity to a practical level. As with
the study of the statics of textile materials, which is ahead
by a few decades, the study of the dynamics of textile processes
shows isolated early investigations, and then the beginnings of
systematic and continuing research (once again pioneered in
Massachusetts, with Backer's work on texturing). But,again, it
is necessary to move from the separate study of different processes to the development of general techniques which are applicable
to a variety of problems.

The role of the computer now becomes central. It is not just a matter of using the computer for the arithmetical chores at the end of elegant mathematical analysis. The tactics of attack on any problem should be through the information-handling capacity of the computer. The strategy for advancing the whole subject should be modular, so that any given problem can be tackled by putting together sub-programs which represent identifiable unit processes of textile operations, such as the application of tensile, twisting, bending, surface, thermal and chemical forces by the separate components of a machine.

We have followed this approach at UMIST in research by Featherstone (9,10) and Overington (11) which is specifically aimed at computational modelling of the false-twist texturing process, but adopts methods which will enable the procedures to be applied to other processes. The work divides into two main areas. One is the macroscopic framework for simulating the whole process, and the other is the detailed modelling of elementary interactions. Because of the history-dependence of the behaviour of polymeric fibres, it is necessary to combine these in a way which follows the movement of successive elements through the process.

There are many interesting technical problems. For example, at the macroscopic level, the transport of yarn through input and output rollers makes elongation the independent variable, but within any zone the mechanical equilibrium (neglecting inertial, surface, or body forces) makes equality of tension the independent parameter: this leads to the need for an optimisation routine in which tension is adjusted until the length fits. And, at the microscopic level, there is the very limited knowledge of thermomechanical responses of synthetic fibres, in tension, torsion, and bending, which we are trying to handle through a four-element spring and dashpot model with variable parameters, as well as the geometry and mechanics of twisted yarns, and the interaction between the yarn and a friction-twister of designed geometry.

If research along the lines proposed is successful, it should provide computational tools to aid the optimum design of machines and components; and to help design and select process conditions which may lead to improved properties, economics, and uniformity in yarn and fabric manufacture, or may lead past such apparent technical limitations as surging at a critical speed in false-twist texturing.

5.   THE INTEGRATING ROLE OF A COMPUTER SYSTEM

5.1 The industrial and commercial network

A major advantage of the adoption of a computer system is the way in which it can liberate the flow of information in a circuit around a company.

The creative concepts in the design studio may justifiably be regarded as the start of the process, although the designers will need to be fed through the network with information on the market, on raw material prices, on availability of stocks and machinery, and other factors which influence a successful

commercial design choice. As the design develops, iterative
calculation will generate more specific feedback on cost and
performance, and iterative sample production will show the
reality of the material.

Of course, the design department does not operate in isolation,
and there will be contacts with marketing and other members of
the managerial team, and with customers, before decisions are
taken to manufacture. A computer system can contribute particularly to this interaction by providing information both as a
starting package for discussion and interactively during meetings.

With the final design selected and details held in the computer,
the necessary information can flow round the company. Hardly seen
by human operatives will be items such as: machine control instructions; purchase orders; production planning; and the handling
of repeat orders. Other parts will feed into the system through
the provision of samples and specifications to the sales office,
cash-flow information to the finance director, and so on.
On a longer time-scale, there will be links to R and D on the
needs for better computer packages, and on the opportunities
generated by technical innovation.

5.2 The links to machinery

The potential for linking the design information in a computer
to control information for machines is clear. An important area
is sample production, which is an essential part of the design
process but is also part of the selling process, with samples
being made for distribution to customers. This indicates the
need for computer-controlled sample machines as part of a CAD
system, with the high probability that the requirements will be
of the same order (less demanding in speed, more demanding in
versatility) as the machine control required for production
machines.

An example of the type of machine currently available is the
Millitron carpet printing machine, which may be used for production or sampling. This machine is computer-controlled with an
instantaneous change-over from one design to another during full
speed production with no reduction in rate of production and
only a six-inch gap between carpets of different designs.
It is therefore possible to run the commercial machine with short
sample lengths interspersed between production runs. Sampling is
made relatively easy by the fact that the substrate carpet on
which printing is carried out is unchanged through the range of
designs. However the designer is not totally freed from constraints because the designs are limited to the range of dyes
on the machine, and to the choice of substrate carpet.

Other textile processes will have greater difficulties in sampling, since the design of a textile fabric incorporates appearance and properties, including colour and structure in its
specification. For weft-knitted fabrics, there may need to be
changes in a small number of yarn packages, but a more significant change in machine gauge. For a woven fabric, a change in
the warp yarns and setting is a major operation. With the
increasing difficulty of change in the fabric parameters, there
is an increasing incompatibility between the speed of supply of

pattern information between the CAD equipment and the speed of change of raw materials and machine parameters which are not at present automated. For the future, one can envisage a sample machine in which the knitting gauge is adjustable and the supply yarn is spun to requirement in conjunction with knitting. In spite of this there may still be a considerable benefit in removal of the setting-up chore if the pattern information is changed from mechanical to electronic control. Developing the interface to achieve this requires considerable effort, but many examples of successful electronic patterning are emerging from the machinery makers, intended for commercial production but of benefit to textile designers.

One project which has been carried out at UMIST has been the development of an electronically-controlled jacquard sampling loom (12, 13). The production of a jacquard fabric to a partic-ular design requires the making of a warp with the correct counts, sett and design of yarns, the cutting of the jacquard cards, production of weft packages, and the weaving of the sample. Each of these operations is time-consuming. The sample loom was designed to alleviate some of these problems. It incorporates the following features:

(a)   a standard full width loom running at normal speed;

(b)   a standard fine pitch jacquard mechanism, with the card cylinder replaced by an advanced electro-mechanical controller;

(c)   the usual provision for weft yarn changes;

(d)   an on-line dyeing arrangement for the warp threads, incorporating dye baths and a microwave drier prior to entry to the loom;

(e)   microprocessor control of the weave and yarn selections.

Although design and development of the individual components have been carried out, construction of the pattern loom system has not yet been completed. When it is available, there should be the possibility of a fast turnover of jacquard patterns, coupled with the possibility of colouring a specified length of a standard undyed warp to the required shade. Although change of warp sett and counts is not possible, the features that have been incorpor-ated should result in a liberating prospect for design students.

5.3 The links to fashion design

Except perhaps for decorative hangings, the textile fabric is not an end in itself. It is a raw material for the fashion designer to cut and sew into a garment or the interior decorator (amateur or professional) to fit into a room. Here there is another possibility for computer linkage to be explored.

Already there are systems which can take a carpet design and impose this, with the appropriate perspective transformation, on a video-picture of a furnished room. As a somewhat more difficult problem, it would be possible to take a video-picture of a standard print cloth, printed with a standard grid, and made up into curtains or a dress, and then, by digital manipulation, replace the grid by information from a print design.

At a more advanced level still, requiring a major input from textile mechanics, it will become possible to simulate the actual folds and drapes of a woven or knitted fabric of new design.

Another possibility through the use of CAD-CAM is in making the design fit the cutting pattern of the final garment. For example, a panelled skirt could have a complete, enclosed and bordered figure in each panel - with automatic adjustment of the pattern to fit different sizes. At the top end of the market, this sort of technique would be liberating to the fashion designer; at the lower end it could lead to economy in cutting and the saving of costs.

6. CONCLUSION

Although progress has in some ways been disappointingly slow during the last decade, there can be no doubt that by the beginning of the next century the textile industry will regard computer-aided design as a commonplace and productive tool. The central need is now, as it was when we first formulated our ideas over 15 years ago, to promote a combination of research, education and exploitation to bridge two cultural gaps. The first is between the analytical expert in applied mechanics and the practising engineer and technologist. The second is between the hardware and software of the computer systems engineer and the sensual creativity of the artistic designer. Apart from the need for imaginative and inventive solutions to problems of considerable complexity and difficulty, the main barrier to progress is the considerable cost of writing good software, and then testing and developing it over a period of time, in order to develop methods which practising textile designers and design engineers find friendly and productive.

REFERENCES

(1)   J.W.S.Hearle, M.Konopasek and A. Newton in 'New Ways to
      Produce Textiles'. Textile Institute Annual Conference,
      Lucerne, 1972, p.133.

(2)   M.Parsey. Seminar at UMIST, March, 1984.

(3)   M.Konopasek in 'Interactive Systems', Online Conferences Ltd.,
      Uxbridge, 1975, p.217.

(4)   J.W.S.Hearle and W.J.Shanahan. J.Textile Inst., 1978, 69,
      81, 92.

(5)   M.Konopasek and S.Jayaraman. 'The TK Solver Book. A guide
      to problem-solving in science, engineering, business and
      education'. McGraw-Hill, 1984.

(6)   S.R.Moghe in 'Mechanics of Flexible Fibre Assemblies'
      (edited by J.W.S.Hearle, J.J.Thwaites and J.Amirbayat).
      Sijthoff and Noordhof, 1980, p.159.

(7)   M.Konopasek and W.D.Cooke. Textile Inst. and Industry,
      March, 1976, p.97.

(8)   H.Panagiotalidis. Ph.D thesis, University of Manchester, 1980.

(9)   A.M.Featherstone. Ph.D thesis, University of Manchester, 1982.

(10) A.M.Featherstone, J.W.S.Hearle and P.E.Wellstead in 'Texturing
      Today'. Shirley Institute Conference, 1982.

(11) M.Overington. Current research.

(12) D.S.W.Tjong. Ph.D thesis, University of Manchester, 1981.

(13) H.C.Inyiama. Ph.D thesis, University of Manchester, 1981.

Department of Textiles,
University of Manchester Institute of Science and Technology,
P.O. Box 88,
Sackville Street,
Manchester M60 1QD,
England.

COMMERCIAL DATA PROCESSING IN THE CLOTHING INDUSTRY: FUTURE DEVELOPMENTS

A.D. Harverd and D. Booth

ABSTRACT

Recent developments in the use of computers within the clothing industry are reviewed. Integrated computer systems covering all operations from order intake to accounting and management information have been developed. These and their benefits embrace:

1. Computerised order processing, stock, production and delivery control. The systems provide high savings in reducing stock levels and better customer service by a quicker delivery response.

2. Integration of the order system with materials procurement and stock control provides a smoother flow of goods to production. Materials and sub-assemblies can be related to the required production flow, which in turn can be tied in with piece-work administration.

3. Integration of order processing and accounting enables effective credit control mechanisms to be established.

4. Integration of standard costing and variance analysis yields improved financial control.

New developments in computerisation are considered and their benefits evaluated. These include automating the work recording aspects of production control, linking computers between large distributors and their suppliers for the transmission of orders and progress chasing, and the control of factories on various sites.

1. DEFINITIONS
1.1 Commercial Data Processing

This paper is concerned with commercial data processing in the clothing industry and probable future developments in this field. Commercial data processing deals with the administration of the business rather than the use of computers to run production machinery or aid the design process. It embraces processing the information which management requires to manage the business.

1.2 Clothing Industry

In this paper, any reference to the clothing industry should also be understood to include the footwear industry.

19

2. CHARACTERISTICS OF THE INDUSTRY

What are the special characteristics of this industry which create a need for a specialised type of data processing?

2.1 Diversity of Products

The industry supplies a mass consumer market created by the diverse needs of people, the conditions in which they live and the activities in which they take part. It has to take account of climatic conditions, fashion trends, the working environment and sporting and leisure activities.

2.2 Variety of Sizes

There is not only a demand for many different categories of clothing, but each type has to be supplied in many sizes to fit the varied dimensions of the consumer. The problems associated with size information present a serious problem to the operation of computer systems.

2.3 Channels of Distribution

The differing needs of consumers are matched by the varied requirements of a wide range of channels of distribution through which the products are marketed. Some distributors require goods to be made specially to meet their exact requirements, whilst others require stocks to be held so that an immediate delivery service can be given.

2.4 High Volumes

Production is often in very high unit volumes which cause special problems of control and measurement.

2.5 Seasonality

The industry is seasonal with much of the range being replaced twice a year.

2.6 High Fashion Content

There is often a high fashion content which requires the frequent introduction of new lines and new raw materials. The data base must, therefore, be capable of frequent change.

2.7 Competitiveness

The industry is highly competitive, so cannot dictate commercial terms to its customers or suppliers. Systems have to be very flexible to cater for this situation.

2.8 Piece-Work Systems

There is widespread use of piece-work payment systems which produce a large volume of transactions which have to be processed rapidly.

2.9 Labour Intensive

The industry is labour intensive, although in many sections raw materials constitute the largest proportion of costs. The added value and average profit margins tend to be low.

3. COMPUTER SYSTEMS TRENDS

3.1 Costly Early Systems

Until recently, the average clothing manufacturer could not afford the high cost of computer equipment and associated software development required to provide a viable system capable of meeting his needs. The use of computers in the clothing industry has, therefore, been rather limited in comparison with their adoption in other industries.

3.2 Reduced Equipment Costs and Increased Software Costs

Because of recent technical development, the cost of hardware has been reducing whilst at the same time technical capabilities have increased. This trend continues. Whilst there has been an opposite, upward trend in the cost of software development, packages have been developed specially to meet the needs of the clothing industry.

3.3 Specialised Software

Early software was developed to meet specific needs, such as piece-work wages processing, and used on small dedicated micro computers. It was not designed to become part of a larger system aimed at meeting the data processing needs of the whole business.

3.4 Economic Mini Computers

More recently, mini computers have become available at much reduced prices. They have adequate and reliable storage capabilities which are able to operate a large number of programs simultaneously and can utilise any number of video terminals and printers.

3.5 Integrated Systems

Integrated computer systems have been developed for the industry which are capable of meeting nearly all the needs of a clothing business.

3.5.1 Definition of an Integrated System

An integrated data processing system is a composite of sub-systems covering all the information processing requirements of an organisation, so that all data are accessible to all parts of the system without unnecessary duplication. Each sub-system accepts, processes and stores data and provides information derived from that data in the form and at the time required by the user.

The development of reliable disc storage methods and advanced computer operating systems (the internal programs that make the computer work) has removed the need to depend on batch processing. Instead, when data are entered, interactive processing can immediately execute the work to which they logically relate. Accuracy checks, calculations, the use of existing stored data, storage of new data and the provision of information to the user can all follow from an entry of data or the execution of a computer process.

The integrated, interactive system depends on the way the storage of data in the computer is organised. The reduced cost and increased reliability of disc storage have made it possible to hold virtually all the information concerning a whole business in a manner that is immediately available to the computer, thus enabling all procedures to use the total file structure whenever required. This is not only possible but it can be provided at a cost acceptable to the average firm in our industry.

3.5.2 Package Integrated Systems

Package integrated systems already exist which have been written specially to meet the needs of the clothing and footwear industries. The several hundred thousand pounds sterling capital cost of creating this software is shared by many users, each benefiting from the years of expert effort involved in producing the packages. All can take advantage of continuing development work and share in the software support available without the need to employ their own, expensive, computer experts.

3.5.3 Validation of Input Data

Many problems associated with data processing systems result from the use of inaccurate information. Every item of data entering a system must be checked very carefully. Complex programs for checking are required which take up much computer time. In an integrated system checking is carried out once only, so the verification process can be more rigorous. There is no duplication of storage and the whole system then benefits from a high level of data accuracy. As the most expensive hardware is that required for data storage, the unified data base also provides a cost advantage.

3.5.4 Comprehensive Reports

The integrated system can provide, in one report, information on all aspects of its subject whatever the source. With other systems several reports might have to be used for the same need. Also, several small specialised documents may replace the large multi-copy form which often holds much more data than any one user requires. In some areas the use of screen enquiry methods removes the need for printed documents altogether.

3.5.5 Quick Response

The immediate response of the integrated system is beneficial when dealing with continually changing data. One transaction might affect another, for instance, when accepting orders against limited supplies or when providing stock availability reports. A single integrated system is less expensive to install and run that several separate systems with the same objectives. Each part of the system also benefits from the greater processing power and higher storage capacity available on the integrated system. More room for growth is available before it becomes necessary to add further equipment.

3.5.6 Need for Clever Computer Operating Systems

A major advantage of the mini computers used for integrated systems is the sophistication of their operating systems. These make the system much easier to use, have better security safeguards and are easier to program than the smaller, micro based systems. Minis are also better able to communicate via telephone lines with many types of equipment at remote sites. The integrated system offers a co-ordinated solution to the information needs of a business, with all parts operating in harmony.

Having considered the specialised needs of our industry and examined the characteristics of interactive, integrated computer systems we can now examine in more detail some particular applications of such systems which are already in use in the industry.

4.   INTEGRATED ORDER PROCESSING, STOCK PRODUCTION AND
      DELIVERY CONTROL

4.1 Main Categories of Clothing Manufacturer

There are two main types of clothing business. Make to order and the stockholding company. Sometimes both categories are found in the one organisation.

4.2 Delivery from Stock

Usually sales are to a large number of small customers with frequent deliveries in relatively small quantities. Often, a proportion of the sales is for future delivery but against standard stock ranges on a seasonal basis. This results in conflicting requirements for the use of available stock. To provide a balanced range, there is a wide mix of many styles, each in several colours and all in many sizes, with possibly several different sizing systems being used in one company. These factors multiply into many thousands of individual stock heads each with the need for several balance records. Forward orders are gradually accumulated, whilst stock must be available for servicing immediate orders. The latter must not pre-empt supply made to meet the forward order book. In companies operating on a large scale, it is impossible to carry out this task efficiently without the use of a computer. It is often the case that many orders are not delivered on time and the level of stocks held is far too high. The computer systems must provide all the required details of each product, including stocks, work in progress by individual size and delivery date, and balances available for sale. Naturally, the account details of each customer will be held on the system and will be available to those concerned with processing sales orders.

When an order is received, it is possible for the operator to enter its details in the system. During this process, rigorous checks are carried out to ensure that all the information entered is accurate. At the same time, the customer's credit is checked and approved. Stock availability, price and delivery date will also be checked. Frequently, such orders carry many different lines from the range.

24

Once a valid order is placed in the system, it forms the basis for all further transaction processing related to the order, through to the ultimate despatch and delivery to the customer. Facilities are also provided to permit orders to be amended or cancelled should the customer change his mind. It is not uncommon for such a system to hold tens of thousands of orders on file.

The records of orders may later be processed to produce summaries of the goods required, by delivery date, product and size, as a basis for forecasting and production planning.

The system must be able to review the order book against available stock by delivery period, product and size to determine which orders should be delivered. This ultimately allows for the printing of delivery instructions and, following despatch, the production of a sales invoice and a posting to the customer's sales ledger account. Such a

system permits the most efficient use of stock and leads to a reduction in stocks held whilst, at the same time, providing a better delivery service. There will also be considerable savings in the cost processing of the thousands of transactions involved.

4.3 Credit Control

Because integrated systems have all the data in the system available to all parts of the system at all times, it is possible to exercise rigorous control over the credit allowed to customers. The allocation of resources to orders for customers whose credit is doubtful, without the knowledge that this is being done, can be prevented. At the latest point, delivery can be stopped if the credit status does not justify the risk. This is possible even when dealing with thousands of customers and many thousands of orders in any period.

4.4 Made to Order Business

The made to order business is spared the problems of processing very large numbers of small orders and of manufacturing stock before it is sold. The scheduling of orders into production without the ability to produce stock orders to fill gaps when they arise at inconvenient times, is a disadvantage. Also, a small number of large customers with very rigorous delivery requirements will form the bulk of the business. Sometimes, large manufacturing orders must be broken down into quite small delivery quantities which must all be despatched at one time to the customer's many branches. A suitable order processing system can help control this activity.

Although the size of customer's order is larger, the management of the control of production, materials and deliveries are very similar to the stock business.

Proposed or actual manufacturing orders may be placed in the system and using a product related parts explosion, the quantity of each material required to satisfy the order can be calculated. This forms the basis of a purchasing requirement. Details of all materials in use are stored and deliveries entered, producing a stock balance.

Some materials are required in sizes related to the size of the garments, although the relationship may not be size for size. The system will convert product quantities to material size quantities, to cover single or groups of manufacturing orders. Similarly, the purchasing and stock records must relate to these sizes.

The importance of materials varies with their value or their availability. Important materials are issued from stores and the exact quantity recorded. This will be the basis of the stock issues entered in the system. For these materials, accurate stock listings can be provided. For less important materials, the quantity used can be estimated from the quantity on the manufacturing order and the usage in the parts list, as a basis for maintaining estimated stock records.

In both cases, there will be facilities for amending the stock records, to correct stock discrepancies which arise.

The existence of accurate material stock and 'on order' records in the system enables checks to be made for potential shortages against existing manufacturing orders and proposed quantities to be scheduled. As a result, less frequent interruptions to production, due to shortage of materials, will occur and higher plant efficiency will result.

The movement of manufacturing orders into and through the production processes will be recorded on the computer at successive control points. Tables of 'lead times' provide the data needed to calculate the time when each point should be reached and the final delivery made. Exception reports of orders running late can be provided. These may trigger management action to restore the desired situation on the shop floor. These same data permit the accurate listing of the quantity of work in progress at each point, which is useful for production control and as a basis for financial evaluation. They are also an essential pre-requisite to realistic production planning.

4.5   Piece Work Payment Systems

In companies using piece-work as the payment system,
detailed records of the operations used on each style, with
their standard minutes or money rates, will be stored on an
operations file. This will be used to produce the payment
tickets for each works order to be collected by the piece-
workers. Job instructions may also be included. After each
operator has collected his/her tickets, they will be used to
calculate the earnings and can also be used as a basis for
detailed efficiency measurement and progress reporting. The
high speed of processing these tickets permits the
production, early each day, of efficiency reports, by
section and factory. These form the basis for effective
action before the causes of shop floor problems are
forgotten. This type of system can reduce excess costs by
making savings in direct labour costs.

The records of piece-work output produced are also useful
when comparing factory performance to budgets.

In production systems, where the identify of works orders is
lost at an early stage, the piece-work tickets will provide
the information required to control the progress of orders
through production.

4.6   On Line Production Control

High volume factories with very fast throughput times
require the control of production to be much more frequent
that once daily. Systems are available whereby the operator
records directly into the computer, by the use of special
cards and readers at the work place, exact details of the
work done. This permits production control to be carried
out on an hour by hour basis. In addition, wages may be
calculated automatically. Such systems are, however, very
expensive.

5.   STANDARD COSTING AND VARIANCE ACCOUNTING

Standard costing and variance accounting may be built up
using data in the integrated system. If material standard
costs are added to the details already in the system,
detailed material lists can be produced giving the material
standard cost for each product.

Standard labour costs may be stored by style in summary
form, or be calculated in detail from the operations data in
the piece-work system. When overhead costs are added,
accurate standard costings can be produced automatically for
all products. Those on file for one season may form the
basis of reworked data, possibly with percentage additions,
for the following seasons or on a trial 'what if' basis for
price fixing purposes. The vast number of calculation
normally involved in producing standard costings for a
complete range are thus fully automated.

The existence of accurate standard costings in the system may then be related to work in progress movements entered in order to calculate the value of standard costs recovered during production. When integrated with the computerised nominal ledger, full variance accounting becomes a practical possibility for a very modest effort.

6. FUTURE DEVELOPMENTS

Many industries are increasingly able to benefit from techniques developed in the space and defence industries where development costs are not under the same restraints as in commercial organisations.

The clothing industry has the opportunity to utilise many of these developments, particularly in the areas of light technology, improved communications and micro-electronics.

6.1 Equipment

The rapid advancement of developments in micro-electronics has resulted in equipment costs being reduced to a level where the majority of organisations can now afford some form of computerised systems.

Whilst this leads to many benefits being derived from an installed computer system, there are many pitfalls relating to the selection and implementation of the system which need to be avoided.

Micro computers manufactured by companies lacking a good record or whose financial stability is uncertain should be avoided, as should special offers of obsolescent models.

Management should ensure that the longer term problems are understood, before authorising the installation of inexpensive micros. These might take up a great deal of the expensive time of computer enthusiasts amongst staff, but much of this work could have to be repeated when larger equipment is required.

6.2 Software

The most important ingredient in any computer system is the software. Selection of the most appropriate software will often automatically lead to the right choice of the hardware. This is particularly true in the apparel industry.

As already noted, the industry has many diverse needs not seen in other commercial organisations. Though packages exist for many purposes, they often involve the user either making expensive changes in traditional and well tried working methods, or in developing expensive amendments to the software itself.

Flexible packages are now becoming available which, simply by changing the program control parameters, can be set up to provide a better match to the users' needs.

More sophisticated computer operating systems and software aids such as report generators are making the task of producing new programs and amending existing programs easier and cheaper. Most modern systems use methods which simplify the operational use, so that the necessity of expensive specialist data processing staff are no longer essential and the care of the system can be left in the hands of the more experienced clerical staff.

6.3 Micro computers

Some professional computers can now use programs written in languages which will also work on larger mini computers. They can also function as terminals to mini computers and have considerable storage ability for independent use. They can be used as an inexpensive means of communication between locations. This means that the entry level for computer systems can be such that the small company can invest without the need for costly replacements at a later date. The system and the software can expand with the business without the original investment being lost.

A combination of such micros and a small mini computer will provide a very powerful system at reasonable cost especially for the company with more than one location.

6.4 Automatic input

The high volume of data required to be input to give meaningful and effective results has inhibited the use of detailed control of manufacturing operations.

The light and laser technology succesfully developed over the last few years has made such systems more practical. Technical developments in producing bar-coded tickets and the practical means of reading them, with either small portable readers or directly into a computer, will increase their use in the industry. Applications will include piece-work tickets and material stock labels. The latter is a much more economic alternative to the miniature punched tickets which require very expensive processing equipment.

The use of encoded tickets for automatic re-ordering should not be ignored. They will provide an easy to use system for both supplier and retailer to save clerical effort and to provide a better and efficient service to the end customer.

6.5   Communications

Communication between computers via dialed telephone lines
is now more reliable and easier to arrange. This permits
customers to pass data direct to their suppliers, and
central offices to communicate with remote factories, sales
offices or sales staff.

Computer software may be transmitted or amended and faults
rectified by support organisations.

Attendance time recording equipment will feed data directly
to operator records on the computer.

Modern teletex systems using conventional broadcasting
equipment, interfaced via standard telephone lines to
sophisticated computer systems, the costs of which can be
shared between users, are now able to offer a reliable and
accurate information and ordering service to many users. By
providing up to date stock information with the latest
market trends, the farsighted supplier will be able to
provide a fast and efficient ordering system, using much
standard equipment, to their customers.

6.6   Production control

A combination of the recent technical developments with
suitable software will greatly enhance the value of
computers in production scheduling, planning and control.

The use of bar-coded documentation will permit the rapid
measurement of materials movements through production
processes. This will provide a detailed knowledge of
balances in the factory, which will facilitate a much better
level of service to the customer.

Frequent accurate factory line balancing systems will use a
combination of data from the piece work ticket, progressing,
time recording, wages and order systems. This will lead to
a truly integrated system.

7.   CONCLUSION

High equipment costs and inflexible systems have in the past
inhibited the more general use of computers by all but the
largest clothing manufacturers.

Better, cheaper, flexible systems are becoming available
which will overcome the cost obstacles and provide more
cost-effective applications to assist in the operation of
the modern business. The limited computer knowledge of some
managements has sometimes delayed decisions to investigate
their more general use. The cost-benefit equation is moving
in favour of the computer user, at a time when companny
operating costs are constantly increasing.

The intelligent use of computers will reduce costs and
provide a better service to customers.

Hacker Young Fraser Williams Limited,
St. Alphage House,
2, Fore Street,
London, EC2Y 5DH,
England.

AN INTERACTIVE DATABASE FOR WOVEN TEXTILE DESIGN

J.A. Hoskins and M.W. King

ABSTRACT

The creation of novel figured weaves challenges the textile
designer to find a unique sequence of yarn placements and
interlacements that will produce a fabric with an innovative
appearance. At the same time, the designer must work within
the constraints of the number of shafts and the type of loom
attachments available, as well as meet the requirement of
weaving a fabric with structural integrity.

We believe there are two important ways in which the computer
scientist can provide assistance to the textile designer in
achieving these objectives. Firstly, he can develop algorithms
which define particular sequences of interlacements, and use
them to generate exhaustive databases of archived designs.
Secondly, he can provide the software that not only enables
the designer to draw from a database all the designs that
apply to a given set of constraints, but also to retain the
successful designs for future use and modification, and to
provide an interactive environment for the display, creation
and alteration of point diagrams.

This type of computer-aided textile design system has recently
become commercially available. This paper describes the software architecture of one such system. By way of an example,
it is demonstrated how on algorithm has been developed to
create a unique database of all the twills, twillins, and
twill derivatives possible on a loom with up to 16 shafts. This
database contains in excess of a billion archived designs.
Among the options available, the user may select some or all
the designs with any size of repeat element ranging from 4 x 4
to 16 x 16. The success of the system relies on the efficient
storage and retrieval of design data and on a large memory
capacity which can now be provided by low cost microcomputers.

1. INTRODUCTION

The process of designing figured woven textile structures and
patterns is a complex one, requiring both artistry and meticulous
attention to detail (1). Successful textile designs must exhibit
a pleasing visual appearance as well as maintaining a satisfactory
level of structural stability. This means that a textile designer
must be in a position to construct and modify a graphic representation of the interlacement pattern which he is creating while, at
the same time, applying computational algorithms to this data to
assess its suitability for producing a woven fabric with specified
properties, on a given loom. A computer-based interactive textile
design system can provide the perfect environment for the execution of these various design operations.

The purpose of this paper is to outline the significant functions
and features required by the designer of figured, single and

multi-layered weaves and to discuss the manner in which a
computer-based system can fulfill these requirements. Conceptually,
such a system can be thought to consist of three major components,
namely the design environment, archives and library storage, and
direct control of the loom. Subsequent discussion is grouped
under these headings. Where appropriate, illustrative references
are made to a specific system, called Pattern Master, which has
been developed according to these principles. The system
described (2), is a software package implemented on an Apple II+
microcomputer with 48K of RAM, with a hardware interface to an
AVL Compu-Dobby loom (3).

2. DESIGN ENVIRONMENT

It has always been important for the designer to be able to
visualize woven design data, regardless of whether the surface
pattern or the structure is documented. This is the main reason
why designers rely so heavily on the traditional point diagram
which corresponds to a graphical representation of the warp/weft
intersections in a rectangular region of the fabric, and this is
why it is clearly essential to include some form of graphical
display as an integral part of any computer-based interactive
design environment (4). In fact, one of the main advantages of
a computer-based system is that it has the facility to rapidly
create a precisely rendered point diagram, while at the same time
developing the underlying data structure.

2.1 Design Input

In the Pattern Master system, the method of design input is
graphical. A grid is drawn on the high resolution graphics
screen, along with a cursor which can be moved under keyboard
control. An individual cell is selected or de-selected by a
single keystroke and the corresponding element is updated in
the data file. Editing functions are also integrated into the
design environment which enable more substantial changes such
as transposition of the design, deletion of an entire row or
column, insertion of a new row or column, or tesselation of
the design region with a finite repeat, to be quickly and easily
achieved. The graphic display and corresponding data file are
of course updated as changes are made, so that there is continuous feedback as to the visual appearance of the pattern.

2.2 Factorization

Up until this point the textile design process has been viewed
entirely as a process of graphical manipulation to achieve a
satisfactory visual result. Although some consideration may
have been given by the designer as to the interlacement properties of the image, this has not been a major focus of this first
stage. Having developed a point diagram however, there arises
a need to determine whether this design can be produced on the
loom available and, if so, precisely what threading and pegging
plan are required.

The algorithm for factoring an interlacement array into its
corresponding threading and pegging plan (or threading, tie-up
and treadling) is not necessarily complex, but it is tedious and
time-consuming and must be completely free of errors (5,6).

It is thus a task which is ideally suited to computer processing.

The inverse process, that of developing an interlacement array from a given threading and pegging plan and displaying the corresponding point diagram is also easily carried out computationally. The combination of these two functions is an extremely powerful feature of a computer-based design system, in that an iterative method of structural development is now possible. A point diagram is created and factored. Perhaps it is found to require too many shafts. Changes are made to the threading draft to accommodate this constraint and the data file is updated and displayed. If the resulting design is acceptable, the process is finished, but if it is not, then further modifications can be made to the point diagram which is then re-analyzed. This sequence of steps is repeated until the designer is satisfied that the final structure is not only visually satisfactory, but also physically achievable.

2.3 Reducibility and Cross-Sectional Representations

The further concern arises as to whether the developed design will produce a structurally stable fabric or whether areas will contain distinct layers of non-interlaced yarns. An algorithm to determine the potential reducibility of fabric structures into disjoint yarn and cloth layers has been developed which is based entirely on the relative size of the row and column sums of the interlacement array interpreted as a binary matrix (7,8). The level of computation and data handling required in this process is sufficient to render it unacceptable as a hand algorithm, for all but very small patterns. This is another area in which a computer-based system can be of great assistance.

The problem of assessing the structural integrity of the fabric corresponding to a given interlacement array is further considered in this design environment, with the implementation of cross-sectional representations (9,10). Much insight into the nature of a fabric structure is to be gained by examining a rendering of the design as sections cut through the warp ends between successive weft picks, or through the picks between successive ends. While this is useful in highlighting yarn floats which may be excessively long in a single layered fabric, the extreme utility of such a function occurs in the consideration of multi-layered fabrics. The interlacement arrays for each fabric layer are normally merged into a single homogeneous point diagram, in keeping with the physical reality of an integrated threading draft and pegging plan (11). It becomes extremely difficult to detect pattern effects in one particular cloth layer and even more difficult to determine the presence or absence of stitching points between the layers. Graphical displays of the interlacement data mapped to a set of cross-sectional output primitives for multi-layers can provide considerable information on both of these subjects.

The Pattern Master system provides the capacity for mapping the constructed data file through the appropriate set of output primitives to cross-sectional representations of up to four fabric layers, and has the capacity to vary the yarn density in a two layer representation. Since it is common, as for

instance in a doublecloth, for the layers to be held together
by the interchange between the face and back of entire regions
of the fabric, a coding scheme has been included to indicate
situations in which this exchange takes place. Figures 1 - 4
illustrate this form of graphical display.

3. ARCHIVES AND LIBRARY STORAGE

3.1 Data base of Twills

Woven textiles have been found which date back to at least
2500 B.C. (12) and woven textile designs have been well documented over the years. These rich traditions and this wealth
of classical and historical reference material can supply the
modern textile designer with invaluable sources of inspiration
and information, provided it is available in some form which is
readily accessible. A computer-based interactive design system
is ideally suited to the storage and retrieval of large amounts
of this data when it is organized as a coherent well-structured
database.

The family of twill structures has long been recognized as being
an important part of this heritage (13) and the need for exhaustive classification and enumeration of these weaves has been
expressed (14). Many attempts have been made at this type of
classification (eg. (15)) but it has been said of the twills
that the "variety...is so considerable as to render an exact
classification of them impossible" (16).

Relatively recently a formal definition of twill structures has
been developed which is based on the group of symmetries of the
corresponding binary interlacement array (17). The combination
of this unambiguous mathematical definition and the advent of
powerful computing facilities has enabled the enumeration and
creation of an exhaustive catalogue of twill structures (18).

The classification scheme developed by Grünbaum and Shephard
involves establishing the first row of the corresponding binary
interlacement array and the rule for obtaining all subsequent
rows from this first row. Each row is required to have an
equivalent interlacement sequence, with complementation, reversal,
cyclic rotation, or any combination of these operations being
defined as leaving a sequence invariant. As well, each column
is required to have an equivalent interlacement sequence and in
addition, the row and column sequences are required to be
equivalent. Finally, the relationship between each row and
its neighbours and each column and its neighbours must be
constant, with the row and column relationships being the same.
Structures, such as the twills, which exhibit all of these
properties are said to be isonemal.

In developing a twill array from an initial binary interlacement
sequence, the rule to get from one row to the next is a simple
shift through one position, with cyclic wrap-around. Thus, the
number of possible twills with a given repeat size is defined
completely by the number of inequivalent first rows. This
number also of course, specifies the number of different twills
that can be woven on a given number of shafts. The numbers of
different twills possible on multiples of four shafts, up to

sixteen, are given in Table 1.

Consequently, in creating a twill database one need store only
the inequivalent first row sequences. The twill designator for
the file unambiguously defines the mapping from each of these
sequences to the corresponding binary interlacement array. In
the Pattern Master system, each interlacement sequence is stored
as a bit string in two bytes of storage, with sequences shorter
than sixteen bits being padded with zeros. The sequences themselves are arranged in a canonical form such that the lowest
order bit is always non-zero. It thus becomes a simple matter to
find the first sequence of a given order by performing a count
of the number of leading non-zero bits in each byte pair up to
the required number. Having found this beginning point, an
individual record can be readily isolated by counting forward in
units of two bytes.

3.2 Database of Twillins, Color Alternate Twills and Color Alternate Twillins

The formal definition of isonemal structures, of which twills are
an example, has led to the introduction of a general class of
weaves called twillins (17), which actually include a number of
classic structures known as satineer (19), re-arranged twills
(20), oatmeal and crepe weaves (21), as well as the regular satins.
These isonemal structures are constructed from a binary interlacement sequence first row, where each row is obtained from
the previous one by a shift of some number of places S. Twills
can obviously be considered a specific case of twillins, in
which the value of S is always one but since this set of
structures is itself so large and diverse, for convenience we
have considered them separately.

Color Alternate Twills and Color Alternate Twillins comprise the
only remaining types of structure which are isonemal and use a
single rule for their generation. In both cases, the rule in
going from one row to the next is a shift of S places and
complementation of the sequence. For Color Alternate Twills,
of course, S always equals one.

The total numbers of Twillins, Color Alternate Twills and Color
Alternate Twillins that are possible on any number of shafts up
to twenty have been enumerated (22) and a subset of these values
is contained in Table 1. All of the elements of these classes
have been catalogued and the implemented database contains
complete files of Twillins, Color Alternate Twills and Color
Alternate Twillins for up to sixteen shafts.

This data is stored in large binary files in a similar format
as for the twills, where for example, the file designator of
Color Alternate Twillins indicates that complementation is
required in the matrix generation rule. In the case of the
Twillins and Color Alternate Twillins, because the order of
these structures is restricted to sixteen shafts in the database,
and because there is only one shift value which produces an
isonemal array for any given sequence length, it is not necessary
to store the number of places through which a given sequence is
to be shifted in generating each new row from the previous one.

3.3 Database of Compound Twillins

The only remaining class of possible isonemal structures is the
Compound Twillins, in which one rule is used to generate all
the even numbered rows from the odd numbered rows and another
rule is used to generate all the odd numbered rows from the even
numbered rows. Each of these rules corresponds to a reflection
of the particular row sequence about a fixed point in the
sequence (23). Compound Twillins can also have complementation
as a part of one, or both or their generating rules.

The Compound Twillins, with and without complementation, have
been enumerated for up to sixteen shafts (24) and the values for
four, eight, twelve and sixteen shafts appear in Table 1. In
addition, all of the elements of these classes have been determined, and are contained in three files in the Pattern Master
database. To simplify the generation algorithm, the first and
second rows for each of these structures have been stored as
bit strings, and again the file designator indicates the presence
or absence of complementation in the generating rules. Representative examples of these structures are illustrated in Figures
5 - 11.

Table I

Order	4	8	12	16
Twills	4	18	122	1162
Twillins	0	9	53	197
Color Alternate Twills	2	6	20	74
Color Alternate Twillins	0	10	32	198
Compound Twillins				
- no complementation	0	29	216	2154
- single complementation	0	10	1	392
- double complementation	0	16	95	656

3.4 Generation of Point Diagrams

Any of these structures can be used to generate a point diagram
quickly and easily, by simply using the chosen interlacement
array as a tie-up matrix and invoking the point diagram generation algorithm. Obviously an appropriate threading and treadling matrix must also be supplied, and this is another area in
which the twill database can be of considerable assistance.

Each of the inequivalent binary sequences used to generate the
twills can be used to define all of the possible threadings and
treadlings with a given number of breaks (18). Each element of
the sequence can be interpreted as a directed line segment of a
specified length, so that the entire sequence defines the points
and straight runs in a particular threading or treadling. In
the Pattern Master system, the run length is specified by the
user. This value is then checked by the program to determine
that it is a divisor of the number of shafts or treadles,

whichever is appropriate.

By way of an example to illustrate this capability, the design
in Figure 12 was developed by first selecting a 16 x 16 compound
twillin as a tie-up matrix. Next a threading was selected from
the database. The particular one chosen had a sequence of
0 0 1 0 1 1 0 1 1 1 1 1 and a run length of four. Finally, a
treadling was selected, corresponding to the sequence 0 0 0 1 0
1 0 1 1 0 0 0 1 1 1 1, also with a run length of four.

3.5 Block Profile Substitution

In designing block weaves such as damask and doubleweave, it is
often convenient to interpret the point diagram as a representation of the gross structure of a fabric rather than the actual
intersections between the warp and weft yarns. In such cases
the graphical data defines only the profile of the design in
terms of the relative size and relationship of the gross design
elements. Implicit in this shorthand description is that the
complete detailed design can be generated by the substitution
of some interlacement array, or block, for every black square
in the point diagram, with a different interlacement array, or
counter-block, for every white square.

A computer-based textile design system can prove of considerable
assistance to the designer of such weaves. In the Pattern Master
system, a library of commonly used blocks and counter-blocks has
been created and stored on disk, with the facility for input of
user defined arrays, as well. When the profile substitution
option is invoked, the created or retrieved interlacement data
is automatically mapped in software through the designer specified
block and counter-block to produce the corresponding detailed
interlacement array. This feature can be used to create and
store the detailed data of an expanded interlacement array, to
graphically represent the fabric corresponding to a given profile
and specified structure (Figures 13 and 14), or to provide the
loom control program with the sequence of lifts required to
weave a particular block design.

This facility is extremely valuable in that the textile designer
need only create a macro-design and specify or develop an appropriate block and counter-block. The tedious, time-consuming
and error prone task of mapping the profile design to the interlacement array is handled automatically in software. Much time
can be saved by this division of the development process into
two stages, where only the first stage, being the creation of
the actual pattern, requires the designer's direct attention.
The second stage, that of providing the design with the necessary
structural integrity and fine pattern detail is handled separately
and independently of the designer.

4. DIRECT LOOM CONTROL

Many of the developmental aspects of a woven textile design can
be accomplished using graphical representations such as point
diagrams and cross-sectional illustrations. As has been
discussed, this process is further aided by the facility for
rapid and accurate structural analysis. Having adapted a classical structure, developed a pattern and used profile substitution,

or created an entirely new design, there comes a point at which
a sample of the actual woven fabric is required. It is desirable
therefore for the design process to provide an integrated link
between the creative and analytical aspects and actual control
of the loom.

The Pattern Master system was implemented to interface directly
to the AVL Compu-Dobby loom, in which the mechanical dobby head
is replaced by a bank of sixteen solenoids connected by a ribbon
cable to a custom interface card within the Apple computer.
Having computed the pegging plan corresponding to the designed
fabric structure, each row of this pegging plan is interpreted
by the software as the decimal equivalent of two eight bit
binary integers. These two integers are stored in two bytes of
memory and passed to the solenoid box where the corresponding
pattern of solenoids is activated. The dobby mechanism is
equipped with a light emitting diode and the sweep arm which
actuates the shafts incorporates a mirror which reflects the
emitted light back to an optical sensor. In this way, the
position of the sweep arm is detected by the hardware which is
thereby able to determine when the solenoids should be re-set
for the next pick.

An inherent limitation of mechanical dobby looms is that every
row of a design repeat requires a lag in proper sequence and
little advantage can be taken of pattern regularity. Special
purpose hardware attachments have been constructed to enable
highly structured block weaves to be handled more easily
(25,26), with varying degrees of success. The computer interfaced dobby loom, with its library of block structures and
automatic substitution algorithms, is ideally suited to over-
coming this limitation.

When weaving designs that include a structural ground weave and
a supplementary pattern weft the Pattern Master system has an
algorithm for automatically computing the two plain weave picks
from the threading draft and for interleaving these sequences
as required between the pattern rows of the pegging plan. In
addition, any pegging plan can be interpreted as a profile
with the possibility of automatically substituting any block
and counter-block pair from the established library as weaving
proceeds. Each time that a new pattern row is read, as many
"virtual lags" as there are rows in the substitution blocks are
generated and sent in sequence to the solenoids. This feature
saves in the amount of time, storage and display space required
in creating block weaves, as well as eliminating an obvious
source of designer error and increasing the flexibility of any
single design.

5. CONCLUSIONS

Designers of figured and multi-layered woven textiles are
confronted with the problem of creating and manipulating large
amounts of data, both graphically and computationally, with a
high degree of interaction between the various operations. The
nature of this process is such that it is perfectly suited to a
computer-based design environment where point diagrams can be
quickly and easily created and graphically displayed, with any

required structural analysis being handled independently of
the designer by the software system. This system is further
enhanced by the facility for long-term storage of personally
developed designs, as well as extensive archives of structures
with known and desirable properties. Finally, the provision
of a direct link between the computer and the loom ensures
that fabric samples of new designs can be woven and made available for marketing, sales and production personnel with a
considerable saving of time and resources. Indeed, by shortening the delay between design conception and realization stages,
we foresee the designer being able to contribute a more dynamic
and effective role in the process of developing novel woven
structures.

REFERENCES

(1) Z.J. Grosicki. 'Watson's Textile Design and Colour:
     Elementary Weaves and Figured Fabrics', Newnes-Butterworths,
     London, 7th edition, 1975.

(2) Pattern Master IV. J.A. Hoskins. Winnipeg, Canada, 1984.

(3) AVL Looms. 601 Orange Street, Chico, California, U.S.A.,
     95926.

(4) J.A. Hoskins and M.W. King. Proceedings - International
     Color Graphics Conference, Tallahassee, March 1983.

(5) J.A. Hoskins and W.D. Hoskins. Ars Comb., 1981, 11, 51.

(6) J.A. Hoskins and W.D. Hoskins. Ars Comb., 1983, 16-B, 341.

(7) C.L.J. Clapham. Bull. London Math Soc., 1980, 12, 161.

(8) J.A. Hoskins, S.S.&D., 1981, 13, 76.

(9) J.A. HOSKINS. Cong. Num., 1983, 40, 63.

(10) J.A. Hoskins. Ars Textrina, 1983, 1, 137.

(11) Z.J. Grosicki. 'Watson's Advanced Textile Design: Compound
     Woven Structures', Newnes-Butterworths, London, 4th edition,
     1977.

(12) S.E. Held. 'Weaving: A Handbook of the Fiber Arts', Holt,
     Rinehart and Winston, New York, 1978, 2nd edition, p. 9.

(13) J. Murphy, 'A Treatise on the Art of Weaving With Calcula-
     tions and Tables for the Use of Manufacturers', Blackie &
     Son, Glasgow, 1836, 5th edition, p. 22.

(14) A.F. Barker, 'An Introduction to the Study of Textile
     Design', Methuen & Co., London, 1903, p. 100.

(15) I. Emery, 'The Primary Structure of Fabrics', The Textile
     Museum, Washington, 1980, p. 92.

(16) H. Nisbet, 'Grammar of Textile Design', Benn, London, 1927,
     3rd edition, p. 24.

(17) B. Grünbaum and G.C. Shephard. Mathematics Magazine, 1980, 53, 139.

(18) W.D. Hoskins and A.P. Street. J. Australian Math. Soc. (Series A), 1982, 33, 1.

(19) U. Cyrus-Zetterstrom, 'Manual of Swedish Handweaving', translated by Alice Blomquist, Charles T. Branford Co., U.S.A., 1977, p. 19.

(20) H. Nisbet, p. 44.

(21) G.H. Oelsner, 'A Handbook of Weaves', Dover Publications, Inc., New York, 1952, p. 175-218.

(22) J.A. Hoskins, W.D. Hoskins, A.P. Street and R.G. Stanton. Ars Comb., 1982, 13, p. 3.

(23) W.D. Hoskins and R.S.D. Thomas. J.L.A.A., to appear.

(24) J.A. Hoskins, R.G. Stanton and A.P. Street. Cong. Num., 1983, 38, 3.

(25) P. Collingwood, 'The Techniques of Rug Weaving', Faber and Faber, London, 1968, p. 333.

(26) S.L. Gustafson. Ars Textrina, 1983, 1, 235.

Department of Computer Science,
University of Manitoba,
Winnipeg, Manitoba,
Canada R3T 2N2.

Department of Clothing and Textiles,
University of Manitoba,
Winnipeg, Manitoba,
Canada R3T 2N2.

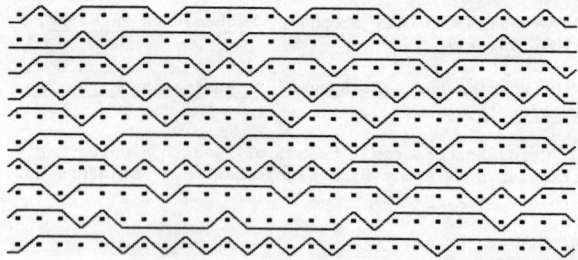

Figure 1

Cross-Sectional Representation
Single Layered Fabric

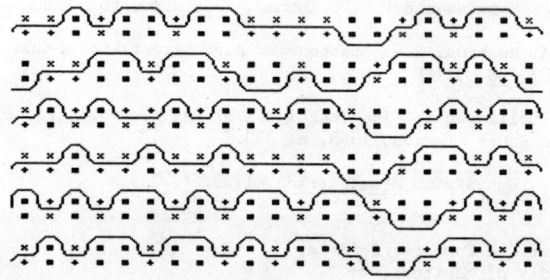

Figure 2

Cross-Sectional Representation
Double Layered Fabric

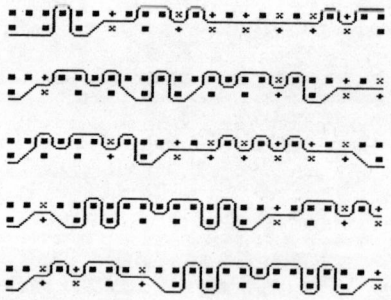

Figure 3

Cross-Sectional Representation
Double Layered Fabric
2:1 Warp Proportion

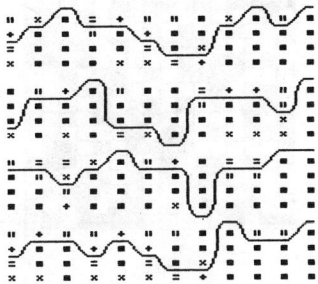

Figure 4

Cross-Sectional Representation
Four Layered Fabric

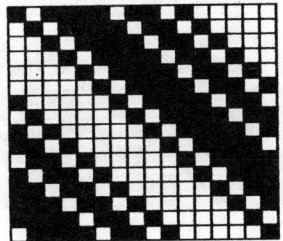

Figure 5

Twill

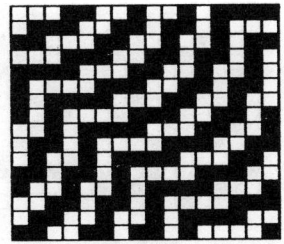

Figure 6

Color Alternate Twill

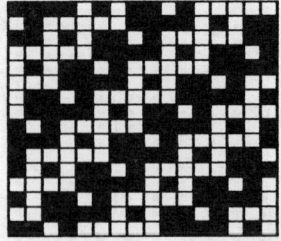

Figure 7
Twillin

Figure 8
Color Alternate Twillin

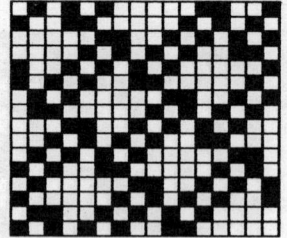

Figure 9
Compound Twillin
No Complementation

Figure 10

Compound Twillin
Single Complementation

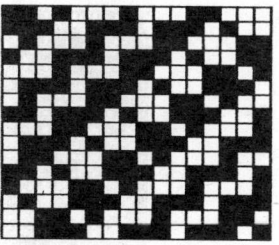

Figure 11

Compound Twillin
Double Complementation

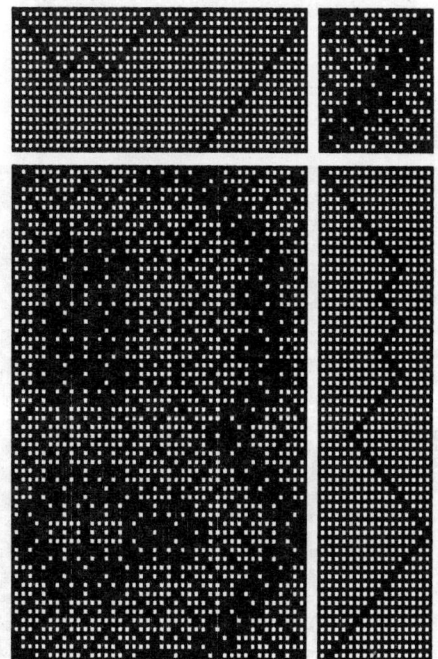

Figure 12

Design Created From Database Elements

Figure 13

Point Diagram As Design Profile

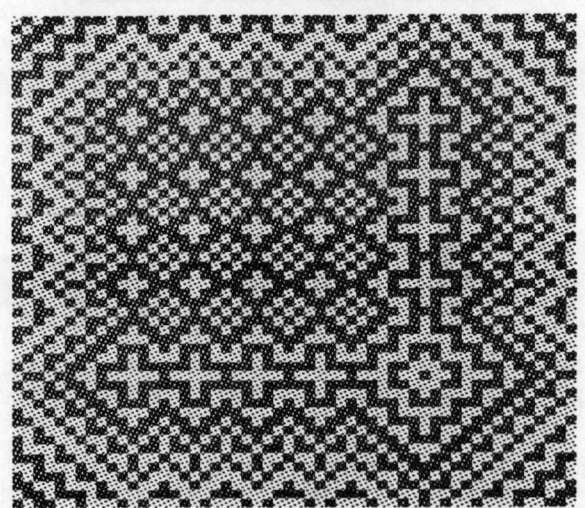

Figure 14

Block Substitution:

5 Shaft Satin Block
5 Shaft Sateen Counter-block

COMPUTER-AIDED PATTERNING OF SURFACE DESIGN

M. KOŠEK, B. KOŠKOVÁ

ABSTRACT

The regularity and the symmetry of textile patterns indicate
that the contents of the patterns are controlled by strict
physical laws and the theory of the two-dimensional crystals
can be applied without any limitations to the mathematical
description of the pattern symetry.This theory namely puts
restrictions on the possible forms of patterns, for a given
motif only 17 patterns exist with different symmetry. The
theory also gives the prescription how to prepare pattern of
a desirable symmetry. The contents of the motif are unlimited.

The possibility of general algorithm for the computer-aided
textile pattern designing follows from the strict mathematical description of surface textile patterns. In general
the design is ambiguous so that the algorithm should take
into accout all the possible patterns for a given motif.
The programmes based on this algorithm must consider the
present computer technical possibilities. The mathematical
theory of a surface pattern is outlined with reference to
the computer-aided patterns designing;the general algorithm
of an authomatic preparation of permitted pattern is briefly
described, the technical means of patterns realization by
computers are discussed and some obtained patterns are
presented.

1. INTRODUCTION

There are two extreme possibilities of the computer-aided
design of a surface textile pattern that are in principal
contradictory. The first method creates the pattern quite
randomly, for example in the simplest form as a line
consisting of small direct segments with both random lengths
and directions (1,2). This approach is suitable namely to
a product of a relatively small size. The second possibility
is based on the strict mathematical description of laws
valid for a usual regular pattern of products with a relatively large size.

The results of the random pattern designing are almost
independent on a designer, who, however, can choose the
properties of the random quantities. On the other hand,
the systematic pattern designing requires from the designer
to prepare a basic motif which can be systematically drawn
by a computer according to the prescribed requirements.
It is typical for both cases that once the designer made
the decision, the following drawing is quite independent on
them.

Between these two extreme cases there are many modifications
that use both the random generated elements and the basic
symmetry operations, for example a mirror reflection,
a translation, and a rotation. These symmetry operations,
however, are not made systemmaticaly by a computer, but
randomly or individually by a designer during the pattern
designing (2). This approach is usually called the interactive design.

The random and interactive compute-aided designing of
a surface pattern were intensively investigated in the past
years (2). To our knowledge a small attention was devoted
to the systemmatical design. It is a purpose of this work
to describe the mathematical fundamentals of the regular
surface patterns, which enable to prepare the general algorithm of a computer -aided design of any regular surface
pattern. The real possibilities of computer designing are
discussed and some results are shown. The work begins with
a simple introduction into the two-dimensional crystal-
lography.

2. DESCRIPTION OF A REGULAR SURFACE PATTERN

Some very simple schematic examples of surface patterns are
shown in Fig. 1. These designes are supposed to be spacially
unlimited. The more complicated pattern is in Fig. 2. From
the Figures two principal properties of the surface patterns
follow: periodicity and symmetry.

The pattern has a two-dimensional periodicity; it can be
made by repeated translations of a motif in two different
directions. The motif is a flower in Fig. 1a, the pair of
flowers in Fig.1b and 1c and a group of four flowers in
Fig. 1d. In the last three cases there are more possibilities
of a choice of the motif. In Fig. 2 the motif consists of
8 flowers.

The second general property is the symmetry, for example the
patterns in Fig. 1b is symmetric with respect to a line shown
in this Figure and the pattern in Fig. 1d can be turned
through 90°, 120°, and 270° with respect to some points and
the resulting position is by no means distinguishable from
the starting one. We shall formulate these properties
mathematically in agreement with the theory of two-
dimensional crystals (3).

2.1. Lattice

Let us choose an equivalent point in every motif of a pattern.
This point is unambiguously defined with respect to the
motif. These equivalent points form a lattice. Its general
form, for the pattern in Fig. 1a, is shown in Fig.3. This
lattice has the property that each point has the same
environment.

The vectors $\vec{a}$, $\vec{b}$ in the lattice are one possible choice of
elementary translations. Their linear combination defines
each point of the lattice. The parallelogram formed by

vectors $\vec{a}, \vec{b}$ is an elemetary cell. More choices of the elementary cell exist, some of them are in Fig. 3. If the lattice points are in the corners of the elementary cell only, this cell is called the primitive one. The second important choice is the elementary cell in addition with one point in its centre; it is called the centered one.

If we restrict only to the primitive cells, its possible forms are summarized in Table I. Every cell and lattice are described by two elementary translations a, b and an angle α between them. Only geometrical figures given in the Table I allow to cover a plane without both empty spaces and over-lappings.

It shoud be noted that in the literature (3) the Bravais lattices are currently used. Their elementary cells are a rhomboid, a primitive rectangle, a centered rectangle, a square, and a hexagon. The comparition of these two groups shows that the primitive cells are more suitable for an authomatized designing of patterns.

The choice of an elementary cell in a given lattice is in some extent artitrary, see Fig. 3. As the mutual correspond-ence between motifs and lattice points exists, the edges of the elementary cell in the lattice are the boundaries of the motif and the area of the elementary cell is the maximum one that the motif can occupy. Therefore in a given lattice the motifs of a different shape can be placed. This statesment has the meaning for the pattern design.

2.2. Symmetry elements

A general symmetry element is defined as an operation that transforms the pattern so that the final form is indistingui-shable from the starting one. The principal symmetry elements are a mirror axis, a n-fold point, a glide axis and a transla-tion. Both symbolic and geometrical reprezentation of these operations are in Table II. The mirror axis divides the pattern into two parts so that one part is the mirror reflection of the other. An example of this symmetry is the pattern in Fig. 1b. The n-fold point is the operation of the rotation arround a given point through the angle of $360°/n$. It can be shown (3) that in the case of an unlimitted pattern n can have only values 1, 2, 3, 4, and 6. The pattern of Fig. 1d exhibits an 4-fold point. The translation moves the pattern in a new position. The glide axis is a two step operation, the first step is a translation to a half distance between the neighbouring motifs; the second one is the mirror reflection this new pattern position with respect to the glide axis. An example is in Fig. 1c.

The symmetry of the pattern is the collection of these basic symmetry elements. For example the centre of symmetry is the combination of a 2-fold points and a mirror axis. From the mathematical point of view the combination of symmetry elements forms a group. The pattern can be described by two types of groups: a point group, and a plane group.

2.3. Point group

The collection of symmetry elements related to a point in
a body that transforms the body into the positions that
are indistinguishable from the original one, forms a point
group. The body can be the motif or the whole pattern. As
the symmetry operations also refer to the symmetry elements,
the new symmetry elements can be created. For example the
4-fold point creates the new mirror axis perpendicular to
the original one, if exists.

An example of a point group of a square is in Fig. 4a. This
point group is denoted by 4 mm. The symbol 4 means the
4-fold point, the first m denotes the system of mirror axes
perpendicular to edges, and the second m is another system
of mirror axes that lie in diagonals of the square. This is
the point group of the motif in Fig. 2, too.

In the plane only ten point groups exist (3)

$$1, \; 1m, \; 2, \; 2mm, \; 3, \; 3m, \; 4, \; 4mm, \; 6, \; 6mm \; .$$

The point group can contain symmetry elements of only two
types: the mirror axis and the n-fold point. If should be
noted that the motif, as an individual, can have other
symmetry elements too, for example the 5-fold point of
rotation. But when this motif is placed into a lattice, the
point group of the pattern created in this way must be
given in the list mentioned above. In the rhomboid lattice
irrespective of the 5-fold point motif symmetry, the point
group of the pattern should be 1, e.g. no symmetry.

Let us suppose that the symmetry of the motif is described
by any point group except the point group 1. In this case
a certain part can be found in the motif form which all other
parts can be made by symmetry operations included in the
point group. It is called the independent part of the motif.
With exception of the point group 1, e.g. the motif has some
symmetry; the independent part can occupy maximally half
of the motif area. When the motif has no allowed symmetry,
(the point group 1), the motif and its independent part are
identical. In some cases the independent part of the motif
is not defined by the point group only. The independent part
of the motifs in the patterns in Fig. 1 and 2 is one flower.
In all the cases the independent part has the same dimensions.

Only the design of the contents of the motif independent
part is a creating part of the designer's work. The other
parts of his work during the creation of a pattern are
routinery and can be in principal made for example by a
computer.

2.4. Plane group

The symmetry elements of the point group can be allocated
to every motif in a pattern. These symmetry elements
(n-fold point and mirror axis) create a pattern. The pattern
of all symmetry elements belonging to a given plane pattern

is called a plane group. In the literature (3) the term
space group is used but we mean that the term plane group
respects the reality of plane patterns in a better way. The
plane group contains the symmetry elements of the motif point
group and in some cases the glide axis defined in the part
2.2. All this symmetry elements are repeated two-dimensionally
by lattice constants. The plane group of Fig. 2 is in Fig.4b.

The plane group describes the symmetry of a surface pattern
completely. The given surface pattern contains all the symmetry elements of a certain plane group and no other ones.
The group theory proves that only 17 plane group exist, 13
of them contain only the symmetry elements of the motif
point group and in the remaining 4 groups there are the glide
axes in addition. In these last 4 cases the motif independent
part depends both on the symmetry elements of the point group
and on the glide axes.

This result has an important practical meaning. For a given
independent part of the motif only 17 surface patterns with
different symmetry described by a plane group are possible.
Four simple examples of them are in Fig. 1 and one more
complicated example is in Fig. 2. The lattice constants
depend on the shape and the dimensions of the motif. No restrictions are laid on the contents of the motif independent
part.

3. BASIC IDEAS OF A GENERAL ALGORITHM

The purpose of the computer-aided designing of surface
patterns is to transform a given independent part of a motif
into other parts and to translate the whole motif to all
equivalent points of a given lattice. Before writing a programme some general problems should be solved, namely a
number and forms of independent parts of a motif in a given
lattice, constants of an elementary cell and lattice for
a given shape of a motif, and formulae for symmetry operations.
In this chapter the solution of this problem is briefly
described.

For the design or more generally for the synthesis of a surface pattern, general well-known rules are valid. The analysis
of a given surface pattern is straigtforward, unambiguous,
just one plane group exists. The synthesis is ambiguous.
Seventeen patterns with a different symmetry can be found to
a given independent part of a motive. Furthermore, the
patterns with a higher symmetry can have some modifications.

3.1. The independent motif part

The independent part of the motif was defined in section
2.3. This depends on the symmetry elements of a plane
group in the general case and it was found for every lattice
and cell listed in Table I. As an example the motif independent parts in the square lattice are in Fig. 5. There are
shown as hatched areas. The Figure contains the independent
parts belonging to lower symmetry too, for example 2-fold

point, because this symmetry element is included in the place group. Only three last independent parts in Fig. 5 correspond to the plane groups of a square lattice. Taking this situation into account the possible number of patterns for a given independent part is greater than 17.

3.2. A choice of a lattice

To a given independent motif part and a chosen plane group symmetry an elementary primitive cell be found which is listed in Table I with the use of Fig. 5 and similar Figures for other lattices. The choice of the lattice is ambiguous. For example the square and the rhombic lattices can be found for the square shape motive in Fig. 5. The values of lattice constants are easily computed from an element cell by simple geometrical considerations.

3.3. Mathematical description of symmetry operations

The symmetry operations (a n-fold point, a mirror axis, and a glide axis) transforms every point of the independent motive part into equivalent points of its dependent parts. The translations move the motif as a whole into the equivalent positions in the lattice. The mathematical formulaes for symmetry operations can be easily derived using the analytic geometry, hence they are not given here.

4. REALIZATION OF THE ALGORITHM

Technical possibilities of the present computers do not allow to realize the algorithm outlined in the preceding section in its general form for a general motif. The main restriction refers to the contents of the motif. Surface patterns can be prepared easily by a computer only in the case of a very simple form of the independent part of the motif.

Two different well-known graphical methods can be used:
a) a vector generated image on a memory screen (a memory oscillograph),
b) a point generated image on a standard screen (a television system).

4.1. Principles, properties and limitations

The memory oscillograph allows to display a pattern when the motif independent part is represented by broken lines. Choosing a sufficient number of segments on the broken line, its direct sections may be made sufficiently short so that the independent part consisting of rather complicated general system of lines can be treated by a computer without a distortion. The independent part of the motif is decomposed into a system of points that are read by a standard input device of a computer.

The television method decomposes the pattern into a system of small areas of typical dimensions about 0,5 mm depending on the technical parameters. The details with a critical dimension of this order or a less order cannot be shown.

52

Namely the lines are approximated by a step system of points.
If dimensions of the motif are reduced during the preparation
of a pattern, some details of the original form of the motif
would be generally lost. If a pattern with many motifs should
be displayed on the screen, the individual motifs   exhibit
little details. The motif independent part is prepared in
the form of a picture and a special equipment transforms
its contents into digital data.

4.2. Comparison of methods

The possibilities of the two discussed methods are contradictory in some sense. The memory oscillograph displays the
lines by sufficient accuracy, but cannot display the areas.
The television system displays large areas very well, but
loses some details where lines or other parts of an image
with at least one small dimension should be displayed. The
memory method requires the decomposition of the motif
idependent part into a system of points, but these input data
use standard input devices of a computer. The television
system treats the motif independent part in a natural form,
but requires a special input device. Two programmes for the
surface pattern design based on the general algorithm
were prepared.

4.3. Programmes

Both the programmes can form a surface pattern with any
possible plane group of symmetry, see part 2.4. The contents
of the displayed pattern is controlled by a type and a form
of a lattice, by number of motifs on the screen, by a form
and dimensions of boundaries of the motif independent part,
and by a plane group of symmetry. From these data the
programmes compute the element cell of the lattice. The
contents of the motif independent part are treated by two
ways.

The memory oscillograph method treats the motifs in the
form of lines only. The lines in the motif independent part
are approximated by broken ones and the points at which
the lines are broken define the independent part for the
programme.

The programme reads coordinates of these points and transforms them into equivalent positions in depending parts of
the motif for each symmetry element of the motif included
in the prescribed plane group of symmetry. Using the lattice
translations the points of the reference cell can be transformed into the other cells on the screen. Finally, the
corresponding groups of points transformed from the independent
part are connected in a given order by straight lines and
the pattern is displayed on the memory oscillograph or
sketched by a plotter.

The television system method forms the surface pattern from
a system of small squares with the defined brightness. In
our realization the screen contained 256 x 256 squares. The
independent motif part, which occupy only a small part of

53

the screen, is decomposed by a special input device into
the squares (in our programme 64 x 64 squares maximally)
and the brightness of these squares is read.

The programme computes the brightness of each square
supposing that the coordinate of its centre is equal to
its indexes. After the input data are read, the brightness
of the independent part in the reference motif is known.
The programme transforms the coordinates of the squares of
the independent part into the dependent parts of the
reference motif in the pattern for every given element of the
motif symmetry.

In general the transformed square does not exactly overlap
ahother square in the dependent part of the reference motif.
The programme takes it into accout so that the only portion
of the original square brightness is added to brightness of
the not exactly covered square. This portion is equal to the
relative value of overlaping these two squares. The same
algorithm determines the brightness in squares of other
motif, once the brithtness in all the squares of the reference motif is known.

From the description of the algorithm follows that the
contrast of the dependent part in the reference motif is
somewhat worse than in its independent part. This relation
also valid for the contrast of reference motif and the other
motifs in the pattern.

4.4. Applications

The programme for the memory oscillograph method was prepared
and tested on the computer ICL 4-72 and the patterns were
displayed on the memory oscillograph Tektronix with the
possibility to make hard copies.

The digital form of the motif independent part for the
television system method was prepared on the equipment of
Czechoslovak Academy of Sciences. The same equipment was
also used for an inspection of the prepared patterns. The
computations were made on a computer similar to IBM 360. The
digital data were stored on a magnetic tape.

5. EXAMPLES OF COMPUTER-AIDED SURFACE PATTERNS

Patterns were prepared by both programmes. Because of
a difficult reproducibility of the patterns prepared by the
television system method and their somewhat lower quality
only some results from the memory oscillograph method are
presented. Interesting results are seen for a great number
of the motif independent parts and their increasing dimensions
with respect to the lattice.

Fig. 2 shows the pattern of high symmetry in the square
lattice. The patterns of high symmetry in the hexagonal
lattice are in Fig. 6 - 8. As it is seen from Fig. 6, the
very simple independent motif parts were used, the pattern
situated higher has the point group 6 and the point group of

54

the lower one is 6mm. The patterns in Fig. 7 were obtained
by increasing the dimensions of the independent part twice
while the lattice did not change. Finally, in Fig. 8 there
are the patterns with the independent parts magnified 4
times. If the independent part of the motif is also outside
the boundaries of the **elementary cell, as in Fig. 7 and 8,**
a quantitatively new pattern may appear, as it may be seen
in these Figures.

6. CONCLUSION

The computer-aided pattern designing can in principle be
used by two ways:

a) by designing a real pattern of a chosen symmetry and
   a lattice from a given independent part of motif that
   respects the dimension of the lattice,

b) by designing an abstract pattern by increasing the
   dimension of an independent part of a motif while the
   lattice dimensions remain constant.

The first possibility allows the designer to transfer to a
a computer the mechanical part of his work connected with
drawing the motifs into the pattern and allows him to devote
himself to designing the independent part of the motif. The
second possibility enables to prepare the different abstract
patterns from a given independent part. The details of the
independent part in this case are not important.

At present both the possibilities are limited to the simple
independent parts as a result of a technical equipment of
a computer. It can be expected that these limitations will be
not so strict in the future.

REFERENCES

(1) J. Vlietster and R.F. Wieling. 'Principes of Computer
     Aided Design ', North Holland, 1973.

(2) W.K. Glioi. 'Interactive Computer Graphics. Data,
     Structures, Algorithmus, Languages ', New Jersey, 1979.

(3) C. Kittel. 'Introduction to Solid State Physics ,
     John Willey and Sons, New York, 1956, 2nd edition.

College of Mechanical and Textile Engineering
46 1 17 Liberec, Hálkova 6.
Czechoslovakia

Table I. List of lattices and primitive cells

Lattice	Geometrical constants	Point group
rhomboidal	$a \neq b$, $\alpha \neq 90°$	1m
rhombic	$a \neq b$, $\alpha \neq 90°$, $\alpha \neq 60°$	2mm
rectangular	$a \neq b$, $\alpha = 90°$	2mm
square	$a = b$, $\alpha = 90°$	4mm
hexagonal	$a = b$, $\alpha = 60°$	6mm

Table II. Symbols of symmetry operations

Symmetry operation	Symbol	Graphical symbol
1-fold point	1	none
2-fold point	2	⬮
3-fold point	3	▲
4-fold point	4	■
6-fold point	6	⬢
mirror axis	m	▬▬▬
glide axis	g	--------
translation	none	none

Figure captions

Fig. 1. Simplified patterns of low symmetry:
a) no symmetry, b) mirror axis, c) glide axis,
d) 4-fold point.
In parts b) and c) one position of axis is shown.

Fig. 2. Simplified pattern of high symmetry - the point
group 4mm.

Fig. 3. Definition of a lattice and a primitive **elementary
cell**

Fig. 4. Examples of a point group (a) and a plane group (b).

Fig. 5. Independent parts of a square shape motif.

Fig. 6. Patterns with high symmetry - point groups:
(a) 6, (b) 6mm

Fig. 7. Abstract patterns with the independent part
magnified twice.

Fig. 8. Abstract patterns with the independent part
magnified 4 times.

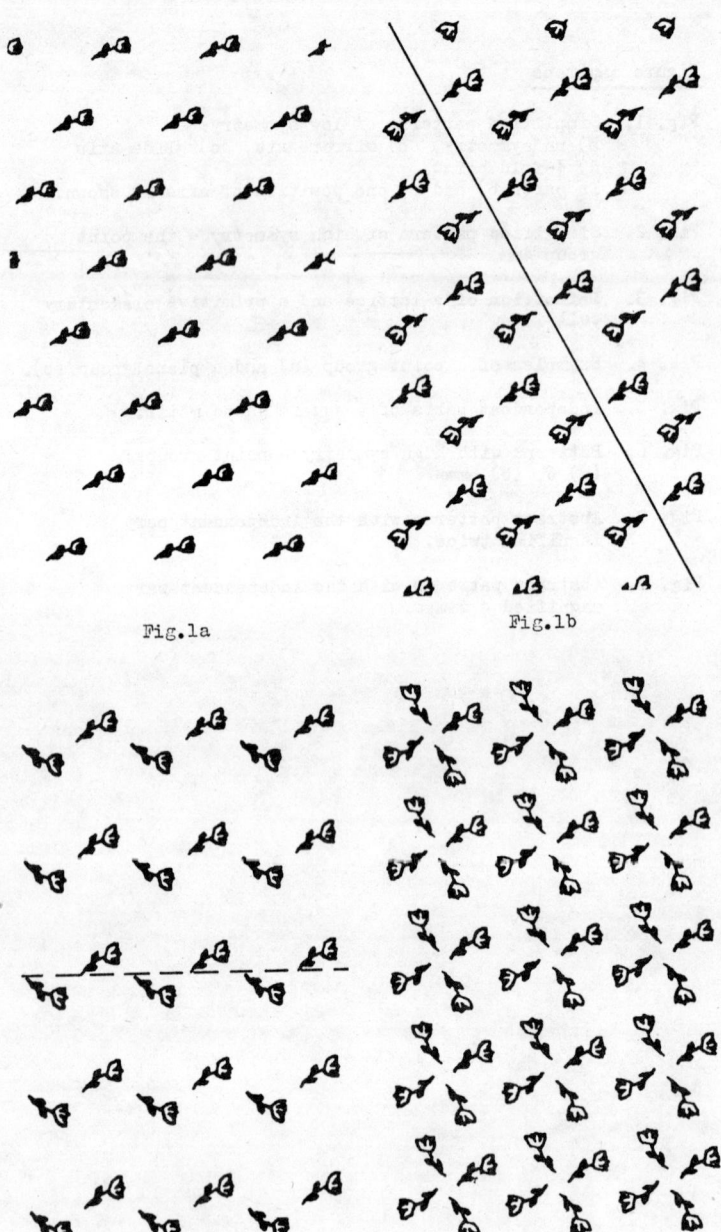

Fig.1a

Fig.1b

Fig.1c

Fig.1d

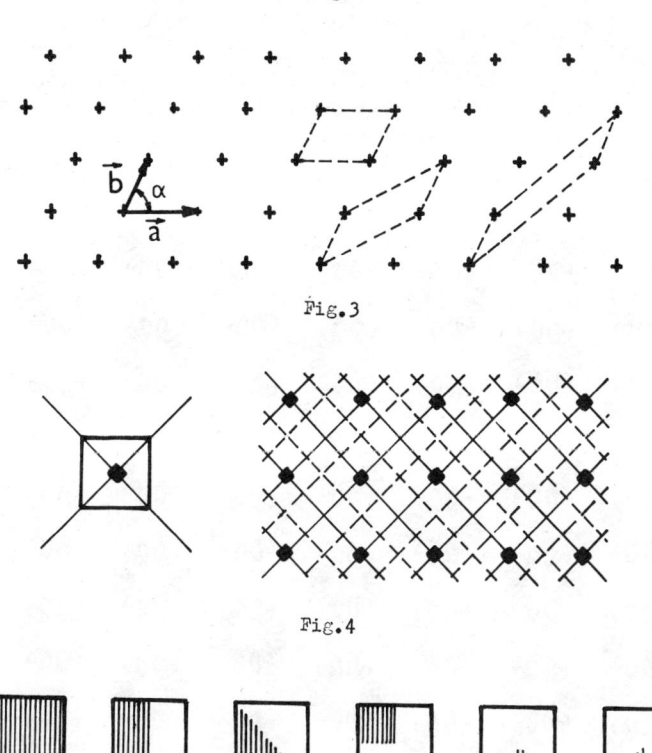

Fig.2

Fig.3

Fig.4

Fig.5

Fig. 6a

Fig. 6b

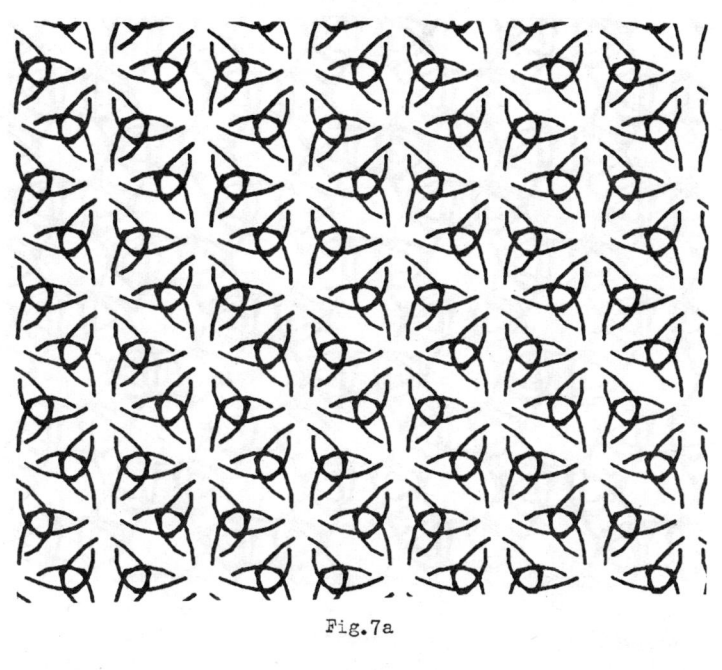

Fig.7a

Fig.7b

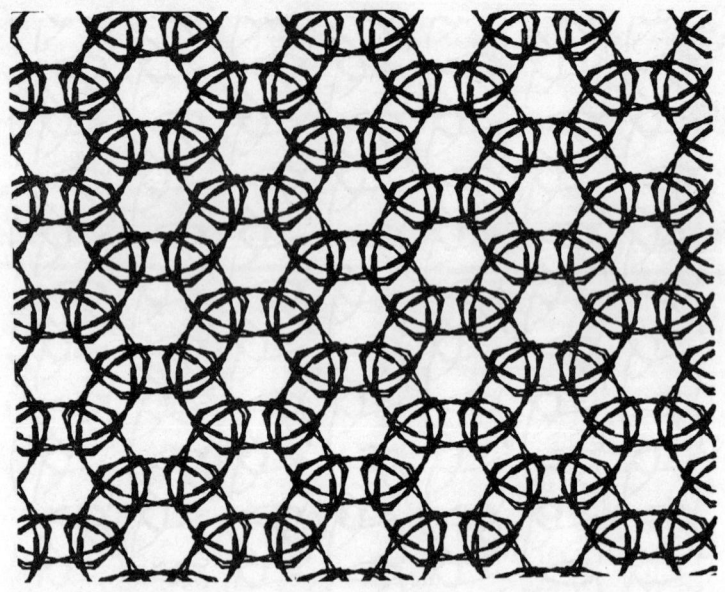

Fig.8a

Fig.8b

A COMPUTER SIMULATION OF A DYE EFFECT ON BLEND YARN WEAVES

Brian J. Hill

ABSTRACT

The computer program was developed to simulate the colour
effects which were achieved by cross-printing flax/
polyester fabrics with a reactive/disperse dye system.
The paper outlines, the initial textile production and the
effects achieved, the development of the computer program
to simulate these effects and how the program was used to
produce new "fabrics". The difficulties which occurred in
operation are stated and solutions to some of these
problems are indicated. The next stages of development of
the system are outlined. Samples of fabric and the computer
simulation will be shown at the conference.

1. INTRODUCTION

It is well known that cross-dyed effects can be achieved by
combining two or more fibre types in a fabric construction
and then dyeing the fabric in a single bath or multiple
baths with a mixture of classes of dyes, each dye class being
substantive only to one of the fibres in the pre-selected
combination. The effect produced depends on the distribution
and proportions of the different fibres, the fabric
construction and the colours selected for dyeing. The fabric
production used this knowledge but the fabrics were printed
using a single screen with a print paste containing the
different classes of dye.

The project concentrated on yarns spun on a semi-worsted or
long staple system made from blends of flax and polyester or
viscose and polyester. These combinations and the method of
yarn production were chosen firstly because blend yarns spun
on this type of system exhibit a characteristic defined fibre
grouping which is utilised in the final product and secondly
these particular combinations of fibres are suitable for
cross-printing (cross-printing is the name given to the effect
achieved by printing rather than dyeing with combined dye
classes on fabrics containing mixtures of fibre types).

2. TEXTILE PRODUCTION

A restricted series of both plain and slub yarns were spun
mainly on a conventional dry spinning system ranging in count
from 25 tex to 175 tex and varying in blend from 15/85 to
85/15. Within this series a limited range of yarns were
deliberately constructed so that the intimate type of blend
normally associated with long staple systems was not produced.
This was achieved by spinning the yarn from undoubled
assembled slivers or by spinning conventionally produced
slivers on a long staple machine which is capable of injecting
fibres in various places along the length of a yarn and hence
provide the potential for gross differential colour effects.

Only plain weave constructions were woven because it was
considered that the colour effects, the yarn characteristics
and the applied surface pattern should be the main design
elements. At a later stage some knitted fabrics were
produced.

After weaving the fabrics were processed prior to printing.
The fabrics were printed with a reactive/disperse dye system.
The paste containing both the reactive dye which is
substantive to the cellulose component and the disperse dye
which is substantive to the polyester component together with
the necessary printing assistants. Some care was taken with
the selection of the reactive dye to ensure that it was
compatible with the disperse dye. In special cases where
high light fastness was a requirement, then the range of
suitable dyestuffs was further reduced. With certain colour
combinations it was essential that the residual traces of
disperse dye were removed and in these cases it was necessary
to use a special range of disperse dyes. The different dyes
on each fibre produce colour effects. To achieve the most
marked colour effects it was best to use contrasting colours.
With fabrics made from plain yarns, the choice of colour for
each fibre component of the blend was not critical. However,
with slub yarns it was better to select the dyes so that the
lighter colour was substantive to the slub component thereby
highlighting it against the mainly darker contrasting colour
of the background. The fabrics were dried, cured and washed
off to remove the non-substantive dye and chemicals.

The designs selected for printing contained elements of mass,
fine line and texture to see how each of these elements would
be affected by the combination of fibre proportion and
distribution, fabric construction and colour. They were all
"single" colour designs (ie those which would normally be
produced in one colour using a single screen). However, the
use of a single screen with a blend yarn fabric and a dye
paste containing a mixture of dye classes allows for the
production of a two or three colour effect. The process is
not limited to single screen designs, nor is it necessary
when using more than one screen to apply colour to more than
one component of the blend or mixture or to produce cross-
printing effects from each screen. A range of plain weave
fabrics had been produced which varied in yarn count, yarn
character, fibre distribution, fibre proportions and on these
fabrics designs had been printed which examined the effect of
the yarn characteristic on the elements of mass, fine line
and texture. The distribution of colour, which varied
according to the yarn parameters just described, produced an
overall effect of scintillation. Having established some of
the effects which could be achieved and how each parameter
played its part in bringing about this scintillant effect,
the question was how to proceed. Should more yarns be spun,
fabrics woven and printed and after examination, continue with
this process.

When considered in detail it was a massive task and not a
sensible line of approach. Therefore it was decided to
attempt to produce a computer program which would simulate
some of the effects which had been achieved and from this
create new "fabrics" by changing some of the yarn and fabric
parameters. The equipment used could not superimpose printed
designs on fabrics, but it could reproduce overall colour
effects and the distribution of these effects would hopefully
give us an indication of the scintillation.

3. COMPUTER PROGRAM

The equipment used was a Research Machines 380Z type microcomputer with a capacity of 56K equipped with 5¼" "floppy"
disc drives, high resolution graphics and a colour board
linked to an Hitachi TV colour monitor. The input to the
micro was through a keyboard. The total cost of the equipment was about £4000. This is not a high powered system and
therefore limited the amount of information which could be
stored and retrieved, but nevertheless it will be shown that
with such equipment it is possible to achieve simulation of
colour effects on woven fabrics. Initially we used the
colour monitor alone because it was more versatile and it was
quicker and easier to change colours. Problems of obtaining
exact photographic representation from the screen were not
envisaged and it was only at a later stage that a plotter was
used in conjunction with the colour monitor.

A program was developed which could produce six simple woven
constructions:

(a) plain weave
(b) 2/2 twill
(c) 2/3 twill
(d) 2/1 twill
(e) 2/2 cord
(f) 2/2 rib

The data necessary to draw the correct weave pattern was held
in data sets and transferred to array form as and when needed.
In order to simulate any pattern, the screen was divided up
into a number of rows and columns which would eventually
represent the warp and weft threads. The thickness of both
warp and weft threads was not fixed but could vary about a
mean within certain limits depending on the standard
deviation of the yarn count. For this simulation only plain
yarns were considered and as yet slub yarns have not been
reproduced.

The colouring of the threads depended on the colouring of the
individual pixels. The intensity range of each pixel depends
on its size in bits, in this case two bits per pixel. Three
intensities were made available for colouring the warp and
weft threads separately and the fourth the background colour.
The distribution of colour within a yarn depended not only on
the proportions of each fibre, but also on the distribution
of each fibre within the yarn. A sub-routine was set up
which took both fibre proportion and fibre distribution into
account.

The method for doing this was to consider each and every pixel on the screen (318 x 191) in turn. Hence there was a considerable delay in producing a complete picture. In the original system there were only three colours available for colouring the yarns, but at a later stage the palette was increased to 256 colours, but because of the amount of space taken up on the discs by information about warp and weft yarns, blend proportions and fibre distributions, only four could be produced on the screen at any one time. This, however, is not a problem in the case where single screen prints using a two-colour dye paste system are used.

During the production of a pattern the program could be interrupted and new colour data inserted and the program allowed to continue.

Using this program on the relatively cheap and simple equip- ment, it was possible to reproduce some of the colour effects created on the printed fabrics. The program was then used to create new "fabrics" and display these on the monitor. Those which gave a pleasing effect were photographed and the relevant information about yarn, fabric and colour was noted. The practical simulation of the fibre distribution was reproduced as closely as possible bearing in mind that there are limitations in production methods. The yarn was produced, fabric woven and printed. The scintillant effects produced on these fabrics were very similar to those which had been created by the computer program. A number of the more interesting "fabrics" were stored on a separate program and were available for immediate transfer to the monitor. This speeded up the simulation process for demonstration purposes as it by-passed the laborious building up of a "fabric" pixel by pixel. Faster methods for the creation of new "fabrics" are being investigated.

Photographs of the fabric simulation taken from the television monitor did not truly represent the colour effects displayed on the screen. Therefore in these cases where interesting colour effects were found it was decided to produce hard copy on a plotter. However, the production of good quality hard copy proved to be extremely difficult.

A new program was designed to provide a hard copy of the design which had been created on the monitor.

This involved reading each screen intensity (colour) from the screen memory and to use this value to select the respective pen colour. The colour was then plotted using an appropriate increment (ie pen step size).

Two methods of plotting were attempted:

(i)   Plot each point and change the pen type as the
      colour changes. One problem was that the plotting
      mechanism had to constantly select pens and as the pens
      worked wet-on-wet some streaking was induced on the hard
      copy drawing.

(ii) Plot one colour at a time. This allowed the colour to
      dry before the next colour was plotted. This method was
      faster than that above and was subsequently used.

In both cases the major problem was a "spreading effect".
This was caused by ink spread on the paper when the pen was
raised or lowered. This is illustrated in Fig 1.

Fig 1 (a)

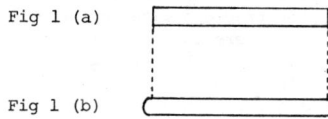

Fig 1 (b)

l(a) shows the desired plot
l(b) gives the actual plot

It can be seen that when the pen was raised or lowered at
each end of a plot the ink spreads slightly. Therefore it
was at its most extreme when the intensity or colour
constantly changed as in the case when there were equal
proportions of each fibre in the warp and weft yarns and the
fibres were intimately blended. This produced the worst
quality hard copy output, whereas simulating fabrics
containing two or more fibre classifications but each yarn
being spun from one type produced the best quality hard copy
output. Nevertheless even the best simulation whilst
conveying colour effects did not really simulate a textile.

4. SOLUTION TO SPREADING OF THE INK

An algorithm was designed to examine intensities before
plotting. If the intensity was the same as the previous then
the pen continued to draw, but if a new intensity was read
then the plotter stopped just short of the required position
to allow for ink spread. Thus by looking at the next
intensity value before plotting it was possible to adjust
the plotting increment (ie a pixel representation) to ensure
that overlapping of the colour was reduced to a minimum or
eliminated. Whenever an intensity changed, the increment
before lifting the pen could be reduced to allow for ink-
spread in the plus x direction and when lowering it with a
different pen it could be increased to allow for ink spread
in the minus x direction. This is illustrated in Fig 2.

Fig 2 (a)    Normal plot (takes no account for spreading).

Fig 2 (b)    Incremental plot compensating for spreading.

An adjustment can also be made to the increment between lines (ie in the y direction). This allows lines to be drawn close together to produce a solid colour effect or separated leaving gaps between each line. In neither case is actual yarn appearance simulated, but textural effects are achieved. The best textural effects are created by plotting the intensities as dots, but this creates problems with the types of pen which can be used. At present there is a restriction of the quality of the hard copy or on the number of colours which can be plotted. With liquid ink pens exact colours can be mixed, but the pens produce poor quality hard copy, due to limitations on the speed of plotting and needle sizes, fibre tipped pens tend to produce a better quality hard copy. The best quality was achieved using Calcomp Ceramicron pens with a very fine tip. Using these pens it was not possible to mix colours and therefore there was a restriction on the number of colours which could be used for hard copy.

Good quality hard copy would come from an ink jet plotter, but this would require rewriting the program for a much more expensive computer system, or trying to interface the two systems. It would also solve the problem of the limitation in the number of colours which could be used to produce good quality hard copy.

Creation of a quality hard copy with the appearance of a textile is important if the paper representation is to be used to demonstrate the type of fabric and colourways which can be produced from specified yarn type. As yet this problem has not been solved, but at least the textural effects which have been produced go some way towards giving the appearance of a textile.

5.   CONCLUSIONS

The program designed for the Research Machines 380Z micro-computer simulates the scintillant effects produced on cross-printed fabrics. The display on the monitor gives a very good visual representation. However, the production of a good quality representative hard copy is difficult. Photographs, especially slides, taken from the monitor are not representative of the colour effects because the sensitivity of colour film does not correspond to the sensitivity of the human eye, especially in the blue/UV area. The colour film is sensitive to UV, the human eye is not. So, if a dye emits radiation in the UV area it will record as blue on colour film so distorting the colour balance of the photograph.

The hard copy produced on a plotter is of variable quality
because of the types of pen used and in some cases the
limitations in the number of colours which can be used.
The copy did not produce a simulated textile, but it was
possible to create textural effects which may possibly be
able to be used to eventually recreate textile simulation.

ACKNOWLEDGEMENTS

The author wishes to acknowledge the facilities put at his
disposal in the Faculty of Art and Design at the
Ulster Polytechnic.

School of Textiles/Fashion
Ulster Polytechnic
Art & Design
Belfast
N. IRELAND

THEORETICAL AND PRACTICAL CONSIDERATIONS OF AN INTEGRATED CAD/CAM SYSTEM FOR FABRIC DECORATION AND PRODUCTION

R. E. Griffith, R. G. Pongrass and W. B. Wilson

ABSTRACT

Embroidery has a long history as a means of fabric decoration. It is both aesthetically and technically demanding in its effective execution. The variety of machinery used extends the complexity of creating and implementary embroidery designs. An integrated CAD/CAM computer system has been developed which integrates the tools used for design and manufacturing such that the more tedious aspects of the process are eliminated. The software in the system is user oriented, enabling enhancement of creativity whilst increasing productivity. The main problems which are addressed by the system are described together with the theoretical basis for the system design. Software features are described in relation to the problems they solve. Application of the CAD/CAM system to other fabric forming processes is under development and the direction of this development is described relative to the embroidery system.

1. HISTORY OF EMBROIDERY

Embroidery is a decorative art. The origins of embroidery are thought to be in the East, in China and India. Western countries introduced embroidery through trading with the East, with records of embroidery in ancient Egypt. It would appear that the Jews learnt embroidery whilst in Egypt, taking that knowledge with them in the exodus. The Greeks and Romans acquired embroidery through their conquests. Then the early Christians started to use embroidery on church fabrics. The Mohammedans took up the use of embroidery in approximately the seventh century. From the ninth to the sixteenth century the main use for embroidery was for ecclesiastical purposes with various countries introducing embroidery and being prominent in its production. This ranged from Italy in the tenth century, England in the twelfth century, the Swiss in the thirteenth, France in the fifteenth and Germany in the nineteenth century.

2. EMBROIDERY PRODUCTION

2.1 Creation of the Design

Embroidery design is multi-dimensional in its potential creativity and its demands. Its structure is three dimensional, with stitching effects permitting the designer to create an impression of depth. As a textile process it is used for embellishment of base materials; creation of lace structures by chemically etching the base material; and production of simulated lace by creating holes with boring effects. In all instances the method of embroidery is as critical as the design itself, especially in the creation of lace where the embroidery finally creates the fabric structure.

In creating an embroidery the designer has to consider not only the design itself but also those tools with which he will create that design. These include the selection of background material, colours, thread types and thicknesses, and the texture of the finished product. Added to these are the specific techniques such as using appliques, creating eyelets, sequins, chenile and other specific effects.

When considering the actual stitching of embroidery, the number and types of stitching effects are limitless. Whereas designs utilise to a great extent the fundamental stitching methods, centuries of embroidery have created many individual stitching techniques.

Embroidery can be applied to piece goods or continuous fabric. It is used in the fashion industry for garments, for furnishings, for emblems and identification, throughout the world.

2.2 Machine Embroidery

Machine embroidery commenced in approximately 1865 when Isaak Groebli invented and produced the original Schiffli machine, a hand and foot powered apparatus. In approximately 1880 he added to this a Jacquard-type mechanism, called the Automat. Whereas embroidery has a long history, machine embroidery is thus relatively new. From the late nineteenth century through to the present time the major exponents of machine embroidery have been the Swiss and the Austrians. In these countries there are schools for training embroidery designers and punchers. However, as recently as twenty years ago, students in some of these schools were forbidden from taking notes in case the information and skills of embroidery design were transmitted to someone outside that country. Even today there are virtually no texts or papers on the subject of embroidery design.

2.3 Present Methods

The sequence involved in the traditional method of producing embroidery patterns is shown in Figure I. The design starts with a sketch or idea, which is then turned into artwork on a one to one scale with the finished product. When this artwork is approved and any modifications completed an enlargement is produced in 6X scale. It is not uncommon to find that where fine detail is required in the embroidery that a 9X scale enlargement is made of those sections. For embroidery of continuous fabric the scaled-up design can be extremely large, often several metres long. When the enlargement is complete the stitches to be embroidered are individually drawn on the enlargement in the desired positions. Since some designs can extend to one hundred and twenty thousand (120,000) stitches, the complexity and time consuming nature of drawing these individual stitches can be appreciated. The person drawing these stitches must also keep count of the number of stitches that have been drawn so that a price can be established for the design.

The enlargement, complete with stitches and instructions is
then passed on to the puncher. The puncher places this
enlargement on a mechanical digitising machine which
generally has a rollover facilty whereby these very large
patterns are progressively passed over the surface of the
digitiser from one roller to another. The puncher must
mechanically digitise the end points of each stitch, such
that the stitch is generated between those points. The
digitiser motion is reflected in a mechanism which produces
a Jacquard card and in most cases is able to stitch a
sample concurrently with the punching. Typically a top
class puncher will be able to produce up to 8,000 stitches
per day. When the punching is complete the roll of
Jacquard card must be checked visually and if a sample
has not been produced in parallel on the punching machine
then the Jacquard card must be run on a sampling machine
to provide a sample of the pattern for checking.

Operation of the punching machine is a physically demanding
activity. Whilst the digitising machine has counterbalances
and in recent times electrical assistance, the operation of
the digitiser mechanism, which is similar to a pantograph,
requires physical strength and endurance. The accuracy and
repeatability of punching is very dependent on the physical
condition of the puncher.

2.4 Embroidery Machinery Today

From the original Schiffli machine, embroidery machines have
developed in two directions.   There has been continual
development of Schiffli machinery for large scale and large
size of manufacturing, and development of multihead
embroidery machines employing individual sewing heads for
smaller scale and size of embroidery. Table I lists
machine types, manufacturers and types of control codes
required for these machines.   Apart from those listed,
there are several brands of machines still in use though
not being produced.

3. STRUCTURAL CONSIDERATIONS IN EMBROIDERY

In the embroidery process, the method of application is as
critical as the design itself.   Whereas in weaving and
knitting a design is mapped onto a grid, with some
compensations for the fabric structure, in embroidery
the problem really begins on completion of the design.
The application of embroidery is not a continuous process
but a batch process, which requires that the design be
broken down into sections, these sections being determined
by change in colour, sequence of sections, covering of
joining stitches between sections and matching pattern
in motifs which have been broken into sections.

Factors which must be considered include:-

(a) Base Material Extensibility

Embroidery is created on a base material. The physical

properties of the base materials can vary greatly across the
broad spectrum of textile fabrics.   For the application of
the embroidery, the base material is put under tension in a
frame, which is then positioned in the machine for the
needle penetrations. When the base material is released
from the frame and is permitted to return to its unelongated
state, the embroidery is forced to follow the contraction of
the base material.   Thus, if a design has been applied
which appears to be correct on the stretched fabric, on
shrinkage it will more than likely distort. Further,
dependent on the fabric structure, the base material
usually has different rates of extensibility in each of the
co-ordinate axes and so the design may very well distort
unequally relative to those axes.

(b)   Base Material Structure

Woven or knitted base materials can vary considerably in
tightness or density.   The positioning of stitches
relative to the grid of the base material may lead to
stitches falling into holes and disappearing from the
design.

(c)   Machine Geometry

In Schiffli machines, the shuttle which contains the bobbin
thread moves in a fixed direction with each needle penetration.
If the direction of frame movement is opposed to the direction
of shuttle movement, this constitutes a restriction on the
release of bobbin thread and so effects the stitch production.

(d)   Change in Stitch Direction

The feeding of top thread and bobbin thread varies as a
function of the type of stitch which is being applied. For
example, a geflect is a type of running stitch used for
filling areas, which creates a woven effect. The stitches
applied in a geflect continue in one direction, with reversal
of that direction only on reaching the shape boundary of the
design.   This provides an even tension on both top and
bottom threads.   However, in the case of a steil, which is
a satin stitch type with short stitch length and reversal
of stitch direction between alternate stitches, threads are
subjected to tension reversals from the reversals in stitch
direction.

(e)   Thread Thickness

The selection of thread thickness determines the fineness of
detail which can be achieved in the representation of the
design.   Since embroidery amounts to building a surface
cover using stitches, the thickness of the thread determines
the spacing between the stitches.   The objective with
embroidery is to produce the best effect (coverage) with
the fewest stitches (least cost) within the desired quality
range.   Schiffli machines usually use heavier threads
than multihead machines, but in each case, compensation
is necessary for various thread counts.

(f) Stitch Density

Cyclic speed in embroidery is independent of stretch length,
except for extreme cases, where the machine is slowed down
for abnormally long stitches. Thus productivity in terms
of apparent coverage increases with stitch length. However,
longer stitches in fact have less covering power than short
stitches, and will need to be placed closer together. This
in term may lead to bunching and thread breakage. A
compromise must therefore be reached in terms of stitch length
and stitch density in order to optimise aesthetic and
productivity requirements.

4. CED SYSTEM DESIGN PHILOSOPHY

The design philosophy for the embroidery CAD/CAM system
was developed from the previous experiences of the system
designers in the field of engineering CAD/CAM. The main
points of the design philosophy were:-

(a) A Tool for the User

The system as a whole was considered as a tool for embroidery
design and manufacturing. Every effort was made to
minimise the need for computer specific knowledge.

(b) Different Users/Different Uses

To be effective the system had to respond to the different
methods of operation utilised in different countries. For
example, embroidery is a major industry in Switzerland,
Austria, France, Italy, Japan and the USA. Each of these
countries has a different approach to designing and
manufacturing embroidery, thus the system had to be flexible
to adapt to different users. Also, since embroidery is
extremely varied in its applications, varying from lace
through to emblems produced on a variety of Schiffli and
multihead machines, it was essential that the systems be
flexible enough to cater to the variety of uses and machines.

(c) Graphics

It was fundamental that since embroidery is a graphic art, it
should be displayed graphically as a visual feedback for
proofing of designs. For that reason it was considered
important to use the highest resolution colour graphics
screens to best represent the end result.

(d) Market Oriented

From experience it is the end user who best knows what is
required. A major consideration was to "hear" what the
end user wanted rather to impose on him the perceived
solutions of the system builder.

(e) Modularity and Expandability

It was critical that the system be built in such a way that
new technology and devices could be incorporated at any time.
Similarly, the program structure was to be such that modules

could be added or deleted as required by the user. For
example, monogram lettering is not required by manufacturers
of all-over embroidery.

(f) Top Down Approach

When the system was first conceived the computer equipment
utilised, mini computers and high resolution graphics screens,
were expensive.   This also applied to hard disks as opposed
to floppy diks.   However, the approach taken was that
computer and electronic equipment would come down in price in
the future, whereas labour costs involved in software would
always increase.   The use of powerful mini computers ensured
that there were no physical limitations to program size or
complexity.

(g) Protection of Knowhow

In an industry as secretive as embroidery, the question of
knowhow always arises.   The approach taken was to provide
generalised programs where specific parameters which
consituted the individual knowhow in embroidery, could be
inserted by the user of the system.   In this way the
system builder was unaware of the knowhow and was not in a
position to pass that knowhow on, either knowingly or
unknowingly, to other embroiderers.

5.   INTEGRATED CAD/CAM FOR EMBROIDERY

It would be more appropriate to call the system CED/CEM,
Computer Embroidery Design and Computer Embroidery
Manufacture.   The system which has been developed by
Wilcom is a truly integrated CAD/CAM system starting from
graphic input and finishing with machine control. Complete
integration is evident through the use of electronic media
for storage of design data and transmission of
pattern information electronically to the machinery, with
the interface between design and machine coding contained
within the CED system.

6.   CAD OR CED (COMPUTER EMBROIDERY DESIGN)

CED is a multi-user, multi-tasking computer graphics system
for the design of embroidery patterns and production of
embroidery tapes and Jacquard cards for electronic data
media.   This sytem is schematically represented in Figure II.
The system consists of graphics workstation, computer, and
input and output devices.   The computer is programmed so
that several workstations and several input/output devices
can operate simultaneously but independently in true multi-
user, multi-tasking operation.

6.1 System Description

Functionally, the CED system is divided into four components:-

(a) Workstation

(b) Computer

(c) Output Devices

(d) Converting Devices

The workstation comprises a computer graphics display with
keyboard and an electronic digitiser tablet.   The graphics
display is normally of the medium to high resolution type
and can be black and white or colour.   Since embroidery
is the production of stitches, and stitches are represented
as vectors on the graphics display then the graphics
displays which are used are relatively unrestricted in
vector display capability.   The digitiser is generally
large enough to provide for the enlargements required
and provides space for a moveable menu through which
the operator is able to pass instructions to the system.

The computer which is used is either a 16 bit or 32 bit
mini computer with hard magnetic disks.   The memory is a
minimum of 256 KB with disk storage capacity being from
20 MB up to 200 MB.

The output devices on the system are of two kinds:-

(a) Graphic output, and

(b) Pattern output.

The graphic output from the machine comes in various forms
such as photocopy of the graphics screen, plotter output,
ink jet output for colour display, printer output of graphic
display.   The choice of graphics output depends on the
type of graphics screen which is being utilised and the
speed required for the output as well as the type of
information to be displayed.   Pattern information is
outputted onto the desired form of data medium.   For
example, 8 channel paper tape punch, one of the three
different kinds of Jacquard card punches, floppy disk,
magnetic cassette, etc. may be used.

Converting devices are paper tape or Jacquard card readers,
which permit existing patterns to be read and inputted
in electronic form into the system for subsequent use
or editing.

6.2 Operation of CED System

Entry to the system is initiated from the graphics display
keyboard.   Operator name and password are entered and the
system is then ready for work.   A moveable menu is
positioned on the digitiser tablet.   This menu contains
control commands, embroidery functions and machine functions
which can be executed by placing the digitiser cursor on the
appropriate square.   When the system is being used in menu
mode, there is no need to refer back to the keyboard but
only to the graphics display to see the results as they are

generated.   The desired position of the menu is indicated
by digitising the origin.

The artist's design, a sketch or enlargement drawing, is then
placed on the digitiser tablet and the window for that design
is indicated to the computer by digitising two corner points.

Since the sequence of embroidery is critical, it is desirable
at this stage to have pre-planned the method by which the
design will be encoded.   The final design is created by
superimposing sections created during this punching process.
These sections can be colour elements, individual motifs,
repeats of previously generated motifs, or sections which must
be individually created so as to eliminate embroidery
distortion.

With this plan in mind, the puncher starts to create the data
base from which the embroidery will be created. From the
digitiser menu the puncher selects the type of stitch which
he wishes to use.   He then digitises the outline of the
desired shape. The CED program uses quadratic spline curves
to describe shapes, thus complex shapes can be described
with few points and the computer is utilised to provide
smoothed curves.   If a running stitch is required, then
selection of the running stitch type on the menu will permit
the designer to describe lines or shapes which will be
created with a nominated stitch length.   Selection of
manual stitching on the digitiser menu permits the puncher
to input individual stitches as he would normally do on a
mechanical digitiser.   As the stitches are being created
by the computer (which is calculating the envelope shape
from the spline points and then calculating the necessary
stitches to fill them) the resultant stitches and input
points are being displayed on the graphics screen.   If at
any time during this process the puncher makes an error,
he is able to delete individual stitches in a backward
sequence or to delete complete sections.

When a section has been completed, it may be stored away or
redisplayed and the number of stitches generated in that
section calculated and shown.   If precise detail is required
the puncher may take a window of the section he has created
and see an enlargement within that section on the graphics
screen.   This window may be as small or as large as desired,
so that very fine detail can be magnified to the full dimensions
of the graphics screen.

The puncher is free at any time to change stitch spacing, type
of stitch or any of the various machine functions.   If for
example, the puncher requires the selection of a borer, then
the computer will keep track of the borer depth and the offset
position between the embroidery needle and the borer.
The borer is represented as a diamond shape on the graphics
screen with the size of the diamond indicating the depth of
the borer.

Each section that is created is named or numbered depending on whether it will be re-used or stored away for future reference. The program keeps track of the numbers of sections which have been created and at any time will list the numbers and names of the sections together with the stitches in each section.

Several sections can be combined and displayed on the graphics screen to check the design itself. At any time the contents of the graphics screen or the details of any section may be produced on hard copy as previously described. Colour plotters or ink jet printers will reflect the colour changes generated within the design. Similarly, a colour screen will represent the different thread colours as they are generated.

Up to this time the design is in an internal data format without specific reference to any type of machine. When the design is complete the type of machine for which the design should be coded may be selected and the appropriate machine coding will be generated by the computer. Since the design is still maintained in an internal data format, this design may be produced in any or all different machine codes availabe to the system. Thus, it is possible to generate an 8 channel tape for a multihead embroidery machine to produce a sample and then generate a Jacquard card for a Shiffli machine for production of the same design.

6.3   Software Features and Stitch Programs

6.3.1   Automatic Stitch Generation for any Shape

A minimum number of points can be used to define any shape, which can be regular or irregular. (Note: this is an exact representation of the shape, not an approximation using arcs and straight lines). By nominating stitch type, stitch length, stitch spacing and other parameters, the defined shape may be outlined or filled with stitches, automatically. Overstitching to compensate for material pull can be nominated and is automatically generated. (overstitch or pull compensation allows for shrinkage of the base material).

6.3.2   Stitch Types

Manual, running, satin (blatt or steil), zig zag, ceeding (geflect), E, bean, split, cross stitches are all available. Any outline may be defined for running stitch, with adjustable stitch lengths. Ceeding (Geflect) matches different sections, has adjustable stitch length, minimum stitch and pull compensation.

6.3.3   Outline Repeat/Backtrack

A particular shape or group of stitches is defined once only and the outline or stitches may be repeated in the forward or reverse stitching sequence as many times as required.

6.3.4 Automatic Underlay

This feature allows underlay stitch patterns, without extra
input. Many standard underlay patterns are available, from
simple zig zag to double zig zag with centre and edge
running stitch. Adjustable underlay parameters include
understitch compensation, pull compensation and zig zag
stitch spacing. (Underlay stitching provides a base for
the covering stitches and permits building of bulk for three
dimensioanl effects. It is critical in stabilising the base
material and reducing distortion).

6.3.5 Programmable Stitch Type (Tessillations)

A series of stitches which constitute a design may be imputted
and stored. This series may be repeated with automatic
spacing and variable size along any curve, which can be
specified like running stitch. The series of stitches can
include machine functions, such as boring, speed changes,
etc.

6.3.6 Automatic Boring

Automatic programming of borers in Schiffli and multihead
machines are accommodated.   Borer movements and depths are
shown with a symbol and the borer number on the graphics
display at the actual position of the borer hole.   Speed
changes, needles in/out, tension changes, clutch actions,
compensation for offset between borers and needles, frame
position to last stitch and resetting of machine functions
are all automatic.

6.3.7 Shuttle Pull Compensation

This facility is used to compensate for shuttle pull, mainly in
Schiffli looms, due to unfavourable direction of stitching
relative to shuttle movement. This can be compensated for
independently for all combinations of stitch directions. The
amounts of compensation for different stitch lengths may be
nominated by the user.

6.3.8 Auto Schiffli Jump Stich

The user can nominate a jump stitch length and when this length
is exeeeded, CED generates a jump stitch, automatically
taking care of speed changes, needles in/out.   This is similar
to jump stitch on multihead machines and can be engaged,
disengaged or stitch length varied as and when required.

6.3.9 Variable Offset Ceeding (Geflect)

The value of the offsets, one for forward and the other for
return stitching, may be nominated.   This provides infinite
variation in regular ceeding (Geflect) effects.

6.3.10 Variable Irregular Ceeding (Geflect)

To create an impression of irregularity as may occur with
manual punching, the stitch length and stitch spacing may
each be randomly varied by a nominated percentage.

6.3.11 Additional Input Methods

Additional input methods which enable easier and faster input
of points for stitch generation are available.   These
methods, referred to as B and C, require less input points
to define shapes and are better suited for complex shape
definition.

6.3.12 Stored Motifs

A design or part of a design may be stored away as a motif
for use as frequently as required in other motifs or
designs.   By giving the motif a name and two reference
points it may be recalled in any number of different patterns
with unrestricted positioning, rotation, mirror imaging
and scaling.   There is no limit to the number of stitches
in a motif.

6.3.13 Editing

Permits manipulation, correction and changing of part or all
of new or previous patterns.   Thus, sections of a pattern
may be reviewed, deleted, added, repositioned or redisplayed.
Parts constituting a pattern may be listed.
The number of stitches in a section may be changed.

6.3.14 Stored Crests

Crests are basic shapes which are stored in the computer,
Positioning is accomplished with a single point definition.
Outline stitching including underlay, compensation, stitch
length, stitch spacing and stitch type can be varied
independently of crest dimensions.   The crest dimensions
can be varied in 'x' or 'y' directions or both.   Crests
can be programmed by Wilcom for customer requirements.

6.3.15 Basic Lettering

CED stores variable automatic lettering in the computer.
The letters may be varied in their height, width, degrees
of italics (slant), stitch length and stitch spacing.
Given a baseline, which may be a straight line at any
angle to the lettering or a circular arc, the words made
up by typing letters into the computer are automatically
spaced along that baseline.   If the letters don't fit
the baseline, CED automatically reduces the letter width
to fit.   Each letter is compensated according to the
shape of the following letter.   Tie-off stitches on the
last letter, thread tension and speed changes between
underlay and top stitches for Schiffli machines are
automatic.   For this basic lettering, joining is along the
bottoms of the letters.   Block upper case letters are
standard with options for block lower case and script
(upper and lower case)

6.3.16 Extended Lettering

This feature offers extended joining possiblities for letters,
particularly important for Schiffli applications.   By using

80

multiple entry/exit points for each letter, the letters can
be joined at selected points, closest point, jumping to a
common point or common line between each letter, jumping
to a point or line at the start or end of a word but closest
point joining within the word.   Tie-off stitches may be
automatic for each letter, dependent on joining method.
For Schiffli, needles in/out for jump stitch and jump
stitch slack in nominated direction are automatic.

6.3.17 Automatic Shading (Jagged Stitch)

This stitch program, used with any shape of design, permits
the designer to automatically provide artistic shading
effects using most stitch types such as blatt, steil,
geflect and other CED autuomatic stitch programs such as
turn fill, parallel fill, slope fill as well as circles,
ovals, rings.   The program permits selection of the
length and regularity of the of the shading (jaggedness),
internally, externally or on both sides of any shape.

6.3.18 Condensed Format

A section or a complete pattern may be created and stored in
a condensed format, allowing the design to be varied in
size with automatic adjustment of the number of stitches.
When size is varied, the number of stitches can be decreased,
increased or kept the same.   It is also possible to
alter the number of stitches without changing the size
of the design.   A whole pattern may have the number of
stitches changed with independent adjustment of each
different type of stitch.   For example, if a design
contains blatt, zig zag, geflect or lettering, the
number of stitches for each of these stitch types, can be
adjusted separately.   The complete pattern may be
mirrored or rotated to any angle.   Use of condensed
format can reduce pattern storage space by up to 80% and
permits editing, conversion to tape codes or modification
of the number of stitches any time the pattern is recalled.

6.3.19 Automatic Change of Stitch Spacing (Wheels, Radeli)

This program provides automatic change in stitch spacing
(wheels, radeli) as the stitch length changes, for every
individual stitch.   The values of stitch spacing for a
given stitch length can be pre-selected by the designer
from an almost infinite range of possibilities.

Several different combinations of automatic stitch spacing
(or sets of wheels, radeli) can be programmed by the
designer for instantaneous use.   Changing from one
combination to another can be used to increase or decrease
the number of stitches in a design, for any section or
colour. Changing combinations can also be used to vary
the amount of stitch coverage.   This automatic function
provides faster punching by reducing the time consuming
changes of stitch spacing (wheels, radeli), and permits
higher quality embroidery with less stitches.

6.3.20 Graphics Display

The graphic system can display input points, outlines of
shapes and stitches as they are being generated.   The
scale of the display can be altered to permit zooming
to show more or less detail of stitching. Existing
patterns may be recalled from memory and displayed as and
when required.

6.3.21 Colour Graphics Software

The feature enables the use of a colour graphics terminal
in the CED System, where each colour thread can be
represented.

6.3.22 Additional Workstations

Extra workstations (i.e. graphics terminal and digitiser)
may be added onto CED systems with the use of this option.
The extra workstations, operating simultaneously, share
all the features of the CED system options and capabilities.

6.3.23 Production Worksheet

The graphics terminal displays the following information:
pattern number, pattern description, hardcopy scale, stitch
count, number of colours, number of appliques, machine
code, maximum stitch length, jump stitch On/Off, details
of framing, position of starting point, colour sequence
and special instructions.   If the hardcopy option is
included with the system, then this information may be
printed on demand.

6.3.24 System Reporting

The CED computer stores data related to stitches generated
and time used by each operator.   A summary may be viewed
on the graphics terminal and/or hardcopy unit.

6.4 Machine Functions

All machine functions may be set and recorded during CED
operation.   All Schiffli functions are available.

6.4.1 Tape Coding

Plauen, Saurer, 8 channel and 68mm Jacquard codes are
available for all Schiffli and multihead machines.
Special tape codes can be provided for particular uses.

6.4.2 Tape Punching

Punching takes place simultaneously but independently of
designing on CED.   8 channel paper tape is punched with
pattern number, description and date. Plauen,   Saurer or
68mm Jacquard is directly punched from the computer with
automatic blank card and test patterns for punch servicing.

6.4.3 Stitch Count

Stitch counts are displayed for parts of patterns as they are being generated and totals are displayed at the end of a complete pattern.

6.4.4 Tape/Jacquard Card Reading

Paper tape or Jacquard cards may be read into the CED system and stored on disk.   The pattern can be decoded, redisplayed and a Wilcom code created.   The pattern can be reproduced, allowing additions, revisions, repositioning of sections, and changes to the stitching sequence, with tape coding and punching to the same and/or other machine codes.

7. CAM OR CEM (COMPUTER EMBROIDERY MANUFACTURE)

The CEM activity is represented by machine coding and the on-line electronic control of embroidery machines.   (A direct analogy of CAM in engineering machinery).   The first part of CEM is carried out by the software which converts design data to machine code in the computer. The more specific part of CEM relates to on-line control of machines.

As outlined in Table I, there are a number of different types of machines each with different control media. In addition to this, each manufacturer tends to use a different machine coding to control special machine functions that they provide.   Since the new machines now being produced by manufacturers tend to utilise more modern data such as cassettes or paper tape, and the production of new machinery represents less than 5% of the machinery available for use in the market place, it was decided to concentrate the area of on-line control of embroidery machines on existing machinery in the field.

A major consideration in the design of an on-line control system was to utilise existing machine control.   This also left open the opportunity to use existing patterns on the existing data media.   As always cost was a major consideration, so that systems dictating major alterations to existing machinery were ruled out.

It was decided to proceed in the direction of emulating existing control media, thereby leaving the machine itself intact and still permitting use of existing control media. The emulation facilities are provided by a micro computer, such that this then serves as a building block for addition of future intelligence to the control device.   The future intelligence and facilities which will be added relate very much to the practical requirements of the machine user. As their confidence and ability to utilise the control grows they tend to make more and more demands to optimise their production.

The on-line control of embroidery machines was divided into two different types.

(a)   machines driven by 8 channel paper tape

(b)   machines driven by Jacquard card.

7.1 Paper Tape Emulation PTE (8 Channel Paper Tape)

A paper tape emulator was constructed utilising a micro-processor to provide the necessary intelligence. This device communicates with a computer on a serial line and on the other side interfaces behind any general 8 channel paper tape reader.   Software can be added or modified to allow for the variations between different brands of paper tape reader.   With the addition of a control switch the PTE can be added to any device which utilises paper tape and the switch permits the user to select whether he wishes to communicate with the computer via the PTE or operate in local mode, whereby the machine can utilise conventional 8 channel paper tape.   It is possible to provide additional memory to the PTE such that those machines which are of the older generation and do not have memory, requiring the paper tape to be run continuously, can be enhanced.

The PTE has been designed and produced in such a way that it is completely general and could be easily adapted to machines other than embroidery machines, knitting machines for example.

7.2 Electronic Jacquard EJ (Jacquard Cad Emulation)

The electronic Jacquard is more complicated than the PTE, since the emulation of the Jacquard card needs to be carried out in a mechanical rather than electronic fashion.   The electronic Jacquard consists of two major components:-

(a)   an electro-mechanical black box which physically functions to emulate the Jacquard card, and

(b)   the control computer which is a micro computer with a screen and keyboard.

The black box fits exactly where the conventional Jacquard card feeder would sit on a normal machine.   It is a relatively easy task to remove an existing Jacquard card feed and install this black box.   The Automat, or Jacquard mechanism of the machine is left untouched. The black box functions in such a way that when the platines from the Jacquard mechanism advance to detect whether or not a hole is present in the Jacquard card, the black box provides either unimpeded progress as would be the case with a hole in the Jacquard card or an impediment to progress of the platine as would exist with the absence of a hole in the Jacquard card.

The control computer provides many features which are not
available with conventional Jacquard card. The software
provides a visual display on the screen of the Jacquard card
as it would appear. It also provides decoding of the card
and display of machine functions. The frame position of the
machine is displayed with every stitch, thread breakage
indications are kept, pattern rewind is electronic and frame
positioning is also carried out electronically. Further,
the control enables the operator to stitch manually with an
electronic push button. The memory of the controller is
modular, such that several different patterns can be stored
in the machine at one time and selected as required.

The pattern in memory may be edited in any fashion required,
such that adjustments of tensions and incorrect stitches can
be done immediately. When these changes have been made it
is possible to transmit this back to the computer from whence
the pattern originated. The control computer has communication
with any other computer or device via a serial interface.
Thus, it is possible to read patterns into the electronic
Jacquard from paper tape readers, magnetic cassettes or
Jacquard card readers. The data format for input is selected
on the screen. The program data may also be outputted to
any device which permits compatible serial line access.

The initial cost justification for on-line control is the
saving in production of control tapes and Jacquard cards.
This stems from the cost of the media, cost of production,
storage and insurance, cost of errors in punching and
reading and the replacement of worn media. However, it is
already obvious from results in implementation that the
added intelligence provided at the machine will be a vehicle
for increasing machine output by reducing non-operating time.

8. BENEFITS OF INTEGRATED CED/CEM

8.1 Increased Productivity

This can be represented either by the reduction of the number
of people involved in the design process or by the increased
production of the same number of people. The productivity
increases are highly dependent on the type of design and
type of embroidery. Overall productivity increases vary
from 4 to 12 times.

8.2 Increased Design Potential

Many effects which would normally be too costly to
produce as a consequence of time consumption, can be easily
produced by the computer. This allows the designer
increased flexibility in the expression of design ideas in
embroidery applications.

8.3 Improved Quality

The consistency and accuracy of the computer in calculating
stitch positions has led to improved quality. Additionally,

the ability to progressively view the design as it is being
punched, and easily edit errors or achieve better implementation, has improved the quality of the embroidered product.
Use of automatic stitch spacing puts sophisticated embroidery
design tools in the hands of designers who need not have
detailed knowledge of embroidery processes.

8.9 Increased Cost Effectiveness

A design can be reproduced for any type of machine, the
number of stitches (and thus the cost) may be varied, the
same design produced in different sizes, all without re-
punching a design.   Motifs which have previously been
designed, may be re-used.   The features permit matching
of a design to a price, thus improving cost effectiveness
of embroidery.

8.5 Reduced Lead Times

The whole process is considerably faster than existing
techniques, particularly in creation of the artwork input.
Visual checking of designs minimises the need for checking
embroidered samples.   The combination of other features
reduces the time for production of designs from concept to
finished product.

9. APPLICATION TO OTHER PROCESSES

Whereas each fabric forming process is in itself demanding
in its technical solutions, two factors indicate the benefits
of applying the approach described above to those processes.
Firstly, as shown in Figure 3, the creation of an artwork
database is necessary, independent of the process to which
it is applied.   Thus, much of the existing programming
relating to this artwork database would be common to other
processes such as knitting and weaving.   Secondly, machine
coding and on-line control of machinery, particularly
knitting machines controlled by 8 Channel Paper Tape, has
already been addressed.

Without underestimating the difficulties to be encountered in
other processes, the authors feel that the multidimensional
nature of the embroidery design process places greater
demands on software solutions.   Some of these software
solutions would provide improvements to existing techniques
in CAD systems for these other processes.   These relate
particularly to the use of contours which permit scaling,
rotation and design editing whilst retaining a high resolution of the design.   In particular, the methods of stitching
developed are directly applicable to the filling and out-
lining of designs in raschel knitting.

The fully integrated CED/CEM System for embroidery known as
CED, has proven successful in concept and implementation.
As with most CAD/CAM systems, it is under continuing development for its intended application.   It is also being
extended for use in other fabric forming processes, using the
same basic system and approach.

School of Textile Technology,   (R.E.G)
University of New South Wales,
Kensington , N.S.W., 2033,
Australia

Wilcom Pty. Ltd.   (R.G.P. & W.B.W.)
P. O. Box 147,
Chippendale, N.S.W., 2008,
Australia.

TABLE 1

MACHINE TYPE	MANUFACTURER	TYPES OF MACHINE CODES				
		8 Channel Paper Tape	68 mm Jacq.	138 mm (Saurer) Jacquard	165 mm (Plauen) Jacquard	Mag. Tape
Schiffli	Saurer	X	–	X	–	X
	Zangs	X	–	–	X	–
	Comerio	X	–	–	X	X
	Hiraoka	–	–	–	X	–
Multihead	Tajima	X	X	–	–	–
	Barudan	X	X	–	–	–
	Hiraoka	X	X	–	–	–
	Eltac	X	X	–	–	–
	Pfaff	X	–	–	–	–
	Zangs	X	X	–	–	–
	Marco	X	X	–	–	–
	Marcus	X	X	–	–	–
	Ultramatic	X	X	–	–	–
	Melco	X	–	–	–	–
	Grosse	X	X	–	–	–
Monogram (single head)	Meistergram	–	–	–	–	X
	Melco	X	–	–	–	–
	Barudan	X	–	–	–	–
	Toyoda	X	–	–	–	–

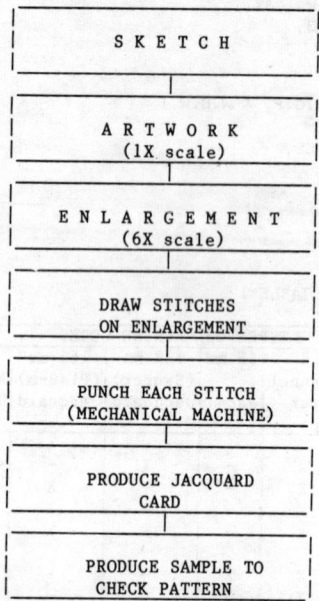

```
┌─────────────────────────┐
│      S K E T C H        │
└─────────────────────────┘
┌─────────────────────────┐
│      A R T W O R K      │
│       (1X scale)        │
└─────────────────────────┘
┌─────────────────────────┐
│  E N L A R G E M E N T  │
│       (6X scale)        │
└─────────────────────────┘
┌─────────────────────────┐
│     DRAW STITCHES       │
│    ON ENLARGEMENT       │
└─────────────────────────┘
┌─────────────────────────┐
│   PUNCH EACH STITCH     │
│  (MECHANICAL MACHINE)   │
└─────────────────────────┘
┌─────────────────────────┐
│   PRODUCE JACQUARD      │
│        CARD             │
└─────────────────────────┘
┌─────────────────────────┐
│  PRODUCE SAMPLE TO      │
│   CHECK PATTERN         │
└─────────────────────────┘
```

FIGURE 1

FIGURE 2

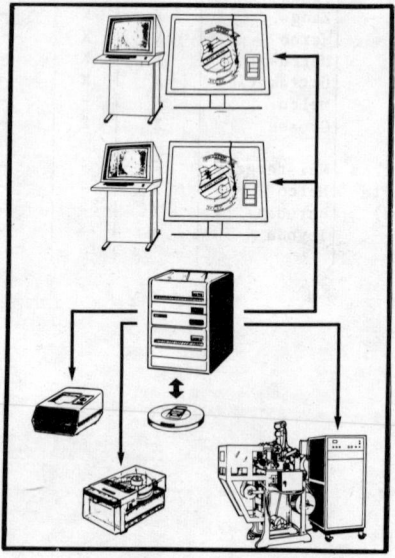

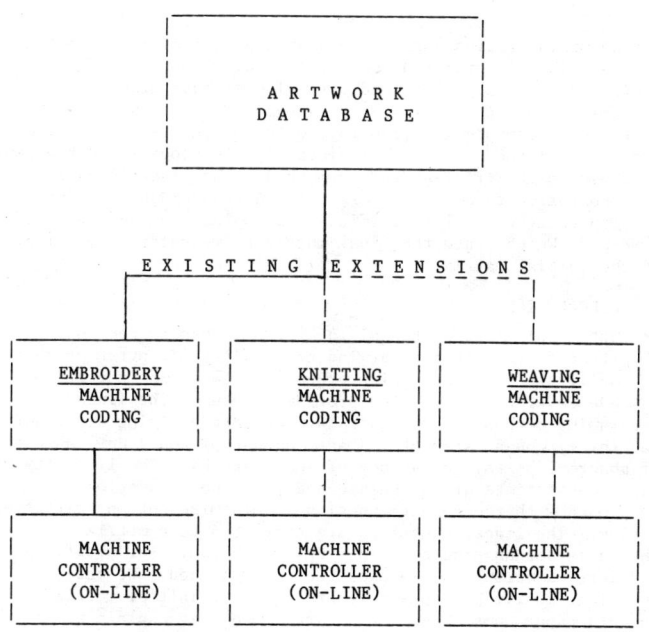

FIGURE 3

LINEAR PROGRAMMING FOR COTTON MIXING

Jae Kon Lee and Young Seok Kim

ABSTRACT

Cotton mixing ratios based on weight that satisfy the constraints such as fiber length, fineness, strength, amount of honey dew, number of abnormal bales, and optimal cost have practically determined in cotton mills by trial-and-error method. We have developed a computer program for cottom mixing using the linear programing method. The constraints in this program are the same as those in the trial-and-error method. The linear equations were converted to a matrix form using Gauss-Jordan procedure in simplex tableau. For artificial variables, we used the big M method. We obtained the final matrix by repeated conversion of the initial matrix.

1. INTRODUCTION

In cotton spinning, cotton mixing ratio is one of the most important factors that determine the quality of cotton products. To facilitate decision-making process to determine the ratios we have developed a computer program by use of the linear programing method. The constraint for cotton mixing are fiber length, fineness, strength, grade, amount of honey dew, number of abnormal bales, and number of small stocks. The linearity of these constraints are discussed and the linear equations are developed with the object function to minimize cotton cost after mixing. The linear equations are converted to a matrix form by the Gauss-Jordan procedure in simplex tableau. For artificial and surplus variables, we used the big M method. We obtained the final matrix by repeated conversions of initial matrix. In this paper some case studies are shown that explain how to determine cotton mixing ratios based on weight using computer program.

SYMBOLS

LM_i	:	lot mark of each lot
X_i	:	cotton mixing ratio based on weight of each lot
N_i	:	number of cotton fibers in each lot
N	:	number of cotton fibers after mixing
L_i	:	mean cotton fiber length of each lot (.793mm, 1/32in)
L	:	fiber length constraint (.793mm,1/32in)
M_i	:	micronaire reading of each lot (μg/in)
M	:	micronaire reading constraint (μg/in)
P_i	:	Pressley Index of each lot (10^3lb/mg)
P	:	Pressley Index constraint (10^3lb/mg)
G_i	:	grade index of each lot
G	:	grade index constraint
C_i	:	cost of each lot (¢ /lb)
S_i	:	number of bales in each lot
YS	:	required bales to be mixed
CL_i	:	color of cotton in each lot
$CL(j)$	:	color constraint in data
$ZCL(j)$	:	color constraint in practical use
AN_i	:	abnormal bale in each lot
$AN(j)$	:	abnormal bale constraint in data
$ZAN(j)$	:	abnormal bale constraint in practical use
HD	:	honey dew in each lot
HD	:	honey dew constraint in each data

ZHD   : honey dew constraint in practical use
SSL   : limited number of small stocks of a lot

2. CONSTRAINTS AND LINEAR EQUATIONS

2.1 Fiber length

The linear equation for cotton fiber length can be expressed by

$$L = \sum_{i=1}^{n} X_i L_i \; , \qquad \sum_{i=1}^{n} X_i = 1 \qquad - - - - - - - - 1$$

The validity of equation 1 is discussed here. The weight equilibrium of cotton before and after mixing is

$$LMN = \sum_{i=1}^{n} N_i M_i L_i \qquad - - - - - - - - - - - - - - - 1\text{-}1$$

Therefore,

$$L = \sum_{i=1}^{n} \frac{N_i M_i}{N \, M} L_i \qquad - - - - - - - - - - - - - - 1\text{-}2$$

The coefficient $N_i M_i / NM$ is equivalent to mixing ratio on weight
base. Hence, equation 1 holds true.

2.2 Fineness

The linear equation for cotton fineness can be expressed by

$$\frac{1}{M} = \sum_{i=1}^{n} X_i \frac{1}{M_i} \qquad - - - - - - - - - - - - - - 2$$

The validity of equation 2 can be found in reference (1).

2.3 Strength

The linear equation for cotton fiber strength can be expressed by

$$P = \sum_{i=1}^{n} X_i P_i \qquad - - - - - - - - - - - - - - 3$$

The validity of equation 3 is given by the fact that Pressley
Index is a quotient of bundle strength in pound divided by
bundle weight in milligrams. By the definition of Pressley
Index, it can be intuitively known that equation 3 holds true (2).

2.4 Grade

Grade of cotton fiber is evaluated by the degree of trash content,
color and preparation. Preparation, however, is trifling due
to the similarity of ginning process in every cotton gin,
therefore, in this paper, we express the grade of cotton fiber
by the degree of trash content and color, discarding preparation.

2.4.1 Trash content

The linear equation for trash content can be expressed by

$$G = \sum_{i=1}^{n} X_i G_i \qquad - - - - - - - - - - - - - - 4$$

The validity of equation 4 can be seen intuitively by the fact
that the degree of trash content on the basis of color contributes
proportionally to the mixing ratio (2).

2.4.2 Color

It is not necessary to develop a linear equation for color

constraint. But, in practice, number of bales, after mixing, in each color is uniquely designated. Therefore, in this paper, color constraint is designated.

2.5 Honey dew

It is not necessary to develop a linear equation for honey dew constraint. But, in practice, the maximum number of honey dew bales after mixing is uniquely designated. Therefore, in this paper, honey dew constraint is designated.

2.6 Abnormal bale

It is not necessary to develop a linear equation for abnormal bale constraint. But, in practice, number of abnormal bales after mixing is uniquely designated. Therefore, in this paper, abnormal bale constraint is designated.

2.7 Number of small stocks in a lot

Small stocks of a lot should be used up for inventory control in a warehouse. Hence, the limited number of small stocks is defined. If a lot fewer than the limited number of small stocks is presented, it should be picked up preferentially. In this paper, the limited number of small stocks is designated.

3. FORMULATION OF MATRIX

Linearity of the constraints was discussed in the foregoing section and it was found that this cotton mixing problem satisfied the conditions of proportionality, additivity and deterministic nature of linear programing problem. The formula of cotton mixing can be represented as the following.

3.1 Data form

Table I shows the data of each lot in a warehouse. Additively, conditions for constraints shoul be given for the practical purpose of this programing. The conditions of each constraint are shown in table II.

Lot mark	Color	Honey dew	Abnor -mal	Weight ratio	Length (1/32 in)	Fine- ness (μg/in)	Streng -th (10^6 lb/mg)	Grade index	Cost (¢/lb)	Stock (bales)
LM_1	CL_1	HD_1	AN_1	X_1	L_1	M_1	P_1	G_1	C_1	S_1
LM_2	CL_2	HD_2	AN_2	X_2	L_2	M_2	P_2	G_2	C_2	S_2
LM_3	CL_3	HD_3	AN_3	X_3	L_3	M_3	P_3	G_3	C_3	S_3
LM_i	CL_i	HD_i	AN_i	X_i	L_i	M_i	P_i	G_i	C_i	S_i
LM_n	CL_n	HD_n	AN_n	X_n	L_n	M_n	P_n	G_n	C_n	S_n

Table I   Data for cotton stock

Cost	To be minimized	White (bales)	CL(1)
Bale to be picked	S (bales)	Light spotted (bales)	CL(2)
Limited number of small stock	SSL (bales)	Snotted (bales)	CL(3)
		Tinged (bales)	CL(4)
Length (1/32 in)	Greater than Lmin Less than Lmax	Light grey (bales)	CL(5)
Fineness(μg/in)	Greater than Mmin Less than Mmax	Grey (bales)	CL(6)
Strength(10^6 lb/mg)	Greater than P		
Grade Index	Greater than G	Abnormal bale 1 (bales)	AN(1)
Honey dew (bales)	Less than HD	Abnormal bale 2 (bales)	AN(2)
		Abnormal bale 3 (bales)	AN(3)

Table II   Data for constraints

3.2 Conversion of constraints and cotton mixing formulae

Number of small stocks does not influence the constraints such as length, fineness, strength and grade. However, the constraints such as color, honey dew and abnormal bale are affected by the number of small stocks. Therefore, constraint conversion should be done by the number of small stocks as shown in table III. From the preceeding discussion, cotton mixing formulae were set as shown in table IV.

* No. of bales of color, honey dew and abnormal bales respectively.		
Color	: CL(j)	(j=1,2,3,4,5,6)
Honey dew	: HD	
Abnormal	: AN(j)	(j=1,2,3)
* The conversion of number of bales.		
Color	: $CL(j) - \sum S_i = ZCL(j)$, if $ZCL(j) > 0$ for S_i of j-th color $<$ SSL	
Honey dew	: $HD - \sum S_i = ZHD$, if $ZHD > 0$ for $S_i <$ SSL	
Abnormal	: $AN(j) - \sum S_i = ZAN(j)$, if $ZAN(j) > 0$ for S_i of j-th abnormal bale SSL	
* The conversion of number of bales to be mixed.		
Number of bales to be mixed	: Put $S - \sum S_i = YS$, if $S_i <$ SSL	

Table III Constraint conversion by the limited number of small stocks

Lot mark	LM_1, LM_2, LM_i, LM_n
Object function	; Minimize cotton cost C after mixing $C_1X_1 + C_2X_2 + \ldots + C_iX_i + \ldots + C_nX_n = C$
Constraints	; L, M, P, G, CL, HD, AN
Length	$L_1X_1 + L_2X_2 + \ldots + L_iX_i + \ldots + L_nX_n \geqq L_{min}$ $L_1X_1 + L_2X_2 + \ldots + L_iX_i + \ldots + L_nX_n \leqq L_{max}$
Fineness	$\frac{1}{M_1}X_1 + \frac{1}{M_2}X_2 + \ldots + \frac{1}{M_i}X_i + \ldots + \frac{1}{M_n}X_n \leqq \frac{1}{M_{min}}$ $\frac{1}{M_1}X_1 + \frac{1}{M_2}X_2 + \ldots + \frac{1}{M_i}X_i + \ldots + \frac{1}{M_n}X_n \geqq \frac{1}{M_{max}}$
Strength	$P_1X_1 + P_2X_2 + \ldots + P_iX_i + \ldots + P_nX_n \geqq P$
Grade Index	$G_1X_1 + G_2X_2 + \ldots + G_iX_i + \ldots + G_nX_n \geqq G$
Color	$\sum X_i$ (If X_i is white) $= ZCL(1)$ $\sum X_i$ (If X_i is light spotted) $= ZCL(2)$ $\sum X_i$ (If X_i is spotted) $= ZCL(3)$ $\sum X_i$ (If X_i is tinged) $= ZCL(4)$ $\sum X_i$ (If X_i is light grey) $= ZCL(5)$ $\sum X_i$ (If X_i is grey) $= ZCL(6)$
Honey dew	$\sum X_i$ (If X_i is honey dew) $\leqq ZHD$
Abnormal 1	$\sum X_i$ (If X_i is abnormal 1) $= ZAN(1)$
2	$\sum X_i$ (If X_i is abnormal 2) $= ZAN(2)$
3	$\sum X_i$ (If X_i is abnormal 3) $= ZAN(3)$

Table IV Practical cotton mixing formulae

3.3 Matrix

Practical cotton mixing formulae shown in table IV can be
converted to a matrix form as shown in table V using the simples
tableau method of linear programing. (3-5)
Table VI shows the details of the matrix, to which the slack,
artificial, surplus variables and the big M values are added.

A; Length, Fineness, Strength, Grade index.	C; Big M value		F; Constraints
	D; Variable		
B; Color, Honey dew, Abnormal bales.		E; Variable	

Table V   Initial matrix of cotton mixing formulae

$C_1 C_2 C_3 .. C_n$	M	M	M	M M M M M M	M M M	
$L_1 L_2 L_3 .. L_n$	1 1					Lmin
$L_1 L_2 L_3 .. L_n$		1				Lmax
1 1 1 1			1			1
$\bar{M}_1 \bar{M}_2 \bar{M}_3 .. \bar{M}_n$						$\bar{M}$min
1 1 1 1		-1 1				1
$M_1 M_2 M_3 .. M_n$						$\bar{M}$max
$P_1 P_2 P_3 .. P_n$			-1 1			P
$G_1 G_2 G_3 .. G_n$				-1 1		G
$\Sigma X_i (X: WH)$				1		ZCL(1)
$\Sigma X_i (X: LS)$				1		ZCL(2)
$\Sigma X_i (X: SP)$				1		ZCL(3)
$\Sigma X_i (X: TI)$				1		ZCL(4)
$\Sigma X_i (X: LG)$				1		ZCL(5)
$\Sigma X_i (X: GR)$				1		ZCL(6)
$\Sigma X_i (X: HD)$					1	ZHD
$\Sigma X_i (X: AN)$					1	ZAN(1)
$\Sigma X_i (X: AN)$					1	ZAN(2)
$\Sigma X_i (X: AN)$					1	ZAN(3)
$\Sigma X: (S: less than YS)$					1	S_i/YS

Table VI   Details of initial matrix shown in table V

3.4 Matrix conversion

The matrix shown in tabel VI can be converted to a final matrix
by the Gauss-Jordan procedure in the simplex tableau method.
The first is the big M matrix conversion, the second is the
simplex tableau conversion, or the conversion can be executed
using the two phase method. Repeating the conversions, the final
matrix can be obtained. Consequently, the cotton mixing report
can be obtained from the final matrix.

3.5 Flow chart

Fig. I shows the general flow chart of computing matrices of
table VI.

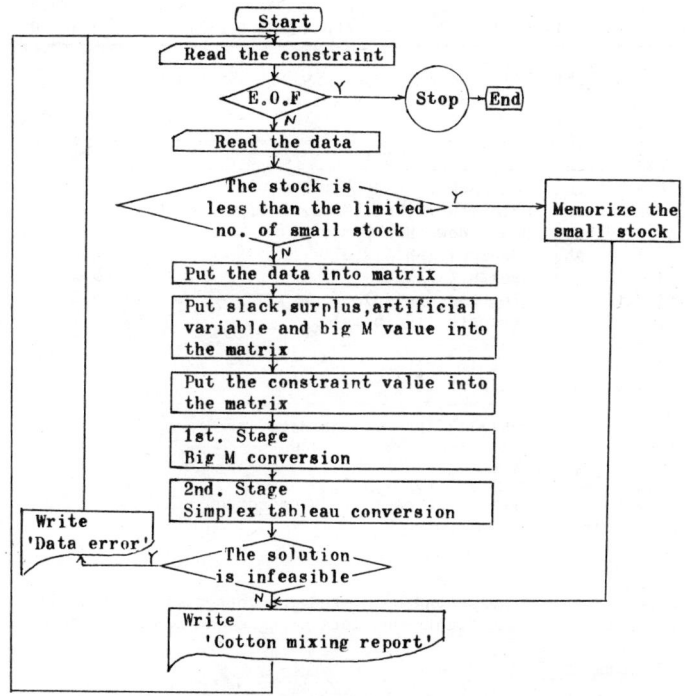

Fig I   The general flow chart of the program

4. CASE STUDY

Data cards consist of two constraint cards (Table VII and VIII)
and several stock list cards showing stock list data (Table IX).

Column		Data	Format
1 - 5	L_{min}	Length (min) (1/32in)	F5.2
6 - 10	L_{max}	Length (max) (1/32in)	F5.2
11 - 15	M_{min}	Fineness (min) (μg/in)	F5.2
16 - 20	M_{max}	Fineness (max) (μg/in)	F5.2
21 - 25	P	Strength (10^3 lb/mg)	F5.2
26 - 30	G	Grade Index	F5.2
31 - 36	S	Stock (bales)	F6.2
37 - 41	SSL	The limited no. of small stock	F5.2

Table VII   Cotton quality constraint card

95

Column		Data (bales)		Format
1 - 18	CL(j) (j=1,2,3,4,5,6)		Color(WH,LS,SP,TI,LG,GR)	6F3.0
19 - 21	HD		Honey dew	F3.0
22 - 30	AN(j) (j=1,2,3)		Abnormal (1,2,3)	3F3.0

Table VIII   Color, Honey dew and Abnormal
bale constraint card

Column			Data	Format
1 - 4	LM		Lot mark	A4
5	CL		Color (WH:1,LS:2,SP:3,TI:4,LG:5,GR:6)	I1
6	HD		Honey dew (HD:1)	I1
7	AN		Abnormal (AN:1,2,3)	I1
8 - 12	L		Length (1/32in)	F5.2
13 - 17	M		Fineness (μg/in)	F5.2
18 - 22	P		Strength (10^3lb/mg)	F5.2
23 - 27	G		Grade	F5.2
28 - 32	C		Cost (¢/lb)	F5.2
33 - 37	S		Stock (bales)	F5.2

Table IX   Stock list data card

4.1 Case study 1

Table X-1 shows the first case study of cotton mixing from 1207
bales from twenty-one lots.

4.2 Case study 2

Table X-2 shows the second case study of cotton mixing from 1187
bales from the same twenty-one lots of case one minus twenth bales.

4.3 Case study 3

Table X-3 shows the third case study of cotton mixing from 1262
bales (the number of bales of case two plus seventy-five bales
from two newly added lots).

5. CONCLUSION

In order to develop a computer program for cotton mixing, we
discussed linerity of constraints and set linear equations for
them. Converting linear equations, we developed cotton mixing
formulae expressed in a matrix from using the simplex tableau
method. Matrix conversions were done by the Gauss-Jordan
procedure. From the final matrix some case studies of cotton
mixing based on weight were shown. From these case studies, we
conclude that this computer program can be effectivelv used for
practical applications in cotton mills.

ACKNOWLEDGEMENTS

The authors wish to express their appreciation to Mrs. Young
Sook Lee, Chairman of Junghun Industrial Scholarship Foundation,
Seoul, Korea for her support and encouragement for this study.

REFERENCES

(1) D.S. Hamby. 'The American Cotton Handbook', vol.1,
     Interscience Publishers, 1965, p.174.

(2) E. Lore. 'Manual of Cotton Spinning', vol.2, part 1, Butter
     Worths, 1961, p.217.

(3) S. Hiller, J. Lieberman. 'Introduction to Operation Research',
     Holden-day Inc., 1973, p.1.

(4) S. Kuo. 'Computer Applications of Numerical Method',
     Addison-Wesley Inc., 1971, p.346.

(5) S. Gass. 'Linear Programing Methods and Applications',
     McGraw-Hill, 1975.

Department of Textile Engineering
Seoul National University
Seoul, Korea

(1)   STOCK LIST

	LOT.	MARK	C H A	LEN.	MIC.	P.I.	G.I.	PRICE	NO.OF BALES
1	230301	VWGS	2 1 0	31.9	4.1	83.16	73.25	67.46	25
2	230401	VWGS	3 1 0	31.9	4.1	83.16	73.25	67.46	23
3	230501	VWGS	4 1 0	31.9	4.1	83.16	73.25	67.46	16
4	230601	ROAL	1 1 2	31.9	4.15	83.28	78.3	73	45
5	230701	ROAL	2 1 2	31.9	4.15	83.28	78.3	73	45
6	230801	ROAL	3 1 2	31.9	4.15	83.28	78.3	73	79
7	230901	KSVA	1 0 0	32.9	3.6	82.13	88	75.3	14
8	231001	KSVA	2 0 0	32.9	3.6	82.13	88	75.3	38
9	231101	KSVA	3 0 0	32.9	3.6	82.13	88	75.3	14
10	231201	RKYA	2 0 3	31.8	4.1	81.21	73.7	63.18	43
11	231301	RKYA	3 0 3	31.8	4.1	81.21	73.7	63.18	112
12	231401	RKYA	4 0 3	31.8	4.1	81.21	73.7	63.18	55
13	231501	MOND	1 0 1	30	4.43	82.45	81.78	76.5	170
14	231601	MOND	2 0 1	30	4.43	82.45	81.78	76.5	5
15	231701	YWMZ	1 0 0	31.7	4.16	78.52	75.58	67.46	18
16	231801	YWMZ	2 0 0	31.7	4.16	78.52	75.58	67.46	143
17	231901	YWMZ	3 0 0	31	4.16	78.52	75.58	67.46	209
18	232001	YWMZ	4 0 0	31.7	4.16	78.52	75.58	67.46	104
19	232101	KUAA	2 0 0	32.7	4	88.31	71	62.43	30
20	232201	KUAA	3 0 0	32.7	4	88.31	71	62.43	10
21	232301	KUAA	4 0 0	32.7	4	88.31	71	62.43	10

TOTAL   1207

* C : COLOR,   H : HONEY DEW,   A : ABNORMAL BALE

(2)   REQUIREMENT

NO. OF BALES TO BE MIXED :   20   BALES

COLOR	WHITE	(1)	6	BALES
	LIGHT SPOTTED	(2)	4	BALES
	SPOTTED	(3)	8	BALES
	TINGED	(4)	2	BALES
	LIGHT GREY	(5)	0	BALES
	GREY	(6)	0	BALES

LIMITTED NO. OF SMALL STOCK BALES :   1   BALES
HONEY DEW :   LESS THEN   8   BALES

ABNORMAL BALE   CLASS 1   4   BALES
                       CLASS 2   0   BALES
                       CLASS 3   0   BALES

LENGTH   31.5 - 32.5
MICRONAIRE   3.5 - 4.5
P.I.   82
G.I.   74

(3)   COTTON BALES FROM 1207 BALES OF 21 LOTS

	LOT.	MARK	C H A	LEN.	MIC.	P.I.	G.I.	PRICE	BALE
10	231201	RKYA	2 0 3	31.8	4.1	81.21	73.7	63.18	3
13	231501	MOND	1 0 1	30	4.43	82.45	81.78	76.5	4
15	231701	YWMZ	1 0 0	31.7	4.16	78.52	75.58	67.46	2
19	232101	KUAA	2 0 0	32.7	4	88.31	71	62.43	1
20	232201	KUAA	3 0 0	32.7	4	88.31	71	62.43	8
21	232301	KUAA	4 0 0	32.7	4	88.31	71	62.43	2

SUM   20

(4)   CHECKING OF COTTON QUALITY AFTER MIXING

	LEN.	M.I.	P.I.	G.I.	PRICE
REQUIRED	31.5 - 32.5	3.5 - 4.5	82	74	MINIMUM
RESULT	31.93	4.11	85.09	74.02	65.8595

Table X-1

98

(1)   STOCK LIST

	LOT. MARK		C H A	LEN.	MIC.	P.I.	G.I.	PRICE	NO.OF BALES
1	230301	VWGS	2 1 0	31.9	4.1	83.16	73.25	67.46	25
2	230401	VWGS	3 1 0	31.9	4.1	83.16	73.25	67.46	23
3	230501	VWGS	4 1 0	31.9	4.1	83.16	73.25	67.46	16
4	230601	RQAL	1 1 2	31.9	4.15	83.28	78.3	73	45
5	230701	RQAL	2 1 2	31.9	4.15	83.28	78.3	73	45
6	230801	RQAL	3 1 2	31.9	4.15	83.28	78.3	73	79
7	230901	KSVA	1 0 0	32.9	3.6	82.13	88	75.3	14
8	231001	KSVA	2 0 0	32.9	3.6	82.13	88	75.3	38
9	231101	KSVA	3 0 0	32.9	3.6	82.13	88	75.3	14
10	231201	RKYA	2 0 3	31.8	4.1	81.21	73.7	63.18	40
11	231301	RKYA	3 0 3	31.8	4.1	81.21	73.7	63.18	112
12	231401	RKYA	4 0 3	31.8	4.1	81.21	73.7	63.18	55
13	231501	MOND	1 0 1	30	4.43	82.45	81.78	76.5	166
14	231601	MOND	2 0 1	30	4.43	82.45	81.78	76.5	5
15	231701	YWMZ	1 0 0	31.7	4.16	78.52	75.58	67.46	16
16	231801	YWMZ	2 0 0	31.7	4.16	78.52	75.58	67.46	143
17	231901	YWMZ	3 0 0	31	4.16	78.52	75.58	67.46	208
18	232001	YWMZ	4 0 0	31.7	4.16	78.52	75.58	67.46	104
19	232101	KUAA	2 0 0	32.7	4	88.31	71	62.43	29
20	232201	KUAA	3 0 0	32.7	4	88.31	71	62.43	2
21	232301	KUAA	4 0 0	32.7	4	88.31	71	62.43	8

TOTAL   1187

* C : COLOR,   H : HONEY DEW,   A : ABNORMAL BALE

(2)   REQUIREMENT

NO. OF BALES TO BE MIXED :   20   BALES

COLOR				
	WHITE	(1)	6	BALES
	LIGHT SPOTTED	(2)	4	BALES
	SPOTTED	(3)	8	BALES
	TINGED	(4)	2	BALES
	LIGHT GREY	(5)	0	BALES
	GREY	(6)	0	BALES

LIMITTED NO. OF SMALL STOCK BALES :   1   BALES
HONEY DEW :   LESS THEN   8   BALES

ABNORMAL BALE			
	CLASS 1	4	BALES
	CLASS 2	0	BALES
	CLASS 3	0	BALES

LENGTH   31.5 - 32.5
MICRONAIRE   3.5 - 4.5
P.I.   82
G.I.   74

(3)   COTTON BALES FROM 1187 BALES OF 21 LOTS

	LOT. MARK		C H A	LEN.	MIC.	P.I.	G.I.	PRICE	BALE
11	231301	RKYA	3 0 3	31.8	4.1	81.21	73.7	63.18	6
13	231501	MOND	1 0 1	30	4.43	82.45	81.78	76.5	4
15	231701	YWMZ	1 0 0	31.7	4.16	78.52	75.58	67.46	2
19	232101	KUAA	2 0 0	32.7	4	88.31	71	62.43	4
20	232201	KUAA	3 0 0	32.7	4	88.31	71	62.43	2
21	232301	KUAA	4 0 0	32.7	4	88.31	71	62.43	2

SUM   20

(4)   CHECKING OF COTTON QUALITY AFTER MIXING

	LEN.	M.I.	P.I.	G.I.	PRICE
REQUIRED	31.5 - 32.5	3.5 - 4.5	82	74	MINIMUM
RESULT	31.79	4.13	84.03	74.42	65.972

Table X-2

(1)   STOCK LIST

	LOT.	MARK	C H A	LEN.	MIC.	P.I.	G.I.	PRICE	NO.OF BALES
1	230301	VWGS	2 1 0	31.9	4.1	83.16	73.25	67.46	25
2	230401	VWGS	3 1 0	31.9	4.1	83.16	73.25	67.46	23
3	230501	VWGS	4 1 0	31.9	4.1	83.16	73.25	67.46	16
4	230601	RDAL	1 1 2	31.9	4.15	83.28	78.3	73	45
5	230701	RDAL	2 1 2	31.9	4.15	83.28	78.3	73	45
6	230801	RDAL	3 1 2	31.9	4.15	83.28	78.3	73	79
7	230901	KSVA	1 0 0	32.9	3.6	82.13	88	75.3	14
8	231001	KSVA	2 0 0	32.9	3.6 '	82.13	88	75.3	38
9	231101	KSVA	3 0 0	32.9	3.6	82.13	88	75.3	14
10	231201	RKYA	2 0 3	31.8	4.1	81.21	73.7	63.18	40
11	231301	RKYA	3 0 3	31.8	4.1	81.21	73.7	63.18	106
12	231401	RKYA	4 0 3	31.8	4.1	81.21	73.7	63.18	55
13	231501	MOND	1 0 1	30	4.43	82.45	81.78	76.5	162
14	231601	MOND	2 0 1	30	4.43	82.45	81.78	76.5	5
15	231701	YWMZ	1 0 0	31.7	4.16	78.52	75.58	67.46	14
16	231801	YWMZ	2 0 0	31.7	4.16	78.52	75.58	67.46	143
17	231901	YWMZ	3 0 0	31	4.16	78.52	75.58	67.46	209
18	232001	YWMZ	4 0 0	31.7	4.16	78.52	75.58	67.46	104
19	232101	KUAA	2 0 0	32.7	4	88.31	71	62.43	25
20	232301	KUAA	4 0 0	32.7	4	88.31	71	62.43	6
21	232401	XMPZ	1 1 0	31.5	3.5 '	80	74	60.1	40
22	232501	XMPZ	3 1 0	31.5	3.5	80	74	60.1	35

TOTAL   1242

* C : COLOR,   H : HONEY DEW,   A : ABNORMAL BALE

(2)   REQUIREMENT

NO. OF BALES TO BE MIXED :   20   BALES

COLOR					
	WHITE	(1)	6	BALES	
	LIGHT SPOTTED	(2)	4	BALES	
	SPOTTED	(3)	8	BALES	
	TINGED	(4)	2	BALES	
	LIGHT GREY	(5)	0	BALES	
	GREY	(6)	0	BALES	

LIMITTED NO. OF SMALL STOCK BALES :   1   BALES
HONEY DEW :   LESS THEN   8   BALES

ABNORMAL BALE   CLASS 1   4   BALES
                        CLASS 2   0   BALES
                        CLASS 3   0   BALES

LENGTH   31.5 - 32.5
MICRONAIRE   3.5 - 4.5
P.I.   82
G.I.   74

(3)   COTTON BALES FROM 1242 BALES OF 22 LOTS

	LOT.	MARK	C H A	LEN.	MIC.	P.I.	G.I.	PRICE	BALE
11	231301	RKYA	3 0 3	31.8	4.1	81.21	73.7	63.18	2
13	231501	MOND	1 0 1	30	4.43	82.45	81.78	76.5	4
19	232101	KUAA	2 0 0	32.7	4	88.31	71	62.43	4
20	232301	KUAA	4 0 0	32.7	4	88.31	71	62.43	2
21	232401	XMPZ	1 1 0	31.5	3.5	80	74	60.1	2
22	232501	XMPZ	3 1 0	31.5	3.5	80	74	60.1	6

SUM   20

(4)   CHECKING OF COTTON QUALITY AFTER MIXING

	LEN.	M.I.	P.I.	G.I.	PRICE
REQUIRED	31.5 - 32.5	3.5 - 4.5	82	74	MINIMUM
RESULT	31.59	3.86	83.1	74.63	64.387

Table X-3

100

USE OF MICROCOMPUTERS IN TODAY'S SYNTHETIC FIBRE INDUSTRY

G. Martens

ABSTRACT

For the economical production of high-quality synthetic fibers, in addition to good quality raw materials, excellent production facilities and equipment should be used.

The entire production process, from spinning to take-up and to subsequent processing on drawing and texturing equipment, must proceed smoothly and in a controlled fashion. It also has to be flexible and economical. Consequently, the need for automation in connection with controlling quality is now of primary importance.

Microcomputers are increasingly being used to solve these problems. The long-term objective which is to be achieved by automation and control of quality, is to become and remain economically competitive. To attain these objectives, it is important to develop solutions for the entire system rather than looking at independent solutions for individual segments within the system. The trend towards a well-structured computer hierarchy becomes more and more apparent. Barmag has been actively engaged for many years in automation and control of quality in synthetic fiber production. Consequently, Barmag can offer concepts and solutions based on micro-computer technology which are already well proven under production conditions for spinning lines and texturing equipment.

1. INTRODUCTION

At Barmag, a leading manufacturer of machines for the synthetic fiber industry, I am heading the development group responsible for the implementation of electrical equipment and microelectronics in our machines. From this perspective, I would like to give you a brief illustrated history of the use of microelectronics in Barmag machinery until today.

15 - 20 years ago, this development work concentrated mainly on special aggregates, such as godet heaters and regulators with the corresponding monitoring devices. However, over the years, the demand for greater machine and equipment versatility has resulted in micro-electronically controlled drive technology becoming increasingly important. With these developments, the groundwork was layed for the tasks of automation and quality monitoring of spinning plants and textile machinery that are in the fore today.

Barmag, as a dynamic enterprise, has prided itself in getting an early jump on innovative developments without losing sight of the economic reality, consequently has already carried out extensive pioneering work in the area of automation and quality control. The large international textile machinery shows, for example the ITMA, are the visible milestones of this development.

Today, computers are indispensable in the commercial and management sectors. It is therefore only natural that there has beeing an ever growing demand to make extensive use of the possibilities offered by the computer in the area of production engineering and manufacturing as well. For this reason Barmag began using computers not only in its own manufacturing, but, for the benefit of our customers, computers have been incorporated in the machines manufactured by us, especially in machinery for the synthetic fiber industry.

The demands made on computers for industrial applications are, however, quite different from those in the commercial sector. These are some of these differences:

- Real time operation

- Very pronounced differences in process-interface units

- Strong interference voltage peaks in the industrie power supply lines

- High interference level in the machines area

2. WHICH ARE THE TASKS OF THESE COMPUTERS IN THE PRODUCTION SECTOR?

Let me give you some specific examples:

2.1. Control system for a high-speed winder

In illustration 1, you see a Barmag high-speed winder of the series SW46 with a speed potential of 6000 m/min for winding textile and industrial denier synthetic fibers. What requirements must be met here to operate the winder?

- Since the bobbin drive in this case is achieved by a drive roller, first, the drive roller containing an inside-out motor must be switched on with a push-button.

- The drive for the approved Barmag traverse motion system with traverse cam and grooved roller has also to be switched on with a push-button.

- With higher winding speeds the chuck with the tubes must be run-up by means of an auxiliary drive.

- The sliding carriage containing the drive roller and the traverse motion mechanism must be lowered pneumatically within a preset time.

- Upon reaching the limit speed of the tube the thread must be strung up manually in the traverse motion mechanism.

- By pushing a button, all threads are strung up onto the tubes. There, for a preset, short time, the transfer tail is formed.

- At the same time, the doff timer for this particular position is started, too.

- At the end of the transfer tail winding the threads are laid down over the entire package width.

- The yarn sensors which have been bypassed during string-up have to be re-activated.

This concludes the string-up process. The threads are now wound at a high speed.

At the end of the doffing cycle, the following control functions are required:

- Shortly before the preset winding time expires, a position to be doffed is indicated by an intermittent warning light.

- When this light changes from intermittent to fully on, the exact doffing time has come. The yarn sensors are now switched off and the threads are picked up in a yarn suction gun.

- The sliding carriage lifts off the package and thus interrupts the drive.

- The package is braked.

- When the chuck stands still the individual packages can be pushed off.

- The packages have to be taken off and deposited in the corresponding creel positions.

- Empty standby tubes must be placed on the chucks.

Then, the threading procedure can start again.

These procedures show in a simplified way what takes place during a simple, normal doffing procedure.

These simple control tasks can still be handled with relatively uncomplicated pneumatic logic. With the increasing integration of winders in an overall organizational structure, however, individual microcomputer control is increasingly gaining popularity.

2.2. Improved package structure with RFR

At Barmag, we see our function not only in supplying efficiently operating machinery and equipment but we are continously working on the development of special additional
equipment which will help our customers to continue improving their production procedure. I would like to give you an
example.

Usually, random winding is used for high-speed winding of
synthetic fibers. As opposed to precision winding, this
means that the traverse motion speed remains constant with
increasing package diameter and corresponding decreasing
package speed. This means that the crossing angle remains
constant over the entire doffing cycle.

One of the biggest problems with the random wind is the
build-up of threads in the so-called ribbon formation area
during the winding procedure.
What does that mean?

At certain determined package diameters, when the package
speed reaches an integer multiple of the number of double
strokes, the threads are wound almost on top of one another.
This leads to a very instable package structure in this area.

In order to reduce this problem, various measures have been
suggested and tested. The so-called ribbon-breaking effect
is the most often used at present. This means that the traverse motion speed does not remain completely constant during the entire doffing cycle, but a saw-toothed frequency
change of $\pm$ 1 to $\pm$ 3% is superimposed on the traverse
drive frequency. In many cases this type of ribbon-breaking
effect is sufficient in order to produce packages of acceptable quality. However, with this frequency modification,
although the residence time within the area of the ribbon is
less, the frequency of passing this particular area is greater. With the large package diameters the market now increasingly demands, the problems increase because the total production time spent winding in the area of critical ribbons
(lower integer ratio and/or fractional ratio) increases.

Based on extensive experience in the area of winding and microcomputers, we have now worked out a solution which sets
an end to most of the problems caused by ribbon formation. I
am talking about the RFR (Ribbon Free Random Wind) system.

Illustration (2) shows the package diameter on axis x and
the winding ratio R on axis y. The winding ratio R indicates
the number of package revolutions per double stroke. The integer winding ratio causes the well-known ribbon formation.
However, even intermediate ribbon formations as shown in illustration (3) can still result in winding problems.

For the RFR system, we have basicly two traversing frequencies. The speeds of the traverse cam and the chuck are measured throughout the entire doffing cycle and analyzed by microcomputer system. At a certain predetermined point prior to the approach of a ribbon formation area, the traverse drive is switched over from the first frequency to the second frequency to allow the winding process to operate outside the ribboning zone (illustration 4). At a predetermined point sufficiently well past the original ribboning zone, the traverse drive is switched back to the original frequency. The winding then continues at the original drive frequency until a precalculated point is reached just ahead of the next ribboning. Then the cycle described above is repeated.

The solution of these problems which has led to significant improved package unwinding characteristics in many cases, was possible only by the use of microcomputers.

2.3. Sensors and analysis of the sensor signals

Next to ensuring quality through the use of high-performance machines and equipment, in-line quality control, for instance monitoring of products is becoming increasingly important as well. It is the desire of every synthetic fiber producer to receive unambiguous, clear information at the end of every doffing cycle to learn whether or not the package is of acceptable quality. Therefore, certain quality-determing parameters have to be monitored at the winding positions to determine whether they stay within preset tolerances. Cost is one of the factors that limit the extent of data collected and we must concentrate on significant parameters. These basic statements apply to spinning equipment as well as to machines for subsequent processing, for example texturing machines.

One of these data which can be considered as a major quality indicator, is the yarn tension. However, where can one find a suitable, sufficiently sturdy and economical yarn tension measuring head on the market which can be used economically in multiple positions?

We accepted this challenge and have developed two very solid yarn tension measuring heads for a variety of applications. These work on the electro-pneumatic and opto-electrical principles. I do not want to go into details about these sensors at this point, but I do want to explain you the analysis of the sensor signals with the help of microcomputers.

Based on our experience with yarn tension as quality indicator it was not only our aim to monitor whether the average value of the yarn tension lies within preset limit values. Rather, but we also wanted to measure short-time peaks which may still lie within the limit values.
How has this task been realized?

Proceeding on the assumption that not the entire measuring range has to be monitored in the same way we are focusing on a tolerance range of only 10 or 15% of the entire measuring range (illustration 5). All yarn tension signals lying outside this tolerance range are designated as defects. But if you divide the preset tolerance range into 10 levels for instance and if you lead the measured signal to ten comparators with ten different reference levels, each yarn tension peak, also in this tolerance range, can be measured and stored virtually instantenously. The stored values can be transmitted to a computer with a relatively slowly scanning cycle, e.g. two to three seconds per machine. There the exact analysis takes place. After each scanning the memory bank is reset. Despite this relatively slow scanning method all yarn tension peaks are monitored.

This procedure demonstrates how, with relativly low expenses, an effective signal evaluation can be achieved. In this context, it should be mentioned that Barmag has applied for patent rights for the above mentioned yarn tension sensors as well as for this type of signal analysis.

2.4. Spindle-driven winder

Although high quality packages can be produced on our high-speed winders with friction drive, for special applications there is a certain demand for spindle driven winders. In this type of winding, the thread is supplied to the winder at constant speed and wound at constant circumferential speed respectively yarn tension.

The spindle speed of godet machines is controlled primarily by the yarn tension.

For the control, regulation and monitoring of such a spindle-driven winder, we are using a microcomputer. The direct digital control is supplied in form of a printed circuit board which can be plugged in (illustration 6).

This winder needs an individual frequency converter for the spindle drive. Partly with this application in mind, Barmag has developed the BELTRO-VERT converter system in which all individual converters are equipped with their own serial party line interface for easy data exchange. These converters are already equipped to accept the direct digital control card.

2.5. Control and monitoring of a texturing machine

As early as 1975, on the occasion of the ITMA Show, Barmag was the first machine manufacturer to introduce a texturing machine with an integrated minicomputer. The main function of the computer consisted of the digital in- and output of set and actual values in the automatic monitoring of the various process parameters (illustration 7).

Since the ITMA in 1979, our texturing machines series FK6-80 has been equipped with microcomputer control and monitoring systems as standard. At the beginning there were only three drives - controlled with high-precision - which could be changed independantly from each other through adjustment of set values. At the ITMA 1983, however, Barmag presented a texturing machine model FK6T-80 which was driven by a static frequency converter and individual synchronous motors per shaft. This made it possible to select any machine setting without manual operation (illustration 8).

By setting the specific product-related parameters, such as basic speed, draw ratio or crossing angle, the microcomputer supplied all converters with the corresponding set values by means of optical fibers. The control of the ribbon breaking and stroke modification for the traverse motion mechanism was also effected by input from the microcomputer control system integrated in the machine. It almost goes without saying, that the set values for the temperatures are also given digitally and that the actual values are micro-electronically monitored for out-of-limit values.

2.6. Automatic package handling (Doffing)

Very early Barmag has dealt with the question of automatic package and yarn handling and put this into practice for several years now in a large number of installations (illustration 9). Here, too, microcomputer control systems are used for the solution of complex control problems. This requires a data exchange between the control systems for the package and yarn handling section on one hand and the machine control system on the other. For this operation as well, serial party line interfacing is provided whith the machine control system in the role of "master" and the Doffer control as "slave".

Our extensive experience with Doffer control systems has made it particularly clear to us that the software is of decisive importance in the area of automation. Unfortunately, the quality of software cannot be judged from the outside. But perhaps the following indications may be helpfull in judging the sophistication of a software package:

Normally it can be estimated that only approximately 30% of the entire software package is needed to fulfill the control requirements as such. This means that by far the largest part is dedicated to fulfilling additional demands which cannot be imagined in their variety and therefore cannot be specified ahead of time.

Today, however, a great many sophisticated, nevertheless user-friendly software packages are available in this area of Doffer and Doffer control systems.

2.7. Automation and quality monitoring in the areas of spinning and texturing

In very general terms, automation is aimed at making products economically and of a constantly high quality maintaining flexibility in adapting these products to the changing market needs.

In the equipment so far, Barmag now has at its disposal the prerequisites for automation in the area of spinning and texturing machines.

Since automation of a production plant affects all sectors of an enterprise, automation has to be looked upon from an overall point of view. In all our efforts in this area, it was therefore important to come to the realization that successfull automation is not the sum of individual solutions, independent of each other, but rather, from the beginning, an overall automation concept has to be established.

Although it is usually easier to automate a completely new production line, for us, it is at least as important to make sure that our automation equipment can be incorporated successfully in existing production plants. In many cases, such a step becomes clearly apparent when it comes to modernizing a production plant.

Essential elements of automation - next to machine equipment - are the computers. When selecting them, it becomes increasingly clear that not one large universal process computer can handle the multitude of automation tasks. Instead, the trend towards a well-structured computer hierarchy is obvious.

As shown in illustration (10), we have taken this trend into account by using high-quality microcomputer control systems (PLC) for each winding position to handle automation tasks in the area of winding. It is part of the function of this PLC not only to control the winder functions but also to exchange data with the machine control system as well as with the corresponding individual frequency converters.

The selection of a suitable and economical communication network depends on how independently the individual control systems are supposed to work. This means that the type and extent of the data exchange which is to take place by means of this communication network has to be estimated. As a logical compromise between expenditure and performance, we have chosen fast serial party line interfacing for these tasks, as already mentioned several times. Through this network, the machine PLC transmit to the winder PLC not only control signals, but, among others, also set values for the operation of individual frequency converters. Furthermore, diagnostic information can be transmitted in inverse direction from the individual frequency converters over the winder PLC to the machine PLC .

Besides the possibility of having each winding position work
as an independant unit, some overall machine functions have
also been achieved with microcomputer control, among these
especially the monitoring and analysis of parameters which
influence the quality. Apart from continuously measurable
physical data, such as temperature, pressure, speed and yarn
tension, the measured value of the package weight is of
great importance (illustration 11).

Therefore, we integrated in our Doffer a high-precision
weighing device. In conjunction with a very precise doff timer resp. measuring system, the data are analyzed for each
winding position on each machine. Thus, important quality
information can be derived from the package weight.

Package transport all the way to the packing station is part
of the overall concept we have mentioned. So is relating
production and quality information to the individual packages.

These tasks are normally assumed by a superior host computer
which receives its information through the corresponding machine control systems.

3. KNOWLEDGE GAINED AND CONCLUSIONS

From what is said so far, it may be concluded that the micro-computer technology has become an integral part of our
spinning and texturing machines. Many decisive breakthroughs
were made possible only through the use of the micro-electronics. Today, we can barely begin to imagine what additional possibilities will be open to us in this area in future years.
But one thing should be made clear, and that is that the micro-computer technology in machines and equipment for the
production of synthetic fibers must not become an end in itself. On the contrary, it should always be an efficient tool
in finding economical solutions to specific tasks, as e.g.
in the area of automation and quality monitoring for the benefit of the producers of synthetic fibers, the subsequent
processors and finally, for the benefit of the customer of
these products.

barmag
Dr. Gerhard Martens
Vab - Ltg.
Postfach 110240
5630 Remscheid 11
West-Germany

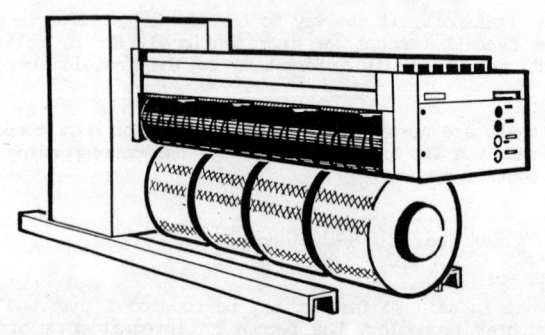

Illustr. 1: Barmag high-speed winder SW46SD

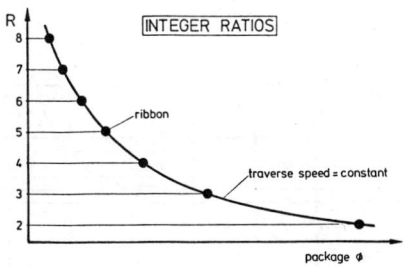

Illustr. 2: Winding graph   Integer ratios

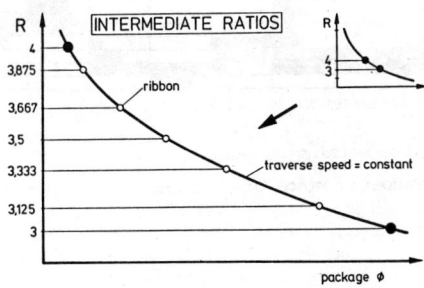

Illustr. 3. Winding graph   Intermediate ratios

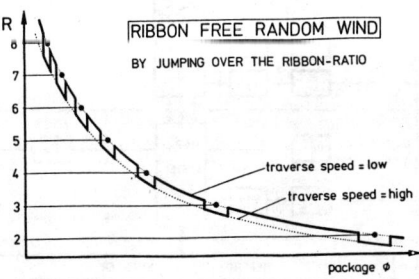

Illustr. 4: RFR (diagrammatic sketch)

111

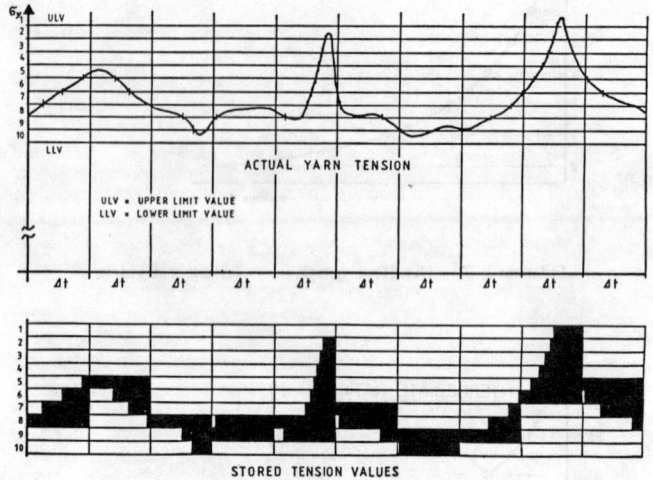

Illustr. 5: Impulse seizing by means of
a graduated range of tolerance

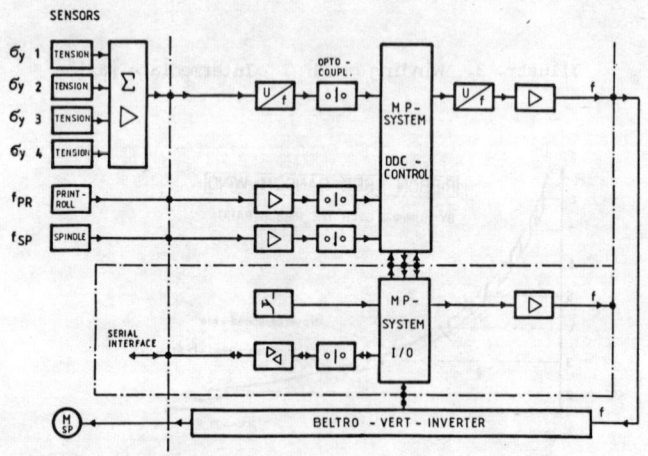

Illustr. 6: Spindle-driven winder (diagrammatic sketch)

112

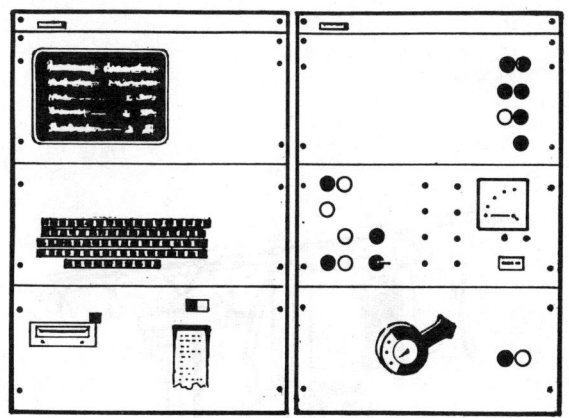

Illustr. 7:   Machine FK6 with minicomputer

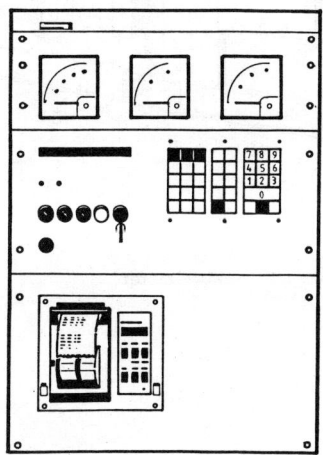

Illustr. 8:   Operating panel FK6M-80

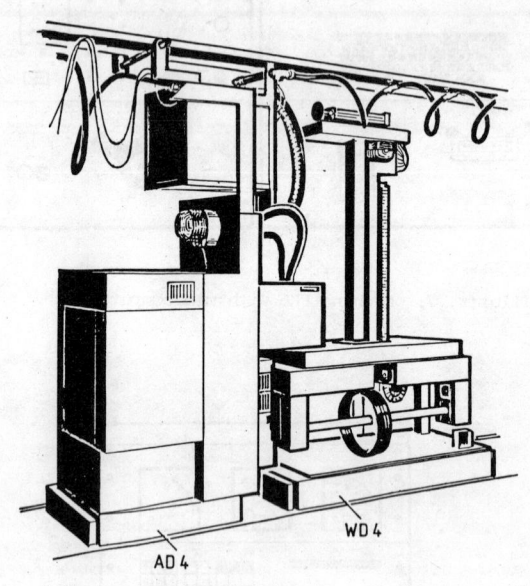

Illustr. 9: AWD4-Doffer

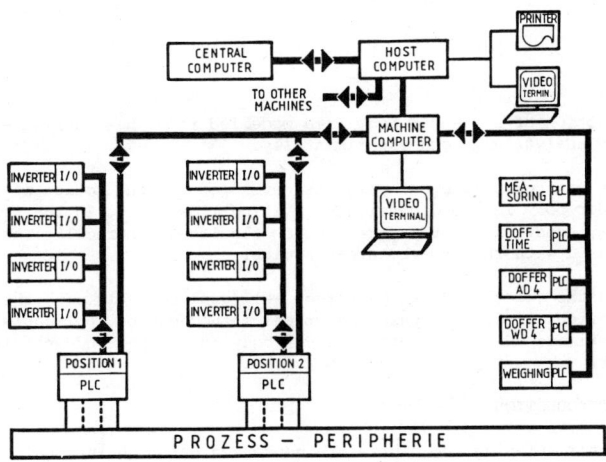

Illustr. 10: Decentralized control systems

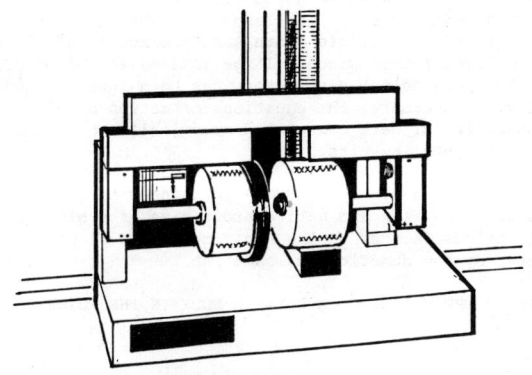

Illustr. 11: WD4-Doffer with weighing device

115

COMPUTER ANALYSES OF OPEN-END SPINNING

O.Yaida

ABSTRACT

The motion of a slender body in a modelled rotor has been investigated analytically and experimentally.

First an approximate analysis was developed for the motion of a slender body in two dimensional rotating flow field. In the next place, equations of the motion were calculated numerically, and compared with the experimental results.

Since the calculated values agreed well qualitatively with the experimental results, this analytical method can be applicable to estimate the motion of a slender body in an open-end-spinning rotor.

1. INTRODUCTION

In rotor spinning the fibres are condensed onto the internal surface of a rapidly rotating rotor which is in the form of a shallow re-entrant frustum(1). In order to improve the characteristics of open-end-spun yarns, it is necessary to control the mechanism of yarn formation, especially the motion of a fibre entering the rotor from the feed tube.

However, it is very difficult to analyze the motion of a fibre in a three dimensional space of open-end-spinning rotor rotaing with a high speed.

In this paper, as the first stage in predicting the fibre motion in an open-end-spinning rotor, a slender body has been used as the simplest model of a single fibre, and the motion of a slender body in a modelled rotor twice as large in size as the practical Toyoda BD-200 open-end spinning rotor, has been investigated experimentally. Furthermore, the equations of motion based on Shiomi's analysis (2) were calculated numerically, and compared with the experimental results.

Since the motion of a slender body is influenced by various factors associated with the flow and native properties of a slender body, effects of various factors on the behaviours of a slender body are estimated by the numerical calculation.

2. ANALYSIS OF THE MOTION OF A SLENDER BODY IN THE ROTOR

2.1 Theory

2.1.1 Equations of Motion

Several workers have investigated the motion of a slender body moving in a parallel current (3,4,5). However, there are only a few reports on the motion of a slender body moving in a rotating flow (6,7). We considered that Shiomi's analysis can be applied to the case of the fibre motion in an open-end-spinning rotor.

Shiomi's analysis deals with the motion of a slender body in a two dimensional flow field under some assumptions. According to this method, the motion of a slender body can be nnalysed sufficiently by using polar coordinates (r, θ) with the origin(0) at the centre of the rotating flow as shown in Fig.1.

The assumptions used in this analysis are as follows.
1) The fluid is incompressible.
2) The slender body moves in a two dimensional flow field.
3) The slender body is a straight rigid body having circular cross section.
4) The gravity and buoyancy can be neglected.
5) The pressure drag acting upon dl and perpendicular to it is given by equation (1).

$$dD = \frac{1}{2} \rho \cdot di \cdot Cd \cdot Vv^2 \cdot dl \quad ------------- (1)$$

where dl = infinitely small length along the slender body
  dD = pressure drag acting upon dl perpendicular to dl
  ρ = density of the fluid
  di = diameter of the slender body
  Cd = drag coefficient of the slender body
  Vv = relative velocity component of flow in direction perpendicular to axis of the slender body.

6) The drag coefficient of the slender body is represented as a function of the Reynolds number(Re_1), and given by equation (2).

$$Cd = (8\pi/Re_1)/[2.0022 - \ln(Re_1)] \quad (Re_1 < 1)$$

$$Cd = -4.078 + 16.631 Re_1^{-0.3778} \quad (1 \leq Re_1 < 5)$$
$$--------- (2)$$
$$Cd = (0.707 + 3.42 Re_1^{-0.5})^2 \quad (5 \leq Re_1 < 37)$$

$$Cd = 0.95 + 4 Re_1^{-0.5} \quad (37 \leq Re_1)$$

$$(Re_1 = \frac{|Vv| \cdot di}{\nu})$$

where ν = kinematic viscosity of fluid.

7) The frictional drag acting upon dl parallel to axis of the slender body is given by equation (3).

$$dF = \pi \cdot \rho \cdot \nu \cdot Vp \cdot dl \cdot Nu \quad --------------- (3)$$
$$(Nu = 0.36 + 0.48 \, Re_2^{0.5}, \text{ and } Re_2 = \frac{|Vp| \cdot di}{\nu})$$

where Nu = Nusselt number
  Vp = relative velocity component of flow in direction parallel to axis of the slender body.

The rotational and translational motion of the slender body in a rotating flow are given by equations(4),(5) and (6).

$$\ddot{\phi} = 6 \cdot \rho \cdot di \, \frac{1}{m \cdot L^2} \int_{-\frac{L}{2}}^{\frac{L}{2}} Vv^2 \cdot Cd \cdot l \cdot dl - \ddot{\theta} \quad ----------- (4)$$

$$\ddot{r} = -\frac{D}{m} \sin\phi + \frac{F}{m} \cos\phi + r\dot{\theta}^2 \quad ----------- (5)$$

$$\ddot{\theta} = \frac{D}{r \cdot m} \cos\phi + \frac{F}{r \cdot m} \sin\phi - \frac{2}{r} \dot{r}\dot{\theta} \quad -------- (6)$$

where $\ddot{\phi}$ = inclination acceleration of the slender body
  $\ddot{r}$ = acceleration of G in radial direction
  $\ddot{\theta}$ = rotation angular acceleration of G
  G = centre of gravity of the slender body
  l = length measured along the axis from G
  L = total length of the slender body
  m = mass of the slender body

D = total pressure drag acting perpendicular to the slender body

F = total frictional drag acting parallel to the slender body

r = radial coordinate of G

$\dot{r}$ = velocity of G in radial direction

$\dot{\theta}$ = rotation angular velocity of G

ϕ = inclination angle of the slender body.

Therefore, the orientation and locus of a slender body in a rotating flow can be obtained by solving the above equations. Since we can use the above equations only when the slender body moves in a clear space of the rotor, these equations require some correction after an end of the slender body contacts the inner wall of the rotor. That is, the slender body is influenced by the reaction and frictional force from the inner wall of the rotor. Hence, the following equations can be obtained on referring to equations (4), (5) and (6).

$$\ddot{\phi} = 6 \cdot \rho \cdot di \; \frac{1}{m \cdot L^3} \int_{\frac{L}{2}}^{\frac{L}{2}} Vv^2 \cdot Cd \cdot l \cdot dl - \ddot{\theta} - 12 \cdot P \; \frac{1}{m \cdot L^2}$$
$$(\frac{L}{2} \cdot \cos(\frac{\pi}{2} - (\phi - \alpha)) + \mu \cdot \frac{L}{2} \sin(\phi - \alpha - \frac{\pi}{2})) \quad \text{---(7)}$$

$$\ddot{r} = - \frac{D}{m}\sin\phi + \frac{F}{m}\cos\phi + r \cdot \dot{\theta}^2 - \frac{P}{m}\cos\alpha - \frac{\mu \cdot P}{m}\sin\alpha \quad \text{---(8)}$$

$$\ddot{\theta} = \frac{D}{r \cdot m}\cos\phi + \frac{F}{r \cdot m}\sin\phi - \frac{2}{r}\dot{r}\dot{\theta} - \frac{P}{r \cdot m}\sin\alpha$$
$$+ \frac{\mu \cdot P}{r \cdot m}\cos\alpha \quad \text{------------------(9)}$$

$$(\cos\alpha = \frac{r + L/2 \cdot |\cos\phi|}{R}, \; \sin\alpha = \frac{L/2 \cdot \sin\phi}{R}, \; \alpha = \tan^{-1}(\frac{\cos\alpha}{\sqrt{\cos\alpha\cos\alpha+1}})$$
$$- \frac{\pi}{2})$$

where   P = reaction applied to the slender body by inner wall of the rotor

R = maximum radius of the rotor

α = angle between straight lines connecting the centre of the rotor with G and with the end of the slender body contacting the rotor wall

μ = coefficient of dynamic friction between the slender body and rotor wall

Moreover, when the end of the slender body contacts the inner wall of the rotor, there exists a quantitative relation between r and ϕ as shown in Fig.2.

$$R^2 = (\frac{L}{2})^2 + r^2 - 2 \cdot (\frac{L}{2}) \cdot r \cdot \cos\phi \quad \text{--------(10)}$$

$$\dot{r}(L \cdot \cos\phi - 2r) = \dot{\phi} \cdot L \cdot r \cdot \sin\phi \quad \text{--------------(11)}$$

$$\ddot{r}(L \cdot \cos\phi - 2r) = \ddot{\phi} \cdot L \cdot r \cdot \sin\phi + 2 \cdot \dot{r}^2 + 2 \cdot \dot{r} \cdot \dot{\phi} \cdot L \sin\phi$$
$$+ \dot{\phi}^2 \cdot L \cdot r \cdot \cos\phi \quad \text{--------------(12)}$$

Consequently, we solve equations (7), (8), and (9) with P=0, only when a slender body moves in a clear space, and solve equations (7), (8), (9), (10), (11) and (12) simultaneously after the end of the slender body contacts the inner wall of the rotor.

118

2.1.2 Velocity Distribution of the Flow in the Rotor

The velocity distribution is required so that the equations described above can be solved numerically. Fortunately, we have already obtained the velocity distribution of air flow in same rotor (8). Fig.3 shows the relation between the radial position divided by R and the circumferential flow velocity divided by the circumferential velocity of the rotor. We obtained the equations of velocity distribution by connecting the measured points in Fig.3 with straight lines.

2.1.3 Numerical Calculation

We solved numerically the above equations of motion under conditions that ρ =101.94 Kg·s^2/m^4, L=40 mm, μ=0.3. The initial values are ri=0.034 and 0.044, ṙi=0, ϕi=π/2, $\dot{\phi}$i =0, θi=0, $\dot{\theta}$i=10(rad/sec).

If the position, velocity and acceleration of s slender body at a certain time is calculated, then each value relating to the motion of a slender body can be obtained over very short time intervals by solving the equations described above. Thus, we calculated the motion of a slender body numerically by dividing the time into ΔT periods.

2.2 Experimental

2.2.1 Apparatus

We have designed and built a model in order to observe the motion of a slender body in a rotating open-end-spinning rotor. This is shown schematically in Fig.4. In this study, we used a modelled one based on a BD-200 Toyoda rotor, because the shape of an actual rotor is not only complicated and small but runs at a high speed.

2.2.2 Materials

We used fine carbon rod as the slender body. The carbon rod used in this study is 40 mm in length and it's density is 166.0 Kg·s^2/m^4. Three different diameters were chosen, those being 0.3, 0.5, 0.7 mm. The carbon rod was finished with a very thin coat of white paint.

2.2.3 Methods and Conditions

The slender body is carried by the air current into the rotor through the feed tube. Due to the centrifugal force in the rotor, the slender body passes to the peripheral groove on the collecting surface through the space of the rotor. The air current originates from the rotor which has ventilation holes. Since the current into the rotor through the feed tube has direct effects upon the flow in the rotor, we observed the motion of the slender body while varying the inlet position of the feed tube. Experimental conditions are tabulated in table 1. The motion of the slender body in the rotor was observed photographically from above and from the side by using a stroboscope. The flash interval of the stroboscope was 0.0033 seconds.

2.2.4 Results

Fig.5(a) and (b) show examples of the photographs obtained; (a) is a case of experimental condition 2 and (b) is of condition 4 (table 1), respectively. Fig.5(a) is an example of the photographs taken from above, and the motion of a slender body until it lies down on the inner wall of the rotor is observed clearly. That is, a slender body is influenced considerably by the flow in the rotor, and moves spirally while rotating, before at last reaching the inner wall of the rotor. Furthermore, a slender body collides with the inner wall of the rotor from its back end, and then falls forward. Fig.5 (b) is an example of the photographs taken from the side. After the slender body leaves the exit of the feed tube, it moves toward the bottom, and then rises to the upper face and at last moves rotationally toward the inner wall of the rotor. From the above photographs, it can be seen that the motion of a slender body in the rotor is in fact three dimensional motion.

3. COMPARISON OF THE EXPERIMENTAL RESULTS WITH CALCULATED RESULTS

Fig.6 shows the comparison of the experimental results with cal-culated results;(a) represents the experimental result and (b) the calculated result obtained by substituting initial values into the equations of motion. Comparing (a) and (b) as shown in Fig.6, close agreement between observed and calculated results is recog-nized in spite of the assumptions which have been used.

Furthermore, in order to compare numerically, the radial coordinate (r), rotation angle (θ) and inclination angle (ϕ) of the slender body were read off the photographs.

Figs.7,8 and 9 show the comparison of the values obtained from photographs with calculated curves. As shown Figs.7,8 and 9, it was verified that the present approximate analysis is capable of estimating the motion of a slender body in the rotor.

4. EFFECTS OF VARIOUS FACTORS ON THE MOTION OF A SLENDER BODY

The motion of a slender body is influenced by various factors associated with the flow and native properties of a slender body.

In this section, by using equations of motion of a slender body derived in the previous section, effects of the density (ρ_a), diameter (d_i), length (L), initial inclination angle (ϕ_i), initial angular velocity $(\dot{\theta}_i)$ of the slender body and rotor speed (n) on the motion of the slender body are estimated by the numerical calcu-lation.

Table 2 shows the conditions of calculation.

Fig.10 shows the calculated results obtained by varying only the diameter of the slender body. Since the density and length of the slender body are the same, the centrifugal force acting upon the slender body increases in proportion to the diameter, and reaches quickly the inner wall of the rotor.

Figs.11 and 12 show the effects of the density and length of the slender body, respectively. Only the radial coordinate is influenced by the difference of the density, the rotation angle and inclination angle are not hardly influenced by the density and length of the slender body.

Figs.13 and 14 show the effects of the initial inclination angle and initial angular velocity on the motion of the slender body, respectively. The initial inclination angle has direct effects upon the inclination angle and radial coordinate of the slender body moving in the rotor, but it can be considered that there is no effect of the initial inclination angle on the rotation angle as shown in Fig.13. It is also shown in Fig.14 that the initial angular velocity has direct effects upon the rotation angle of the slender body.

Fig.15 shows the effects of the difference of the rotor speed on the motion of the slender body. As is obvious from this figure, the rotor speed is the main factor so that the motion of the slender body is dominated by the rotor speed.

CONCLUSIONS

As the first stage in predicting the fibre motion in an open-end-spinning rotor, the motion of a slender body in a modelled rotor was investigated experimentally and theoretically. Furthermore, effects of various factors on the motion of the slender body were estimated by the numerical calculation.

The results obtained are summarized as follows.
(1) A slender body is influenced considerably by the flow in the rotor. After a slender body leaves the exit of the feed tube, it moves toward the rotor bottom, and then rises to the upper face and at last moves rotationally toward the inner wall of the rotor. It reaches the inner wall from its back end, and falls toward on the wall.
(2) In regard to the motion of a slender body in the rotor, the analysis method derived in this paper gives fairly good agreement with the experimental results.
(3) The rotor speed is the main factor which has direct effects upon the behaviours of a slender body moving in the rotor.
(4) It can be considered that there is no effect of the length on the behaviour of a slender body moving in the rotor within this calculation range.

REFERENCES

(1) F.Happey. 'Contemporary Textile Engineering', Academic press, London, 1982,p.200.
(2) A.Shiomi, T.Matsumoto and M.Uno. J.Text. Mach. Soc. Japan, 1982, 35, 135.
(3) J.Ripka. Conference on Open End Spinning, Prague, 1969.
(4) L.H.Bangert, P.M.Sagdeo. Textile Res. J.,1977, 47, 773.
(5) A.Shiomi, H.Kise and M.Uno. J. Text. Mach. Soc. Japan, 1982, 35, 105.
(6) A.Horikawa, K.Chiba, K.Nishitani and T.Ueshima. J. Text. Mach. Soc. Japan, 1980, 33, 118.
(7) J.Ripka and J.Junek. Textiltechnik, 1974, 24, 341.
(8) A.Horikawa, O.Yaida and M.Niida. J. Text. Mach. Soc. Japan, 1980, 33, 78.

Faculty of Science of Living,
Osaka City University,
Sumiyoshi-Ku, Osaka, 558
Japan.

Table 1: Experimental Conditions

Condition No.	di	rf/R	lf/R	Ⓗ	n
1	0.3	0.55	0.30	20	230
2	0.5				
3	0.7				
4	0.3	0.71			
5	0.5				
6	0.7				

Where, rf.= position of insertion of feed tube
lf = length of feed tube inserted into rotor
Ⓗ = angle of insertion of feed tube
n = rotor speed (rpm)

Table II: Conditions of Calculation

Condition No.	Factor	Value
1	di (mm)	0.3
2		0.5
3		0.7
5	ϕ_i	90°
7		100°
8		80°
5	$\dot{\theta}_i$ (rad/s)	10
9		20
10		30
5	L (mm)	40
11		20
12		30
13		50
14		60
5	ρ_a (kg·s²/m⁴)	166.0
15		83.0
16		249.0
17		332.0
5	n (rpm)	230
18		115
19		345
20		460

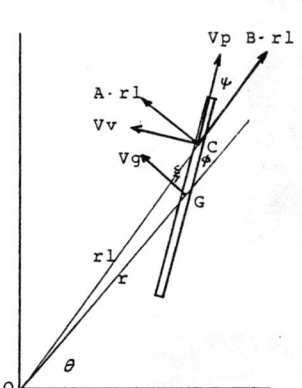

Fig.1 Coordinate System

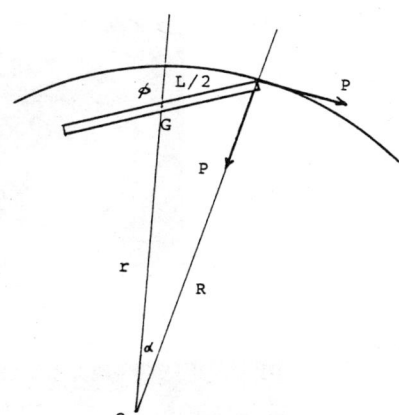

Fig.2 Forces Acting Upon a Slender
Body After It Reaches the Wall

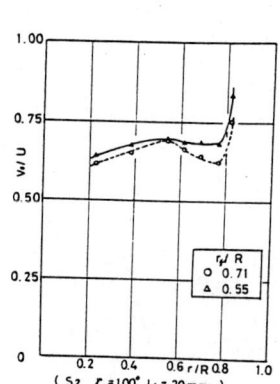

Fig.3 Velocity Distribution
of the Flow in the
Rotor

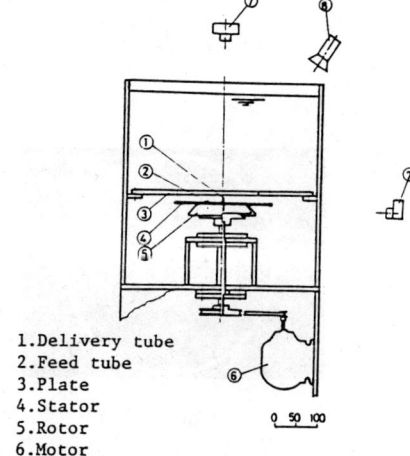

1.Delivery tube
2.Feed tube
3.Plate
4.Stator
5.Rotor
6.Motor
7.Camera
8.Stroboscope

Fig.4 Schematic of the Experimental
Apparatus

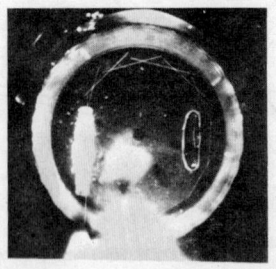

(a)

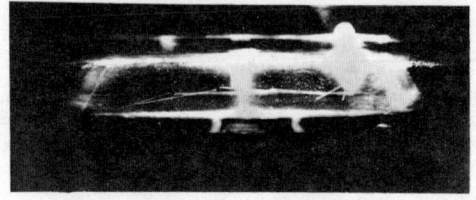

(b)

Fig.5 Motion of a Slender Body: (a) is the
photographs taken from above, (b) is
taken from the side.

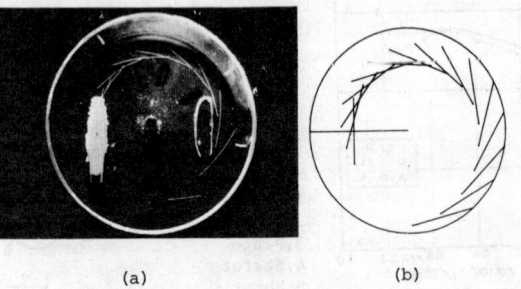

(a)   (b)

Fig.6 Comparison of the Experimental Results
with Calculated Results: (a) is the
experimental results, (b) is the calculated
results.

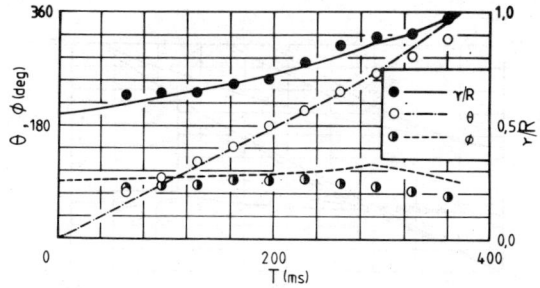

Fig.7 Comparison of the Values Obtained from Photographs
with Calculated Curves (1)
(Condition 1)

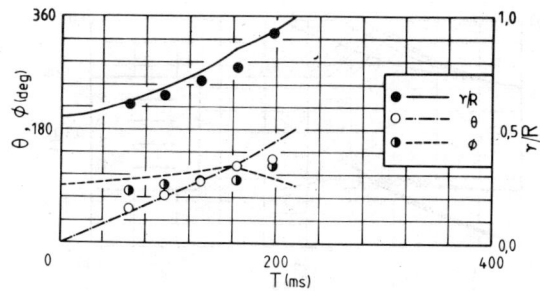

Fig.8 Comparison of the Values Obtained from Photographs
with Calculated Curves (2)
(Condition 3)

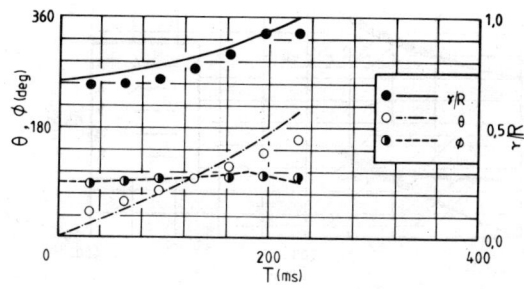

Fig.9 Comparison of the Values Obtained from Photographs
with Calculated Curves (3)
(Condition 4)

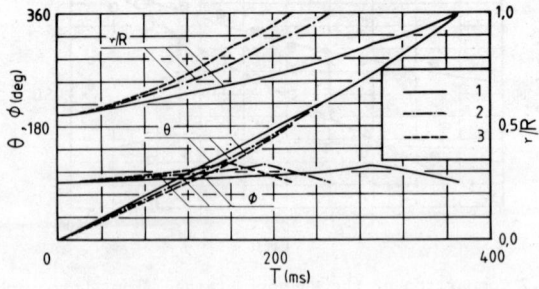

Fig.10 Effects of the Diameter of the Slender
Body on the Motion.

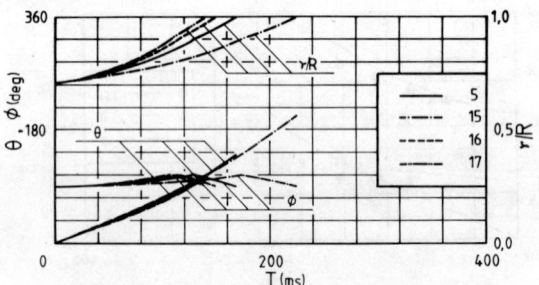

Fig.11 Effects of the Density of the Slender
Body on the Motion

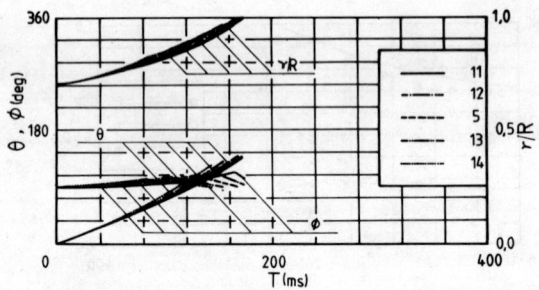

Fig.12 Effects of the Length of the Slender
Body on the Motion

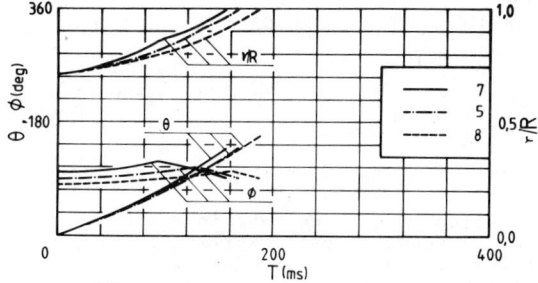

Fig.13 Effects of the Initial Inclination Angle
on the Motion

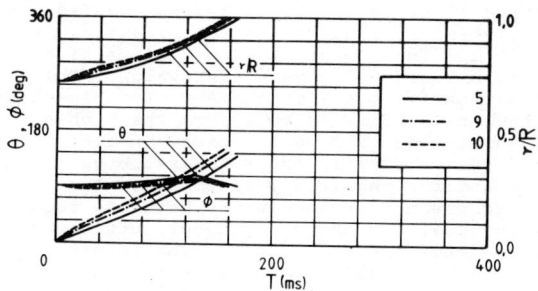

Fig.14 Effects of the Initial Angular Velocity
on the Motion

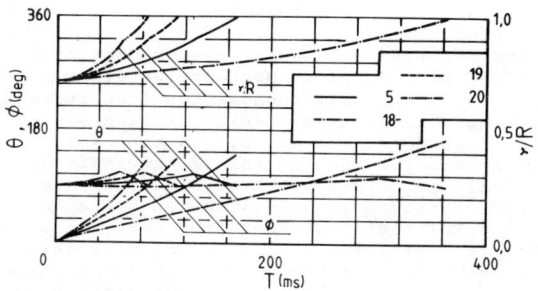

Fig.15 Effects of the Rotor Speed on the Motion

EFFICIENCY AND AUTOMATION IN SPINNING:COMPUTERIZED DETERMINATION OF THE PRINCIPAL TECHNOLOGICAL AND ECONOMIC PARAMETERS

A. Cerretini and G. Godio

ABSTRACT

The simulation of machine behaviour and technological processes represent a valid working instrument for the information and data it can give.
The utilization of these tecniques is very wide and covers all firm activities, from design to production. By means of a simulation model, one can analize the effect of the various parameters on chosing a piecing system.

1. INTRODUCTION

The textile industry has recently changed from an essentially labour industry into an industry based on capital and investment: the cost of machinery per employee is assuming very high values. This transformation imposes a management of the machinery and of the entire firm as to assure the highest quality and the optimum performance. On line control is therefore decisive in order to assure quality standards and the required performances. The simulation of machine performance under both the techno-logical-physical and the managing-productive aspects is used to determine the best working conditions and to evaluate "acceptable" deviations from such conditions in the case of the practical use of the machine. The following case refers to the simulation of a spinning machine, employing a statistical distribution of the aleatory variables:
- (a) moment of end break;
- (b) time elapsed between end break and beginning of repair;
- (c) time necessary for repair;
- (d) doffing time;
- (e) time necessary to change roving bobbins.
The machine efficiency has been evaluated on the basis of the statistical composition (interferences, etc.) of these aleatory variables. Modern systems for machine performance control (in the case of spinning frames for the control of the individual unit: spindle or rotor) allow a relatively simple and a sufficiently precise evaluation of the real distribution of the above mentioned parameters. This data is useful for the following reasons:
- (1) to control the production performance compared with an optimum situation theoretically determined or based on previous reliable data.
- (2) to design for the department more economic and useful lay-outs and structures of organization (e.g. to concentrate end break repairs only

where and when they exceed a certain threshold).
(3) to design automatic piecing devices which
    have the requirements for a correct optimum
    condition.
The following step will be to connect programmes
which simulate machine management with programmes
simulating the physical and dynamic behaviour of
the technological spinning process. For example:
data from studies found in the enclosed references
already allow to foresee power consumption and yarn
tension for ring spinning frames. Similar studies
are being made to simulate the entire rotor O.E.
spinning cycle. The aim is to dispose of valid
instruments to foresee the behaviour of entire
working cycles after the operative conditions have
changed.

2. SIMULATION MODEL

2.1 Description
A textile machine being a multi-position machine
(spindles) may be considered a system requiring
various operations to be carried out by a worker or
automatic device. In the model described below it
will be assumed, for the sake of simplicity, that
the operator shall only piece up the end breaks.
When an end break occurs, and the operatoris busy
somewhere else, a certian period of time will pass
before this end break will be pieced up. The time
elapsed between end break and beginning of repair,
and the consequent loss of production, depend on
various parameters:
- number of spindles looked after by the operator;
- end break frequency;
- operator moving speed;
- the criteriaby which the operator chooses the next
  end break to be pieced up.
This simulation model allows to evaluate the influence
of each of the above mentioned parameters on:
  time between end break and repair;
- operator efficiency;
- machine efficiency.
Furthermore, the time advancement of the model depends
on the duration of the events. Three kinds of events
have been considered:
- end breaks;
- end of operator's moving;
- end of spindle down-time.
In order to establish the time required for end breaks
and   piecing up   it is possible to use both
classic processes (normal, exponential, Poisson, etc.)
and processes realized on the ground of statistical
obeservations.
As far as the operator's moving event is concerned,
this speed is a variable, while the various criteria
for choosing the spindle to be repaired are:
- shortes moving time;
- continuous clockwise or counterclockwise movement

around the machine;
- casual choise (uniform distribution).

2.2 Example of utilization

Figures 1 and 2 illustrate some example of how to employ the simulation model; the results illustrate the operator's efficiency in relation to the number of spindles to be looked after and the various criteria and moving speed. For piecing up times a normal generator characterized by an average $E(t_s)$ (10 s) and a variance $\sigma^2(t_s)$ (3 s) has been used, for end break times a Poisson generator with average frequences of λ_1 (5.5 10^{-6} 1/s) and λ_2 (1.6 10^{-5} 1/s) and for the operator moving-speed values V_1 (0.6 m/s) and V_2 (1.5 m/s).

REFERENCES
(1) P. Citti, G. Nerli, P. Rissone, M. Bona, A. Cerretini.'Calcul du ballon par un method numerique. Application a la filature a anneau au retordage', Proceeding Sixth International Wool Textile Research Institute, Pretoria, South Africa, 1980.

(2) G. Lisini, G. Nerli, P. Rissone. Transactions of the ASME, J. of Engineering for Industry, 1981, 103, 424-430.

(3) G. Godio, G. Nerli, S. Nesti. 'Meccanica della Filatura ad Anello Rotante', Proceeding of Seventh National Congress AIMETA, Trieste, Italy, 1984.

(4) R. Capitani, A. Cerretini, G. Nerli. 'Studio del Sistema di Filatura Open-End a Rotore', Proceeding Seventh National Congress AIMETA, Trieste, Italy, 1984.

(5) F. Angrilli, V. Cossalter, G. Godio, V. Venchiarutti. Selezione Tessile, 1983, 21-22, 12.

CERIMATES S.P.A.
Centro Ricerche Macchine Tessili,
Villanova di Sotto,
33170 PORDENONE
Italy.

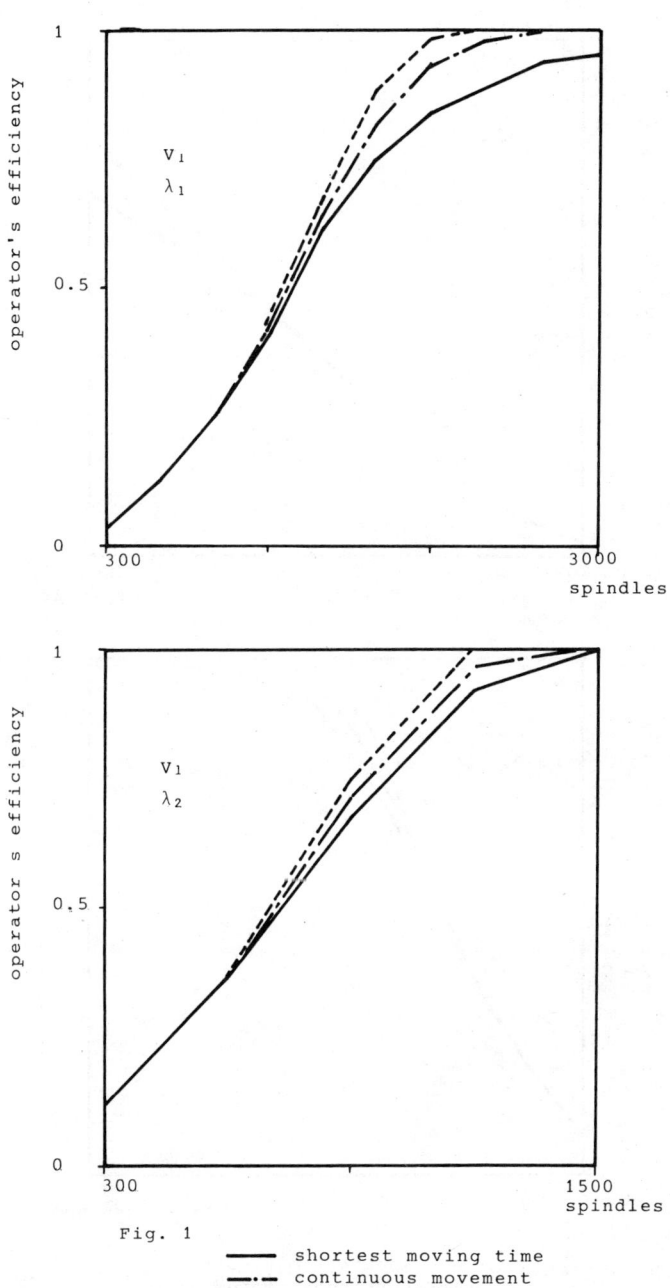

Fig. 1

——— shortest moving time
—·—·— continuous movement
- - - - casual choice

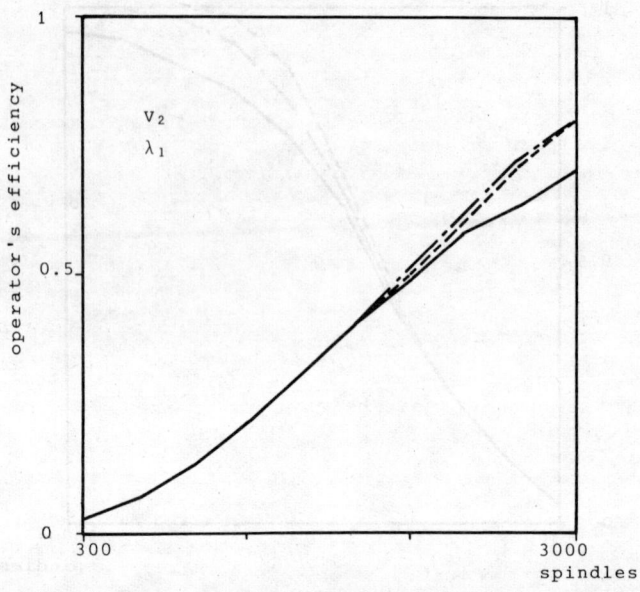

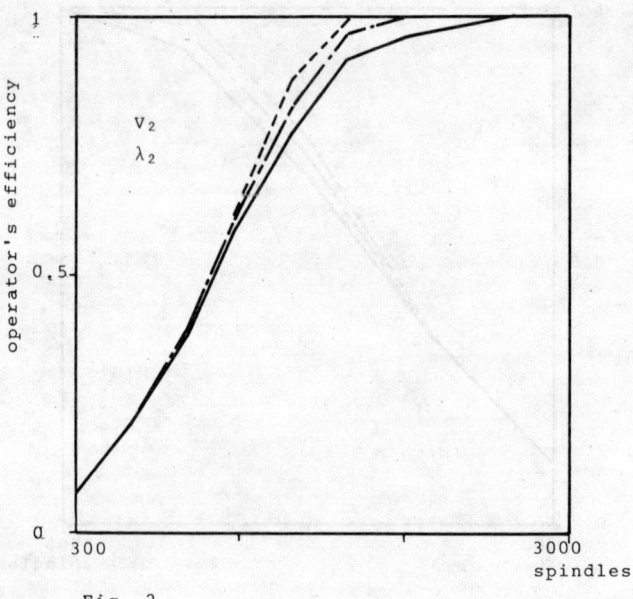

Fig. 2

——— shortest moving time
—·—· continuous movement
- - - - casual choice

132

MICROCOMPUTER-AIDED DATA-ACQUISITION AND PRODUCTION CONTROL IN A ROTOR-SPINNING MILL

J. Rüge

ABSTRACT

For spinning plants which are equipped with the highly
automated Rotor Spinning and Winding Machine Autocoro
the Informator system for computer aided data acquisition and production control is available.

Each Rotor Spinning Machine is equipped with a machine
Informator composed of keyboard, display and printer
which automatically at the end of the shift makes
a print-out as shift report about the actual production
data. Upon demand an intermediate report can be given
at any time about the period since the beginning
of the shift or about the previous shift.

The shift reports appear at will in three forms and
are complemented by an Off-Standard-Report which
gives statistical information about the last four
shifts.

The integrated length measuring device allows the
production of packages of equal length so that the
package remnants in warping are below 1 %.

Up to 100 individual machine Informators can be connected to a Central-Informator by an easily fitted
wire saving link. The Central-Informator offers a
comprehensive installation report and establishes
reports for days, weeks and months. This is done
with consideration of the Rotor Spinning Machines
according to production groups which may be adjusted
according to articles.

One feature of the Central-Informator is that it
can be extended by application of modern software
technology such as Menue-Technique, the High Level
Language BASIC and modular software supplement by
the user.

The principle of distributed processing ensures highest
security against data loss and enables call-up and
print-out of shift data by the machine Informator
as well as by the Central-Informator.

1. INTRODUCTION

Since the middle of the seventies Schlafhorst offers
for their machines data collecting and processing
systems for the textile mill.

Since this time a change in computer technique resulted
by the electronic with a positive reflection upon
purchasing costs, availability and capability of
such data acquisition systems.

We must, however, bear in mind that despite shorter innovation periods and the tendency that electronics soon will be available for everybody as purchasable consumer goods there are still some handicaps for easy application:

Programming capacity is rare and expensive

For the equivalent of one month of manpower for individual software you may get at each corner a complete personal-computer inclusive standard-software.

A free portable high level language is still missing

There have been many attempts and new efforts with personal-computers shall make us hopeful.

We are lacking a standardized applicable interface

which is also suitable for smaller computers.

For the electrical part alone this problem has been solved but this does not allow communication between two computers.

Schlafhorst offers for the Automatic Winding Machine Autoconer and the Automatic Rotor Spinning and Winding Machine Autocoro data acquisition systems with the trade name Informator.

In the following the Informator for the Automatic Rotor Spinning and Winding Machine Autocoro will be explained in respect of system construction, properties and usefulness for a rotor spinning plant.

2. THE SURROUNDINGS OF AUTOCORO ROTOR SPINNING

Rotor spinning is marked by the fact that the three classical processing steps roving frame, ring spinning frame and winding machine are substituted by only one single machine - the rotor spinning machine.

The Rotor Spinning Machine Autocoro for the first time introduced as new quality the high automation of spinning in rotor spinning.

Yarn breaks are repaired automatically by the piecing carriage. Full packages on the spinning positions are automatically exchanged against empty tubes with transfer tail by the package doffer and deposited upon a conveyor belt for each machine side.

Both devices are mobile at their own.

Thus the Autocoro spinning plant shows itself as a production process with several thousand spinning positions and with very few personnel but high and uniform efficiency. Today already there are installations with over 12 000 spinning positions.

The remaining non-automated tasks are:

- providing the spinning positions with supply material
- removal of finished cross-wound packages
- supervision of the quality produced
- maintenance measures

3. SYSTEM SURVEY

For such a rotor spinning installation as described
the data acquisition system Informator has become
to an indispensable tool for the management for the
daily tasks.

The total system consists of the three following
units (figure 1):

3.1 Machine Informator

It is located in the drive-stock of the machine.
It consists of a micro-computer basing upon the Motorola-Processor 6802, display, keyboard, printer and
the necessary transmission devices for the complete
machine.

3.2 Network and Controller

The network is designed as wire-saving link and allows
the connection of up to a maximum of 100 machine
Informators. A commonly available telephone cable
with 4 wires is used which can easily be installed.
At the end is a controller in an 19" housing which
serves as an interface transformer which operates
on one side the network and offers at the other side
the IEEE 488 standard.

3.3 Central-Informator

For the central processing of the data of all connected
machine-Informators we recommend the Technical Personnel
Computer 9010 of Hewlett Packard. The configuration
possesses sufficient storage capacity for data storing
even for longer periods. Furthermore an integrated
communication connecting point RS 232 generally offers
the possibility to convey datas to another computer.

4. CHARACTERISTICS OF THE MACHINE-INFORMATOR

The characteristics of the machine-Informator can
be briefly described as shown in figure 2.

The information is based upon the following machine
signals:
- running signal of the spindle
- fault signal of the spindle (red light)
- full diameter of the spindle
- yarn delivery speed of the machine
- on/off signal of the machine

A signal alteration is acknowleged as correct if
the new condition is identical during two call-up
cycles in sequence.

At a power failure the stored data of the Informator
are secured against loss by a battery-buffer of the
storage for about 720 hours.

The report appears either as shift or intermediate
report according to the desire of the user in one
of the three forms:

Short Report

this contains all summarized data related to the
machine.

Normal Report

this contains all data related to the machine
and to the individual sections.

Long Report

this contains all data related to the machine,
to the individual sections and to the individual
spindles.

Figure 3 shows an example of the shift reports as
short report.

It gives on top the information about the machine
number, the version number of the software, the date
and the time of the shift end.

Below are the important production parameters as
well as the association of the machine to a distinct
production group. In this example it is group 1.
The association is made by the input keyboard.

Between the dotted lines follows afterwards the actual
production information about the machine during the
last shift. In the example it is machine number 7
with 192 rotors. It operated with an efficiency of
97.2 % which corresponds to an average rotor running
time of 466 minutes. Overall there were 372 automatic
yarn piecings registered by the piecing carriage.

Further down some statistical datas are illustrated.
E. g. 494.7 kg yarn have been spun and 273 packages
have been produced. The average breakage free yarn
length was 178.9 km.

At the end of the report the Off-Standard-Report
can be seen which shall be explained as well as the
length measuring device briefly.

4.1 Off-Standard-Report

The Off-Standard-Report registers all spindles which
exceeded limit values within an adjustable number
of subsequent shifts.

This is the case

if the efficiency of one spindle is 25 % or more
below the overall machine efficiency

OR

if the number of piecings on a spindle is higher
than a calculated number of piecings per spindle

$$YPO = \frac{YP}{\text{number of rotors with piecings}} \times 2 + 3$$

This figure results from the total number of piecings
divided by the number of rotors with piecings multiplied by 2 and increased by 3

AND

if this has happened according to the input of the
user 1, 2, 3 or 4 times in subsequent shifts.

Thus efficiency and number of piecings are floating
limit values.

The example shows rotor number 24. Above the dotted
line are the limit values for the efficiency EFF
and the number of piecings YP with the index Ø
for the shift which just ended.

Behind are the limit values for the number of piecings
for the previous three shifts with the indications
1, 2 and 3.

This means that the rotor 24 in the just ended shift
with 9 piecings had a value above the limit value
of 5 piecings. It is understood that the efficiency
drops thus. That, however, was not the reason for
the bad production.

In the previous shift - listed under YP1 - a high
number of piecings was not the reason why the spindle
was in Off-Standard. Therefore it must have been
the efficiency.

In this way everything can be traced.

According to his requirements the user is enabled
to neglect individual exceptions according to his
requirements and concentrate upon repeated and syste-
matical faults.

This is supported by the application of the floating limit values in the Off-Standard-Report.

In case that the complete machine once is operating badly this can be seen on the overall efficiency. Thus the print-out of 216 spindles in Off-Standard is not required which would happen with the input of predetermined limit values.

4.2 Length Measuring

The second remarkable feature is the length measuring device. The Informator with length measuring device allows the production of packages with equal yarn lengths. In comparison with the hitherto applied method of packages with uniform diameter this has the advantage that the package remnants e. g. in warping are drastically reduced.

Up to now package remnants of 6 % to 13 % and even more have been everyday's practice but now the length measuring achieves package remnants less than 1 %.

To reach the goal to produce packages of even yarn length it is obvious that this can be done much more accurately by measuring the length than by measuring the appropriate diameter. The principle applied is shown in figure 4 and is based upon the delivered yarn length as proportional value of the number of revolutions of the take-up-roller.

This information is added up in the Informator and compared with the predetermined target length. As soon as the registered figure matches the predetermined figure the spinning position is switched off and signals to the automatic doffer the demand for package doffing and for repiecing an empty tube.

The absolute deviation of this procedure ranges by about 200 m for each spindle with an actual length of 100 km.

By tolerances in machine adjustments in respect of cradle pressure, yarn tension etc. the deviation may - according to experience - raise to values between 400 and 700 m per 100 km of yarn length.

The practical results show in many cases that, according to figure 5 package remnants are left over with less than half a percent and these remnants are subject to the reference value as shown in the picture.

After withdrawal of the packages in the warping creel the remnants were determined by permissible weight since the length of yarn is directly proportional to yarn count and weight.

The reduction of package remnants has the following advantages:

- reduction of rewinding cost for package remnants
- less stoppages in warping by exhausted packages
- reduction of possible faults by retying exhausted packages

One large Autocoro spinning mill operating with length measuring completely abandoned rewinding of package remnants since the small remnants would require higher rewinding costs than the savings by rewinding the remnants would be. They just sell the remnants.

5. EFFICIENCY CHARACTERISTICS OF THE CENTRAL INFORMATOR

As previously mentioned the Central Informator collects the production data of up to 100 individual machine Informators. This corresponds to a total number of almost 22 000 rotors. Today already collections of 12 000 rotors are realized.

It may not be in the interest of the responsible manager for rotor spinning that he receives e. g. a report from the Central informator about 8 000 rotors. Nobody can read this and nobody can sensibly store this.

Of interest is the total result split-up according to machines, production groups or lots and hints in which respect rotors show a negative result according to the criteria of the Off-Standard-Report.

The conception therefore is based upon condensing the datas to the super-imposed Central Informator. Hints are given to the Off-Standard-Reports which can be printed out on demand of the user.

The features of the Central Informator can be explained with the abstracts shown in figure 6.

The Central Informator also gives a long-term recording of the production combined with a condensation of a daily, weekly and monthly record.

By destination of the Autocoro machines via the machine Informator to groups a summarized production report is available according to lots or other criteria.

6. PERFORMANCE OF THE SYSTEM

In co-operation between the Central Informator and the individual machine Informators some rules in respect of handling by the user as well as from the systematic point of view must be defined to avoid conflicts.

Datas required for setting the rotor spinning machines
are input during adjustment of the machine by the
keyboard of the machine Informator. Here it is possible to receive all information in regard to the
machine.

The Central Informator holds in his concept the date,
the time and the shift-calendar which are downloaded
to the machine Informators.

The Informator-system is based upon the idea of distributed processing and easy extension by the user upon
the level of the Central Informator.

The machine Informator is a completely independent
system with basically the same features - whether
as stand-alone-device or connected to the network.
The machine Informator always has available the datas
of the running and the previous shift and records
them upon call-up at any time, even repeatedly. The
total system with Central Informator thus avoids
a data loss which might be caused by interference
of the Central Informator, the network including
the controller or an individual machine Informator.

The Technical Personnel Computer 9816S of Hewlett
Packard is used as Central Informator. This is a
16-Bit-Computer with the Motorola-Processor 68000
which operates together with a lintproof disc storage
in Winchester-technology. The corresponding software
of Schlafhorst uses the easy learnable programming
language BASIC. The layout of the software is so
that the user easily can make alterations or extensions.
This indeed is possible by the following features:

- easy to supervise data basic which again is basic
  for all further processing
- consequent modularizing of the software
- efficient basic software with the high level
  language BASIC.

This supports to an optimal extent the availability
of the data basis and the application of new data
fields. Writing and inserting of new moduls is possible
without problems. The dialogue correspondence is
supported by the Menue-Technique.

7. EXTENSIONS FOR FUTURE APPLICATIONS

As with any special system of this type naturally
the question arises about further extension and application.

We endeavour here to differentiate between three
qualities of extensibility.

7.1 Extensibility on the Machine Informator Level

Today's situation covers the explained features.
Extensions can be practically made only by Schlafhorst
because of the required knowlege about the machines.

We do see the next step in incorporating the information
about yarn breaks caused by yarn quality control
devices.

In respect of units and devices the connecting conditions on the Autocoro are incorporated by Schlafhorst
in respect of a uniform interface for yarn quality
control devices. It remains to be agreed with the
first users upon the volume of the shift records.

7.2 Extensionability on the Level of the Central
Informator

The capability has been explained.

The actual desire for extension will be related to
the software. The desires are very specifically here
which may result in a lot of handling problems which
grow with the distances of the partners to each other.

The Central Informator - to our knowledge for the
first time - offers a pioneer way which is proven
already successfully in two cases.

The applied principle of distributed processing in-
tentively created by clear arrangement of the software
and the data basis as well as by reserves in the
storage capacity are preconditions for the extension
of the software.

Time-problems by steady polling of all connected
machines are eliminated.

The programming language is the easy to learn high
level language BASIC with a powerful instruction
set and also a powerful operating system which, however, will not be realized by the user.

We utilize here the properties of a modern personnel
computer whereby the software can be extended by
the user. For this we deliver for each system the
complete programme documentation as well as the source
programmes.

Sometimes we are asked whether we could not use the
hardware of another manufacturer.

This thought is understandable. But since we miss
software portability that will not do. To write one-
self the complete software inclusive the communication
to the machine Informators for another computer also
cannot be recommended. A quick calculation of the
costs proves that immediately.

7.3 Connection to the EDP (Electronic Data Processing)

According to our experience it is desirable to leave
things which belong to the EDP there and to leave
things which are necessary for the technical management
of rotor spinning to the Central Informator. There
is often the desire to reduce the cost for one CPU.
In this way, however, neither the manager of the
EDP nor the manager of rotor spinning will be pleased.

The cost for establishing of the software and the
system integration are manifold higher than the CPU
with accessories.

One user of the Central Informator e. g. connected
the Central Informator for transmission of shift
datas on line to his commercial EDP-installation.
For this purpose he utilizes the serial line interface
RS 232 and made the required programme extensions
by himself. The Central Informator thus supplies
by loose coupling the function of a subsystem.

Another possibility is the data transmission by Floppy
Disc.

8. PRACTICAL WORK AND UTILITY

The experiences in rotor spinning equipped with highly
automatic machines such as the Autocoro show that
only the application of a production data acquisition
system enables the full utilization of the production
capacity.

A rotor spinning plant with 20 machines has a production
capacity of about 4 300 rotors available. This could
correspond to a daily production of 40 t for a yarn
with the count 50 tex. In the meantime there are
farther greater installations.

The responsible management for production tries very
hard to chase the causes for efficiency losses very
quickly and to get them in order again as quickly
as possible.

Finding of the fault causes many times is the most
difficult task:

- is it the machine?
- is it the supply material?
- is it the environment?

Then there are more questions whether it was a random
or a systematic fault and so on.

If the management possesses a system such as the
Central Informator it has after shift end immediately
the results available.

All machines will be shown which are running below
the expected efficiency.

For all machines the number of Off-Standard spindles
will be noted and the number of faults where the
piecing automatic could not restart the spinning
procedure.

Reports of such examples are shown in figures 7 and 8.

Basing upon this information the decision can be
made whether and where first of all trouble shooting
must be done.

If a fault on the machine is suspected the maintenance
mechanic will go to the machine and will be informed
by the machine Informator about the detailed report
about the respective spindle. So he will get further
information.

An example out of practice.

We received the following Off-Standard-Report from
one of our customers.

Off-Standard-Report

ROT	EFFO	YPO	YP1	YP2	YP3	SH
	63.2	9	7	7	9	4
13	80.6	17	18	18	14	42
21	71.7	57	53	62	58	19
43	74.5	9	12	17	21	6

NO PRODUCTION

40	95

This recording shows the following negative conditions:

- The yarn breakage limit values are with 7 - 9 very
  high (usually 3 - 5).
- 3 spinning positions went during 3 shifts in sequence
  in Off-Standard-positions, partly up to 42 times.
- A high cumulation of piecings within the first
  section (not demonstrated here but documented in
  the normal shift-print-out).

The reasons could be traced as follows:

- channel plate damaged (13)
- sealing defective (21)
- contamination of the fibre guide channel (43)

Furthermore for the complete machine the following
became obvious.

The rather high yarn breakage limit values without
cumulation to Off-Standard spinning positions allows
the conclusion that the influence is not based upon

winding positions but upon the sliver supply. It
was found out that empty running sliver cans with
a proportion of 30 % of all yarn breaks had been
responsible for the breakages.

The Off-Standard spinning positions with the identification NO PRODUCTION have been investigated systematically. The findings were:

- limit ring missing, so no running signal (40)
- yarn lifter wire missing, so no running signal (95)

The customer made the can change for complete sections.
The remaining remnants were processed on the first
section. This is a measure with very negative consequences since the high yarn break concentration is
upon a few packages only.

The value of the Central Informator can be appreciated
by a comparison with a spinning plant which operates
with machine Informators only.

20 machines without Central Informator means that
per shift there must be 20 print-outs collected and
evaluated. At 3-shift-operation these are 60 print-outs
within 24 hours or 300 reports per 5-day-week. In
case that intermediate print-outs are requested or
if the shift cycle must be altered it is necessary
to go to the machine.

The effort for these tasks is of great weight as
well as the time which is passing until the desired
information is available.

Time is money. Who does not know it. In many cases
the consequences of late information are more expensive
than hardware and software of a micro computer.

Dr. J. Rüge
W. SCHLAFHORST & CO.
Postfach 205
D-4050 Mönchengladbach 1
Germany

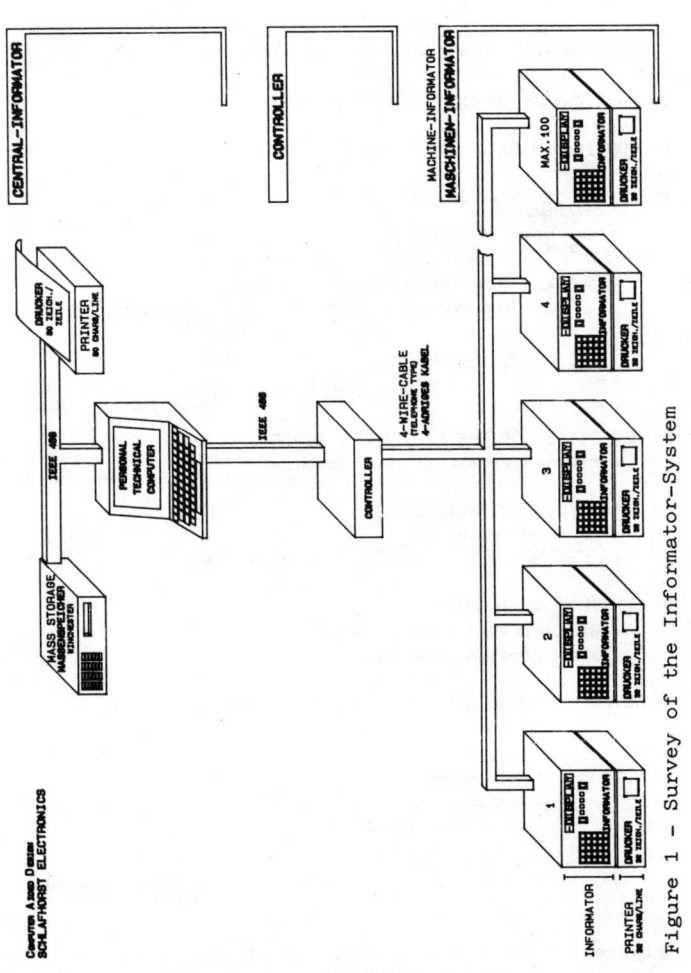

Figure 1 – Survey of the Informator-System

PERFORMANCE FEATURES OF THE MACHINE INFORMATOR

► MAINTENANCE OF DATE / TIME / SHIFT CALENDAR

► CONTINUOUS DATA ACQUISITION

► AUTOMATIC SHIFT REPORT ON METAL PAPER PRINTER
(32 CHARACTERS/LINE)

- FORMAT SHORT : MACHINE DATA
  STANDARD : MACHINE + SECTION DATA
  LONG : MACHINE + SECTION + SPINNING-SITE DATA

- LOG DATA : – FEEDS (YARN COUNT, PRE-SET LENGTH, ETC.)

  – MEASUREMENT DATA (PRODUCTION SPEED, EFFICIENCY, PRODUCTION IN KG,
  NUMBER OF CHEESES, NUMBER OF PIECINGS, NUMBER
  OF RED-LIGHT SWITCHES, ECT.)

  – OFF-STANDARD SPINNING SITES ACROSS 4 SHIFTS
  CRITERIA : EFFICIENCY
  NUMBER OF PIECINGS
  NUMBER OF SHIFTS AT OFF-STANARD

► REPETITION OF THE LAST SHIFT REPORT

- FORMAT CHANGES POSSIBLE BY FORMAT MODIFICATION, TOO

► INTERMEDIATE INQUIRIES

- FORMAT SHORT : MACHINE DATA
  STANDARD : MACHINE + SECTION DATA
  SECTION : SECTION + SPINNING-SITE DATA OF ONE SECTION

► LENGTH MEASUREMENT

- INITIATION OF BOBBIN CHANGES ON REACHING LENGTH

- MONITORING LENGTH MEASUREMENT DEVICE

► NETWORK CONNECTIBILITY (FOR CONNECTION TO CENTRAL INFORMATOR)

- DATA EXCHANGE WITH PARENT COMPUTER

  – DATE, TIME

  – SHIFT CALENDAR

  – SHIFT DATA

  – INTERMEDIATE INQUIRIES

SCHLAFHORST ELECTRONICS
COMPUTER AIDED DESIGN

Figure 2 – Performance features of the
machine-Informator

```
••••••••••••••••••••••••••••••••••••••
MA.     7        1.4.1   3-25.01.84    22.00
**********************************************
***                                        ***
              INFORMATOR  AUTOCORO
***                                        ***
              W. SCHLAFHORST  & CO
**********************************************

                  SHIFT REPORT

MA-T             480          EL-T      480
NM               20.3         TEX      49.3
NE               12.0         ALPHA     125
V-P              128.2        MKG/H    63.7
CAN-KG           18.0         GROUP       1
LM ON!           37800
ROT     192              EFF    RT      YP
--------------------------------------------

MA.     7               97.2   466     372
--------------------------------------------

KG            494.7  -EFF               0.52
DOP            273   CHC                  27
F               72   KM/F              100.9
F/100KG        14.5  F/100KM            0.72
RL              64   RL-T               18.7
OFF STANDARD REPORT
ROT      EFF0   YP0    YP1    YP2    YP3  SH
         72.2    5      5      7      6   4
--------------------------------------------

24       84.1    9      1      8      0   6

NO PRODUCTION !

1
```

Figure 3 - machine-Informator shift report

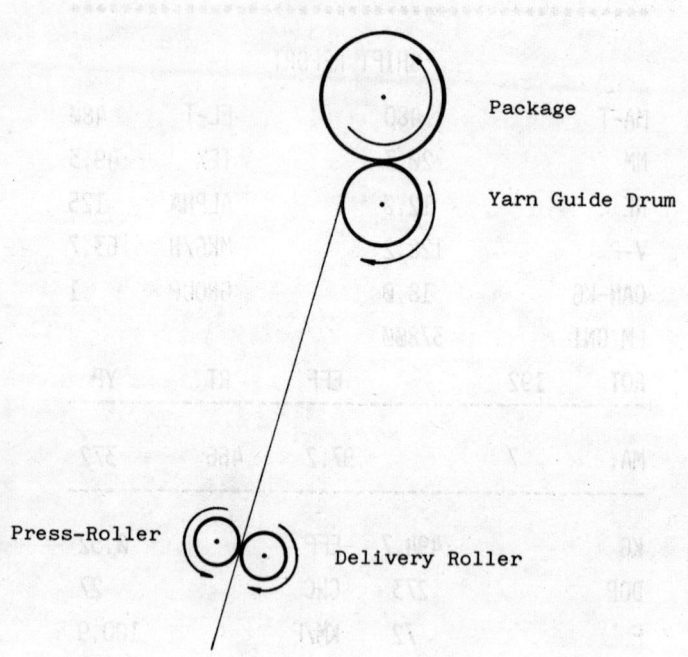

Package

Yarn Guide Drum

Press-Roller

Delivery Roller

length~ D · π · r.p.m. · time (Delivery Roller)

number of revolutions

Figure 4 - Principle of length measuring

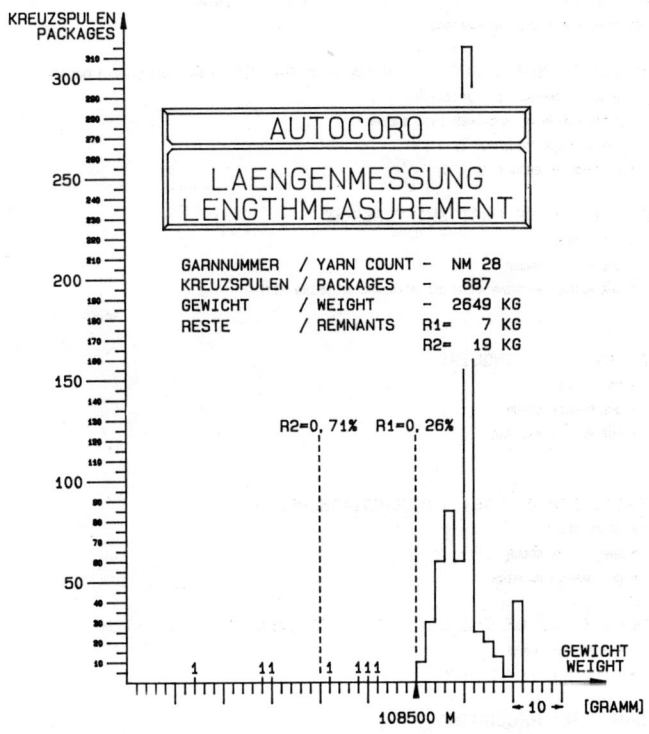

Figure 5 - Results with the length measurement

PERFORMANCE FEATURES OF THE CENTRAL INFORMATOR

▶ MAINTENANCE OF DATE / TIME / SHIFT CALENDAR
  * CENTRALLY FOR ALL INFORMATORS *

▶ AUTOMATIC SHIFT REPORT ON MATRIX PRINTER (80 CHARACTERS/LINE)
  * WITH OFF-STANDARD IDENTIFICATION *
  • SUBDIVISION OF MACHINES INTO GROUPS
  • MAXIMUM 100 MACHINES (1 - 100)
  • MAXIMUM 26 GROUPS (A - Z)

▶ REPETITION OF LAST SHIFT REPORT
  • TOTAL PLANT
  • ONE RANDOM GROUP
  • ONE RANDOM MACHINE WITH OFF-STANDARD SPINNING SITES

▶ INTERMEDIATE INQUIRY
  • TOTAL PLANT
  • ONE RANDOM GROUP
  • ONE RANDOM MACHINE

▶ REPETITION OF LAST INTERMEDIATE REPORT
  • TOTAL PLANT
  • ONE RANDOM GROUP
  • ONE RANDOM MACHINE

▶ PRE-SETTING OF THE LIMIT OFF-STANDARD SHIFT COUNTER
  • FOR ALL MACHINES
  • FOR EACH MACHINE INDIVIDUALLY

▶ LONG TERM RECORDING
  • DAILY , WEEKLY , MONTHLY GROUP REPORT

SCHLAFHORST ELECTRONICS
Computer Aided Design

Figure 6 - Performance features of the Central-Informator

```
***********************************************************************
*****  W.SCHLAFHORST & CO.  ****  CENTRAL-INFORMATOR AUTOCORO  ****  V1.1  *****
***********************************************************************

Date/Time of report      We - 6 Jun 1984  13:33

repeated shift report    We - 6 Jun 1984  06:00    shift C   elapsed time  8:00

GROUP:  3     NM 20.4 ALPHA 140
```

MA	MA-T	NM	AL	N-R	V-P	MKG/H	LM	EFF	F	DOP	KG	F/KG	RL	RL-T	OF
23	479	20.4	140	82	130	82.7	647	94.1	111	199	622.3	.2	58	58.4	4
24	479	20.4	140	82	130	82.6	426	86.7	130	352	572.3	.2	49	33.5	1
30	479	20.4	140	82	130	82.5	426	90.5	339	294	596.4	.6	54	36.7	6

```
GROUP:  OFF-T:  0: 0      EFF-MA:  90.4      F:  580      KG :   1791.0
                          EFF-EL:  90.4                   F/KG:      .3

=================================================================================
PLANT:  OFF-T:  0: 0      EFF-MA:  91.2      F:  3104     KG :   4946.2
                          EFF-EL:  91.2                   F/KG:      .6
=================================================================================
```

Figure 7 - Section of a Central-Informator shift
report. Shown are the machines of group 3
and the production of the complete installation

```
********************************************************
********** MECHANICS WORKSHEET **********
********************************************************

repeated shift report    We -  6, Jun 1984  06:00   shift C   elapsed time   8:00

GROUP :    1    NM 28.4 ALPHA 132        EFF-LIMIT : 91.0 %

MA   27    EFF-MA :  88.1 %

MA   31    EFF-MA :  89.4 %

MA   32    EFF-MA :  91.0 %

MA   33    EFF-MA :  90.3 %


GROUP :    2    NM 24.3 ALPHA 140        EFF-LIMIT : 90.0 %

NO MACHINES DETECTED


GROUP :    3    NM 20.4 ALPHA 140        EFF-LIMIT : 90.0 %

MA   24    EFF-MA :  86.7 %
```

Figure 8 - Section of a Central-Informator shift report. Shown are the machine groups which did not reach the expected efficiency

COMPUTERS ON THE INDIAN TEXTILE SCENE : A CRITICAL ASSESSMENT

P.V.Bhave and A.R.Garde

ABSTRACT

The use of computers by ATIRA over the past 20 years in three distinct areas - research, interfirm comparisons and development of special programme packages for textile mills - is briefly reviewed. A third generation computer has been used for solving intricate equations numerically, for simulations, for plotting profiles of three-dimensional cams etc. in research. The data processing for questionnaire-based IFC survey, with built-in checks for internal consistency of data, has been done annually since 1972. Package programmes have been developed for cost accounting, sales invoice analysis, loomshed efficiency analysis etc. for mill use. The factors that determine the extent to which computers can be used profitably in each of these areas are discussed in the light of extensive experience gained by ATIRA.

The use of Electronic Data Processing units in the Indian cotton-based textile mills has increased considerably in the past 5-6 years. The spread of EDP is gauged on the basis of an industry-wide survey undertaken in 1983. The nature of usage is analysed, giving critical comments on why business type usages are more common and the quantitative analyses for management decisions are not.

A brief outline is given of the directions in which future growth is likely to take place in the usage of computers in Indian textile industry. Such a look into the future has become necessary in view of the rapid growth of the electronic industry in India in the recent past.

1. COMPUTARISATION : THE ATIRA EXPERIENCE 1964-1984

The Ahmedabad Textile Industry's Research Association, known commonly as ATIRA, was the first co-operative research institute to be established by any industry in India. Right from the time ATIRA began to function in 1949, its work pattern has evolved and changed continually in a unique manner.

The basic objective of ATIRA as an industrial research institute was to identify the current and future needs of its member industry and to fulfil them in a timely and cost effective manner. Consequently, ATIRA happened to pioneer the introduction of several new techniques into the Indian textile industry based on cotton type machinery. Starting from the introduction of statistical quality control and the 'training within industry' for supervisory development in early 1950s, ATIRA pioneered applied research and consultancy in the areas of fuel economy by late 1950s and techniques of operations research in early 1960s. At about the same time, ATIRA had already recognised the potential advantages of the computer as a tool for research as well as consultancy and services to its member mills. Not surprisingly, therefore, ATIRA was the first textile research organisation in India to acquire a computer and later, to use one on a large scale in its own work and also for giving services to its member mills. It would be an interesting exercise to review and to assess the experience of ATIRA over the 20-year period from 1964-1984.

1.1 The Early Attempt : 1964-72

In the early 1960s itself, two large textile mills* in India had acquired their own computers, which were of the type suitable for business applications. As the ideas on the probable nature of work to be done with the computer by ATIRA crystallised, it was clear that a scientific type of computer would be more appropriate to ATIRA's needs. ATIRA, therefore, acquired for its own use an IBM 1620 computer in August 1966. Since our own research work could not be enough to keep the computer busy, and since availability of Electronic Data Processing services in India was rather inadequate at that point in time, an early decision was taken to make the ATIRA computer available to its member mills. A series of packages useful to cotton textile mills was developed and a scheme for giving computer services was introduced in 1969 under the title of "Computer Club". A member mills of the club had to pay a very nominal fee per annum in return for which it would get the following :

(a) Training to the mill staff in the usage of computer, including data preparation, card punching, etc.

(b) Help in developing special pacakages to suit their own needs

and (c) An unlimited use of computer time over the year.

Of the 57 member mills in Ahmedabad, 16 mills joined this computer club. Common areas of computer applications were

(i) Cost analysis
(ii) Loomshed Efficiency Analysis
(iii)Damages Analysis (Finished Fabric)
(iv) Payroll
(v) Production Control Records, and
(vi) Inventory Control

The thrust in all these areas was to develop general purpose packages which could be useful to any mill without much change in its own method of record keeping. For example, the programme on Cost Analysis which could generate 12 cost reports covering various aspects of yarn/fabric costs, including marginal costs can be used by any textile mill by using its own method of analysis.

However, the Computer Club did not really grow. The changes needed in the procedures being followed by mills proved to be not so easily assimilable as expected. The total computer usage at ATIRA did not go beyond 4-6 hours per day in spite of the fact that unlimited time was made available to 16 member users and to ATIRA staff for its own work. Considering that IBM 1620 was a relatively slow computer, and had limited capacity, this usage was judged as too little.

---

*Total mills in India at that time were 479

On the other hand, complex problems like production planning by linear programming involving large matrics of over 120 x 40 could not be tackled due to inadequate capacity of the IBM 1620 computer. Consequently, after about three years of existence of the "Computer Club", a decision was taken to dispose off the IBM 1620 unit and to start using IBM 360 computer available in a neighbouring institute. This third generation computer was about 30 times faster than the IBM 1620, and much larger in its capacity. The "Computer Club" Ceased to exist with this change.

1.2 Research Applications

The different divisions of ATIRA are organised around a major discipline but together with members from other divisions depending upon the R & D assignments. Almost all divisions have used the computer for various purposes over the year. (Table I)

TABLE I : Computer Applications for Research in ATIRA

Area		Topic	Division of ATIRA
Fine Structure of Fibres	i)	Crystallanity determination from radial X-ray diffraction scans	Physics Division
	ii)	Resolution of overlapping peak profiles	
	iii)	Structure factor computations	
Drying, Humidification Power Consumption	i)	Simulation for optimum design and process conditions for textile drying, optimum humidity indicator	Engineering Division
	ii)	Optimum area for multiple effect evaporators	
	iii)	Air conditioning plant computations	
	iv)	Thermal efficiency and heat balance of equipments	
	v)	Power consumption at Ring Frames	
Machine Design, especially of cams	i)	Picking cams for overpick looms - 3-dimensional	Loom Design Division

TABLE I (contd.)

Area		Topic	Division of ATIRA
	ii)	Ring Frame cams and shedding tappets	
	iii)	Reverse cams for under-pick looks	
Experimental Design	i)	Multifactor experimental design for optimum conditions in resin finishing.	Chemical Technology Division
Yarn Irregularity	i)	Spectral Density approach to the study of quasi-periodic yarn irregularity	Mechanical Processing
Random events - damages	i)	Optimum cloth cutting for maximising sales realisation - computer simulation	Operations Studies Division
Factor Analysis and multiple correlation analysis	i)	Relationship between end breakage rate and factors affecting it	Mechanical Processing Division

The list given in Table I is by no means exhaustive but indicates the nature of computer usage by ATIRA researchers over the years. A few of these items, especially the work by the Engineering and Loom Design Divisions, have been later used extensively for helping individual mills to improve their humidification and steam consuming equipment and for improving the design features of non-automatic overpick looms.

1.3   Interfirm Comparison Studies

The first ever inter-firm comparison (IFC) study of productivity in spinning and weaving for several units of any industry in India was undertaken by ATIRA in 1950. The results of this study were published in 1952. However, this activity of IFC on various aspects of the working of the cotton textile mills started regularly in ATIRA from 1960s.

Computerisation of two major IFC activities of Productivity Analysis and Financial Analysis was undertaken in 1973-74. The advantages of computerisation were :

(a)   Data could be asked in great details with a view to provide meaningful analysis to individual participating mills.

(b)   Internal consistency checks could be built-in to cross-check validity of data.

(c)   The total work could be so streamlined as to finish the survey within about 4 months of receiving data. Thus, the IFC studies could be made a regular annual feature.

(d)   The entire emphasis of the IFC studies could be changed towards each participating mill not only to assess its relative position, but also to diagnose causes of poor performance in quantitative terms. A special diagnostic individual mill report was prepared and given to each participant. Thus; the annual IFC studies by ATIRA became a management tool for improving their mill's performance.

The productivity reports are prepared separately for Spinning and Weaving. The productivity is split into Machine Productivity and Labour Complements. In each case, a comparison is made with a hypothetical standard mill which produces the same products but on standard machinery appropriate to Indian techno-economic conditions. Thus, the mills position relative to a standard mill is assessed. Information is given also about the level of performance that can be reached with the given type of machinery in the mill. Thus, the mill can assess the gap between the actual and the achievable performance. The annual IFC studies on productivity have also helped ATIRA to establish norms for all parameters related to labour and machine productivity in spinning and weaving.

The IFC reports on financial performance are in two distinct parts - the first consists essentially of financial ratio analysis based on the published annual reports. This analysis is done separately for spinning mills and for composite mills*. The second part deals with those vital aspects of technical performance which affect the profitability of the mill in a big way. This part is based on questionnaire filled in by participating mills on Costs, Productivity at ring frames and looms, and Cloth damages etc. These annual IFC studies have also provided ATIRA with a valuable data base which permits analysis of industry trends over the years and also helps in establishing norms on various critical aspects of a mill's working.

It is necessary to emphasize here that this entire progress has been possible mainly because the facility of a computer was used extensively by the Mechanical Processing and Operations Studies Divisions of ATIRA since 1974.

1.4   Packages for Mill Use

Once the Computer Club was disbanded, ATIRA decided to devote its attention to only such applications which will have a research or a developmental component. Routine programmes such as payrolls were therefore left to the commercial agencies which sprang up in the area of Electronic Data Processing. The work by ATIRA in the area of developing programmes was restricted to applications which needed a specialist

*Composite mills - Vertically integrated units consisting of spinning, weaving and chemical processing facilities.

textile background - A review of our activities shows that the nature of work done by ATIRA for mills falls into three distinct categories :

(a) Specialised Applications Adapted for Use by Indian Mills

Developing on Computerised colour matching service, application of the Linear Programming Technique for cotton blending and production planning (i.e., allocating looms to fabric/sorts or ring frames to yarn counts for maximising contribution, application of network planning for machinery modernisation proposals, etc. are examples of this category.

(b) Programmes Developed in Response to Mill Demand

Examples of this type of packages are efficiency analysis for loomshed to identify poor looms, weavers to sorts; analysis of sales invoice in different ways to improve control on the distribution system; analysis of accosunts receivables; stores accounting and inventory control; yarn quality reports for a group of mills, cost accounting reports etc.

Most of such programmes have been used by a large number of mills, even though these were initiated by an individual mill to begin with.

(c) Programmes Developed for Giving Better Consultation

Over 60% of staff time in ATIRA is spent on consultancy, training and services based on the R & D work done by ATIRA. One major use of the computer in ATIRA has been to give a better quality of consultant reports to the clients. To illustrate: When a financial institute approaches ATIRA to prepare a techno-economic viability report for a mill in distress, it becomes imperative to work out accurately and reliably the working capital requirements of the mill in question. Consequently, a total system of working out cash flow on a monthly basis has been worked out and fully computerised. Similarly, items such as sensitivity analysis for profitability, breakeven analysis, and variance analysis have been developed as aids in better consultation.

These computer applications are not meant for use by mills, because they are needed only once in several years by any individual mill.

1.5 ATIRA Experience Assessed : 1964-84

We can make the following salient observations on the process of adoption of computers at and through ATIRA, based on our experience of past 20 years.

(a) The computer has been really useful in developmental research. A greater awareness on the part of researchers and a better streamlining of computer facilities could have improved the computer usage by at least 50%.

(b) The services given through annual IFC studies on productivity and finance have been well received. The participant strength has increased from year to year, and the spread has been wider all over India. Further standardisation and simplification of questionnaires etc. has helped.

(c)   The Operations Research type of packages have failed to gain entry into the industry. Several complex reasons are responsible for this situation. Important among them are : non-preparedness of ATIRA staff to take a total systems view of the client needs, too early an attempt to introduce sophisticated tools in a culture which is quantitative and intuitive, and inability to get the involvement of the true decision maker in the mills.

(d)   Even the business applications of the type of loomshed efficiency analysis did not really spread in the industry. Here too, not taking a total system view was the main reason for failure, the secondary reason being the speed with which ATIRA could respond to client needs. It was not good enough.

(e)   A major advantage, though intangible, was obtained through the multi-pronged process of computer applications initiated by ATIRA in the Indian cotton textile industry. The industry as a whole become familiar to the computer earlier than it would otherwise become and the 15-20 mills which took active interest in the late 60s, pioneered the adoption of computers in the mills when the cost of computers came down in late 70s.

2.   COMPUTER USAGE IN INDIAN TEXTILE MILLS : 1984

A couple of textile mills acquired computers in early 1960s, as mentioned earlier, but the number of mills using a computer remained less than 10 till the end of 1970. This was admittedly a slow progress. However, some of the companies started utilising their computer installations for doing outside EDP jobs and grew in strength. Since the electronic industry in India made a very rapid progress after about 1975, and since textile mills became more aware of the economic and other advantages of computer installations, the computer usage increased substantially after 1975.

Although no systmatic surveys were conducted on computer usage in textile mills by any agency in India, enough information is available from a 1979 survey by three co-operative research associations of the staffing pattern in Indian textile mills working on the cotton type machinery. The findings based on questionnaires filled-in by 259 mills (39.2% of mills in India) were:

(a)   About 14% of the respondents, were using computers - either their own or on time sharing basis. This means that about 5% of all mills were using computer facilities, if we assume that most of the computer users were amongst those who responded to the questionnaire. [Such an assumption is justified on the basis of authors' familiarity with the 'Indian textile scene']

(b)   A very large proportion of the computer users were
      composite mills; only a few spinning mills had felt
      the need for EDP. Significantly, most of the early
      entrants into the EDP systems as well as the users
      of large computers were mill companies which had diver-
      sified outside the textile production.

As a part of ATIRA efforts towards helping mills to use
computers on a larger scale and for better management controls, a thorough survey was planned. Conducted in late
1983, this survey can be taken as representing the industry
status on computerisation in 1984, since it also included
information on mills which intend to install/use EDP facilities in near future.

2.1   Survey of Computer Usage

In 1983-84, the total number of textile mills in India is
about 800. Of these about 290 are composite mills, while
the rest are spinning mills. The number of large scale processing houses, which independently undertake dyeing, printing and finishing of all types of fabrics, is around 200.
The questionnaire on computer usage was, therefore, mailed
to all these 1000 companies spread all over India. Only
213 mills returned the completd questionnaires, which meant
a response of only 21%. We therefore, supplemented the information available from this questionnaire by using three
secondary sources - Computer Directory of India, Asian Computer Year-Book 1984, and the Annual Reports of the companies (collected annually by ATIRA for Inter-firm Comparison
of Financial Performance). The following facts emerged on
computer usage in 1984 by cotton-based textile units in
India.

2.1.1 Own Installations

The distribution of own installations amongst the different
types of units was as follows :

Spinning Mills	23
Spinning + Weaving Mills	3
Composite Mills	51
Textile Processing Houses	2
Total:	79

These data show that the spinning mills have realised the
need for EDP after 1979, and that the total number of mills
using own EDP installations has increased substantially. The
process houses have just begun to use computer.

Although the questionnaire response shows only 8% (79/1000)
of the mills using computers of their own, information from
other sources show that about 40 more mills have computers.
Thus, the total installations of computers is about 12%.

2.1.2 Shared Use

The questionnaire response showed that 49 mills use computer facilities available with other institutes/companies. Estimates on this type of usage are not available from the other sources mentioned earlier. This raises the total textile users of computers to about 170 i.e., about 17%.

2.1.3 Installations Planned

To the question on plans for EDP installation in near future (1-3 years), the response was interesting. While 32 mills reported that they wish to install a computer system in the near future, 81 mills categorically reported that they do not wish to acquire computers. Further analysis shows that 28 out of 49 shared users plan to install their own compluters, while 4 other companies, not using EDP facilities at present, wish to start using them in near future.

This analysis shows that most mills which start using computer facilities on a shared basis discover the manyfold advantages of EDP and then acquire a computer facility of their own.

2.1.4 Usage Pattern

The pattern of computer usage may be analysed in terms of number of applications in each mills as well as the type of applications. Information obtained from the questionnaire (from 96 respondants) is summarised in Tables II and III.

TABLE II : Extent of Computer Usage by Number of Applications

Number of Applications	Number of Respondents Using	
	Own Installation	Shared Time
1	4	12
2	2	6
3	1	6
4	6	8
5	5	7
6	4	2
7	10	4
8	10	–
9	2	2
10	1	–
More than 10	4	–
Total	49	47

As expected, most of the mills with own installation tend to use the computer for at least 4 applications, and generally between 6 and 10 applications. On the other hand, the mills using shared facility tend to use the computer for 1 to 5 applications.

TABLE III : Nature of Computer Usage in Textile Mills

Application Area/Item	Number of Mills Using the Application		
	Own Instal-lation	Shared Time	Total
Production Management			
Production Accounts	1.8	7	25
Production Reports	30	13	43
Process Control	--	1	1
Colour Matching	3	2	5
General Maintenance	1	--	1
Loom Efficiency Analysis	1	1	2
Sub-total	53	24	77
Selling and Distribution			
Billing	35	14	49
Invoice Analysis	35	16	51
Excise Account	1	--	1
Sub-total	71	30	101
Cost and Financial Accounting			
Stores Accounting	32	23	55
Financial Accounting	33	26	59
Cost Accounting	17	8	25
Cash Flow	2	1	3
Budgetory Control	1	1	2
Dyeing Costs	1	0	1
Sub-total	86*	59*	145
Wage Payment			
Payroll	41	26	67
Provident Fund Accounts	2	1	3
Sub-total	43	27	70
Administration			
Shares Account	23	10	33
Fixed Deposit Account	18	10	28
Debentures	4	0	4
Mailing List	1	1	2
Sub-total	46	21	67
Materials Control			
Raw Material Stocks	5	0	5
Finished Goods Inventory	3	0	3
Sub-total	8	0	8
Management Planning and Control			
Linear Programming	5	3	8
Others	1	3	3
Sub-Total	6	6	12

Note: *Since these values exceed the number of respondents in
each category (own/shared), some overlap in responses
is indicated.

The data in Table III are quite revealing. Most of the usage of the computer is seen to be in substituting computers for clerical work and to improve the records through a more detailed analysis permitted by the electronic data processing systems. Applications which help ˙in management decision making through use of modern tools are rare indeed! Computerised colour matching, loomshed efficiency analysis, linear programming and other similar applications have been mentioned only by a few respondents. From experience in the industry, it is known that even those who have responded to these items do not use it regularly except in the case of colour matching and loomshed efficiency analysis. The Indian cotton textile mills seem to be in the very first phase of computer usage i.e. for substitution of clerical manpower. How likely is this industry to take up computerisation on a large scale and also to graduate into the second phase of using computers for taking better management decisioons?

3. SHAPE OF THINGS TO COME

In attempting to predict the future growth of computer usage in the Indian cotton textile industry, two major trends in the environment must be taken into consideration. The first refers to the rapid growth of the electronic industry in India, with special reference to manufacture and use of computers on the national scene. The second refers to the changes in the socio-economic circumstances, shaped by political realities, which exert an increasingly greater pressure on the textile mills towards improved technical and managerial performance.

The electronics industry in India made a slow but sure beginnning in the late 1960s. By early 1970s, electronic calculators of different types were assembled and sold in India. By mid-70s, the scale increased enormously, the prices of electronic calculators of all types came down by a factor of 3 to 5, the first table-top computers and micro-processors made their appearance in the market. Today, more than fifty companies have entered the manufacture of electronic data processing equipments covering a wide range from table top computers to full-fledged computers of third or fourth generation and the allied equipment/periferals. The computer industry of India in 1983 had a turn-over of Rs.750 millions, and the Government of India has an ambitious plan of raising it to about Rs.20,000 millions by 1990. The Seventh Five Year Plan, beginning in 1985, envisages introduction of computers in 250 schools all over India. This step, taken together with the entry of personal computers on the Indian scene in 1983-84 itself, would go a long way towards spreading widely the awareness of computers and their use in India. Although most of the integrated circuits needed for the development and manufacture of equipments were imported from advanced countries of Europe, United States and Japan, plans are afoot to install large complexes for the manufacture of these basic items in India itself. As a result of this total thrust, a wide variety of low cost EDP equipment will become available to the Indian textile mills also.

The textile industry in India consists of three major sectors - the organised sector consisting of mills and large process houses, the decentralised power loom sector and the handloom sector. About 70% of the country's total cloth production comes from the decentralised sectors of handlooms and power-looms. In 1951, this proportion was only 30% from the decen-tralised sector. The loom capacity in the organised mill sector has been frozen by Government policy, in order to ensure large scale employment through use of powerlooms and handlooms. Subsequently, only the powerloom sector increased considerably, while the production from the hand-looms increased only slowly. At present, the estimated number of powerlooms in the country is about 700,000, compared to only about 210,000 in the organised sector. All spindles are in the mill sector, which supplies yarn to handlooms and powerlooms. The total production capacity of the three sectors together is estimated conservatively to be at least 100% more than that needed at the present per capita consump-tion of fabric in metres. Over the past 10 years, the per capita consumption on textiles in real money terms has in-creased at a rate of about 4% annually (for a 2.2% growth rate of population), but has reduced from about 15 metre to about 13 metres in terms of quantity. Most of this dif-ference is explained by the introduction of synthetic fibre - mainly polyster - on a large scale. The excise duty structure is such that polyester and blended fabrics are much more expensive (100 to 300%) than the corresponding cotton fabrics. This high price and greater durability (3 to 4 times that of cotton), taken together swith the slow rate of increase in the income of the common man and a change in his prefe-rence to consumer durables such as television, radio, cycles, etc. from textiles, have led to an extremely competitive situation for textile mills in India. It is just not possible to pass on the burden of steadily increasing fixed costs and also the inflationery increase in the raw material costs to the consumer. Only the mills which have an excellent technical performance can combat effectively in the product market segment that they operate. The income distribution in India ensures that only a fraction of (about 30% of looms) the mills can operate in the market segment category to fabrics priced beyond Rs.12 per metre at 1984 prices. Rest of the mills must produce fabrics of about Rs.5 per metre on an average, and still be competitive with the power loom sector. The powerloom sector is given several benefits in the current government policy on the one hand, and has to pay much less wages to the worker. The net effect of both these factors is that the cost price of a fabric is less by about Re.1 per metre (in average price of Rs.5 per metre) compared to the average composite mill.

Clearly, the average composite mill today has to be managed much more efficiently than just 10 years ago in order to survive and to make adequate profits to grow in future. Only those who can manage to do so will continue to exist, whether in the nationalised, state, co-operative or private sector of the industry. This environmental pressure towards highly efficient management is less on the spinning mills today, but will increase considerably in near future owing to excess capacity.

It is therefore expected that the pressure from environment towards highly efficient management and the rapid strides in availability of inexpensive computers together will lead to a rapid growth of computer usage in the Indian textile mills. The percentage of mills using computers was about 0.5% in 1960, about 5% in 1978 and about 12% in 1983. It is expected to become about 17% by 1986 itself, if the trend seen from the questionnaire survey is any indication. One can confidently expect about 30% of cotton type textile mills in India to use computer by 1990. Hopefully, the nature of use of computers will be more in the areas of management decision making. The mills which see this need clearly and then change their management practices effectively to permit utilisation of EDP for improved management decisions will have better chances to survive and grow in the increasingly difficult environment in India.

ACKNOWLEDGEMENTS

We thank the Director, and the Council of Administration of ATIRA for permission to present this paper at the conference of the Textile Institute at Hongkong.

ATIRA,
Polytechnic P.O.,
Ahmedabad 380 015,
India.

SELECTED BIBLIOGRAPHY

(1)   ATIRA, ATIRA Silver Jubilee Brochure 1974.

(2)   ATIRA Annual Reports

(3)   Indian Cotton Mills Federation (ICMF) ICMF Handbook
        of Statistics.

(4)   G.H.Trivedi, MIS Frame work : Marketing in a Textile
        Mill. Computerage, November 1982.

(5)   A.R.Garde, K.Jayachandran and C.V.S.Rao, Productivity
        Measurement : Assessment and Development of a New
        Approach, 15th Joint Technological Conference by ATIRA,
        BTRA, SITRA, 1974.

(6)   ATIRA Circular Report, Computerised Cost Analysis,
        1971.

(7)   P.V.Veeraraghavan, P.V.Bhave and G.D.Chitnis, Staffing
        in Textile Mills, A Joint Project of ATIRA, BTRA and
        SITRA, December 1981.

(8)   Computer Directory of India.

(9)   Asian Computer Yearbook 1984.

(10)   CSI (Computer Society of India) Communications, April
        1984.

AUTOMATED VISUAL INSPECTION AND CLASSIFICATION OF TEXTILE MATERIALS AND GARMENTS

A. A. Hashim, M. Lefley, D. Spencer

ABSTRACT

The application of computer vision techniques in the automation of textile manufacturing processes represents a significant introduction of new technology. A prototype for automatic visual inspection of textile materials and garments has been developed by the Image Processing Group at Leicester Polytechnic. The prototype consists of a monochrome TV camera which views the garment. The resulting video waveform is digitised and provides a digital word sample of 512 picture elements along each scanning line. A frame store holds the digitised information from each complete frame scan and it is processed by a microcomputer. Tree-structured Hierarchial image processing techniques based on linear transformations have been implemented, and shown to be sensitive to both localised and widespread defects. Further image analysis algorithms are then employed to extract the appropriate features from the captured image for garment classification and sizing. The prototype has been tested under laboratory conditions, and demonstrated to acurately detect textile defects, and capable of automatically pairing socks into one of nine size classes or one error class with a maximum deviation of + 2 mm. The processing time for each sizing operation is less than 0.5 sec.

1. INTRODUCTION

There is currently a major research effort directed towards the development of the automated factory. Recent developments in both hardware and software have meant that many production tasks involving decision type processes may now be carried out by computer-controlled machinery. Of particular importance is the relatively recent development of devices with the capability of processing visual data received by some form of camera. The amount of information available in a digital image is very large and vision is the basis of human perception, so it is essential that modern industrial computer systems use this facility. Chin and Harlow (1) provide an excellent summary of the work currently being undertaken in the field of computer vision.

There are two particular fields of research into vision applications, visual sensing and visual inspection. Parks (2) shows how inspection is aimed at reducing three forms of overheads;

a) Preventative costs

b) Costs of appraisal

c) Costs of failures

One field that could yield an immediately cost effective implementation is the inspection of materials and garments in the

167

textile industry. This is an area that is currently very expensive to the industry, as it employs intensive skilled labour; Goodman (3) has discussed the situation, and in particular the fact that human inspection is less consistent and less reliable than is desired. This has been further shown by Wang (4) to apply most acutely when the inspection is repetitive and intricate, as in the case of textile materials.

Attempts have been made to improve human inspection and its application; the Graniteville Corporation of America (5) has made a complete documentation of defects and Knoll and Wolfe (6) discuss the use of a 'points system' to cost faults. The human inspector remains the inconsistent element; nevertheless such work is a valuable aid to the implementation of computer processing in this application.

One of the first major considerations of the use of computers in the inspection of fabric was carried out by the SIRA institute by Purll (7). This study provides useful information on the hardware requirements of such a system, although software interpretation was limited since realistic real-time software processing has only recently become viable. Some research has been undertaken into the development of laser inspection systems that work at very high speeds on the simple structure of non-woven goods (e.g. J-Cloths.) This is discussed by Knoll (8) and the use of such a system by Philips (9). Such devices are intended to detect holes and stains that cause major deviations in the impinging laser light, as detected by photocells. However none of these systems have the processing power to be used in handling the more subtle textures, patterns and defects encountered in the knitting industry. Koshimizu (10) showed that defects could be detected on small samples of fabric with a camera-based system, but does not extend the work to full width fabric and made only 2 tests leading to just 4 classes of defect; this work also highlights the need to develop a more software-intensive approach.

To construct a device useful to the knitting industry, a method for the detection of smaller faults and more subtle defects that are spread over large areas (e.g. barre, neppiness) for a range of textures is required. For this the system will require sophisticated software processing techniques, developed from a thorough understanding of the structure of the problem. The system must also be capable of classifying and sizing garments in a way that is compatable with current production processes in the industry.

2. THE PROBLEM

2.1 The structure of defects

Most defects can be recognised and identified by means of visual inspection. In considering the most appropriate way in which to present a classification of defects, the latter have been grouped by their similarities or general appearance and their effect on the visual quality of the fabric. Numerous attempts have been made to construct classifications of defects. These for most part have involved the accumulation and clarification of the many terms which have come into common use throughout the long history of the textile industry. Most recently, The American Society for Testing and Materials (11) published the standard

168

'Definitions of Terms relating to Fabric Defects'. In 1983
the British Standards Institution (12) proposed a new point
system for fault classification. The most common type of
defects are: Holes; Stains; Knots; Fly; Slubs; Neps;
Needle lines; Individual dropstitches; Individual tuckstitches;
Thick ends; Barre; Cuts; and Press offs. All these defects
exhibit one of the following structures:

a) Vertical lines

b) Horizontal lines

c) Area

These structures are used to identify and describe defects.

By far the majority of defects occur during the knitting operation.
Approximately 40% of the total reject garments from factories are
caused by fabric defects. It is important to note at this stage,
that the further the faulty fabric progresses along the
manufacturing route, the more costly the defect becomes. For
these reasons, the knitting operation represents the most
critical area for defect indentification.

2.2 Sock pairing

Socks are produced by the hosiery industry in large batches of
one size. However due to variations in the knitting and other
stages of manufacture, they vary slightly in size. In some cases
this variation may be as much as 12mm in leg or foot length. To
maintain quality control, socks must be paired up so that the
pair consists of two socks which are of the same physical
dimensions. There are two important measurements; foot length and
leg length, and no two socks in a pair may vary by more than 10mm
in these measurements. Socks vary in size in a range from about
40mm for the smallest baby sock to about 500mm for a man's long
sock. They also vary in shade and pattern with the extremes of
white and black being the most common shades. Socks are currently
paired by skilled operators who match socks presented to them in
batches. Socks are removed from a batch one at a time and are
compared to any socks currently on an inspection table in front
of the operator, and if no sock is found to match, the sock under
consideration is placed on the table so that it will be paired
later. As part of the operation the sock is also inspected for
defects, and variations in colour shades.

At any time an operator will have less than ten socks unpaired on
the inspection table. Any greater number would slow the pairing
process due to too many comparisons being made. Pairing to a
resolution of ten sock sizes can be considered to give a grouping
to an accuracy of about +/- 2.5mm on each of the two measurements.
This is because it will give 3 distinct classes of leg length and
3 distinct classes of foot length giving 9 overall possible
sizings. Any sock found to lie outside of the possible classes,
goes into a tenth reject class.

3. THE DEVELOPMENT SYSTEM

A development system somewhat larger than that envisaged for a
target system was used, so that different approaches could be
considered before designing a final version. The frame store
used was a Gresham Lion 214 supervisor which can capture, in real
time, images from a standard T.V camera. The unit was linked by

Q-bus to a PDP 11/23 minicomputer, with 64Kbytes of main memory
and 2Mbytes of disk storage. The Gresham Lion Unit is housed in
a self contained box to which can be added a PDP 11 processor
and memory board. Hence the software developed can easily be
transferred to this hardware, thus reducing the costs involved
in developing a prototype target system.

The raw data was obtained by directing the camera at an
illuminated textile material or sock on a flat surface, with no
initial fixed orientation. As is common with this sort of problem,
illumination can be directed from behind or above the object of
interest.

4. DEFECTS RECOGNITION ALGORITHMS

Since so many defects in the fabric are seen to take the form of
horizontal and vertical lines, an attempt was made to use the
sums of lines across and along the fabric data to detect such
defects, thus developing the work of Koshimizu (10). However, the
variation due to illumination was seen to submerge any deviation
due to defects. To reduce this effect a statistical model of the
variation was developed to allow comparison between the model and
the data, such deviation indicating a line-type defect. A
quadratic model across and along the illuminated surface was seen
to be sufficiently accurate and flexible to model the 'pedestal'
type variation of illumination.

Such a model was observed to reduce the variation by a factor of
about 25 times, and was found to be highly sensitive to defects
in the form of lines which extend right across the surface, as
would be hoped since the statistic was designed to fit such
structures. However they will not find other structures such as
small lines, since each such structure would require a similarly
structured statistical detector.

Ideally speaking a mask is needed for each type and size of
defect. The mask M is an operator of shape similar to that of the
defect, and if M is operated on any part of a given image, it
results in feature F such that:

F approaches the value zero for no defect, and unity, when that
part of the image contains the defect. A possible mask for
horizontal 5x2 picture elements (pixels) defect is given by :

$$
M = \begin{matrix} - & - & - & - & - \\ + & + & + & + & + \\ + & + & + & + & + \\ - & - & - & - & - \end{matrix}
$$

To detect all types and size of defect a large number of masks is
required. This is obviously impractical. A family of basic
masks was developed with a hierarchic tree structured system to
obtain the required features which directly interpret the various
defect structures.

4.1 The Linearly Arranged Tree Structured (LATS) System

Consider a mask M; $M = \begin{matrix} - & + & + & - \end{matrix}$, and a feature F; F results
from the operation of M on 4x2 pixels of a given image. F is
shown to be effective in detecting a 2x2 pixels defect. A larger
length defect may be detected easily by implementing a binary
tree structure of the feature set {F} as shown in Figure 1.

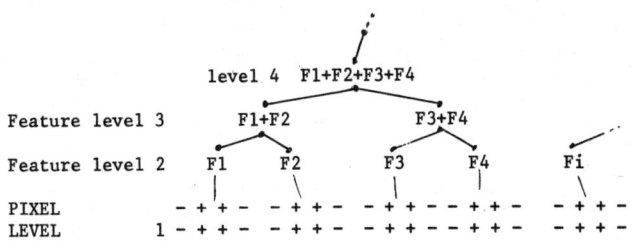

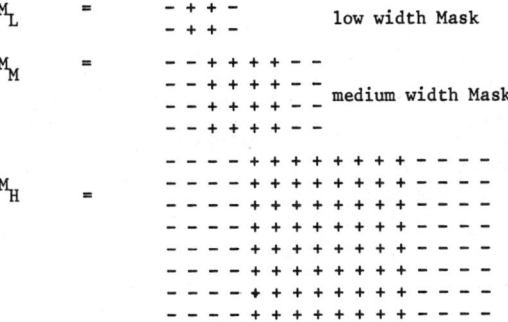

The n-th node of the tree is computed by adding the feature
sets of the two adjacent nodes of level (n - 1). Three basic
masks are used to maximise the tree-structure sensitivity to a
wide range of length and width of defects. The masks are :

$$
M_L =
\begin{array}{cccc}
- & + & + & - \\
- & + & + & -
\end{array}
\qquad \text{low width Mask}
$$

$$
M_M =
\begin{array}{cccccccc}
- & - & + & + & + & + & - & - \\
- & - & + & + & + & + & - & - \\
- & - & + & + & + & + & - & - \\
- & - & + & + & + & + & - & -
\end{array}
\qquad \text{medium width Mask}
$$

$$
M_H =
\begin{array}{cccccccccccccccc}
- & - & - & - & + & + & + & + & + & + & + & - & - & - & - \\
- & - & - & - & + & + & + & + & + & + & + & - & - & - & - \\
- & - & - & - & + & + & + & + & + & + & + & - & - & - & - \\
- & - & - & - & + & + & + & + & + & + & + & - & - & - & - \\
- & - & - & - & + & + & + & + & + & + & + & - & - & - & - \\
- & - & - & - & + & + & + & + & + & + & + & - & - & - & - \\
- & - & - & - & + & + & + & + & + & + & + & - & - & - & - \\
- & - & - & - & + & + & + & + & + & + & + & - & - & - & -
\end{array}
$$

Work is currently being undertaken to be able to construct the
tree-structure to work heirarchically in 2 - dimensions.

4. 2 Defect indentifications

At any node in the tree, the expected value is zero for no
defect. A null hypothesis of no defect is tested by the measure
of the significant deviation from zero. The distribution of the
feature sums is nearly normal, particularly in the lower nodes of
the tree. The t-test was used to make a good/nogood decision
based upon threshold for the statistic. The threshold value may
be tuned to give an optimum trade-off between false alarms and
defects missed. The detector was tested under laboratory
conditions, and demonstrated to be sensitive to both localised
and widespread defects. However, no comparison has been made,
for effectiveness of detection, with a human operator.

5. SOCK PAIRING ALGORITHMS

Using the image processing library which has been built up at
Leicester Polytechnic's School of Electronic and Electrical
Engineering, the nature of the sock images was investigated.
Various simple approaches were used to break down the problem
into smaller, more easily handled units. The socks were seen to
stand out well from the background and thus edge detection was
easily performed, by even the simplest edge operators.

Measurements of simple operators, such as perimeter, area and so
on were tried as solutions to the problem. However all were found
to be far too variable to be useful. Further, these measurements

did not correlate well to the matching procedure currently
used. This was seen to be due to other variations in shape
(e.g variation in leg width) causing large deviations in these
measurements, though such variations are not important to pairing.
It was thus seen to be necessary to design routines which would
take measurements similar to those currently used in pairing
socks. To be able to make such measurements consistently, the
algorithm needs certain reference points which do not vary for
any given sock. To determine such points, the possible
orientations, in practice for a single sock, must be considered.
Ideally the reference points must not alter in relation to each
other, under the possible orientations. That is, for any
practical presentation of a sock to the camera, the measurements
based on the distances between the reference points must be the
same.

5. 1 Sock Orientation

Taking into account the structure of socks, three possible types
of orientatiion need to be considered. These are movement,
rotation and deformation. Movement is the movement of the whole
sock in the field of the view. Rotation is the circular rotation
of the whole sock. Deformation is the movement of just the foot
in relation to the leg. See Figure (2)

FIGURE (2)

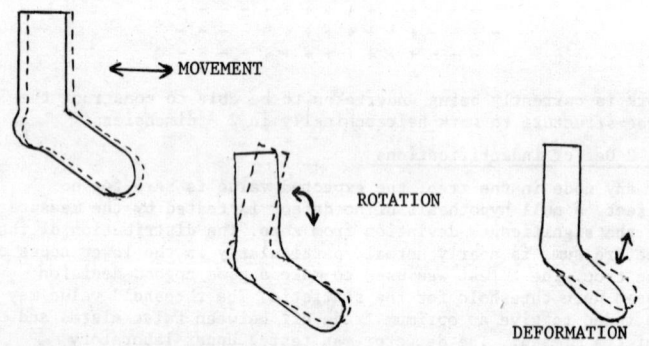

Other deformities are unlikely to occur if the sock is
presented flat for the camera. In all the above cases we are
considering only small deviations in a sock placed flat upon
the conveyor.

5. 2 The selection of reference points

The top centre of the sock is reasonably easy to locate and
define, and this is an essential point in determining the length
of the leg. The end of the foot is not so easy since it is
rounded, yet to find the foot length some point is required here.
The edges of the sock leg and sock foot were found to be quite
reliable to locate, along with their orientation so it was
possible to find the leg and foot besectors, these are
illustrated in Figure (3) as lines A-B and C-D. These lines were

found to be consistent in their position and so could be used
as rules along which to measure the foot and leg. By extending
these lines to the points where they crossed each edge of the
sock, two lines are obtained whose lengths are the measurementsof
leg and foot. However, when these measurements were tested for
consistency, it was found that they were unreliable under
deformation of the sock since points C and D (see Figure 2.)
varied along the edge of the sock. This variation was seen to be
of an order of the required measurements and so this system was
not used.

FIGURE 3.

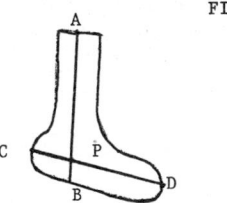

As an alternative the length from the foot and leg ends to the
centre of gravity of the sock were considered since this was
thought to be more stable. However on considering the theory
involved, it is still seen that this point will vary with
deformation of the sock.

5. 2. 2 The centre of rotation

The ideal point to use as a measure along the bisectors was seen
to be one that did not move relative to the foot and leg under
any of the possible orientations, particularly deformation of the
foot with respect to the leg.

Such a point was at the point of intersection of the two
bisectors, at point P (see Figure 3.) since this point seemed to
be very close to the pivot about which the foot and leg moved.
Hence deformation of the sock does not move this point in
relation to the other landmark points and so gives repeatable
translatable measurements. Thus the sock will be measured as
having leg length AP and foot length PD. These can be quite
simply derived from the coordinates of these points, once they
have been found.

5. 2. 3 Finding the edges

To use such a landmarking system the edges of the sock need to be
found in a way that is consistent regardless of real and noisy
variation in orientation or illumination. The choice of edge
detector is very large, ranging from the most simple threshold
operator to the more complex array type operators such as those
suggested by Sobel (13) and Roberts (14).

5. 2. 4 Choice of an edge finding method

To design a measuring scheme that works to the required
accuracy it is necessary to have an edge detector that can
repeatedly find edges to an accuracy of an order of magnitude
greater than the required. In this way calculations of distance
based upon the edge points will be consistent. Since the socks
were to be classified in 5mm groups the chosen precision
selected was +/- 1mm. For an accuracy of 1mm on a full scan size

of 500mm we have;

Required accuracy = 500/1 = 500

To be able to measure this accurately would require an accuracy
of one pixel for an image of resolution 512x512. It was thus
seen that all possible binary type thresholds would be inaccurate
in this measurement, since they can only be accurate to +/-1
pixel, as a change of one grey level in the measurement can move
such a binary threshold one pixel in either direction. An obvious
solution would be to increase the resolution such that this
problem is overcome but it was seen that on the grey level image
the sock edge was certainly not a binary edge but that it was a
gradual change over 2-3mm. Thus increasing the resolution (at
greater cost) was simply increasing this gradient, making the
measurement precision of +/- 1mm no more obtainable. So it was
seen that the edge detector was required to have the following
properties;

i) To make a statistical point estimate of position based on an
array of points

ii) To make a repeatable estimate at any point along the edge

iii)To give a continuouse estimate between the boundaries of
pixels rather than a sharp binary change.

This latter point was very important; it implied that it was
necessary to make a measurement of greater precision than a
single pixel so that a variation in the light or position along
the edge would only cause a variation of less than one pixel.

The position of the sock edge in the centre pixel is given by the
percentage of that pixel that contains sock that is given.

B = light level of background illumination

O = light level of object

E = light level in edge pixel

P = position of beginning of edge pixel.

$$\text{Position of edge} = P + \frac{(E - B)}{(O - B)}$$

This method gives a continuous variation through each pixel as
the sock moves within it, from zero when the sock edge
immediately follows the background pixel to one when the sock is
immediately before the object pixel.

In practice this measurement is not so simple since the edge of
the sock is never so clear that there is a background pixel
followed by an edge pixel followed by an object pixel. In the
final developed prototype a number of pixels are sampled
perpendicular to the edge to determine the centre of change, that
is the location of the edge of the pixel. Once again similar
techniques are applied to make this selection subject to a
continuous rather than instant change.

To make this scheme statistically robust along the varying edge a
group of pixels parallel to the edge are summed to give a more

consistent measure. Practical experiment showed that summing
over 5 pixels gave a measurement that was sufficiently reliable.

5. 2. 5 Measurement to the welt

Since the top of the sock is often thought to be the welt line
rather than the physical top, some way of being able to measure
to this line is required. So far the position of the sock has not
been considered, so what is required is a positioning that can
give the top of the sock as either the physical top or the welt
line. The alternative of having the computer find the welt line
is far too complex, due to the great variety of possible styles
of welt.

Observations in factory environments have shown that alignment
may be made very fast on a moving belt if the alignment marks do
not vary as the belt moves. Thus a line along the belt, parallel
with the direction of the movement was chosen as the only
physical alignment. On this line is placed the chosen top of the
sock (either the physical top or the welt), and this aligns the
sock in the correct position for image capture by the camera.

ACKNOWLEDGEMENTS

The authors gratefully acknowledge the technical assistance of
Mr.P.Clements and Miss M. Prior of Leicester Polytechnic, and the
sponsorship and active support of the SERC and CORAH PLC of the
UK.

REFERENCES

(1) R.T.Chin and C.A.Harlow. IEEE Trans. on PAMI.,
     1982, 4, (6), 557.

(2) J.R.Parks. Proc. Soc. Optical Inst. Eng., 1977, 130, 2

(3) L.R.Goodman. Text. Inst., 1971, 2 , (8), 230

(4) H.C.Wang, Quality, Sept. 1975.

(5) Graniteville Corporation of America - Shirley Inst.
     'Manual of Standard Defects in the Textile Industry'. 1975

(6) A.L.Knoll and R. Wolfe. Tex. Inst., 1975, 13, (5), 138

(7) D. J. Purll. 'Automatic Inspection of Fabrics'
     SIRA Institute, Vov. 1970.

(8) A. L.Knoll Tex. Inst , 1975, 13, (5), 138

(9) J. Philips. Canadian Text. J., 1979, 96, (10), 19.

(10) H.Koshiamizu. SPIE, 1979, 182 , 30.

(11) The American Society for Testing of Materials. The Standard
     Definitions of Terms relating to Fabric Defects
     D3990, ASTM, 1981.

(12) The British Standards. Numerical Designation of Fabric
     Faults by Visual Inspection B.S. 6395. 1983.

(13) I. Sobel. Camera Models and Machine Perception. 1970, 121

(14) L. G. Roberts. Symposium of Optical and Electo-optical
     information processing, 1964.

Leicester Polytechnic
Leicester, U.K.

COMPUTER APPLICATIONS IN TEXTILES : THE NIGERIAN EXPERIENCE

S.C.O. Ugbolue, P.Ng and P.O. Adegbile

ABSTRACT

Nigerian textile industry has pursued aggressive policies in restructuring the manufacturing units and consequently new horizons have been opened in the use of computers. A survey of some of the textile mills in Nigeria revealed a pattern whereby computers of varying hardwares and configurations are being used for specific objectives. Typical applications of computers in the Nigerian textile industry include: payroll costs analysis, process control, production planning, inventory management systems, customer order processing and sales analyses. The impact of computer education and training in the Nigerian textile industry is assessed in relation to the overall textile science and technology programmes. Suggestions and recommendations are proferred to ensure a well sustained industry - academia interaction in the area of computer applications in Nigeria.

INTRODUCTION

Technological advancement has brought in its train considerable pressure and desirability to utilise the computer as a powerful tool in the management-decision processes of corporate organisations. The Nigerian textile industry is made up of about 134 textile mills out of which about 38 are of medium and large scale firms [1,2]. A total of about 75,000 persons now work in the industry which has witnessed a significant decrease of about 25% in the total labour force since the peak period of textile manufacturing in 1980. In recent years, the industry was afflicted with serious economic problems arising from the squeeze on the national economy.

2. STRUCTURE OF THE INDUSTRY

The inner structure of the Nigerian textile industry has been influenced, in the past years, by the development of the primary raw material cotton. The main areas of textile manufacture are in Kaduna, Lagos and Kano. The major difficulty facing the industry in the past has been that of antiquated and obsolete, uneconomic plant but some of these mills are being rapidly replaced by a progressive investment policy although capital is increasingly becoming scarce.

176

A large proportion of the textile industry and, indeed the major mills have foreign investment and are largely controlled by foreign management. Between 1975 and 1980 the textile subsector had a growth rate of 34.5% and contributed about 19% of the total national manufacturing output. For the past 3 years, however, the industry has reported little or no profits and many of them have been running at about 45% capacity.

3. COMPUTER POLICY IN THE NIGERIAN TEXTILE INDUSTRY

There is no identifiable policy on computer acquisition in the textile industry. Indeed, there seems to be a total lack of even a national policy. Our investigations reveal that there are large concentration of computers of varying hardwares and configurations in Lagos, Oyo, Kaduna and Kano States and some computers also in Anambra, Bendel and Imo States. Specifically, as far as the textile industry is concerened, the larger mills have acquired some mini computers and series of microcomputers. This is understandable since the overall cost of processing and installing a computer (large frame or top mini) is quite sizeable. A lot of the mills using these computers feel convinced that despite the slump in our economy they would continue to invest appreciable amounts in their computer installations.

4. COMPUTER APPLICATIONS

In the Nigerian textile industry, various types of computers as shown in Table I are used but the totality of the utility of computers is rather insignificant and limited and mainly concentrated to routine data processing. Many mills are slow in grasping the desirability of adapting the computer power to their organisation. Table II shows the types of computer applications in the Nigerian textile mills. In fact, the largest textile mill in Nigeria which employs about 6,000 persons in one location is also the largest user of IBM/System **3**.

4.1 PROBLEMS ASSOCIATED WITH USE OF COMPUTERS IN NIGERIA

4.1.1 Hardwares

It is estimated that there are about 200 computers (excluding micro computers) in Nigeria, and that Nigeria may spend up to ₦200 million on microcomputers in the next few years[3]. However, the Government continues to charge about 40% duty on the hardware and 38½% on computer stationery.

TABLE I

TYPES OF COMPUTER INSTALLATIONS IN THE
NIGERIAN TEXTILE INDUSTRY

- IBM/System 3
- ICL 1900 series
- ICL ME 29
- WANG VS 80
- APPLE II
- CM Technologies
- PDP 1411

TABLE II

SUMMARY OF COMPUTER APPLICATIONS IN THE
NIGERIAN TEXTILE INDUSTRY

- Staff Payroll costs Analysis and Administration
- Daily Production List
- Sales Analysis by Customer
- Sales Analysis by article
- Raw material Inventory Control
- Cotton Inventory Stock Status Report
- Cotton Year to date Stock Balance Report
- Cotton Inventory Physical Count Adjustment
  transaction Report
- Cotton Reordering Advice Report
- Finished Goods Inventory List
- Production Control
- Invoicing
- Job Classification
- Colour preparation

4.1.2 Need for Dual Electric Generator

The irregular generating and supply of electric
power by the National Electric Power Authority
(NEPA) has reached alarming proportions in recent
years. Consequently, all users of computers must
of necessity install additional electric generators
as stand-by power supply to forestall incessant
power cuts by NEPA.

4.1.3 Importation of Software

It is disheartening to note that in some of major
textile mills employing a reasonable number of
indigenous computer scientists virtually all their
softwares are imported. Sometimes foreign 'experts'
are also imported into Nigeria to develop the software for use in the mills. In most cases, in other
public and private enterprises, "a lot of such software packages are "black boxes" which cannot be
modified to meet the changing needs of the importing
organisation⁵". It is estimated that the average
software package costs about ₦40,000.

4.1.4 Maintenance

It is observed that there is poor, ineffective maintenance facilities for the computers which the vendors supply to the textile industry. There is, therefore, need for vendors to set up proper servicing units in Nigeria to be able to service the requirements of the clients in terms of spares and routine maintenance. One major problem associated with poor maintenance is the dual role of the computer supplier who also acts as the consultant in the procurement exercise.

4.1.5 Shortage of Trained Manpower

The textile industry has found it increasingly difficult to recruit and retain high calibre computer scientists. A few Nigerian universities offer undergraduate and postgraduate courses in computer science. All polymer/textile technologist reading for B Sc Tech at the Federal University of Technology, Owerri and at the Department of Textile Science and Technology, Ahmadu Bello University, Zaria respectively, undertake courses in computing. The HND Textiles students at the Kaduna Polytechnic also take courses in programming. However, very few of such technologists ever seek employment in the computer department of textile mills. There is need to encourage more indigenous manpower training in the area of computer science. Many data processing operators are now trained by the private sector and also by the textile mills themselves.

4.1.6 Financial Constraints for Increased Production

The textile industry has a reputation for being in need of modernisation while at the same time facing abundant opportunities for implementing technological advances. Replacement of losses as well as finance for modernisation, such as procurement of computers, are sanctioned in the form of loans which carry interest. Unfortunately, many Nigerian businessmen are not willing to invest in private textile enterprises. However, it is projected[4] that the population of Nigeria will double by 2000 so that there will be a rise in textile consumption from 136 million kg/year to about 267 million kg/year resulting in expansion of output by 6.5 million kg/year for the next 20 years.

5. FUTURE DIRECTION

There is an increasing drive in some sections of the
Nigerian textile industry to diversify into the
highly specialised areas of high fashion textile
manufacturing. This is because of the increasing
demand for high quality printed and colour woven
shirt fabrics and ladies garments.

There is also the desire to improve productivity in
the industry although many of the medium textile
mills are reluctant to fully automate their
production lines. The greatest scope for computerisation in the Nigerian textile industry is in the
area of chemical processing of textiles. One major
manmade fibre and textiles producer in Nigeria has
invested tremendous capital in microprocessors.
Some of the large textile mills, however, believe
that productivity will accrue through better utility
of their existing plants and equipment rather than
completely rebuilding of the plants. To accomplish
the envisaged productivity, it would be necessary
to have the proper merging of better controls and
better management information retrieval system.

Our view of the future persuades us that the
country's goals and objectives are linked closely
to science and technology and that the ultimate
survival of the Nigerian textile industry lies in
meaningful research and development programmes
performed in Nigeria. An essential and invaluable
tool in accomplishing that goal is the computer.
Emphasis must be directed towards production and
process control/applications of the computer. The
impact of the computer as an effective management
tool must be emphasised in the industry. Our
success in textile industrialisation in Nigeria
demands wider participation and capital investment.
The Nigerian textile industry cannot and must not
allow its operations dismantled and its production
transferred to other sources despite the pressures
and shocks it has continued to receive. Finally,
we wish to suggest that the time is now ripe for
reorganisation, modernisation and introduction of
cost effective measures to ensure a strong, viable
Nigerian textile industry.

REFERENCES

1. S.C.O. Ugbolue. The Nigerian Textile Industry:
    Problems and Prospects. 1981 Kaduna
    International Trade Fair Symposium
    15 February, 1981.

2. S.C.O. Ugbolue. Text Horizons, 2, 32-33

3. S.B. Jaiyesimi. Keynote Address to the
    Conference of the Computer Association of
    Nigeria, Calabar 11-12 May, 1984.

4. African Textiles. August/September 1980,
    Published by Alain Charles Publishing Limited.

ADDRESS

1. Prof. S.C.O. Ugbolue
    Federal University of Technology
    P.M.B. 1526
    Owerri, Nigeria

2. Peter Ng
    United Nigerian Textiles Ltd
    Kaduna, Nigeria

3. Dr. P.O. Adegbile
    Department of Textile Technology
    Kaduna Polytechnic
    Kaduna, Nigeria

MICROPROCESSOR APPLICATIONS IN TEXTILE MACHINERY

E. C. Lear

ABSTRACT

The microprocessor has now become a standard part of a good
textile machine. Applications fall into two main classes -
data collection and machine control. Both of these
applications have been applied to the machines manufactured by
Cobble. The traditional method of buying ready-made hardware
and employing a software house for program writing leaves the
machine manufacturer with a diminishing knowledge of his
machine. A better method is to design amd build all hardware
and software in house. These points are described, together
with details of applications to carpet-tufting machinery,
materials-handling equipment, length measurement, and
carpet-backing lines.

Cobble Blackburn Limited
Blackburn
Lancashire
ENGLAND

WEAVE ROOM EFFICIENCY COMPUTER MODEL

W. A. Berger, D. O. Vess and M. H. Mohamed

ABSTRACT

A basic program has been developed for a micro-computer to determine weave room efficiency, with a given staff assignment, using the Mack, Murphy and Webb model. The Mack, Murphy and Webb model (MMW) will determine the efficiency of machines looked after by an operator who patrols in a fixed path and repairs any stopped machines with a fixed time per repair. The original MMW model resulted in a table which gave loom efficiencies for a wide range of situations likely to be encountered in the weave room. However, these tables only reflected a small percentage of actual weave room situations requiring considerable time to interpolate and find actual efficiencies. The computer program presented in this paper eliminates this interpolation process and allows management to manipulate variables quickly and easily to simulate efficiencies in a wide variety of weave room situations.

The model is interactive with the user inputing data for key variables, such as, the number of breaks or stops per hour, repair time for each type of break or stop (minutes), walking and inspection time (seconds), relaxation time per hour (%) and the number of looms per weaver. From this data the model calculates machine efficiency, time per patrol (minutes) and the time spent on repairs per patrol. The user is also provided with a feature to change variable data and to perform a sensitivity analysis on any of the input variables.

This model is specifically designed for use by weave room managers to determine theoretical machine efficiency providing an accurate measure with which to judge actual performance.

1. INTRODUCTION

Staff assignment in the weave room and the resulting machine efficiency are of particular interest to weave room management as it is the only production variable under the manager's control. When one operative/operator or weaver has more than one machine under his care, there will be an interference factor when the operator is servicing or repairing one machine while another machine has also stopped. This machine interference will cause a decrease in machine efficiency.

Models have been developed to statistically determine the machine efficiency, given a set staff assignment. Ashcroft (1), Benson and Cox (2) and Benson, Miller and Townsend (3) have attempted to develop accurate models but have fallen short. Ashcroft gave the efficiency for variable repair times and tables for constant repair times. This model neglects the effect of walking and servicing time. Servicing is any work performed other than repairs. Benson, Miller and Townsend dealt further into the effect of machine interference. This model assumed that the weaver attends to the machines in the order in which they have stopped, thus systematic patrols are not possible in this model. These models are only reasonable when the number of looms per weaver is very small.

Mack, Murphy and Webb (4) have developed an accurate model for when the number of looms per weaver is large. It is commonly used today. Other models in use today, such as the Palmer model (7), are not statistically based, but are derived from industrial engineering work and time study measurements. The basic assumptions of the Mack, Murphy and Webb model are:

a) The operative/operator patrols his machines in a fixed path repairing any stopped machines he comes across.

b) Stoppages occur at random.

c) The time to repair any stopped loom is constant.

d) In each patrol, the time for walking, inspecting, servicing and relaxation is constant.

This model gives an accurate solution to the problem, as long as the above assumptions hold. However, in practice, the weaver will not consistently patrol in a systematic path. Repair time will vary, as well as the manner in which the weaver performs his subsidiary duties. Therefore, the calculated efficiency is only an approximation.

Mack, Murphy and Webb gave the initial tables for interpolating the machine efficiency from specific variables which will be described later in this paper. Kemp and Mack (5) gave extended tables of the model in order to ease the lengthy interpolation process for the weave room manager to find the same efficiency results without the time consuming interpolation process.

2. DESCRIPTION OF THE MACK, MURPHY AND WEBB MODEL

2.1 Assumptions

The following assumptions were made in the development of the model:

a) The intervals between stoppages, for any one machine, are distributed exponentially in running time. There are two (2) possible states for each machine (running or stopped).

b) The weaver takes a constant time, K, mean walking time, to walk to a loom, inspecting before repairing it or proceeding to the next loom.

c) The time to repair and restart any stopped machine is
a constant, C.

2.2 Definitions

Machine efficiency is defined as the ratio of the average
production achieved to the production rate possible with
no time lost on repairs. A round is defined as starting
when the weaver leaves the first machine and ends when the
weaver leaves that machine again. It was shown that
successive rounds define a Markov process which yields a
unique steady state solution.

2.3 Application of the Model

The quantities that need to be evaluated are:

a) X-Average stoppage rate per loom minute.

b) C-Average repair time per loom minute.

c) K-Walking and inspection time in minutes.

d) N-Number of looms per weaver.

e) The percentage of time (per hour) allowed for
relaxation and subsidiary duties.

Quantity X is calculated from the sum of stoppage
rates per loom per hour divided by 60. The types of
stoppage usually are:

- Warp breaks per loom per hour.
- Weft breaks per loom per hour.
- Slack ends per loom per hour.
- Other stops per loom per hour.

Quantity C is calculated from the sum of the individual
stoppage rates multiplied by their corresponding repair
times, then divided by the total number of stoppages per
loom per hour. Quantity K can be estimated from time or
work studies in the mill and usually runs between .041 and
.133 minutes.

To account for the allowances for relaxation and
subsidiary duties the values of C and K are inflated by
an allowed percentage to C' and K'. The number of
looms per weaver is assumed to be constant since the
assignment is typically fixed for a given shift for
ease of calculating production related pay.

Machine Efficiency (E) is given (by Mack, Murphy and
Webb) as:

$$E = F/\left((X \times NK' \times G) + (X \times N \times C' \times F) \right)$$

Where:

$$F = (b-1) \{1 + \binom{n-1}{1}(ab-1) + \binom{n-1}{2}(a^2b-1)(ab-1) + \ldots\}$$

and

$$G = 1+(b-1)\left\{\binom{n}{1}+\binom{n}{2}(ab-1)+\binom{n}{3}(a^2b-1)(-1)+\ldots\right\}$$

$$a = \exp(XC') \qquad b = \exp(XNK')$$

The combinations calculated are the "number of combinations of N looms stopped R at a time" (4). Due to the memory capacity of a personal computer, R was limited to at most 30% of N (for N > 50) and 50% of N (for 20 >N> 50). Loom stoppages of greater than these percentages would be indicative of some type of problem, either mechanical or preparatory. This limitation does not significantly affect the machine efficiency result.

The time for One Patrol (T) in minutes is given as:

$$T = N \times K' (1 - X \times N \times C' \times E)$$

and the" Actual Time Spent on Repairs" per patrol (U) is:

$$U = (T - N \times K')/T$$

The machine efficiency result is given as a percent, but used in subsequent calculations in its fractional form. The efficiency calculated from the model does not account for mechanical failures so actual efficiency could be slightly less (as much as 3% lower).

4. DISCUSSION

The computer model is interactive with the user inputing data for the key variables listed in the User's Guide. The values are placed into a datafile from which the computer program will read the data. This allows the user to store the information for quick retrieval. The number of variables are small and the values for them can be determined from historical data or from time studies. The user is able to change variables, thus shortening the time to determine efficiency when a few variables change.

The sensitivity analysis section can be an important decision aid to the weave room manager. A sensitivity analysis is performed when there is a degree of uncertainty in the importance of one or more variables. It measures the response of machine efficiency (dependent variable) to changes in one or more independent variables. A popular viewpoint believes that a maximum level of machine efficiency is the most economical state. However, this is not necessarily the case. Capital and labor cost differ, as well as material and preparatory costs. The sensitivity section allows the weave room manager to examine various levels of efficiency, in conjunction with the firms cost models, to determine the minimum cost level of operation.

5. USER"S GUIDE TO WEAVE ROOM EFFICIENCY MODEL

CALCULATES:

MACHINE EFFICIENCY
TIME PER PATROL (minutes)
TIME SPENT ON REPAIRS PER PATROL

5.1 Definition of Variables

5.1.1 Input Variables (from Datafile)

```
 *J$(1)    LOOM SPEED
 *J$(2)    REED WIDTH
 *J$(3)    ENDS PER INCH(or CM)
 *J$(4)    PICKS PER INCH(or CM)
  J$(5)    NUMBER OF WARP BREAKS per LOOM per HOUR
  J$(6)    NUMBER OF WEFT BREAKS per LOOM per HOUR
  J$(7)    NUMBER OF SLACK ENDS per LOOM per HOUR
  J$(8)    NUMBER OF OTHER STOPS per LOOM per HOUR
  J$(9)    REPAIR TIME per WARP BREAK
  J$(10)   REPAIR TIME per WEFT BREAK
  J$(11)   REPAIR TIME per SLACK END
  J$(12)   REPAIR TIME per OTHER STOPS
  J$(13)   WALKING AND INSPECTION TIME(seconds)
  J$(14)   RELAXATION TIME PER HOUR(%)
  J$(15)   NUMBER OF LOOMS PER WEAVER
**J$(16)   TOTAL NUMBER OF LOOMS IN A WEAVE ROOM
```

Variables marked (*) should only be changed in the
sensitivity analysis section. Changing them in the
"CHANGE A VARIABLE" section will not alter the initial
computations. The "TOTAL NUMBER OF LOOMS" is provided
for a more complete description of the weave room but
is not used in any calculation and therefore should not
be a variable to change.

5.1.2 Output Variables

```
H$(1)    AVERAGE NUMBER OF STOPS per LOOM per HOUR
H$(2)    AVERAGE NUMBER OF STOPS per LOOM per MINUTE
         [X]
H$(3)    TOTAL REPAIR TIME per LOOM per MINUTE
H$(4)    WEIGHTED AVERAGE REPAIR TIME(min.) per LOOM per
         HOUR (C)
H$(5)    INFLATED WEIGHTED AVERAGE REPAIR TIME(min.) per
         LOOM per HOUR FOR RELAXATION [C']
H$(6)    WALKING AND INSPECTION TIME (minutes) (K)
H$(7)    INFLATED WALKING AND INSPECTION TIME(min.) FOR
         RELAXATION (K')
H$(8)    AVERAGE STOPS INFLATED REPAIR TIME (XC')
H$(9)    AVERAGE STOPS NUMBER OF LOOMS PER WEAVER
         INFLATED WALKING TIME (XNK')
H$(10)   LOOM EFFICIENCY
H$(11)   TIME FOR ONE PATROL (minutes)
H$(12)   ACTUAL TIME SPENT ON REPAIRS PER PATROL
```

Variables followed by () are the corresponding variables
of the Mack, Murphy and Webb model. All of these

variables are calculated and cannot be used for a
sensitivity study. Loom efficiency is given as a percent.

5.2 Discussion of Data Entry and Output

The Machine Efficiency model uses the statistical model
developed by Mack, Murphy and Webb. Basic assumptions
made were:

a) Weaver has a set number of looms.

b) Weaver walks in one direction and each patrol forms a
    closed loop.

c) Walking time includes the time to walk from the center
    of machine A to the center of machine B, inspecting
    and servicing it before attempting repairs or moving
    or moving on to machine C.

d) The time to repair a stopped machine is constant.

e) Relaxation time is thought to be constant percentage
    per hour. Average repair times and walking times are
    inflated to take this into account.

The machine efficiency model used input variables J(5)
through J(15) to calculate H(10), Machine Efficiency. The
model then calculates H(11), Time for One Patrol, and
H(12), Actual Time Spent on Repairs per patrol. The
values for the output variables are shown in the "STAFF
ASSIGNMENT/MACHINE EFFICIENCY" table.

I. STAFF ASSIGNMENT/MACHINE EFFICIENCY
    LOOM NAME: AIR JET
    FABRIC NAME: PLAIN
    ****

VARIABLE	VALUE	#
AVG # OF STOPS/LM/HR	1.1	1
Avg # OF STOPS/LM/HR	.02	2
TOTAL REPAIR TIME/LM/HR	.74	3
WAVG REPAIR TIME(MIN)/LM/HR	.67	4
INF REPAIR TIME(MIN)/LM/HR	.84	5
WALKING TIME PER MIN	.05	6
INF WALKING TIME PER MIN	.06	7
AVG STOPS *INF REPAIR TIME/MIN	.02	8
AVG STOPS *#LMS *INF WALK TIME	.05	9
LOOM EFFICIENCY	93.08	10
TIME(MIN) FOR ONE PATROL	5.86	11
ACTUAL TIME SPENT ON REPAIRS	3.36	12

    NOTE-MACHINE EFFICIENCY DOES NOT
    INCLUDE MECHANICAL FAILURE, ACTUAL
    EFFICIENCY COULD BE SLIGHTLY LESS

A table of the input variables, from the Datafile, can
also be printed.

II. DATAFILE VARIABLE TABLE
     LOOM NAME: AIR JET
     FABRIC NAME: PLAIN
     ****

VARIABLE	VALUE	#
LOOM SPEED	180	1
LOOM WIDTH	40	2
ENDS PER CM	60	3
PICKS PER CM	60	4
# WARP BREAKS/LOOM/HOUR	.65	5
# WEFT BREAKS/LOOM/HOUR	.3	6
# SLACK ENDS/LOOM/HOUR	.1	7
# OTHER STOPS/LOOM/HOUR	.05	8
REPAIR TIME/WARP BREAK(MIN)	.85	9
REPAIR TIME/WEFT BREAK(MIN)	.33	10
REPAIR TIME/SLACK END/MIN	.5	11
REPAIR TIME/OTHER STOPS(MIN)	.75	12
WALKING & INSPECTION TIME(SEC)	3	13
RELAXATION TIME(%)	20	14
# OF LOOMS PER WEAVER	40	15
TOTAL # OF LOOMS	400	16

5.3 Changing Variable Values

The user has the option to change the values of the input
variables, J$(I). The program will query "CHANGE A
VARIABLE ?(Y/N)". A "Y" response will cause the program to
ask the user "VARIABLE NUMBER", J$(I), and the "NEW
VALUE", J(I). The user will then have the option:

a) Saving the value in the original dataset,

b) Creating a new datafile, or

c) Not saving the changed value.

The program then continues through the calculation
section.

5.4 Performing A Sensitivity Analysis

After viewing the output table, the user will be queried
"SENSITIVITY ANALYSIS ?(Y/N)". A "Y" response to the
question will cause the program to go to the sensitivity
analysis section.

The user will be prompted "NUMBER OF VARIABLE TO STUDY",
J$(I). Any of the input variables can be used for a
sensitivity study. The percentage change of this value is
input by the user through the question "STEP PERCENTAGE."
The user must use care in determining the step perentage
so that the output is not trivial due to a too low or too
high step percentage. If the user enters "3" as the step
percentage the model will compute the variable values as
follows:

189

NEW AMOUNT

```
 88% ORIGINAL VALUE
 91% ORIGINAL VALUE
 94% ORIGINAL VALUE
 97% ORIGINAL VALUE
103% ORIGINAL VALUE
106% ORIGINAL VALUE
109% ORIGINAL VALUE
112% ORIGINAL VALUE
```

For each of the new amounts the model will then calculate
the Machine Efficiency, Time per Patrol and the Actual
Time Spent on Repairs. The original value will not be
changed in the memory.

III. SENSITIVITY STUDY

```
NUMBER OF VARIABLE TO STUDY 15
STEP PERCENTAGE:3
CALCULATING
SS=-12          NEW VAL=35.2
SS=-9           NEW VAL=36.4
SS=-6           NEW VAL=37.6
SS=-3           NEW VAL=38.8
SS=0            NEW VAL=40
SS=3            NEW VAL=41.2
SS=6            NEW VAL=42.4
SS=9            NEW VAL=43.6
SS=12           NEW VAL=44.8
```

IV. SENSITIVITY ANALYSIS RESULTS
     ****
```
LOOM NAME:  AIR JET
FABRIC NAME:  PLAIN
VARIABLE # OF LOOMS PER WEAVER
```

NEW AMOUNT	MACHINE EFFICIENCY	TIME PER PATROL	TIME SPENT ON REPAIRS
35.2	94.06	4.49	2.29
36.4	93.76	4.79	2.52
37.6	93.47	5.12	2.77
38.8	93.14	5.47	3.04
40	93.08	5.86	3.36
41.2	92.11	6.19	3.62
42.4	91.31	6.56	3.91
43.6	91.29	7.04	4.31
44.8	90.72	7.48	4.68

```
ANOTHER SENSITIVITY STUDY?(Y?N)N
STOP (1) OR RETURN (2)?1
```

It is estimated that the relationship between machine efficiency and input variables J$(1) through J$(4) is inversly exponentially proportional to a power of 1.5 (6). Time Per Patrol and Time Spent on Repairs are functions of machine efficiency along with the other input variables. Due to the interaction of these variables, Time Per Patrol and Time Spent on Repairs cannot be accurately predicted from changes in machine efficiency only.

The user will then be queried "ANOTHER SENSITIVITY STUDY?(Y/N)". An "N" response will cause the model to query the user "STOP(1) OR RETURN(2)". A(1) response will cause the program to stop. A (2) response causes the program to return to the "Change a Variable" section and the user will then be able to perform another study.

REFERENCES

(1) H. Ashcroft. J. Roy. Sta. B., 1950, 12, p. 145.

(2) F. Benson and D. R. Cox. J. Roy. Sta. B., 1951, 13, p. 65.

(3) F. Benson, J. G. Miller, and M. W. H. Townsend. J. Text. Ind., 1953, 44, p. T619.

(4) C. Mack, T. Murphy, and N. L. Webb. J. Roy. Sta. B., 1957, 19, 1, p. 166.

(5) A. Kemp and C. Mack. J. Text. Ind., 1961, 52, p. T471.

(6) P. R. Lord and M. H. Mohamed. Textile Recorder, October 1964, p. 67.

(7) W. S. Palmer. 'Production from Multi-Machine Assignments: Calculations for Industrial Engineers,' 1974 (revised), Institute of Textile Technology, Charlottesville, Virginia.

School of Textiles
North Carolina State University
Raleigh, NC 27965-8301

APPENDIX A

EFFICIENCY PROGRAM IN APPLESOFT BASIC

```
10    DIM J(20),H(20),J$(20),H$(20),M(20,20),E(20)
20    DEF FN LA(X) = INT (100 * X + .5) / 100
70    HOME
100   PRINT "NORTH CAROLINA STATE UNIVERSITY"
110   PRINT "SCHOOL OF TEXTILES"
140   PRINT "APPLESOFT BASIC VERSION 8-83"
150   PRINT "*************************************"
160   PRINT
170   PRINT "WEAVING TECHNOLOGY MANAGEMENT"
180   PRINT "MODEL TO CALCULATE:"
190   PRINT "STAFF ASSIGNMENT; MACHINE EFFICIENCY"
203   INPUT "LOOM NAME: ";LOOM$
205   INPUT "FABRIC NAME: ";FABRIC$
220   INPUT "DATAFILE NAME:";F$
230   PRINT CHR$ (4);"OPEN";F$
233   FOR I = 1 TO 16
235   PRINT CHR$ (4);"READ";F$
240   INPUT J(I),J$(I)
250   PRINT CHR$ (4)
260   NEXT I
270   PRINT CHR$ (4);"CLOSE";F$
280   INPUT "CHECK VALUES IN DATAFILE(Y/N)";S$
290   IF LEFT$ (S$,1) < > "N" THEN 310
300   GOTO 700
305   PRINT "VARIABLE"; TAB( 32);" VALUE"; TAB ( 38);"#"
310   FOR I = 1 TO 16
330   PRINT J$(I); TAB( 32);J(I);TAB(38);I
340   NEXT I
350   INPUT "CONTINUE ? ";S$
355   REM SUBROUTINE TO CHANGE A VARIABLE
360   INPUT "CHANGE A VARIABLE?(Y/N)";J$
370   IF LEFT$ (J$,1) < > "N" THEN 390
380   GOTO 700
390   INPUT "ENTER VARIABLE #:";P
400   INPUT "NEW VALUE:";R
410   J(P) = R
420   INPUT "CHANGE ANOTHER VARIABLE?(Y/N)";J$
430   IF LEFT$ (J$,1) < > "N" THEN 390
440   HOME : PRINT "SAVE THESE CHANGES:"
450   PRINT "DATAFILE:";F$;"(ENTER 0)"
460   PRINT "A NEW DATAFILE:(ENTER 1)?"
470   PRINT "DO NOT SAVE:(ENTER 2)"
480   INPUT ">";W: IF W > 2 THEN 700
490   IF W = 2 THEN 700
500   IF W = 0 THEN 520
510   INPUT "NEW FILE NAME?";F$
520   PRINT CHR$ (4);"OPEN";F$: FOR I = 1 TO 16
530   PRINT CHR$ (4);"WRITE";F$
540   PRINT J(I);" , ";J$(I)
550   PRINT CHR$ (4): NEXT I
560   PRINT CHR$ (4);"CLOSE";F$
570   PRINT "DATAFILE FILE SAVED"
580   PRINT "NAME";F$
699   REM NAME OF CALCULATED VARIABLES
```

```
700   H$(1) = "AVG # OF STOPS /LM/HR"
710   H$(2) = "AVG # OF STOPS/LM/MIN"
720   H$(3) = "TOTAL REPAIR TIME/LM/HR"
730   H$(4) = "WAVG REPAIR TIME(MIN)/LM/HR"
740   H$(5) = "INF REPAIR TIME(MIN)/LM/HR"
750   H$(6) = "WALKING TIME PER MIN"
760   H$(7) = "INF WALKING TIME PER MIN"
770   H$(8) = "AVG STOPS *INF REPAIR TIME/MIN"
780   H$(9) = "AVG STOPS *#LMS *INF WALK TIME"
790   H$(10) = "LOOM EFFICIENCY"
800   H$(11) = "TIME(MIN) FOR ONE PATROL"
810   H$(12) = "ACTUAL TIME SPENT ON REPAIRS"
999   REM CALCULATION SECTION
1000  H(1) = J(5) + J(6) + J(7) + J(8)
1050  H(2) = H(1) / 60
1100  H(3) = (J(5) * J(9)) + (J(6) * J(10)) + (J(7) *
      J(11)) + (J(8) * J(12))
1150  H(4) = H(3) / H(1)
1200  H(5) = H(4) * (100 / (100 - J(14)))
1250  H(6) = J(13) / 60
1300  H(7) = H(6) * (100 / (100 - J(14)))
1350  H(8) = H(2) * H(5)
1400  H(9) = H(2) * J(15) * H(7)
1450  T8 = EXP (H(8))
1500  T9 = EXP (H(9))
1550  REM *********SPECIAL MACHINE EFFICIENCY CALCULATIONS*
      ********
1560  N = J(15):N = N - 1:NM = N
1562  IF Z = 3 THEN 1570
1565  FLASH : PRINT "CALCULATING": NORMAL
1570  COUNTER = 0
1575  GOSUB 5000
1580  N = J(15):F = (T9 - 1) * (1 + V)
1590  COUNTER = 1:NM = N: GOSUB 5000
1600  G = 1 + ((T9 - 1) * (J(15) + V))
1610  H(10) = F / ((H(9) * G) + (H(8) * J(15) * F))
1620  REM *****END MACHINE EFFICIENCY CALCULATIONS*****
1900  H(11) = (J(15) * H(7)) / (1 - (H(8) * J(15) * H(10)))
1950  H(12) = H(11) - (J(15) * H(7))
1955  H(10) = H(10) * 100
1960  IF Z = 3 THEN 3220
1973  FOR I = 1 TO 12
1975  H(I) = FN LA(H(I))
1976  NEXT I
2010  GOTO 5999
2999  REM SENSITIVITY ANALYSIS SECTION
3000  PRINT TAB( 12);"SENSITIVITY STUDY"
3010  PRINT TAB( 12);"----------------"
3020  INPUT "NUMBER OF VARIABLE TO STUDY ";VST
3030  IF VST > 15 OR VST < 1 THEN PRINT "INVALID VARIABLE":
      GOTO 3020
3040  INPUT "STEP PERCENTAGE:";K
3050  IF K > 100 OR K < 1 THEN PRINT "INVALID STEP
      PERCENTAGE": GOTO 3040
3060  STUDY$ = J$(VST)
3070  PRINT : FLASH : PRINT "CALCULATING": NORMAL
3080  SC = 1
3090  Z = 3:VH = J(VST)
3095  A = H(10)
```

```
3100 FOR SS = ( - 4 * K) TO (4 * K) STEP K
3110 J(VST) = (VH * SS / 100) + VH
3115 PRINT "SS=";SS; TAB ( 20);"NEW VAL=";J(VST)
3120 IF VST < 5 THEN 5505
3190 GOTO 1000
3220 M(SC,13) = J(VST)
3230 FOR N = 1 TO 12
3240 M(SC,N) = H(N)
3250 NEXT N
3260 SC = SC + 1
3270 NEXT SS
3280 J(VST) = VH:Z = 0:SC = 0
3285 3285 H(10) = A
3305 HOME
3310 PRINT TAB( 6);"SENSITIVITY ANALYSIS RESULTS"
3320 PRINT TAB( 6);"*****************************"
3330 PRINT "LOOM NAME ";LOOM$
3340 PRINT "FABRIC NAME ";FABRIC$
3350 PRINT "VARIABLE ";STUDY$
3360 PRINT
3370 PRINT TAB( 3);"NEW"; TAB( 11);"MACHINE"; TAB
     ( 22);"TIME PER"; TAB( 31);"TIME SPENT"
3380 PRINT TAB( 2);"AMOUNT"; TAB( 10);"EFFICIENCY"; TAB
     ( 23);" PATROL"; TAB( 31);"ON REPAIRS"
3420 FOR ST = 1 TO 9
3425 M(ST,13) = FN LA(M(ST,13)):M(ST,10) = FN
     LA(M(ST,10)):M(ST,11) = FN LA(M(ST,11)):M(ST,12) = FN
     LA(M(ST,12))
3430 PRINT TAB( 2);M(ST,13); TAB( 13);M(ST,10); TAB
     ( 23);M(ST, 11); TAB( 33);M(ST,12):Next ST
3460 INPUT "ANOTHER SENSITIVITY STUDY?(Y/N)";S$
3470 IF LEFT$ (S$,1) < > "N" THEN 3020
3480 GOTO 6270
4499 REM ++++SUBROUTINE 4500++++ COMBINATION CALC.
4500 P = 1:C = 1:S = 0
4520 FOR I = N - D + 1 TO N
4530 IF 1.7E38 / I > = P THEN 4550
4540 PRINT CHR$ (7);"MORE THAN 9.9E62 PERMUTATIONS"
4545 RETURN
4550 P = P * I
4560 NEXT I
4570 IF D = 1 THEN 4600
4580 FOR J = 2 TO D
4590 C = C * J:NEXT J
4600 S = P / C
4610 RETURN
4999 REM ++++SUBROUTINE 5000++++EFFICIENCY CALC.
5000 V = 0
5001 IF N > = 50 THEN TF = .30
5002 IF N < 50 THEN TF = .5
5005 IF N > 20 THEN NM = FN LA(N * TF)
5010 FOR L = 1 TO NM
5020 D = L
5030 GOSUB 4500
5040 IF COUNTER = 1 AND L = 1 THEN NEXT L
5050 V1 = 0:V2 = 1:V3 = 0
5055 IF COUNTER = 1 THEN D = D - 1
5060 FOR J = 1 TO D
```

```
5070 V1 = ((T8 * J) * T9) - 1
5080 V2 = V2 * V1
5090 NEXT J
5100 V3 = V2 * S
5105 IF V3 < .005 THEN RETURN
5110 V = V + V3
5120 NEXT L
5200 RETURN
5505 IF SS = 0 THEN H(10) = A:H(11) = 0:H(12) = 0:
     GOTO 3220
5506 IF SS < 0 THEN 5515
5510 H(10) = A - ((1 - (SS/100))   1.5): GOTO 5525
5515 H(10) = A + ((1 + (SS/100))   1.5)
5525 H(11) = 0:H(12) = 0: GOTO 3220
5999 REM OUTPUT TABLE SECTION
6000 PRINT "VIEW DATAFILE TABLE AND OUTPUT TABLE(ENTER
     0)";Z
6010 INPUT "OR OUTPUT TABLE ONLY?(ENTER 1)";Z
6020 IF Z = 1 THEN 6150
6025 HOME
6030 PRINT "DATAFILE VARIABLE TABLE"
6040 PRINT "LOOM NAME:";LOOM$
6050 PRINT "FABRIC NAME:";FABRIC$
6060 PRINT "***************************************"
6070 PRINT "VARIABLE"; TAB( 32); "VALUE"; TAB( 38);"#"
6080 FOR I = 1 TO 16
6090 PRINT J$(I); TAB( 32);J(I);TAB (38);I
6100 NEXT I
6105 PRINT
6110 INPUT "PRESS RETURN TO CONT";S$
6145 PRINT : PRINT: PRINT
6150 PRINT "STAFF ASSIGNMENT/MACHINE EFFICIENCY"
6160 PRINT "LOOM NAME:";LOOM$
6170 PRINT "FABRIC NAME:";FABRIC$
6180 PRINT "***************************************"
6190 PRINT "VARIABLE"; TAB( 32);"VALUE"; TAB( 38);"#"
6200 FOR I = 1 TO 12
6210 PRINT H$(I); TAB( 32); H(I); TAB( 38);I
6220 NEXT I
6230 PRINT
6240 PRINT "NOTE-MACHINE EFFICIENCY DOES NOT"
6243 PRINT "INCLUDE MECHANICAL FAILURE,ACTUAL"
6246 PRINT "EFFICIENCY COULD BE SLIGHTLY LESS"
6250 INPUT "CONTINUE?";S$
6260 INPUT "SENSITIVITY ANALYSIS?(Y/N)";S$: IF LEFT$
     (S$,1) < > "N" THEN 2999
6270 INPUT "STOP (1) OR RETURN (2)?";V: IF V = 2 THEN 280
9999 END
```

195

APPENDIX B

PROGRAM TO CREATE A DATAFILE

```
3     PRINT "CREATE A DATAFILE"
7     DIM J$(20),J(20)
8     PRINT : INPUT "FILE NAME:";F$
10    PRINT CHR$ (4);"OPEN";F$
20    GOTO 499
30    FOR I = 1 TO 16
32    IF J$(I) = "0" THEN J(I) = 0
34    IF J$(I) = "0" THEN 100
40    PRINT "VALUE FOR: ";J$(I)
50    INPUT J(I)
60    PRINT CHR$ (4);"WRITE":F$
70    PRINT J(I);" , ";J$(I)
80    PRINT CHR$ (4)
90    NEXT I
100   PRINT CHR$ (4);"CLOSE";F$
110   PRINT "DATAFILE: ";F$;" COMPLETE"
120   END
130   PRINT
499   REM VARIABLE NAME ASSIGNMENTS
500   J$(1) = "LOOM SPEED"
510   J$(2) = "LOOM WIDTH"
520   J$(3) = "ENDS PER CM"
530   J$(4) = "PICKS PER CM"
540   J$(5) = "# WARP BREAKS/ LOOM/HOUR"
550   J$(6) = "# WEFT BREAKS/LOOM/HOUR"
560   J$(7) = "* SLACK ENDS/LOOM/HOUR"
570   J$(8) = "* OTHER STOPS/LOOM/HOUR"
580   J$(9) = "REPAIR TIME/WARP BREAK(MIN)"
590   J$(10) = "REPAIR TIME/WEFT BREAK(MIN)"
600   J$(11) = "REPAIR TIME/SLACK END(MIN)"
610   J$(12) = "REPAIR TIME/OTHER STOPS(MIN)"
620   J$(13) = "WALKING & INSPECTION TIME(SEC)"
630   J$(14) = "RELAXATION TIME(%)"
640   J$(15) = "# OF LOOMS PER WEAVER"
650   J$(16) = "TOTAL # OF LOOMS IN WEAVE ROOM"
700   GOTO 30
```

Ms W. Berger., D. O. Vess & M. H. Mohamed
School of Textiles
Dept. of Textile Materials & Management
North Carolina State University
Raleigh
North Carolina
U.S.A.

MACHINE EFFICIENCY FLOWCHART

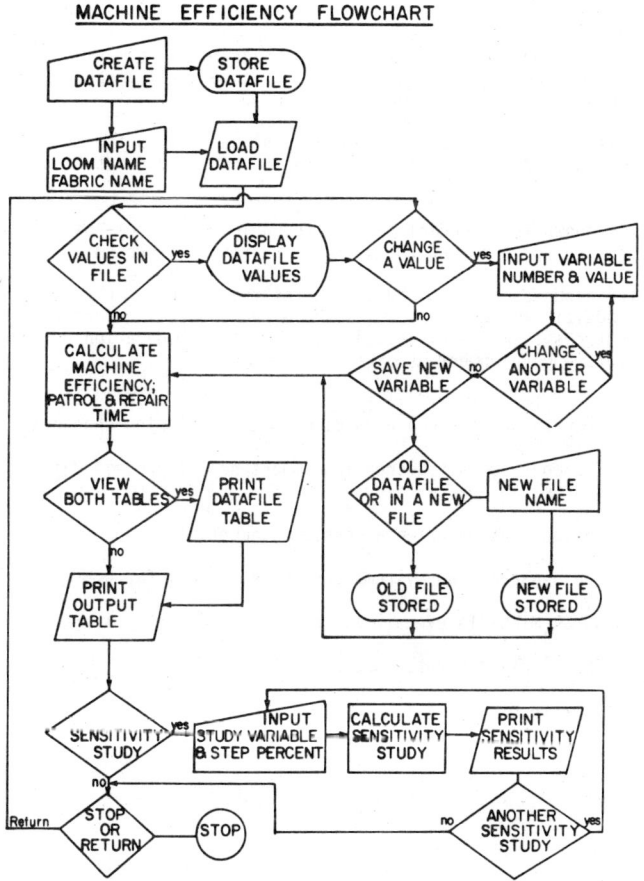

AN INTEGRATED INFORMATION SYSTEM FOR TEXTILE MILLS

H. Howald

ABSTRACT

On-line monitoring of production and quality in textile processing is becoming an established 'state-of-the-art'. This paper
describes a unique solution for an integrated information system
based on decentralized sub-systems. It covers all processes from
spinning preparation to weaving.

Special considerations are given to the quality monitoring
functions and the application-oriented overall concept of the
system.

It is shown that special textile technological 'know-how' is
necessary for ensuring the usefulness of such a system.

After a survey of the specialities of the various sub-systems,
the additional functions fulfilled by an overriding central
computer system are discussed. Finally, a consideration of trends
in future development is given.

The paper is sub-divided according to the following chapters :

1. The continuously increasing importance of process data
   systems in the textile industry

2. An application-oriented system concept

3. The separate sub-systems and their special features

4. USTER MILLDATA overall system

5. Future developments, trends

6. References

1. THE CONTINUOUSLY INCREASING IMPORTANCE OF PROCESS DATA SYSTEMS IN THE TEXTILE INDUSTRY

Process data systems are well on the way to being generally accepted as an unrelinquishable tool in textile production. Originally considered as an 'intelligent' replacement for mechanical production counters, the application range of process data systems has become extended more and more. In some cases, they even fulfil selected machine control functions. Nevertheless, we should continue to consider the following as the principal requirements of a process data system :

° making mill conditions transparent, monitoring of the more important process parameters, continuously 'around-the-clock',

° indicate disturbances and insufficiencies instantly and objectively,

° assist the planning of material and personnel assignments

° automate work-intensive routine tasks necessary in order to collect and evaluate production data.

Why is it then that the importance of process data collection has only recently become of such importance ? The applicable technical means such as, for instance, computers, multiplexers, etc., have been available for quite some time. Computer controlled process data systems were successfully applied in several textile plants more than 10 years ago.

There would seem to be two primary reasons for this development:

° production conditions in the textile industry have changed quite considerably. The application of a much wider scale of high productive and capital-intensive machines has set different and generally higher requirements on personnel and mill management. More and more production is achieved with less and less personnel. Further to this, the market situation necessitates increased flexibility in order to adapt quickly to changing market requirements.

° the evolution of microelectronics has contributed a great deal to making possible the economic manufacture of such process data systems having the necessary reliability.

The simultaneously increasing familiarity with computer technology is primarily responsible for breaking down sentimental barriers which had been established in reaction to such systems.

2. AN APPLICATION-ORIENTED SYSTEM CONCEPT

There are various possibilities to build up an on-line information system for production processing. The concept chosen by
our company is the result of many years experience and a consideration of the various requirements with respect to function,
costs, reliability, extensibility, etc. The main points of the
USTER concept are :

° an integrated solution with decentralized standard sub-systems
  and an overall central system (fig. 1).

° quality supervision as an important part function

° simple operation which can be carried out by the already
  available mill personnel.

° high reliability and assured continuity.

Data systems are dependent primarily on their successful application by the personnel concerned. Accordingly, the concept for
such installations should be adapted to the user. Trained
personnel, particularly at the overlooker or mill manager level,
are few in number and are accordingly fully occupied with their
normal work-load. A data system for this group of users should be
easy to operate, not extensive and, of most importance, reliable.
Only such a system will be quickly accepted and used daily as a
production tool. A concentration on the more important and useful
functions has priority over an unsurveyable flood of data and
possibilities.

With the practical application of process data systems, moti-
vation of personnel should be accorded the most significant
consideration. One method to realize this is to arrange a non-
restricted availability of all collected data. The data
evaluation should also be organized, if at all possible, in the
form of decentralized self-control and not only in the form of a
centralized supervision.

The **sub-division of the complete system into decentralized sub-
systems** per processing stage ensure that the installation is
easily understood and accepted by mill personnel. It is therefore
more readily and correctly applied. In addition, it provides for
an optimum adaptation to the various conditions. As each sub-
system can operate in an autonomous manner, the reliability of
the overall sytem is increased. Last, but not least, the concept
provides for the step-by-step extension of such an information
system by means of clearly-defined investment stages.

Every development of a company is influenced, whether intentionally or otherwise, by its tradition and its other fields of activity. As a consequence, the second important characteristic of our concept came into being. We consider it of great importance, that besides the collection of production data, solutions are also made available for **on-line collection of quality data.**

Productivity and quality are intimately connected in all the multiple stage processes of textile manufacture. Unsuitable quality in the earlier production processes negatively affect, as is known, all subsequent process stages and the quality of the finished product. Furthermore, with modern high production machines, higher requirements with respect to a continuously high quality at the earlier production processes is also extremely important. A well-known example, in this respect, is the increased quality requirements set for the yarn used with the higher weft insertion speeds of modern weaving systems. Certainly, quality data is more difficult to determine and requires more complicated sensor systems than with the collection of production data. A considerable 'know-how' in sensor technology is also necessary therefore.

The third important characteristic of our concept takes into consideration the understandable wish of the user to have a **solution which can be integrated into an overall information system.** Each process data system has its own particular application field. Connecting together the different part-systems, new application possibilities are made available. As, in the normal case, it is not possible for the textile mill to develop its own overall system, we have arranged the modules of our system according to the following considerations :

° each sub-system has a standard interface and software
  for communication with a central computer system,

° connection possibilities to other non-USTER sub-systems are
  provided, e.g., the board computers of modern automatic rotor
  spinning machines.

A characteristic which is becoming of more and more importance for the user in terms of long term considerations, is the **continuity and extensibility** of the system. Technological progress today is such that only by means of continuous development and modular extensibility will the necessary investment be repaid by many years of successful application. To this must be added, of course, the necessary technical support offered by the manufacturer to the user, and also the assurance of many years of customer service.

3. THE INDIVIDUAL SUB-SYSTEMS AND THEIR SPECIAL FEATURES

Each sub-system has been specially designed for a certain process stage (fig. 2). The primary difference between the various systems is a result of the deviating information requirements, and particularely with respect to quality data collection. As it is not possible in this paper to explain each sub-system in detail, only the special features of the various systems will be referred to.

3.1 Data system for processes prior to spinning(USTER SLIVERDATA)

USTER SLIVERDATA is applied right at the beginning of processing. It covers the processing stages from opening to drawing, and upto the production of roving. The quality of a yarn is primarily determined at the processes prior to spinning. Accordingly, the accent in this case is **on on-line quality data collection.**

The most important quality characteristics which can be supervised at cards, combers and drawframes are :

° sliver count (fig. 3),

° evenness and periodicities (fig. 4).

The advantages of on-line data collection compared to conventional sample testing are primarily the much shorter reaction time, which in turn is the result of continuous "round-the-clock" supervision. The system provides for an automatic alarm with any irregularities and an automatic stopping of the machine with serious faults.

A speciality of this system is a new sensor, the Fibre Fineness Monitor (fig. 5). This unit is able to determine the short wavelength variations. The patented measuring principle is free of any disturbing influences brought about by drift or fibre fineness. The last referred to property makes possible a further extension stage (in combination with a special version of the active-pneumatic measuring unit) to provide an on-line supervision of the fibre fineness.

The **production data collection,** on the other hand, is applied at
all machines of the processes prior to spinning. The most important production data are :

° efficiency

° machine stops

° doffings (e.g., can changes)

° production amounts

° production speeds.

Frequent machine stops indicate disturbances in production. By
means of an early enough signalisation of production bottlenecks,
deteriorations in the complete spinning process can be avoided.

Although USTER SLIVERDATA is now going through the market introduction phase, practical experience has been obtained over a
number of years in the American market with the specially-
developed arrangement, USTER DFM. This experience has indicated
the following main advantages of the system :

° avoidance of quality deviations and costly complaints,

° reduction of the amount of testing in the mill laboratory,

° better control over the conditions in the processes prior to
  spinning.

3.2   Data systems for spinning

3.2.1 Data system for ring spinning (USTER RINGDATA)

Practical experience has indicated that USTER RINGDATA has
resulted in quite considerable improvements in quality and
productivity in ring spinning. The speciality of this system is
the end break detection at each separate spinning position. This
is undertaken by means of a travelling sensor on each side of the
machine which checks the rotational movement of the traveller
(fig. 6). The frequency of end breaks value shows quite clearly
how close quality and productivity of the textile production processes are interdependent :

° end breaks result in production downtimes as a result of stopped
  spindles, material losses due to the roving being suctioned off
  to waste and in higher operator work-load as a result of increased supervision and end break piecing.

° analyses comparing cops with and without end breaks show significant relationships between end break frequencies and yarn
  quality (see ref. 1).

A reduction in the number of end breaks can be achieved, primarily, in two ways :

° reduction in the number of end breaks which are the result of
  outsider or "rogue" spinning positions. Results obtained under
  practical conditions show that only a small percentage of the
  spindles are responsible for more than 30 % of all the end
  breaks.

° determination of optimum conditions with respect to machine
  settings, the choice of critical machine elements (traveller,
  drafting elements, travelling blower, etc.), ambient climatic
  conditions, and the raw material (see ref. 2).

Success as a result of reducing the end break level can be used to
achieve, step by step, higher production speeds (fig. 7). Important in the assessment of productivity is the characteristic of
'grams per spindle hour'. The experience values with reference to
European RINGDATA installations offer a possibility of assesssing
what could be considered as 'technological limits for the 80ties'
(fig. 8).

An important quality-determining aspect offered by the USTER
RINGDATA is the measurement of yarn twist. The detection and
achievement of optimum conditions of twist is important as each
reduction results in a proportionally-increased production output.
With each separate spinning position, losses in traveller speed
below those of the nominal (as a result of slip) can be critical.
Accordingly, supervision of rotational speed at each spinning
position is an important characteristic of the USTER RINGDATA. In
this way, quality deficiencies as a result of unsuitable twist
values can be determined and corrected at the place where they
are produced.

A further speciality of the system is an indication of end breaks,
which is arranged by means of lamps on each side of the machine
and at each spindle section. It serves as a guidance for the operating personnel. Practical application has shown that a reduction
of patrol time by one half can be achieved (see ref. 8). The end
break indication can be applied successfully where the end break
level is low enough as compared to the patrol time (fig. 9).

3.2.2 Data system for rotor spinning (USTER ROTORDATA)

In the modern rotor spinning mill, end breaks are a seldom event.
In a similar way as in the ring spinning mill, accumulations of
end breaks provide valuable directives with respect to disturbances and insufficiencies. The end break supervision with a data
system makes possible a process-oriented maintenance and an optimum setting of the rotor spinning elements.

A speciality of the USTER ROTORDATA is the **length measurement**
arrangement. This provides for a reduction in length variation
between packages such that with subsequent processing (e.g.,
beaming), it is not necessary to take into consideration the
processing of yarn rests (fig. 10). It should be mentioned here,
however, that many modern automatic rotor spinning machines are
already equipped by the machine manufacturer with systems for
length measurement and data collection. USTER ROTORDATA also
provides for an integration of such machines into an overall
system.

For mills with automatic rotor spinning machines and special
quality requirements, systems for **on-line quality supervision**
are being universally applied. The USTER OE-INSPECTOR, for
instance, detects short and long thick place
faults, thin place faults and moiré faults at each spinning position. With a disturbing yarn fault, it stops the feed to the
rotor. The automatic piecing unit then extracts the respective
length of yarn, cleans the rotor, and starts up the spinning
procedure. With repeated yarn faults within a certain yarn
length, the supervisory system blocks the respective spinning
position. Simultaneously, an alarm lamp at the measuring head of
each spinning position and per machine head is activated in order
to call up the supervisory personnel. The USTER OE-INSPECTOR is so
arranged that it can be integrated into the board computer of the
particular type of spinning machine and into the USTER ROTORDATA
installation. It serves, therefore, not only for eliminating
disturbing yarn faults directly at the production process, but in
providing valuable on-line quality data.

3.3 Data system for cone winding (USTER CONEDATA)

In the winding department, we use the electronic yarn clearer as
the measured value sensor. In this way, we combine two advantages:

° as the signals from a complete machine can be taken from a
central position at the control unit of the yarn clearing
installation, no complicated auxiliary cabling is necessary,

° the yarn clearer provides not only production data but also
quality information. The yarn fault cuttings give an indication
of the quality of the incoming yarn and the number of knots,
respectively the number of splices, gives an indication of the
cones produced (fig. 12).

For this low cost and quickly installed solution, a certain compromise in terms of summarized information per winding machine
section as a result of the clearer cabling arrangement has to be
taken into consideration. In spite of this limitation, experience
has shown already that well over 100 mills have achieved significant improvements in efficiency and knot frequency with this
system (see ref. 3).

3.4 Data system for weaving (USTER LOOMDATA)

Weaving is that branch of textile processing which has the longest
tradition in process data collection. This is due primarily to
the following reasons. The investment per work place is, traditionally, relatively high and the automatic signal determination
does not provide any special technical problems. With most types
of modern weaving machines, the signals can be taken directly
from the machine control (see ref. 4).

Also with this system, we have concentrated our efforts on providing a simple and reliable operation. An example of this is the
optional Machine Entry Station for coding downtimes. This does not
necessitate any form of switches or push-buttons but is activated
magnetically by plug-in cards. The coding can therefore be selectively allocated to certain personnel groups and reasons for
stops. The advantages of this system, in contrast to code entries
at a central terminal, are the distances from the machines which
have to be taken into consideration and an improved detailing of
the long-term stops (e.g., separation of waiting time and actual
working time).

The software of USTER LOOMDATA, although standardized, can be
adapted to specific customer requirements by means of a large
number of parameters. An extensive collection of standard reports
provides for an application-orientated selection and sorting of
the required information. A speciality of the system is the
extremely flexible stop time analysis provided in the form of
lists and diagrams (fig. 13). Also in the course of development
of the USTER LOOMDATA, the extended number of functions in terms
of warp planning have resulted in a universal acceptance and
application of this installation.

3.5 Data system for the textile laboratory (USTER LABDATA)

The laboratory data system has the primary task of on-line
collection of measured values from testing instruments, and
analysis of this data for application-orientated use. Accordingly,
the requirements of this installation do not differ in principle
from those of the "normal" process data systems.

What are the basic justifications for a computer-controlled system
in the modern textile laboratory ? In this respect, one should
first of all take into consideration the requirements of the
modern textile mill quality control laboratory. The main task of
the laboratory is certainly to check the quality parameters in a
systematic manner of the machines at all production stages in the
mill. In this respect, a large amount of data is accumulated which
contains various types of reports, diagrams, etc. A laboratory
data system offers, therefore, advantages mainly in terms of data
collection and evaluation :

° the laboratory personnel are dispensed from time-consuming
  routing work and can concentrate their efforts on the more
  important test procedures (see ref. 6),

° exception conditions are indicated immediately. Additionally,
  directives can be provided for a more purpose-orientated fault
  investigation process.

° the data are automatically concentrated in a form which can best
  be applied by the respective user,

° graphical representations facilitate the long-term control of
  quality standards and provide an indication of trends.

The system has been arranged initially for the connection of all
USTER testing instruments. As a further extension stage, a so-
called "comfort variant" is in preparation which fulfils, besides
other, the following additional functions :

° contral control of the testing parameters of the connected
  testing instruments

° preparation of further quality data as provided by instruments
  outside the testing laboratory

° setting-up and supervision of the sampling plans.

A speciality which is becoming of increasing importance is the
possibility of setting out yarn certificates per order or per yarn
quality (fig. 14). These contain a summary of the more important
quality parameters and provide, therefore, a basis for discussion
between the yarn producer and the yarn processor.

4. USTER MILLDATA OVERALL SYSTEM (fig.15)

USTER MILLDATA, which was shown for the first time at the ITMA 83 was universally assessed as a significant development in data collection technology. The system integrates the decentralized sub-systems into a complete information system covering the overall manufacturing range. The main functions of this installation are :

° long-term storage and collection of data from the sub-systems

° quality control over several production stages

° order supervision and control of delivery times

° material management

° graphical representations (fig. 15).

USTER MILLDATA is primarily a software package that can be implicated by means of standard computers of various manufacture. It applies the latest generation of software technology, particularly with respect to the operating system and the databank. The hard- and software package delivered can be adapted to customer requirements. It covers a range from the basic software package to the overall system including computer, peripheral units and individual software.

The network which is formed by the sub-systems and USTER MILLDATA extends the function possibilities of such sub-systems in several directions. One example is the addition of functions at sub-system level by means of direct access from sub-system terminals into the MILLDATA computer.

USTER MILLDATA will become available in 1985 for a more extended circle of customers.

5. FUTURE DEVELOPMENTS, TRENDS

The possibilities which are offered by modern microtechnology and software are by no means fully exhausted. We will continue to extend and complement our systems. However, it will always be necessary to take into consideration the relationship between expense and return on investment. We must, nevertheless, not loose sight of the main task of data collection systems, i.e., to support personnel and management in their efforts to economically run their high production and capital-intensive machinery installations (see refs. 7,8).

Process data systems initiate new ideas and requirements in
terms of new application possibilities. We are, therefore, always
very open-minded to such considerations. In general, we see that
development is running, primarily, in the following directions:

° on-line quality control at all process stages

° board computers on every processing machine

° integrated information systems

° extension of data systems to become process control systems,
  e.g., for the centralized control of machine settings, material
  transportation, etc.

6. REFERENCES

1. E. Felix, I. Harzenmoser 'Fadenbrueche in der Ringspinnerei'
   Melliand Textilberichte, No. 10/1978

2. K. Douglas (Editor), 'The detection of end breaks in ring
   spinning', USTER NEWS BULLETIN No. 27, August 1979

3. K. Douglas (Editor), 'The USTER system of yarn fault control'
   USTER NEWS BULLETIN No. 29, November 1981

4. H. Howald, 'Wirtschaftliche Prozessdatenerfassung mit dezen-
   tralen Subsystemen', Texil Praxis, No. 3, 1983

5. G. Mierzowsky, H. Wöhler, 'Prozessunterstützung durch EDV in
   Spinnerei, Weberei und Veredlung', Textil Praxis, Nos 3,5,6 and
   10/1983

6. K. Douglas 'Quality control and data logging techniques',
   CONTEMPORARY TEXTILE ENGINEERING, (Editor, F. Happey),
   Academic Press, 1982

7. I. Harzenmoser 'Betriebserfahrungen mit automatischen Faden-
   brucherfassungsanlagen' Deutsche Wolltertigungsinstitut an
   der Technischen Hochschule, Aachen, 10. Tagung, Sept. 1983

8. K. Douglas (Editor) 'USTER Prüf- Regulier-, Ueberwachungs- und
   Datenerfassungsanlagen'; USTER NEWS BULLETIN, No.32, Juli 1984

ZELLWEGER USTER LTD
CH-8610 USTER
Switzerland

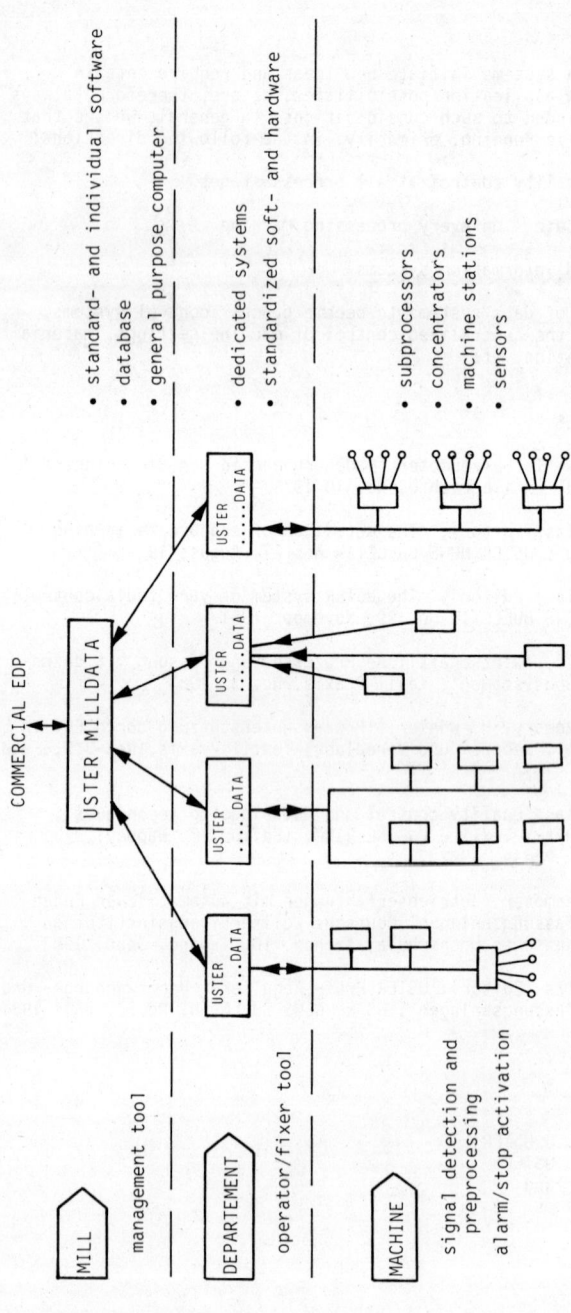

Fig 1.
3-level information system with purpose-oriented distribution of computing power.

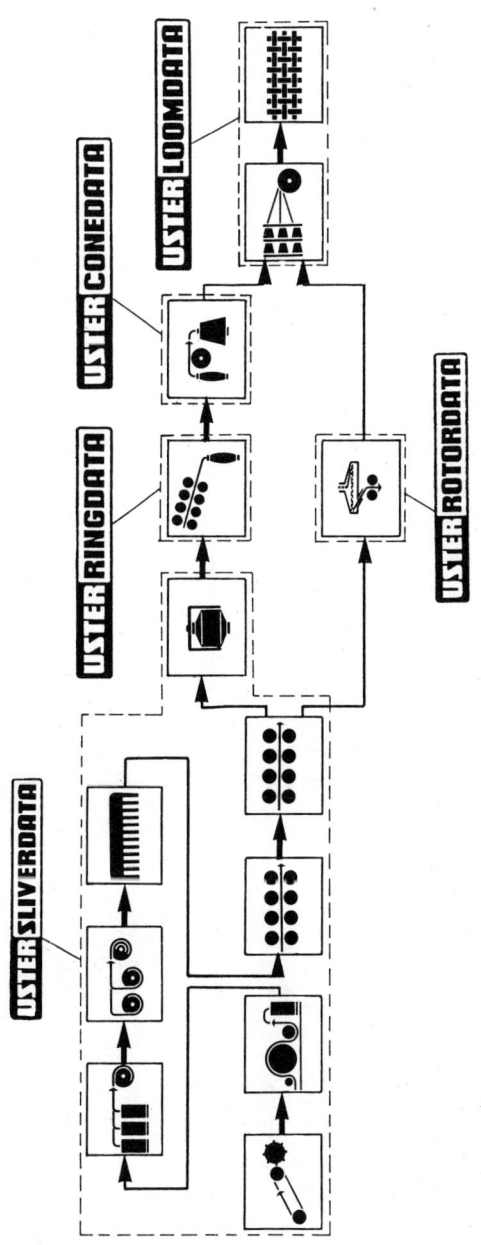

Fig 2.
Arrangement of the sub-systems according to the various production processes.
(Example: Cotton spinning mill)

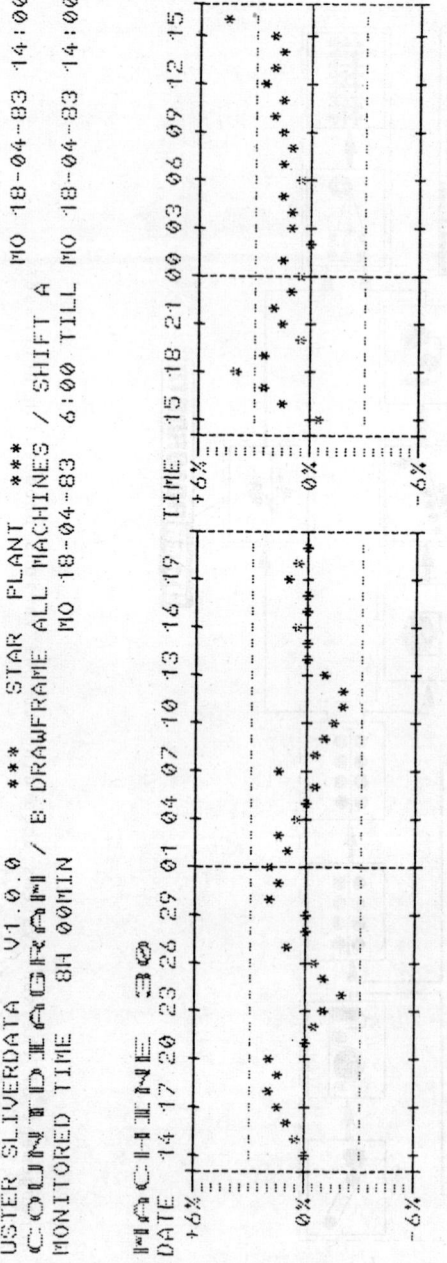

Fig 3.
USTER SLIVERDATA count diagram for machine no. 30 over a period of 40 days, and in detail over the last 24 hours.

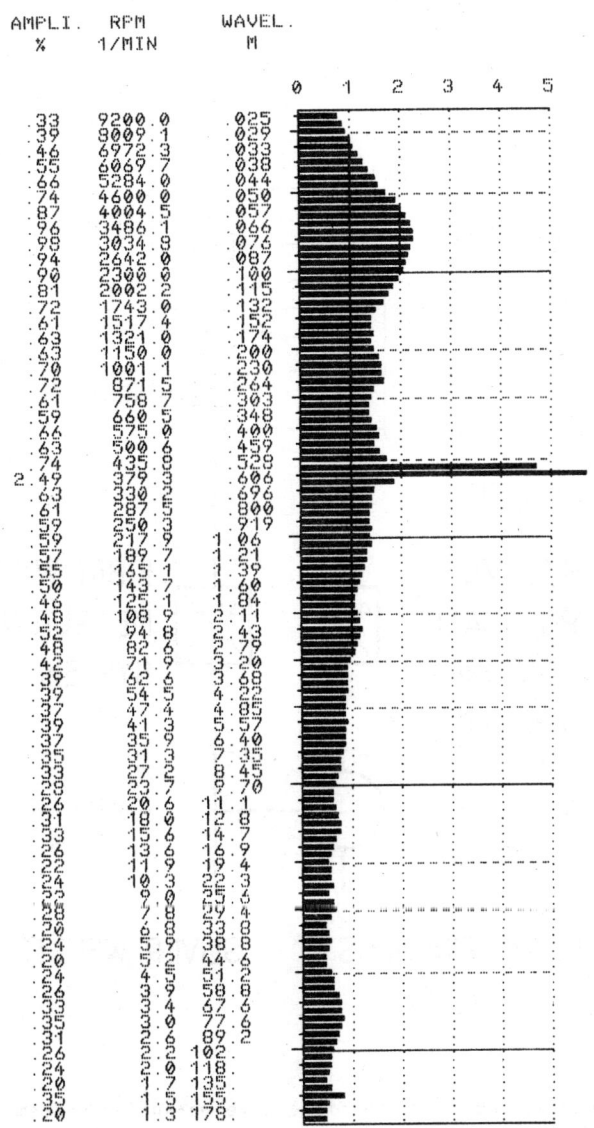

Fig 4.
On-line SPECTROGRAM of finisher drawframe sliver
indicating a periodic fault of wavelength approx.
60cm resulting from a defective middle roller.

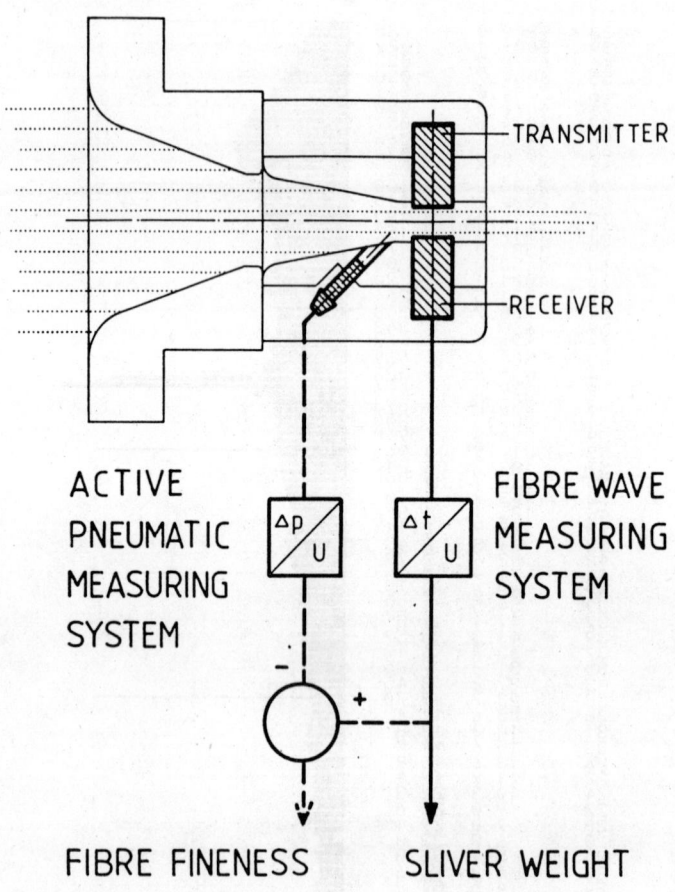

Fig 5.
Measuring trumpet with fibre wave measuring system
for sliver weight determination and optional
pneumatic system for assessing fibre fineness.

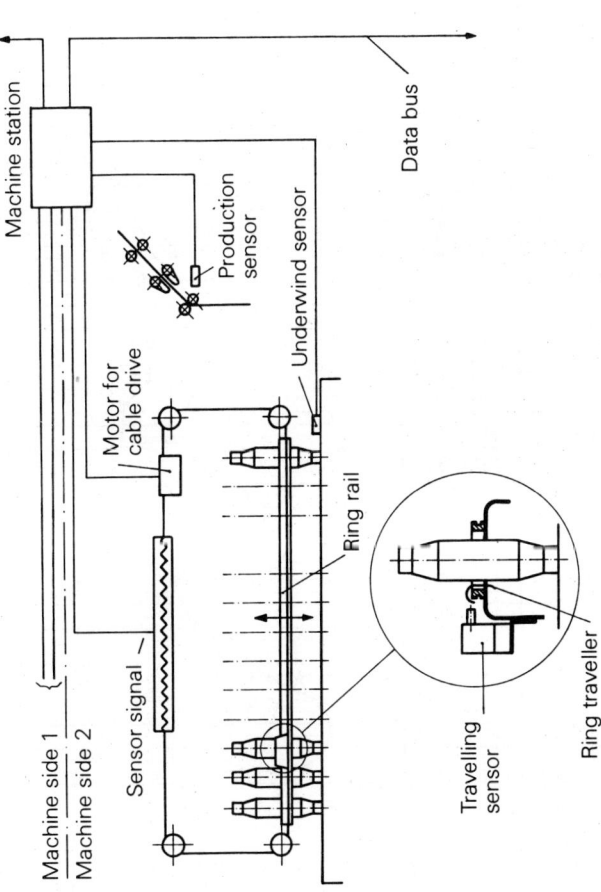

Fig 6.
Schematic arrangement of
the USTER RINGDATA data
collection installation.

Machine station

Data bus

Production
sensor

Underwind sensor

Motor for
cable drive

Ring rail

Sensor signal

Machine side 1
Machine side 2

Travelling
sensor

Ring traveller

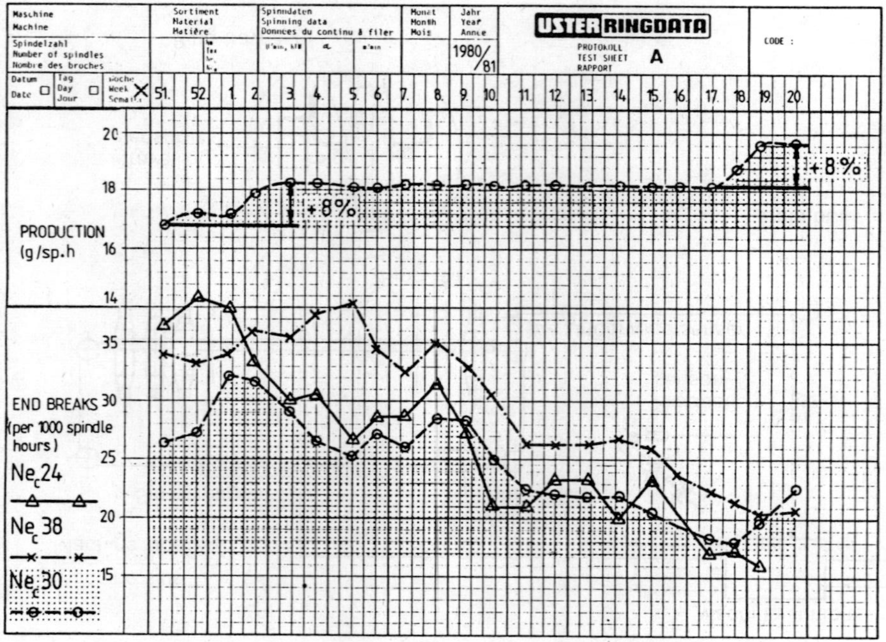

Fig 7.
Resulting from a reduction in the overall end break rate, it was possible to increase spinning speed and thereby production.

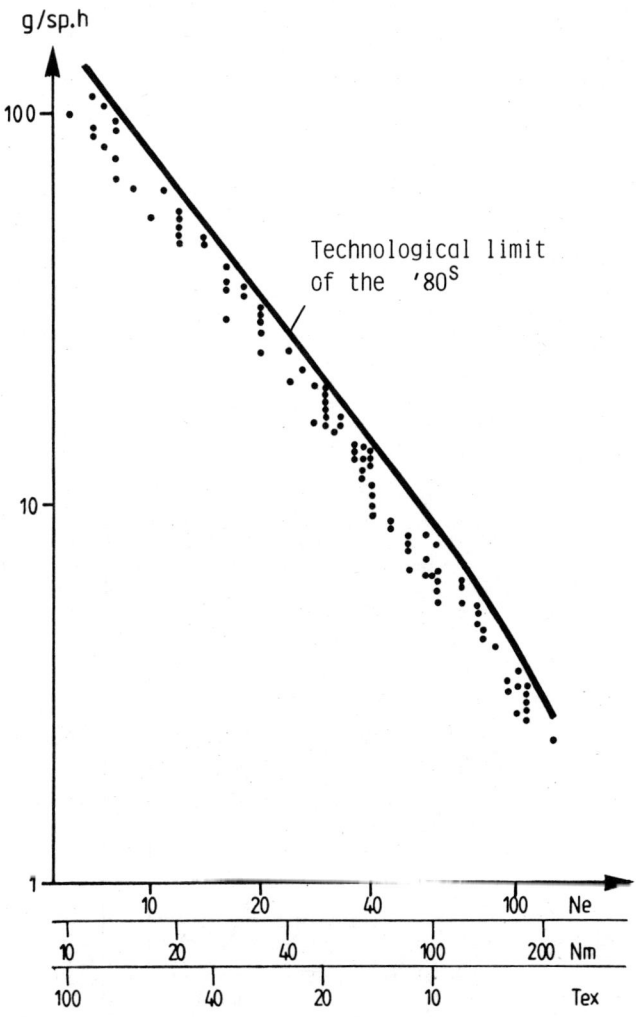

Fig 8.
USTER RINGDATA experience values for the specific
production in short staple ring spinning (in grams
per spindle-hour, considering an actual efficiency
of 100 %).

Ringspinning machine with 500 spindles

Fig 9.
Diagram for investigation of applicability
of sectional end break indication lamps
(ex. for machines with 500 spindles). With
20 end breaks per 1000 spindle hours and
a patrol time of 40 minutes, the end break
indication is acceptable. On the average
only 4 to 5 lamps (of a total of 12 per
2 machine sides) will be alight when the
operator arrives at the particular machine
corridor.

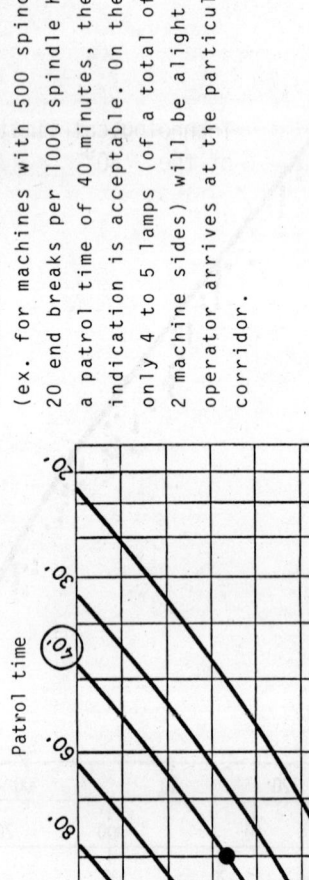

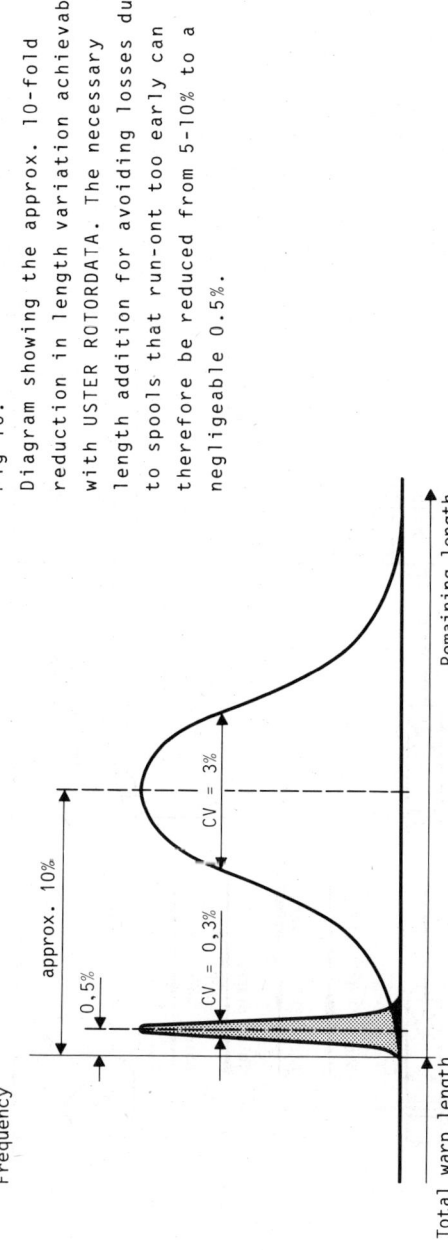

Fig 10.
Diagram showing the approx. 10-fold reduction in length variation achievable with USTER ROTORDATA. The necessary length addition for avoiding losses due to spools that run-ont too early can therefore be reduced from 5-10% to a negligeable 0.5%.

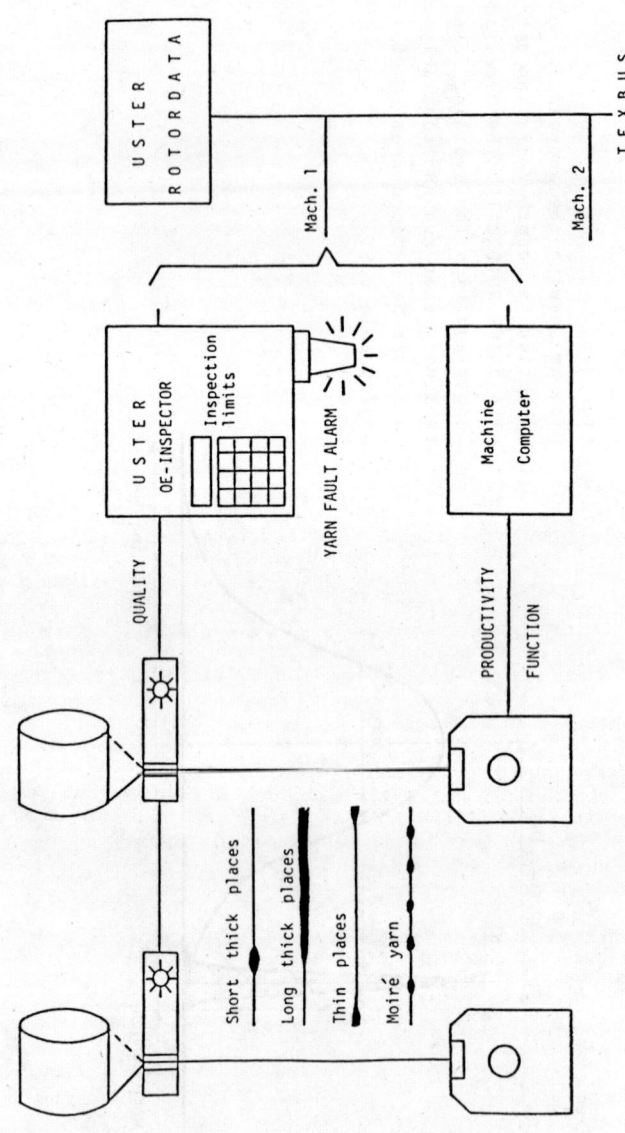

Fig 11.
Quality inspection and process monitoring on automatic rotor spinning machines.

220

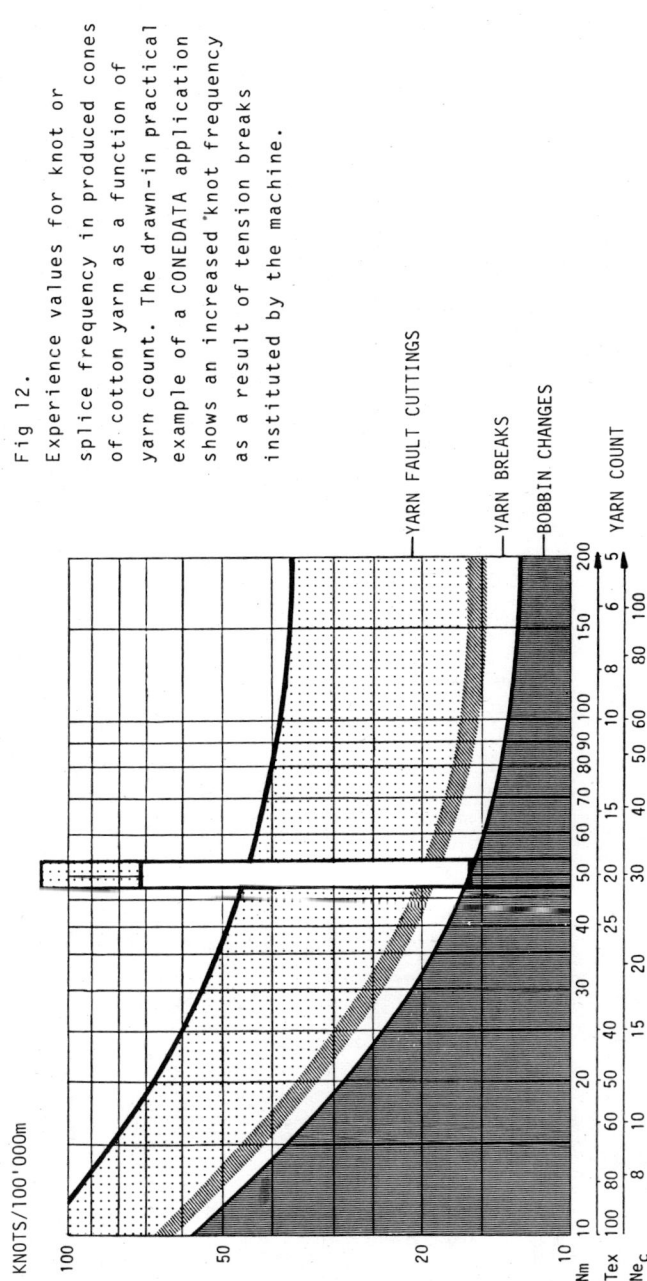

Fig 12.
Experience values for knot or splice frequency in produced cones of cotton yarn as a function of yarn count. The drawn-in practical example of a CONEDATA application shows an increased knot frequency as a result of tension breaks instituted by the machine.

```
USTER LOOMDATA   V2.2.0   ***WEBEREI MUSTER AG, WERK USTER***      TU 28-02-84 12:53
FIXER 2 / MACH WITH OPH)0 / OP-DIAGRAM / L8
MONITORED TIME 12H 20M          TU 28-02-84 00:33   TO   TU 28-02-84 12:53

FIXER 2
TIME     02:00     04:00     06:00     08:00     10:00     12:00
MACH
5      :.........:.........:.........:.........:...35.....:.........:
9      :.........:.........:31*.......:.........:.........:15**********
14 ****:.........:.........:.........:..10......:.........:15**********
23     :.........:..$......:.........:..P.......:..60......:..21......:
38     :......##13***.:.........:.........:..P.......:..60......:.........:
52     :.$.......:10****....:.........:10****....:.........:.........:
75     :.21*.....:.........:.........:..P...35..:..P...35..:$.........:
88     :.........:10**......:.........:.........:.........:15**********
106    :.........:.31*:.....35...:.10*......:.........:10..##13***:
127 **************************:.P********************:.P********:10.##13***:
128    :.........:.31......:.........:.P********:..60......:15**********
149    :10**.....:.........:.........:.P.......:..60......:15**********
162    :.........:####17*..:.........:.P.......:.........:.........:
197    :.21......:.........:.........:.P.......:..60......:.........:
```

10,35,. Code for stop reason (P = power down)
***...* waiting time
###...# work time

Fig 13.
Graphical representation of the 'out-of-production' conditions as a function of time. Example refers to machines in overlooker (fixer) group no. 2 which were out of production within a time period of approx 10 hours.

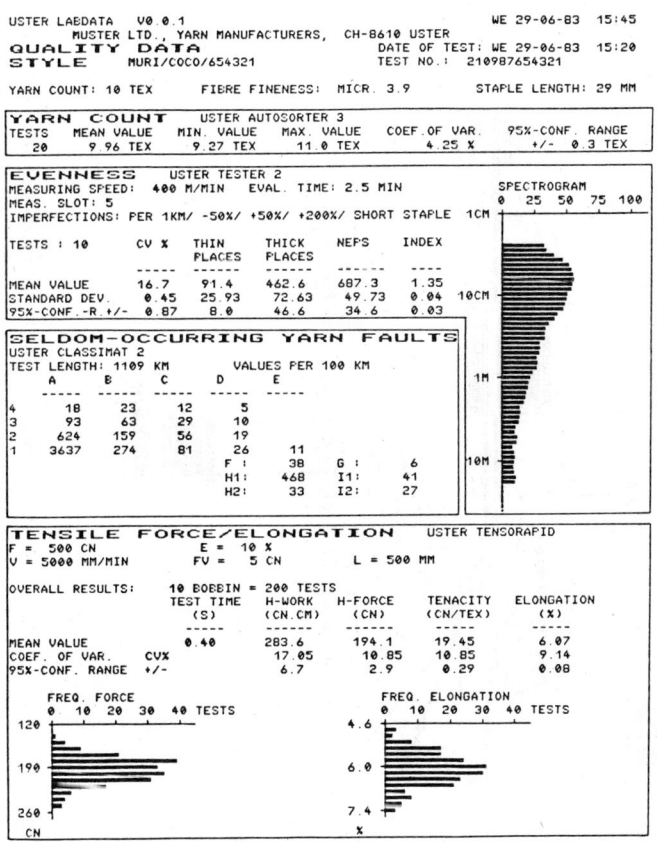

Fig 14.
USTER LABDATA print-out showing a yarn certificate
with the result of count, evenness, fault frequency
and strength testing.

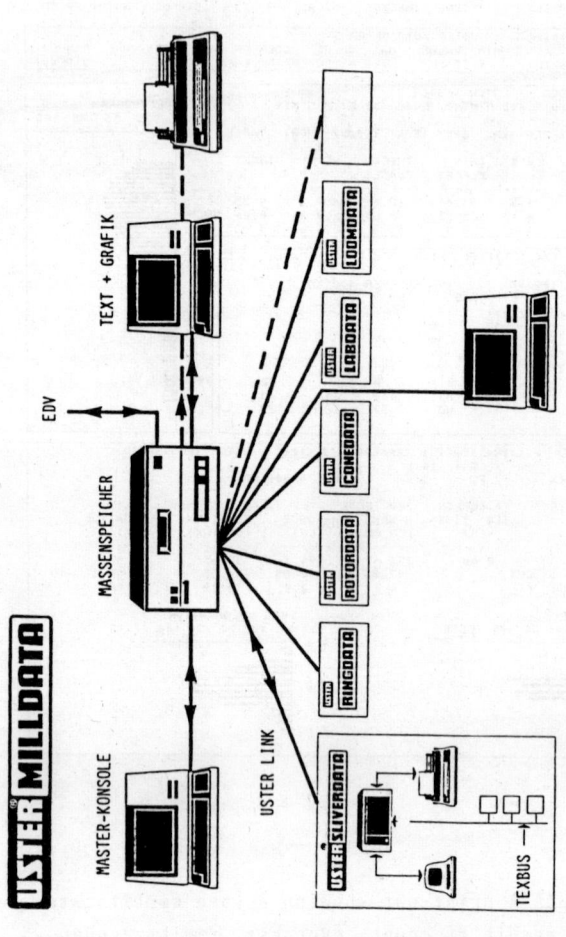

Fig 15.
Arrangement of the USTER MILLDATA communication system showing on-line connections with subsystems and EDP. MILLDATA terminals serve for centralized and decentralised DATA input/output.

Fig 16.
Graphical representation of out-of-production times divided into 3 main categories for analysis of the corresponding efficiency losses over a period of one year.

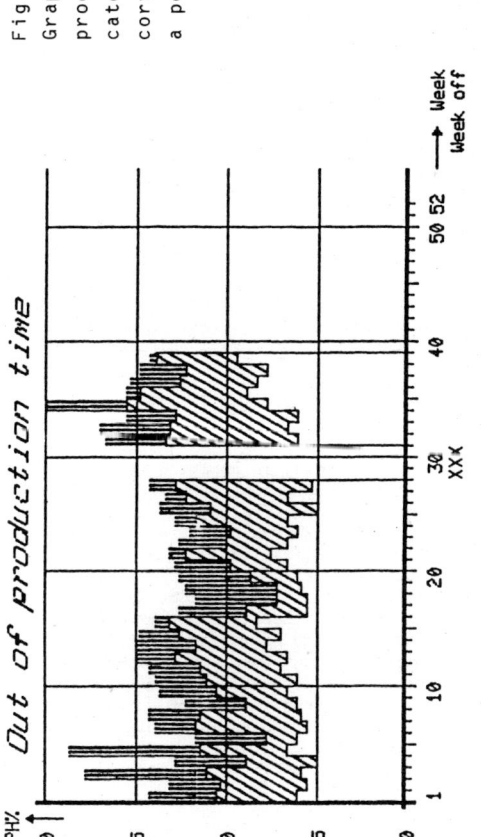

Out of production time

OPH%

CD 30 ... 39   REPAIRS : 2.8 %

CD 20 ... 29   WARP / STYLE CHANGE : 4.5 %

CD 12, 14, 16   WAITING FOR MATERIAL / ORDERS; OTHERS : 6.7 %

CONTINUOUS QUALITY CONTROL IN MODERN YARN PRODUCTION

P. R. Lord, W. C. Stuckey and A. A. Marathe

ABSTRACT

Conventional practice utilizes manual sampling of the product and subsequent testing; whatever economical sampling plan is used, there are delays which permit the manufacture of undesirable quantities of faulty product and a strong chance that batches of faulty material will escape detection. Failure to eliminate faults at an early stage compound the problems because these faults often generate others in subsequent operations.

Improvement of product quality may be measured in terms of the cost advantage in dollars/lb. The productivity of a machine can be used to estimate how much can be spent on a given control system. On this basis, very little could be spent per spindle of a ring-frame, whereas considerable sums could be profitably spent in carding, drawing or other high-productivity machines.

The twin developments of microelectronics and computer technology are leading to a revolution in quality control. Continuous monitoring provides data streams which permit reporting by exception. Out-of-tolerance material can be found very quickly and the defects remedied more easily than before. The present systems use computers, but the possibility exists of using low-cost electronics instead. To obtain complete control of the production system it is necessary to develop transducers capable of measuring more than just linear density; in all probability this will require simultaneous measurement of several parameters at an early stage in the process line.

1. INTRODUCTION

Manual sampling and testing at a place remote from the place of production leads to delay in applying remedies when faulty material is found. Economical sampling plans run the risk of missing faulty material altogether. Errors that become continuous as mechanical faults develop are found eventually. Transient faults, such as those due to inclusions of faulty fiber, trash or malprocessed material, are frequently missed. As the productivity of the machines increases, there is need for better quality of feed material and the quantity of faulty material increases unless the delays in response are reduced accordingly. Furthermore, developments in machinery used to process the yarn lead to a need for better quality if the machines are to realize their potential; this includes winding, beaming, weaving, etc. It follows that errors formerly ignored now have to be detected and corrected.

2. MONITORING

Continuous monitoring of the output from the production
machines is beginning to be established. Some of the
systems merely record whether or not the machine is
producing, but others measure some attribute of the output
in a continuous manner. The continuous measurements can
be used to operate a control system or merely sound an
alarm when the material is out of tolerance. When the
system is connected to a computer, the patterns of failure
and/or performance can be used to control and manage both
machinery and personnel. The happy conincidence of the
availability of continuous data streams and the powers of
data manipulation of modern computers provide a powerful
tool, and this is an important development in textile
technology.

Modern monitoring systems have been very successfully used
to control the effects of mechanical failures. Early
warning of the onset of machine-component damage can often
be recognized by the characteristic defects produced as
soon as they start to appear. The fixers can be required
to "punch-in" the times when they acknowledge the defect
and when they complete their work. The history of
particular operators, fixers and machines can be used to
rank their performance. Accurate records of failure rates
help the stocking of spare parts and the determination of
maintenance schedules. The near-certainty that adequate
warning of failure will be given, permits operations with
skeleton crews at unpopular and expensive working times.
Thus, in many ways, monitoring with the equipment
available today provides many advantages. However, there
is a major untapped potential still ahead.

In staple yarn production, it is rare to find the
continuous measurement of any parameter except linear
density. In commercial filament yarn production, it is
rare to find measurement of anything other than
temperature and yarn tension. Complete control is not
possible unless all the important parameters are measured.
These parameters include the variables introduced by the
feed material and it is here that resides the potential
for a major advance in control technology. Means of
measuring the fiber-borne influences and the relative
importance of them must become one of the important
objectives of research in the future.

3. AUTOLEVELLING

Autolevelling has been known in the textile industry for
many years. Continuous measurement provides error signals
which are used to actuate changes in the operation of the
machine in such a way to reduce the error. If a feed-
forward system is used, it is necessary to delay the error
signal until the material reaches the proper position at
which the change is made. For example, in roller drafting
it is required that the draft be changed at the precise
instant that the faulty material reaches the acceleration
point in the draft zone (point V in Figure 1).

Unfortunately, the acceleration point is ever-moving as drafting waves pass through the system. To fine-tune the system, there is need to predict the delay as well as measure the linear density. If feed-back systems are used, the regenerative nature of them tends to automatically set the sensitivity, but these systems cannot deal with short random errors. A random error arriving at the transducer has already passed through the processing stage and cannot be altered by it; indeed any attempt at alteration only produces a negative error further along the strand. Thus a feed-back system tends to produce a series of echoes of the short random transients. When errors are strictly periodic, or are long, then the feed-back system can operate satisfactorily. Often combined systems are used. There is an evident need to be able to predict which of the errors are periodic and which are random so that the spurious responses can be eliminated. This is a challenge to the instrumentation people in our industry.

There are further difficulties. In staple processing, the blend proportions affect the nature and magnitude of the errors produced in the roller drafting systems. The blend changes constantly and there are random and periodic components of the variation. A steep change in blend composition passing through a roller drafting system is associated with a longitudinal migration of the short fibers with respect to the long. As depicted in Figure 2, this provides a mechanism by which changes in blend become translated into changes in linear density. Thus even though a strand is perfectly autolevelled as far as overall linear density is concerned, but contains inhomogeneities in blend, errors re-erupt as the material passes through subsequent machines. This sort of error is usually reduced by doubling but the doubling of uneven strands can in itself produce blend errors. Hence even when doubling is used, there is every reason to make the component strands as uniform as possible.

4. ECONOMICS

It is theoretically possible to install monitoring systems on any machine, but cost has to be considered. Let us consider the allowable cost of equipment. If the savings due to improvement in quality and efficiency amount to $x/lb, the productivity of a unit is p lb/h, and the number of working hours needed to pay off the equipment is t hours, then the allowable cost is $(xpt-k), where k is any additional cost incurred in operating the monitoring equipment. Thus a ring-frame spindle producing 0.02 lb/h over 20,000 h at a saving of $0.02/lb would justify an expenditure of only $8/spindle. A texturing machine producing 150 denier yarn at 1000 m/min with the same saving over a similar period would justify a little less than $900. A drawframe running at 8 lb/h with the same savings and period would justify $3,200 per head. A normal card would justify about $32,000. A bale milling machine running at 1000 lb/h might justify up to $400,000 outlay if it could be demonstrated that accurate

228

microblending could result in $0.02/lb saving in the final product.

These simple calculations make it clear that it is advantageous economically to operate the quality control equipment as near to the beginning of the process as possible providing the control is effective at all stages in and beyond the yarn manufacturing plant. This is not to say that there should be no control systems on later machines, only that their cost should be lower than that of the earlier machines. One important issue is that of prediction of the performance of the machines downstream. Once mechanical problems are under control, a major source of error is in the material being transferred from machine to machine. If these incipient errors can be controlled, then there is a chance of realising some of the economic gains projected above.

5. THE PROGRESSION OF ERRORS DURING PROCESSING OF STAPLE FIBERS

Errors generated by machines early in the process line are carried with the fiber and many of these errors become elongated by drafting as they pass through successive machines. Improper fiber separation and cleaning, or inhomogeneous blending, can lead to outbreaks of drafting waves and imperfect movement of fibers in drafting. These often lead to slub-like assemblies of fiber embedded in the strand or to concentrations of a particular fiber-blend component along the length of the strand. Often, when these imperfections pass through a roller drafting zone, they are broken up as drafting waves are formed. The sub-concentrations might be smaller in absolute terms, but as a percentage of the number of fibers in the cross-section of the output, they are often greater because the base has been changed by drafting. The sub-concentrations are strung out like a string of beads and, as they pass through the next drafting zone, they cause bursts of drafting waves. Yarn defects are often associated with these irregularities as shown in Figure 3. The outbreaks seem to occur randomly, but within any one outbreak there is usually a significant degree of organisation. Within the outbreak, the disturbances often appear to be periodic; the number of oscillations is usually limited, but the periodicities frequently agree with those found from measurements from Uster spectrograms.

It is interesting to note that the transient blend composition changes during processing and these variations in composition can often be related to drafting waves in the particular machine and in earlier ones. Some experimental data illustrating such variations is shown in Figures 4 and 5.

Doubling usually reduces these errors but drafting increases them, and where there is doubling there has to be a corresponding amount of extra drafting over that needed for attenuation. One can find periodicities in most fiber parameters in card sliver with wavelengths that

might be attributable to the frequency of presenting the
flats, and to the rotation of the doffer, cylinder,
licker-in and feed roll. With manual methods of testing
discrete samples, there is little hope of obtaining
sufficient data for a truly acceptable harmonic analysis,
but these quasi-harmonic variations have been observed
sufficiently often to establish a prime facie case for
their existence. In roller drafting the case is a little
stronger because Fast Fourier Transforms have been made
over many cans full of drawframe sliver, and from time to
time there are distinct harmonics with frequency
distributions which are consistent with Uster spectrograms
made on the same material.

6. TRANSDUCER DESIGN

Several systems of measuring linear density or strand
diameter are available. The tongue-and-groove roller
measures the volume of a continuously moving short length
of the strand at a specific compression. The pneumatic
trumpet measures the air permeability of a compressed
moving strand and the trumpet reaction device measures the
drag on the trumpet caused by the flowing strand. Various
optical devices measure the diameter or its equivalent.
Beta gauges or capacitive elements can be used to measure
the mass of material in an ever-changing length of the
material. All measure more than one parameter and, on
their own, are unable to discriminate between the
component parameters.

Many of these devices require that the strand be
compressed, especially if the strand be a sliver. The
stress/strain curves for compression are non-linear but
Figure 6 shows that the reaction forces arising when
sliver is pulled through trumpets of different sizes, are
almost linear with changes in sliver weight. A change in
fiber type alters the relationship, and the sensitivity of
the device depends on the degree of compression. The air
permeability of a strand passing through a trumpet is non-
linear as shown in Figure 7, and there is a component
which varies with speed. Furthermore, experience shows
that changes in fiber fineness also has a significant
effect. In each of these cases the device has to be
calibrated for the given conditions. In other devices
there are other reasons for non-linearity and abiguity,
but the point of the need for further development still
remains, especially in view of the evidence of varying
strand composition.

Ultrasonic beams in combination with one or more of the
conventional measurements of "linear density" have
resulted in signals which seem to be related to fiber
fineness. This leads to thoughts regarding simultaneous
measurements. In mathematics, a complete solution of
simultaneous equations is possible only when there are as
many equations expressing unique elements of information
as there are unknowns. All practical measurements are
likely to contain random signals, and if the signals are
too noisy, it is difficult to resolve the simultaneous

signals into primary components. If the transfer
functions of each transducer are similar to the others, it
is also difficult to resolve them. It is desirable to
have linked transducers in which each element has a
predominance in one major basic parameter, and the noise
level should be as low as possible.

In laboratory measurement, there is noise generated from
random sampling and random selection of feed materials.
Often the input and output are not measured concurrently
and this adds noise to the process of analysis. With
continuous monitoring, there is a better chance to
correlate the data and to generate larger quantities which
permit noise reduction by superposition of repetitive
phenomena. This adds pressure to interest in developing
new transducers and it is likely that new ones will emerge
because of this.

7. SIGNAL PROCESSING

All textile materials are variable and an important
parameter is the standard deviation of the variables.
Errors arise from (1) the machines being sampled, (2) the
feed material, and (3) sampling. Sampling errors can be
minimized by continuous monitoring at the production point
and the errors generated within the machine being
monitored can be diagnosed with fair accuracy, but the
errors (and sources of error) carried by the textile
material pose some problems.

If the feed materials are chosen randomly from a pool, it
is difficult to correlate errors with prior processes
unless some tracking system is used. If the feed material
contains randomly dispersed "fault triggers", such as
foreign fibers, trash particles or discrete concentrations
of short fiber, etc., then the errors occur in bursts and
both the primary parameters and their variances change
irregularly. It is no longer possible to typify
production with single values of averages and CV's. It
becomes evident that as we make more demands on our
quality control systems, the more complicated it becomes.

Fortunately computers can be programmed to solve
mathematical and computational problems, but if the
computer is linked up to a network of machines, the system
can become rather expensive. Again, fortunately, progress
with microelectronics has made available low-cost semiconductor devices with incredible power. Not only can the
output of a transducer be amplified with extremely small
amplifiers which consume very little energy, but it is
relatively easy to differentiate, integrate or transform
the transducer signal on the spot. One of the
possibilities is to carry out Fast Fourier Transforms
right at the measuring point to give diagnostic capability
by means of identifying the error wavelengths. Another
possibility is to use low-cost RMS chips to transform the
data. The root mean square (RMS) of a continuous function
is closely related to the standard deviation of a series
of discrete measurements along the "length" of that

231

function. The mean of the squares implies that there must
be an integration length, and in this case, it is
analogous to the sample length. With a computer it is
possible to use a true sliding average of the squares, but
even wtihout one it is possible to use an RC integrator
with a fading memory to achieve almost the same result.

To simulate the familiar length/variance curves, an RC/RMS
device was connected to the output of a capacitance type
transducer whose output gave the difference between the
direct signal and a smoothed version of it for different
integration lengths. A set of results is shown in
Figure 8. Yarns, roving, drawn sliver and carded sliver
have been tested in this way. All have shown variation in
the RMS values and the amplitudes of those variations have
also varied in an organised manner. Figure 9 shows some
traces for sliver and it will be noted that the RMS value
does indeed fluctuate in the manner discussed earlier.
Such devices have been incorporated in various transducers
and they show promise in achieving the aim of developing
low-cost effective monitoring devices.

8. CONCLUSIONS

Textile quality control is moving, and must move, towards
continuous error measurement coupled with reporting by
exception. A range of sophisticated devices is expected
to emerge which will be capable of simultaneous operation
to remove some of the ambiguities which exist in present-
day systems.

A range of sophistication will emerge giving the user the
choice between complex computer systems capable of machine
and personnel management on the one hand, and low-cost
alarms systems with diagnostic capabilities which operate
only when out-of-tolerance material is being produced, on
the other hand. The tolerances can be expressed in terms
of any parameter which can be measured, including the
variance.

The justifiable cost is related to the productivity of the
machine to which the system is to be applied and to the
effectiveness with which it operates. Where a line of
machines is used with highly productive early machines,
there is financial incentive to develop control systems
which will obviate later problems. This involves research
to predict the ultimate responses to the control devices
used.

9. ACKNOWLEDGEMENTS

Grateful acknowlegements are made to Girish Grover and
Xiuye Yu for their experimental work in connection with
Figures 4 and 5.

P. R. Lord, W. C. Stuckey and A. A. Marathe
Department of Materials and Management
School of Textiles, North Carolina State University
Box 8301
Raleigh, NC 27695-8301

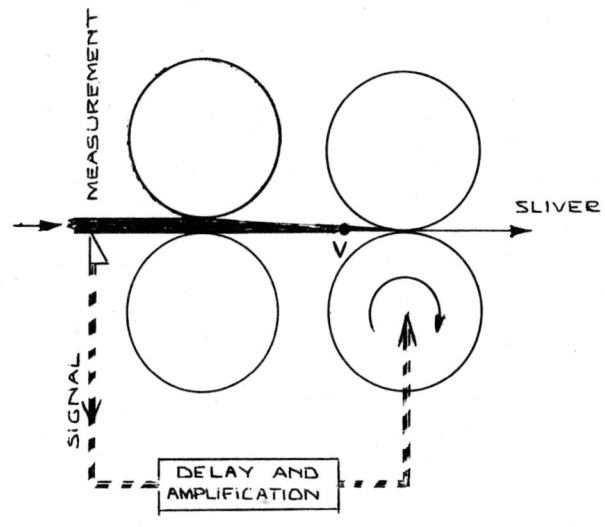

FEED-FORWARD AUTOLEVELING

FIGURE 1

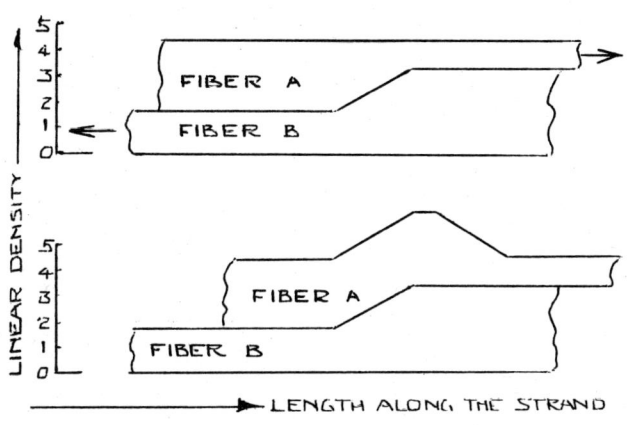

EFFECT of FIBER SHEAR on LINEAR DENSITY

FIGURE 2

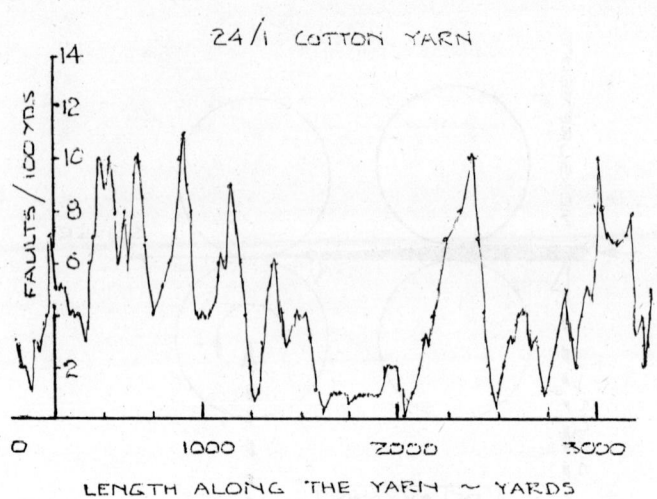

24/1 COTTON YARN

N₂ FAULTS WERE COUNTED WHEN RMS TRANSIENTS ≯ 70 UNITS

INTERMITTENT FAULTS IN YARN

FIGURE 3

FIBER VARIATIONS

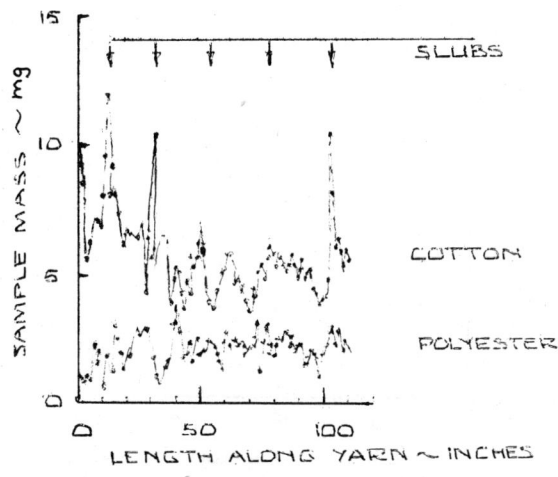

BLEND CHANGES IN A YARN

FIGURE 4

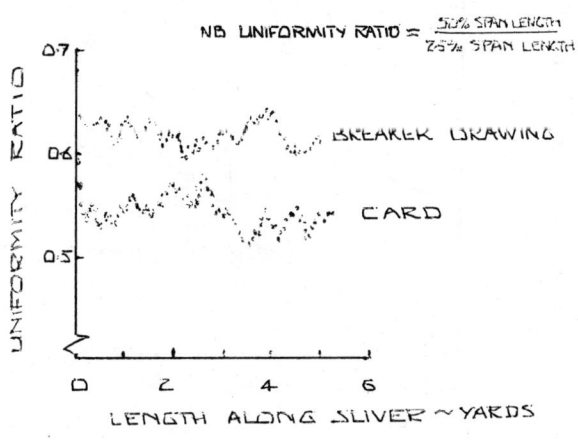

VARIATION IN FIBER UNIFORMITY RATIO

FIGURE 5

TRANSDUCERS

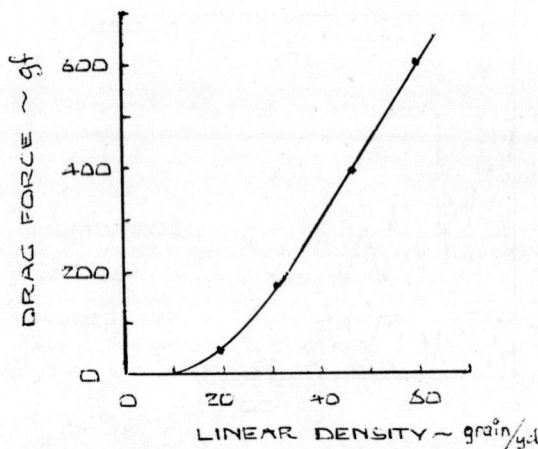

DRAG FORCE OF COTTON SLIVER PASSING THROUGH
A 4 MM DIAMETER ORIFICE

FIGURE 6

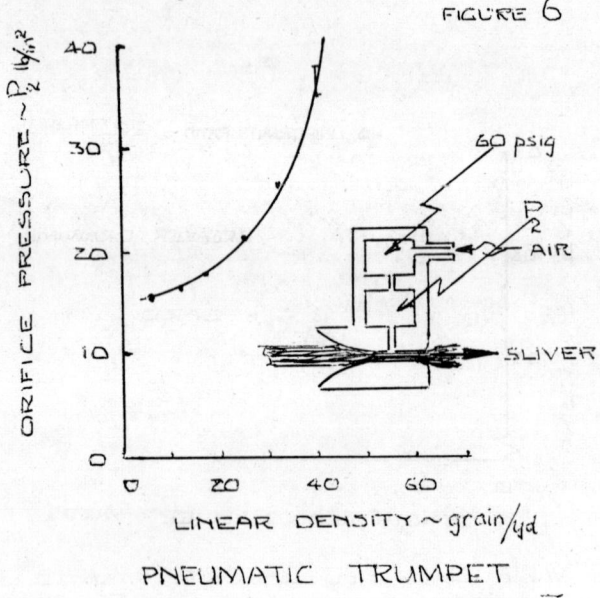

PNEUMATIC TRUMPET

FIGURE 7

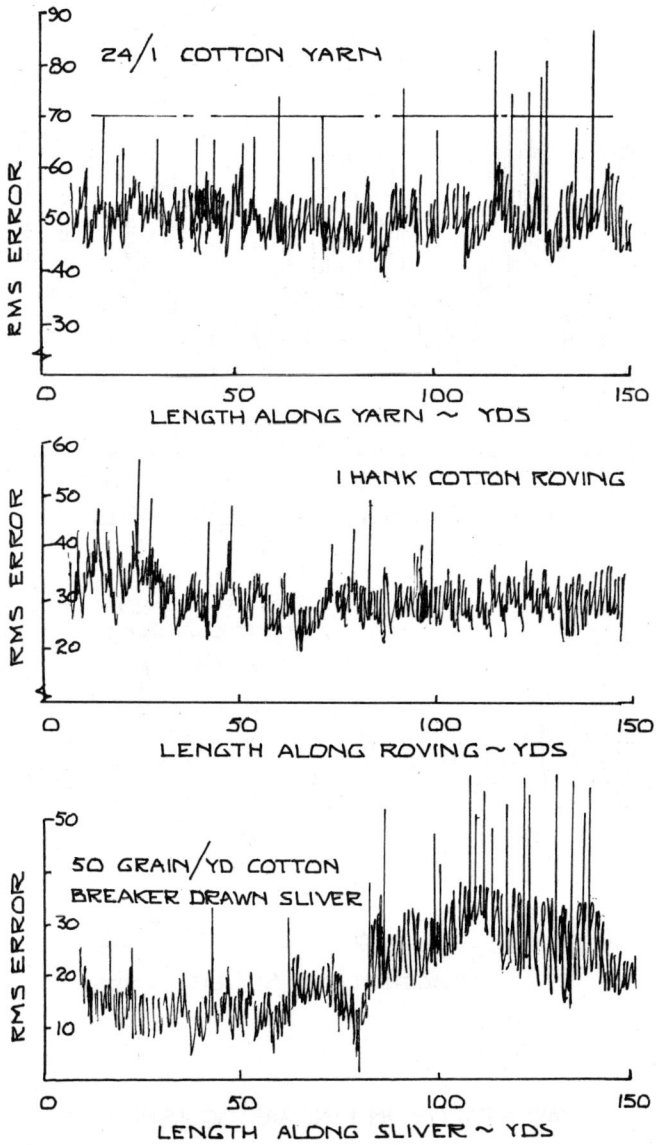

RMS ERRORS in LINEAR DENSITY

FIGURE 8

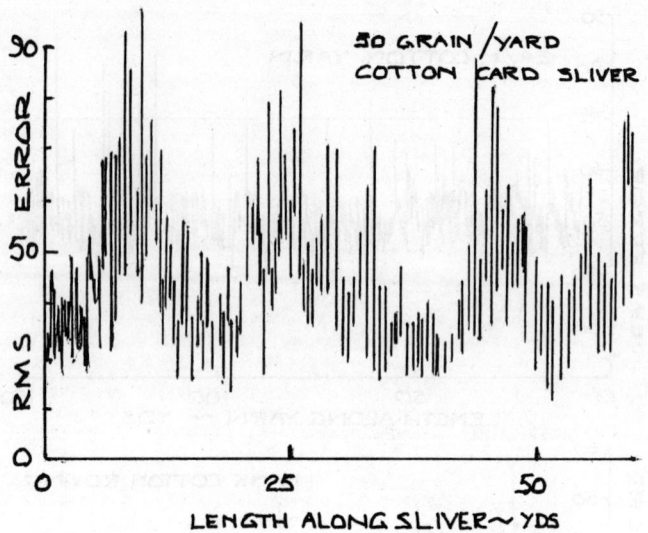

50 GRAIN /YARD
COTTON CARD SLIVER

LENGTH ALONG SLIVER ~ YDS

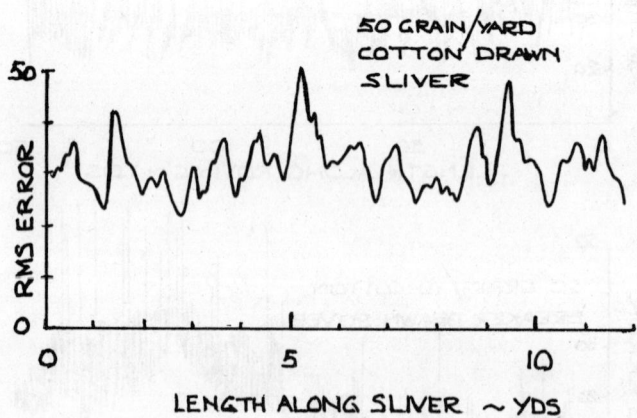

50 GRAIN/YARD
COTTON DRAWN
SLIVER

LENGTH ALONG SLIVER ~ YDS

VARIABILITY IN LINEAR DENSITY

FIGURE 9

238

MICROELECTRONIC - THE CHALLENGE FOR THE TEXTILE MACHINERY MANUFACTURER

M. Zuend

ABSTRACT

The Textile Industry is one of the oldest industries. In contrast, microelectronics is one of the youngest industries and is today initiating the next industrial revolution.

The influence and application of microelectronics in textile machinery design is unmistakable and is a necessity for modern and competitive textile machines.

The replacement of machine elements by electronic systems is proceeding rapidly. However it is still of decisive importance to determine how good the mechanical and textile technological performance of machine components is. Only rational combination of mechanical and electronic elements will bring reliable and economic solutions, which can survive the hard demands of spinning practice.

Latest technology from raw material up to fabric, with simultaneous high productivity and quality, is possible today only with the aid of microelectronics.

This paper will attempt to show that "microelectronic" is not simply a catchword but that RIETER has taken up this challenge and is meeting it.

MICROELECTRONICS

The term "microelectronics" is in use only since the start of the 1960's, that is since the individual building components of a circuit (transistors, diodes, resistors etc.) together with their control devices and connector leads could be integrated in a microscopically small form on silicon wafers ("chips") a few square millimeters in area.

Such integrated circuits (IC) are not only several magnitudes smaller than the corresponding circuits made up of individual elements, they are also substantially more reliable, require less power input and are above all better value.

The State of the Art will be presented for the most important fields of application of microelectronics in construction of textile machinery, namely

- Control Systems
- Automatic Devices, Handling Equipment
- Man-Machine-Interface
- Transport Systems
- Data Handling

Future developments will also be refered to. Further, the
hardware-technology used by Rieter will be presented.

In connection with microelectronics, the increasingly important aspect "Software" must also be dealt with.

1.   INTRODUCTION

In the development of new machine types the complete process
must increasingly be borne in mind. Development is proceeding
now from more-or-less fully automated machines to fully automated process stages.

Exchange of information between the machine control systems
enables optimisation of the operating performance, efficiency is raised and quality is improved by continual production.

Aside from the main purposes of the electronic machine,
such as

- process control
- safety
- operating and indication functions

several other functions can be achieved, usually without
additional expenditure on hardware.

Examples:

- monitoring of limit values
- self-monitoring of the microcomputer
- self diagnosis
- plausibility test
- statistics of all available machine data
- preparation and storage of machine data
- transfer of machine data to a control
  data processing facility
- etc.

This means that the use of efficient microcomputer systems
in the machine control enables in many cases the elimination
of additional monitoring systems.

Where this is not possible or useful, the machine control
system is for example prepared therefor, in that the appropriate interfaces are built in during series production.

Early contacts with system suppliers of quality and process
data handling systems are becoming increasingly important so
that the interfaces can be defined in the development phase.
Thus it is ensured that machines already delivered can subsequently be fitted with such systems without substantial
additional expenditure.

Many of the currently available mechanical functions would
not be possible without additional electronics. Besides the
actual control of the machine operation, a variety of monitoring steps are required. Additional auxiliary functions are

incorporated in series machines for commissioning and servicing purposes.

Extensive self-testing functions are integrated into the machine control for safety and reliability of the machine. Besides the indication of important operational data such as efficiency, coefficient of variation etc., detailed fault signals, enabling rapid elimination of the cause of the fault, are today considered as "state of the art".

The proportion of electrical equipment in spinning machinery is continuously increasing. This development will be illustrated with the example of the Drawing Frame (fig. 1).

2. THE DEVELOPMENT OF THE TEXTILE INDUSTRY IN COMPARISON
    WITH MICROELECTRONICS

To what extent has the rapid development in the semiconductor industry exerted an influence on the functions and efficiency of spinning machines?

If in the year 1800 approximately 10 working hours were needed for the production of 1 kg of yarn, then in 1984 only 2 minutes would be needed for the same result. This corresponds to an increase in efficiency by the factor 1.5/year (fig. 2).

A comparison with the increase in the integration density in the semiconductor industry gives a value of 1.7/year. (Fig. 3.)

2.1 EFFECTS OF MICROELECTRONICS ON THE FUNCTIONS AND
    EFFICIENCY OF SPINNING MACHINES

Inprovements in performance such as those provided by the latest generation of spinning machines are to be attributed not only to the use of microelectronics.

The use of electronics is also required because of increased process demands, for example

- soft start and controlled acceleration to operating
  speed ⟶ electronic drive equipment
- on-line monitoring of quality due to high material throughput and to enable high efficiency ⟶ new measurement systems
- monitoring of all machine functions and rapid reaction in
  the event of faults, emergency stops (safety technology)
- input of machine data and process parameters
- status and fault indications in legible text (display,
  printer)
- complex doffing systems because of high material throughput
  and interconnection with transport systems
- collection of operating data and production statistics for
  service personal, production manager and general management

2.2 STATE OF THE ART

The extent to which microelectronics has gained access to a
spinning mill equipped with modern machines is shown by the
spin plan on fig. 4.

3. MAN-MACHINE-INTERFACE (MMI)

Provided the machine operates in accordance with its designed
functions and free of faults it is usually of no importance
to the machine operators what type of electronic technology
is provided under the machine covers and in the control panel.

As viewed externally, predominantly the operating and indicating units have changed since the introduction of microelectronics. This very important point does not always receive
adequate attention.

The Man-Machine-Interface has the following tasks:

- input of machine functions such as on/off, manual, change
  etc.
- input of operating parameters such as production, sliver
  count, yarn length etc.
- indication of operating conditions, machine timing, fault
  location, fault cause

Exactly because machine controls are becoming ever more complex and expensive Man-Machine-Interfaces must be maintained
simple and comprehensible. Large control panels with rows
of buttons and lamps belong to the past.

PROGRESS OF MMI-TECHNOLOGY

Yesterday	Today	Tomorrow

- Many buttons
- Many lamps
- Analog Indi-
  cations
- Potentiometers
- Decade Switches
	- Few buttons
	- Few indicator
	  Lamps
	- Decade Switches
	- Keyboard (decimal,
	  hexadecimal)
	- Indications in
	  Man-readable text
	- Printer output
		- Keyboard
		- Display
		- Video Screen
		- Spoken input
		       -output
		- Remote ope-
		  ration via process
		  data handling sys-
		  tems

EXAMPLES:

Operating Unit of OE Machine M2/1: (fig. 5)

- plug-in on the front plate of the machine control
- low cost
- universal and flexible
- input via function keys and decimal keyboard
- alphanumeric display, test output

- all input and output is interactive, controlled from the
  microcomputer system of the machine control

Operating unit of Unifloc Al/2: (fig. 6)

- Functionally and ergonomically designed
- comprehensible and simple lay-out
- easily readable display
- simple programming through interactive operating guide
- control via microcomputer
- text output in various languages (selectable)

4. ON-LINE PROCESS CONTROL AND QUALITY MONITORING

The output of individual process stages is today so great
that disturbances in the process can produce quite large
quantities of defective material. The resultant damage is
correspondingly high, especially if this is first recognised
in the succeeding process stages.

These high performance machines force the machine manufacturer to develop reliable and self-monitoring electronic systems. Often it is not the technical possibilities but the
rapidly rising costs which make the inclusion of redundant
systems uneconomic.

Practically all manufacturers of textile machines are now replacing their relay controls and discrete digital or analog
systems with microcomputer systems. The quantity of data
available, and the quantity of data to be processed on machines of the latest generation, is so high that the use of
microcomputers is unavoidable for technical and economic
reasons (fig. 7).

4.1 BLOWING ROOM

In the blowing room, extraction of fibres and blending of
cotton bales takes place automatically. A microcomputer system controls and monitors the bale opening machine Unifloc
Al/2. Programming of the operating parameters is performed
interactively via an operating unit with a key board and
display. Status and fault indications are given in man-
readable text and in 5 different languages.

The reduction in price for semiconductor memories enabled
the development of a program in a higher program language
(PASCAL) and the integration of extensive self-test and
auxiliary programs for service purposes. The patented production control enables optimisation and maintenance of
efficiency.

4.2 CARDING ROOM

The basis for the quality of the end product is lead down in
the carding room. Control systems for holding sliver count
constant are part of the standard equipment of all modern

spinning mills. Rieter has exerted every possible
effort in developing a control system which sets new standards in exactness, long term constancy and robustness.

A microcomputer controls the infeed speed so that a sliver
count as constant as possible is obtained at the delivery.
The control algorithm used for this purpose is self-optimi-
sing, that is the control system automatically adapts the
control parameters to changing operating conditions.

The doffer speed is continously adjusted to the delivery by
a frequency converter (TEXINVERT). A starting and braking
control prevents sliver breaks.

These and other special features (eg. CV of the C4 control)
are possible only with the aid of microelectronics or programmable systems.

Future developments aim for a continuous material flow from
bale opener to card. In comparison with the currently normal,
discontinuous processing in the various cleaning and blending stages, improved performance will be obtained from the
plant with the same specific machine performance, and with
higher quality.

4.3 DRAWING FRAME D1 (fig. 8)

The salient performance characteristics, such as

- delivery speed maximum 800 m/min
- automatic adjustment of the control parameters to
  the delivery speed
- regulated start/stop
- regulation range ± 25 %
- intermediate term regulation with minimum evening
  length of 2 m
- infeed measuring element for evening length ~ 50 cm
- reduction of CV_B (10 m) to < 1 %
- etc.

can be achieved only with correspondingly high expenditure
on electronics.

An efficient 16-bit microcomputer system processes the signals of the infeed and delivery measuring devices. Since the
delivery speed is constant, the control action of the regulating system is exerted on the main draft of the drafting
mechanism via a fast-acting servo-drive system.

The display for "CV %" and the instantaneous control deviation are built into the series machines. A programmable controller controls and monitors machine operation. For drawing
frames without regulation, a so-called sliver-controller is
offered for average value monitoring. This low cost monitoring device automatically switches the machine off if a set
sliver count is exceeded. Simultaneously it indicates via a
printer the cause of the stop and the time of the fault.

A portable microcomputer system can be connected to the
machine for on-line checking of the drafting mechanism. The
output signal of the delivery measuring device is analysed
into its frequency spectrum and printed out in a wavelength
range of 3.15 ÷ 200 cms.

The regulating system and the electronic shift and production figures can be fed to a control process data handling
installation.

4.4 ROTOR SPINNING MACHINE M2/1 (fig. 9)

The new rotor spinning machine M2/1 is a typical example of
a machine with various, more or less closely coupled control
systems.

The machine control together with the length control and statistic system form the central unit. Automation elements,
such as the following, are coupled to the control unit:

- Piecing automat
- Tube feeder
- Package handling
- Section electronics
- Box electronics

The M2/1 system is supplemented by connection possibilities
built into the series machines such as

- process data handling system (eg. ZAG)
- quality monitoring systems (eg. ZAG, Peyer)

The use of latest technology such as single chip microcomputers, optical fibre leads etc. bring advantages such as,
for example:

- simpler, more comprehensible system design
- less mechanical parts
- high functional reliability
- simple and speedy elimination of faults
- system capable of extension and development
- low cost

4.5 FILAMENT MACHINES (fig. 10)

The proportion of electronics is also steadily increasing in
the field of filament machines. 40 ÷ 70 % of the complete
installation cost is no longer unusual.

In addition to mechanical processing components for spin-
draw-wind machines Rieter delivers the complete electrical
and electronic equipment. In contrast to electronics in
staple fibre machines, the main emphasis is on distribution,
conversion and control of relatively large quantities of
power. All of the power fed into the process at this processing stage, approximately 30 ÷ 40 kW per threadline, is
controlled electronically. The draw rolls are accurately
maintained at their operating speeds by frequency converters

245

(TEXINVERT) ($\pm$ 0.1 %!). A microcomputer control regulates and monitors the automatic winders. All system components have data interfaces so that they can be connected to central data processing installations.

The set values for speed and temperature of the draw rolls and the doffing times for the automatic winders are fed in over a central system for all threadlines.

5. TRANSPORT SYSTEMS

New standards have been set by the new fully automatic, high performance machines such as

- bale opener Unifloc A1/2
- card C4
- drawing frame D1
- rotor spinning machine M2/1

However, the high material throughput and production rates thereby achieved cause new problems.

The supply and removal of cans, laps, packages etc. must be coordinated at such high rates, and the weights of the bodies of textile material involved are sometimes so large, that transport systems become imperative as machine-linking systems.

Already existing machine-doff-stations have to be adapted for connection to a transport system.

Future machine control systems must be prepared not only for process data handling but must also have a communication interface with a transport or handling system. If the machine supplier is not also the supplier of the transport system then corresponding software and hardware adaptations on the machine control system are unavoidable.

Linking of several process stages requires in addition to the actual control system also the control system and data handling system superintending transport and process so that the plant efficiency can be optimised and possible weak points eliminated.

6. HANDLING OF PROCESS DATA

The ever increasing investment per job, and the maintenance of quality, cause ever more spinning mills to connect part or even the whole of the mill process to process data handling systems. Under cost pressure, many plants are operated with 3 or 4 shifts. On the other hand, development is proceeding in the direction of full automation of process stages.

The following categories of process data are to be distinguished: (fig. 12)

- condition data
- production data
- quality data

In this line of development Rieter can offer the following
solution:

- All machines of the newest generation are prepared for
  connection to a process data handling system. (Fig. 13.)

What does this mean in practice?

- All machine control systems with a microcomputer system
  are equipped with a serial data interface and a corresponding interface program (the interface specification will
  be provided on demand)
- Machine control systems without serial data interfaces
  (even older machines) can in the future be equipped with
  a special device to enable the connection.

Transfer of machine data from an interface plug-in device of
the machine manufacturer brings the following advantages:

- cheaper, because no extra sensors are required. All important machine data is already stored in the microcomputer system of the machine control
- the data is exact and relevant (the machine control also
  operates on it)
- uniform interfaces in respect of software and hardware
- as compared with retro-fitting of sensors, all data available from the machine is available for processing; the
  central process data handling system decides which data
  is to be processed.

Previous data handling systems operate mostly with only a
few machine conditions, such as machine operating/machine not
operating. From such data the following information can be
derived:

- running time (machine producing)
- down time (machine not operating)
- efficiency [%] $(\frac{\text{Running Time}}{\text{Running Time + Down Time}}) \cdot 100 \%$
- if a pulse infeed is also connected (eg. doffer speed)
  then production rate can also be derived

Important information such as

- causes of defects (no feed material, lap, safety switch
  operated, operating range exceeded etc.)
- quality data (twist, CV %, thread breaks etc.)

can be derived only with correspondingly large additional
expenditure on hard- and software, unless the control system
used by the machine manufacturer already has this data and
feeds it to a corresponding interface.

Remote operation and programming of selected operating and
production parameters on the machine from a central data
processing system will also become important for future process control systems.

The main emphasis in relation to process data handling systems lies in the future not in the installation of sensors
but in the extraction of data via defined interfaces, data
transfer via suitable interfaces and bus systems, practical
data preparation and concentration and comprehensible display and alarm upon deviations from predetermined set limits.

Fig.11 provides a summary of process data on Rieter machines
as already available today via a specific interface for
central process data handling systems.

7.   HARDWARE

Hardware development proceeds so rapidly that a fully developed product is often already obsolete from the point of
view of the electronics specialist. Nevertheless, clear emphasis for application of various fields of technology can
be identified.

7.1 RELAY TECHNOLOGY

For small, simple controls without specialized functions,
eg. counters etc., up to   about 10 relays.

7.2 PROGRAMMABLE CONTROLLERS (PC)

This type of control is

- flexible
- extendable
- economic
- reliable
- programmable
- space saving

Memory programmable controllers are today replacing relay
controls for a large part. On the other hand they are also
clearly invading the operating field of the microcomputer
systems. Functions such as

- counters
- arithmetic
- closed loop control
- word processing
- parallel programs
- etc.

are already state of the art.

248

7.3 MICROCOMPUTER SYSTEMS

This term refers to systems which have a single-board computer and transfer data via a system bus with various memory and peripheral units.

The strength of such systems lies in

- productivity (16-bit processor)
- speed
- program store (4-48 KB)
- data store (1-16 KB)
- various programming languages (Assembler, PASCAL)
- flexibility
- serial interface for process data handling
- etc.

Microcomputer systems together with programmable controllers form the backbone of the Rieter control systems. (Examples: Unifloc A1/2, Contimeter/Mixcontrol B0/M, Card C4, Drawing Frame D1, Ringspindoffer G5/1D, Rotor spinning machine M2/1.)

7.4 MICROPROCESSORS

Microcomputers for specific applications are also being developed at Rieter to an increasing extent. So called chip solutions (Computer, Memory and Input and Output elements) are often technically and economically the best solution when large quantities are involved (fig. 14).

We regard as especially important the tendency away from large, complex and central systems to smaller ones with distributed "intelligence" (Single-chip-microcomputer). The connection between individual sub-processors is made eg. over a disturbance-free optical fibre system.

In manufacture of textile machines, the highest demands are made on the hardware regarding reliability and safety.

Under severe operating conditions, such as high operating temperatures, dust, power supply failures, high humidity, badly trained operating and maintenance personnel etc., the microelectronic systems must fullfil their tasks in 3-shift operation over years, disturbance and fault free.

Rieter's own electronic production, above-average quality standards, and extensive tests, check and preparation steps (burn-in) provide the customer with the assurance of high operating reliability.

The modular design in easily exchangeable units and self-test auxiliary programs for simple diagnosis aid service in the event of faults.

7.5 DEVELOPMENT TENDENCIES

- Replacement of analog technology by microcomputers
- Signal processors for on-line quality monitoring
- Microcomputers also for control and optimization of drive
  systems
- Optic fibres in place of electrical connections
- Replacement of hardware by software
- IC's specific to the customer (Semi-custom IC)
- Network-IC's for the construction of low cost micropro-
  cessor systems for handling process data (Local Area Net-
  works)
- In the next 10 years the development of activities is not
  going to slow down; in other words every second year doubling of function densities could be achieved with halving
  of the cost.

8. SOFTWARE

The success of microelectronics is due largely to the fact
that practically any desired function can be realised with
standard components such as microprocessors, stores and
peripheral units, together with software, which is stored
in coded form in the program memory.

With the same microcomputer configuration, through mere
adaptation of the input/output interfaces to the circumstances of use, a variety of machine control system can be designed with the appropriate programs.

The development effort of the machine manufacturer is shifting increasingly from hardware (circuit design) to software. On average, program development already represents
about 30 ÷ 50 % of the total development time of a machine
control.

The fact that Rieter has opted completely for programmable
microcomputer systems brings the following advantages:

- Standard hardware, that is for several machine types (from
  the bale opener to the rotor spinning machine) the same
  hardware components and thus smaller stocks of replacement
  parts.
- Further developments and improvments can be offered to the
  customer subsequently - simply by exchange of the program
  memory (EPROMs).
- Auxiliary functions such as
  - diagnostic programs, several languages for display
  - single step and test programs, rapid fault location and
    elimination
  - self-test programs for the complete control system during
    acceleration and operation
- So-called "intelligent machines" with
  - interactive man-machine-interface
  - self optimizing algorithms
  - communication between process stages and hence process
    optimization
  - individual collection of data on each machine

9. OUTLOOK AND SUMMARY

Today already, after only 10 years of experience with micro-electronics, the question arises, how a spinning mill could look in the year 2000?

Simple extrapolation of the last 10 years would mean:
- less process stages; instead more highly integrated machines
- processes completely electronically controlled and monitored
- use of new sensors for material transport, measurement of production and quality etc.
- new processing methods
- process data handling from blowing room to end product with automatic process optimisation
- ghost-shifts, that is practically no operating personnel
- material handling with robots specific to the application
- hierarchical information systems for the levels operating and maintenance, foreman, production manager, general management, sales dept. etc.

Developments in microelectronics to even higher function densities will bring in the future still more productive and complex components.

For the textile machinery manufacturer there is thus the chance to substantially improve once more textile processes with regard to productivity, quality, energy demand and reliability. Inevitably connected therewith is the linking of process stages with fully automated transport systems. High material throughput requires continuous monitoring of quality.

The large quantity of available machine data must be extracted via predetermined interfaces and represented comprehensibly as far as possible in accordance with purpose of use.

New technology brings in addition to many advantages also new problems. From the viewpoint of the textile machine manufacturer the following should be mentioned:
- high development expenditure associated with a short life-span (typical product lifespan in the field of electronics is 5 years)
- the electrical equipment of the machines becomes more complicated and the number of possible sources of faults is thereby increased. From the exterior the machine must be as simple to operate as before and in spite of much higher performance the machine must be at least as reliable.
- the requirements laid on the customer and the machine operators are raised
- understanding of the machine and the process with the head rather than skill in manipulation is becoming steadily more important

- the training of the customer and of the manufacturer's
  erectors is becoming of central importance in conjunction
  with the sale of machines and processes
- replacement parts service for electronic systems must be
  adapted to the changing circumstances.

Marcel Zuend
Rieter Machine Works Ltd.
8406 Winterthur
Switzerland

Changes in Proportion of Electronics with Machine Performance

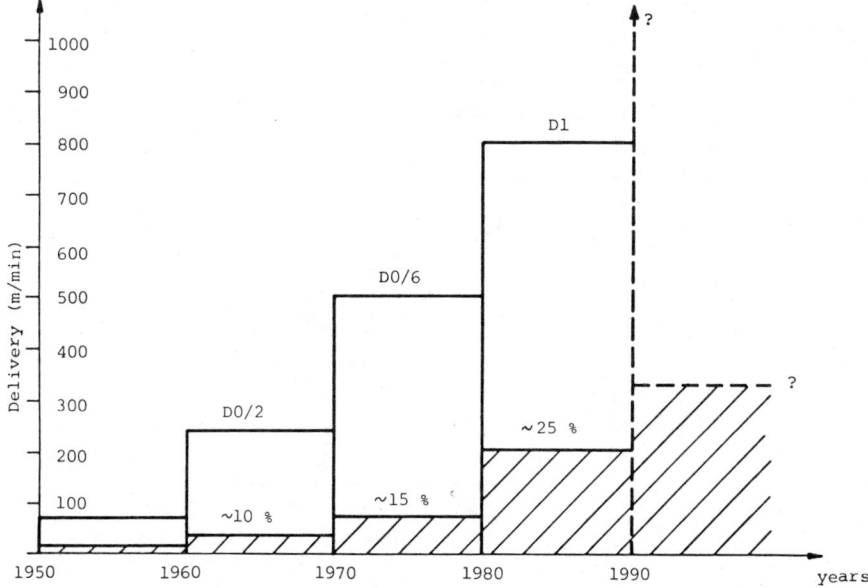

Fig. 1

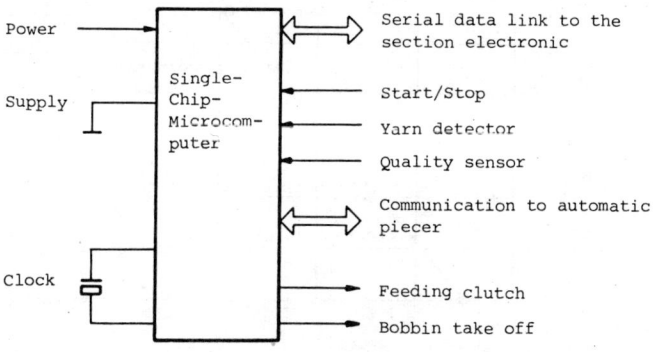

Fig. 14

RIETER	M2/1 Box Electronic	

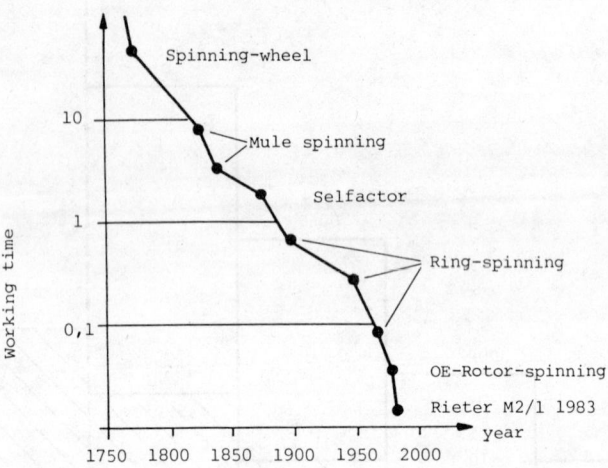

Fig. 2

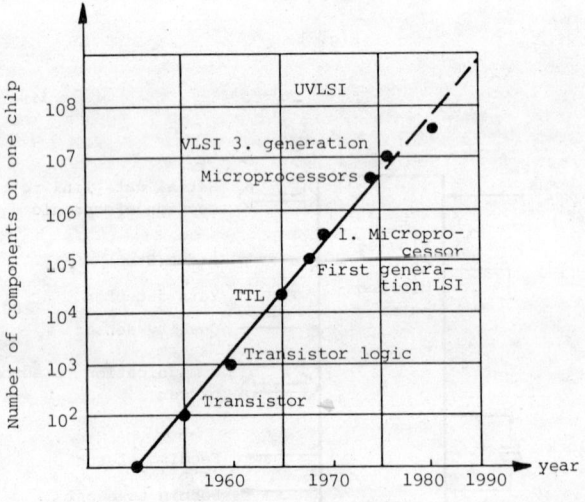

Fig. 3

| RIETER | Innovation rates in comparison
Textile Semiconductor Industries | |

254

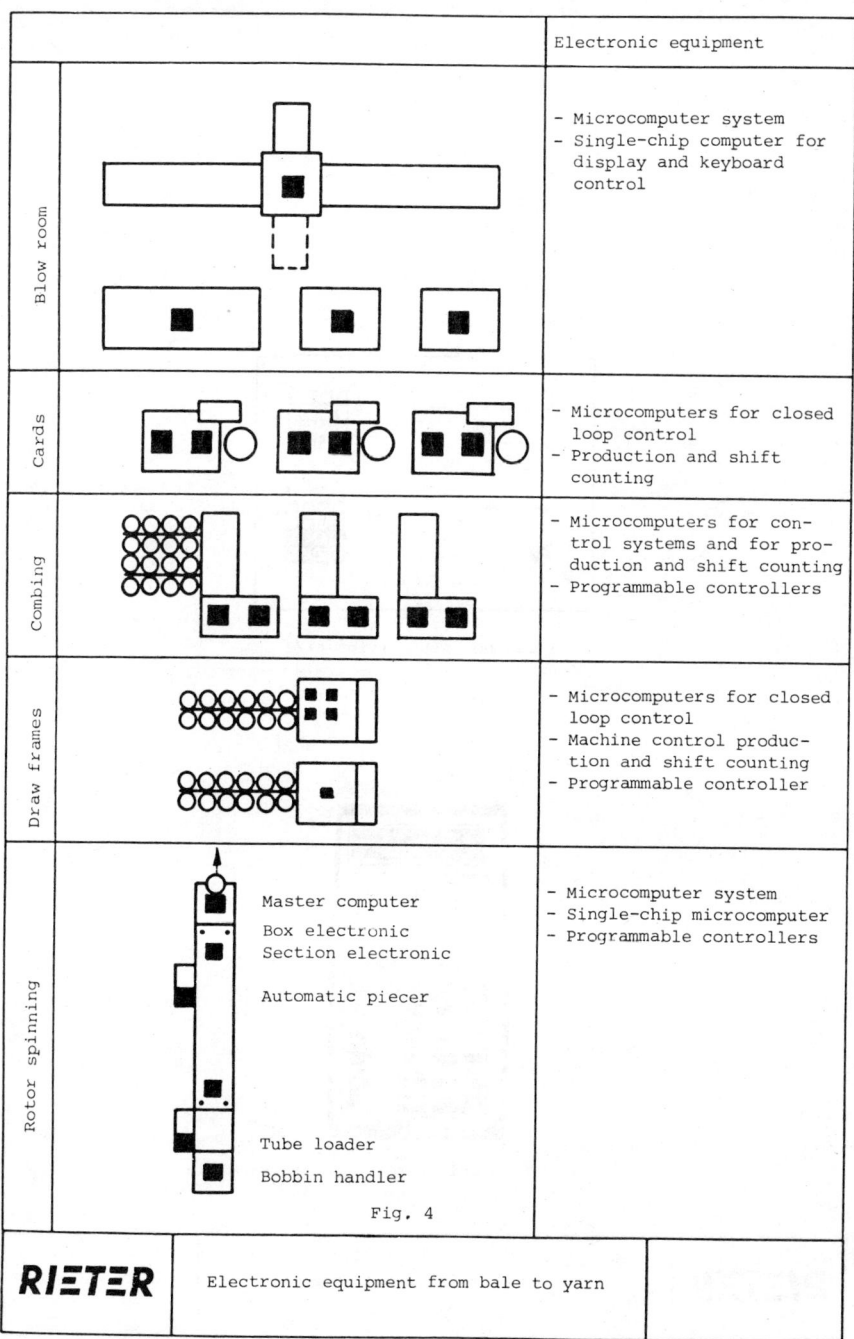

		Electronic equipment
Blow room		- Microcomputer system - Single-chip computer for display and keyboard control
Cards		- Microcomputers for closed loop control - Production and shift counting
Combing		- Microcomputers for control systems and for production and shift counting - Programmable controllers
Draw frames		- Microcomputers for closed loop control - Machine control production and shift counting - Programmable controller
Rotor spinning	Master computer Box electronic Section electronic Automatic piecer Tube loader Bobbin handler	- Microcomputer system - Single-chip microcomputer - Programmable controllers

Fig. 4

RIETER   Electronic equipment from bale to yarn

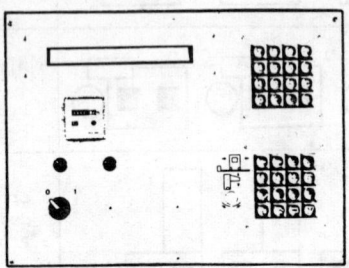

Operating unit Unifloc A1/2

Fig. 6

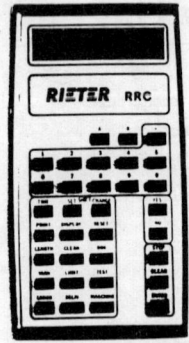

Operating unit Rotorspinnmachine M2/1

Fig. 5

RIETER	Man-Machine-Interface	

256

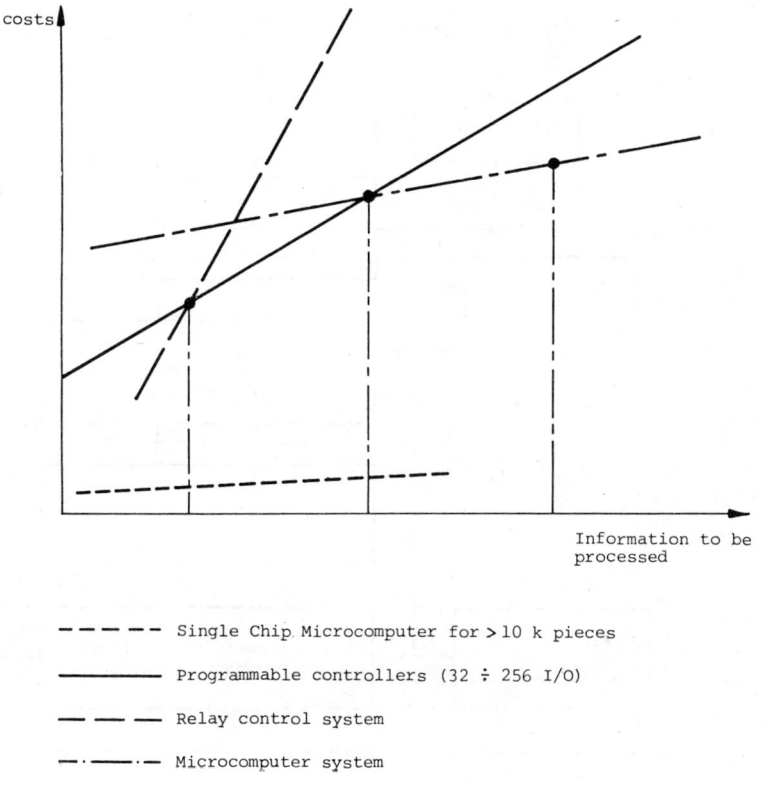

costs

Information to be
processed

- - - - - Single Chip Microcomputer for > 10 k pieces

————— Programmable controllers (32 ÷ 256 I/O)

— — — Relay control system

—·—·— Microcomputer system

Fig. 7

RIETER	Comparison of Technology	

257

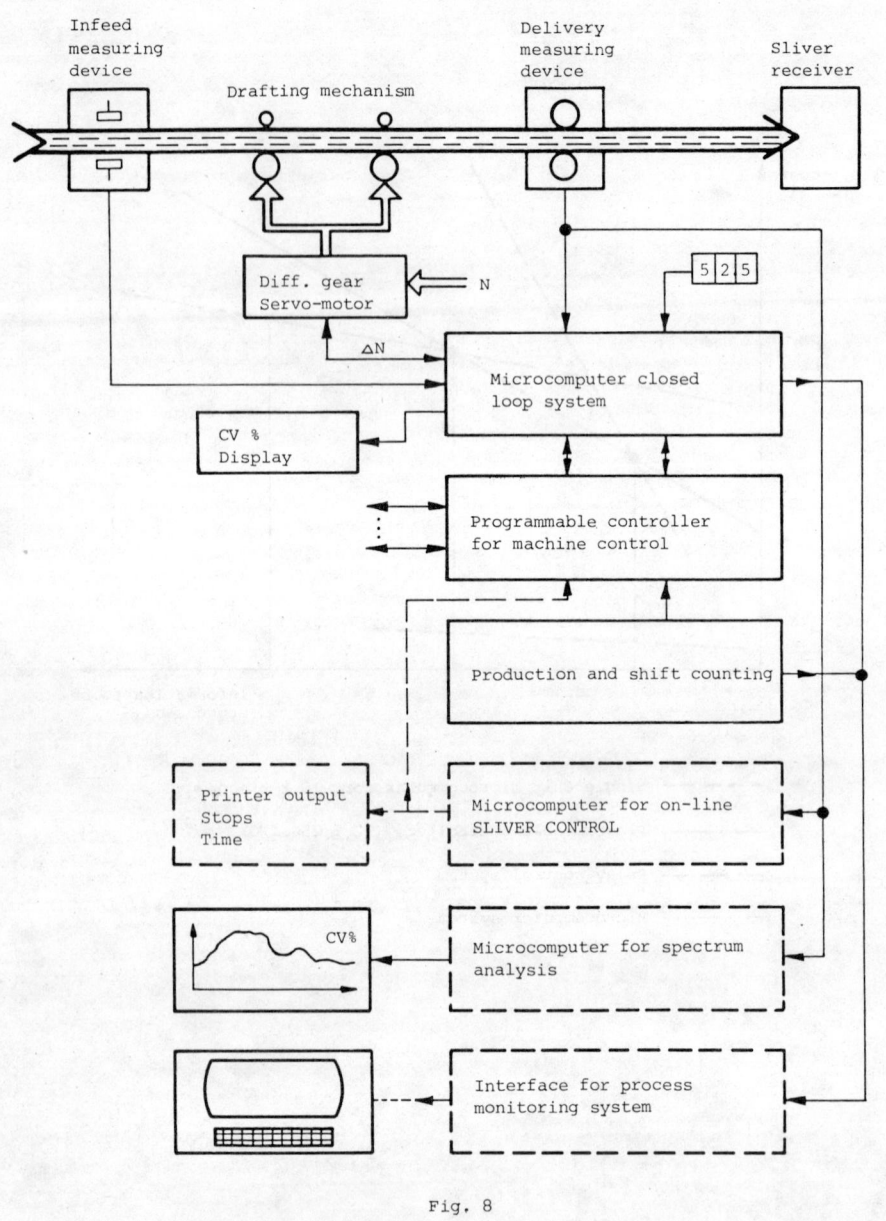

Fig. 8

RIETER	Draw Frame D1 Electronic Equipment	

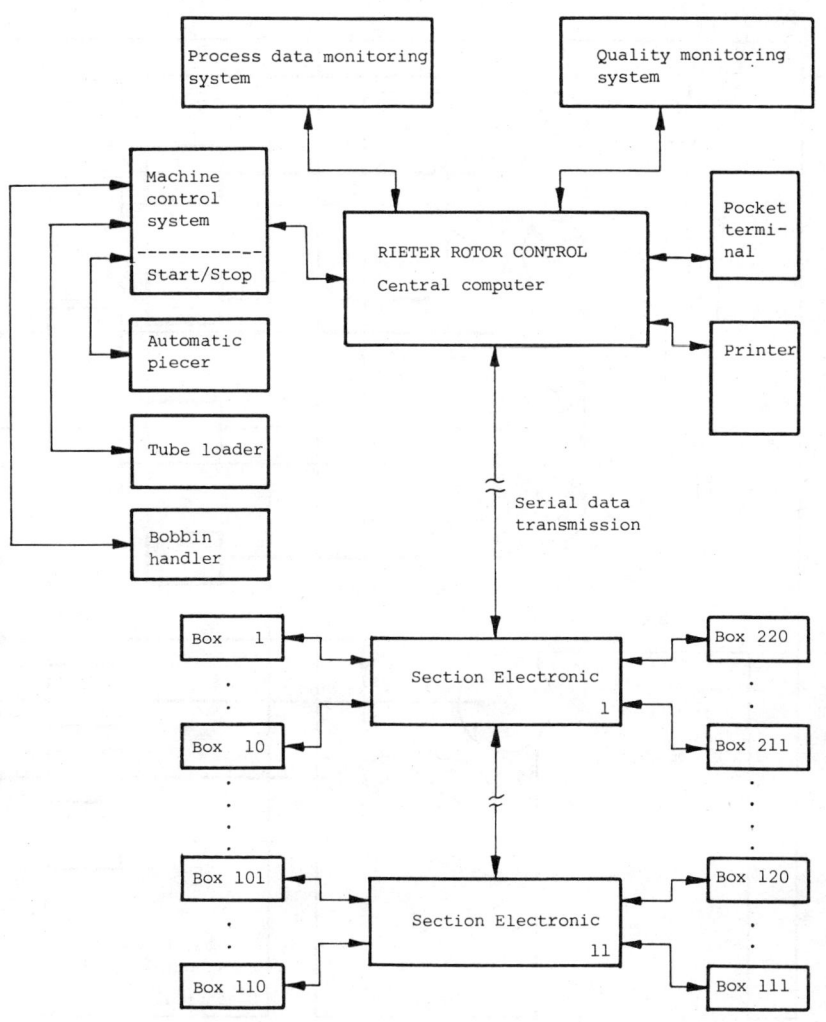

Fig. 9

RIETER	Control System Rotor spinning machine M2/1	

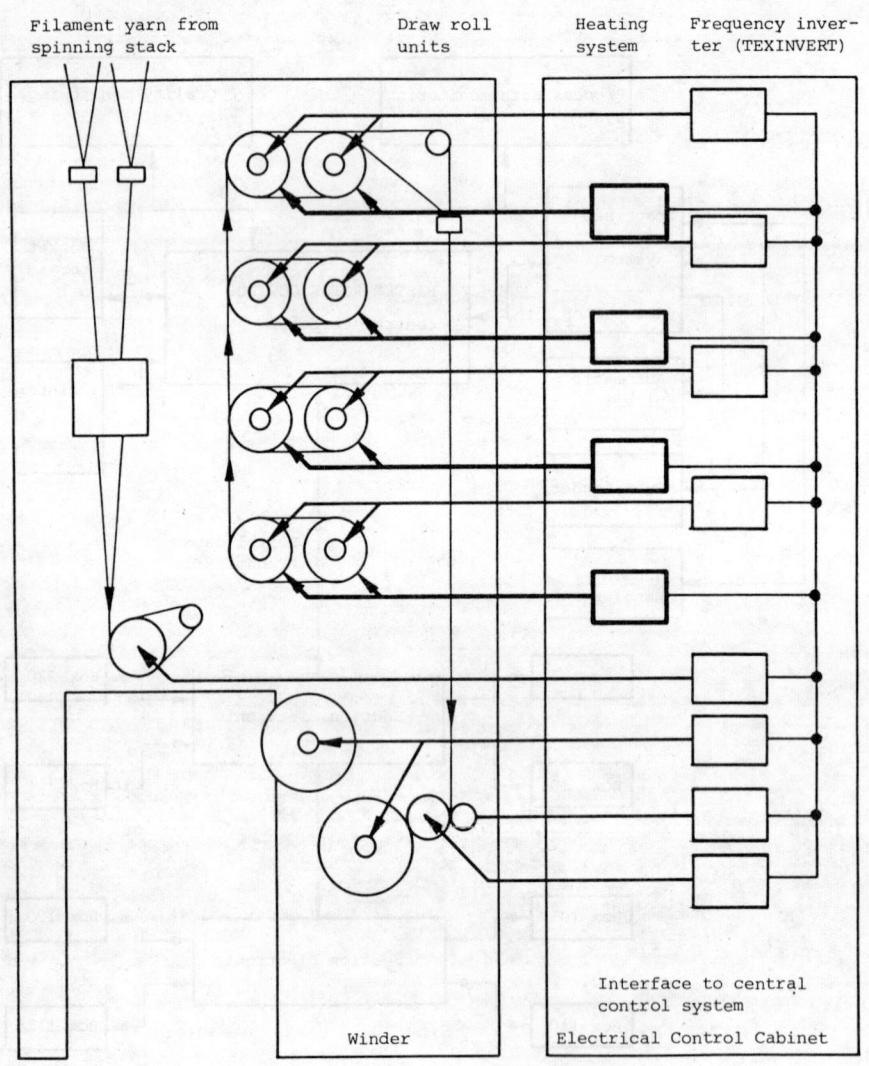

Filament yarn from spinning stack

Draw roll units

Heating system

Frequency inverter (TEXINVERT)

Interface to central control system

Winder

Electrical Control Cabinet

Fig. 10

RIETER   Spin Draw Process J7/8

= Rieter / = other syst. / = future	Blow Room	Card Feeding Card	Combing Preparation	Combing	Drawing Frame	Rotor Spinning Machine
Speed	Rieter	Rieter	Rieter	Rieter	Rieter	Rieter
Delivery	Rieter	Rieter	Rieter	Rieter	Rieter	Rieter
Twist	Rieter	Rieter	Rieter	Rieter	Rieter	Rieter
Production	Rieter	Rieter	Rieter	Rieter	Rieter	Rieter
Length counter	Rieter	Rieter	Rieter	Rieter	Rieter	Rieter
Shift counter	Rieter	Rieter	Rieter	Rieter	Rieter	Rieter
Shift number	Rieter	Rieter	Rieter	Rieter	Rieter	Rieter
Cans, package	Rieter	Rieter	Rieter	Rieter	Rieter	Rieter
Coefficient of variation		Rieter			Rieter	
Thread breaks counter						Rieter
Moirée						other syst.
Thick/thin places		Rieter			Rieter	other syst.
Blend	Rieter					
Fibre fineness						
Wavelength spectrum		other syst.			Rieter	
Operating condition	Rieter	Rieter	Rieter	Rieter	Rieter	Rieter
Cause of stop	Rieter	Rieter	Rieter	Rieter	Rieter	Rieter

RIETER Available Process Data on Rieter Machines — Fig. 11

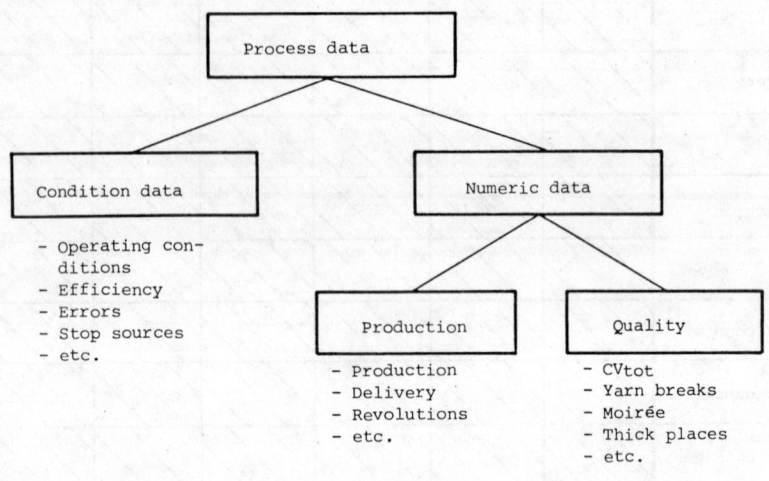

Fig. 12

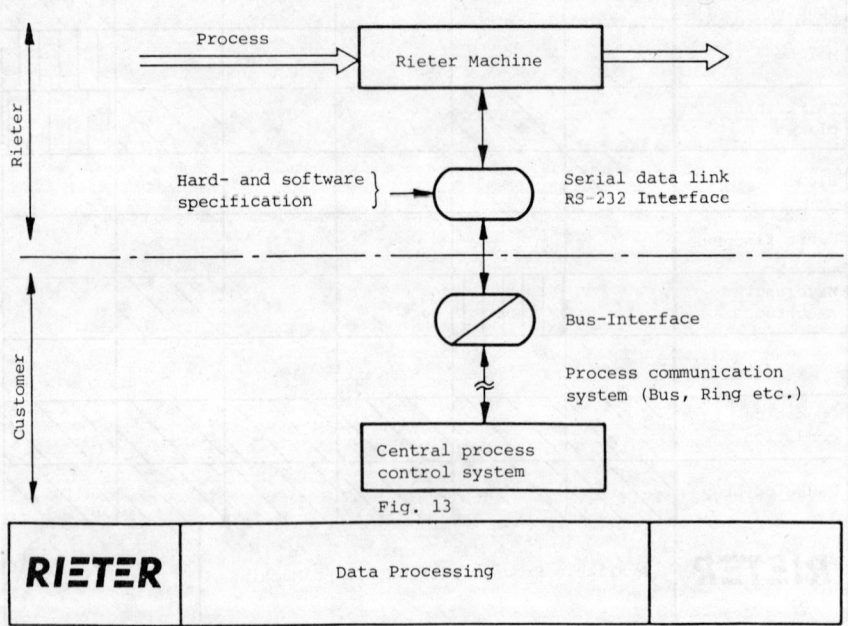

Fig. 13

COTTON BLENDING FOR SPINNING MILLS USING COMPUTER ASSISTED OPERATION RESEARCH MODEL

Devinder Sharma

ABSTRACT

Cotton exhibits high variation from fibre to fibre, bale to bale, cotton area to cotton area and season to season. New strains tend to blow resource set and with market becoming increasingly cost-quality conscious the resource/product situation is becoming more competitive and uncertain. Consequently success of a spinning mill depends upon its ability to purchase right type of cottons at right time at right price and efficient formulation of mixings. In the emerging scenario it has become imperative for managements with modern outlook to replace traditional mixing methods which have become costly, wasteful and unpredictable with scientific approaches and methods for economy, consistency, quality and reliability. It is possible to build and use computer based Operations Research models for efficient and consistent blending of cottons which provides scope to effect 5% to 12% savings vis-a-vis traditional mixing methods.

1. INTRODUCTION

Linear programming as an OR modelling technique enjoys great popularity and success in industry from a host of mathematical programming models for solving allocation problems. Allocation problems concern themselves by trying to identify a unique, best method of alloting available (scarce) resources to competing activities to meet required objectives in an environment characterized by definite resource constraints and or other technical restrictions. In a cotton spinning mill available cottons are the resources, the varieties of yarn expressed in equivalent of a cotton mix the competing activities. In the treatment following, the cottons are viewed as resources which are allocated to various products which are synonymous to the various mixes formulated. Each constituent cotton is identified qualitatively through its fibre properties. Products to be manufactured may be limited, though cotton varieties are large in number with varying quantities of even larger number of lots. The mix must meet the norms set for it and must be constructed based upon individual fibre properties with the prime objective of least cost mix.

2. NOTATION PERTAINING TO MODEL

2.1 Let N — Number of cotton varieties in stock

   K — Number of products for which mixings have to be constructed

Then $X(I,J)$ is the proportion of the Ith cotton in the Jth product/mixing, with I varying from 1 to N and J varying from 1 to K.

2.2 $C(I)$ is the cleaned cotton cost per bale of the Ith cotton variety computed by adding for trash content present in the cotton to purchase price.

2.3 $AQ(I)$ is the available quantity in bales of the Ith cotton.

2.4 Symbols used for fibre properties of cotton and their
meanings alongwith the variable field are described below –

SYMBOL	UNITS	FIELDWIDTH	PROPERTY OF ITH COTTON
SL(I)	Inches	9.999	2.5% Span length measured by Digital Fibrograph
STH(I)	Gms/Tex	99.999	Strength measured using Stello-meter
FINE(I)	Micronaire	9.999	Fineness measured using Fibre Fineness Tester
UR(I)	Percentage	99.999	Uniformity Ratio computed using 2.5% & 50% Span lengths
MC(I)	Number	.999	Maturity coefficient measured using Projection Microscope or indirectly with Fibre Fineness Tester
FFI(I)	Number	99.999	Floating Fibre Index, computed
TR(I)	Percentage	99.99	Trash content, computed
FQI(I)	Number	999.999	Fibre quality Index, computed as

$$\frac{SL(I)*UR(I)*STH(I)*MC(I)}{FINE\ (I)}$$

2.5 Symbols for expressing the norms or standards (quality requirements) for a mix are described below –

SYMBOL	NATURE OF REQUIREMENT	PROPERTY OF JTH PRODUCT
SLMX(J)	Equal to or less than (maximum)	2.5% Staple length
SLM (J)	Equal to or greater than (minimum)	2.5% Staple length
STHM(J)	Equal to or greater than (minimum)	Strength
FINEMX(J)	Equal to or less than (maximum)	Fineness
FINEM (J)	Equal to or greater than (minimum)	Fineness
URM(J)	Equal to or greater than (minimum)	Uniformity Ratio
MCM(J)	Equal to or greater than (minimum)	Maturity coefficient
FFIMX(J)	Equal to or less than (maximum)	Floating Fibre Index
FFIM(J)	Equal to or greater than (minimum)	Floating Fibre Index
TRM(J)	Equal to or less than (maximum)	Trash content
FQIM(J)	Equal to or greater than (minimum)	Fibre quality Index

2.6 BQ(J) is the batch quantity in bales, required for the Jth
product and is the sum of bales of different cottons going into
the Jth mix.

3. THE BASIC LP MODEL FOR BLENDING COTTON
The aim of the LP cotton blending model is to identify a unique
best solution given the conditions represented in the model. The
model is structured as –

Minimize

$$TMC = \sum_{J=1}^{K} \sum_{I=1}^{N} X(I,J) * C(I)$$

where TMC is the sum of the individual mixing costs of different products/mixings, subject to the following constraints-

(1) $\sum_{J=1}^{K} \sum_{I=1}^{N} X(I,J) * SL(I) \leq \sum_{J=1}^{K} SLMX(J)$

(2) $\sum_{J=1}^{K} \sum_{I=1}^{N} X(I,J) * SL(I) \geq \sum_{J=1}^{K} SLM(J)$

(3) $\sum_{J=1}^{K} \sum_{I=1}^{N} X(I,J) * STH(I) \geq \sum_{J=1}^{K} STHM(J)$

(4) $\sum_{J=1}^{K} \sum_{I=1}^{N} X(I,J) * 1/FINE(I) \leq \sum_{J=1}^{K} 1/FINEMX(J)$

(5) $\sum_{J=1}^{K} \sum_{I=1}^{N} X(I,J) * 1/FINE(I) \geq \sum_{J=1}^{K} 1/FINEM(J)$

(6) $\sum_{J=1}^{K} \sum_{I=1}^{N} X(I,J) * UR(I) \geq \sum_{J=1}^{K} URM(J)$

(7) $\sum_{J=1}^{K} \sum_{I=1}^{N} X(I,J) * MC(I) \geq \sum_{J=1}^{K} MCM(J)$

(8) $\sum_{J=1}^{K} \sum_{I=1}^{N} X(I,J) * FFI(I) \leq \sum_{J=1}^{K} FFIMX(J)$

(9) $\sum_{J=1}^{K} \sum_{I=1}^{N} X(I,J) * FFI(I) \geq \sum_{J=1}^{K} FFIM(J)$

(10) $\sum_{J=1}^{K} \sum_{I=1}^{N} X(I,J) * TR(I) \leq \sum_{J=1}^{K} TRM(J)$

(11) $\sum_{J=1}^{K} \sum_{I=1}^{N} X(I,J) * FQI(I) \geq \sum_{J=1}^{K} FQIM(J)$

(12) Batch quantity constraint: the sum of bales of different cottons alloted to a mix should be equal to the batch quantity, BQ(J) for that product/mix; mathematically the sum of proportions of different cottons going into the mix should be unity and is modelled as -

For Product P_1 : $X(1,1)+X(2,1)+X(3,1)+\ldots X(N,1) = 1$
For Product P_2 : $X(1,2)+X(2,2)+X(3,2)+\ldots X(N,2) = 1$
For Product P_3 : $X(1,3)+X(2,3)+X(3,3)+\ldots X(N,3) = 1$

.
.
.

For Product P_K : $X(1,K)+X(2,K)+X(3,K)+\ldots X(N,K) = 1$

(13) Availability constraint: the sum of same cottons alloted cannot exceed available quantity on stock and is modelled as -

For Cotton V_1 : $X(1,1)*BQ(1)+X(1,2)*BQ(2)+\ldots X(1,K)*BQ(K) \leq AQ(1)$
For Cotton V_2 : $X(2,1)*BQ(1)+X(2,2)*BQ(2)+\ldots X(2,K)*BQ(K) \leq AQ(2)$
For Cotton V_3 : $X(3,1)*BQ(1)+X(3,2)*BQ(2)+\ldots X(3,K)*BQ(K) \leq AQ(3)$

.
.
.

For Cotton V_N : $X(N,1)*BQ(1)+X(N,2)*BQ(2)+\ldots X(N,K)*BQ(K) \leq AQ(N)$

In the above model for 'N' cotton varieties and 'K' product types there will be 'N*K' number of decision variables. Decision variables are proportions of cotton varieties alloted to various products and describe the objective function and the constraining equations. There will thus be 'N' elements in the objective function and 'K' sets of equations for each group of constraints with each constraining equation comprising 'N' number of elements. The model assumes no forbidden allotments, i.e. any cotton may be alloted to any mix. Real life situations will generally however impose restrictions.

4.EXTENDED MODEL CATERING FOR FORBIDDEN ALLOTMENTS

4.1 Economic and productivity related issues force inclusion of waste cottons into mixings judiciously where possible. At the resource end mills negotiate this by collecting in process waste generated or by purchase or by both methods. While at the usage side certain products permit complete usage of waste, some partial while others do not permit inclusion of any waste. The objective for extending basic model is that by incorporation of sufficient and necessary rules, mixings meeting above real life conditions can be declared. Consequently, scope of model is greatly enhanced and can cope with virtually any situation in any mill.

4.2 Retaining notation set out in Section 2 and the basic model as in Section 3, consider a scenario where 'K' products are to be constructed from 'N' varieties of cottons. Let resource/product set be characterized as −

K_1− Products which do not use waste at all,
K_2− Products which use waste partially,
K_3− Products which use waste wholly;
Such that $K = K_1 + K_2 + K_3$

And N_1 − Now waste varieties of cottons,
N_2 − Waste varieties of cottons comprising mill generated and purchased from market;
Such that $N = N_1 + N_2$

4.3 It must be ensured that 'N_2' cottons should not be alloted to 'K_1' products and similarly 'N_1' cottons should not be alloted to 'K_3' products. While 'K_2' group of products will pick from 'N_1' and 'N_2' cottons. The dimensions of allotment dynamics are illustrated in Table 1. The model can now be extended. The objective function and the constraining equations remain unchanged, described in section 3. Additional constraining equations brought into the model begin from constraint nos.14 and onwards in the ensuing treatment.

(14) It is necessary to prevent 'V_{N_1+1} ', 'V_{N_1+2}', 'V_{N_1+3} ' ....
.... '$V_{N_1+N_2}$' waste varieties of cottons being alloted to non waste products P_1, P_2, P_3, ... P_{K_1}. These conditions are modelled as −

$X(N_1+1,1) = 0$, $X(N_1+1,2) = 0.........X(N_1+1,K_1) = 0$
$X(N_1+2,2) = 0$, $X(N_1+2,2) = 0.........X(N_1+2,K_1) = 0$
$X(N_1+3,3) = 0$, $X(N_1+3,3) = 0.........X(N_1+3,K_1) = 0$

.
.
.

$X(N_1+N_2,1) = 0$, $X(N_1+N_2,2) = 0........X(N_1+N_2,K_1) = 0$

(15) Similarly it is necessary to prevent 'V_1 ', 'V_2 ', 'V_3 '...
... 'V_{N_1}' non waste varieties of cottons being alloted to products '$P_{K_1+K_2+1}$' ,'$P_{K_1+K_2+2}$', '$P_{K_1+K_2+3}$' .... '$P_{K_1+K_2+K_3}$' constructed entirely from waste products and these conditions are modelled as −

$X(1,L) = 0$, where $L = K_1+K_2+1$, K_1+K_2+2 ..... $K_1+K_2+K_3$
$X(2,L) = 0$, where $L = K_1+K_2+1$, K_1+K_2+2 ..... $K_1+K_2+K_3$
$X(3,L) = 0$, where $L = K_1+K_2+1$, K_1+K_2+2 ..... $K_1+K_2+K_3$

$\bullet$
$\bullet$

$X(N_1,L) = 0$, where $L = K_1+K_2+1$, K_1+K_2+2 ..... $K_1+K_2+K_3$

(16) Additional batch quantity constraints to ensure that products P_{K_1+1}, P_{K_1+2} ..... $P_{K_1+K_2}$ pick up that quantity of regular and waste cotton combination so as not to violate batch quantity requirements of K_2 family of products and is modelled as —

For product P_{K_1+1} : $X(1,K_1+1)+X(2,K_1+1)+X(3,K_1+1)+$ ....
$X(N_1,K_1+1)+X(N_1+1,K_1+1)+X(N_1+2,K_1+1)+$
$X(N_1+3,K_1+1)+......X(N_1+N_2,K_1+1) = 1$
For product P_{K_1+2} : $X(1,K_1+2)+X(2,K_1+2)+X(3,K_1+2)+$ ....
$X(N_1,K_1+2)+X(N_1+1,K_1+2)+X(N_1+2,K_1+2)+$
$X(N_1+3,K_1+2)+......X(N_1+N_2,K_1+2) = 1$

$\bullet$
$\bullet$
$\bullet$

For product $P_{K_1+K_2}$: $X(1,K_1+K_2)+X(2,K_1+K_2)+X(3,K_1+K_2)+......$
$X(N_1,K_1+K_2)+X(N_1+1,K_1+K_2)+X(N_1+2,K_1+K_2)+$
$X(N_1+3,K_1+K_2)+......X(N_1+N_2,K_1+K_2) = 1$

(17)Additional availability constraints to ensure that waste varieties of cotton allocated do not exceed the available quantities and will be modelled as —

For cotton V_{N_1+1} : $X(N_1+1,1)*BQ(1)+X(N_1+1,2)*BQ(2)+$
$X(N_1+1,3)*BQ(3)+...... X(N_1+1,K_1)*BQ(K_1)+$
$X(N_1+1,K_1+1)*BQ(K_1+1)+X(N_1+1,K_1+2)*BQ(K_1+2)+$
$...... X(N_1+1,K_1+K_2)*BQ(K_1+K_2)+$
$X(N_1+1,K_1+K_2+1)*BQ(K_1+K_2+1)+$
$X(N_1+1,K_1+K_2+2)*BQ(K_1+K_2+2)+........$
$X(N_1+1,K_1+K_2+K_3)*BQ(K_1+K_2+K_3) \leqslant AQ(N_1+1)$
For cotton V_{N_1+2} : $X(N_1+2,1)*BQ(1)+X(N_1+2,2)*BQ(2)+$
$X(N_1+2,3)*BQ(3)+..... X(N_1+2,K_1)*BQ(K_1)+$
$X(N_1+2,K_1+1)*BQ(K_1+1)+X(N_1+2,K_1+2)*BQ(K_1+2)+$
$...... X(N_1+2,K_1+K_2)BQ(K_1+K_2)+$
$X(N_1+2,K_1+K_2+1)*BQ(K_1+K_2+1)+$
$X(N_1+2,K_1+K_2+2)*BQ(K_1+K_2+2)+........$
$X(N_1+2,K_1+K_2+K_3)*BQ(K_1+K_2+K_3) \leqslant AQ(N_1+2)$

$\bullet$
$\bullet$
$\bullet$

For cotton $V_{N_1+N_2}$: $X(N_1+N_2,1)*BQ(1)+X(N_1+N_2,2)*BQ(2)+$
$X(N_1+N_2,3)*BQ(3)+...... X(N_1+N_2,K_1)*BQ(K_1)+$
$X(N_1+N_2,K_1+1)*BQ(K_1+1)+X(N_1+N_2,K_1+2)*BQ(K_1+2)+$
$...... X(N_1+N_2,K_1+K_2)*BQ(K_1+K_2)+$
$X(N_1+N_2,K_1+K_2+1)*BQ(K_1+K_2+1)+$
$X(N_1+N_2,K_1+K_2+2)*BQ(K_1+K_2+2)+ ......$
$X(N_1+N_2,K_1+K_2+K_3)*BQ(K_1+K_2+K_3) \leqslant AQ(N_1+N_2)$

(18)Sometimes there is a requirement that members of 'K_2' family use waste cotton uniformily as a definite percentage, say $a_1\%$ of total batch quantity. The requirement could take the shape of an equality or an inequality. Additional constraints to meet these requirements are modelled as —

$$X(N_1+1,K_1+1)+X(N_1+2,K_1+1)+X(N_1+3,K_1+1)+\ldots\ldots\ldots\ldots$$
$$X(N_1+N_2,K_1+1) \lessgtr a_1/100$$
$$X(N_1+1,K_1+2)+X(N_1+2,K_1+2)+X(N_1+3,K_1+3)+\ldots\ldots\ldots\ldots$$
$$X(N_1+N_2,K_1+2) \gtrless a_2/100$$
$$X(N_1+1,K_1+3)+X(N_1+2,K_1+3)+X(N_1+3,K_1+3)+\ldots\ldots\ldots\ldots$$
$$X(N_1+N_2,K_1+3) \gtrless a_3/100$$

.

.

.

$$X(N_1+1,K_1+K_2)+X(N_1+2,K_1+K_2)+X(N_1+3,K_1+K_2)+\ldots\ldots\ldots\ldots$$
$$X(N_1+N_2,K_1+K_2) \lessgtr a_n/100$$

(19)Similarly it is possible to allot different percentage
of waste to different products of 'K' family. Thus it is
possible to prevent any cotton variety – regular or a waste
type – from being alloted to any product whenever a requirement so demands.

4.4 Outputs declared by the LP package for mechanizing the
foregone models will be proportions as against the total quantity
in bales to be constructed, which these models assume as one.
These proportions must be converted into bales outside the LP
package into integer or whole numbers. This can be achieved by
using the algorithm described in Appendix I. The algorithm could
be programmed and run through the computer by plugging it into
rear end of the LP package or used manually. Alternatively recourse may be had to Integer Programming. Conceptually the Integer
Programming (IP)model differs from the LP model as regards the
decision variables. The decision variables used in the IP model
will be interpreted as the 'quantity in bales' of a cotton variety
alloted to a mixing as against the LP model which interpreted it
as 'a proportion of a cotton variety' alloted to the mixing. In
the IP model, the objective function remains unchanged while the
RHS of constraints (1) to (11) will be multiplied by $BQ(J)$, all
batch quantity constraints will also be multiplied by $BQ(J)$ in the
RHS while other constraining equations remain the same. Additional constraint is included to force decision variables to take
integer values only, by setting the condition $X(I,J) = 0,1,2,3 \ldots$
$\ldots$ only for all values of I and J.

5. DETERMINATION OF NORMATIVE/TARGET VALUES FOR A MIX

5.1 Vast empirical data is regularly published covering interrelationships between yarn counts and process parameters as
spindle speeds, twist multiplier (TM), efficiencies, production
per spindle, yarn contraction and other in process issues. Each
mill by the virtue of their experiences and perception, product
range, extent and quality of machinery abstract and maintain data
of interest. Values vary from mill to mill. In spite of variations it is desirable and also possible to have target values which
mills should try to aim at.

5.2 For those who mix and spin must have prior knowledge of end
use and expected strength of yarn. Based upon expected tensile
strength of yarn production per spindle and machine efficiency
could be targeted. These and associated factors enable
selection of TM. For a given count the TM and TPI (turns per inch)
are related as $TPI = TM\sqrt{COUNT}$. TPI is generally specified by

customer or picked up from relevant yarn specifications.
Estimated CSP (count strength product) for the yarn can
be ascertained. The FQIvalue of the mix required for different
counts and levels of CSP of yarn under good or standard working
conditions can be computed by the relation −

$$CSP = (K - COUNT)\sqrt{FQI}$$

where K is a constant, varying from mill to mill taking a value
between 270 to 330. For mills with good working conditions it
can be safely set between 295 and 315. The final figure can be
arrived at for a given mill by regression analysis.

5.3 The problem now reduces to −"obtain initial normative values
of SLMX(J), SLM(J), STHM(J), FINEMX(J), FINEM(J), VRM(J), MCM(J)
FFIMX(J), FFIM(J), TRM(J), for the computed FQI(J) or an FQI
range corresponding to a given count, TM and CSP values". A
mill has to select initial norms by virtue of its past experiences.
Past data for each product/mix must be analysed over a two year
period for eventual selection. Table−2 exhibits a scheme for
analysis of past data.

5.4 Exercise of past two year data reduction will yield initial
norms albeit with qualifications. Values change over time
reflecting insight into processing, changes in process results,
varying resource/product matrix as also through continuous process
of machinery replacement and or degradation. With initial set of
norms, blending by computer can commence and values tuned over time.
Data used by way of illustration in Table−2 is now reduced to
initial norms in Table−3.

5.5 Reference Table−3, all norms except TRMX(J), FFIMX(J) and
FFIM(J) have been initially set. TRMX(J) will have to be
targeted as percentage trash which the mix must not exceed. No
absolute figure can be given and each mill must select a normative
value based upon its experience tempered by its sources of cotton
purchases. This constraint could be included at a later stage
also as cleaned cotton cost is covered by the objective function.
Experience indicates that it is wise to set an FFI limit with a
maximum and a minimum constraint. FFI spread for example in
Table−3 is wide − 8.40 to 54.56, while the average value is 17.00.
It is suggested that the mill first arrive at the minimum
constraint and the maximum value can then be set as +15% to 30%
of the minimum value. As experience is gained and resultant
yarn results analyzed over a period TRMX(J), FFIM(J) and FFIMX(J)
could be finely tuned mix/product wise.

6. MODEL VALIDATION

6.1 Validation phase is a logical succession to model formulation
stage and the most appropriate methodology is to conduct an
controlled experiement with the objective − " assess effectiveness of model in encountering any situation that it might be
expected to handle under real life conditions". It implies
simulation for a definite span of time, and experiment to be
carried out in isolation so that disturbances extraneous to
model do not effect sequence of experiment. Discrete
simulation in a benign environment is indicated.

6.2 Cotton cycle comprises of purchase committment, cotton
arrival, testing and purchase confirmation, decision upon

production schedule and what cottons to be issued to what
products, actual issue, manufacture and testing of yarn
and finally updating cotton stock positions and its systems
dynamics is illustrated in Fig.1. For validation real life
situations is bounded by taking only those events which
immediately precede or succeed model per se as depicted in
Fig.2.

6.3 Of the two validation options open, either use the
computer for mixing decisions in parallel to current mixing
methods or simulate for a selected past period the later
is preferred. Past being a historical fact makes it possible
to compare without prejudice the computer suggested mixings
with the manual ones constructed over the reference period.
Comparison will enable a direct assessment of savings possible.
While parallel simulation is likely to biase subsequent mixings.
Also, in real time experimentation mode an error or unpredictable
model behaviour will lead to a set back. Thus using the later
option the experiment could always be discontinued and restarted
without any serious dislocation.

6.4 A 3 month reference period is suggested and the period used
for the validation/experimentation being reported was 1st April,
1983 - 30th June, 1983. This should be so selected that there
are no drastic changes in cotton procurement - usage practices
and the time for which data is collected and experiment designed.
A system is devised to collect and organize data for experimentation and the resultant data organization achieved in various
files is described in Table-4. The mechanics of experimentation
follow.

6.5 Run for 1st April, 1983

(1) Set cotton (resource) availability:
To FILE#2 add records for 1-4-1983 from FILE#3. When adding
to or subtracting from a file, lots having the same lot
identifiers can be added or subtracted otherwise not, in
which case a new record results. This will yield complete
resource availability for 1st April, 1983. It is suggested
to make use of FILE#6 for such records.

(2) Set production requirement :
Extract from FILE#1 the product/mixing sought to be made
for 1st April, 1983.

(3) Set product/cotton matrix :
Using FILE#6 and production requirements set up product/
cotton matrix as shown in Table-1.

(4) Set up objective function and constraining equations:
The objective function can be set up using product/cotton
matrix and the constraining equations using the matrix and
norms from FILE#4 as applicable. Set up constraints for
forbidden allotments.

(5) Feed equations set to LP package, execute and store
results.
Execute model and obtain solution for all mixings. Convert
model outputs into integer bales using algorithm at
Appendix-I if LP package is used. If IP is used the results
will be in integer bales. Store results in appropriate
result file mentioned in Table-5.

270

6.6 Runs for balance reference period (2-4-1983 -30-6-1983)

(1) Set cotton (resource) availability :
From FILE#6 subtract corresponding bales of cotton chosen
by the previous day's selection using appropriate result
file and comming up with the cotton availability set as on
the previous date. From FILE#3 add or introduce cotton
records for that day.

(2)Step (2) through Step (5) are executed in the same way
as outlined in 6.5 above.

6.7 The computer suggested mixing must now be validated which
implies checking the truth of the result. The result is true
if suggested mixing is spinnable for the product and mixing
desired yield good working. Confirmation of a mixing's spinnabili-
ty must be on questionnaire basis with an expert panel of judges
as respondents, and importantly the questionaire should not force
the decision maker with a Yes/No choice. Recommendations of
experts for the same mixing will be resolved and one common value
judgement arrived at and progressively entered in RESULT FILE#7.

6.8 At the conclusion of the experiment statistical testing of
results is done to gain confidence of model and that of the
users. Two hypothesis are framed —

(i) Computer does not give valid and adequate spinnable
blends,

(ii) Computer suggested mixing are more costly than
manually declared mixings.

Using Chi squared or F-test the above hypothesis could be negated
using RESULT FILE#6, RESULT FILE#7, RESULT FILE#9 and DATA FILE#5.
The results could be further analyzed to obtain ratios like :
percentage of computer suggested mixings falling in the Gaussian
distribution, percentage of adequate mixings to poor/rich as
perceived by panel and number of mixings deemed to be spinnable
to total number of mixings declared.

7. DEVELOPMENT AND IMPLEMENTATION OF COTTON BLENDING PACKAGE
AND IMPLICATIONS THEREOF

7.1 Once the basic LP model has been validated and found to work
satisfactorily it can be implemented. Normally real life, large
OR models are installed and run on computers. It must be ensured
that the output of the model, in whatever form they are used must
be fed back to the computer. This implies that, feed back
mechanism be devised and implemented for regular use. Requirements
and availability change from period to period. This calls for
regular administration of the model. Efficient administration
is dependant on information about the way the model output are
being used. It includes follow up of model outputs, ensuring
feedback of information concerning events taking place, overseeing
that all desired inputs flow to the computer in time with
requisite accuracy. It also includes human intervention with the
model behaviour as and when necessary. For example one or
more of the mixings declared by the LP model may be used by the
decision maker with some modification. Thus the actual drawl
of cotton must be fed back to the computerised blending package
to update cotton availability file to correctly reflect real
stock position.

7.2 LP models when implemented on the computer use the concerned software package that can be run on the available computer. The software package will have its own format for input data as well as output reports. Often these formats are rigid, though comprehensive to account for very large varieties of situations the package is likely to encounter. While using these generalized models, often interface programs have to be devised which will take data in the form it is being used in the company and convert it to the form acceptable by the input file of the model. Similarly new or revised outputs may be desired in the formats the company is used to.

7.3 No OR model can run on its own steam for long. It must keep evolving, firstly towards producing more accurate results close to real life situations and lastly to account for new realities resulting from the ever changing and dynamic environment it tries to describe and bound. In the industrial world a real life situation is portrayed by a mathematical model by establishing interrelationships between entities which are primarily endogenous. However, some entities/variable viewed by a decision maker as endogenous may force a model builder to treat them as exogenous with little or no effect upon the decision surface or rules and providing excellent decision support. Interestingly some endogenous variables may change over time due to variety of reasons. Thus model behaviour must be monitored and recorded to facilitate future changes.

7.4 From the utilisation point of view and increasing the productivity of the model the by-products must be looked upon as desirable and the outcome of committing additional marginal computing resources. Cleverly used they will provide closer control over the cotton cycle. Cotton cost forms the single largest component - 50% to 60% of total cost of yarn, thus even a small saving or increased productivity means a compensating increase in the gross profits of mill in absolute terms. Also at the other end is the requirement of the decision maker for more information using the same data base as that of the model for enhancing decision quality. When there are more than one model user the information requirements of both the primary and secondary users should be satisfied as far as possible.

7.5 In light of the above considerations the cotton Blending Package when implemented has a number of programs enveloping the basic LP model. These programs are arranged in layers one upon the other, are interconnected with the flexibility of individual execution or continuous execution in sequence. In the Cotton Blending Package developed the core or the kernel is a manufacturer supplied LP package with a number of programs around it. Structurally the package is composed of three parts, viz.-

    (a) top of LP model or front end
    (b) LP model
    (c) bottom of LP model or rear end.

Each part further includes programs for data input and validation, data movement, master file updating, maintenance and routine compacting, input file creation and maintenance, output/report file generation and program to link the rear end to the front end for movement of selected data.

7.6 At the current level of package design following constituents are being used —

$\sum_{i=1}^{6} D$	Source documents	(1) purchase document,(2) cotton received documents, (3) cotton issue document, (4)cotton test report,(5)yarn test report and (6)production schedule.
$\sum_{i=1}^{6} M$	Master Files	(1)processing norms master,(2)purchase contract master,(3)receipts and issues master,(4)mixings suggested master, (5)mixings used master &(6)cotton history master
$\sum_{i=1}^{2} I$	Input Files to LP Model	(1) production schedule file &(2)cotton properties file and cost data
$\sum_{i=1}^{3} O$	Output files from LP Model	(1) Basic LP model outputs,(2)extended model outputs &(3) sensitivity analysis and shadow prices output.
$\sum_{i=1}^{n} R$	Reports	prepared by Cotton Blending Package (hard copy available selectively on request)

Master files can be interrogated using interactive querry language. A more elaborate description covering the intricacy of design and the results obtained as also the computing resources employed forms the theme of another paper under preparation.

8.CONCLUSION

8.1 The mill is situated in a cotton region and procures cotton from over 100 different stations. Waste generated during process-ing is collected and purchase of waste cotton is also resorted to ensuring that adequate waste cottons are always in stock. All cottons — regular or waste are tested and a test report issued lot wise. The experiment to validate model was conducted on an B-1955 Burroughs mainframe computer working under operating system MCP I & MCP II with a 512 KB primary memory, 200 MB mass disk storage using manufacturer supplied data sensitive LP package called TEMPO. The extended model was selected.

8.2 Average number of products/mixings per day was 10, the maximum number of cottons (regular and waste) was 240 the average being 200 with the waste cottons within 40 varieties. The largest initial matrix extended to a size of 1100 columns and 900 rows. To handle a matrix of this size the LP package must possess the capability of virtual arraymanipulation. It took on the average two trained programmers 3 to 5 hours to set up and input data on discrete basis for each day's run. Execution took between 20 and 30 minutes of CPU in a multi programming, multitasking mode in a time sharing environment. By including maximum and minimum staple length and fineness norms the first iteration results in a reduced matrix which speeds up next series of iterations. Initial runs validated the model indicating savings in excess of 7%. For the complete Cotton Blending Package an algorithm was designed and implemented to deliberately prevent certain cottons from being considered for particular products based upon technical considerations. This resulted in introducing a large number, upto 30% of zero elements in the initial matrix. Such a matrix can be installed on smaller computers and reducing execution time. By integerating model into purchasing and stock control functions further economies can be expected.

8.3 Further analysis of results collected in result files could be made for ascertaining impact upon inventory holding, inventory turnover ratio, capital blocked and opportunity cost, issues of quality, thumb rules for purchasing etc. These could gradually be developed into a high reliability on-line early warning systems. After the experiment is found to be significantly successful model can be implemented and results carefully monitored to achieve the above desirable features. Different mills are likely to come up with different implementation strategies with different systems and procedures.

8.4 Once the front and rear end for the package are developed and integerated into the LP package it is possible to build up a very comprehensive data base on cotton cycle in general with emphasis on cotton blending. Also, programs should be developed so that addition to or subtraction from availability files is done incrementally day to day automatically to drastically cut down time spent on data input. Intelligent use of data base will enable improved quality of decisions, higher yarn realisation, deterministic purchase, tighter inventory control, realistic production economies and thereby provide information a tap and thus go a long way in introducing flexibility in the firms operations to react in a superior fashion to changing market forces. Potential for realizing all round improvement in terms of savings and increased productivities connected with the cotton cycle are phenomenally high.

ACKNOWLEDGEMENTS

The author gratefully acknowledges the encouragement and support of Mr.D.J.Madan, Managing Director and Vice Chairman of Gokak Patel Volkart Ltd. and Mr. D.E.A.Paul the Mills General Manager.

The author also acknowledges the active association and assistance of System analyst and programmers Mr. P.K.Philip and Mr.Rengarajan. Thanks are also due to Mr. M.R.S.Gupta for providing laboratory test data and to Dr. Dilip Das for the use of computing resources.

REFERENCES

(1) J.E. Booth. 'Principles of Textile Testing', Butterworth group, London, Fourth édition.

(2) T.V.Ratnam and R.Rajamanickam. 'Norms for Productivity in Spinning', South India Textile Research Association, Coimbatore, Sept.1978.

(3) A.R.Garde and T.A.Subramanian. ' Process Control in Cotton Spinning', Ahmedabad Textile Industries Research Association, Ahmedabad, 2nd edition, 1978, P16.

(4) F.F.Martin. ' Computer Modelling and Simulation ', John Willey and Sons, New York, 1968.

(5) K.Bhaskar, P.Pope and R.Morris. 'Financial Modelling with Computers', Economist, April 1982 (EIU Special Report No.120), P 62.

(6) A.Kaufmann. 'Methods and Models of Operations Research', Prentice Hall, New York, 1963.

(7) A. Schenek. 'Methods for Estimating Short Fibre of Cotton', Melliand Textilberichte – International Textile Reports, Volume II, Nos.8, August, 1982.

(8) G.D.Chitnis and C.V.Modi. 'Computer Application in Textiles', The Indian Textile Journal, Oct.1982, P.79.

(9) K.N.Krishnaswamy. 'Systematic Formulation of Cotton Mixing', The Indian Textile Journal, Oct.1982, P.91.

(10) D.Hsiao and F.Harary, 'A Formal System for Information Retrieval from Files', Communication of the ACM, Volume 13, Number 2 (February, 1970), P 67.

(11) D.Hsiao and N.S.Prywes. 'A System to Manage an Information System', Proceedings of the IFIP Joint Conference on Mechanized Information Storage and Retrieval, Rome, 1967, P 637.

(12) D.L.Caldwell. 'Managing Information Resources', Information and Records Management, April 1980, P 14.

Manager (EDP)
Gokak Mills, Gokak Falls,
Dist. Belgaum. Pin. 591 308.
INDIA.

APPENDIX I

ALGORITHM FOR CONVERSION OF NON INTEGER BALES TO INTEGER BALES

STEP 1: Add all fractional parts to obtain a whole number as 1,2,3

STEP 2: Sort the quantities (Q_i) in ascending order of cost/bale ignoring fractional or non integer part.

STEP 3: Starting from the first cotton in the series, take as many cottons as the whole number in STEP 1, and add 1 to these selected cotton quantities making an upward shift.

Example	Q_i	Bale quantity	Cost/Bale (Rs.)
	Q_1	1.3	2,200
	Q_2	2.8	1,900
	Q_3	1.9	1,975
Step 1	.3 + .8 + .9 = 2		
Step 2	Form series in ascending order as –		
	Q_i	Bale Quantity	Cost/Bale
	Q_2	2	1,900
	Q_3	1	1,975
	Q_1	1	2,200
Step 3	Make upward shift		
	Q_2	3	1,900
	Q_3	2	1,975
	Q_1	1	2,200

STEP 4: Construct a mix with this series of cottons obtained in STEP 3. Check if the mix now satisfies all the constraints imposed by norms. If yes, then take this as the solution otherwise get into STEP 5.

STEP 5: Revert all cottons whose quantities were stepped up back to their original whole numbers. Now beginning with the second cotton in the series taking as many as the whole number obtained in STEP 1 and add 1 to these selected cotton quantities.

Example Suppose the above situation did not satisfy the constraint, then applying STEP 5 would yield a situation as –

Q_i	Bale quantity	Cost/Bale
Q_2	2	1,900
Q_3	2	1,975
Q_1	2	2,000

STEP 6: Again construct a mix as outlined in STEP 5 and check if constraints imposed by norms are satisfied or not. If yes, then the solution is as now constructed otherwise get into STEP 7, as under.

STEP 7: As in STEP 5, now begin upward shift from third cotton and construct series. If constraints are satisfied then take this as the mix solution, otherwise make upward shift beginning from the fourth cotton series and check. Keep doing recursively till the solution is obtained.

Real life situation indicate that 95% of the time satisfactory mix is achieved within 2 upward shift.

276

TABLE-1 DIMENSIONS OF ALLOTMENT DYNAMIC

I \ J (Jth PRODUCT →)		1	2	3	---	K_1	K_1+1	K_1+2	---	K_1+K_2	K_1+K_2+1	K_1+K_2+2	---	$K=K_1+K_2+K_3$
Ith COTTON		P_1	P_2	P_3		P_{K_1}	P_{K_1+1}	P_{K_1+2}		$P_{K_1+K_2}$	$P_{K_1+K_2+1}$	$P_{K_1+K_2+2}$		$P_{K_1+K_2+K_3}$
1	V_1	$X(1,1)$	$X(1,2)$	$X(1,3)$		$X(1,K_1)$	$X(1,K_1+1)$	$X(1,K_1+2)$		$X(1,K_1+K_2)$	$X(1,K_1+K_2+1)$	$X(1,K_1+K_2+2)$		$X(1,K_1+K_2+K_3)$
2	V_2	$X(2,1)$	$X(2,2)$	$X(2,3)$		$X(2,K_1)$	$X(2,K_1+1)$	$X(2,K_1+2)$		$X(2,K_1+K_2)$	$X(2,K_1+K_2+1)$	$X(2,K_1+K_2+2)$		$X(2,K_1+K_2+K_3)$
3	V_3	$X(3,1)$	$X(3,2)$	$X(3,3)$		$X(3,K_1)$	$X(3,K_1+1)$	$X(3,K_1+2)$		$X(3,K_1+K_2)$	$X(3,K_1+K_2+1)$	$X(3,K_1+K_2+2)$		$X(3,K_1+K_2+K_3)$
4	V_4	$X(4,1)$	$X(4,2)$	$X(4,3)$		$X(4,K_1)$	$X(4,K_1+1)$	$X(4,K_1+2)$		$X(4,K_1+K_2)$	$X(4,K_1+K_2+1)$	$X(4,K_1+K_2+2)$		$X(4,K_1+K_2+K_3)$
5	V_5	$X(5,1)$	$X(5,2)$	$X(5,3)$		$X(5,K_1)$	$X(5,K_1+1)$	$X(5,K_1+2)$		$X(5,K_1+K_2)$	$X(5,K_1+K_2+1)$	$X(5,K_1+K_2+2)$		$X(5,K_1+K_2+K_3)$

N_1	V_{N_1}	$X(N_1,1)$	$X(N_1,2)$	$X(N_1,3)$		$X(N_1,K_1)$	$X(N_1,K_1+1)$	$X(N_1,K_1+2)$		$X(N_1,K_1+K_2)$	$X(N_1,K_1+K_2+1)$	$X(N_1,K_1+K_2+2)$		$X(N_1,K_1+K_2+K_3)$
N_1+1	V_{N_1+1}	$X(N_1+1,1)$	$X(N_1+1,2)$	$X(N_1+1,3)$		$X(N_1+1,K_1)$	$X(N_1+1,K_1+1)$	$X(N_1+1,K_1+2)$		$X(N_1+1,K_1+K_2)$	$X(N_1+1,K_1+K_2+1)$	$X(N_1+1,K_1+K_2+2)$		$X(N_1+1,K_1+K_2+K_3)$
N_1+2	V_{N_1+2}	$X(N_1+2,1)$	$X(N_1+2,2)$	$X(N_1+2,3)$		$X(N_1+2,K_1)$	$X(N_1+2,K_1+1)$	$X(N_1+2,K_1+2)$		$X(N_1+2,K_1+K_2)$	$X(N_1+2,K_1+K_2+1)$	$X(N_1+2,K_1+K_2+2)$		$X(N_1+2,K_1+K_2+K_3)$
N_1+3	V_{N_1+3}	$X(N_1+3,1)$	$X(N_1+3,2)$	$X(N_1+3,3)$		$X(N_1+3,K_1)$	$X(N_1+3,K_1+1)$	$X(N_1+3,K_1+2)$		$X(N_1+3,K_1+K_2)$	$X(N_1+3,K_1+K_2+1)$	$X(N_1+3,K_1+K_2+2)$		$X(N_1+3,K_1+K_2+K_3)$
N_1+4	V_{N_1+4}	$X(N_1+4,1)$	$X(N_1+4,2)$	$X(N_1+4,3)$		$X(N_1+4,K_1)$	$X(N_1+4,K_1+1)$	$X(N_1+4,K_1+2)$		$X(N_1+4,K_1+K_2)$	$X(N_1+4,K_1+K_2+1)$	$X(N_1+4,K_1+K_2+2)$		$X(N_1+4,K_1+K_2+K_3)$

$N=N_1+N_2$	$V_{N_1+N_2}$	$X(N_1+N_2,1)$	$X(N_1+N_2,2)$	$X(N_1+N_2,3)$		$X(N_1+N_2,K_1)$	$X(N_1+N_2,K_1+1)$	$X(N_1+N_2,K_1+2)$		$X(N_1+N_2,K_1+K_2)$	$X(N_1+N_2,K_1+K_2+1)$	$X(N_1+N_2,K_1+K_2+2)$		$X(N_1+N_2,K_1+K_2+K_3)$

FORBIDDEN ALLOTMENT

COUNT-X SPINDLE SPEED -1200 rpm CSP-Y TWIST MULTIPLIER-Z
MACHINE EFFICIENCY -90%   PRODUCTION PER SPINDLE PER 8 HOUR SHIFT - 180 gms

MIXING NUMBER / STATISTICAL MEASURE	SL in inches			STH in gm/tex			UR as percentage			MC as a number			FFI as a percentage			FINE in micronaire			No of coteins in min	FQI
	MAX.	MIN.	DIFF.	MAX.	MIN.	DIFF.	MAX.	MIN.	DIFF.	MAX.	MIN.	DIFF.	MAX.	MIN.	DIFF.	MAX.	MIN.	DIFF.		
- - - - -	1.052	0.948	0.104	21.08	17.06	4.02	49.96	47.47	2.49	.74	.66	0.08	21.19	12.77	8.46	4.91	3.69	1.02	6	39.43
- - - - -	1.064	0.950	0.114	22.54	17.50	5.04	49.05	46.65	2.86	.76	.70	0.06	19.22	13.08	6.14	4.82	4.04	0.78	6	42.84
- - - - -	1.048	0.941	0.107	23.95	16.66	7.29	48.89	47.67	1.28	.75	.71	0.04	18.71	8.44	10.29	4.93	4.02	0.91	9	40.09
- - - - -	1.073	0.978	0.095	23.95	17.54	6.41	49.29	47.95	1.34	.77	.70	0.07	27.99	15.19	12.60	4.93	4.04	0.89	11	43.78
- - - - -	1.044	0.894	0.150	24.36	13.27	11.08	52.13	45.48	6.65	.83	.56	0.27	49.76	18.73	31.03	5.69	2.90	2.79	4	39.22
- - - - -	1.031	0.911	0.120	25.19	18.68	6.51	53.78	47.95	5.83	.83	.74	0.09	21.17	12.71	8.46	5.74	4.28	1.46	5	39.49
- - - - -	1.004	0.948	0.056	22.00	20.84	1.16	50.84	49.00	1.84	.77	.73	0.04	19.22	12.81	6.44	5.02	4.81	0.21	6	39.03
- - - - -	0.966	0.947	0.019	21.96	16.59	5.37	48.83	43.45	3.38	.81	.64	0.17	21.19	12.66	8.53	5.61	3.72	1.89	7	36.97
- - - - -	0.968	0.918	0.050	20.89	20.10	0.79	54.45	50.28	4.17	.82	.73	0.09	18.71	12.71	6.00	4.66	4.27	0.39	7	37.45
- - - - -	0.966	0.830	0.036	21.96	17.67	4.29	52.83	48.69	3.14	.82	.64	0.18	22.28	13.24	9.04	5.72	3.72	1.89	5	36.07
MEAN VALUES	0.951	0.900	0.051	22.376	17.033	5.54	51.86	47.35	4.51	.795	.675	0.120	24.32	12.67	11.65	5.24	4.06	1.18		37.61
MODAL VALUES	0.960	0.895		23.000	16.850		52.50	46.55		.800	.655		21.50	12.30		5.25	4.05			39.00
AVERAGE = (MAX+MIN)/2	0.9255			19.775			49.605			0.7275			18.500			4.650				
SPREAD	.834 to 1.075			13.500 to 24.625			44.460 to 65.000			0.500 to 0.830			8.400 to 51.360			3.650 to 5.740			4 to 11	34.75 to 44.26

TABLE-2 ANALYSIS AND REDUCTION OF PAST TWO YEAR DATA

TABLE-3 DEVELOPING INITIAL NORMS/TARGETS

VARIABLE	DATA SPREAD	INITIAL NORM	CONSIDERATION	TUNNING
SLM(J) & SLMX(J)	.83 to 1.078 with modal value .988 & .90; mean values .906 & .885 & SLMX(J) and average value .9825.	SLM(J)=.980 & SLMX(J) =+.20%	Alternatively SLM(J) & SLMX(J) could be set as +.20% of average value.	Based upon experience and yarn tests, norms could be further tuned. A stabilized value is not expected to change for long periods.
FNEMX(J) & FNEM(J)	3.640 to 5.860 with modal values 4.08 & 5.28; mean values 4.484 & 5.62 and average value 4.650.	FNEMX(J) =5.25 FNEM(J) =4.05	Process route, machinery condition, desired spindle speed will modify norm.	Based upon experience and yarn testing, value could be tuned for a set of stabilized values for different values of FRT. Preferable to have a set of values than a single Valued norm and use as per requirement.
URM(J)	44.450 to 55.000 with modal values 46.55 & 53.50; mean values 47.45 & 51.85 and average value 49.605.	47.00	Alternatively an initial value of 49.605 may be set.	As experience is gained a stabilized value could be arrived at. A stabilized norm is not expected to change for long periods.
MCM(J)	.500 to .810 with modal value .698 .655 & .800; mean values .698 & .795 and average value .7295.	.655	Seasonal and agricultural conditions determine the raw values of cottons entering market.	Based upon experience and yarn test results for specific requirements a range of values under different conditions could be arrived at. Values once established may remain stable for under periods.
STHM(J)	13.590 to 20.860 with modal values 16.00 & 23.00; mean values 17.03 & 23.575 and average value 19.775.	20.00	This value could be chosen for sum of A's will many featuring. Value is based upon mills perception of quality.	Norms will change as for customer/market requirements.
FQI(J)	26.75 to 44.25 with modal value 39.00 and mean value.	38.00	Any value between 36.00 & 42.00 could be set, depend-ing upon mills perception of product desirability and characteristics. So could be chosen for but manufacturing & marut to suit specific requirements.	For but manu featuring over acceptable value is chosen to further tuning may be required to ensure consistant quality. Suggested FQI longer vis-a-vis products to arrived at.
FFI	8.60 to 19.860 with modal values 10.60 & 21.90; mean values 12.05 & 19.45 and average value 15.900.	See Section 8.5	See Section 8.5	

DATA FILE #	FILE NAME	FILE REQUIREMENTS	FIELDS/CONTENTS
FILE #1	PRODUCTION SCHEDULE	List products/mixings made over 2f frames period. One date multiple records. Key - date, product/mixing nos.	Date, mixing/product Identifier, B@(x), waste usage qualifications, staple fibre usage qualifications.
FILE #2	COTTON STOCK POSITION AS ON 31st MARCH, 1983	List all cottons - regular, waste (purchased or collected) along with proportion and connected data as on error of 31st March, 1983	Original nos. of Bales, Cost/Bale, ?R(x), Lot Identifier Variety Name, A@(x), SL(x), UA(x), STN(x), FINE(x), 4/FINE(x), MC(x), FF(x), F@1(x), cleaned cotton cost per bale.
FILE #3	DAILY ADDITIONS TO USEABLE STOCK	List all cottons on daily basis (date on which it can enter reserve stock) depending upon mill stocking and issuing policies. One daily multiple records. Key - date, Lot No.	Date, cost/bale, cleaned cotton cost for Bale, ?R(x), Lot Identifier, Variety Name, A@(x), SL(x), UA(x), STN(x), FINE(x), 4/FINE(x), MC(x), FF1(x), F@1.
FILE #4	NORMS & TARGETS	List norms decided for each product/mixings for experiment after analysis of past data. Key - Product/mixing name	Product/mixing name, F@1N(x), SLMX(x), SLN(x), STNN(x), FINEM(x), FINEMX(x), MCM(x), UAMC(x), FF1M(x), FF1MX(x), TRMX(x).
FILE #5	DAILY ISSUES FILE	List actual constituent Cottons issued date wise for FRAMES over reporting period. For one date, multiple records. Key - date, Product/mixing nos.	Date, product/mixing name, total nos. of bales, total cost; various cotton varieties going into mix, bales issued of each, cost/bale of each, mixings for which they were prepared, its lot no. (identifier).
FILE #6	COTTON AVAILABILITIES FILE	Constructed. List actual cottons (regular and waste) available for each duration day. For one date, multiple records. Key - date, Lot No.	Bale, Cotton variety, Lot Identifier, cleaned cotton cost for Bale, A@(x), SL(x), UA(x), STN(x), 4/FINE(x), MC(x), FF1(x), SF(x), F@1(x).

TABLE-4   ORGANIZATION OF DATA FOR EXPERIMENT

280

RESULT FILE#	FILE NAME	FILE PURPOSE	FIELDS/CONTENTS
FILE # 6A	DATEWISE SIMULATION HISTORY FILE	Contains computer declared mixings for product/mix list on daily basis over reference period. For each date multiple mixing records. For each mixing record multiple bottom records. Key - date, product/mixing name, lot no.	Date, product/mixing name, total cost of blend, cotton variety for each variety, Lot identifier, nos. of bales, cost/bale, $SL(CD)$, $UR(CD)$, $STR(CD)$, $FBRR(CD)$, $UI(CD)$, $MIC(CD)$, $FFI(CD)$, $FEI(CD)$.
FILE # 7	VALIDATION OF COMPUTER SUGGESTED MIXING	Prepared after receipt of questionnaire from members of expert panel; opinions resolved and single judgement arrived at. Key - Date, Product/mixing name.	Date, product/mixing name and against each Expert Reference, Recommendation, Experts qualification (if any), Interpreted Judgement.
FILE # 8	DAILY COMPARISON FILE	Brings out all essential data to enable essential properties/technical comparison of computer suggested mix constituents with actual mix constructed and effect. Key - Date, product/mixing name.	Date, Product/mixing name, desired (CSP, FQI), Expert Recommendation for each product; Computer suggested mixing (Variety used for each variety - nos. of bales, cost/bale, $SL(CD)$, $STR(CD)$, $FEI(CD)$ $FEI(CD)$); Actual mixing used (variety and each variety - nos. of bales, cost/bale, $SL(CD)$, $STR(CD)$ $FEI(CD)$, mixing formulated for); Total mixing cost in each case.
FILE # 9	CUMULATIVE COMPARISON FILE	Extension of above to bring out cost comparisons and compute absolute savings on daily and cumulative basis over reference period Key - Date, product/mixing name.	Date, Product/mixing name, and for each product; Computer suggested mixing (edg's cost, cumulative cost); Actual mixing used (edg's cost, cumulative cost); Cost difference Calculy ($+/-$), Cumulative ($+/-$).

TABLE-5. ARRANGEMENT OF RESULT FILES AFTER SIMULATION

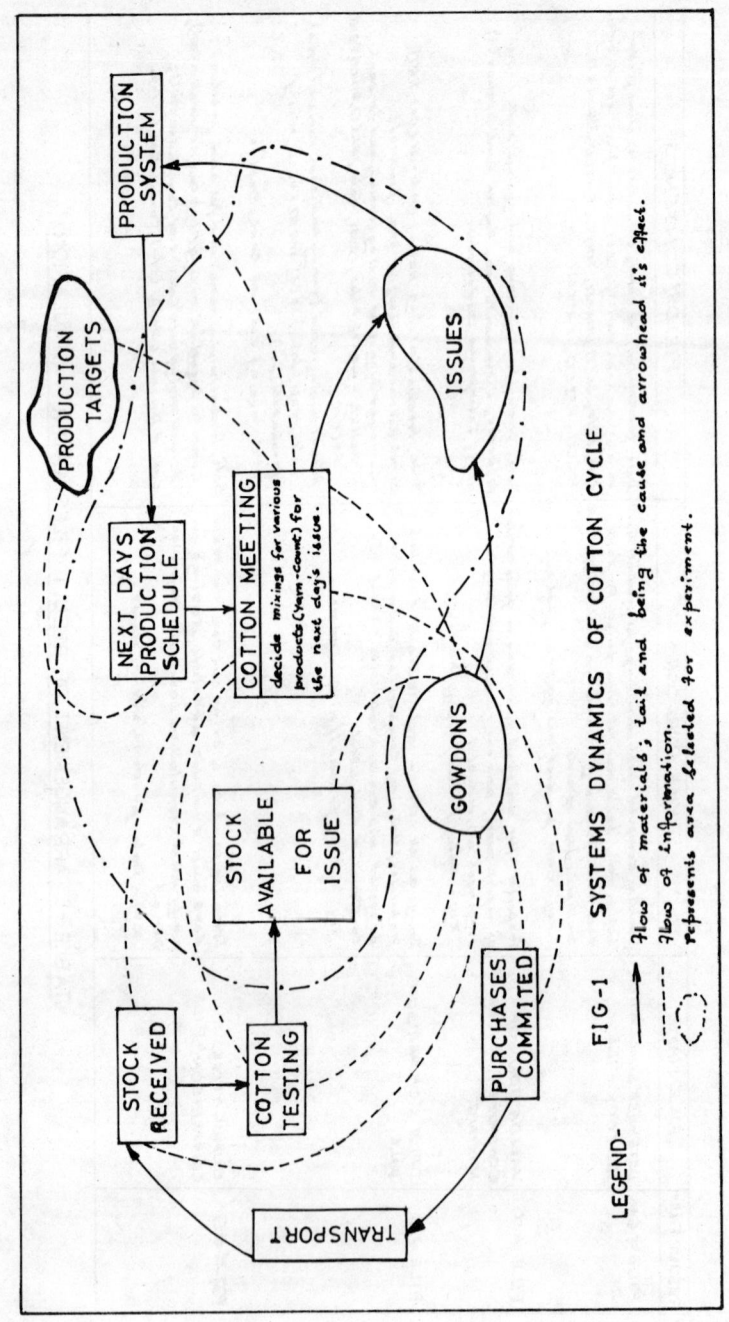

FIG-1   SYSTEMS DYNAMICS OF COTTON CYCLE

LEGEND-

→ Flow of materials; tail end being the cause and arrowhead it's effect.

--- Flow of information.

⟨⟩ Represents area selected for experiment.

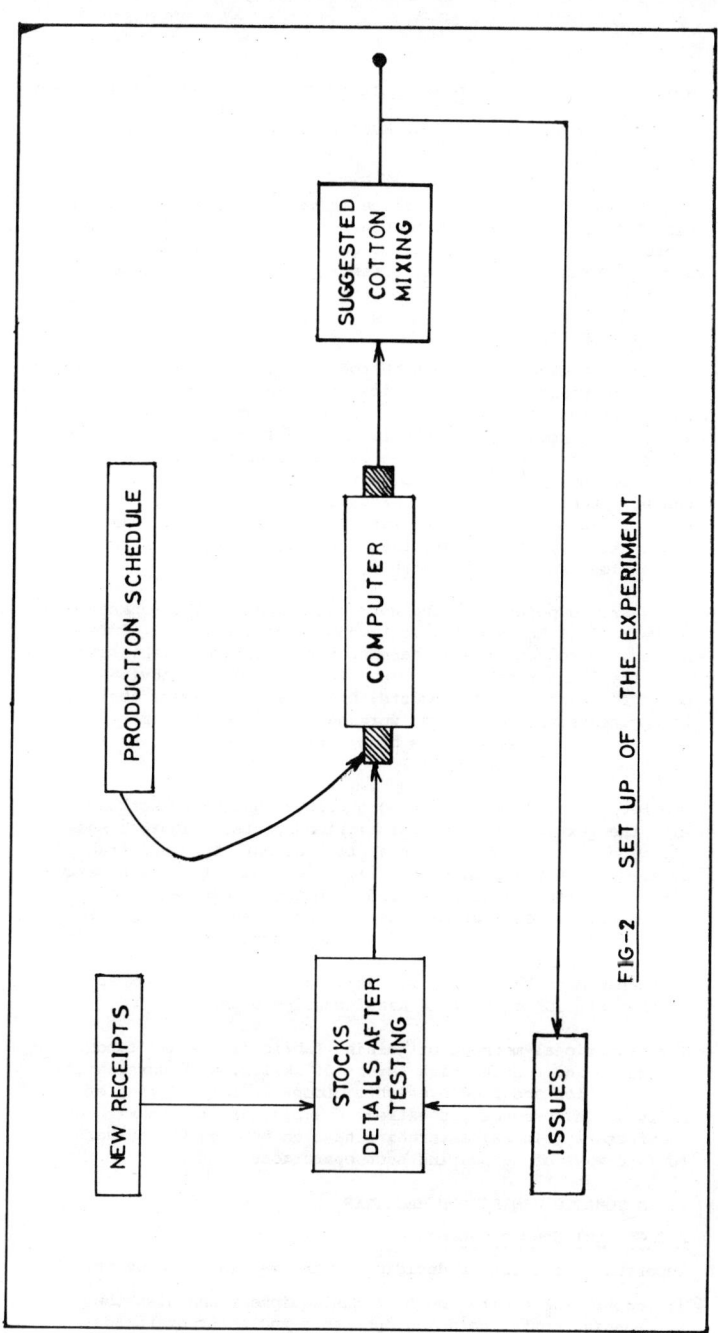

FIG-2 SET UP OF THE EXPERIMENT

COMPUTER CONTROLLED MACHINERY FOR GARMENT MANUFACTURE

R. Vitols, G.R. Wray, B.J.M. Murphy, J.E. Baker and T.G. King

ABSTRACT

This paper includes a comparison of various methods for achieving automatic control of machines, a discussion of alternative
approaches to the automation of garment making-up operations
and a description of two different applications of computer
control.

1. INTRODUCTION

Clothes are made to be worn in todays comfort seeking society.
It is important that the fabrics they are made from retain
their flexibility during and after making-up. Progress on
automatic garment assembly will be very limited, unless methods
can be found to take advantage of the pliable properties of
textiles, so that edges of different lengths and curvatures
can be matched, in order to produce complex three-dimensional
shapes. Such making-up systems will only be useful commercially if they can perform these functions within an acceptable time and for a favourable cost.

The starting point, for the work undertaken in the Department
of Mechanical Engineering at Loughborough University of Technology, is to accept that garment materials are pliable and
that they must remain that way. This may seem an obvious
point to Textile Technologists, but it is not always obvious
to engineers who are used to working with more rigid materials.
"Fabric rigidification" has been seriously suggested as an
aid to garment assembly [1].

The Mechanical Engineers at Loughborough have been working
with the Textile Industry for eighteen years. Figure 1 shows
the wide range of textile projects that have been undertaken
by members of the Department [2]; they range from yarn texturing to garment inspection, and from the investigation of
individual elements of machines to the invention and development of complete processes (e.g. the 'Locstitch' pile fabric
machine [3,4] and developments arising from it [5]). Therefore,
the Department has a very realistic and practical approach
to the solution of textile manufacturing problems.

The traditional methods of joining fabric pieces are labour
intensive and require high levels of skills, with unrelenting
concentration and good eyesight. Loop-for-loop linking of
knitwear is, perhaps, an extreme example, and knitwear
manufacturers in Leicestershire have encouraged the authors
to find ways of automating such operations.

2. AUTOMATIC CONTROL OF MACHINES

2.1 General Considerations

Important criteria for deciding on any machine concept are:

i)   cost: the capital cost of the equipment and also the
     running cost, including operators and their overheads;

  ii) flexibility: the ability to accept variations in
        workpieces;
 iii) speed: the overall output of the system, and
  iv) availability: whether the necessary techniques and
        equipment have reached a suitable stage of development.

Figure 2 is a qualitative indication of how the various ways
of achieving automatic control of machines compare when
related to the above criteria.

2.1.1 Rigid sequence

Such a system may be controlled by cams or limit switches;
the changes required to alter the sequencing will often
involve skilled fitters and may keep the machine off the
production line for long periods. Therefore, the system
rates badly for flexibility. On the other hand, it is likely
to be relatively fast as well as being cheap to buy and run,
because it involves well understood technology. These very
important advantages tend to get lost in the move away from
rigid automation. The fact that manufacturers are prepared
to accept this loss, shows how important flexibility is to
them.

2.1.2 Preset sequence

The use of controllers of various kinds can permit changes to
be made in a very much shorter time than in a rigid mechanical system. This will improve the flexibility considerably,
but the cost and speed will be affected adversely, depending
on the extent to which special motor-driven movements or
adjustments are used in place of preset cams and switches.

2.1.3 Operator/machine interaction

Typical examples are computer controlled patterning on a
knitting machine and nesting of shapes for cutting. The
cost is high and the speed is low for on-line operation.
Once the sequence has been established and the operator is
satisfied, it may be possible to switch over to 'preset
sequence' operation; this combined approach increases the
speed of operation but the extra hardware for interacting
with the operator is not fully utilised.

2.1.4 Intelligent systems

Computers can be given sufficient knowledge to make decisions.
If this knowledge can be kept simple and specific, even small
computers can make decisions fast enough to control machines
during their operation. Hence a different range of flexibility is possible, such as the ability to respond to detailed
differences in workpieces as well as to overall style changes.
The speed and cost are likely to be comparable with the previously mentioned systems and the technology can be developed
with existing hardware.

2.1.5 Expert systems

This heading is used to cover the range of computer developments which will increase the flexibility of machine control
in the future (6,7); at present, though, they are either
too costly or too slow and are not readily available
as attractive possibilities for immediate use in garment manufacture.

2.2   Application to Knitwear

The above systems are valuable, separately or in combination,
but the old adage 'norses for courses' must be applied in
order to achieve an optimum solution to a particular problem.
For example, different approaches will be used for automatic
linking according to whether the loops can be kept under control by transferring them to a carrier, or the loops have
to be located by some means before they can be operated on.
It is preferable to retain control of the loops, if possible
(Once you have found them never let them go!). This approach
was used by the Loughborough team when they developed machines
for running-on ribs for the fully-fashioned knitting process.

3.   LOUGHBOROUGH 'ART' MACHINE

Automatic Rib Transfer (ART) machines are available from
various machinery manufacturers. The basic V-bed principle
is used for making the ribs and each trim is automatically
transferred from the knitting elements to a magazine bar,
instead of sequential trims being joined to each other.
These systems are only available as complete, integral
machines.

The terms of reference for the work which led to the Loughborough ART machine were that it should be a 'bolt on'
attachment which would operate with any V-bed knitting
machine (8).   The design was applied originally to a Dubied
DRC-2 V-bed machine to allow the knitting and automatic
loading onto magazine bars of two body ribs or four sleeve ribs
in one pre-programmed operating cycle. A microcomputer controls the number of layers of ribs, between 1 and 24, that
are loaded onto the magazine bars. When tne preset number
of ribs has been loaded, a signal to the operator indicates
that the loaded bars are to be replaced by empty ones.

The cycle of operations of the ART conversion begins with a
standard hook-up element bar rising to a position between
the needlebeds to control the formation of the welt edge.

During the knitting of the first few courses of the rib, the
hook-up element bar is withdrawn through the needlebed in
a series of pre-selected increments, controlled by a microcomputer according to a preset program. The purpose of the
pre-selected increments is to allow for varying the take-
down tension to accommodate different yarn types. Up to seven
of the initial courses can be knitted with the take-down tension controlled to very fine tolerances; this is particularly
useful when knitting delicate yarns. After the first few
courses, adjustable weights on the hook-up bar provide the

take-down tensions.

When the required courses of the rib have been knitted, all
the loops are transferred to the needles on the front bed.
The microprocessor then initiates and controls the transfer
of the rib onto a magazine bar. Figure 3 is a diagrammatic
illustration of eight stages in the transfer of one loop:

Stage A represents the starting point where the loop is shown
in the latch needle on the front bed.

At stage B the traversing cam mechanism clears the latch
and sets the needle.

Stage C shows the needle and its loop in the required attitude,
with the front bed in the dropped position. The novel transfer
element has been raised to its upper position.

Stage D is the important, transient relationship of the transfer
element to the loop held on the closed latch of the needle.
The front bed has risen with a slanting movement from the
position of stage C to place the loop over the sloping tip
of the transfer element.

Stage E indicates a transient position of the loop which
results from another passage of the traversing cam mechanism.

Stage F shows the loop resting on a barb at the rear of the
transfer element. The loop is pulled down by the tension in
the rib and held there by the take-down weight. The front
bed has dropped to its lowest position and the transfer element
is ready to lower the loop to the unloading area.

Stage G illustrates the engagement of the transfer element
with the magazine bar element, and the approaching pusher blade.

Stage H shows the loop pushed up to the previously transferred
ribs on the magazine bar. The pusher bar and the magazine bar
are about to be withdrawn to enable the hook-up bar to rise
for the start of the next rib.

The above complicated sequence of movements is controlled by
the microcomputer. This is achieved by operating the normal
functions of the machine intermittently so that the new mechanisms,
which are powered by an intermittently indexed camshaft, can
combine with the knitting elements to collect and transfer
the ribs. The computer is able to control the sequence at slow
speed for setting up (9).

In addition to controlling the transfer cycle and the initial
take-down tension, the computer controls the yarn cut and clamp
devices; the release of take-down tension and the unhooking
of the transferred ribs from the hook-up elements; the counting
of the knitted rib courses; monitoring draw-thread and knitting
yarn quality and breaks; as well as ensuring crash-free running
of the interacting mechanisms.

Low cost electronic controls for the trial machines were developed by members of the Department; variability of settings
was achieved by switches. During trials it was realised that
a more flexible control system would be required for the production machines. The Stonefield Electronics 'Mini-Micro' system
was selected for reliability, low cost and suitability for
extending the control to other machine operations. The Stonefield
system contains a 'programmable logic controller' which has
two particular features:

i)   standard modules can be connected to suit the specific
     requirements of the application. When the development
     system has proved satisfactory, a single board can be
     created, easily and cheaply, in the same form as the
     modules, thus avoiding another development and test
     stage and the use of multiple connectors between the
     boards.

ii) a special language is used for the programming; this
     was developed so that non-computer experts can quickly
     learn to understand it and then write new sequences
     in order to vary or expand the capabilities of the
     system. Up to sixteen different tasks can be run simul-
     taneously under the commands of the system. The commands
     are used to turn on and off individual channels, to set
     and start timers, to wait until specific conditions
     occur and even vary the sequence under certain condi-
     tions; the controller can also carry out some logic
     and arithmetic functions if required.

This control system performed well at the prototype stage
and the authors are informed by the machine manufacturers
that the capability for plant engineers to modify and extend
the controls is proving a useful feature.

An associated development is a manually controlled Gauge Changing and Doubling Unit which has been developed to assist
the transfer of ribs from one machine to another (10,11).
Both the ART machine and the Re-gauging machine are currently
being manufactured and marketed by Jordan, Lovatt and Jones
Ltd, Thurmaston, Leicester.

4.   TOE CLOSING OF SOCKS AND TRIM ATTACHING

4.1 Preliminary Research

The ART machine uses its computer in a pre-programmed manner.
However, the current research, into toe closing and trim
attaching, is at a much earlier stage of development but will
make use of the 'intelligent control' possibilities of computers.
It is concerned with knitted components having loops which
cannot be retained on rigid carriers between knitting and
linking; therefore another way must be found to relocate
the loops, after they have been removed from the needles on
which they were knitted. A control system is required which
makes use of the flexibility of the computer and its ability
to make decisions.

Research studies are being made into two operations; these
are the toe linking of socks and the linking of collars and

stoles to outerwear. Although they may seem to be very different operations, both processes require machines which are able to:

   i) present the fabric pieces to be worked on;
  ii) sense the pieces and recognise important areas and shapes;
 iii) position the pieces with appropriate manipulators;
  iv) interface with, or include, mechanisms to perform the operations involved, and
   v) unload the worked-on fabric pieces in a convenient manner.

The resulting machine would be sophisticated and would require the solution of a wide range of new problems. It was decided that sensing of the linking course would be crucial to the progress of this research, with likely applications in areas other than linking. Unless the recognition of particular loops and the calculation of the positions of their centres could be done reliably and quickly without large computing capacity, the project would not be practicable; by contrast all the other problems, although very complex, appeared to be soluble by traditional engineering techniques. Therefore it was decided that the scanning, recognition and centre-line calculation of particular courses of loops would be the priority area of investigation.

A wide variety of sensing methods was investigated; the criteria used for choosing a system were:

   i) it must use a property which is, or can be, included in the fabric without problems. It must not affect the customer acceptability of the product, add to the cost or cause problems in manufacture;

  ii) it must be reliable and hence not deteriorate with use. For example, 99.5% reliability on a sock knitted on 200 needles would, on average, miss one loop per linking operation which is clearly unacceptable;

 iii) it must have a sensing head which will not impede the manipulating mechanisms. This means that the head must be small or able to operate at a distance;

  iv) it must be able to transfer information rapidly and reliably to the manipulator control system;

   v) it must not be so expensive or complicated as to be inappropriate for the final product; and

  vi) in addition, it must be able to work on fabrics in the flat or in the round and be able to recognise its own position without causing disturbance or damage to the fabric nor rely on measurement from an uneven edge.

With these criteria in mind, vision seems an obvious choice (12,13). However, a good deal of thought and some testing was applied to the use of touch, which contributes significantly to the ability of operators to locate loops manually at surprisingly high speeds. Consideration was given to equipping manipulators with appropriate touch sensors, but

this was not pursued, because of the likelihood of wear and
speed problems (14). In any case, it was foreseen that vision
would be required to obtain some of the necessary information;
therefore it was decided to test whether vision alone would
be sufficient.

Consideration was also given to including special yarns or
yarns with special treatments, for detection by electrical
or other means, but this appeared to offer no advantages
over straightforward optical detection; it would be undesirable to use a yarn that made knitting more difficult. However, the task of the vision system could be made simpler
by knitting the first waste course with a yarn of a different
appearance.

A research rig has been built which is capable of scanning a
piece of fabric in a way that meets the requirements. It
uses a Fairchild ' charge coupled device ', which has a line
of 256 closely packed sensing elements, each of which is 17
microns wide by 13 microns long (15). The information from
one scan of the sensor can be read by a desk-top computer
in a quarter of a millisecond and the calculations necessary
for following a line of loops and finding particular loop
centres can be completed in half a millisecond. The work is
supported by the UK Science & Engineering Research Council .

4.2 Toe Closing of Socks

Work was concentrated initially on the toe linking of socks
because of the firm encouragement of a local sock manufacturer.
So far, only a conceptual study, economic analysis and some
preliminary design work have been done on this proposal. The
intention was that the machine should operate on socks which
have been knitted in a continuous string. An operator would
load a string of socks onto a mandrel; then the machine would
turn the socks inside out and feed the string along the mandrel,
while a sensing device would search for the toe pouch corner
and indicate the approximate position for the start of the
linking course. Another sensing device would scan along the
linking course, recognise the loops which would need to be
linked, calculate the positions of the loop centres and control
the engagement of points with the loops. With points inserted
in all the linking loops, the sock would be separated so that
the machine could index the sock, part of the mandrel and the
point carrying mechanism through 180 degrees, to bring the
scanned sock to the linking position and, at the same time, index
another set of linking points to the scanning position. The
points would be matched and aligned in pairs, and then the
toe would be linked. This sock would then be unloaded as
the next sock is indexed into position.

Recently the emphasis of this work has changed. The authors
realised that machinery for toe-linking socks would have special
features which might not suit other garment assembly operations.
Therefore, they looked for another operation which would lead
to systems likely to be more widely applicable to garment
assembly automation, as well as having an immediate application.
With the cooperation of Corah plc, it has been decided to

concentrate on the linking of collars and similar trims to outerwear.

4.3 Collar and Trim Attaching

The basic sensing system for finding loop centres will be much the same as before, but some of the programs which make the decisions will be different, although working to the same principles.

The machine concept would, of course, be very different. Collars or trims would be knitted in a conventional manner whereby each one would be joined to the next with a draw-thread, providing a continuous supply for the next stage. A machine of a new design would feed these collars forward, then monitor and approximately position each slack course. The linking course would then be scanned, and transfer points inserted into the appropriate loops. After removal of the draw-thread, a separate mechanism would transfer the collar onto a magazine bar which would be capable of accepting a large number of collars for subsequent linking to the body of the garment.

The functions under computer control would include the following:

  i) the initial feeding of trims;
 ii) sensing and recognising the linking course;
iii) controlling the engagement of points;
 iv) catering for widths of trims which vary with styles;
  v) the loading of magazine bars, and
 vi) interacting with the operator for changes of bulk supply.

An economic study of the proposed system, using projected figures for machine costs and outputs, is very favourable, not only in comparison with manual linking, but also when compared to the lower quality, approximate linking systems.

5.   CONCLUSION

A report on "the state of the art of assembly of apparel products", prepared for the Commission of the European Economic Community in 1979, stated that "80% of the direct operative work force spends 90% of its time picking-up, positioning, manipulating and removing one or more pieces of fabric around a stitch making device" (1).

The above statement emphasises the importance of automation in this area, but it makes it all sound very simple. It is true that computers offer new opportunities, but they do not make all the problems disappear. The authors of this paper are well aware that due to the pressures of fashion, runs are often short, changes are frequent and small operating plants are common; this is why emphasis was put on the need to apply the criteria of cost, flexibility, speed and availability when considering alternative ways of achieving automation.

Although the work described in this paper is specific to knitwear, the authors expect to use the same basic approaches and accrued knowledge to further the general progress towards wider automation of garment assembly.

LIST OF FIGURES

ACKNOWLEDGEMENTS

Most of the research work referred to in this paper has been
funded by the UK Science and Engineering Research Council;
the most recent work is under the auspices of that Council's
'Robotics Initiative' and this support is gratefully
acknowledged.

The authors gratefully acknowledge the support and assistance
given to them over a number of years by Corah plc, in particular,
as well as by several other UK textile manufacturing and machinery
companies, many of whom are named in Figure 1.

In addition the authors wish to acknowledge the expertise of
Stonefield Omicron Electronics Limited, Denne Parade, Horsham,
West Sussex, RH12 1DL England in developing a production version
of the microprocessor control system for the ART machine.

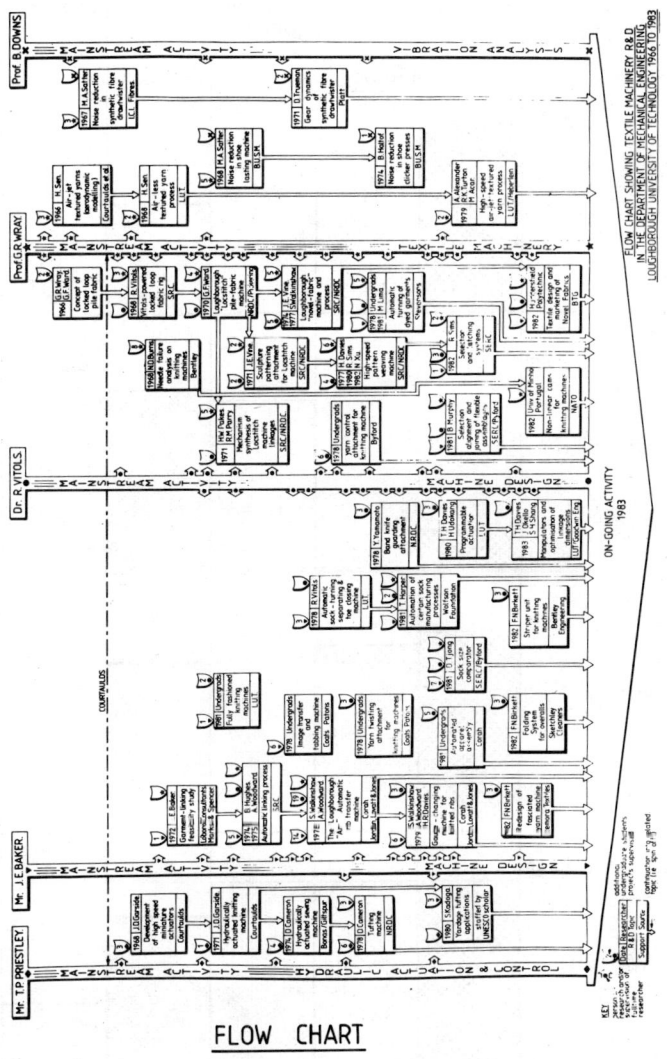

FLOW CHART

Figure. 1.

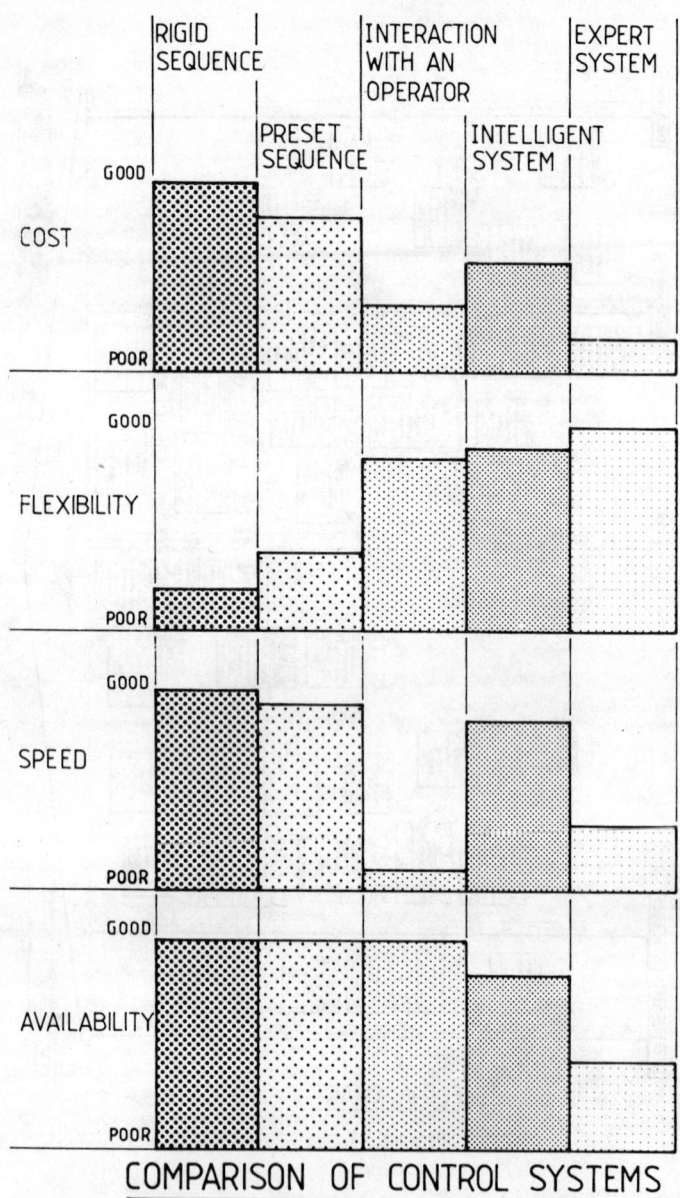

Figure. 2.

COMPARISON OF CONTROL SYSTEMS

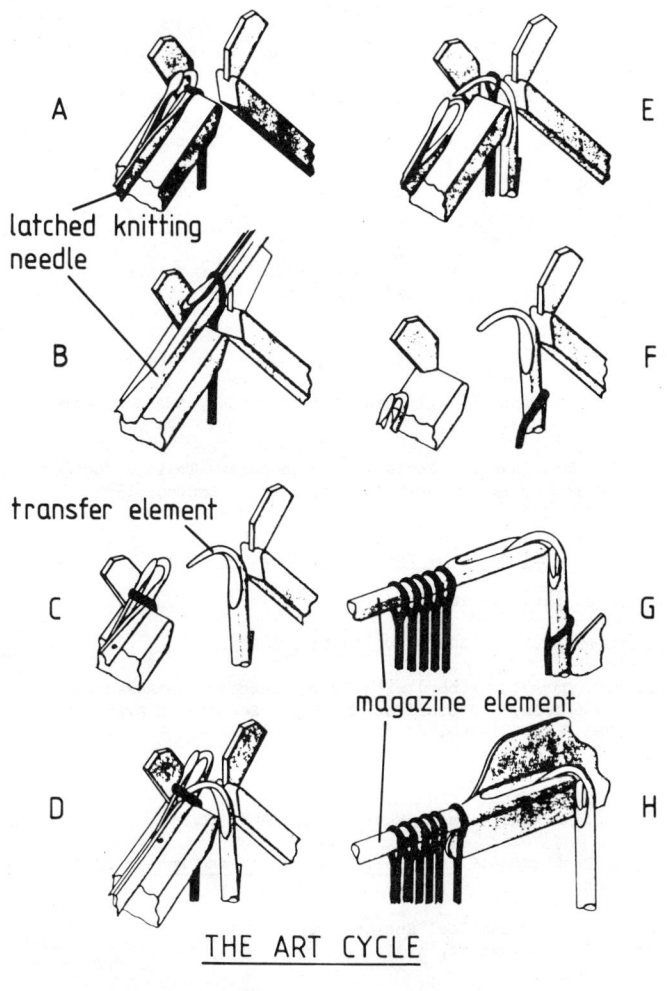

THE ART CYCLE

Figure. 3.

REFERENCES

(1) Kurt Salmon Associates. 'The 1980's: the Decade for Technology?' Report for the Commission of the European Economic Community, Dec. 1980.

(2) G.R. Wray in 'Engineering Challenges to the 1980's', Cambridge Information and Research Services Ltd. Royston, Herts. Vol. 1, Ch. 2.

(3) G.R. Wray, G.F. Ward and R. Vitols in 'Studies in Modern Fabrics', The Textile Institute, Manchester, 1970, pp 30-39.

(4) G.R. Wray. Proc. IMechE 1976, 190, pp 367-378.

(5) R. Vitols, J.E. Vine, S. Walkinshaw and G.R. Wray in 'The Fabric Revolution', The Textile Institute, Manchester, 1981.

(6) R. Johnston. Computer Talk, 4.11.1983, p. 16.

(7) P.H. Winston. 'Artificial Intelligence', Addison-Wesley, 1979, p. 237.

(8) G.R. Wray and R. Vitols in 'Contemporary Textile Engineering', (edited by F. Happey), Academic Press, London, 1982, pp 375-409.

(9) Anon. Knitting International, 1981, 89, No. 1057, p. 96.

(10) Corah plc. EP 10982. (6 Nov. 1978).

(11) Corah plc. BP 2080837. (2 Aug. 1980).

(12) P.G. Davey. 'Robots with Common Sense! The Research Scene Today', Journal of the Royal Society of Arts, Oct. 1983, pp. 671-685.

(13) I. Clark. Sensor Review 1981, Jan. p. 20.

(14) L.D. Harmon. Sensor Review 1981, April.

(15) M. Trowbridge. Engineering Materials and Design 1981, Sept.

Department of Mechanical Engineering
Loughborough University of Technology
Loughborough
Leicestershire
LE11 3TU
England.

AUTOMATED PARTS LAYOUT PLANNING IN GARMENT INDUSTRY BY USING GROUP TECHNOLOGY

M. Nakajima and K. Hayashi

ABSTRACT

Algorithm for optimum solution of parts layout problem for garment industry are proposed to obtain new optimum solutions using the Group Technology Concept. Four techniques aimed for reduction of waste are proposed and computer programs are prepared to determine parts layout. The computed results are examined and compared with actual parts layout planning examples. The percentage of waste attained for a specified waste loss and the computing time required to make calculation of parts layout for a specified output rate are used as the measure of effectiveness. The main results of this study show that there are significant differences among the effectiveness results achieved by the proposed techniques.

1. INTRODUCTION

The marking operations for parts layout in the garment industry requires to fit many kinds of parts to original cloth, aiming to minimize waste. The operation is called "the parts layout" for cloth cutting operation, and is usually done manually by experienced operators in the garment industry (1,2,3). Rrcently, the marking operation has been automated by using computers to save operating and job time (2,4). Computer algorithms aiding layout operations have been developed for the Japanese garment industry (2,3). However, the process is not fully automated, and still needs some further improvement. Tanaka and Wachi (1) have developed a computer algorithm for parts layout. The main contribution of Tanaka and Wachi's paper is to discuss the use of the mathematical induction method for solving combinational layout problem. The Tanaka and Wachi did not guarantee the optimal solution as for the parts layout. The purpose of this paper is to improve on the algorithm of Tanaka and Wachi using Group Technology Concept[5] for data input aiming to decrease waste and also to apply an actual parts layout by using this algorithm, and to compare the wastage of cloth to the wastage using Tanaka and Wachi's algorithm.

2. BASIC CONCEPT OF PARTS LAYOUT

2.1 Assumptions and Prerequisites

Three assumptions are made as proposed by Tanaka and Wachi (1):
(1) All parts can be laid out anywhere within the boundaries of the original cloth provided.
(2) The parts are laid out in one direction only.
(3) The part's layout starts from the edge of the original cloth.
The purpose of this paper is to develop an algorithm that minimizes the waste of original cloth based on the

above assumption and satisfying the following three
conditions:
(1) Overlapping of parts are not permitted.
(2) The layout will minimize waste of the original
    cloth and will fit within the boundary of the
    original cloth.
(3) All parts must be laid out with the same direction
    of warp and weft.

2.2 Conditions of the Operation of Parts layout

The following conditions are also imposed:
(1) Select a part from the set of all parts to be laid
    out.
(2) Select orientation of the first part in the layout
    area.
(3) Choose a location for the selected part in the
    layout area.
To meet the above conditions, the following four variables
are difined:

$$P_n : P_n = {}_n(A)$$

$$T_r : T_r = {}_n(B) \tag{1}$$

$$X, Y : x \; \varepsilon \; X, \; y \; \varepsilon \; Y$$

where P_n is the number of parts in event (A), designated
as $_n(A)$, T_r equals the direction of the part to be laid
out and is designated as $_n(B)$. x, y is a cartesian
coordinates in layout area X, Y.
It is supposed that the parts to be laid out are located
on the cloth. Then the symbol of "Γ" maps from an event
(B) to an event (A), Γ is given as:

$$\Gamma = P_n \cdot T_r \tag{2}$$

and may be expressed as the location of the parts to be
laid out in the layout area by defining Γ, X and Y, then
layout the parts means to solve the following function
f:

$$f = \xi \; (\Gamma, \; X, \; Y) \tag{3}$$

where Γ, X and Y are variables needed for laying out parts.

2.3 Representation of the Parts

In order to represent the basic operation of layout
satisfying the above prerequisites, based on the
assumptions of inside location in layout area during
layout operation of part, it is necessary to describe
the following items.
Let us define point A "0-cell", line a with length u
"1-cell", a regular square area with one side of line a
"2-cell". A "cellular complex R" is defined as a set of
"0-cell $\{A_\varepsilon\}$", "1-cell $\{a_j\}$ and "2-cell $\{\alpha_k\}$" of finite
number in N-dimensional Euclid space $E^{(N)}$,

$$R = \{A_1, \; A_2, \ldots, \; A_n, a_1, a_2 \ldots, a_u, \alpha_1, \alpha_2, \ldots, \; \alpha_r\} \tag{4}$$

Using above mentioned notations, a layout area and parts
to be laid out are presented by the cellular complex.
The layout parts are approximated by sets of 2-cells
with length of 1 cm.

2.4 Convex Representation of Parts

Using the cartesian coordinates X-O-Y, a measure of each coodinate renders as integer multiple of 1-cell with a, coordinates are cellular complex such as:

$$x = a\ n,\ y = a\ n' \qquad (n,n' = 1,\ 2,\dots) \tag{5}$$

Curve F_p of part renders coordinates X-O-Y satisfying the following three conditions:

(1) Curve F_p has to take either coordinate $(x_0,\ y)$ with $x = 0$ or coordinate $(x,\ y_0)$ with $y = 0$.
(2) Each coordinate is non-negative.
(3) The weave direction coincides with the direction of the X-axis.

Assuming sets that succesive y coordinates in the part curve F_p are of equal values (see Figure 1), $\{x_{ij}\}$ is placed for its sets, where "i" is suffix for y-coordinates, "j" is one for x-coordinates. Then R_i and F_i give:

$$R_i = \max\ \{x_{ij}\}\ ,\ F_i = \min\ \{x_{ij}\} \qquad (6)$$
$$i = 1,\ 2,\dots,\ y_{max} \qquad j = 1,\ 2,\dots,\ n$$

$$F_p = \{F_i,\ R_i\} \qquad i = 1,\ 2,\ \dots,\ Y_{max} \tag{7}$$

In general, letting $F = (y_i,\ x_i)$, $R = (y_1',\ x_1')$ then
$$F_p = (F\ U\ R) \tag{8}$$

The parts can convexly be represented by obtaining equation (8) from (5) and define the part which is convexly represented as the "layout part". Therefore, all possible parts were represented in "cellularal complex" by taking small "1-cell" lines, plus a layout operation of parts become an easy task. The algorithm does not calculate the big concave sort of parts.

2.5 Transfer of Parts

Two kinds of transfer are allowed:
(1) Parallel motion; this is moving along the x or y axis. The moving along the x-axis is called "Transfer", and the moving along the y-axis is called "Lift up".
(2) Rotation; this is rotation around the origin.

Therefore, deciding on "location" of parts means determination of the distance (X,Y) from the origin after the results of Transfer and Lift up. Deciding on "direction" is determined by the amount of part rotation.

Letting the distance moved along the x and y axes is represented by $t_x = n_x a$ and $t_y = n_y a$, the coordinates are equal to:

$$F_t = (y_i + t_y,\ x_i + t_x)$$
$$R_t = (y_i' + t_y,\ x_i' + t_x) \tag{9}$$

and the parts layout after coordinates transfer becomes:
$$F_p = (\ F_t\ U\ R_t) \tag{10}$$

then, the following three types shown in Figure 2 are considered for the rotation of a part.

(1) Symmetry by rotation around the y-axis: From equation (8), we obtain:
$$F_B = (y_i,\ x_{max} - x_i)$$
$$R_B = (y_i',\ x_{max} - x_i') \tag{11}$$

where suffix B means y-axis symmetry.
Using the same procedure,
(2) Symmetry by rotation around the x-axis:

299

$$F_c = (y_{max} - y_i, x_i)$$
$$R_c = (y_{max} - y_i', x_i') \tag{12}$$

(3) Symmetry by rotation around the origin:
$$F_D = (y_{max} - y_i, x_{max} - x_i)$$
$$R_D = (y_{max} - y_i', x_{max} - x_i') \tag{13}$$

2.6 Basic Concept of Parts Layout

Procedure of parts layout can be expressed as follows.
(1) The set of all given parts $P_1, P_2, ..., P_n$ is expressed by
$$U = \{P_1, P_2, ..., P_n\} \tag{14}$$
(2) Any combination comprised from all parts in U puts
$$P = P_1, P_2, P_3, ..., P_n \tag{15}$$
(3) After parts layout of n-times, if one combination P determines, we express this P by
$$P_{(n)} = P_1, P_2, P_3, ..., P_n \tag{16}$$
(4) And, in this case, inside situation of layout area expresses by $Q_n(n)$ as following.
$$Q_{(n)} = P_1, P_2, P_3, ..., P_n \tag{17}$$
(5) Function which takes out n_ith natural number from $x_{(n)}$ gives the following:
$$D_i n(x_{(n)}) = x_i \tag{18}$$
(6) Convex representation of layout with function $D_i^n(x_{(n)})$ is put in $s_{(i)}$.

Assuming that inside situation of layout area determines, by hysteresis $H_{(n)}$ of layout area, the following equation has to exist.
$$R_{(n+1)} = F(H_{(n)}, S_{(n)}) \tag{19}$$

where, $R_{(n+1)}$ is cycle of output operations, therefore, the basic concept of parts layout is given as described below.

Inside situation $Q_{(n+1)}$ of layout area determines by the representation $S_{(n+1)}$ of parts laid out and the just before inside situation $Q_{(n)}$ of layout area. This relation can be expressed as follows:
$$Q_{(n+1)} = G(Q_{(n)}, S_{(n+1)}) \tag{20}$$
And, by the above same concept, cycle $R_{(n+1)}$ of layout operation and many decision $D_{(n+1)}$ for layout also determine by the representation $S_{(n+1)}$ of parts laid out and the just before inside situation $Q_{(n)}$ of layout area, therefore we obtain:
$$R_{(n+1)} = F(Q_{(n)}, S_{(n+1)}) \tag{21}$$
$$D_{(n+1)} = D(Q_{(n)}, S_{(n+1)}) \tag{22}$$

2.7 Envelopes

In order to display a transition of the inside state in layout area accompanying with the layout, the concept of "Envelopes" is introduced.

Envelopes based on parts layout and of convex representation of parts is generally expressed as follows. If parts of n-pieces are laid out, Envelopes are given by

$$E_{(n)} = \{y, x_{(y)}\} \qquad (y = a, 2a,...,ia,...,W) \qquad (23)$$

where W is width of original cloth. If one part is laid out, so Envelopes is rewritten. Therefore, the more parts that are successively laid out, the more Envelopes that are developed. Envelopes $E_{(n+1)}$ is defined by just before Envelopes $E_{(n)}$ and optimal value P_o which is designated in state variable Γ, X, Y, that is,

$$E_{(n+1)} = T (E_{(n)}, P_o) \qquad (24)$$

It is necessary to decide on P_o to satisfy layout conditions. In order to prevent an overlapping between a new part and an Envelopes which is just previously drawn by layout operation, let us put a new part in location of F_n shown in Figure 3, length ρ difines as follows:

$$\rho = E_{(n-1)} - F \qquad (25)$$

And then, let us search the maximum length of $\rho (= \rho_{max})$ in total domain y (y = a, 2a,..., na). In searching ρ_{max}, F is lifted up in pitch of 1-cell with line a. ρ_{max} means the minimum value which has to move along to x-axis in order to prevent an overlapping. To lay out completely, pick up the part with minimum of ρ_{max} from parts of Γ - (n-1) pieces which are not yet laid out, "Transfer"ρ_{max} and the amount "Lift up" give t_x and t_y of part which is next put, that is,

$$D_i^n(P_{(n)}) \equiv \min_{\Gamma} (\max_{\Gamma,Y} (E_{(n-1)} - F))$$
$$\equiv \xi (\Gamma, t_y, t_x) \qquad (26)$$

Envelopes is modified by using t_x, t_y which is given by the equation (26), and the Envelopes is newly displayed then the new Envelopes is successively registered by this procedure.

2.8 Performance Measure

The effect of parts layout is related with complexity of shape of the new part. In this paper, the following performance measure, $\Phi(W,x)$, in order to evaluate an effect of layout gives:

$$\Phi(W,x) = (1 - \frac{A}{W \cdot x}) \cdot 100 \qquad (27)$$

where 'x' is the necessary amount minimum length of cloth to be measured in x-direction, 'A' is total area of all part. Let us call this performance measure, the "Percentage of waste".

3. IMPROVEMENT OF BASIC CONCEPT

3.1 Various Improvement of Algorithm

There are two questionable points in Tanaka and Wachi (T,W) algorithm. It is possible that the right side edge of the part to be finally laid out sticks out too much by reason in determination of only "ρ" without consideration of largeness and shape of individual parts. Percentage of waste increase largely by this reason. Also, as parts layout is determined by moving for the

sake of prevention of overlapping, waste between
individual parts which are laid out is not considered.
It is doubtful that parts layout which is determined
by the concept of "ρ" give a minimum percentage of waste.

Some improvements were made by applying Group Technology
Concept. One improvement is to classify parts into
several groups according to size of the part. If the
part is circumscribed by a rectangle as shown in Figure
4, the shaded portion of Figure 4 is designated as
"Rectangle of Part". A second improvement is to classify
parts into several groups according to the ratio of
(Waste area of part/Rectangle area of parts: W/S). It
is well-known through experiments that if the parts are
laid out beginning with the largest area proceeding to
the smallest one, we can get a small "percentage of
waste". The number of classification of parts is
determined by the number of parts. This algorithm is
denoted as Classification (C) technique.

Another improvement made is to calculate the area of
shadow portion of the part which is moved in order to
prevent an overlapping of parts as shown in Figure 5.
In this case, location enclosed by the broken line in
part 4 is not selected. The location enclosed by the
full line for part 4 is selected, because the area of
hatched portion is smaller than the area of the one
dotted chain line portion. The technique is called F.W
technique.

After the first part is laid out, the next step is to
select a certain part, and calculate an area of shadowed
portion as shown in Figure 6. Then we select the part
that minimizes the shadowed area. In the case of Figure
6, the first part laid out is larger than the second part
laid out. Figure 7 shows the reverse case. This technique is called "Second Waste (S.W) technique".

3.2 Various Methods of Application and Sequences of Algorithm

It is proposed that various techniques (C, F.W & S.W)
for part layout improving the T.W's algorithm in the
previous section. Then it is proposed to consider five
kinds of technique (T.W, T.W + C, F.W, S.W and S.W + C),
where (T.W + C) means that C-technique is introduced into
T.W technique.

An example of the flow diagram for the algorithm is shown
in Figure 8. The computer program for parts layout is
prepared in FORTRAN-language and used for actual parts
layout planning.

4. APPLICATION AND CONSIDERATION

4.1 Numerical Example

In an attempt to clarify the various improved techniques
for determing the parts layout, a numerical example is

presented. Table 1 shows parts datum for input.
Table 2 shows the shape of parts and their shape
after transfer. Data for classification by the ratio
(W/S) are shown in Table 3. Computation is carried out
by using of the FACOM 230-28(128KB) computer. In this
example, with the use of various improved techniques,
eight parts are processed. Table 4 shows a comparison
of the results of layout. An example of parts layout
by the S.W technique is illustrated in Figure 9.

4.2 Discussion

The result in the case of 78cm-width cloth is shown in
Table 4. The table shows the following. Percentage of
waste by applying the T.W technique is obtained (36.19
(%)) but when the C technique is applied to T.W, its
value is reduced to (30(%)), a saving of 1638 cm in
cloth area (8.09(%)). The percentage of waste by
applying S.W technique is (29.43(%)), a saving of 9.58%
over the T.W technique. The percentage of waste by the
F.W technique is (40.94(%)); this is bad results in
comparison with the other techniques.

Computing time is reduced by 38 seconds when C technique
is used to modify the T.W's techniques. This means
that the cycle of computation required for search of
parts is decreased by using the C technique based on
Group Technology.

The effect of the width of the original cloth on the
marking length (necessary minimum length in longitudinal
direction of original cloth) and on the percentage of
waste are shown in Figure 10 and 11. Figure 10 and 11
show that each marking length based on each various
technique decreases with the increase of width of
original cloth. If marking length is short, it means
the technique is good. Therefore, it is obvious that
the best technique is (T.W + C), and using this technique, we can find out the marking length which minimizes percentage of waste. In this example, a minimum
percentage of waste is obtained using 90 cm width of
original cloth. By using the (T.W + C)technique,
minimum value for the percentage of waste is (20.3(%)).
Figure 12 shows the parts layout giving best results.

5. CONCLUSIONS

An improvement of Tanaka-Wachi(T.W) technique is
presented. Four improved algorithms are proposed to
illustrate the improvement, and computer programs are
prepared to determine parts layout. The proposed
algorithms are applied to parts layout planning. The
effectiveness of a "Classification" technique that
classifies parts into several groups based on Group
Technology Concept is shown. The best result in
percentage of waste is (20(%)).
The proposed algorithms may also be applicable to
pattern layout problems of steel plate in shipbuilding,
the problem of arrangement rooms in house design,

facility layout problems in a production plant, or packing problems of products and layout of sheet aluminium in the aircraft industry.

ACKNOWLEDGEMENT

The authors wish to thank Prof.Emeritus H.Noshi, Kyoto Industrial & Textile University for his contribution.

REFERENCES

(1) M. Tanaka and T. Wachi. J. Text. Mach. Soc. Japan, 1973, 26, No.7, 121.

(2) T. Wachi. J. Text. Mach. Soc. Japan, 1976, 29, No. 8, 375.

(3) H.Tada. J. Text. Mach. Soc. Japan, 1974, 27, No.10 610.

(4) G. M. Cokes. Textile Inst. and Indus., 1975, 13, No.108, 108.

(5) M. Nakajima. ' Production Management Systems by Group Technology ' (edited by K. Hitomi), Nikkan Kogyo Shinbunsha , Japan, 1st edition, 1981, p.5.

Kyoto Industrial & Textile University
Faculty of Textile Science,
(KOUSENDAI)
Matsugasaki, Sakyo-ku, Kyoto-shi,606
Japan

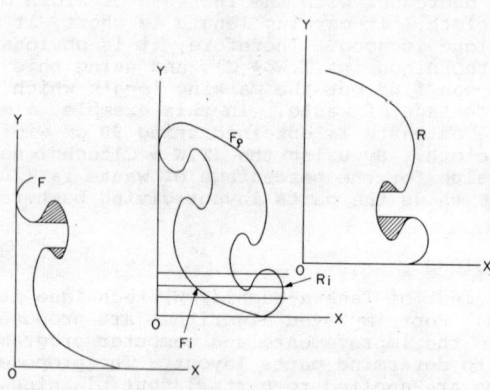

Fig.1 Convex Representation of Part

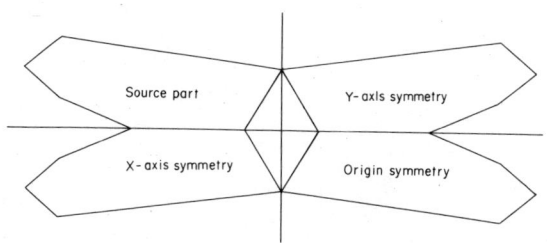

Fig.2 Transfer of Part

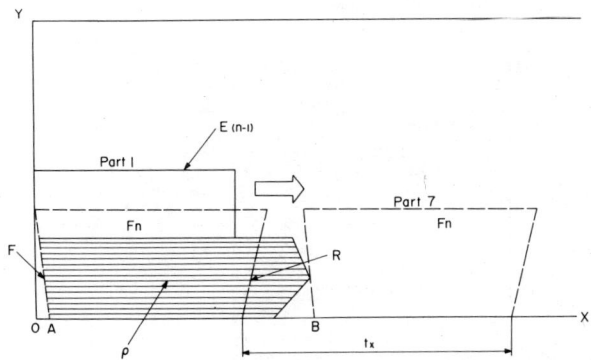

Fig.3 Envelopes

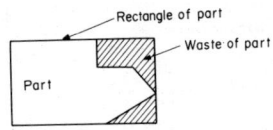

Fig.4 Rectangle and Waste of Part

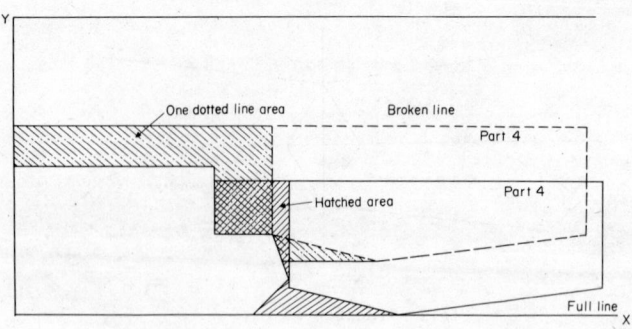

Fig.5 First Waste (F.W) Technique

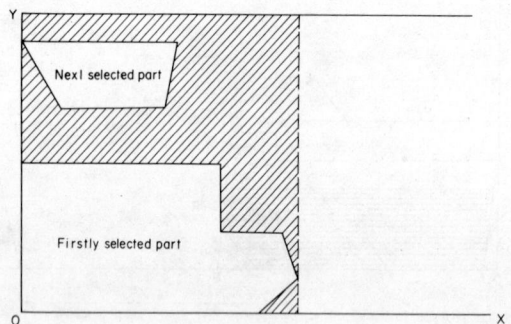

Fig.6 Second Waste (S.W) Technique

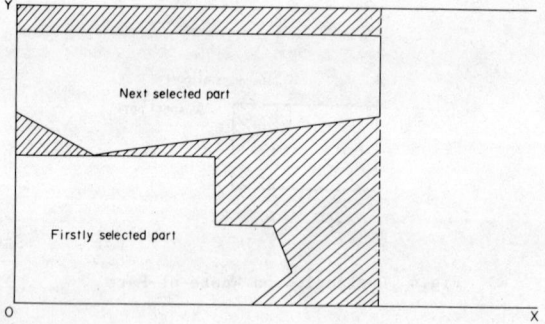

Fig.7 Second Waste (S.W) Technique

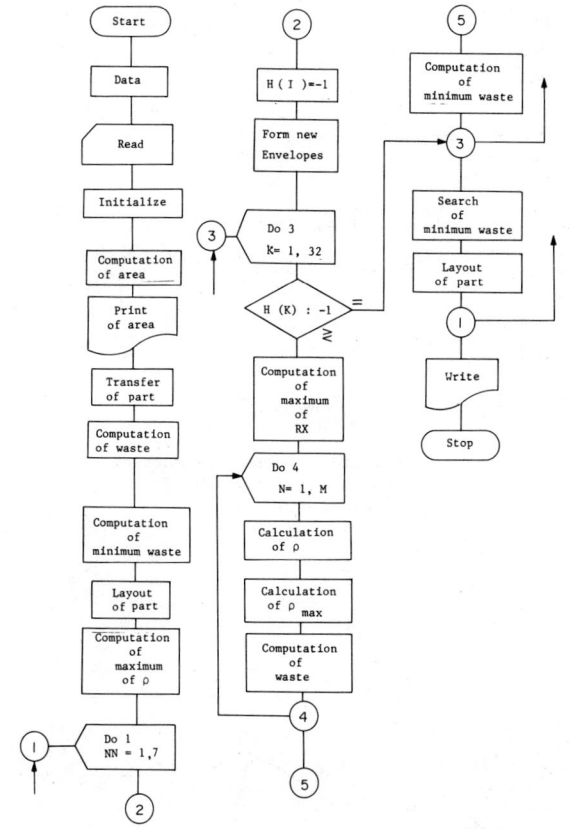

Fig.8   Flow Diagram

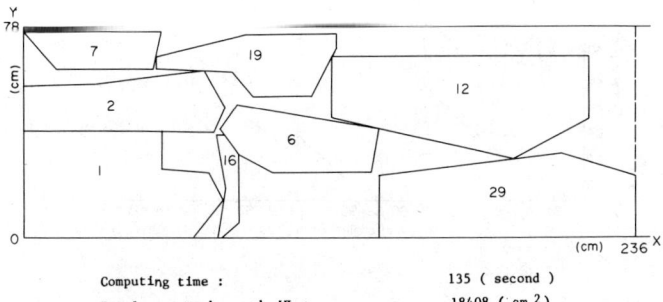

Computing time :	135 (second)
Total area to be used, WL :	18408 (cm^2)
Sum of area of part, A :	12990 (cm^2)
Total area of waste, WL – A :	5418 (cm^2)
Percentage of waste, (1 – A/WL) x 100 :	29.4 (%)

Fig.9   An Example of Parts Layout (by S.W)

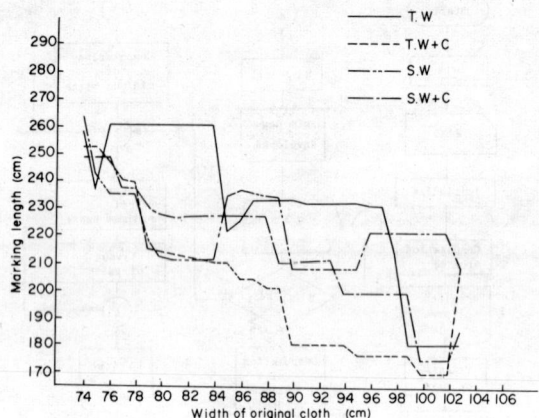

Fig.10 Relation Between the Marking
Length and the Width of
Original Cloth

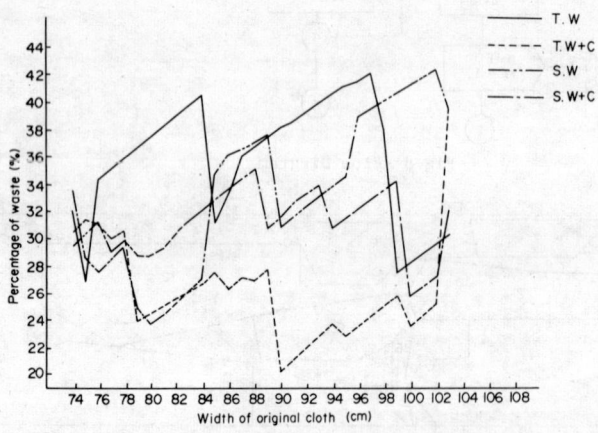

Fig.11 Relation Between Percentage of
Waste and Width of Original
Cloth

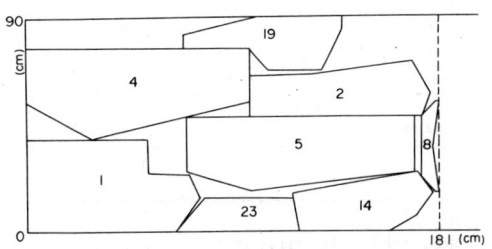

Total area to be used, WL:	16290 (cm^2)
Sum of area of parts , A:	12990 (cm^2)
Total area of waste, WL - A:	3300 (cm^2)
Percentage of waste, (1 - A/WL) x 100:	20.3 (%)

Fig.12 Parts Layout of the Best Result (T.W + C)

Table 1. Input Data of Parts

No. of part	1	2	3	4	5	6	7	8
Area of part (cm^2)	2622	1491	1072	3062	2721	1121	682	219
Area of rectangle, S (cm^2)	3003	1794	1587	3762	3069	1525	756	304
Waste, W (cm^2)	381	303	515	700	348	404	74	85
W/S x 100 (%)	12.7	16.9	32.5	18.6	11.3	26.5	9.8	28.0

Table 2   Transfer of Part

Source part	Y-axis symmetry	X-axis symmetry	Origin symmetry
1	9	17	25
2	10	18	26
3	11	19	27

309

Table 3(a). Classification by Size of
Area of Parts

Area of part	Small	Large
No. of part	2, 3, 6, 7, 8	$1^*, 4^*, 5^*$

Table 3(b). Classification by (W/S) Ratio

Percentage of waste	Small	Large
No. of part	$1^*, 2, 4^*, 5^*, 7$	3, 6, 8

Table 4. Comparison of the Results of Various Techniques

Techniques Items	T.W.	T.W.+ C	F.W.	S.W.	S.W.+ C
Computing time (second)	118	80	154	135	101
Cloth length to be used (cm)	261	240	282	236	238
Total area to be used (cm^2)	20358	18720	21996	18408	18564
Total area of waste : WL- A (cm^2)	7368	5730	9006	5418	5574
Percentage of waste : (1- A/WL) x 100 (%)	36.19	30.61	40.94	29.43	30.03

A PROTOTYPICAL ALGORITHM FOR COMPUTER PRODUCTION OF INDIVIDUALLY FITTED PATTERNS

F. Heisey, P. Brown, R.F. Johnson

ABSTRACT

A conceptual framework was developed for a quantitative methodology to accurately and rapidly produce patterns for specifically fitted garments. The framework was based upon modeling the underlying mechanisms of fit. It separates body specification, garment form specification and projection of the pattern into discrete steps. A prototypical algorithm for a basic skirt was produced using the methodology.

1. INTRODUCTION

The most satisfactory garment is one that has been specifically fitted to the individual who wears it. At the present time there is no accurate, rapid method of producing specifically fitted patterns. Fitting a garment is a time consuming art. The purpose of this research was to develop a conceptual framework for a quantitative methodology which could be used to accurately and rapidly produce patterns for specifically fitted garments.

2. CONSIDERATIONS IN DEVELOPMENT OF A NEW METHODOLOGY

2.1. <u>Traditional Methods of Producing Specifically Fitted Patterns</u>

Traditionally there have been two major methods of producing a specifically fitted garment pattern, vis., drafting and draping.

2.1.1. Descriptions

Draping is the process of forming a cloth pattern directly on the body or body substitute; the fabric is smoothed over the body, shaping near bulges by the insertion of fitting devices, e.g., darts, gathers, seams. Designing, fitting and pattern making are accomplished simultaneously.

Drafting is the process of producing a pattern from a set of body dimensions. The shape and size of the pattern are a function of selected principal dimensions. Body dimensions are generally obtained by measuring lengths and girths directly on the surface of the body with a tape measure and/or a hand held anthropometer.

2.1.2. Cost and Benefits of Traditional Methods

Draping is the more accurate method of producing a specifically fitted pattern. The primary disadvantage of draping is cost; it is expensive in both human and material resources.

Drafting is a more mechanistic approach to pattern making. The use of formulae in drafting patterns reduces both the level of

311

training required by the pattern maker, and the amount of time
needed to produce a pattern. The major disadvantage of drafting
is that no drafting system consistently produces patterns that
fit as well as those that have been produced by draping. Nearly
all garments constructed from drafted patterns must be altered.

2.1.3. Reasons for Performance of Traditional Methods

There appear to be two major reason for the superior fit
produced by draping: 1) the pattern is formed in direct
relationship to the three-dimensional body, 2) fabric is used in
the pattern forming stage. Forming the pattern directly on the
body produces a pattern that not only accommodates the magnitude
of the body's principal dimensions, but also their spatial
distribution. Using fabric in the pattern forming stage allows
immediate adjustments to be made in response to its physical and
mechanical properties.

The primary reason for the failure of drafting systems appears
to be the inability of currently used data collection systems to
comprehensively and unambiguously specify the form of the
individual body. Patterns are derived primarily from girth and
length measurements, which contain little three-dimensional
information. Although the geometry of the body can be
accurately inferred if the distances between enough reference
points are measured, the number of distances that can be
measured in practice is far fewer than the number needed to
adequately specify such a complex form. The use of as many as
fifty lengths, breadths and circumferences, all two-dimensional,
to reconstruct a body requires considerable interpolation to
fill in the missing details (1). The number of measurements
actually used to make a pattern is limited by time, precision,
and accuracy.

Due to difficulty in measuring the body, data used for drafting
patterns is limited to a few principal dimensions. To produce a
pattern from this amount of information the drafting system must
contain assumptions about both the spatial relationships of the
principal dimensions and the magnitude of the dimensions not
measured. These assumptions are rarely stated explicitly, but
are contained implicitly in the basic formulae of the system.
The assumptions produce an accurate pattern for an individual
whose body is identical to the system standard, but fail as the
individual's body deviates from the standard.

2.2. Overview of Attempts to Improve Drafting

Interest in the systematic investigation of the relationship
between pattern shape and body form is a relatively recent
development.

2.2.1. Major Approach

The major approach to improving drafting systems has been to
increase the number of body dimensions used in drafting a
pattern. The earliest drafting systems that were published
derived all pattern dimensions from a single principal
dimension. Pattern makers soon discovered that utilizing more

312

than one principal body dimension increased the accuracy of fit.
A large number of systems have been developed that attempt to
improve fit by measuring more and/or different lengths and
girths. The accuracy attainable with this approach is limited
by its inability to adequately specify body form.

2.2.2 Other Approaches

As early as the nineteenth century, pattern makers recognized
the need to specify the form of the body more completely.
However, this approach was hampered by the fact that instruments
that could quantitatively measure the geometry of the body were
very cumbersome. For this reason the majority of the drafting
methods that are based on attempts to more completely specify
body form use a combination of traditional measurements and
qualitative schema for classifying individual body form. The
shape of the pattern produced by this type of system is a
function of the principal dimensions of the body and the
category into which the body is classified. Although this type
of system can be quite useful, it has a major flaw: body
variation is continuous, attempts to artificially categorize the
geometry of an individual body will inevitably lead to a loss of
information.

A quantitative approach is necessary to specify the geometry of
a form as complex as the human body. A variety of alternative
measuring techniques have been developed that attempt to more
fully specify body form. These alternative measuring techniques
include mechanical frames, electronic probes, automated tape and
caliper devices and photogrammetric methods.

Most of the alternative techniques for measuring the body used
in drafting patterns yield little or no more three-dimensional
information than traditional techniques. Drafting systems based
on alternative measuring techniques that produce essentially
two-dimensional data fail for the same reason that traditional
systems do: too many assumptions must be made about the body
form. Many of these assumptions have not been recognized as
such because the act of measuring the body does not specify its
form, as is usually assumed, but actually produces a
two-dimensional abstraction of it. These abstractions are
fundamentally empirical, the underlying geometric explanation
for their success or failure has rarely been investigated.

Rapid non-contacting techniques based on photographic
principles, such as stereophotogrammetry, suggested by Herron
(2), Bourachkov (3) and Appel and Stein (4), appear to be most
appropriate for completely specifying body form. From two sets
of stereopairs, it is possible to determine Cartesian
coordinates for nearly any point on the body.

Although techniques that can completely specify the
three-dimensional body form have been available for some time,
they are rarely used to collect data for the production of
specifically fitted patterns. Hutchinson (5) suggested that
three-dimensional data is not used more frequently because the
relationship between the three-dimensional body form and the
two-dimensional pattern shape is not understood very well. He

investigated the relationship statistically. Bourachkov (6) and
Appel and Stein (4) investigated the same problem with a more
geometric approach.

Bourachkov produced a pattern for a second skin by unrolling the
body form to form its "involute". The pattern consisted of 36
strips. Bourchakov discussed how examination of the strips
might be useful in further research, but never produced a
garment pattern. From coordinates for twenty-seven points on
the body, Appel and Stein modeled a bodice as a polygonal form.
The polygonal model was developed into a pattern. The fit of
the bodice produced by their method was not entirely successful.
More work is needed to understand the relationship between the
three-dimensional body form and the two-dimensional pattern
shape.

3.   ALGORITHM DEVELOPMENT AND EVALUATION

3.1. Approach

The approach of this research to developing a quantitative
methodology for producing specifically fitted patterns was based
upon modeling the physical and mechanical aspects of fit in
order to relate the three-dimensional body form to the
two-dimensional pattern shape. A modeling approach was
considered preferable to statistical "curve fitting" because it
allows direct examination of the underlying mechanisms involved
in fitting a garment.

The objective was to develop a methodology that combines the
advantages that were identified for both draping and drafting,
viz., accuracy and speed, respectively. Therefore a
quantitative three-dimensional specification of the body form
was used in developing new formulae to systematically relate
three-dimensional body form to two-dimensional pattern shape. A
data set for complete and unambiguous specification of body
form is quite large, e.g., 2900 points for a woman of average
size. Due to the large amount of data, computer manipulation
was assumed to be an integral part of the methodology.

Several systems have already been developed that use computers
to produce specifically fitted patterns, however, most of these
systems are merely traditional drafting methods that have been
encoded. The ability of computers to quickly manipulate large
quantities of data offers the potential to develop new
algorithms. The data from which a pattern is produced no longer
needs to be limited to a few principal dimensions, or points.
It is not necessary to form a crude two-dimensional abstraction
of the body as part of the measuring process. New algorithms
should separate body specification and abstraction. A garment
pattern is really the garment form flattened, not the body form
flattened, thus a three-dimensional garment form should be
specified and then the pattern produced from it. The term
"last" will be used to designate a three-dimensional
specification of a garment form.

The fact that a garment is not a replica of the skin is
generally accepted, but little work has been done toward

314

developing a method to quantitatively describe a properly fitted garment form. The polygonal bodice modeled by Appel and Stein (4) was the only incidence found in the literature of last specification.

Once a last is specified, it should be systematically projected onto a planar surface. Factors that determine conformation of fabrics to irregular surfaces should be included in the projection algorithm.

Only Appel and Stein (4), and Bourachkov (6) attempted to produce a pattern by geometrically projecting a three-dimensional form onto a plane. Appel and Stein's method appears to be dependent upon defining the bodice as a set of polygons that are large enough so that each is bounded by fitting devices or garment boundaries. This resulted in a last specification that did not very closely approximate the curvilinear form of a real garment. Bourachkov more closely approximated a three-dimensional form, but he produced a pattern that consisted only of narrow strips, which were not and probably could not be combined into a real garment. The approach in this research was to closely approximate the last surface in a way that allowed it to be projected onto a plane to produce a traditional pattern.

3.2. Algorithm: Projection and Development of a Last Onto a Planar Surface

3.2.1. Last Specification

A spherical last was used during the initial stages of algorithm development. Although a sphere is somewhat less complex than the surface of a typical garment last, it has the most essential attribute needed for algorithm testing; it is not applicable to a planar surface. Use of the spherical last simplified data collection and verification of the algorithm. The use of a last that could be mathematically generated eliminated confounding evaluation of last modeling and verification of the projection algorithm.

The surface of the spherical last was specified using a cylindrical coordinate grid. Coordinates were calculated for the intersections of forty equally spaced longitudes and sixteen latitudes.

3.2.2. Algorithm Overview

The algorithm for projecting the last onto a planar surface involved three steps. The surface of the last was approximated as a mesh of n-quadrilaterals.[1]

------

[1] A closed convex figure with four or more sides need not be coplanar. When it cannot be assumed that such a figure is planar it will be referred to as an n-polygon or an n-quadrilateral, a planar figure as a p-polygon or a p-quadrilateral.

Individual n-quadrilaterals were projected onto a plane.
Following projection, the planar representation of the last was
composed of many p-quadrilaterals, one p-quadrilateral for each
element of the original mesh. Finally the p-quadrilaterals were
combined to form a pattern.

3.2.3. Approximation of the Last

A standard technique for approximating a curved surface is to
represent it as a mesh of polygons (7). Use of p-polygons with
more than three sides requires fairly elaborate techniques to
locate the vertex points on the form (8). Estimation by
triangles seems to be the most popular technique because
coplanarity of the polygons is ensured. For this research
n-quadrilaterals having approximately equal length and breadth
were used, because they were considered to model the
micro-structure of woven fabric.

It is essential that the n-quadrilateral size be chosen so that
the curvature of the surface approximated by the n-quadrilateral
is no greater than that which can be accommodated by the
elasticity of the fabric. Within an n-polygon the ability of
fabric to conform to a three-dimensional surface is dependent
upon the degree and directions of surface curvature. If
curvature is around only one axis, fabric bending is sufficient
to produce conformation. However, if curvature of the surface
is around more than one axis the material must be capable of
extending and/or compressing in selected areas. For woven
fabrics, which have little potential to stretch or compress
along the warp and weft, accommodation must occur by shearing
(9).

It was assumed that most woven fabrics can shear more than
enough to accommodate the curvature that occurs within a 2 cm
square on most areas of the body. Therefore n-quadrilaterals
used in this research were approximately 2 cm square.
Intersections of the cylindrical coordinate grid on the last
were used as vertices for the n-polygon mesh. Further work is
needed to determine optimal n-polygon size.

3.2.4. Projection of the Last Onto a Planar Surface

Grid vertices resulted in n-quadrilaterals that were not
necessarily coplanar. Therefore each individual n-quadrilateral
was projected onto a planar surface to form a p-polygonal
representation of the last. Due to being non-applicable the
scale in some regions will be compressed while in other regions
it will be stretched. This means that an object on a curved
surface may not have the same size and shape on a plane.

Three options were identified for projecting an n-quadrilateral
onto two-dimensions. Option 1: The proportional relationship
between all four angles and the length of one side would be
preserved. The length of the other three sides would vary
depending on the extent to which planarity was violated by the
n-quadrilateral. Option 2: The length of all four sides and

the proportional relationship of one angle would be preserved. The size of the other three angles would vary depending on the extent to which planarity was violated by the n-quadrilateral. Option 3: A projection which minimizes some error function for the vertices. The most common of such projections is an orthogonal projection where the error function which is minimized is the sums of squares between the original points and their representation on the projection plane (pers. com. D. Heisey). This produces a polygon with the least total error, but the size of all of the angles and the length of all of the sides may vary from the original depending on the extent to which planarity was violated by the quadrilateral. Error functions other than sums of squares have also been advocated (10).

At first glance the orthogonal projection seems to be the most attractive because it would involve the smallest amount of error in a certain sense. However, Option 2 was judged to be the most useful for pattern production. Once the polygons have been projected, they must be fitted together edgewise to make the final pattern. Adjacent polygons must fit together precisely, therefore the exact length of the original sides must be preserved.

The following method was used to project the n-quadrilaterals. The length of each side was computed as the Euclidean distance between the vertices. The Euclidean distance is a straight line approximation of the actual distance over the curved surface. The error involved in this approximation should be very small for a 2 cm square n-quadrilateral on most areas of the body. Next, the angle of each n-quadrilateral corner was determined. If the four vertices were coplanar the sum of the four angles would be equal to 2 * pi radians. If they were not coplanar the total would be less than 2 * pi radians; the difference is an indication of the violation of planarity. To determine a scaling factor for the angle 2 * pi radians was divided by the sum of the four n-quadrilateral angles. To calculate the single p-polygon angle that was to be proportional to its counterpart in the n-quadrilateral, the n-quadrilateral angle was multiplied by the scaling factor. Each polygon was then plotted.

The projected polygons were tested in fabric. The covering produced for the spherical last appeared to fit like a "second skin". From this evidence mesh approximation of the sphere and projection of the n-quadrilaterals was tentatively judged to be a success.

3.2.5. Forming the Development

The next step in producing a realistic pattern was to combine

the polygons[2] to form a "development". Appel and Stein (11)
defined a development as "unfolding of the surface of a solid
onto a flat plane". If the surface approximated by the polygons
is applicable to a planar surface the polygons can be unfolded
so none of them overlap, and so there are no gaps between them.
For example, the polygons for a cone form a sector of a circle,
or the polygons for a cylinder form a rectangle. Generally only
prisms, cones, or cylinders can be unfolded to produce a
continuous development (11). If the surface of the object is
not applicable to a plane, such as a sphere, the polygons either
overlap, or have gaps between them. This is the problem that
Bourachkov (6) encountered with his strips. The amount of
overlap or gap is an indication of the non-applicability of the
two surfaces.

Two polygons can be developed to form a single piece by
translating and/or rotating one of them so their common sides
are adjacent. An entire vertical or horizontal strip of
polygons can be developed in the same manner. A horizontal and
a vertical strip of polygons that intersect can also be
developed by a combination of translating and/or rotating.

It is not so easy to develop two parallel strips of polygons.
For example, if four polygons, two adjacent polygons from each
of two parallel vertical strips, are to be developed, any three
of them can be developed simply by rotating and/or translating.
However, the fourth polygon cannot be developed so that it
contacts both of the polygons adjacent to it. By rotating
and/or translating, it can be aligned with either the polygon
that is vertically adjacent to it, or the one that is
horizontally adjacent to it; it cannot be aligned with both.
In order to fit the fourth polygon into position, it must be
selectively compressed and stretched. To preserve the length of
all sides of the fourth polygon, while fitting it into position,
it was pseudo-sheared. Pseudo-shearing consisted of pivoting
the sides around their end points until both the horizontal and
vertical sides of the polygon were aligned with the adjacent
polygons. This resulted in two of the angles being stretched,
and the other two being compressed, e.g., a square polygon that
is pseudo-sheared will become a parallelogram.

Pseudo-shearing of the polygons was an attempt to model on the
macro level, fabric shearing that occurs on the micro level in a
garment. Pivoting the sides of a polygon around their end
points does not perfectly model shearing that occurs in fabric.
Yarns remain parallel to each other when a fabric is sheared; in
the polygon model the sides of the polygon will

---

[2]For this section polygons and quadrilaterals will be
assumed to be planar unless otherwise noted.

not necessarily remain parallel. However, if the pseudo-shear angle remains relatively small, polygon shearing appears to be reasonably consistent with the mechanism that allows woven fabric to conform to three-dimensional surfaces.

There is a limit to the degree to which a polygon can be pseudo-sheared. The polygon can only be pseudo-sheared as long as it has four separate sides. Triangles cannot be pseudo-sheared, therefore the limit to pseudo-shearing is reached when two sides become one.

There is another limit to pseudo-shearing that is usually more restrictive. Polygon pseudo-shearing may not exceed the amount of shear that can be accommodated by the fabric. The limit imposed by the fabric is usually lower than the geometric limit. If a polygon is pseudo-sheared farther than the fabric can accommodate, the fabric will buckle, causing wrinkles in the garment.

The only shear angles we found for actual garments were reported by Mahar et al. (12). They measured localized shear angles in the region along the shoulder of a man's suitcoat. The shear angles ranged up to approximately 13 degrees. The maximum angle that the polygons can be pseudo-sheared will probably vary depending upon the specific fabric that is to be used in constructing the completed pattern.

A polyester/cotton broadcloth was used to test the development algorithm. The maximum allowable pseudo-shear angle to be used for this fabric was determined empirically. A series of coverings for the spherical last were constructed. Each covering in the series used fewer pieces to cover the sphere, e.g., the first covering was made of forty pieces, one piece for each vertical row of polygons, the second covering was made of twenty pieces, two vertical rows of polygons were developed to form each piece. The largest pseudo-shear angle in the pattern was increased each time another strip was added. The series was continued until a pattern was produced that caused the completed covering to buckle unacceptably. The pseudo-shear angle of the polygon immediately before the one which buckled unacceptably was used as the maximum. The maximum pseudo-shear angle before buckling occurred was determined to be 13.25 degrees.

A polygon cannot be pseudo-sheared into position if it will be pseudo-sheared more than the maximum pseudo-shear angle. In such a situation the remaining side cannot be aligned. Two different developments will result depending upon which side of the polygon is aligned with an adjacent polygon. Either a vertical or horizontal gap or overlap will result.

Gaps that result from rotating to avoid exceeding the maximum pseudo-shear angle are fitting device precursors. The type of pattern to be produced determines which of the two possible developments will be used, and what kind of fitting device the precursor will become.

The algorithm for development produced patterns that appear to
fit in all aspects except one. The bottom of the second skins
were slightly scalloped. This seems to be a result of pseudo-
shearing the polygons into position during development. When a
polygon is pseudo-sheared into position one diagonal of the
polygon is shortened and the other is lengthened. This
combination of lengthening and shortening produced the scallops.

The amount that the vertical boundaries were shortened was
dependent upon the number of polygons within the piece and the
amount they had to be sheared. To correct this situation the
amount shortened or lengthened cannot be simply summed and added
to the bottom of the lateral edge of the development, because
adjacent development pieces must remain the same length so they
can be sewn together. Further work is needed to determine the
best approach to compensating for the distortion resulting from
pseudo-shearing.

The effect of sequence is another point that needs further
investigation. Different developments result depending upon
which polygon is used as the starting point and the sequence of
development. This has major implications for final pattern
shape, and is the basis for style variation. The term
development definition will be used to denote the sequence of
development and the rules that are used for inserting fitting
device precursors to form a particular development.

In spite of the need for further research on some points, the
algorithms used for projection and development were tentatively
judged to be successful. The next step was to extend the method
to produce a real garment.

3.3. Algorithm: Prototypical Garment

3.3.1. Body Specification

A Wolf size 12 hanging mannequin was used for testing last
specification. The primary reason for using a mannequin rather
than a person was that a mannequin's form would be more
constant. Fluctuations in body form would have confounded
errors in last specification.

A mechanical instrument built by the University of Minnesota
shop was used to determine cylindrical coordinates for points on
the mannequin surface. The instrument consisted of a frame
which supported a Siber Hegner Anthropometer model GPM-101 and
the mannequin. The mannequin was fastened to a rotating table
that was graduated in degrees. The location in three-space of
any point on the body could be specified by three values: the
angle of rotation, the vertical distance in centimeters from the
base to the point, and the horizontal distance in centimeters
from the anthropometer to the point on the body surface.

The area of the mannequin measured was limited to that which was
required to specify a last for a basic skirt. The same type of
cylindrical coordinate grid was used for measuring the

body that had been used to specify the sphere. Vertical cross sections were spaced at 10 degree intervals; horizontal cross sections were spaced at 2 cm intervals parallel to the floor.

3.3.2. Last Specification

The term last is used to denote a three-dimensional model of the space that is enclosed by a garment. It is analogous to a wooden last used to manufacture shoes. Garment details such as fitting devices determine the shape of the development and the final pattern but they are not part of the last specification. The ideal garment last should be defined as a function of body form.

A basic skirt last was preliminarily modeled as a convex form that rests on the body 1/2 inch (1.25 cm) below the waist. The waist circumference of the last was set equal to the circumference of the body 1/2 inch (1.25 cm) below the natural waist.

Cylindrical coordinates for each horizontal cross section of the last were calculated using the following method. Each cross section was determined from the set of body coordinates that included those from the corresponding level of the body and all levels between it and the waist. The convex hull was calculated for the set of body coordinates. Next points were calculated for any vertical cross sections that did not have a point on the convex hull. These points were calculated as the intersection of a line connecting the two convex hull points on either side of the missing values and the plane that defined the vertical cross section.

3.3.3. Approximation, Projection and Development

Approximation by an n-polygon mesh, projection of the n-polygons onto a plane, and construction of the development from the p-polygons were accomplished using the same algorithms as for the sphere. The same fabric was used to test the skirt patterns, so all parameters were the same.

3.3.4. Development Definition for the Basic Skirt

The last was developed into six pieces bounded by the center front, five fitting device precursors and the center back. The five fitting device precursors corresponded to the two front waist darts, a side seam, and the two back waist darts of a basic skirt. Center front was defined as the vertical cross section that included the center front seam on the mannequin at the waist. Center back was defined as the vertical cross section closest to the center back seam on the mannequin. On a body where a seam would not conveniently mark center back, center back could be located 180 degrees from center front.

The side seam precursor was located along the vertical cross section that contained the point on the waist that was farthest from the sagittal plane. This vertical cross section was 80 degrees from center front. The two front skirt darts should

divide the space between the center front and side seam
approximately into thirds. Their precursors were located at 30
and 60 degrees from the center front. The inner back dart
precursor was located along the vertical cross section 10
degrees toward the side seam from the vertical cross section
that passed through the fullest part of the buttocks. The
fullest part of the buttocks was defined as the data point
farthest from the coronal plane in the posterior direction.
This cross section was 140 degrees from center front. The side
back dart should evenly divide the space between the center back
dart and the side seam. Its precursor was placed along the
cross section 100 degrees from center front. The length of dart
precursors was determined by the distance of the relevant
prominence from the waist. Any fitting needed below the bottom
of each dart precursor was accommodated by the side seam.

Development started at the upper medial edge of each of the six
development pieces and proceeded in a lateral and downward
direction. All parts of the development definition could be
accommodated by the computer program except one. The program
could not accommodate setting a specific length for a fitting
device precursor. Therefore the preliminary developments
produced by the computer had fitting device precursors that
extended through the entire length of the development. The
preliminary developments were manipulated using flat pattern
techniques to move any fitting device precursor that occurred
below the defined levels into the side seam precursor.
Modification of the program used in this research would be
needed to allow shorter fitting device precursors, but no change
would be needed in the basic development algorithm.

3.3.5. Forming the Skirt Pattern

The completed developments were not a pattern for a basic skirt.
Three development pieces were combined to form each of the skirt
pattern pieces. Fitting device precursors were transformed into
fitting devices, and ease for space occupied by the fabric and
seam allowances was added. Patterns were manually produced from
the developments. Production by computer would require a
trivial extension of programs used to produce the developments.

Two basic skirt patterns were produced. The one pattern
included only enough ease to accommodate the thickness of the
fabric and seams. An additional 1/2 inch (1.25cm) ease was
added between the side and center development pieces in the back
panel of the second pattern. When both patterns were tested in
fabric, they appeared to fit well, except, the side seam stood
away from the body a little just below the waist. This was
probably due to the pseudo-shearing, which had caused scalloping
in the spherical coverings.

Additional work is needed on particular details of the
algorithm, most notably on pseudo-shearing. However, the basic
conceptual framework which separates body specification, last
specification and pattern projection seems to be useful for
pattern production.

REFERENCES

1. R. Herron. <u>Yearbook of Anthropology</u>, 1972, <u>16</u>, 18.
2. H. Steinberg. <u>Development of a National Anthropometric</u>
       <u>Data Base: A Preliminary Study Report</u>. Technical
       Analysis Division Institute for Applied Technology
       National Bureau of Standards, 1974, NBSIR74-506.
3. V. Bourachkov. <u>Teknol. Likoi Prom.</u>, <u>58</u>, 1972, 104.
4. A. Appel and A. Stein. <u>Proceedings: Paperless Apparel</u>
       <u>Management</u>, American Apparel Manufacture Assoc.
       Atlanta, USA, 1978
5. R. Hutchinson. Master's Thesis, University of Leeds, 1977.
6. V. Bourachkov. <u>Teknol. Lekoi Prom.</u>, <u>58</u>, 1972, 103.
7. H. Gouraud. <u>Computer Display of Curved Surfaces</u>, Garland
       Press, New York, USA, 1971.
8. J. Foley and A. Van Dam. <u>Fundamentals of Interactive</u>
       <u>Computer Graphics</u>, Chapter 13, Addison Wesley,
       Reading, Mass., USA, 1982.
9. J. Hearle, P. Grosberg and S. Backer. <u>Structural Mechanics</u>
       <u>of Fibers, Yarns and Fabrics</u>, Wiley-Interscience,
       New York, USA, 1969.
10. A. Siegel and R. Benson. <u>Biometrics</u>, <u>38</u>, 1982, 341.
11. A. Appel and A. Stein. <u>Proceedings: First USA-JAPAN</u>
       <u>Computer Conference</u>. AFIPS, Tokyo, Japan, 486.
12. T. Mahar, R. Dhingra and R. Postle. <u>Proceedings:</u>
       <u>Objective Specification of Fabric Quality, Mechanical</u>
       <u>Properties & Performance</u>, The Textile Machinery
       Society of Japan, Osaka, Japan, 1982.

F. Heisey
1300 Linden Drive
University of Wisconsin
Madison, WI   53706
USA

P. Brown & R.F. Johnson
McNeal Hall
University of Minnesota
St. Paul, MN   55108
USA

COMPUTERIZATION IN A GARMENT FACTORY

E. Y. Cheng, J. H. Wong, and D. W. Poon.

Abstract

Traditional computerization of a garment factory would utilize the expertises of mainframe computer companies and software consulting firms which involves large investment, tremendous extra effort of everyone throughout the organization and management commitment to complete the project. This paper reports an alternative way using the microcomputers and available software, which costs only a fraction of the above mentioned investment cost, job by job implementation which can cease at the any time and will not upset the normal operation of the factory.

1. INTRODUCTION

The Darwinian Law of Evolution - Survival of the Fittest, can be applied to the garment industry in Hong Kong. A manufacturer must be highly competitive in order to stay in the field. This means that besides having to excel in product design as well as production technique and quality, a manufacturer must also achieve a high degree of operational and management efficiency.

The rising complexity of the garment trade, however, has made the task of efficiency improvement increasingly difficult. The market demand of a wide variety of product stylings in an equally large variety of raw materials to be manufactured in diminishing time allowance has placed tremendous pressure on every operation of a factory. While workload in order processing, material requirement planning, inventory control, production scheduling, has risen inevitably, one must exploit the advantages of using computer. The traditional approach is to use customized software supplied by consulting firms. However, the cost is high due to the service involved and the sophisticated hardware required. In addition, both management and staff are heavily burdened with supplying detailed specifications of all operations in the system design stage.

We propose an alternative approach to computerize the commonly encountered problematic areas of most garment factory as shown in exhibit 1, by using relatively inexpensive but increasing powerful microcomputers and commercially available software. The process requires no specialized personnel and integration.

There are several stages necessary for the successful
implementation of the systems. Firstly is the initial planning
stage which includes the analysis of the current situation,
outlines of the required areas of automation, specifications of
the equipment and staff needed and identification of the costs
and benefits. Secondly is the concept development stage which
includes the determination of the package required and the design
of output and input. Finally comes the stage of implementation.
Here we are concerned with the design of the system procedures,
system testing and training of the staffs. We will emphasis on
the areas of application using microcomputer and commercially
available software and the possibilities of systems integration.

2. THE MICROCOMPUTERS AND COMMERCIALLY AVAILABLE SOFTWARE

2.1 The Microcomputers

Microcomputer is the newest and most popular product of computer technology. The very low cost of microcomputers, their readily availability and their ease of use revolutionize the application of computers and increase its popularity exponentially.

The microcomputer is built around a powerful microprocessor which is a LSI (Large scale integrated circuit) implementing the function of an ALU (Arithematic and Logic Unit) plus its associated control unit in a single chip. A microprocessor may also be defined as a CPU (Central Processing Unit) in a chip. Generally, the microcomputer would have a cassette or diskette storage unit, a printer and a visual display unit. However, with the advancement of microcomputer, some models are compatible minicomputer and use line printers, hard disc storage and multiple input stations. Hence, it is somewhat difficult to draw the line between the super microcomputer and minicomputer.

2.2 Advantages of Microcomputers

a.) Size - The CPU of the traditional computer requiring several square meters of space has been replaced by a small microprocessor. Hence a great deal of computer power has been made possible to occupy a very small area.

b.) <u>Cost</u> - Lower cost to purchase is possible because of the mass production technique and lower operating cost is possible because of its small power consumption (120W) and less heat generated.

c.) <u>Reliability</u> - The high reliability of the chips and the reduced number of interconnection on the circuit boards reduce the failure rates.

d.) <u>Environment</u> - Based on point (b) and (c) above, microcomputer requires less critical air conditioning and other environmental controls.

e.) <u>Portability</u> - Portability is increased because of smaller size and weight.

f.) <u>Peripherals</u> - Nearly all types of peripherals mentioned can be connected to microcomputer. Though they may be slower, they are much cheaper than the large computer.

g.) <u>Ease of use</u> - Because of the adequate software and system support, a person with no computer training can use microcomputer either without the need to write a program at all or if necessary can write one in natural language rather than the complicated computer language. Many software houses provide system packages catering to a different aspect of the apparel industry e.g. production system, management system. On the other hand, some packages allow one to create a complete program by answering questions posted by the microcomputer in natural languages.

Another factor contributing to the use of microcomputer
is that it provides a processing facility wherever it is
needed. The low cost makes it possible to install microcomputer in different sites and thus eliminate disadvantages
of centralization e.g. divoicing user staff from the processing of their work and creating delay while data and output
are moved. However, the installation at different site can
also be linked to form a system network.

2.3 Basic Components

The basic components of most microcomputers include a
keyboard, a VDU (Video Display Unit), a printer and a disk
drive.

a) Keyboard

Generally, the keyboard is very similar to the common
typewriter with standard alphanumeric layout plus some
special functions keys and a calculator-type numeric keypad
for ease of entering numerical values.

b) VDU (Video Display Unit)

The VDU is similar to a television set which we often
refers to as the monitor or screen. The screen displays 80
characters per line with 24 or 25 lines. Monitors of the
monochrome type comes in amber, green, and black and white.
However, the high resolution color monitors are particular
useful for graphic display.

c) Printer

Dot-matrix type is the most widely used printer today.

It can produce graphics and is fast and inexpensive.
Bidirectional printing is often feasible at about 160
characters per second with an average price of US$600.
Another type of printer often known as letter quality printer
employing a daisywheel for its functioning. It can produce
limited graphics, however, the speed is very slow and
operating at approximately 50 characters per second.

d) Disk and Disk Drive

Early microcomputers used magnetic tapes for off-line
data storage and is extremely slow. Now we can use diskettes
to remedy this situation. They are in the form of flexible
or floppy diskette with diameters 5-1/4 or 8 inches. Such
diskettes may be single or double density and single sided or
double sided which mainly increase their storage capacity.
Most double sided and double density disketes can hold
320,000 characters (320K bytes) of information. Some may
even hold as much as 1 mega (1M) bytes on an 8" diskette.

Due to limited storage capacity of a 5-1/4 inches floppy
diskette, frequent human intervention of diskette swaping is
necessary to store huge quantity of information. To remedy
this problem, there are now Winchester and other hard disk
drives which can store as much as 500 times of data as a
floppy. While, they cost at least US$2,000 against US$5 per
floppy and $300 for each floppy disk drive, their vast
storage capacity and fast data transfer will be appreciable.

2.4 Commercially Available Software

A lot of application packages being sold today still goes into mainframe computer used by banks, airlines, government and other large corporations. Traditionally, such package are leased instead of sold from the computer manufacturer which can cost as much as US$200,000(1)a year.

Previously, due to a lack of software for the microcomputers, plenty software firms are formed and reaching out to market their own brands of package for different classes of application. Besides the standard application packages such as general ledger, accounts receivable and payable and inventory, other excitements for the industry are programs for spreadsheet, database management, statistics, graphic plotting and word processing, which contributed to the accelerating popularity of microcomputers.

2.5 Outlines on different types of packages

a) Spreadsheet

There are many kinds of spreadsheet packages available, for example, VisiCalc is a trademark of VisiCorp and SuperCalc is a trademark of Sorcim. Although the brands and the versions are varied, their principles, functions and features are more or less similar, basically, a number processor. The average price is around US$200.

The program is based on the simulation of a worksheet that consists of columns and rows. Columns are numbered across the top in alphabets and rows are numbered down the left side of the display in numbers. The space where a

331

column intercepts a row forms a box, the building block of the spreadsheet. These boxes are called as 'cell' which can hold texts, numerical values or formulae.

Spreadsheets are used in a similar manner as the paper worksheet. Tabulated tables with sums and averages as a listing of inventory with price and quantity in variable columns and dollar values and total value can be computed by inserting the appropriate formulae in cells. A change of value in the variable column will instantly activate the program to re-calculate all related values in each cell.

Besides, there are lots of other features and functions of the program which allow us to manipulate data and produce reports in the most efficient and convenient ways.

b) Database Management

Firstly, we have to disscuss what is a database management system (DBMS). Conceptually, a database is a specially designed, supported and controlled set of related data. The system integrates the data and makes it much easier to get useful information from the records, rather than just reams of data. Diagrammatically, a DMBS looks something like exhibit as exhibit 2.

DBASE II, trademark of Ashton-Tate, is one of the most widely used database programs currently available. It costs only about US$700 which provides file creation commands such as CREATE, COPY TO, SAVE TO AND INDEX ON, file manipulation commands such as DO, APPEND, SELECT and SORT, and creating,

332

editing and displaying data commands such as CHANGE, DELETE,
RECALL, PACK, EDIT, FIND, INSERT, LOCATE, READ, REPLACE, SUM
and TOTAL to handle all the nitty-gritty of a DBMS. It is
used for creating a data file for storing valuable information. And later using the above mentained commands to
manipulate the data in the file.

c) Statistics/Plotting

VisiTrend/VisiPlot, trade mark of VisiCorp, is an
effiecient and popular statistics/plotting program.

Conceptually, the plotting program provides the
advantage of creating a visual representation of data.
Comparing two sets of values on a screen will be much more
attractive and useful than two sets of figures. The charts
furnish us with the capability to see the relationships just
at a glance. The statistic program elaborate the graphic
measures with those scientific methodologies for statistical
purposes. With the aid of this kind of package, it turns a
stack of numbers into a chart and perform desired
mathematical analysis which are most time-consuming and
error-prone if they are to be performed by hand. This
package can read data created by the VisiCalc spreadsheet
program and costs about US$300.

d) Word Processing

One of the major use of the microcomputer is word
processing. WordStar, a product of MicroPro International
Corporation, probably is the most widely used word processing

333

program costing about US$300. As stated in its manual, it is
a screen-oriented system with the capability of integrated
printing(2). Both initial entry of text and subsequent
alteration are displayed directly on the screen. Most
formatting functions take place immediately enabling a true
print image; additional enhancement are performed during
printout. The MailMerge option adds form letter generating
capabilities. With the help of a good word processing
program, we can produce error-free documents.

3. APPLICATIONS

We shall illustrate the principles and steps to computerization giving one example for each application with inputs, outputs and programming steps.

3.1 Production Planning

To establish production time standards are usually time-consuming due to the great varieties of product range and manufacture approach. However, without these information, capacity planning and scheduling becomes conjectural and even erroneous. In order to establish the time-standard, we are looking for a convenient index which could be obtained from a readily available datum - wage rate.

We will use commercial available spreadsheet program to illustrate this application and will divide the Production Planning System into two parts, namely, the Time-Rate Index Analysis System and the Sample Costing System.

3.1.1 Time-Rate Index Analysis System

The input data to the system are the payroll and time information readily available from the Accounts Department. We will divide the process departments into:

a.) cutting,

b.) sewing,

c.) stitching (including hemming, finishing),

d.) pressing, and,

e.) packing (including inspection, button sewing and cleaning).

The wages for individual worker under each wage period
coupling with the time incurred available from the time card,
are entered into the spreadsheet. The wage per hour are
computed for every worker. (See Exhibit 3, example for sewing
department.)

Columns A and B are used to accomodate the worker's name
and the item names of wage/period, hours/period and wage/hour
respectively, are entered as text data. Starting from column
C and row 5, all cells are used to enter data or formula.
Cell C5 up to cell Z5 are used to store wage/period of the
first worker for the most recent twenty-four wage periods.
Similarly, cell C6 up to cell Z6 are used to store
hour/period. While, cell C7 up to cell Z7 are used to store
the formula to calculate the wage/hour by dividing the
wage/period by hours/period. (C7=C5/C6, D7=D5/D6, ...,
Z7=Z5/Z6.

On the other corner of the table. Cell AA11 and AA12
are the total wage and total hour respectively for 12 months
of the last worker. Cell AA13 is the wage/hour taking into
consideration of the 24 wage periods by dividing AA11 by
AA12. Cell AA14 and cell AA15 accomodate the total wage and
hour for all workers during that specified period. While
AA16 and AA17 store the formula to compute the wage/hr for
the department and the Time-Rate Index respectively. In
fact, the index is only the reciprocal of the wage/hour.
Those formula used are exhibited in Exhibit 4.

Using a different file for every department, we compiled
a summary Time-Rate Report as in Exhibit 5. These indices are
used to compute the workload for each work centre.

3.1.2 Sample Costing System

In this system, data are originated from the sample
department. When a sample is made, its labour cost is
estimated in accordance with the production method,
manufacture approach, machine and fabric type. The costs
are, however, classified into cutting, sewing, stitching,
pressing and packing, which correspond to the classification
of the time-rate system. These information are entered into
the sample costing file and is updated when a new sample is
made.

At this stage, the system sorts and adds all costs by
process for all orders to be shipped in a stipulated period.
It is the usual practice for the company to plan a week ahead
one month's production in accordance to delivery priority,
finanical necessity, quota deadline and material
availability. And those orders that cannot meet the delivery
schedule in the previous month are carried over to the
following month. Then, all labour costs classified by
process for the month are calculated by multiplying the
individual process total cost by the relevant time-rate index
to obtain the total working time required for the month's
production.

And from the time available (including overtime) for
each department in the period, the number of workers required
is computed by dividing the total working time required by
the time available.

These manipulations can be done by using the spreadsheet
program which we are not going to illustrate again as the
principles are similar as previously discussed. Thus this
implementation can be used by the planner to pinpoint the
overload and underload conditions for each work centre. He
therefore can make adjustments to minimise work queue lengths
(by reducing lead time), to ensure that labour will not run
out of works and to analyse those overloads and underloads so
as to help determine which orders can be subcontracted.

3.2 Order Listing

A complete list of the order status can be a useful
managerial tool throughout the organisation. A simple listing of
such information as order number, style number, quantity, fabric
and delivery date not only acts as a reference look-up table, but
also serves as a guideline for order intake and production
planning.

When updating the list, majority of the content will be
unchanged. It is mainly a mechanical process by reiterating most
of the old content and the addition of new information to compile
a new list.

The value of a computer in combatting this problem is obvious
and will turn the system efficient, timely and accurate together
with reduced clerical costs. Using a commercial available data

338

base package, we can generate different lists by the program's
report writer feature to add, interrogate, modify or delete
informations in the data file. We use dBASE II package to
accomplish this job. The program listing and data file structure
are illustrated in exhibit 6.

3.3 Purchases and Inventories

To serve the high end of the market, factories need to
accept orders of smaller quantity and numerous colours.
To deliver merchandises on time and to minimise overstock and
understock of the tremendous amount of fabric and trim
materials, we need an efficient purchase and inventory
management system. We can design such system using the database package of dBASE II. The underlying principles will be
similar to the set up in the order list, but the procedures
will be much more complicated. Numerous reports are designed
to serve those purposes aforementioned.

3.3.1 The System Inputs

The informations entered to the system can be classified
into the following six categories.

a. Material Requirement Input - When a new manufacture
order is issued, the client information and order quantity
should be entered. Then the estimated unit consumptions for
different materials in code form are entered to provide the
quantities needed accordingly.

b. Purchase Order Entry - From the above information and
thosefrom the inventory file, the balance quantities to order

can be computed. We can then make out the purchase orders

and enter the revelant data into the inventory file.

c. Material Receipt Entry - When the ordered material

arrives, the quantity received is entered to update the

inventory status report.

d. Material Issue Entry - The materials received are

issued to the shop floor for production. This entry will

record all those data accordingly.

e. Material Return Entry - Coupling with the issue entry

will be the return entry. The materials returned, if any,

should be entered in connection with the individual issuance.

f. Adjustment Entry - Adjustments are inevitable for all

system. This entry is essential to provide corrections on

quantity, description and value.

3.3.2 The Output Reports

With all the information provided by the input system,

the output reports should cover the inventory status report,

the committment report, purchase overdue report, purchase

receipt report and material requirement report.

a. The Inventory Status Report - It provides an

exhaustive report on the current status of all inventory

items. A brief description, stock quantity, value, average

price and date of last movement are the integral part of the

report.

b. The Committment Report - It highlights all out-

standing materials requirement not yet ordered. When there

is material requirement input, the quantity needed will be

updated. The outstanding quantity will then be calculated by subtracting the stock on hand from the quantity needed. It should be noted that when an issue entry is made, the relevant quantity needed must be deducted accordingly.

c. The Purchase Overdue Report - This report is used to isolate all outstanding overdue pruchases. It shows the vendor, P/O number, material code, scheduled delivery and other relevant details enabling us to follow up accordingly.

d. The Purchase Receipt Report - This report is similar to the previous one, except there are two additional columns. One is the invoice number, and the other is the payment term. Furthermore, the quantity, amount and scheduled delivery are superseded by the quantity received, invoice amount and actual delivery respectively. The program should be written so that all transaction amounts within a particular fiscal period are added up to provide accounts payable information for the accounts department.

e. The Material Requirement Report - It provides a complete listing on all information from the materials requirement input. It is paramount for checking purposes because any corrections and adjustments can be traced after all data are initially input to the system. Every single item consumption and total quantity needed for all M/O are listed to give a complete summary.

f. Purchase Summary Report - To list all current purchases in addition to the overdue purchases.

g. Purchase Performance Report - To list all purchases received with simple analysis on varience in delivery and quantity etc.

341

h. Issue Status Report - To give an overall view on the shop floor material acquisition.

i. Return Status Report - To give record on materials returned and provide simple analysis in relation to the issuance data.

j. Adjustment Report - To list all adjustment made.

The benefits thus obtained using this computerized system may be summarised as follows:

a. Fast and accurate - Comparing the manual and computerized systems, similar work can be accomplished in a shorter time and greater accuracy. When a client places ten orders, the manual system will 4 hours to compute materials needed for individual order, make summaries and check the stock book to calculate the quantities required to order. With the computerised system, all we have to do is to enter the unit consumptions and order quantities. It is not incredible to obtain those information in less than half a hour.

b. Management Report - Various reports can be prepared to serve specific purposes which are difficult to obtain with the manual system.

c. Centralising of Information - The staffs in the purchase and inventory department as well as other departments are now working with the same information. The result improvement in speed and delivery, minimal over and under stock and elimination of duplicate orders.

3.4 Payroll

The highly repetitive nature of payroll with its well-defined rules of computation is a logical target for automation. It is often one of the first operation to be computerized in order to reduce the high clerical costs required to perform the function manually.

Either a spreadsheet or database management system can be used for payroll. Since the garment industry often uses a piece-rate system, the starting point is to establish codes for all the production processes. The required codes are then grouped under a specific manufacturing order and payment rates are assigned to them.

3.4.1 Typical Payroll Output

Generally, the payroll output should consist the piece rate summary, worker earning ledger, worker earning summary and department earning summary.

a. Piece Rate Summary - In this report, all processes for every style are listed together with the respective piece rate. It is mandatory for checking purposes.

b. Worker Earning Ledger - It lists all manufacturing
orders, piece rates and quantities involved for every workers
and the total direct wages computed accordingly for every
specified wage period.

c. Worker Earning Summary - It consists a complete
listing on the total wage and hours incurred for every
worker. Then, wage per hour is calculated by dividing the
former by the latter. Those data are important for period-
to-period self-comparison and worker-to-worker comparison.

d. Department Earning Summary - It consists the summary
on total wage, hours incurred and wage per hour for every
department. Those data are necessary for period-to-period
comparison and department-to-department comparison. We can
use commercial available statistics/plotting package to
vitalise the payroll system. Using this kind of package, we
can measure and hence control the performance of individual
workers and departments by manipulating the data obtained
from the payroll system. Furthermore, we can also forecast
the labour cost for the coming budgetary period and work out
its inflationary trend.

There are, in fact, several kinds of statistics/plotting
package. However, we must use the package which can read the
data obtained from the payroll system described above. For
example, if we are using dBASE II for payroll, ABSTAT and
dGRAPH will be the solution. While VisiTrend/VisiPlot will
be the answer for VisiCalc. With these types of packages and
the payroll data, we can calculate and generate tables of
statistical measures such as minimum, maximum, mean and

variance etc, display charts on the screen or print them on
the printer.

We can make the following analysis.

a. <u>Worker</u> <u>Hourly</u> <u>Rate</u> <u>Analysis</u> - in this report, the
average hourly wage, say, for the past 12 months and the
current hourly wage are presented in a pictorial manner.
There can be many difference types of graphic presentations,
but we feel that combined comparative bar chart will be the
most suitable format to highlight the over/under earning
workers. Management can then take suitable actions to
regulate performance of the workers. (See exhibit 7.)

b. <u>Worker</u> <u>Working</u> <u>Hours</u> <u>Analysis</u> - In addition to the
last report, this analysis shows the number of working hours
for each worker. Since the previous analysis shows the
efficiency of the worker, this chart (exhibit 8) plots the
working hours to reflect their attendance.

c. <u>Department</u> <u>Total</u> <u>Wage</u> <u>and</u> <u>Control</u> - In this analysis,
we uses the line chart (see Exhibit 9) to show the department's
total wage for every month and the trend line is plotted
using statistic's "Best fit straight line" approach. This
best-fit straight line can be extended for a specified number
of periods to forecast the trend, thus management can use
this information for budgetary control purpose.

d. <u>Department</u> <u>Hourly</u> <u>Rate</u> <u>Forecasting</u> <u>and</u> <u>Control</u> - It
is similar to the worker hourly rate analysis. The hourly
rate for a particular period, say 6 months, for each
department is used instead and the best-fit line is plotted.

This chart shows the inflationary trend for each particular process and deviation can be isolated and investigated accordingly. (See exhibit 10).

Such statistical and graphic reports can be produced manually but the clerical work involved outweighs the benefits obtained. In this case, it is only an extension of the computerised payroll system using the data previously entered via the payroll system by the statistic/plotting package.

3.5 Export Documentation

One of the major uses of the microcomputer is word processing which prepares letters and documents of error-free and variable layouts. As competition grows, the controls excercised by the importing countries are becoming tighter and tighter, prompt action must be taken immediately to apply for the relevant permit and license when information are available. If the documents are prepared by the computer, the clerical work load is reduced and documents prepared fast and accurate.

One potential application of the word-processor is when a lots of similar document is required in a short time, such as shipping documentation. It is not uncommon to have ten copies of them. The word-processor plus the printer will help to print the contents clearly even using carbon papers, which eliminates repeated typing when a typewriter is used.

4. SYSTEMS INTEGRATION

With the application examples so far discussed, we are
actually using a job by job approach to automate the manual
systems. The logical sequence is to acquire the proper packages
to computerise the existing manual procedures. However, when we
later discover new applications, we are then facing lots of
duplications of repeated data entries of the same kind. If the
new application can use the same package and data previously
collected and entered, it is only an extension of the system
which we termed as 'system extension'. If the new application
involves manipulating data entered using other package, it will
be the 'software integration'. If we can build the systems into
a net-work, it will be the ultimate 'hardware integration'.

4.1 System Extension

Due we are neither professional computer people nor
experienced system analyst, it is difficult to have a
thorough study in planning and materialising an exhaustic
integration system. Therefore a piece meal approach is
almost an inevitability but also a panacea to computerization. In the earlier stage of computerization, the applications are rather fragmented, and using of the packages are
confined to specific areas without any definite and tentative
relationships.

As different processes are automated, more applications
will be explored. The payroll and the production planning
systems of which both used the spreadsheet program, is a good
example to illustrate the merging of the different systems.

347

We may also call it as 'system extension' because the production planning system is just an extension of the payroll system.

The suggested output/input for the payroll and production planning system respectively are reiterate as in exhibit 11. We can see that the inputs of the production planning system is actually the outputs of the payroll system. By using the same package (Spreadsheet), the two systems can be integrated as one. Thus, we can avoid data reentering and hence save us the unnecessary duplications.

4.2 Software Integration

Strictly speaking, it is similar to the system extension discussed except that we use other types of software package for the extension. Since early commercial softwares are written by different firms under different operating systems, the data files from each package is not interchangeable between these packages. For example, data file created by a spreadsheet program cannot be used by the data base program. Therefore, the efforts involved in integrating the systems of this nature would mean searching for or writing a program to transfer data from one package to another which provides information management, spreadsheet processing, statistical and graphic analysis using a common data structure. The second generation software is designed to overcome this situation. New packages such as LINK, Lotus 1-2-3, APPLEWORKS, JACK II, etc will open up new areas of compute-

348

rization.

4.3 Hardware Integration

As the system grows, one or two computer will not be
enough. Five or six will not be uncommon depending on size
of the company and degree of computerization. However, it
will not be economical if each computer owns its own printer
which lies idle most of the time. Furthermore, how can we
interchange data between these computers if each has its
individual disk drive. By that time, we can imagine that
passing the floppy disks around is only little better than
the manual system. Hence the best solution would be hardware
integration.

By this, we link up the computers as a network in a
local environment enabling them to communicate through the
use of network peripherals, therefore each computer will
still be working on its own while sharing and assessing the
same hard disk data storage unit (a common data base) and
printer. In addition, the advantage of these will be no
total system failure.

5. SUMMARY

The use of computer is not well appreciated in the local
clothing industry because of the following classic problems:

a. Most of the manufacturers feel that their factory is so
    complicated and sophisticated that can hardly be com-
    puterized.

b. The manufacturers doubt if computer can help in pro-
    duction and management to acheive a strong return.

c. Even if they are willing to computerize, the cost
    incurred using the traditional approach of contracting
    customised softwares will deter potential users.

Here we proposed an alternative approach to computerization,
using inexpensive but powerful microcomputers and available
software. As we have pointed out, the process requires no system
analysts and involves a job by job automation with an aim of
ultimate integration. Substantiated by the examples, their
justifications and outline of system integration proposed, we
believe this is an inexpensive and good approach to computerization. Although fragmented, the result is instantenous when a
manual process is computerized which may take only a week.
Another advantage is the management can cease the computerization
project at any stage and what had accomplished is not wasted.
When comparing to the traditional approach using mainframes, once
the commitment is made, the project must continue and the result
will depend on the project's successfulness which may be many
months or a year later.

REFERENCE

1. Time   April 16,84, page 34

2. WordStar General Information Manual, Section 1

3. dBASE II User Manual, page 96

(E. Y. Cheng & D. W. Poon)
Institute of Textiles and Clothing
Hong Kong Polytechnic
Hung Hom
Kowloon
HONG KONG

(J. H. Wong)
Twiga Knitting Corp Ltd
Blk A & B
Kwin Tong
Kowloon
HONG KONG

SCOPE	PROBLEMS	PACKAGE	REMARK
PRODUCTION			
Planning	conjectural & subjective	spreadsheet	objective (info from order status, payroll & pricing system)
Control	time consuming	spreadsheet	fast (from payroll system)
SALES			
Order Status	erroneous and time-consuming	DBM	fast & accurate, provide info for production planning and export
Pricing	"	spreadsheet	fast & accurate, provide info for production planning and costing
Sales Report	"	spreadsheet/ Statistics/Plot	fast & accurate, provide info for sales analysis by client, market and country
Correspon- dence/Telex	"	Wordprocessor	fast & accurate
PRUCHASING			
Inventory	incomplete, exhausting	DBM	enable on-line enquiry, highlight late delivery, provide receiving info and maintain stock ledger for A/C purpose
ACCOUNTING			
General Ledger	time consuming & high clerical	std G/L	accurate, fast, cost reduced, enable on-line enquiry, report & statement
Account Payable	"	std A/C payable	"
Account Receivable	"	std A/C receivable	"
Payroll	time-consuming, high clerical cost & incomplete details for other system	DBM, Statisticas/ Plot	fast, accurate, provide info for production planning & control, costing and wage analysis
Costing	erroneous, time-consuming	spreadsheet	timely & accurate (info from payroll & inventory system)
SHIPPING			
Import	untimely info	spreadsheet	timely processing (info from inventory)
Export	untimely info & time-consuming	Wordprocessor	faster issuing of documents, timely info obtained from order status and production control

Exhitit 1. Table on problematic area

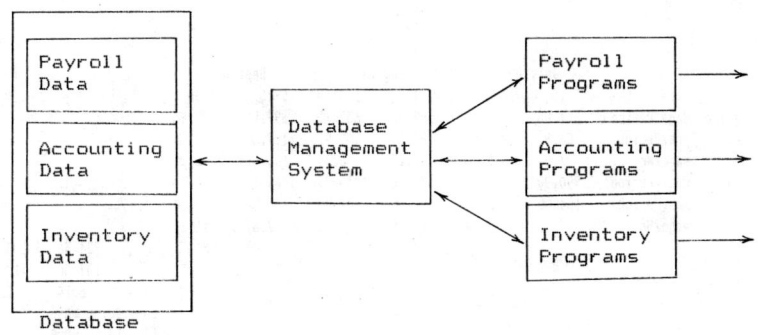

Exhibit 2. A database management system(3)

	A	B	C	D	E	F	G	H	I	Y	Z	AA
1												
2												
3			July 82		Aug 82		Sept 82					
4	Worker	Item	1-15	16-31	1-15	16-31	1-15	16-30				
5	Wong Fung Yee	Wage/Period	614.00	585.40	582.30	652.70	699.80	683.95				
6		Hrs/Period	86.91	101.85	80.91	102.92	107.50	109.50				
7		Wage/Hr	7.06	5.75	7.19	6.34	6.51	6.25				
8	Lee Mai Chun	Wage/Period	990.90	1065.90	1131.10	1033.20	1069.20	1316.30				
9		Hrs/Period	104.00	114.15	96.00	104.00	139.50	113.50				
10		Wage/Hr	9.53	9.34	11.78	9.93	7.67	11.60				
11										724.36	883.95	14049.60
12										107.50	117.54	1705.05
13										6.74	7.52	8.24
14										TOTAL WAGE		44277.90
15										TOTAL HOUR		5166.12
16										WAGE/HOUR		8.57
17										INDEX		0.12

Exhibit 3. Time-wage Analysis Screen Input/Output for Sewing Department

354

	Y	Z	AA
11	724.36	883.95	SUM(C11:Z11)
12	107.05	117.54	SUM(C12:Z12)
13	Y11/Y12	Z11/Z12	AA11/AA12
14	TOTAL WAGE		AA5+AA8+AA11
15	TOTAL HOUR		AA6+AA9+AA12
16	WAGE/HOUR		AA14/AA15
17	INDEX		AA15/AA14

Exhibit 4. Formula Display for Time-wage Analysis

PERIOD:JULY 1, 82 TO JUNE 30, 83

PROCESS	INDEX (Hrs/$)
Cutting	0.08
Sewing	0.12
Stitching	0.08
Pressing	0.10
Packing	0.20

Exhibit 5. Time-Rate Index Report

Exhibit 6. Data File Structure and Program Listing

(Order Listing)

Data Base File for the Order List

In order to computerise the order list, we must first determine the data fields required. Generally, the underneath will suffice.

MO - the manufacture order number

STY - the style number of the order

QTY - the quantity of the order

FAB - the fabric used

DELIVERY - the intended delivery date

CANCEL - the cancelled/not-cancelled statuse of the
          manufacture order

dBASE is then entered to create the database structure.

FILENAME:ORDERLST

ENTER RECORD STRUCTURE AS FOLLOWS:

FIELD   NAME,TYPE,WIDTH,DECIMAL PLACE

001   MO,C,8

002   STY,C,8

003   QTY,N,5,0

004   FAB,C,6

005   DELIVERY,C,8

006   CNACEL,L

007   (cr)

INPUT NOW?N

Now we are in a position to write a series of command files which are used like a program written in a more classical language. It consists of one controlling file, MENU and

356

three subordinate files, ENTER, CANCEL, AND LIST.

The MENU Command File

First the MENU command file is entered so that the user can select his next step.

```
*PROGRAM - MAIN MENU
ERASE
SET TALK OFF
SET COLON OFF
SET EXACT ON
DO WHILE T
    SET FORMAT TO SCREEN
    ERASE
    @ 5,30 SAY"ORDER LIST MENU"
    @ 6,30 SAY"==============="
    @ 8,30 SAY"0 - Exit"
    @ 9,30 SAY"1 - Enter New M/O"
    @ 10,30 SAY"2 - Cancel M/O"
    @ 11,30 SAY"3 - List"
    STORE T TO A
    DO WHILE A
    STORE 0 TO CHOICE
    @ 20,20 SAY"Enter desired action";
    GET CHOICE PICTURE "#"
    READ
    IF CHOICE<0 .OR. CHOICE >3
        STORE T TO A
    ELSE
```

357

```
        STORE F TO A
    ENDIF CHOICE
    ENDDO A
    DO CASE
        CASE CHOICE=0
                ERASE
                CLEAR
                SET TALK ON
                CANCEL
        CASE CHOICE=1
                DO ENTER
        CASE CHOICE=2
                DO CANCEL
        CASE CHOICE=3
                DO LIST
        OTHERWISE
        LOOP
    ENDCASE MAIN MENU
ENDDO
```

The ENTER Command File

Second, the ENTER command file is entered so that we can
enter new orders to the list.

```
*PROGRAM - M/O ENTRANCE
ERASE
USE ORDERLST
@ 22,0 SAY"Enter M/O Number of 0 to Exit"
STORE T TO BA
DO WHILE BA
```

```
STORE "          " TO mMO
STORE "          " TO mSTY
STORE 0 TO mQTY
STORE "       " TO mFAB
STORE "          " TO mDEL
@ 1,0 SAY "M/O No:";
        GET mMO PICTURE "XXXXXXXX"
READ
@ 1,40 SAY"Style No:";
        GET mSTY PICTURE "XXXXXXXX"
@ 2,0 SAY "Quantity of Order:";
        GET mQTY PICTURE "#####"
@ 2,40 SAY"Fabric Used:";
        GET mFAB PICTURE "XXXXXX"
@ 3,0 SAY "Scheduled Delivery:";
        GET mDEL PICTURE "XX/XX/XX"
IF mMO="0"
    STORE F TO BA
    CLEAR GETS
ENDIF mMO="0"
READ
APPEND BLANK
REPLACE MO WITH mMO, STY WITH mSTY, QTY WITH mQTY,
        FAB WITH mFAB, DELIVERY WITH mDEL, CANCEL WITH F
ENDDO BA
DELETE
PACK
RETURN
```

The CANCEL Command File

Then the CANCEL command file is entered to allow
cancellation.

```
*PROGRAM - M/O CANCEL
ERASE
USE ORDERLST
@ 22,0 SAY"Enter M/O Number of 0 to Exit"
STORE T TO CA
DO WHILE CA
    STORE "        " TO mCAN
    @ 1,0 SAY"Enter Cancelled M/O no ";
        GET mCAN PICTURE "XXXXXXXX"
    READ
    IF mCAN="0"
        STORE F TO CA
    ELSE
        GO TOP
        LOCATE FOR MO=mCAN
        REPLACE CANCEL WITH T
    ENDIF
ENDDO
RETURN
```

The LIST Command File

Finally, the LIST command file is entered to print hardcopy
of the order list in the conventional manner.

```
*PROGRAM - CANCEL M/O
USE ORDERLST
STORE 0 TO CURRENT
```

```
SUM QTY TO CURRENT FOR .NOT. CANCEL

SET PRINT ON

SET FORMAT TO PRINT

@ 1,0 SAY"M/O"

@ 1,10 SAY"STYLE"

@ 1,20 SAY"QUANTITY"

@ 1,30 SAY"FABRIC"

@ 1,40 SAY"DELIVERY"

GO TOP

STORE 2 TO POS

DO WHILE .NOT. EOF

    IF CANCEL

        SKIP

    ELSE

        STORE POS+1 TO POS

        @ POS,0 SAY MO

        @ POS,10 SAY STY

        @ POS,20 SAY QTY

        @ POS,30 SAY FAB

        @ POS,40 SAY DELIVERY

        SKIP

    ENDIF CANCEL=T

ENDDO .NOT. EOF

@ POS+2,10 SAY "TOTAL QUANTITY = "

@ POS+2,30 SAY CURRENT
SET PRINT OFF

RETURN
```

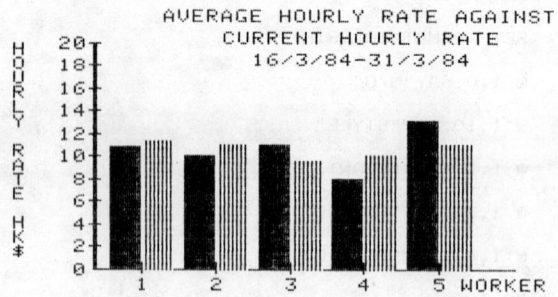

EXHIBIT 7. WORKER HOURLY RATE ANALYSIS

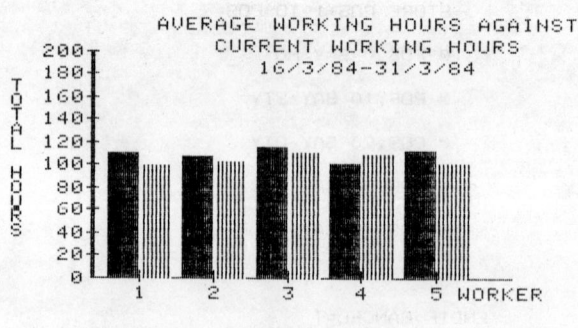

EXHIBIT 8.   WORKER WORKING HOURS
ANALYSIS

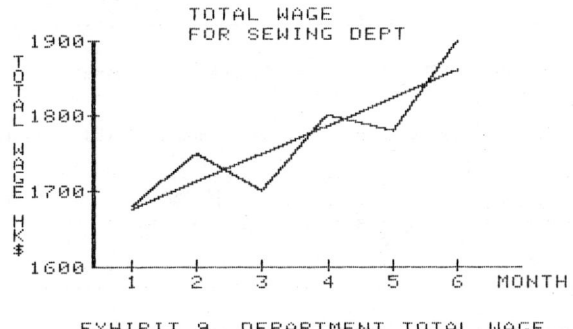

EXHIBIT 9. DEPARTMENT TOTAL WAGE
             AND CONTROL

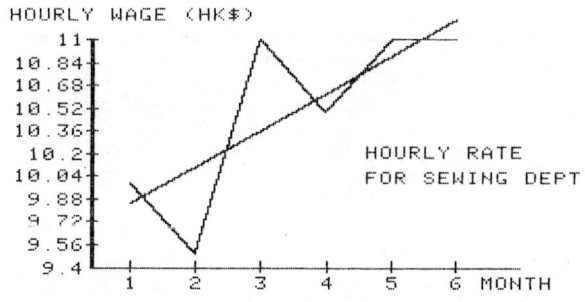

EXHIBIT 10. DEPARTMENT HOURLY RATE
              FORECASTING AND CONTROL

```
!--------------------------------------------------------------------!
!                                                                    !
!         A. Worker Earning Summary (Payroll System)                 !
!                   Department: -------                              !
!                                                                    !
!  Worker Code     Period      Wage/Period    Hours/Period    Wage/Hr !
!                                                                    !
!    ------        ------        ------         ------          ---- !
!                                                                    !
= - = - = - = - = - = - = - = - = - = - = - = - = - = - = - = - = - ==


!--------------------------------------------------------------------!
!                                                                    !
!  B. Time-Wage Analysis Screen Input (Production Planning System)   !
!                   Department: -------                              !
!                                                                    !
!    Worker            Item        Period    Period    Period        !
!    -----             Wage/Period   ----      ----      ----        !
!                      Hours/Period  ----      ----      ----        !
!                      Wage/Hour     ----      ----      ----        !
!                                                                    !
!= - = - = - = - = - = - = - = - = - = - = - = - = - = - = - = - = - =
```

Exhibit 11. An Output/Input for the Payroll and Production Planning System

364

THE USE OF MICROCOMPUTERS FOR PRODUCTION CONTROL IN THE GARMENT INDUSTRY

E.Teague, B.Clarke and M.Gray

ABSTRACT

Powerful low cost, desk top microcomputers are universally available. Suitable specialised software is now available for the garment manufacturer to provide effective control over labour and material utilisation and work in progress. A typical system is outlined and the associated benefits to be expected explained.

1.WHY USE MICROCOMPUTERS ?

A typical desk top microcomputer costs approximately one third the price of a typical sales representative's car and has virtually no running costs. It can be operated by present clerical staff with the minimum of training and requires no specialised knowledge or staff to use or maintain it. Such a machine will also operate in the typical office environment, (although this may not always apply in tropical countries).

Just as it would be eccentric to employ clerks to copy handwritten correspondence in commercial matters, management would be handicapping their office staffs by denying them the use of modern office equipment. Although the office is often the most under-automated part of the factory the use of printing desk top calculators,electric and electronic typewriters , photocopiers are now accepted as standard.

The typical desk top microcomputer combines the functions of three familiar items of office equipment:

A Filing Cabinet

A very sophisticated typewriter

An Electronic Calculator

2.1 Filing Cabinet

Dispensing with the need for paper , information or data can be held in magnetic form on tape or floppy disks. This means that electronic information or data storage : -

Reduces physical storage space required

Reduces storage costs

Is easily accessible

Is easily copied

Is easily available as printed or hard copy

Can be easily transmitted via the telephone and telex networks

Large volumes can be handled and transmitted if required by posting <u>Floppy Disks</u>

Can be easily and quickly processed

Can be simply and easily protected

1.3 Fancy Typewriter

Despite the many benefits of electronic storage and transmission of data it is still necessary to prepare information in a printed form as reports,labels,graphs,balance sheets etc.,

Typical printers operate at printing speeds of 250 characters per second in a range of print sizes and can also incorporate <u>intelligent</u> two colour printing so that certain information may be printed in a second colour if it falls outside certain pre-determined reporting criteria.

1.4 Electronic Calculator

Schoolchildren as late as the mid sixties would have been incredulous when told that it would be possible to simply press the numbered keys on a small oblong of plastic and metal in the appropriate sequence to see the correct arithmetical result displayed. All at the cost of a couple of weeks pocket money °

Whilst the electronic calculator is a familiar item of equipment in the office many are unfamiliar with the calculating capacity of microcomputers which can now outperform the mainframe computers of only a few years ago.

As an example,an article in the November 1983 issue of BYTE reports a physicist performing experiments on bubbles who had to perform extensive calculations.He was hiring time on a CRAY super-computer,currently the world's largest and most powerful computer,costing in excess of 20 Million Dollars.This required the use of telephone lines and hire charges of thousands of dollars per hour. A typical calculation run was performed in 9 seconds.A desk top microcomputer performed the identical calculations in 7 minutes.

Although slower by a factor of over 1000 it was of course perfectly acceptable as the alternative manual calculations would have been measured in man weeks.

1.4 Speed

The principal feature of microcomputers is <u>speed</u> :

Speed of **access** to information held electronically

Speed of **calculation**

Speed of **output**,printed or through visual display

Indeed the slowest thing attached to any computer is the human operator - consequently there are many attempts to remove the need for human operation especially for **Data Input**.

1.5 Data Input to Microcomputers

Microcomputers need information or data to process,this is usually entered through the keyboard. There are several ways for a computer to read information in a semi automatic way which are relatively familiar :

Bar Coding

Now a familiar site on packaging,equipment to produce bar codes and to read them is costly and failure of equipment brings any system to a halt. Such codes are not of course directly "human" readable and so need duplicating in a suitable form.

Optical Character recognition

Although less costly to produce printed codes,and readable by "humans" the reading equipment is expensive and subject to high levels of error increased by handling of paper - grease marks,creases etc.,

Mark sensing

Very sophisticated systems can be designed that detect the presence or absence of a mark. Probably the widest use is in the reading of Football Coupons.Such systems are very expensive and not very flexible.

Magnetic stripe

Limited applications where a standard code is frequently read and may need to be changed - Credit cards,clock cards etc.,

Punched cards

A now outdated method of data entry in which the cards were manually punched but has still some very wide applications. The American elections use a clever punched card system where voters register their vote on many issues simultaneously - such systems also have wide application in market research.

Digitised Pads

Pressure pads can "read" the location of a pen using simple X and Y co-ordinates.Suitable overlays on the pad can be used so that handwritten data can be translated into data entry. Although expensive this can be used for very regular data entry for such items as payrolls.

For staff unfamiliar with keyboards it may be used for such procedures as stocktaking or goods receipts on portable equipment. Again the cost of equipment is high compared with microcomputers.

1.5 Ease of use

Every quantum jump in the information revolution has been characterised by certain noticeable features:

1 Attempts to restrict access to new techniques – hence the priestly acolytes who controlled the production and dissemination of written material.

2 Deliberate attempts to conceal the mysteries and methods of production – the establishments of guilds etc.,

3 Deliberate attempts to restrict circulation – Stamp duties on publication etc.,

The early post war history of computers in Europe and North America followed a similiar pattern as the white coated priests (now called data processing managers) frightened managements with their arcane knowledge aided by a gullible press to whom computers will either accidentally start global conflict or send Gas Bills for millions of pounds.

The microcomputer revolution has been entirely different.Free from the restraints of a tiny heirarchy intent on non revelation, (and the maintenance of their power bases within corporate structures)it is difficult to believe that there is a manager anywhere, unaware of the benefits that microcomputers can provide as a management tool.

1.6 Decision Support Tool

Increasingly ,effective managers are seen to be those who can most efficently employ assets by taking the correct decisions.

Ideally every manager knows that he should not make a decision until he has assembled all the relevant information and tested every course of action.

Practically everyone knows this is so much nonsense. Surrounded by querulous customers,failed delivery promises,ringing telephones and the demands to meet budgets the succesful manager is often seen to be the one who "flies by the seat of his pants".

Just as such an approach to the flying of aircraft was acceptable with the string and paper planes of World War 1 they are inadequate when flying supersonic jet fighters.

To be competitive internationally such haphazard management techniques, whilst widely admired in some sections of the textile industry are nonetheless unacceptable.

The microcomputer is therefore emerging as the greatest asset to the overworked line manager because it presents him with information :-

Fast

In an intelligible and easily read,legible format

Provides the facility to disseminate information, instructions, orders etc clearly and accurately

Is low cost,easily used and infinitely flexible

1.6 Working Disciplines

"I don't care how bad the system is - at least let's have a system"

Traditional Lancashire saying

The installation of microcomputers instills a working discipline.Unlike manual systems they cannot easily be overridden or ignored (if designed correctly). This will in itself improve management effort and understanding because regular reporting and consideration of such reports will in itself ensure the continued and detailed review of production systems.

The systems considered later all are designed to provide improved working disciplines with :

Very fast entry of data with full validation

Simple easy to use systems that require the minimum of training

Flexible structures to allow verying levels of integration

Modular systems to allow for systems development

Complete integration of data entry routines on all systems to improve familiarisation and speed training

2.A TWO PRONGED ATTACK ON COSTS

Universally garment manufacturers have pre-sold production to major retail groups or similiar buyers. This means that production management is continually struggling to maintain production costs because there is no flexibility over the end selling price.

Microcomputers therefore provide the hard pressed and progressive production manager with simple and effective control over the two major variables which will affect profitability :-

Utilisation of Labour

Utilisation of major fabric components

The data from such systems will also provide a detailed historical actual cost basis for preapring future accuarte costings.

2.1 Low Cost

Typically a complete system for a typical factory with 200 sewing operatives making garments with 20 to 40 operations per garment such as jeans,ladies outerwear,shirts etc.,would cost in Western Europe between ten and fifteen thousand pounds sterling. Payback times would vary between six and eighteen months.

3.FABRIC UTILISATION

Major fabric components constitute 30 to 40 percent of the end selling price of most garments.

Factors affecting the utilisation of cloth :-

1 Faults in weaving / knitting

2 Faults in finishing

3 Faults induced by handling - stains,rips etc.,

4 Wastage during cutting

5 Faults in assembly of garments or using faulty fabric

The first two factors are beyond the control of the production manager but any system introduced must adequateley document such faults to substantiate subsequent claims onn the manufacturer or finisher etc.,

The third and final factors are subject to control by training,improved work aids,handling equipment and form part of the normal managerial function of continuous improvement of labour training.

The fourth factor aggregates all the wastage caused in the cutting room by :

Lays too long for the marker

Excessive joins at roll changes

Incorrect number of plies laid down

It is these causes of wastage which provide the greatest waste of fabric andf which can be effectively controlled on a simple system.

Such a system can provide (with a Cutting Records System) a powerful and comprehensive control over the issuing of cutting orders and the flow of work through the cutting room.

3.1 Setting the System up

Files are maintained with details of:

1.All sales contracts with details of style/colours/quantity to deliver of each size.

2.Fabric description and cost (for contract costing).

3.Panel description.(A panel is all the componnents of a garment cut out of the same fabric at the same time)
4.All markers used with details of length/width/sizes and panels.(This may include,where available details suitable for calculation of labour times/efficiencies etc.,)

It is possible to link this with data about markers from computerised lay planning such Gerber or Laser Lectra equipment.

3.1 Printing Cutting Orders

It is possible to raise and print either a single cutting order or to raise batches of cutting orders to print as and when required.

All that is required is to enter the style/colour/panel details with the marker detail and total quantity required.

The system will validate Cuttting Orders produced by comparing with the files:

Style / Colour / Panel / Marker

The system prevents the use of any invalid style/colour/panel combinations or the use of a marker that has not been allocated to that style/panel combination.

3.4 Printing the Cutting Order

Cutting orders are printed on plain or pre-printed three part NCR stationery with the following details:

Unique incremental Cutting Order Number
Date of issue
Style/colour/panel to be cut
Fabric to be used with full description
Panel Description (i.e. Hood Lining etc.,)
Optional comments (i.e. Corduroy one way lay)
Marker to be used with Length/Width
Quantity of each size and total to be cut
Number of plies required
Total length of fabric required (Marker length X Number of plies)

The form provides for the cutting room staff to enter:

Plies laid
Quantities cut per size
Length and roll numbers of fabric used
Time lay started and finished
Time cutting started and finished
Names of operatives
Any remarks required (i.e. Fabric faults etc.,)

3.5 Using the Cutting Order in the Cutting Room

The readily legible Cutting Order imposes a simple discipline on cutting room staff and merely requires them to fill in times of start and finish, roll numbers used, plies laid and amount of fabric used (in Kilograms or metres).

Because the Cutting Order production system is self-validating it is impossible to produce or use an illegal Cutting Order and thus cut the wrong parts out of the wrong fabric.

3.6 The Cutting Order as part of a Cutting Records System

The Cutting Order forms the basis of a system for recording the output of the Cutting Room and the performance can be reported as a series of variances from standards.

The Basic standards are :-

Marker Specification = Usage of fabric per garment taken as Length of Marker divided by number of garments cut on Marker

Analysis of this variance shows the excess (shortage) of cloth used against theoretical minimum,excessive use due to faults,too long lays etc., is soon apparent.

Work Specification = Usage of fabric per garment taken as Total of fabric ordered for Contract divided by Total of garments on contract

Analysis of this variance continually shows the way fabric is being utilised against the contract and will alert management to shortages or excessive stock build up so that extra fabric may be ordered/dyed/quilted etc., (or cancelled).

Standard Cost = Usage of fabric determined as Standard Cost basis,this may vary from either of previous values.

This may be used for Standard Costing purposes.

By using the actual elapsed times of laying up and cutting this system can be used to form the basis of a cutting room labour reporting system similiar to the labour reporting system of the sewing operatives Labour Reporting System .

3.6 Maintaining the Records

Maintenance of the system merely requires entry of the Cutting Order number,Style/colour/panel,quantities cut per size and total length of fabric used.

The system then calculates and displays variances based on:

3.6.1 Marker Variance

Fabric used in excess of Marker Length X Plies.
The above amount expressed as a percentage.
The value of fabric used in excess.

3.6.2 Work Specification Variance

Fabric used in excess of fabric purchased for contract divided by total quantity of garments on contract.
The above amount expressed as a percentage.
The value of fabric used in excess or saved.

3.6.3 Standard Cost Variance

Fabric used in excess (or short) of standard cost usage.

The above amount expressed as a percentage.
The value of fabric used in excess or saved.

Variances are calculated and displayed and can be written onto the original cutting record by the operator. The cutting room supervisor/manager signs to accept the level of variance. Copies of the cutting record can be used by different departments.

It may be remarked that all this can be done manually , but it requires roomful of clerks or reports produced so long after the event that they cease to be useful. The use of the microcomputer provides however, instant recording and analysis allowing management to take fast and effective action.

3.7 Printed Reports

Once entered the cutting records form a comprehensive database which can be used to prepare reports in a variety of ways for different purposes.

Several standard reports are normally available on demand :

1 **Standard** report showing all work cut and contract balances by selected style or for all styles showing all cutting orders or just summary totals.

2 Report for **Materials Requirement Planning** showing summary of all work cut showing contract balances,costs of fabric,total fabric used,current actual usage and projected fabric requirment to complete contract.

3 Report for **Selected period** (i.e. week) showing all work cut for all styles with analysis of variances,excess costs,cost of variances,fabric used.(Effectively a weekly cutting room report)

4 Where incorporated **Labour Efficiency** reporting will be possible to show actual labour costs compared with calculated labour costs.

Further reports can be generated that analyse other aspects of the cutting room performance,especially labour efficiency , comparative marker yields,fabric fault analysis etc.,

4.WORK TICKET PRINTING

This system prints workshop orders as a **bundle ticket with a series of individual self adhesive operations tickets** which are used both as the basis of payment for operatives and also for monitoring the flow of Work in Progress.

A central ticket stub lists the operations performed with a space for signing by the operative on completion of their operation on the bundle.

Control Tickets can be prepared for any number of Control Points which are used in conjunction with a Work in Progress System.

4.1. Setting the System up

The system maintains a style file which consists of a list of labour operations with their time values. Issuing tickets is simple and straightforward and consists of simply entering the style required,the number of plies per lay,the garment sizes and ratio per lay and the colour per lay.

The system is unique because lays can consist of as many plies /colour splits/and sizes per lay as the operator wishes.

Once the instructions have been entered in a "ticket printing queue" they can be printed whenever required.

Such a system can also integrate with an operations file built up on a database using a synthetic work study system such as General Sewing Data (a proprietary system also available on microcomputers from Methods Workshop in Europe,North America and Australasia).

4.2 Printing the Tickets

The tickets are printed in 3 lines on self adhesive stationery and can incorporate whatever information is specified by the user from: -

	No of characters	
Operation No	2	Alpha / Numeric
Operation Description	20	Alpha
Style	6	Numeric
Colour	8	Numeric
Size	8	Alpha / Numeric
Length	6	Alpha / Numeric
Bundle Number	4	Numeric
Bundle Quantity	2	Numeric
Customer	8	Alpha / Numeric
Order Number	6	Numeric
SM's per operation	6	Numeric (to 3 decimal places)
SM's per bundle	7	Numeric (to 3 decimal places)
Pence per operation	6	Numeric (to 3 decimal places)
Pence per bundle	7	Numeric (to 3 decimal places)

Extra instructions (of any length) can be entered on each bundle ticket to supplement the above if required.

The design of the work ticket can be varied quite simply and can be reduced to a 2 line ticket (with less information) to improve printing speeds by a factor of over 100%.

This extra speed means that tickets are available quicker and that the computer is released for other uses.

Tickets are printed in pairs,so where there is an uneven number of work tickets a void ticket is automatically inserted to prevent the issue of blank tickets ,which could be overwritten and misused.

Ticket printing can be interrupted at any time and can either be continued or stopped to be restarted at some future time.

The use of a large printer buffer (up to 260.000 characters) provides the facility to send a ticket queue to the printer and release the computer for further work.

4.3 Printer Facilities

Many different types of printer are available each providing different speeds and facilities such as two colour printing. The choice of printer may depend upon other uses for which it is required such as printing box and bag labels,correspondence etc.,The usual rule applies that the more you pay the greater the speed and range of facilities available.

5.WORK IN PROGRESS

Ultimately the demand on any garment producer is to produce the styles/colours/sizes in the ratios desired by the end customer and on time.

As a consequence any system must provide a comprehensive and easily handled system for giving senior management control over large contracts,by providing accurate,detailed up to the minute reports for management action.

Such a system merely requires a daily input of:

A) Work loaded on machines

B) Work off machines

C) Work out of examination

D) Work into Finished Goods Warehouse (plus seconds)

E) Garments despatched

All simply recorded by Style/size/colour.

If required further Control points between A and B can be introduced to control work on machines.

The details of A,B,C are controlled by using the control tickets generated by the Work Ticket program.

The details of D and E are controlled by use of internal transfer notes and delivery (despatch advices) notes.

Note that this allows the control of work to be done in singles,tens or dozens irrespective of the size of work bundles on the sewing floor or of the size of cartons etc., in the finished goods warehouse.

Note that such a system using simple manual control tickets overcomes the problems associated with bar coded tickets because it provides for control when the work cease to be a bundle and also when the quantity in the bundle changes (because of

375

seconds/rejects or the return of part of the bundle for repairs).

5.1 Printed Reports

A variety of reports can be produced on demand which show:

    A) All transactions (usually only run as an "audit trail")

    B) Weekly Totals and Grand Totals

    C) Grand Totals for each Style/Colour/size/length

Each Total line shows the total singles passed through each department and the balance of work in each department.

Seconds can be shown both as a _quantity_ and as a _percentage_ of total production for each style.

5.3 Work in Progress Valuation

A report can be produced on request which shows for each style/colour/size/length :

    A) Contracted quantity

    B) Total quantity passed through each department

    C) Total in each department

    D) Balance left on contract

    E) Value of work in each department based on a percentage of finished goods valuation (other forms of valuation can be provided for if required).

It is expected that such a valuation report would be run at quarterly or half yearly stock takes.

6.LABOUR REPORTING AND PAYROLL CALCULATION

The Work Ticket system provides self adhesive work tickets that show :

    Standard Minutes per operation
    Total Standard Minutes per bundle

These are attached by the operative to a daily worksheet which is also used to record "off standard" work categories.

Offstandard categories include those categories of work which are paid at average or basic pay rates when no piece work is done — machine breakdowns,waiting for work etc.,

The work tickets may also where required display for the operative the total pay for the bundle (Total SM's per bundle X Yield Rate in pence per SM).

6.1 Setting up a system

No two systems of pay are identical and therefore the standard payroll requires adjusting to adopt the pay rules agreed for the factory.

Two static files require to be maintained.

6.1.1 Personnel File

A file is held for all personnel containing ,clock number,name,normal attendance times,pay rates etc.,This may be updated at any time.Clock numbers of any size may be used.

There is considerable flexibility in the design of the Personnel file which may incorporate as much detail as required for normal personnel requirements.

6.2.2 Sections

Details of each section require to be held

6.3 Daily Payroll Entry

Any system of Labour reporting is necessarily historical.It is therefore vital that such reports are produced with the minimum of delay.The speed with which data can be entered is therefore of paramount importance to the effectiveness of the system.

Many systems of data collection and entry have been evaluated – to date our experience shows that although there are many automatic or mechanical systems available they are unsatisfactory for a variety of reasons.

For example it is possible to have time recording clocks which read the attendance and off standard times straight into the computer – these cost in the region of £3.000 sterling in the UK (the price of the average microcomputer). Therfore a 200 girl factory would require at least 4 in use with a fifth unit as backup and so merely recording the times automatically would cost in excess of the whole of the rest of the system°

Every automatic system of data entry also requires a manual override in case of breakdown,this places a very high overhead on the software and memory capacity of the computer and sever limitations on the system. It also introduces the possibility of deliberate fraud,in a system designed to eliminate it. For example if a bar coded work ticket system allows for manual entry as a result of greasy,folded,cut, or mutilated tickets it also allows for a manual override if someone wishes to enter tickets fraudulently.

6.4 Automatic Data Entry

As a result of considerable effort and research we remain sceptical about the use of automatic data recording with microcomputers in a working environment at the present stage of systems development. Such things are possible but perfectly acceptable systems are available at very much lower cost and less susceptible to failure.

There are many determined efforts aimed at providing a real time,on line control system to provide management with information instantly.Such systems are quoted to cost in a range of £500 - £700 sterling per operative compared with £50-60 sterling per operative for a typical microcomputer system.

It is not our experience that such an increase in initial costs can be justified or payback expected in reasonable time.It must also be remembered that such elaborate systems often require the need for highly skilled full time in house staff.It is these data processing staff who have seen the preparation and handling of data as an end in itself rather than as a means to an end, who have given the use of computers in industry such a bad name and increased the threshold of fear in senior management faced with the need to computerise.

6.5. Simple, Fast, Effective Data Entry

The daily payroll entry requires the entry for each operative of:

Clock Number
Attendance times
Start and finish times of unscheduled unpaid breaks
Start and finish times of any "off standard" work
Total number of Standard Minutes produced

Where necessary the operative may change sections

Absence is recorded in a variety of categories ,maternity/ illness/holiday/statutory holiday etc.,(Weekly Report for SSP purposes can be produced).

Overtime is calculated according to the prevailing rules.

Operative details may be entered in any order so that no lengthy and time consuming manual pre-sorting is required.If required entry can be stopped at any stage and recommenced and any pay record can be examined at will.

6.5 Complete Daily Pay Record Displayed

The complete daily payroll entry is displayed to the operator on a single screen allowing visual checking of the complete record before filing,thus eliminating manual errors in entry.

Every pay record is subject to a variety of validation procedures before filing.

By using programmable keys the system eliminates multiple key stroking,thus if an operative attends for normal hours of work one key strokes accepts the normal attendance times,individual keys are used for each off standard work category and a single key files the record.

(Such simple data entry procedure taking perhaps 20 seconds may be compared with a typical wage clerk who may be requird to write down over 100 characters of information manually and perform some 10 arithmetical calculations,manually.)

6.6 Daily Reports and Pay slips

Upon completion of entry of the operatives pay sheets all clerical effort has finished,which for a 200 operative factory would be bewteen 1 and 2 hours depending upon the complexity of the payments system.

The automatic production of labour reports for each work section and factory reports is fast and immediately follows the end of payroll entry.

Typically a daily payslip for each girl is produced showing all the times taken,the work produced and payment for it.The distribution of these to operatives for the preceding days work leads to the elimination of wage rate arguments.It is our view that a better informed work force is a better motivated work force.

Should it be necesary the pay details can be altered by **direct access to a single pay record.**

The section and factory reports can be designed to show the labour efficiency reporting in any way required.

6.7 Weekly Pay Calculation and Reports

After all the daily pay records have been entered for the whole week and all alterations agreed and made the weekly operative pay record can be produced.

This when signed and agreed with the operative is the Weekly Gross Pay.

Reports for each section and for the whole factory can be produced which aggregate the information from the daily reports.

6.8 Data Transmission using the Public Telephone and Telex

Such reports can be automatically transmitted over Publicly Switched telephone Networks or by Telex to Administrative centres etc.,

Data can also be transferred using cassette tape and floppy disk where inter company transport is readily available.

7.BENEFITS TO BE EXPECTED

The system outlined is typical of several available at present and widely used in Western Europe.

Major savings in direct costs of clerical staff can be expected which are relatively easy to quantify. There are also attendant savings due to the elimination of errors due to illegibility,imperfect calculations,deliberate fraud which are less easy to quantify but easily demonstrable.

Improved and effective monitoring of material and labour utilisation provides major cost benefits which are again difficult to quantify. It is evident that in themselves such systems only provide management with suitable information for taking effective decisions. Management bear the responsibility to take the necessary action to maintain and improve profitability.

It is our experience that such systems can yield a payback time of from 6 to 18 months.Such is the speed of development of the equipment available that the computer purchased today will be obsolete after two years of installation . To predict the path of development is difficult but it can be said with absolute certainty that faster,new generation equipment with improved features will be available probably at half the cost of present equipment.

Cautious management or merely the timid may delay the installation of such systems claiming to wait for newer faster equipment to become available. Whilst such a delay may appear beguiling at present ,it might be pointed out that you might not be around to make that decision in two years time.

Shiloh Software Systems Limited
Holden Fold
Royton
Near Oldham
England
OL2 5ET

THE ACCURACY OF COMPUTER COLOUR MATCHING WITH FIBRE-BLENDS

T. F. Chong

Abstract

Computer colour matching with fibre-blends has found to be less accurate than single component fibre. The main problems associated with fibre-blends match prediction are examined and examples are illustrated. Several methods described in the literature for match prediction with fibre-blends are discussed. It is selectively tested against a proposed method which has found improved accuracy.

1. INTRODUCTION

In spite of the fact that the basic method of colour measurement was established more than half a century ago, it is only during the last fifteen years that the application of colour measurement is particularly substantial and significant because of the advancement of the computer technology and the revolution in the equipment design. This has brought the colour science from a scientific exercise in the research laboratory to a widely used commercial and industrial tool.

Among the applications of colour measurement, the use of computer colour matching (CCM) has been playing a very important role. In textiles and others, the main objective of CCM is the calculation of colorant concentrations necessary for matching. Because of the speed and the availability of the multiple choices of the predicted recipes, CCM can provide optimum and economic recipes (1) and is therefore more attractive than the use of the traditional approach which is based on trial and error method.

The application of the CCM technique has been quite successful on single component fibre. The basis of CCM for textiles is relied on the use of Kubelk-Munk theory (2),(3),(4). The author has demonstrated this technique under controlled conditions and less controlled conditions (5). A typical step by

381

step approach of CCM is illustrated by a flowchart
in Figure 1. As time goes by, the textile
market of single fibre substrate is gradually
replaced by substrates of fibre-blends for the
purpose of unique physical properties or for
economic reasons. For example, we can improve the
handle, the strength or lustre by blending the fibre
concerned with other types of fibres. Normally, in
the case of the coloration of fibre-blends, the
individual type of fibre has to be dyed with
different classes of dyes. This presents some
problems to the CCM technique. The following
describes the problems of CCM with fibre-blends and
the methods that tries to reduce these problems.

2. PROBLEMS OF CCM WITH FIBRE-BLENDS

To produce a solid shade on a fibre-blend, the
individual components of the blend should be dyed to
the same colour. The job of CCM is therefore to predict
dye recipes separately for each of the fibre components
and the resulting colours of the dyed fibre components
would match the standard colour. The accuracy of such
CCM could be reduced to a large extent due to the
folowing possible sources of errors in addition to those
limitations experienced with single component fibre >
CCM (6).

2.1 Variation in Dyeing Conditions

This is the difference in the dyeing conditions during
the primary calibration dyeings of single component
fibres and that during the dyeing of fibre blend such
as changes in liquor to goods ratio, pH and the effect
of blocking by the other fibre component. To
investigate this effect, two almost identical dyeings
(same recipes and process conditions) on the cotton
part of two forms of substrates using the same reactive
dyes were carried out. The two dyeings only differ in
the following manner:

(a) In the first dyeing, a polyester-cotton blend
(65:35) knitted fabric were used.

(b). In the second dyeing, a pure polyester knitted

fabric and a pure cotton knitted fabric were used.
The ratio of the polyester fabric weight to the
cotton fabric weight were 65:35 (i.e. same component
ratio as that of the blend in (a).)

The raw fibres used in manufacturing the fabrics in
(a) and (b) are the same and so are the spinning
and knitting process. To measure the colour of the
cotton part of the blend in (a), the polyester part
was removed using a standard burn out method with a
solution of Potassium Hydroxide in Ethanol. Figure 2
shows the difference in the spectral reflectance
factors for the dyed cotton parts in both cases.

2.2 Cross-Stainings

Normally, the dye class used for the differnt
components of the blend is different for optimum
fastness and physical properties. As a result,
cross-stainings of the dyes on the opposite components
of the fibre-blend occur during dyeings. Hence,
this effect will not be accounted for during the
preparation of the primary single fibre calibration
dyeings.

Figure 3 shows the spectral reflectance factor curves
of the staining on the polyester part of the
Polyester-Cotton (65:35) fabric obtained by dyeing
the blends with increasing concentration of a
Reactive dye (Drimarene Dis. Orange X-31G) and then
remove the cotton part by treatment with Sulphuric
Acid. In comparison with the top curve which is
the undyed Polyester fabric, one can easily observed
the presence of the staining and the degree of
staining increases with increasing Reactive dye
concentrations.

Figure 4 shows a similar situation except that the
staining is on the cotton part of the blends and
is obtained by dyeing the blends with increasing
concentrations of a Disperse dye (Terasil Br. Red 4G)
and then remove the polyester part by treatment with
Potassium Hydroxide in Ethanol.

2.3 Effect of the Fibre Separation Process

In order to evaluate the colour of the individual

dyed components of the blends, a fibre seperation
process is necessary. To investigate whether
the separation process has any effect on the colour
of the dyed components, dyed fabrics of pure cotton
and pure polyester were treated in the appropriate
fibre separation solutions for the opposite fibres
i.e. dyed pure cotton is treated in the burn out
solution for polyester and vice versa.

Figure 5 shows the spectral reflectance factor curves
for a pure polyester knitted fabric dyed with a
mixtures of disperse dyes before and after the
burn out treatment. Figure 6 shows similar
information for the case of a pure cotton knitted
fabric dyed with a Reactive dye. It can be
observed from these curves that the burn our treatment for the dyed polyester has no effect on the
colour change while the burn out effect on the
dyed cotton is small.

However, it should emphasised that the dyed
material should be properly aftertreated prior to
the burn out process. Furthermore, the separation
process may affect the degree of staining on the
other component of the fibre-blends.

All of these sources of errors would not occur in
the CCM of single component fibre.

3. PRESENT METHODS FOR CCM WITH FIBRE-BLENDS

In discussing the following methods, the polyester-
cotton (65:35) blend is sometimes used as an
example for illustration.

3.1 Method 1

In this method, the primary calibration dyeings is
created separately for the polyester component and
for the cotton component using suitable dye classes
such as Disperse dyes and Reactive dyes respectively.
Then, recipes are predicted separately for the

polyester part and for the cotton part*. The final
recipes will be adjusted according to the blend ratio.

Any commercial CCM system can use this method. The
drawbacks are that all the previously mentioned
errors may exist. Furthermore, the substrates used
to creat the primary calibration dyeings may not be
the same as that of the components present in the
blends that leads to further problems. The accuracy
of this method may be improved by selecting dyes of
less staining power on the other component of the
blend. However, the selection of recipes is usually
dominated by other factors such as fastness and
economy.

3.2 Method 2

In this method, emphasis is placed on the calibration
of the staining information (7). Basic information
about the dyeing and staining behaviour of the
individual dye is created. Then recipes are predicted
for each fibre separately. These recipes and the
primary staining information are then used to
calculate the stain on the fibres. Finally, the
recipes are corrected for the contribution of
the stainings. However, the details of this method
was not published and therefore will not be examined
by this paper. This method tries to correct the
the error due to cross-stainings.

[*   Most commercial CCM systems allow the recipes
     to be weighted by factors. In this case, the
     values of the factors depend on the expected
     degree of cross-stainings and hence depend on
     the dyers' experience. However, this technique
     of trying to correct the staining effect is
     by no means reliable.]

3.3   Method 3

Matched pairs of two classes of dyes are preselected
for each fibre component of the blend i.e. members of the
Disperse dyes for dyeing the polyester should match in
colour with the corresponding members of the Reactive
dyes for dyeing the cotton(8),(9).   Then, recipes are
predicted for the individual component.of the blend
separately based on Method 1.   The choice of recipes
are limited to the extent that the two recipes for
both components of the blend should contain the
corresponding 'matched pair' of the dyes.

Another similar method is based on the use of pre-mixed
dyes.   The dye manufacturer supplies physically
mixed dyes of two classes and when applies to a certain
fibre blend with a certain blend ratio will dye both
components to the same colour.

This method still have the possible errors mentioned
in section 2 although the cross-staining may be corrected
more easily during the correction stage.   Furthermore,
the choice of recipes, which is a main attractive feature
of CCM, is very much limited.   On the other hand, the use
of premixed dyes may reduce the error due to differences
in the dyeing conditions since the calibration dyeings
can be developed directly onto the fibre-blend.   Yet,
the use of this method has other similar problems and is
limited to specific application process and blend ratio
In view of these limitations, Method 3 will not be
tested against other methods.

4.   PROPOSED METHOD FOR CCM WITH FIBRE-BLEND

In this method, the calibration dyeings are created
directly onto the blend with one dye class and then
this process is repeated for the other dye class.

The undyed component of the blend is then removed
using an appropriate separation process.   They are
then used as the corrected primary calibration
dyeings.

Then recipes are predicted separately for the
individual component of the fibre-blend using the
corresponding corrected primary calibration dyeings.

The recipes predicted by this data bank is used to
obtain the stained samples of each fibre components.

Finally, recipes for each fibre component is adjusted
for this staining effect.

This method tries to minimise the errors due to
variation in dyeing conditions (e.g. blocking effect)
and the cross-staining effect. Furthermore, the
pure fibres of the individual component of the fibre-
blend, which is not always available, are not required
for the preparation of the calibration dyeings.

4.1 Preparation of Data Bank

The following describes the preparation of the data bank
to evaluate the accuracy of Method 1 and the Proposed
Method.

4.1.1 Preparation of Textile Substrates

Pure polyester fibres and pure cotton fibres were spun
into polyester yarn and cotton yarn respectively. The
same Polyester and Cotton fibres were also mixed in the
ratio of 65:35 and spun into a blended yarn. The three
kinds of yarn (30 s each) were individually knitted into
plain fabrics. They were then properly pretreated.

4.1.2 Calibration Dyeings - Disperse Dyes

Three Terasil Disperse dyes were used for preparing the
calibration dyeings. These include Ter. Yellow 2GL,
Ter. Br. Red 4G and Ter. Navy Blue BGL. Calibration
dyeings were carried out for these dyes at suitable
concentration levels using the Linitest Laboratory
dyeing machine. The liquor to goods ratio was 12:1.
All the chemical auxiliaries employed were laboratory
grade. The dyeings were carried out for both the pure
polyester fabric and the blended fabric. The dyeing
method is shown in Figure 7.

4.1.3 Calibration Dyeings - Reactive Dyes

Four Drimarene Reactive dyes were used for preparing the
calibration dyeings. These include Drimarene Rubinole
X-3LR, Drimarene Discharge Orange X-3LG, Drimarene Blue
X-3LR and Drimarene N-Blue X-RBL. The preparatory
work is similar to that of the Disperse dyes. The
dyeing method is shown in Figure 8.

387

4.1.4 Skeleton Calibration Dyeings

The calibration dyeings that were carried out on the
Polyester-Cotton blend were subjected to a fibre-
separation process to remove the undyed component of
the blend. Sulphuric acid (70%) was used to burn out
the cotton component while a solution of Potassuim
Hydroxide in Ethanol was used to burn out the Polyester
component.

4.2 Colour Measurements

The Zeiss RFC3 spectrophotometer was used for the
measurement of the spectral reflectance factors at
20 nm intervals in the range 400 to 700 nm. The
spectrophotometer is calibrated with the Merck Barium
Sulphate using the Tungsten source and a diffuse/8 deg.
geometry. The specular component was included. Each
sample was measured several times at different areas
and directions and at complete opacity.

Figures 9, 10 and 11 show a typical calibration dyeing
curves for the Disperse dye (Ter.Br. Red 4G) being
applied on to the Polyester, the blend and the dyed
skeleton respectively. Similar information is given
in Figures 12, 13 and 14 for the Reactive dye
(Dri. Discharge Orange X-3LG).

4.3 Colour Standards for Matching

Four colour standards (A-D) were prepared and their
spectral reflectance factor curves are given in Figure
15.

Based on the Kubelka-Munk (single constant) theory and
the established calibration dyeings data bank,
formulations for both components of the polyester-
cotton blends were created according to Method 1 and
the Proposed Method to match the four colour standards.
Dyeings were carried out onto the blends with a
normal two-baths two-steps process using the
same dyeing conditions as that of the calibration
dyeings. Finally, colour differences (ΔE_{ab}^{*}) were
measured between the colour standards and the
corresponding dyed colours of the blends. These colour
differences provide some indications of the degree of

accuracy of the methods.

4.4 Result and Discussion

The spectral reflectance factor curves of the colour
standards and their corresponding matchings for each
method are given in Figures 16, 17, 18 and 19 for
the standards A, B, C and D respectively. Table 1
summarises the colour differences of these matchings
for each method using the 1976 CIELAB colour difference
equation, standard illuminant D65 and 10 degree standard
observer.

The average colour difference between the standards and
the matchings based on the Proposed Method is 2.2 units
while the corresponding figure based on Method 1 is 3.6
units. The poorer result obtained by Method 1 is
expected as this method suffers from all the drawbacks
mentioned in section 2 whereas the major drawback of
the Proposed Method is the error involved during the
fibre separation process. Table 2 compares the two
methods with regard to the possible sources of errors.

The improvement in the accuracy of the Proposed Method
over Method 1 is expected to be more significant in
practice . This is because in utilising Method 1, it
is necessary to creat calibration dyeings on the pure
single component fibres which should be identical to
the individual component of the fibre-blend for best
performance. This point has been taken care of for
this project. However, it would be very difficult in
practice, if not impossible, for the dyer to obtain
the pure fibres of the individual component of the
blends that he is told to color.

ACKNOWLEDGEMENTS

The author thanks the Hong Kong Polytechnic for
financial support of this project. Special
acknowledgement goes to Dr. Y.C. Siu and Mr. K.M. Li
for their technical assistance. The author would
also like to thank the many dyestuff manufactures
who have contributed both the chemicals and the
technical information for this project.

REFERENCES

(1) D. Cox. 'How a Knitter Slashes Dyeing Costs',
     Textile World, 1977 (Aug.).

(2) Kubelka,P., and Munk,F.. Z. Tech. Phys., 1931,
     12,p593-601.

(3) E. Allen, J.O.S.A., 1966, 56, p1256.

(4) R.P. Best, Golden Jubilee of COLOUR in the CIE,
     (Pub. by S.D.C.),1981,p139-155.

(5) T.F. Chong, Proceedings of the 4th Congress of
     the International Colour Asso., 1981, pC2

(6) A. Brockes, J. of Amer. Asso. Tex. Chem. & Col.,
     1974 (May),6, p21-38.

(7) R.St. John, Color 73, 1973, p431.

(8) S.S. Patwardhan, 'Instrumental Colour Matching
     for Textiles', Wool Research Asso., India.

(9) ICI, Technical Information, Ref 22811.

Institute of Textiles & Clothing
Hong Kong Polytechnic
Hung Hom, Kowloon
Hong Kong

FIG. 1 FLOWCHART FOR COMPUTER COLOUR MATCHING

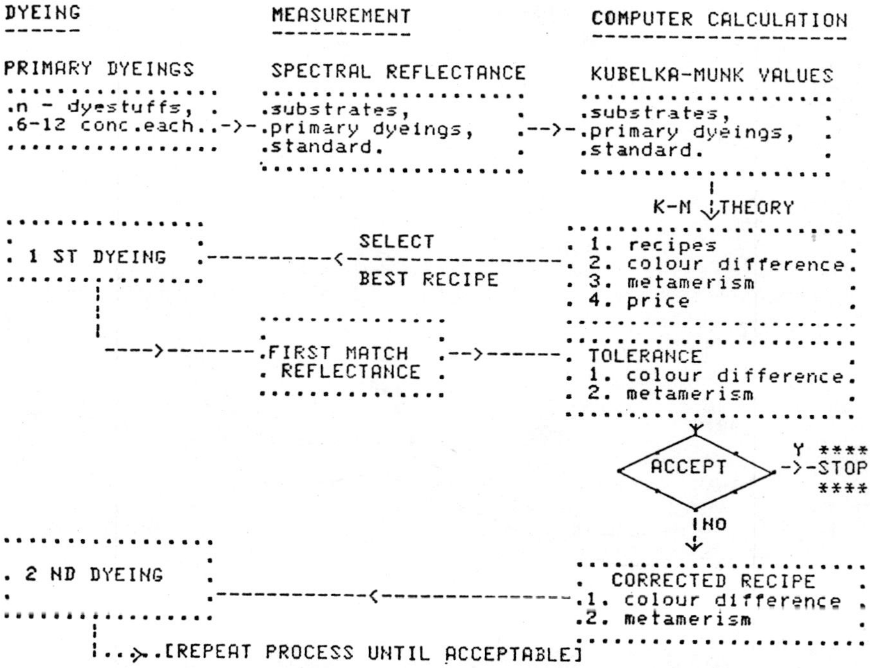

```
DYEING                    MEASUREMENT              COMPUTER CALCULATION
------                    -----------              --------------------

PRIMARY DYEINGS           SPECTRAL REFLECTANCE     KUBELKA-MUNK VALUES
...................       .....................    .....................
.n - dyestuffs, .        .substrates,        .    .substrates,        .
.6-12 conc.each..->-.primary dyeings,    .-->-.primary dyeings,  .
...................       .standard.          .    .standard.          .
                         .....................    .....................
                                                             ¦
                                                    K-M ↓THEORY
...................                              .....................
. 1 ST DYEING    .------------<---------------. 1. recipes         .
...................          SELECT             . 2. colour difference.
        ¦                 BEST RECIPE           . 3. metamerism      .
        ¦                                       . 4. price           .
        ¦                 ...............        .....................
    ---->-------.FIRST MATCH .-->------.TOLERANCE           .
                . REFLECTANCE .              . 1. colour difference.
                ...............             . 2. metamerism      .
                                            .....................
                                                       ╱╲
                                                      ╱  ╲   Y ****
                                                     ⟨ACCEPT⟩-->-STOP
                                                      ╲  ╱      ****
                                                       ╲╱
                                                       ¦NO
                                                        ↓
...................                             .....................
. 2 ND DYEING    .                             . CORRECTED RECIPE  .
.               .-----------<---------------.1. colour difference .
...................                            .2. metamerism      .
        ¦                                      .....................
        ¦..>.[REPEAT PROCESS UNTIL ACCEPTABLE]
```

FIG. 2 VARIATION IN
DYEING CONDITIONS

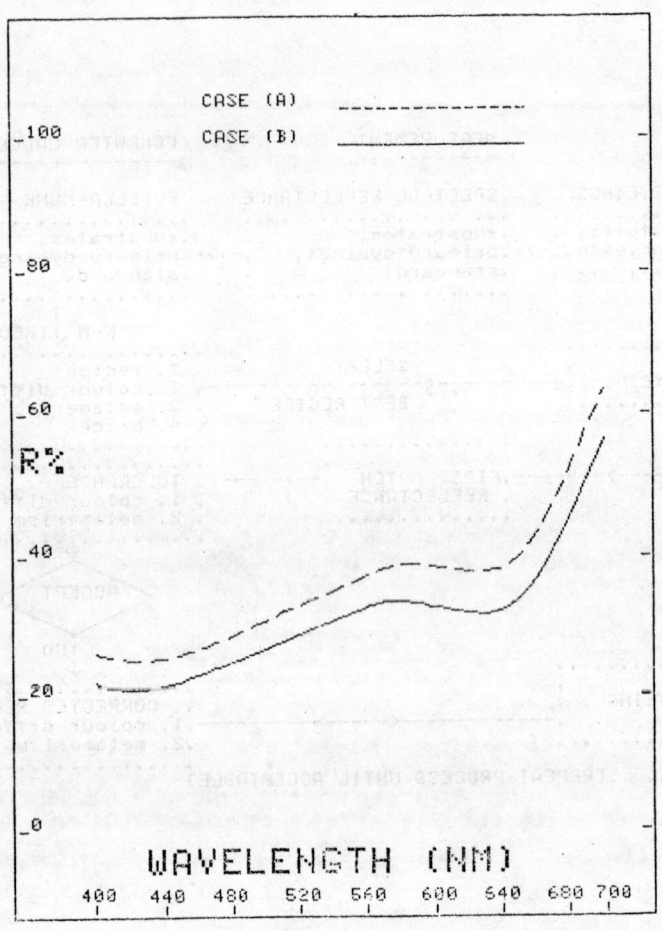

FIG. 3 CROSS STAINING OF REACTIVE DYE ON POLYESTER

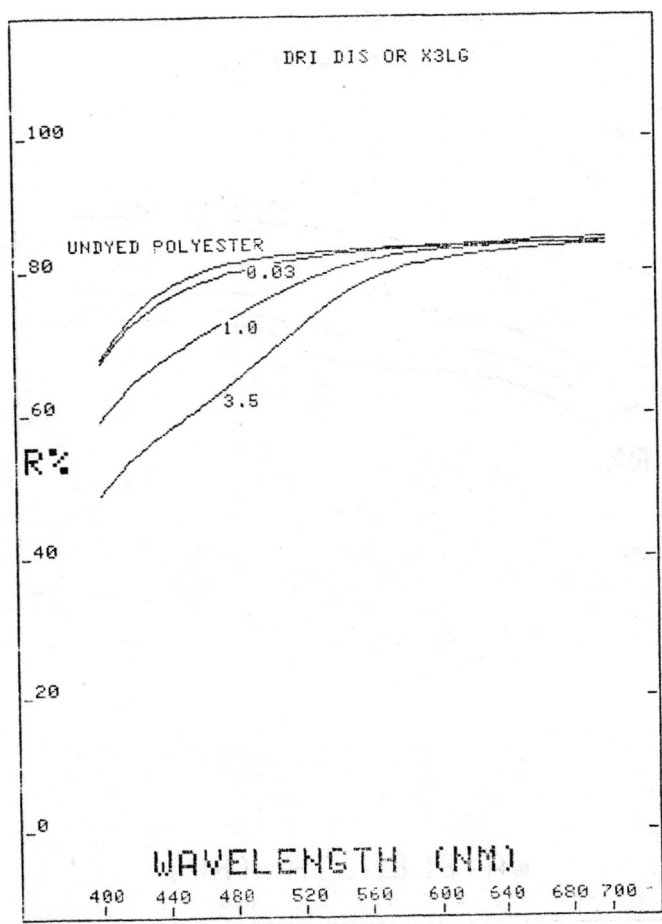

FIG. 4 CROSS STAINING OF DISPERSE DYE ON COTTON

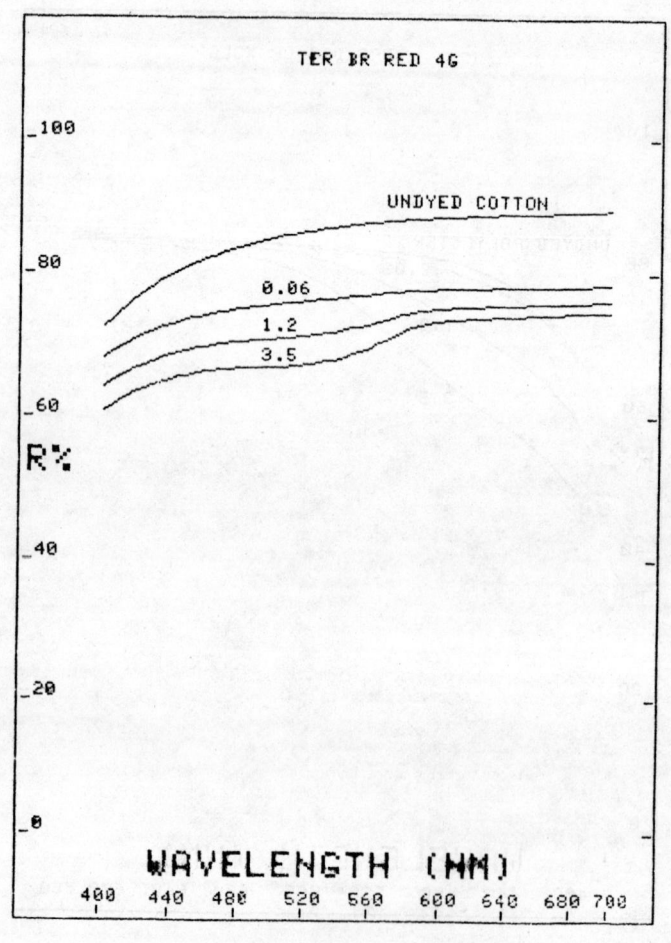

TER BR RED 4G

UNDYED COTTON

0.06

1.2

3.5

R%

100

80

60

40

20

0

WAVELENGTH (NM)

400 440 480 520 560 600 640 680 700

FIG. 5 EFFECT OF BURN OUT TREATMENT ON ON THE COLOUR OF DYED POLYESTER

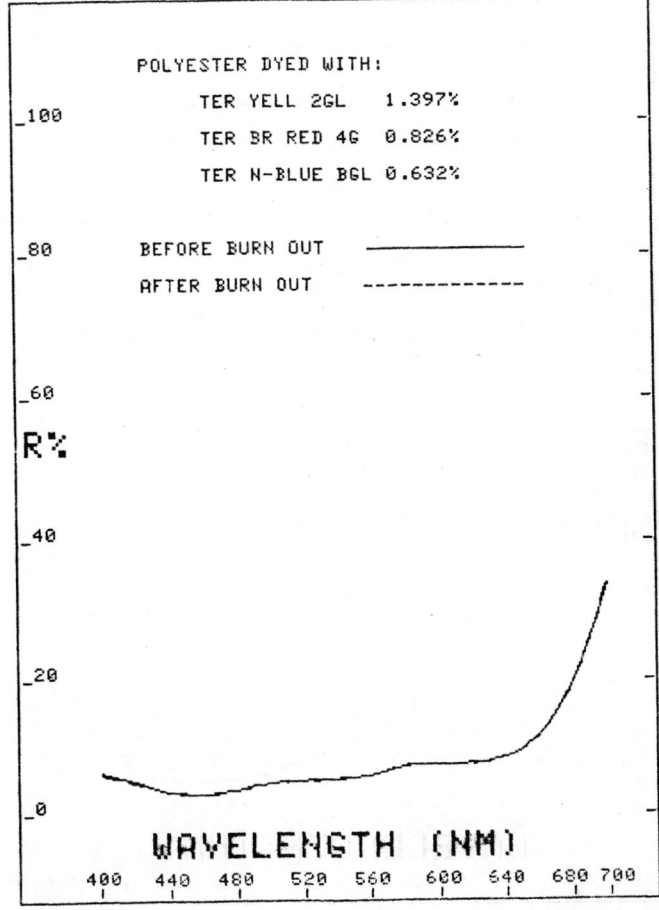

POLYESTER DYED WITH:

TER YELL 2GL   1.397%

TER BR RED 4G   0.826%

TER N-BLUE BGL 0.632%

BEFORE BURN OUT ——————————

AFTER BURN OUT -------------

R%

WAVELENGTH (NM)

400 440 480 520 560 600 640 680 700

FIG. 6 EFFECT OF BURN OUT TREATMENT ON THE COLOUR OF DYED COTTON

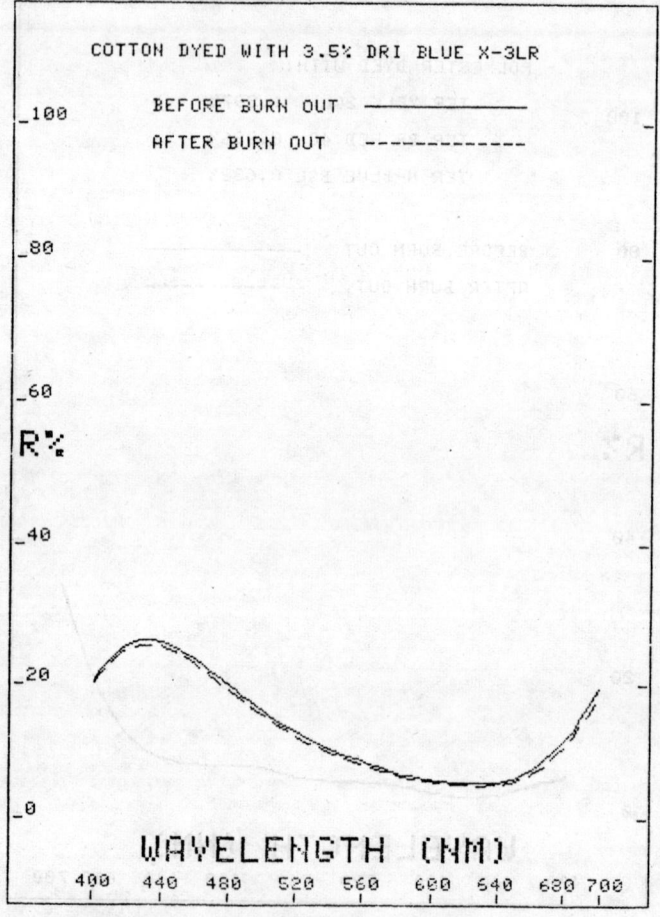

COTTON DYED WITH 3.5% DRI BLUE X-3LR

BEFORE BURN OUT ————————

AFTER BURN OUT — — — — — — —

R%

WAVELENGTH (NM)

FIG. 7 DYEING METHOD FOR DISPERSE DYE ON POLYESTER

PREWETTED SUBSTRATE

DYE

BUFFER (pH 5)

DISPERSING
 AGENT

L.R - 12:1

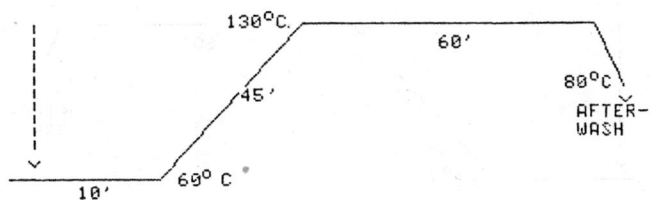

AFTERWASH: RINSE COLD
            RINSE HOT
            REDUCTION
             CLEARING
            RINSE HOT
            NEUTRALIS-
             ATION
            RINSE HOT

FIG. 8 DYEING METHOD FOR REACTIVE DYE ON COTTON

PREWETTED SUBSTRATE

DYE

SALT

SODA ASH

PROTECTIVE
 COLLOID

L.R - 20:1

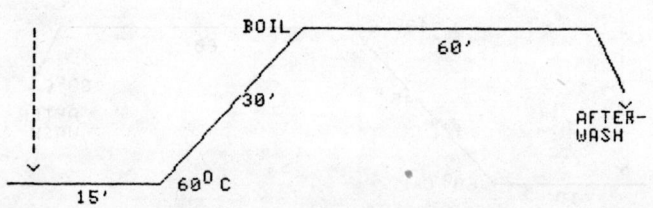

AFTERWASH: RINSE COLD
            RINSE HOT
            SOAPING
            RINSE HOT
            RINSE COLD

FIG.9 CALIBRATION DYEINGS OF A DISPERSE DYE ON PURE POLYESTER

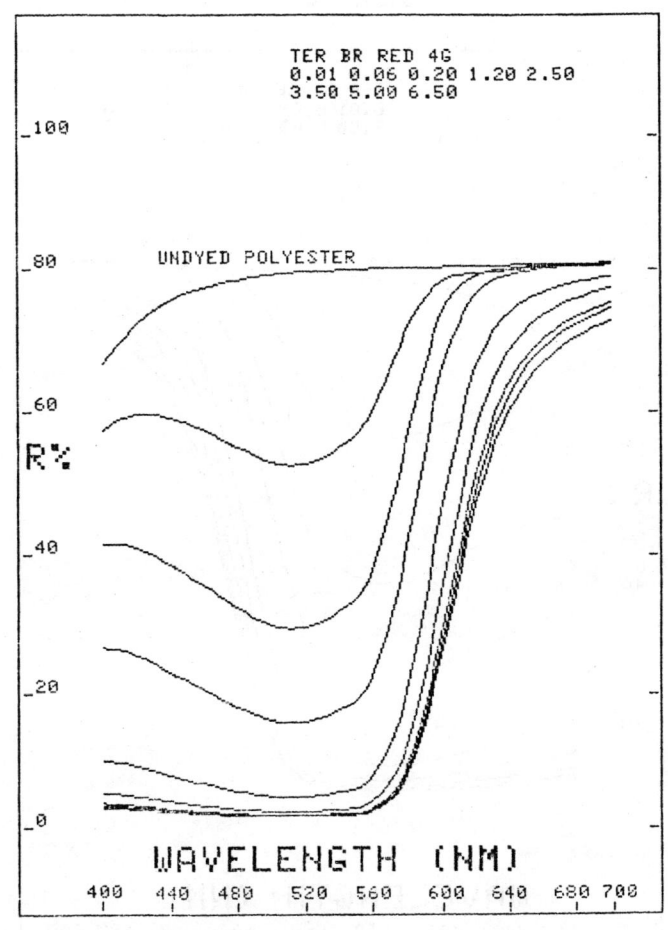

TER BR RED 4G
0.01 0.06 0.20 1.20 2.50
3.50 5.00 6.50

UNDYED POLYESTER

WAVELENGTH (NM)

FIG. 10 CALIBRATION DYEINGS OF A DISPERSE DYE ON POLYESTER-COTTON BLEND

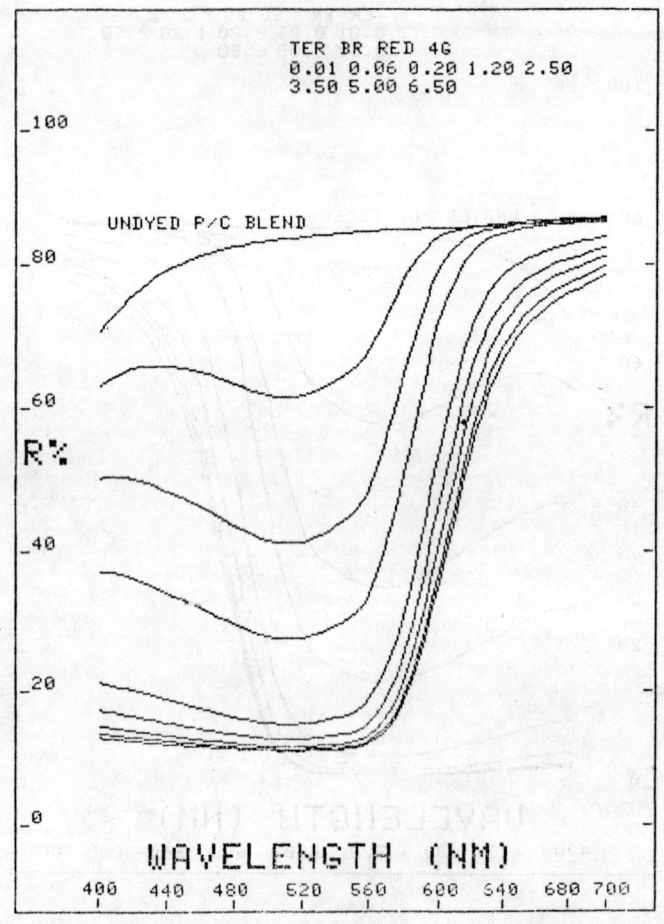

TER BR RED 4G
0.01 0.06 0.20 1.20 2.50
3.50 5.00 6.50

UNDYED P/C BLEND

R%

WAVELENGTH (NM)

FIG.11 POLYESTER SKELETON CALIBRATION DYEINGS OF A DISPERSE DYE ON P/C BLEND

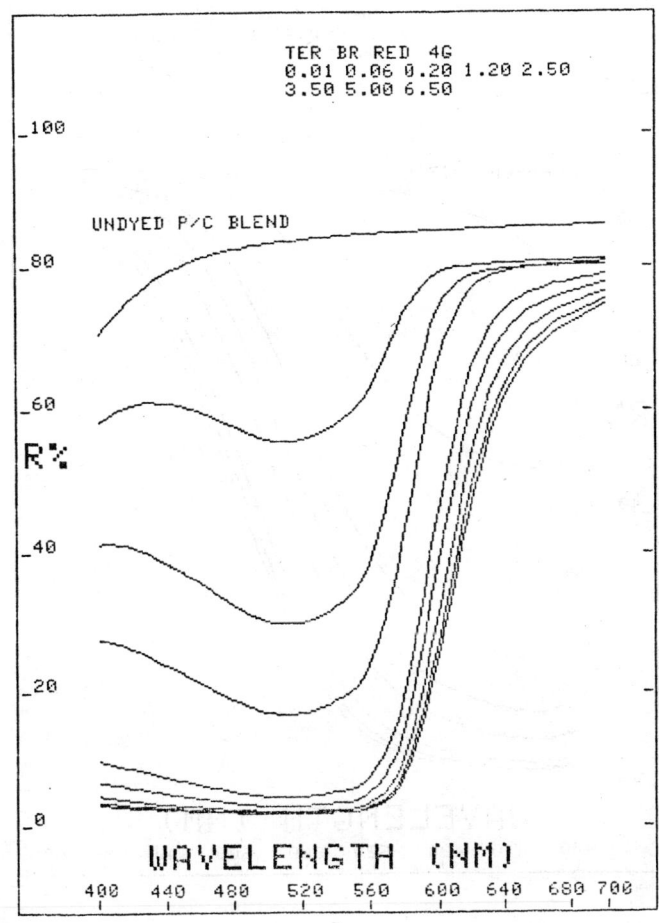

TER BR RED 4G
0.01 0.06 0.20 1.20 2.50
3.50 5.00 6.50

UNDYED P/C BLEND

R%

WAVELENGTH (NM)

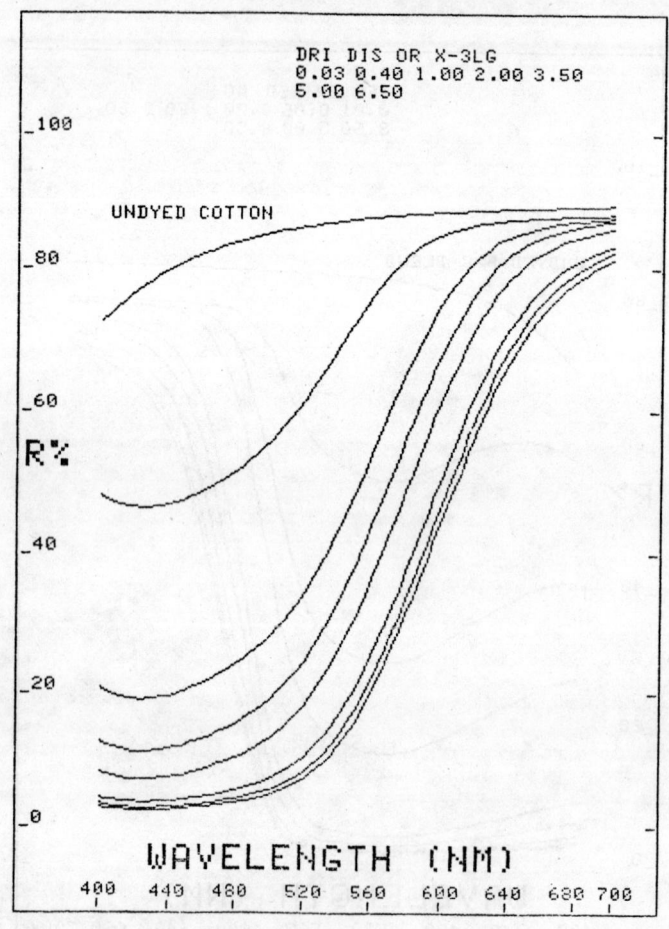

FIG. 12 CALIBRATION DYEINGS OF A REACTIVE DYE ON PURE COTTON

DRI DIS OR X-3LG
0.03 0.40 1.00 2.00 3.50
5.00 6.50

UNDYED COTTON

FIG. 13 CALIBRATION DYEINGS OF A REACTIVE DYE ON P/C BLEND

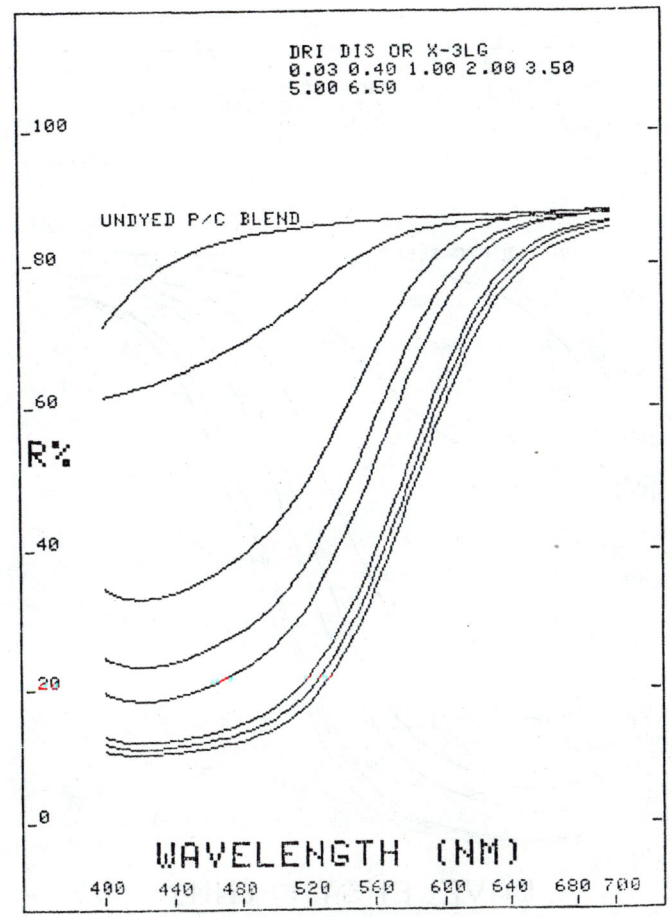

DRI DIS OR X-3LG
0.03 0.40 1.00 2.00 3.50
5.00 6.50

UNDYED P/C BLEND

R%

WAVELENGTH (NM)

FIG. 14 COTTON SKETETON CALIBRATION DYEINGS OF A REACTIVE DYE ON P/C BLEND

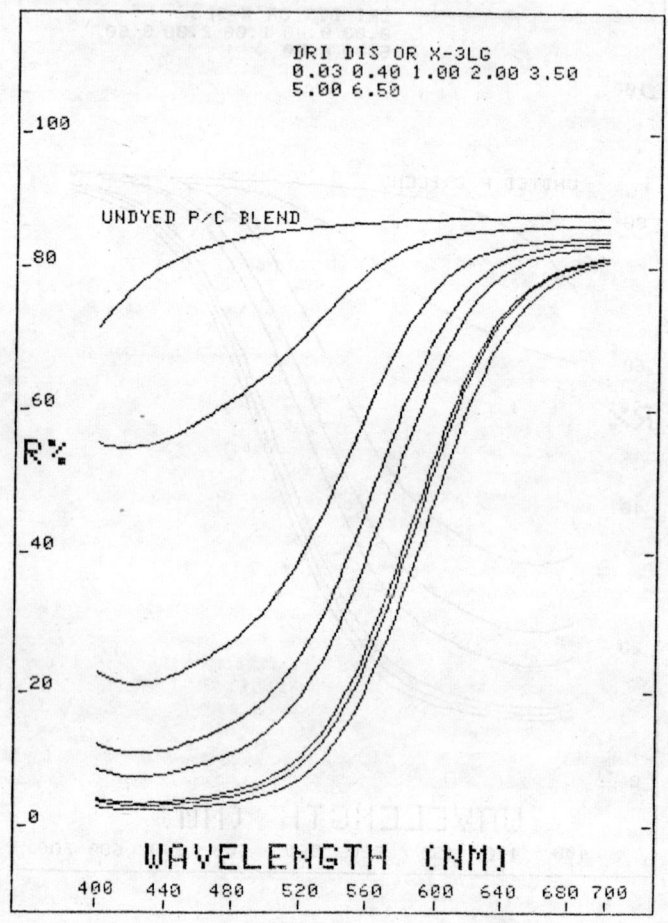

DRI DIS OR X-3LG
0.03 0.40 1.00 2.00 3.50
5.00 6.50

UNDYED P/C BLEND

R%

WAVELENGTH (NM)

FIG.15 SPECTRAL REFLECTANCE FACTOR CURVES FOR COLOUR STANDARDS A-D

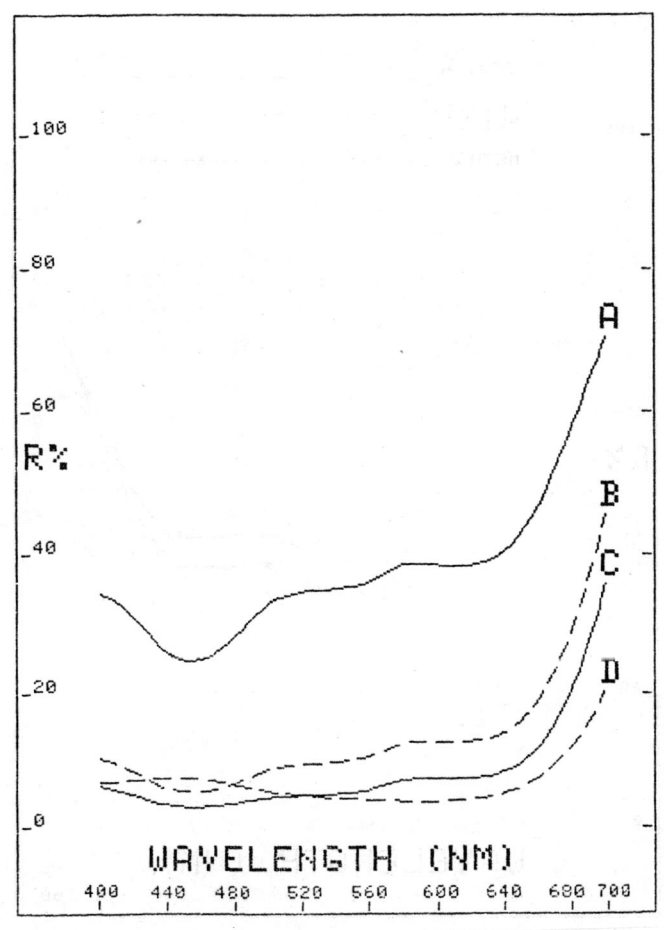

FIG.16 SPECTRAL CURVES OF THE MATCHINGS BY THE PROPOSED METHOD & METHOD 1 FOR STD. A

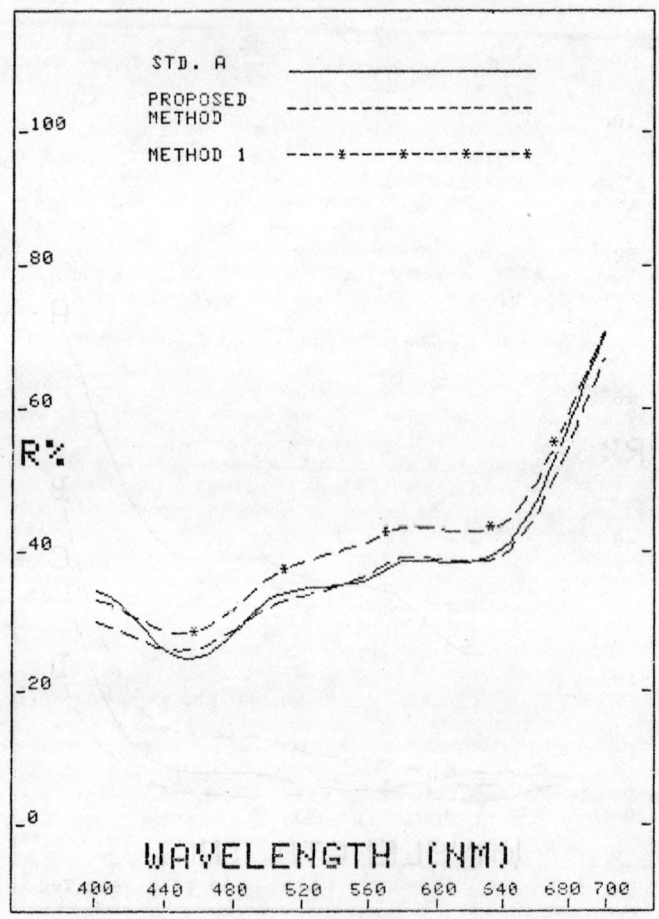

FIG.17 SPECTRAL CURVES OF THE MATCHINGS BY THE PROPOSED METHODS & METHOD 1 FOR STD. B

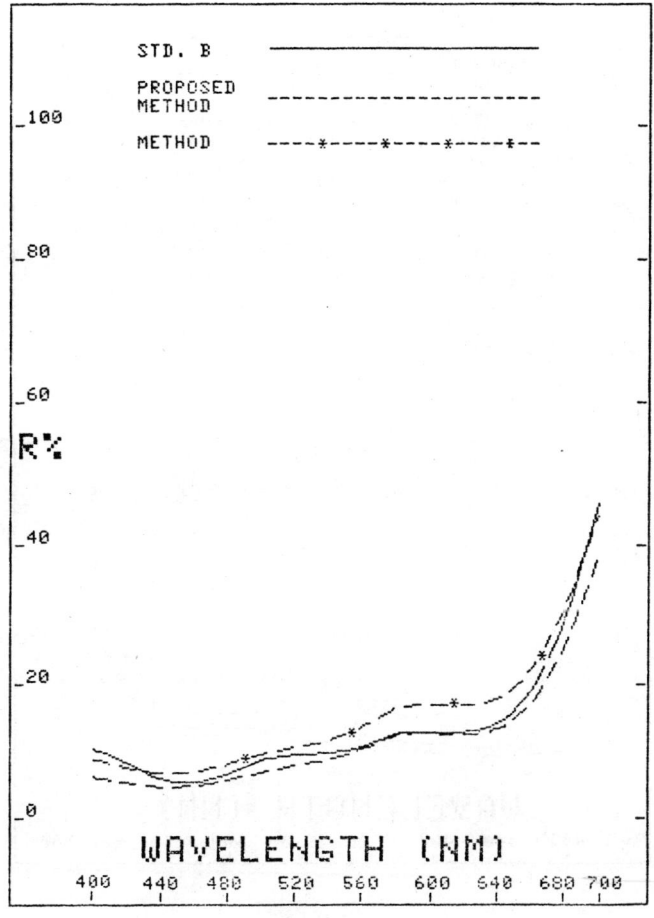

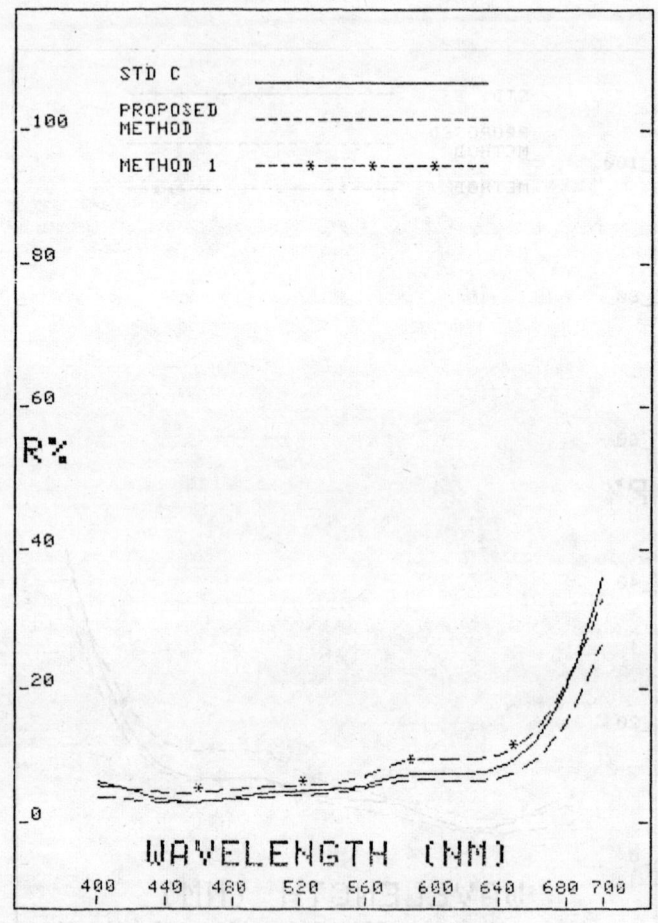

FIG.18 SPECTRAL CURVES OF THE MATCHINGS BY THE PROPOSED METHOD & METHOD 1 FOR STD. C

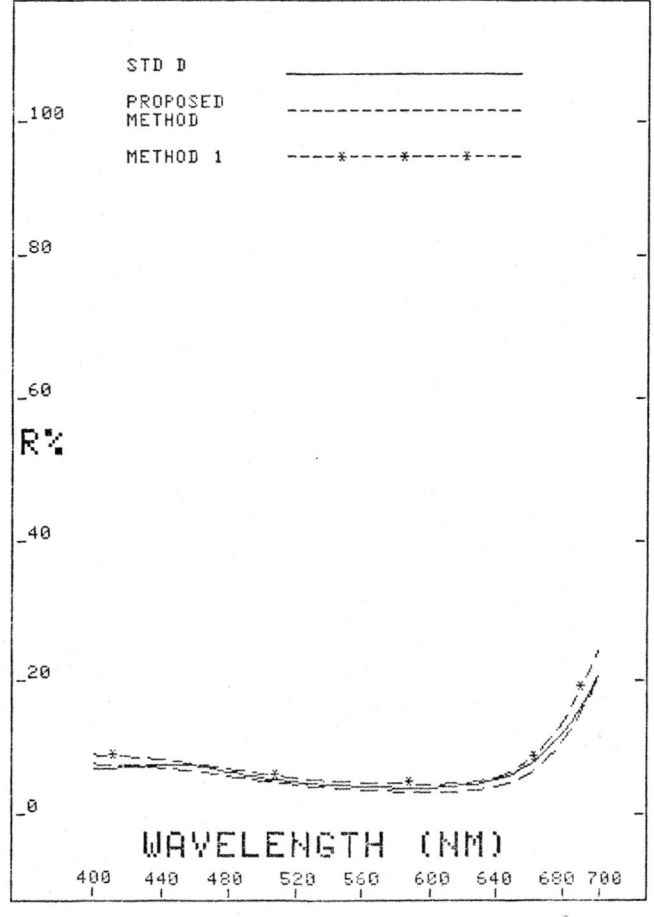

FIG.19 SPECTRAL CURVES
       OF THE MATCHINGS
       BY THE PROPOSED
       METHOD & METHOD 1
       FOR STD. D

Table 1   Accuracy of CCM on Polyester-Cotton Blend
———————   Using Method 1 and the Proposed Method

	STD A	STD B	STD C	STD D	AVE
PROPOSED METHOD	0.4	3.8	2.4	2.2	2.2
METHOD 1	3.5	5.5	3.7	1.7	3.6

(NOTE: THE COLOUR DIFFERENCES PRESENTED ARE BASED ON
THE 1976 CIELAB EQUATION, STD. ILL. D65 AND 1964 10
DEGREE STANDARD OBSERVER.)

410

Table 2.   POSSIBLE SOURCES OF ERRORS

METHOD	VARIATION IN DYEING CONDITIONS	CROSS-STAININGS	FIBRE SEPARATION PROCESS	VARIATION OF THE FIBRES USED FOR CALIBRATIONS FROM THAT OF THE FIBRE-BLEND COMPONENTS
1	POSSIBLE	POSSIBLE	POSSIBLE	POSSIBLE
PROPOSED	LESS POSSIBLE	LESS POSSIBLE	POSSIBLE	NOT POSSIBLE

411

MICROCOMPUTERS IN PRODUCTION CONTROL IN TEXTILE FINISHING

M. Stuart and A. Maclean
Shirley Institute, Manchester

ABSTRACT

Microcomputer based data-processing systems can be used to improve upon manual methods of production planning and control in small and medium sized textile dyeing and finishing enterprises, but lack of suitable software is a major drawback. Development of software which aids decision making and performs routine clerical tasks, and which would be acceptable to finishers with a minimum of tailoring to suit specific individual requirements has therefore been the major objective.

The resulting system details shop floor activity, e.g. location of orders, size of queues at machines, and listing of late orders. It permits the reprocessing and splitting of orders. Completed orders can be analysed to provide valuable management information on market trends and factory performance. By monitoring and analysis of process faults quality inspection can be integrated with order progress. Movement of grey and finished goods has been linked to work-in progress to give an accurate up-to-date stock position. Detailed recording of grey stock allows orders to be traced to source to verify material usage and to control quality.

The longterm workload on machines can be displayed for committed orders to help plan new orders into work and so smooth machine loading. The effect on load profile of altering the sequence of jobs on the shop floor can be studied to optimise the use of key resources.

1. INTRODUCTION

Rapid developments in microelectronics over the past few years have seen the proliferation of low-cost desk-top computers, a proliferation and cost reduction in hardware terms which show little sign of slowing down. The availability of computing power at low cost opens up vast scope for the productive use of information, from rudimentary accounting packages to specialised data handling specifically linked to the operations and needs of a company with a unique set of control, or operational, or development needs.

The covering of the globe with this availability of data handling capacity has been heralded by countless examples of man's technical ingenuity; the provision of ever more lines on a single chip, the pandering in one sense to the sensational record-breaking features of engineering skills represented by the current increasing number of data channels, blinds many to the inescapable fact that the microprocessor, the enabling step in all this, is power-less unless linked to a microcomputer, and the micro-

412

computer, however cheap and capacity-laden it might be,
has also to be programmed before it can be put to work
doing useful jobs; there is little sign that the costs of
supplying software are subject yet to any manufacturing
learning curve equivalent, and the costs of provision of
packages continues to escalate. Not only does that feature
emerge as important, but the unpalatable fact is that there
are qualities of software as there are qualities of hardware, only the qualities of software are much more difficult
to determine. This is certainly true in principle, but
additional practical problems arise since problems due to
software inadequacy are not easy to extract from problems
which might be intrinsic to the application. Nor is there
any guideline on efficiency by which the lay user can
establish whether any particular programme is making
excessive demands on the application power available.
Thus the provision of suitable applications software, which
may, in fact, require a fundamental change akin to the
development of the microprocessor as a universal chip, is
lagging far behind developments in hardware. It is maybe
a less glamorous field, maybe there is more personal
fortune to be made in undemanding provision of video games,
but the need is basic to making full beneficial use of
computers in industrial environments.

2. SOFTWARE CONSIDERATIONS

To obtain suitable software for any particular application,
the range of software available, given in order of probable
increase in cost, and hence decreasing desirability,
provided qualities are similar, is:

(a) Purchase a complete off-the-shelf software package
(b) Purchase an off-the-shelf package, and have it tailored
    in - hence to suit particular needs
(c) As (b) but tailored by the software package supplier
(d) Use in-house programming skills to write the required
    software
(e) Have the required software specially prepared by a
    software house

At the risk of offending in-house specialists, this order
probably also represents the increasing probability of
getting what you want, certainly the more complicated and
specific an application becomes. There are numerous off-
the-shelf packages available for standard office uses,
notably basic business accountancy packages, covering
nominal accounts, payroll, sales ledger, purchase ledger
and so on, varying greatly in cost, complexity and general
applicability. But beyond universal office uses, where
the development of fully professionally accepted codes of
practice are an essential pre-requisite to such universality,
off-the-shelf software for management of production is often
of limited use and applicability without major modification.
This can hardly be surprising, for two substantial reasons.

First, much of the software available today has been developed

for engineering applications, where factories or workshops
produce complex manufactured articles, built up from components and sub-assemblies, and satisfying a fairly predictable medium and long-term demand. In this kind of
environment the main requirements are to balance orders and
capacity, and to ensure timely release of sufficient
materials while maintaining satisfactory inventories.

Secondly, reference has been made earlier to the costs of
software development. When the chip was first developed,
it application was very limited, since powerful though the
device is, provision of custom-made chips is an expensive
business, and difficult to justify in the absence of a
mass market.

Likewise, the larger the available market for a piece of
software development, the more likely the cost is to be
justified. Hence off-the-shelf packages will tend to
offer a lowest common denominator level of acceptability
in the interests of satisfying to some extent a wider
client base.

The dyeing and finishing industry, particularly those elements
which operate on commission base which is widespread in the
UK, do not operate in the fixed framework of manufacture
of artifacts, and the welcome opportunities to plan
production, equipment use and stock requirements well ahead
are frequently few, overridden as they are by the un-
predictability of demand and uncertainties of processing
time which are the dominant characteristics of a commission
based industry. Flexibility is the key characteristic of a
commission finisher's business; and this means responding to
changes in product mix, volume, and demands or priority
instances in as cost-effective and efficient a way as
possible.

It also means ability to deploy labour in a number of
work centres, not implying total versatility, but sufficient
spread of skills to ensure that expedient labour scheduling
is possible; it means the ability to alter working hours;
and it means that the balance of equipment between those
dedicated to specific product types, and those which can
process several products is appropriate to his pattern of
business. Operation of a software of which variation, and
not uniformity, is a key feature, demands an information
system which enables plant management to exercise maximum
control over day-to-day operations, and hence will provide an
up-to-date and accurate position of what is actually happen-
ing at shop floor level.

Few textile firms have the expertise, the time or maybe the
determination to develop their own software, and hence the
only option left available to them is that of external software development, with its attendant direct cost which can
easily lead to the cost of implementing a computer solution
being unacceptably high. There is a vital additional cost

which is too often overlooked, namely, the costs of the
user's time in educating the external agent about the
nature of the system with which he is to deal, and perhaps
in actually thinking through what it is he aims to achieve
by using a computer-based solution to his problems.

The need for appropriate and custom-built software in the
areas of production planning and control has been made clear
from Shirley Institute's contacts with industry, and with
the ever increasing specific nature of software requirements,
expert knowledge of one sector can enable such development
for a number of users to take place.

3. STRUCTURAL CONSIDERATIONS

The dyeing and finishing industry in the United Kingdom,
particularly that section of it related to cotton and allied
textiles, the classification of the sector nationally
recognised, is characterised by its commission nature, and
the general absence of its incorporation in large vertically
integrated operations. The resulting fragmentation of the
industry and its commercial activities has resulted in
survival of individual operations being achieved by individual
responses to business situations, and not by a generalised
approach on the part of the industry. Many countries do
not, in fact, distinguish their cotton and allied textile
finishing in the same way as the United Kingdom does, and
prefer to classify their industries according to company
type, whether integrated, merchant or commission; to company
operation irrespective of fibre type, or by geographical
region. In practice, this restriction of definition hardly
represents the activities undertaken by many such companies;
areas of overlap with other classifications of industrial
sector have developed, e.g. with knitted goods; as a result
of the growth of non-wovens and coated fabrics; and as a
result to other changes in the structure, markets and
technology of the textile industry. The slightly paradoxical
outcome has been that the process of developing a more strongly
vertical structure for the total textile industry has resulted
in outcome in a preferential reduction in concentration of
ownership of available dyeing and finishing capacity, with
larger integrated groups closing down finishing capacity,
leaving some opportunities for the extension of commission
and merchanting operations. This has happened even to the
extent that apparel printing operations closed down by larger
groups as unsuited to their corporate purposes have reopened
as independent commission operations as a result of, for
example, management buy-out. The initial fieldwork in this
project therefore covered a sector characterised by variety,
in some cases by an idiosyncratic approach to business requirements, in most cases by the expediency born from needs for
survival in the adverse business circumstances generated by
the specific UK problems in the 1980/81 period, expediency
which made some nonsense of official industrial classifications.

The first step taken was to classify firms in the sector in a
way which could represent the main features of the activities
and give some ordered framework within which work could be
carried out. A sample of firms was then selected, and
management interviews were conducted to establish

(a) what information the management of these companies used
    at present to control their production operations

(b) what information management, given freedom from cost
    constraints, would wish to use to control their production
    operations in the future

(c) what the realistic scope for the adoption of microprocessor/
    microcomputer based information systems was for these
    companies.

Any general categorisation of the firms worked at was that
they were relatively small with a range of employee number
from 50 to 400. Management of these firms was anxious to
make full use of microcomputer based information, within
limits, and the main restriction was that of cost; the
exercise therefore had to be practical, not tailored for the
ideal but for the useable.

4. FIELD WORK

The activities carried out by the firms interviewed in the
first instance were as follows

(a) dyeing of apparel and industrial fabrics on own account
    and on commission

(b) printing of furnishing fabrics on own account and on
    commission

(c) dyeing, proofing and coating of apparel fabrics on own
    account

(d) laminating of foam and textiles on commission

(e) application of specialised industrial finishes to fabrics
    on commission

All the firms operate manual systems of production control
which demand considerable clerical effort in the preparation
of works and customer documentation. Where priority is given
to information relating to raw material supply into the
works, and product dispatch from the works, dissemination
of information relating to work-in-progress which represents
the change from former to latter does not get the attention
it merits. It is in this transition which poses to firms the
greatest problems in maintaining accurate stock records,
especially when the product mix includes goods to be finished
on own-account and on commission, and hence renders difficult
the running of a production operation at maximum efficiency.

In addition to using a computer for handling normal
production control functions, management generally
considered that the following two items of control information represented valuable additions to those which they
deploy manually at present.

(a) Recording and analysing material losses which occur
in processing, as an aid to quality control

(b) Generating trend information based on completed
production orders. This could be useful to other
departments e.g. cost accounts and marketing.

Next we worked closely with firm (e) above to gain
first hand experience in designing and implementing
a computerised production control system in an industrial
sector not catered for by software houses. The chosen
firm found it difficult to produce accurate shop floor
information quickly using present procedures, mainly due
to the diversity of process routes. The quite complex
nature of their activities helped to ensure that the
outcome of the collaboration could be carried over to
other finishers with minimum tailoring. The firm's
activity can be summarised as follows:

Orders received per week	60
Production cycle	4 - 5 weeks
Finishing machines	30
Machines per route	4 - 20
Routes	150

The system was intended to satisfy three broad
requirements -

1. Supply the production office with an up-to-date
picture of work in progress including the loads
on each machine.

2. Supply accounts with information on stock levels
and customers with information on goods, held on
their behalf.

3. Generate statistics such as machine utilisation and
orders received by product category.

5. OUTCOME

It is essential for any operational management team to
recognise at the outset that any derived production control
system is still an information-supplying system, not a
decision-taking system. A service is offered, and
should enable management decisions to be taken on sound,
timely and relevant information; no substitute for management decision-making and accountability is on offer here.
This might sound a trite observation to make, but the

417

credulous side of man's nature is very apparent when faced
with the output of a computer-based information system.
The key factor, to our mind, is that such systems are the
most ill-equipped to deal with the abnormal, and it is
dealing with the abnormal, preferably before its impact
has become of any significance, that constitutes the
majority and the most important of management's tasks.

There is still no substitute for knowledge of the
operation; while artificial intelligence capabilities and
experience-based systems are under development, we can be
confident that their use will remain for some time yet
beyond the needs and capabilities of the companies our
project was aimed to help.

As a result of the survey and on-site collaboration it
emerged that a production control system should perform
certain basic functions. It should -

1. Log new orders into the system and signal their
    completion.

2. Generate at least part of the documentation usually
    associated with processing orders.

3. Feed information on the status of WIP and machine
    loadings to all relevant and involved management
    activities, e.g. the production office, shop floor,
    personnel, sales and customers.

4. Interface WIP back to grey goods and forward to
    finished stocks.

5. Permit the scheduling of orders to optimise the use
    of resources, both equipment, materials and labour.

6. Provide performance/market statistics to aid business
    strategy.

Accordingly software has been developed to handle six areas
of production planning and control, on a modular basis.
Development was undertaken on a microcomputer with twin
floppy disks and running under the CP/M operating system.
This system provides good program portability, i.e.
programs developed for one machine can be run without
modification on other CP/M machines and so applications
are not limited to one computer manufacturer. The
programming language used is Microsoft BASIC which has
excellent file handling capability.

The modules consist of the following individual elements.

5.1 Order Processing

This is the most basic part of any production control
system and one which was handled manually by all of the
samples of companies initially approached. The system
maintains a file of customer orders and generates the
necessary documentation. Creating a works order is a
two step process. An incoming request is first logged
into the system. Then before a job is released as work
in progress, production parameters are added and copies
of the works order printed. When a job is completed the
computer will generate the delivery note and invoice.

5.2 Stock Recording

In addition to work in progress the system maintains a
grey stock and a finished stock file. The grey stock
file is updated on receipt of a grey lot and when an order is
instructed into work. Similarly when an order is completed
the processed quantity is added to the finished stock
file where it remains until called for by the customer.
A stock print-out for one customer is shown in Fig. 1.

In commission finishing it is common practice for a
customer to call off over a period, several orders from
a single grey lot held on his behalf. The system will,
therefore, print out a history of cloth usage for that
lot which can be used to reconcile differences between the
quantity received and the quantity put into work.

Reports: Grey, WIP and finished stocks
           Works order history of grey lot

5.3 Progressing Orders

By assigning a route and completion dates for each stage
of the route using the scheduling module (see below)
the progress of an order can be monitored to provide
status and workload information for production staff and
customers. In-works orders may be selectively sorted to
yield action reports for specific personnel or departments. Examples are given in Figs. 2, 3 and 4.

Other features of this module are the ability to track
orders which are (a) sent back one or more stages for
reprocessing and (b) split up during processing. The
magnitude and origin of process losses can also be
recorded as the job progresses. It is thus possible to
build up a history of losses distinguishing between those
chargeable to processing and those to substandard cloth.

Reports: Orders due out in selected week
           Location of orders by quality/pattern/job number
           Loads on work centres
           Work programme by department

5.4 Scheduling

This permits a process route to be built up for the order
in hand from available work centres. A new route may be
appended to the routes file and recalled for future use.
Once a route has been defined a timetable, consisting of
dates by which each process stage should be completed, is
input. Route and timetable data are added to other
production data held in the record for that order.

5.5 Capacity Planning

This module aims to make the best use of resources. It
is in two parts.

(i) Medium range planning. Based on confirmed orders the
    system maintains a load profile for each work centre
    up to the planning horizon, typically nine weeks ahead.
    The effect of provisional orders can be examined by
    entering order quantity and schedule. By varying the
    mix and/or schedule of these orders loads can be more
    readily be matched to available capacity.

Reports: Weekly load in hours on work centres (Shown Fig. 5)
          Extra load on work centres due to provisional
          orders

(ii) Short range planning. A routine has been developed
     to help with short range planning on the shop floor.
     The routine simulates the arrival and departure of
     jobs at one or more work centres. The aim is to
     predict the magnitude of the queue over-time at the
     work centre so as to provide early warning of an
     over or under load situation. Computer simulation
     provides a rapid means of studying the effect on
     queue size, of altering the sequence in which jobs
     are processed at an earlier stage in the production
     cycle. Load profile can have an important bearing
     on the value of WIP and the economics of machine
     operation.

Reports: Predicted buffer stocks over-time at a process
          junction

5.6 Statistics

This module recognises the fact that orders by virtue of the
raw data they contain are a rich source of statistical
information valuable for indicating market trends and how
well capacity is being managed. Periodic analysis of
recent orders thus provides a vital check on the state
of the business. e.g. the length processed is automatically
recorded against the appropriate work centres whenever an
order is progressed. This information is used to maintain
a table showing throughput by work centre for the last
ten periods ending in the current period.

(Fig.6)

Similarly completed orders will provide raw data for a
table of volume of orders by product group provided
product group is one of the data items entered on the
order file.

Reports: Volume of orders by product group/customer by
            Machine utilisation

            Process yields by work centre/cloth quality

The modular aspect set out above makes it possible to offer
a potential user rough guidelines on the choice of system
depending on the size and complexity of finishing activities.
For short production cycles of 2 or 3 days, monitoring the
precise location of a job is of limited interest. Here
simple order processing without detailed progress monitor-
is probably sufficient.

The clerical effort needed to process customer orders is
considerable partly due to repetitive typing of the same
order details. The justification for computerised order
processing is that the computer need only store a data
item once and can quickly generate works order documentation,
delivery note and invoice, freeing office staff to get on
with other tasks.

As the production cycle increases, due to more complex
routing, there is a need to keep track of orders. Often
the task is cumbersome using manual procedures. Computerised
progress monitoring combined with a scheduling facility can
then offer a real improvement in the speed of presentation
and accuracy of shop floor information.

6. CONCLUSIONS

The whole field of computerisation and information technology
is fascinating and diverse; but by that very nature it is
prey to the kind of technological fashion which can appear
to be fundamental but ends up down a short term side-
alley of no long term significance but of brief excitement.
Technological resources are precious, and their optimum use
still requires strict discipline. Against that background,
the work here reported is relatively unexciting. There is
little novel in what we have done; no uncharted territory has
been explored; no fundamental changes in production philosophy
or management practice have been made. But we must not lose
sight of the fact that many small and medium sized enterprises,
unable to afford the costs of being at the head of the high-
tech race, not interested in advantages which could only be
gained with expenditure of large amounts of capital, can
still make considerable improvements to their business
management by taking advantage of applications which the
technically sophisticated now aiming at a 21st century
of artificial intelligence would treat with disdain. There
is still a great deal of benefit to be gained by the application of microcomputer-based systems to give incremental
improvements in existing management operations. The way

ahead is neither necessarily nor exclusively along one
broad sunrise highway; the side-roads and country lanes
are still routes to be profitably fr'lowed. In this
case, a microcomputer based production control system has
been developed for small and medium firms in textile
finishing. The system will improve the flow of information leading to greater efficiency in the management of
production. We have placed emphasis on providing job and
machine status information in an easy to read format to aid
decision making and enable management to respond quickly to
exceptions. The system can also generate historical trend
information which should benefit other departments, and
with the modular nature of the soft-ware, it is adaptable to
a variety of production environments.

ACKNOWLEDGEMENTS

This work was carried out with the assistance of the
Textile and Other Manufactures Requirements Board of the
United Kingdom Department of Industry under a shared-cost
contract.

The help and guidance of contributing firms is acknowledged,
especially that of Melland and Coward with whom the detailed
programmes were established.

A Maclean & M. Stuart
Shirley Institute
Didsbury
MANCHESTER

FIG 1   Maclean

CUSTOMER STOCK

AMTEX
  14/12/83

	Order	Length	Quality	Next process	Delivery
Work in progress					
	421	4700	1	MUR	50
	311	6400	2	Dye	1
	312	5200	3	Dye	1
	555	1100	1	Finish	52
	2100	1400	2	Prep	51
	432	3790	1	Finish	50
	142	360	1	Stent	49
	Total	22950			
Finished stock					
	151	255	1		49
	567	3000	1		52
	181	1500	3		49
	100	4000	1		52
	Total	8755			

Grey stock

Lot No	Width	Length	Pieces	Constrn	Grey ref	Date
MS9	56	7000	5	WGK	GR456	12/83
MS11	60	2400	5	45/32	GT45	12/83
MS12	42	2217	9	NW	FR4	12/83
	Total	11617				

FIG. 2

Work in progress summary

Week 49

Order	Grey	Prep	Bleach	Stent	Dye	Wash	Finish	Exam	MUR
151	255	255			255		255	255	255
143	*	470			470	470		470	470
125	*	*			2340	2340	2340	2340	2340
131	*	*				*	900	900	900
555	1100	1100			1100		1100	1100	1100
133	450					450			450
134	1100	1100			1100		1100	1100	1100
142	360		360	360			360	360	360
162	1200	1200		1200	1200		1200	1200	1200
163	1300		1300						1300
171	*		*						1200
172	1200		1200						1200
181	*	*			*		*	*	1500
99	*	*			1000		1000	1000	1000
220	680	680			680			680	680
49	1350					1350			1350
988	1200	1200			1200		1200	1200	1200
567	*	*			*		*	3000	3000
344	4000		4000	4000					4000
789	5000		5000					5000	5000
100	*	*			4000		4000	4000	4000
513	*	*	2400	2400					2400
299	870	870			870			870	870
343	1100	1100			1100			1100	1100
2100	1400	1400			1400			1400	1400
300	840	840			840			840	840
Queues	23405	470	2400	0	7340	0	900	3000	270

- A row of the table indicates the process route,
- A queue is total metres immediately behind a process,
- A numerical entry represents a load on the process at the head of the column,
- * means that the order quantity has passed through that process
- A space means that that process is not part of the route

FIG. 3

Orders due out next week

Week	49								
Order	Grey	Prep	Bleach	Stent	Dye	Wash	Finish	Exam	MUR
220	680	680			680			680	680
421	4700	4700	4700	4700	4700		4700	4700	4700
425	3200			3200		3200	3200		
426	5300			5300		5300	5300		
427	4000			4000		4000	4000		
428	3800			3800		3800	3800		
428	6300			6300		6300	6300		
430	5200			5200		5200	5200		
432	3790			3790		3790	3790		

FIG. 4   Maclean

Work scheduled for week 50

Week   49

	Order	Length	Quality	Delivery
Grey				
	555	1100	1	52
	99	1000	3	52
	49	1350	3	51
	988	1200	3	52
	311	2100	1	4
	430	5200	1	50
	432	3790	1	50
Prep				
	220	680	2	50
	421	4700	1	50
Bleach				
	421	4700	1	50
Stent				
	421	4700	1	50
	430	5200	1	50
	432	3790	1	50
Dye				
	220	680	2	50
	421	4700	1	50
Wash				
	430	5200	1	50
	432	3790	1	50
Finish				
	421	4700	1	50
	430	5200	1	50
	432	3790	1	50
Exam				
	220	680	2	50
	421	4700	1	50
MUR				
	220	680	2	50
	421	4700	1	50

426

FIG 5.

PLANNED WORKLOAD (hours)

Week	49	50	51	52	1	2	3	4
Grey	66	16	19	0	0	0	0	0
Prep	8	20	7	12	5	4	0	0
Bleach	0	17	7	12	5	0	0	0
Stent	31	22	7	8	5	0	0	0
Dye	8	16	0	15	0	9	0	0
Wash	31	12	0	0	0	0	0	5
Finish	6	49	0	7	8	0	0	5
Exam	8	23	0	0	15	0	4	0
MUR	0	35	0	0	15	0	0	4

FIG. 6

Machine throughput in last 10 periods (thous.m.)

	Week	10	11	12	13	14	15	16	17	18	19
Grey		2.0	0.0	0.0	0.0	0.8	5.5	0.0	0.0	0.0	59.2
	Total	67.5									
Prep		2.4	0.0	0.0	0.0	0.8	5.5	0.0	0.0	0.0	50.0
	Total	58.7									
Bleach		0.0	0.0	0.0	0.0	0.0	3.2	0.0	0.0	0.0	4.0
	Total	7.2									
Stent		0.0	0.0	0.0	0.0	0.0	0.0	0.0	0.0	0.0	9.2
	Total	9.2									
Dye		1.4	0.0	0.0	0.0	1.8	1.8	0.0	0.0	0.0	50.0
	Total	55.0									
Wash		0.0	0.0	0.0	0.0	0.0	0.0	0.0	0.0	0.0	5.2
	Total	5.2									
Finish		0.0	0.0	0.0	0.0	1.0	0.0	0.0	0.0	0.0	5.2
	Total	6.2									
Exam		2.4	0.0	0.0	0.0	1.0	5.0	0.0	0.0	0.0	50.0
	Total	58.4									
MUR		2.4	0.0	0.0	0.0	1.0	1.8	0.0	0.0	0.0	54.0
	Total	59.2									

SAVINGS BY DYEBATH-COMPOSITION CONTROL : SOME COMPUTER-BASED ANALYTICAL APPROACHES

L. Bettens

ABSTRACT

Computers can now be used in the discontinuous dyeing of textiles to reduce energy and water and dyestuff consumption. The methods for reducing consumption are based on the control of exhaustion from the bath by regulating the chemical equilibria and the equilibrium repartition on one hand and on the recycling of rising baths and exhausted dyebaths on the other.

The application of these methods is based on knowledge of the chemical composition and of the variation of this composition by pH-regulation.

A computer model of the chemical equilibrium is presented, wherein the total and individual concentrations as well as the relations of proportionality are the elements of the different matrices.

The mathematical models of the chemical equilibrium are continuously being expanded and have been developed to simulate and test low-temperature dyeing processes.

To complete the concentration and equilibrium constants, a dynamic data base has been developed, and computerized analysis techniques are used.
These analysis techniques are : titroprocessing, spectrophotometric multicomponent analysis, and three-dimensional chromatography.

Although fairly completely automatic, the laboratory is very flexible, with a high degree of interaction.

Experience on an industrial scale has proved that recycling and controlled exhaustion have an economic and ecological use and that computers have an important function in this.

1. INTRODUCTION

Microcomputer technology has come to play an increasingly important part in our laboratory for the visualization, interpretation, and subsequent reporting of data accumulated in research on process water and dyebath composition (figure 1a, 1b).
With the help of computer-controlled analytical instruments and personal computers, researchers are now able to rapidly transform raw data into clear and easily surveyable representations.
Software has been expanded in different directions, mainly to extend our knowledge of the exact chemical composition of process waters. Only a few of the many examples form the subject of this paper.

Computer systems are used to achieve the following aims :

- energy savings by lowering the dyeing temperature and by
  reducing migration time or dyebath reuse;
- dyestuff savings by increasing bath exhaustion and by lowering
  the consumption of auxiliaries such as levelling and retarding
  agents;
- water savings and the reduction of environmental pollution by
  the reutilization of dyebaths;
- the complete automation of exhaust dyeing.

These goals cannot be realized in practice without a knowledge of
the distribution of the active bath components over the different
equilibrium states.

2. SAVINGS BY LOWERING THE TEMPERATURE, INCREASING BATH EXHAUSTION AND THE REUSE OF THE EXHAUSTED DYEBATH

2.1 Principles

The production of level and batch-to-batch-reproducible dyeings
can only be achieved by controlling one or more of the variables
involved in the dyeing process. Level dyeing can be obtained
either by controlling the rate at which the dyes exhaust onto the
substrates or by redistributing initially randomly absorbed dye
by means of migration as dyeing proceeds. The latter is a very
energy-intensive process and should be replaced.

It is possible to control exhaustion by using a constant, or
nearly constant, temperature during the dyeing cycle, a controlled
change in dyebath composition being effected by adding acid, base,
salt, or other chemicals.

In the dyeing of wool and nylon fibres, for example, decreasing
the pH-value in a controlled manner as dyeing proceeds is advocated for the control of environmental pollution. This is a
method of dyeing control that is particularly pertinent for automation. Characteristically, the dye adsorption should be an
exponential decrease in the rate of adsorption (5).

In contrast to temperature-controlled dyeing, the value of the
initial exhaustion in a pH-controlled process must be selected
in such a way that the initial unlevelness is no more than what
can be rapidly corrected by migration of the dye. pH-control
operates by determining the exhaustion at equilibrium, and the
higher this exhaustion, the higher is the rate of dyeing. Equilibrium, ion activity, and exhaustion can be altered throughout the
course of dyeing by external control. The addition of salt, acid,
base, or other appropriate chemicals is to be made continuously
in response to a preset program or through conductivity and pH-
measurements and closed-loop control.

2.2 Savings

In pH-controlled dyeing processes, for example, the final exhaustion can be very high. This saves energy, dyes, and chemicals.

Reusing the water several times more saves a considerable amount
of energy, chemicals, and, of course, water. This is possibly
based on the titration of a strong base with a strong acid with a

closed-loop control, as in the pH-controlled process for nylon
and wool dyeing with acid dyes.

2.3 Importance of a computer model

Knowledge of the exact composition of the dyebath and of how to
control the exhaustion of dyes and other chemicals, is an interesting area for development. It may be used, in the future, to
maximize the rate of dye uptake commensurate with obtaining
satisfactory levelness. Knowing the chemistry of the acid-base
system may enable dyers to make use of any residual dye left at
the end of the dyeing cycle in the next bath by measuring and
carrying out the appropriate topping up for the next dyebath.
pH-controlled dyeings using NH_4OH, acetic acid, or other weak
bases and acids produce buffers and a build-up of buffers.
Reusing such dyebaths is possible, but the precise control of
equilibrium exhaustion necessitates a computer model showing the
influence of chemical composition on dyeing equilibrium and
kinetics (2).

2.4 Knowledge needed to realize the savings

It is possible to achieve savings by lowering the temperature,
by increasing the bath exhaustion or by reusing exhausted dyebaths
or rinsing baths if one makes use of a computer model showing
the chemical equilibrium of the dyebath as well as of sufficient
analytical data.

The key to savings lies in the knowledge of :

1° the repartition of the individual components over the different
   equilibrium states;

2° the variation of the equilibrium relations as a consequence of
   the variations in process parameters, temperature, ion activity, pH;

3° the resultant equilibrium state produced by mixing part of the
   reused dyeing bath with fresh process water;

4° the variation of the bath composition and distribution as a
   consequence of the addition of dyestuff, auxiliaries, and
   textile material in the dyebath.

3. COMPUTER MODEL OF THE CHEMICAL-EQUILIBRIUM STATE OF A PROCESS WATER CONTAINING SEVERAL COMPONENTS

3.1 Presentation of the chemical equilibria in water

L. Bettens and M. Van Lancker (1) have described the formal presentation of the chemical equilibrium, which is based on the
basic principles proposed by J. Hissel (3).

Table I shows an example of the mass balance and the chemical
equilibria of process water for the dyeing of polyamide.

431

Table I.

Chemical equilibria

$$H_2O \quad \longleftrightarrow \quad H^+ + OH^- \qquad K_1 = \frac{[H^+]\,[OH^-]\gamma_1{}^2}{[H_2O]}$$

$$H_2CO_3 \quad \longleftrightarrow \quad H^+ + HCO_3^- \qquad K_1 = \frac{[H^+]\,[HCO_3^-]\gamma_1{}^2}{[H_2CO_3]}$$

$$HCO_3^- \quad \longleftrightarrow \quad H^+ + CO_3^{--} \qquad K_2 = \frac{[H^+]\,[CO_3^{--}]\gamma_2}{[HCO_3^-]}$$

$$HAc \quad \longleftrightarrow \quad H^+ + Ac^- \qquad K_1 = \frac{[H^+]\,[Ac^-]\gamma_1{}^2}{[HAc]}$$

$$HD \quad \longleftrightarrow \quad H^+ + D^- \qquad K_1 = \frac{[H^+]\,[D^-]\gamma_1{}^2}{[HD]}$$

$$(donor) \quad \longleftrightarrow \quad (particle) + (acceptor)$$

Mass balance

$$[H^+ total] \;=\; [H_2O] + 2[H_2CO_3] + [HCO_3^-] + [HAc] + [HD] + [H^+]$$

$$[CO_3 total] \;=\; [H_2CO_3] + [HCO_3^-] + [CO_3^{--}]$$

$$[Ac\ total] \;=\; [HAc] + [Ac^-]$$

$$[D\ total] \;=\; [HD] + [D^-]$$

In this model, it is assumed that the dyebath is composed of the following co-ordinates : water, carbonate, acetic acid and acid dyestuff, and the H^+-ion as exchangeable particle. The model can be extended with more particles, more co-ordinates, and more phases (water, micelles, air, textile fibres). Its practical realization is the subject of further investigation. Proposals for the presentation of a dyebath with several co-ordinates and particles are cited in the literature (1, 2, 3, 4).

3.2 Matrix presentation of the chemical equilibria (Table II)

a. The various total co-ordinate concentrations are presented together with the concentrations of each of the particles in the column marked matrix A.

b. Matrix B contains the concentrations of the individual components.

c. The elements of matrix C are the total potential concentrations of the exchanging particles.

d. The elements of matrix D indicate the relationships between the individual and the total concentrations : B = D.A.
   The elements having a value different from 1 or 0 are functions of the pH.

e. Matrix E contains the number of particles in each of the individual components; it contains as many rows as there are particles and meets the relation C = E.B.

f. Matrix F is obtained by the product E.D = F, so C=E.D.A = F.A.

Table II.

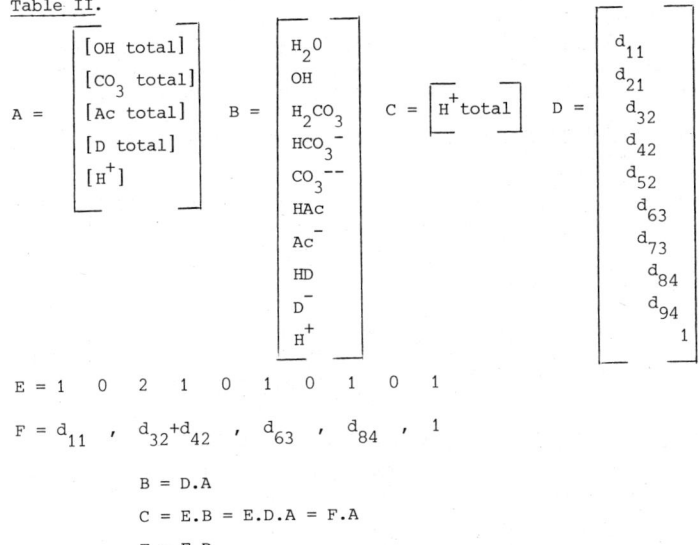

$$A = \begin{bmatrix} [OH\ total] \\ [CO_3\ total] \\ [Ac\ total] \\ [D\ total] \\ [H^+] \end{bmatrix} \quad B = \begin{bmatrix} H_2O \\ OH \\ H_2CO_3 \\ HCO_3^- \\ CO_3^{--} \\ HAc \\ Ac^- \\ HD \\ D^- \\ H^+ \end{bmatrix} \quad C = \begin{bmatrix} H^+total \end{bmatrix} \quad D = \begin{bmatrix} d_{11} \\ d_{21} \\ d_{32} \\ d_{42} \\ d_{52} \\ d_{63} \\ d_{73} \\ d_{84} \\ d_{94} \\ 1 \end{bmatrix}$$

$$E = 1 \quad 0 \quad 2 \quad 1 \quad 0 \quad 1 \quad 0 \quad 1 \quad 0 \quad 1$$

$$F = d_{11} \quad , \quad d_{32}+d_{42} \quad , \quad d_{63} \quad , \quad d_{84} \quad , \quad 1$$

$$B = D.A$$

$$C = E.B = E.D.A = F.A$$

$$F = E.D$$

Table III shows the individual elements of the F-matrix.

Table III : F-matrix elements for a typical process water.

$$f_{11} = \frac{1}{1 + K_w/(f_1 . 10^{-pH})} \qquad \rightarrow OH$$

$$f_{12} = \frac{2f_2 . 10^{-2pH} + (f_2/f_1) . K_1 . 10^{-pH}}{f_2 . 10^{-2pH} + (f_2/f_1) . K_1 . 10^{-pH} + K_1K_2} \qquad \rightarrow CO_3$$

$$f_{13} = \frac{1}{1 + K_{Ac}/(f_1 . 10^{-pH})} \qquad \rightarrow Ac$$

$$f_{14} = \frac{1}{1 + K_{HD}/(f_1 . 10^{-pH})} \qquad \rightarrow Dye$$

$$f_{15} = 1 \qquad \rightarrow [H^+]$$

3.3 <u>Computer program of the chemical equilibria in a process</u>
<u>water</u>

For the representation of the chemical equilibria, a PASCAL
program has been developed, which offers the following possibilities :

1° <u>Calculation of $[CO_3$ total$]$</u>

It is sufficient to analyse the temperature, pH, conductivity,
alkalinity, and total concentrations of the other components in
order to calculate the total carbonate concentration.

2° <u>Calculation of the concentration of the individual components</u>
<u>in matrix B</u>

3° <u>Calculation of the quantity of acid or base</u> needed to bring the
bath to a desired pH-value ($\Delta[H^+$ total$]$ or $\Delta[OH^-$ total$]$).

4° <u>Calculation of the pH</u> by addition of acid or base (e.g.
$\Delta[H^+$ total$]$ or $\Delta[OH^-$ total$]$).

5° <u>Calculation of the pH</u> and the <u>chemical composition</u> of a <u>blend</u>
of two different waters, such as the composition of a dyebath
obtained by an exhausted bath, supplemented with fresh process
water and the chemicals required.

4. ANALYTICAL DATA : COMPLETION OF THE MATRICES

The computer model for the calculation of the chemical equilibria
has now to be completed with analytical data.

4.1 <u>The element of the matrix D and F</u>

On the basis of the measurement of the electrical conductivity and
the temperature, the average activity coefficient γ_n can be calculated for the n-valent ions.

The concentration of the hydrogen ions $[H^+]$ can then be found on
the basis of the pH and the average activity coefficient γ_1 of the
monovalent ions : $[H^+] = \dfrac{10^{-pH}}{\gamma_1}$. To complete the D and F matrix, it

will be sufficient to know the acidity constants K (fig. 2). The
activity coefficients and acidity constants depend on, among other
things, the temperature. The data contained in the files can be
consulted as a function of the temperature. Missing information,
such as the K-value of a certain acid at a given temperature, is
requested in an interactive way by the program when required.
New information is placed in a dynamic list and the acid-file is
automatically updated. The flow chart of the program, shown in
fig. 3, illustrates the approach.

Acidity constants can be determined by means of two totally
different computerized analysis techniques : spectrophotometry
and potentiometric titration.

The spectrophotometric pK-determination is based on a different
specific absorption spectrum of the acid (HA) and basic (A^-) form
and can be made completely automatic. For this purpose a program

has been written in PASCAL, which controls the pH, temperature, conductivity, and concentration of the sample. The program also measures the spectra as a function of the pH, establishes the spectra of the acid and basic forms to be determined, and calculates for each intermediate pH the activity of the acid and basic forms.

The algorithm is :

- first, automatic control of the pH, temperature, concentration, and ion-activity;

- a spectrum is then taken at extreme pH-values to determine the specific spectrum of the acid and the basic form;

- spectra are next taken at intermediate values, and the activity of the acid and basic form is calculated by means of multicomponent analysis;

- finally, the pK is calculated on the basis of $pK = pH + \log \frac{a_{HA}}{a_A}$.

The potentiometric pK-determination is based on the same relationship between the activities of an acid/base-pair, the pH-value, and the dissociation constant or pK-value, respectively,

$$pH = pK + \log \frac{a_b}{a_a} = pK + \log \frac{[A^-]\gamma_1}{[AH]}.$$

When the acid-activity a_A is equal to the base-activity, $pH = pK_A$. This acidity constant can be obtained from the titration curve at the pH corresponding to half of the end-point (fig. 2). As the ion force is here not taken into account, the pK thus obtained is only an approximation. If a more accurate value is required, titrations have to be repeated with decreasing ion force, and the results of the pK-values have to be extrapolated to a zero ion force. The pK_A is determined with a titroprocessor by a dynamic titration. The titroprocessor is a microcomputer-steered titration automate with built-in software for the determination of the acidity constants from dynamic titration curves. In contrast to the titration with constant-volume steps, the dynamic titration uses variable-volume steps, and the end-point of the titration can be obtained from the differentiation curve.

The Metrohm-titroprocessor is, like the HP-spectrophotometer, computer-controlled. With a PASCAL program, pK_A can be accurately determined. Not only are the activity coefficients taken into account, but, by using the titroprocessor and computer, the results obtained are more reliable and cover a larger pK area than before.

The determination of the acidity constants of dyestuffs and auxiliaries is extremely important, not only for controlling the final exhaustion but also to select the compatibility of dyestuffs and auxiliaries.

We have attempted above to explain our ideas concerning pK and the elements of matrices D and F. It is obvious that this kind of work belongs to the textile research laboratory. Once the pK-values are known as a function of the temperature and have been stored in the database, they must not be redetermined, and the

information can be used by the application laboratories.
Centexbel's database now contains dozens of pK_A-values of acids
and is constantly being updated with information about dyestuffs
and auxiliaries.

4.2 The elements of the A-matrix

The A-matrix is composed of the total concentrations of the
co-ordinates or acceptors and of the concentration of the exchanged hydrogen ion $[H^+]$.

To fill in the A_i-elements, the process water must be analysed.
$[OH\ total] = [H_2O] + [OH^-]$ is made equal to 55,3 mol/l at 25°C.

The determination of the total concentrations such as phosphate,
ammonium, silicate, and even acetate (Ac) does not require further
details; they are current colorimetric determinations carried out
in analytical laboratories.

$[H^+]$ is obtained from the pH, conductivity, and temperature.
$[H^+] = 10^{-pH}/\gamma_1$.

Determination of the total carbonate concentration $[CO_3\ total]$
requires the analysis of the alkalinity by potentiometric titration up to pH 8.2 and pH 4.5. The algorithm for the determination
of the total carbonate concentration is amply described in the
literature (3, 4).

4.2.1 Potentiometric analysis

This determination of $[H^+]$ and $[CO_3\ total]$ is best done by means
of the titroprocessor, simultaneously with the alkalinity determination. The titroprocessor guarantees temperature compensation
of the electrode-response. The temperature can be considered as
a parameter or be measured directly with a temperature probe.

The titroprocessor is controlled by a computer with control charts
and a keyboard. The microprocessor program in ROM makes it an
automatic titrator. After each determination or titration, the
titroprocessor transfers reports to a freely programmable HP 9826
desktop-computer via an HPIB-interface. The titroprocessor operates in combination with a balance and a sample-exchanger. Its
application covers the complete area of potentiometry : acidi-
metric (pH), ion-selective (p-ion), redox (U/mv), precipitation,
and complexometric titrations. For the control of a low-temperature dye process and for the recycling and maximum exhaustion of
a dyebath, the titroprocessor is an extremely useful instrument.
Thanks to a certain number of built-in routines, even the most
complex and particular determinations can be made completely
automatic.

4.2.2 UVIS-multicomponent analysis

Process waters possibly contain many other components, such as
tensio-active products and dyestuffs. To determine their total
concentrations, tremendous efforts have been made. Two techniques
have been developed : the multicomponent analysis of dyestuff
blends and three-dimensional chromatography for the identification
and quantitative determination of auxiliaries in process waters
containing different amounts of similar components.

The spectrophotometric determination of the dyestuff concentration by multicomponent analysis by means of a computer-controlled parallel-access spectrophotometer has been described by L. Bettens (1). The multicomponent analysis of a dyestuff blend (figure 4) in a fresh bath, in an exhausted bath, or in rinsing waters is of primary importance for maximum use of the dyestuff.

The analysis method is based on the Beer-Lambert laws :

Absorption = path length Σunit absorption$_i$.concentration$_i$.

For each component, a regression equation $A_\lambda = X_\lambda \beta + \in$ is established.

Where A_λ = absorption at wavelength λ

X_λ = absorbtivity

β = component concentration

$\in$ = error term.

By parallel measurement of the absorption (A_λ) at 200 wavelengths in the field 400 - 800 nm, the concentrations can be found by a maximum-likelihood estimator (1). We have succeeded in doing the measurements in such a way that Beer's law and the conditions for an ML-estimation are fulfilled.

This can be done successfully by a unique method of sample conditioning. Before analysing the sample by means of multicomponent analysis, it is brought into a constant physico-chemical environment so that the pH, conductivity, temperature, and solvent concentration remain independent of the nature and dilution of the sample (figure 5).
This sample conditioning is achieved by means of six microprocessor-controlled peristatic pumps. The conditioning is automatically regulated by an external computer via a Data Acquisition Control System. Interfacing has been realized by Centexbel by means of six completely independently programmable pulse-train generators and a control program written in PASCAL on an HP 9826 table computer.
At the moment, the conditioning and multicomponent analysis of acid, metalcomplex, reactive, direct, indigo, and vat dyestuffs are available. Figure 6 illustrates the importance of the conditioning. One can clearly see how a rise in temperature moves the maxima to a shorter wavelength, which indicates that dyestuff dissolves from aggregates.

The spectrophotometric multicomponent analysis is strongly disturbed by the presence of turbidity. It is impossible to avoid this problem, particularly if the remaining concentration of an exhausted bath has to be determined (figure 7).

To correct the measured spectrum for turbidity, a computer program has been developed. The first of the two methods used is based on Rayleigh's law, which states that the apparent absorption caused by turbidity is a function of the wavelength of diffused light. Here, a theoretical spectrum is generated which gives the absorp-

437

tion as a function of the wavelength for the entire turbidity. A second method is the measurement of a characteristic spectrum of the turbidity component. In both methods an extra component, the characteristic absorption spectrum of which has been generated, is included in the multicomponent analysis. The computer program is strongly interactive and enables certain routines on the spectrophotometer to be programmed without having the computer program adapted or interrupted.

4.2.3 Three-dimensional liquid chromatography

For very complex dyebaths, even the highly sophisticated UVIS-multicomponent analysis does not allow the quantitative determination of each dyestuff component. For this reason, a three-dimensional chromatographic technique has been developed. This technique, also called wavelength chromatography, gives the UVIS-light absorbency in terms of time as well as wavelength.

With this system, it is possible to identify dyestuffs and auxiliaries, and to determine their concentration, even for very complex dyeing or finishing baths.

The system includes a High Performance Liquid Chromatograph, a parallel-access diode-array spectrophotometer, a 32-bit personal computer with peripherals (figure 8). The software has been written in the higher programming language PASCAL. A flow chart is given in figure 9.

The graphics program can be used to present a display of the chromatograms at any preselected wavelength (figure 10). The program can also present total spectral information from a chromatogram or at any selectable retention time (figure 11) in the form of a three-dimensional graph (figure 12).

The presentation of data in this form provides a unique fingerprint of any particular sample, making possible the critical comparison of small differences between closely related samples. This new form of presentation also offers tremendous potential for positive sample identification.

5. CONCLUSION

Various computerized analysis techniques are available to complete the D- and A-matrix. This makes it possible for the program to calculate, from the chemical equilibrium, the concentration of each of the individual elements. The program is extended to include the calculation of the concentration of each of the species and the total concentrations when two process waters are blended and known quantities of recipe and pH-regulating chemicals are added to fresh or recycled process water.

With such a computer model and on the basis of the analytical techniques described, the composition of a process water can be predicted and accurately regulated.

Encouraging results have been obtained during the industrial dyeing of polyamide-fibre carpets at 40°C, the dyeing of wool in a standing bath with acid dyestuff, and the dyeing of viscose fabric in a standing bath with direct dyestuffs.

Computers are a tremendous help in optimizing energy and water and chemical consumption.

ACKNOWLEDGEMENTS

This lecture is based on a research programme granted by the I.W.O.N.L. (Institute for Encouragement of Scientific Research in Industry and Agriculture).

REFERENCES

(1) L. Bettens. Note Technique, March 1982, 16, Les mesures spectrophotométriques de transmission et leurs applications, Centexbel.

(2) L. Bettens, M. Van Lancker. Modèles mathématiques de quelques processus discontinus de teinture. Une aide lors de l'optimisation et le développement de nouvelles recettes de teinture, Congrès FIATCC, London, September 1984.

(3) J. Hissel. Micro-informatique et équilibres chimiques dans les eaux, ISBN 2-87080-006-1, Ed. CEBEDOC - Liège Belgique, 1982.

(4) L. Bettens, Note Technique, 1979, La mesure et la neutralisation du pH des effluents, Centexbel.

(5) L. Bettens. V.C.V. tijdingen, 1982, 9, Optimalisatie van het verven van Polyamide met zure kleurstoffen.

Centexbel,
rue Montoyer 24,
1040 Brussels,
Belgium

Figure 1a

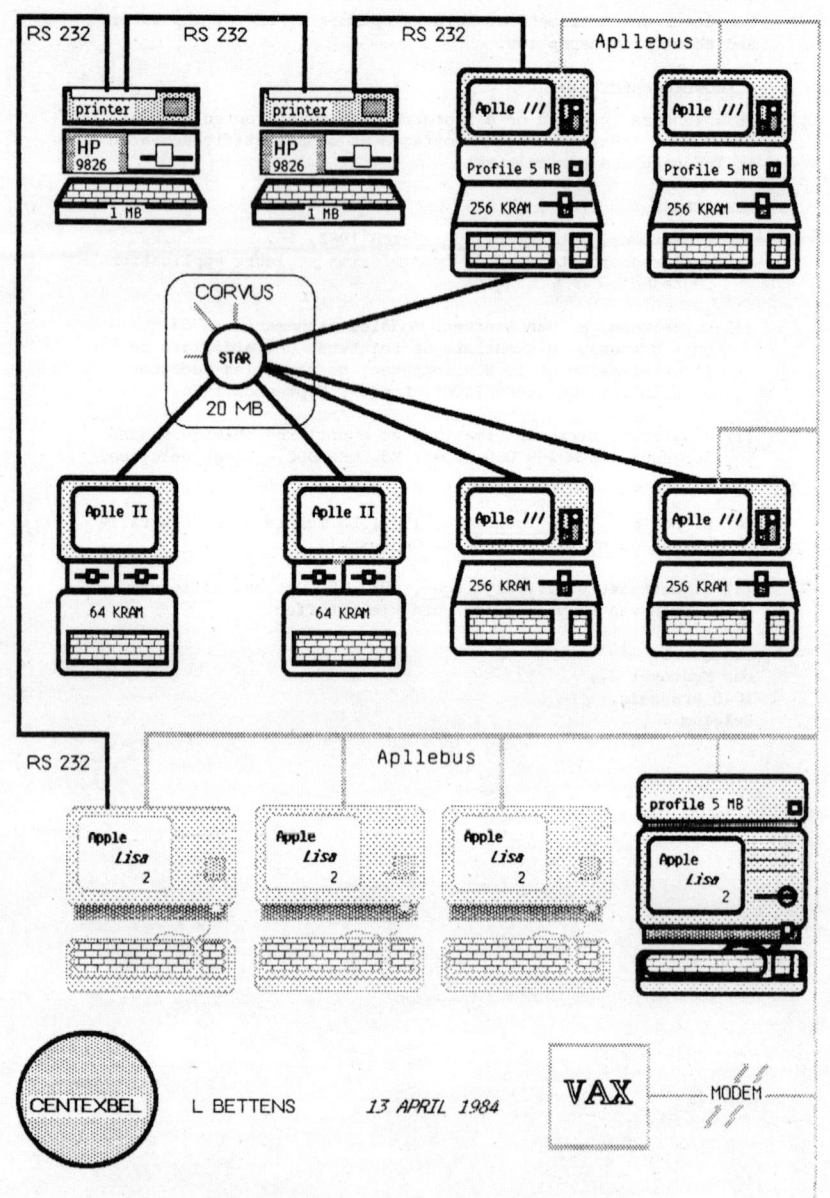

computer systems and local area network in the analytical laboratory

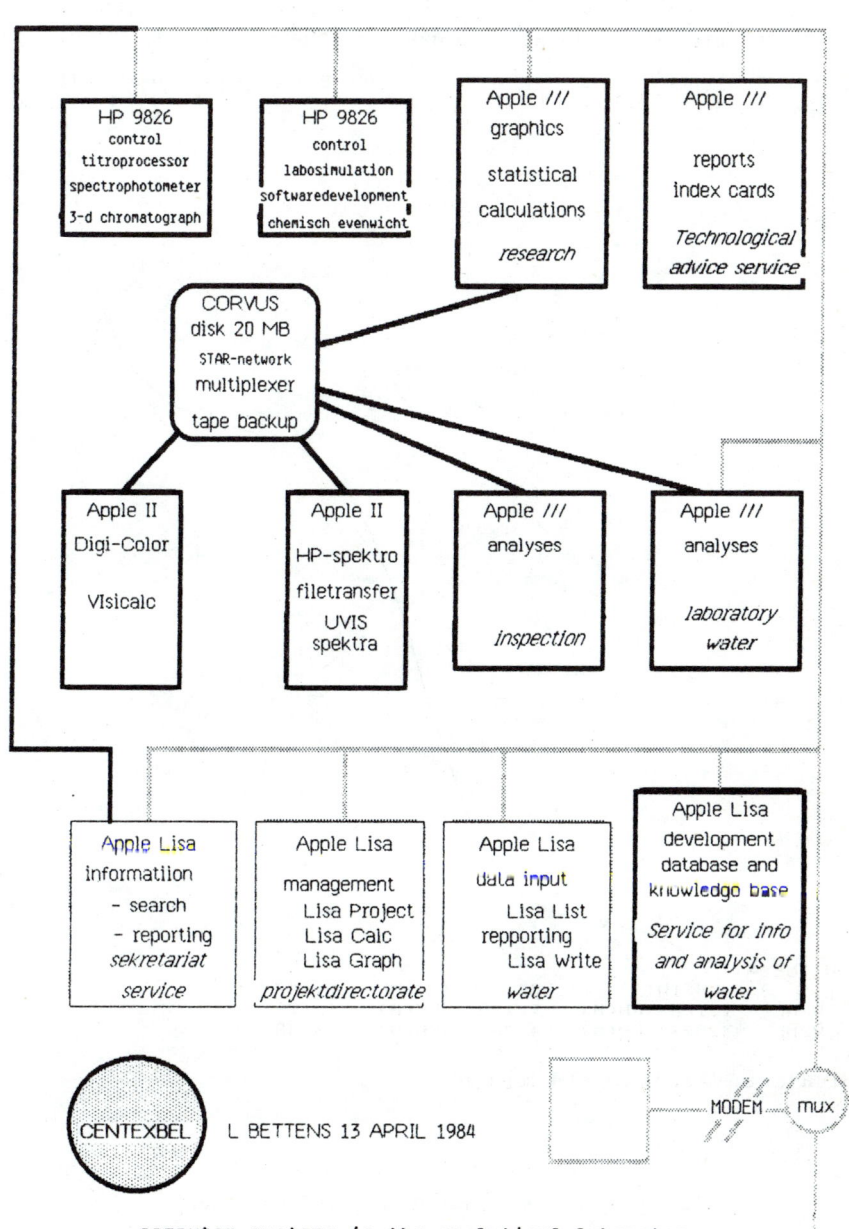

computer systems in the analytical laboratory

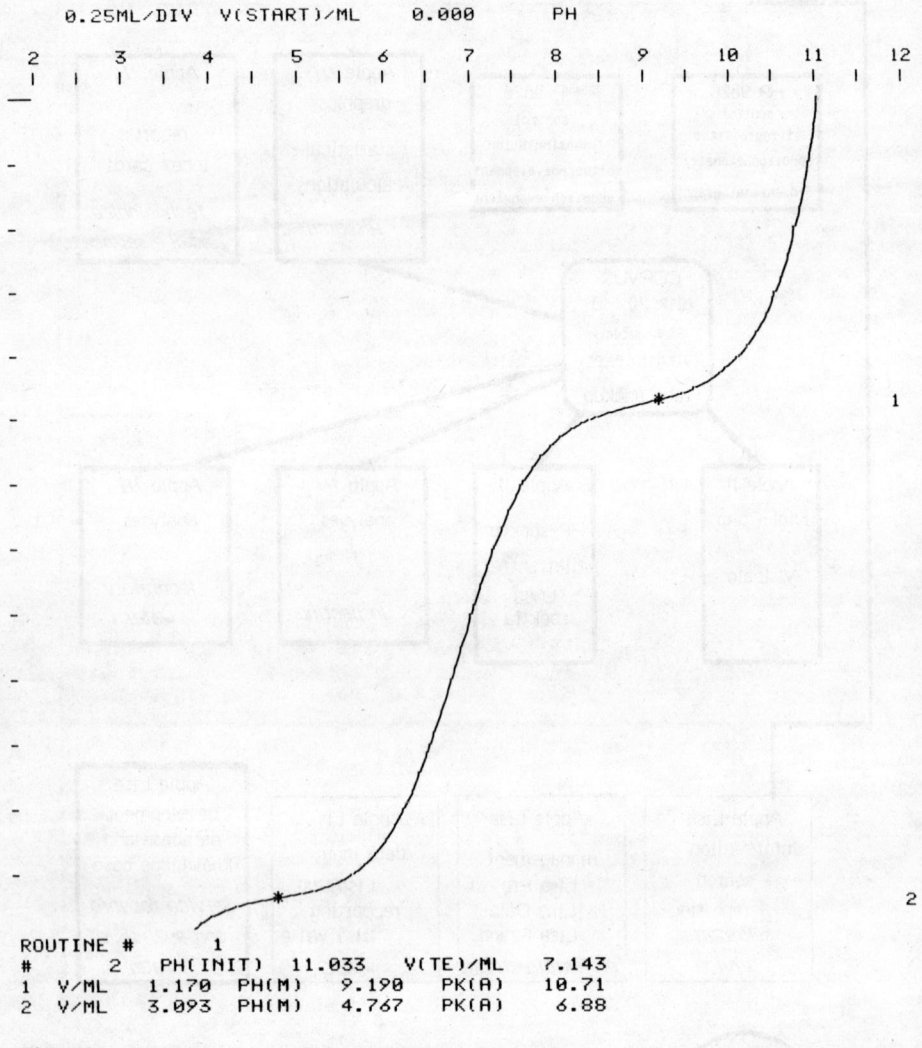

```
      0.25ML/DIV  V(START)/ML     0.000     PH

  2         3         4         5         6         7         8         9        10        11        12
  |    |    |    |    |    |    |    |    |    |    |    |    |    |    |    |    |    |    |    |    |
 ___

  -                                                                                                    1

  -

  -

  -

  -

  -

  -

  -

  -

  -                                                                                                    2

 ROUTINE #      1
 #       2   PH(INIT)   11.033    V(TE)/ML    7.143
 1  V/ML   1.170   PH(M)    9.190   PK(A)    10.71
 2  V/ML   3.093   PH(M)    4.767   PK(A)     6.88
```

Titration curve of Na_3PO_4 with HCl 0,1N

<u>Figure 2</u> : pK-determination of phosphoric acid.

442

Fig 3 Computer model of the acid-base equilibria

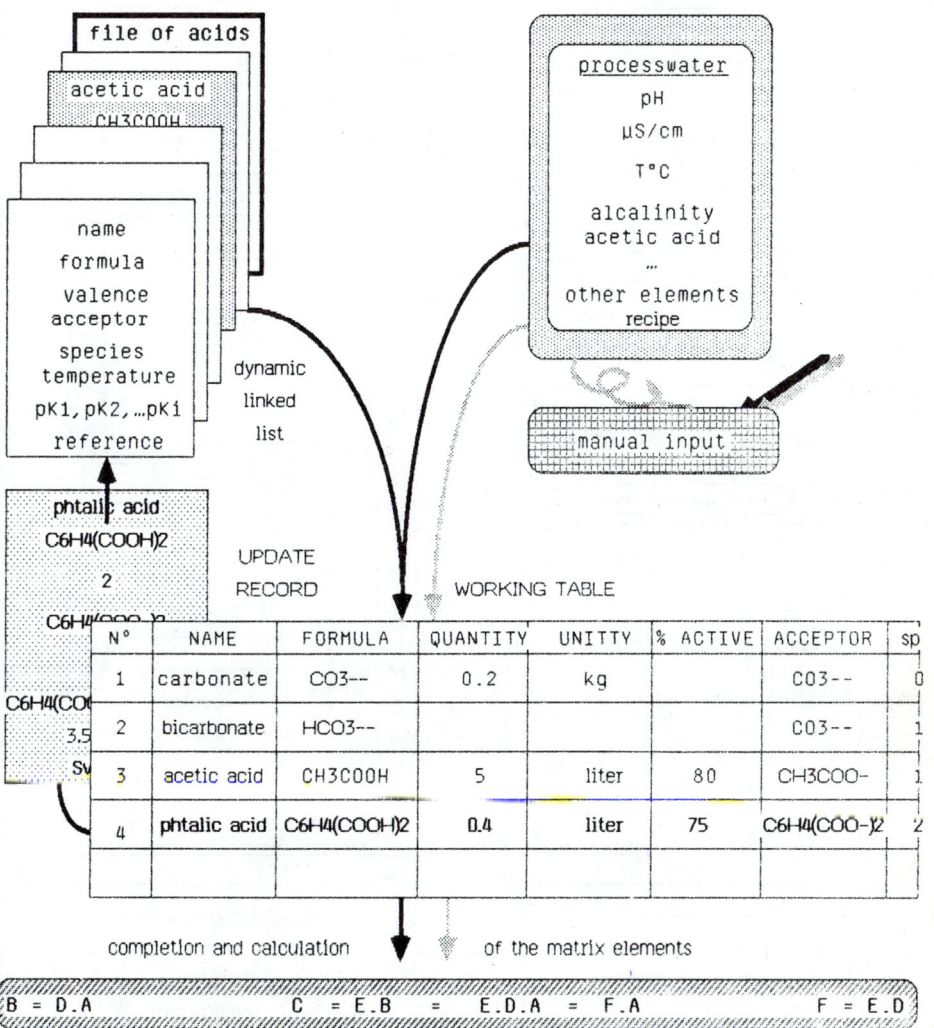

Fig 4 Specrophotometric Multicomponent Analysis

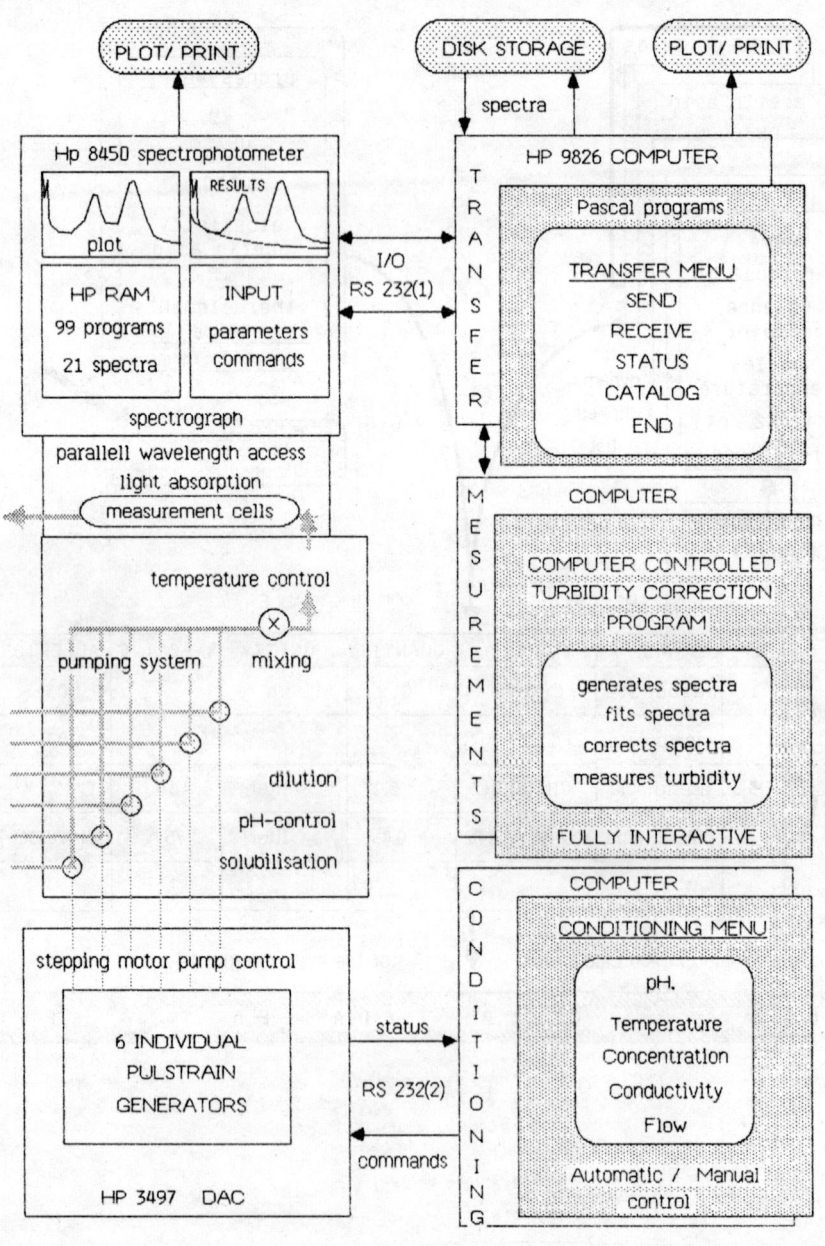

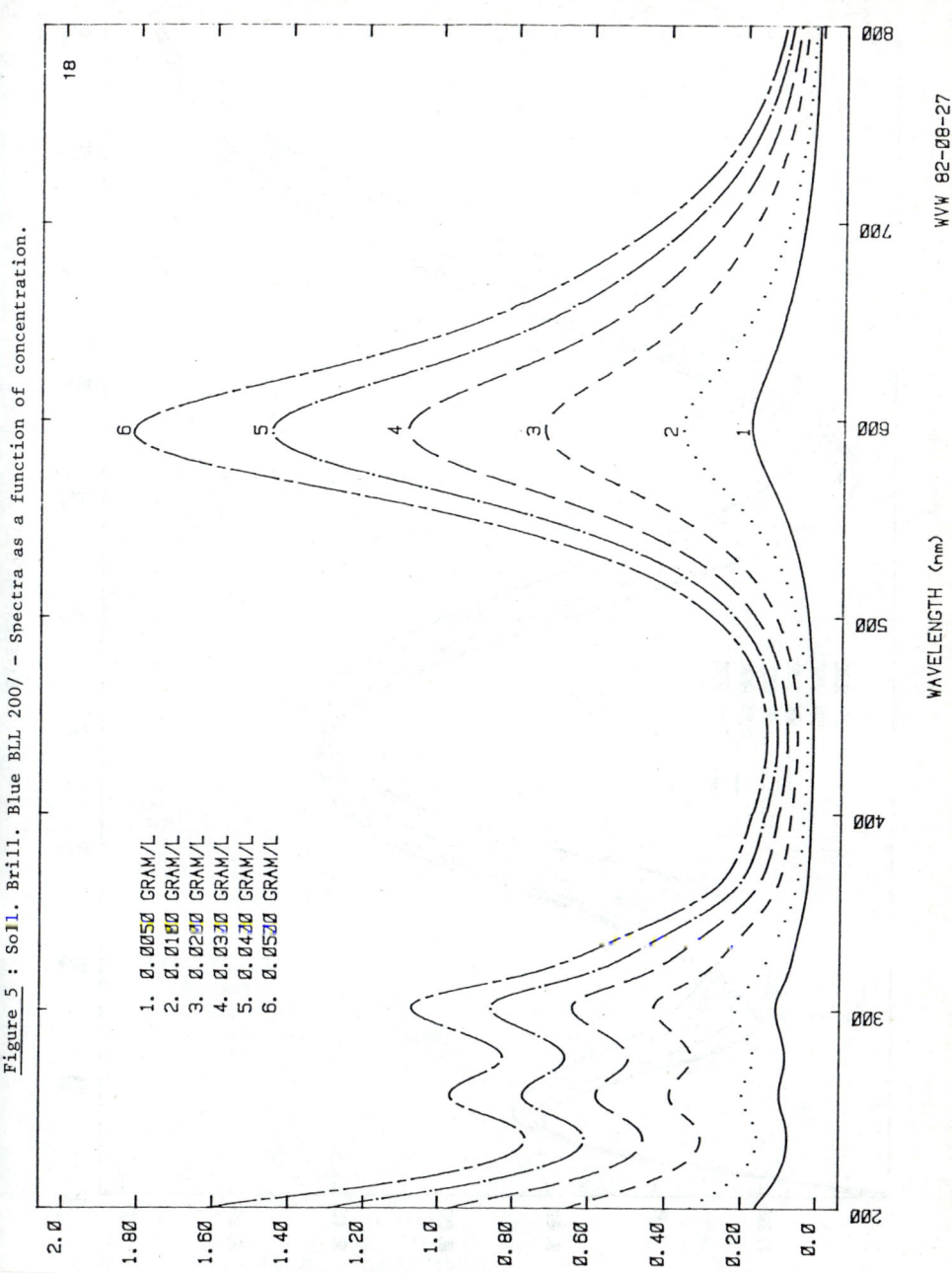

Figure 5 : Soll. Brill. Blue BLL 200/ - Spectra as a function of concentration.

1. 0. 0050 GRAM/L
2. 0. 0100 GRAM/L
3. 0. 0200 GRAM/L
4. 0. 0300 GRAM/L
5. 0. 0400 GRAM/L
6. 0. 0500 GRAM/L

WVW 82-08-27

WAVELENGTH (nm)

ABSORBANCE

Figure 6a : Sirius Green BLL - Spectra as a function of the temperature.

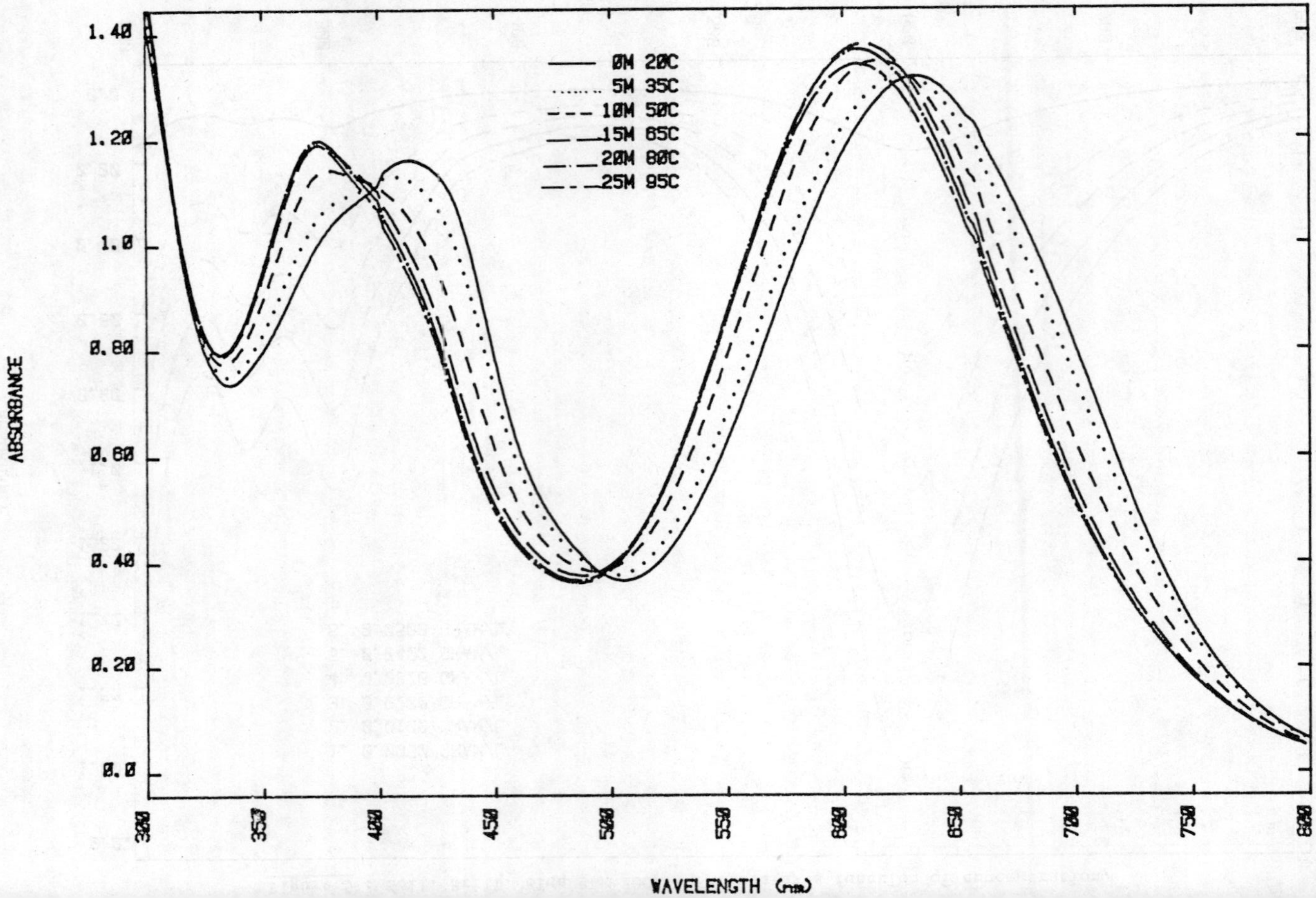

446

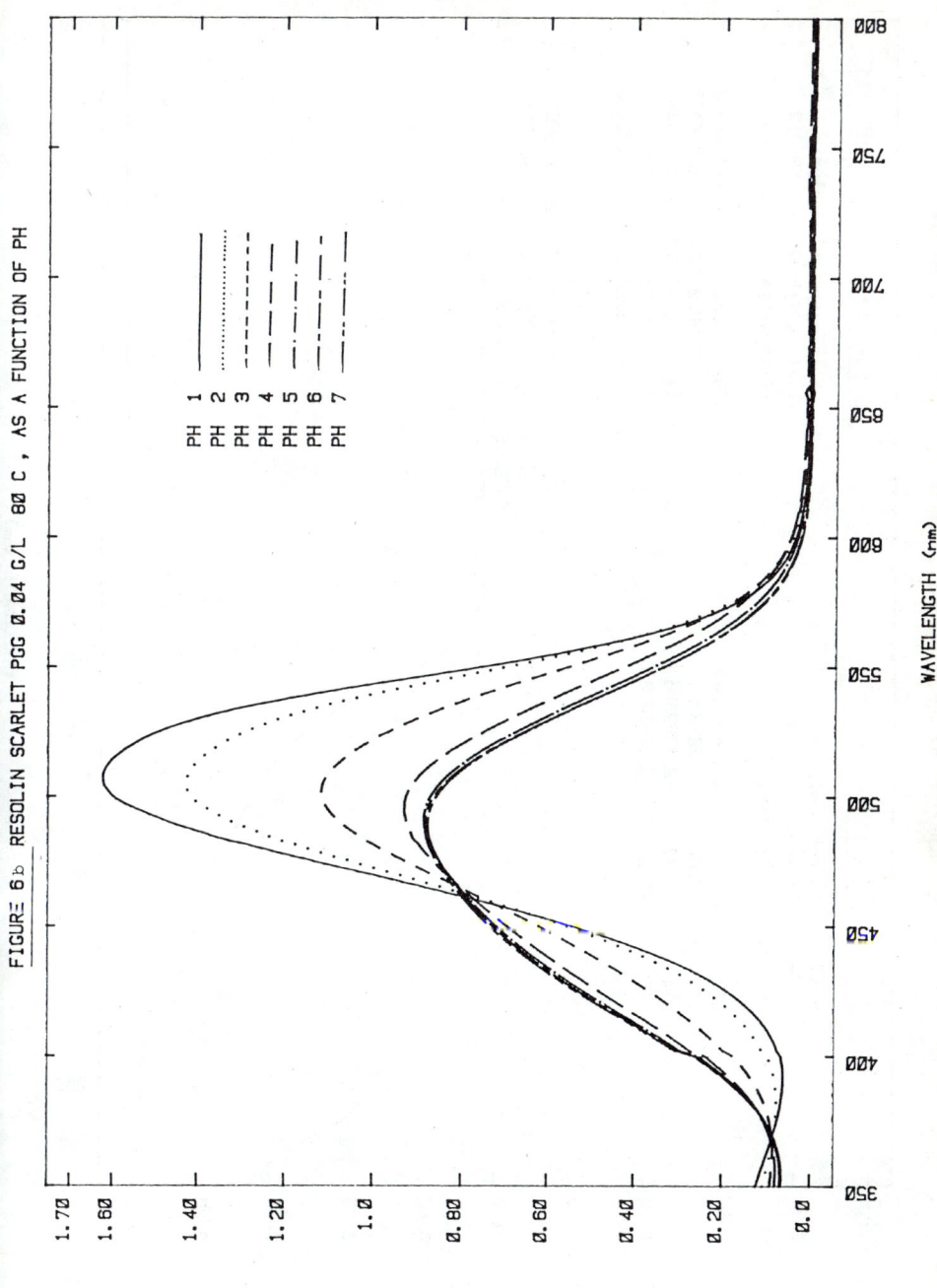

FIGURE 6 b RESOLIN SCARLET PGG 0.04 G/L 80 C , AS A FUNCTION OF PH

PH 1
PH 2
PH 3
PH 4
PH 5
PH 6
PH 7

WAVELENGTH (nm)

ABSORBANCE

447

Figure 7 : Starting bath-final bath - Influence of turbidity on the absorption spectra.

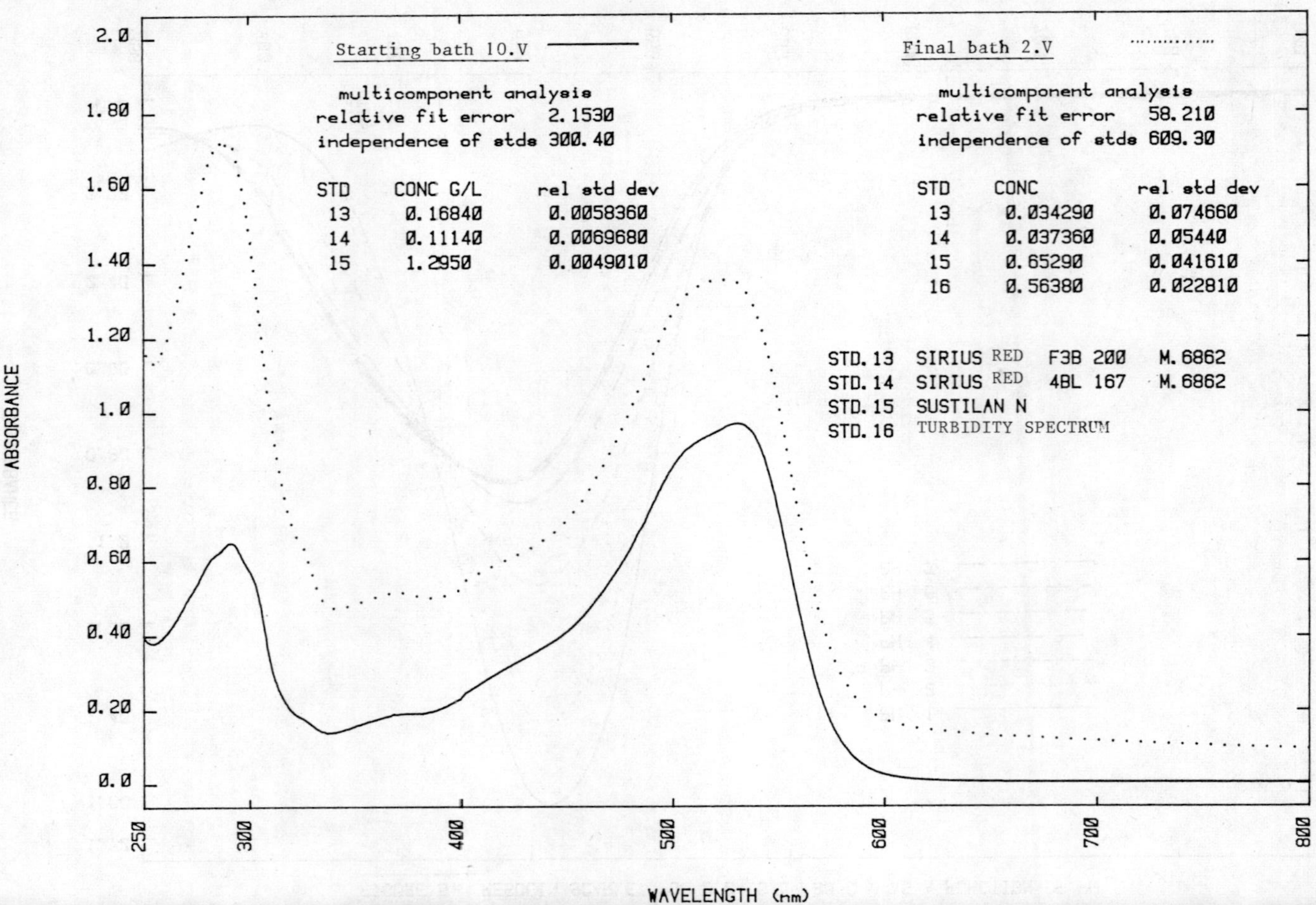

Starting bath 10.V
multicomponent analysis
relative fit error 2.1530
independence of stds 300.40
STD CONC G/L rel std dev
13 0.16840 0.0058360
14 0.11140 0.0069680
15 1.2950 0.0049010
Final bath 2.V
multicomponent analysis
relative fit error 58.210
independence of stds 609.30
STD CONC rel std dev
13 0.034290 0.074660
14 0.037360 0.05440
15 0.65290 0.041610
16 0.56380 0.022810
STD. 13 SIRIUS RED F3B 200 M.6862
STD. 14 SIRIUS RED 4BL 167 M.6862
STD. 15 SUSTILAN N
STD. 16 TURBIDITY SPECTRUM
ABSORBANCE
2.0
1.80
1.60
1.40
1.20
1.0
0.80
0.60
0.40
0.20
0.0
250
300
400
500
600
700
800
WAVELENGTH (nm)

Fig 8 : 3- dimensional Chromatography

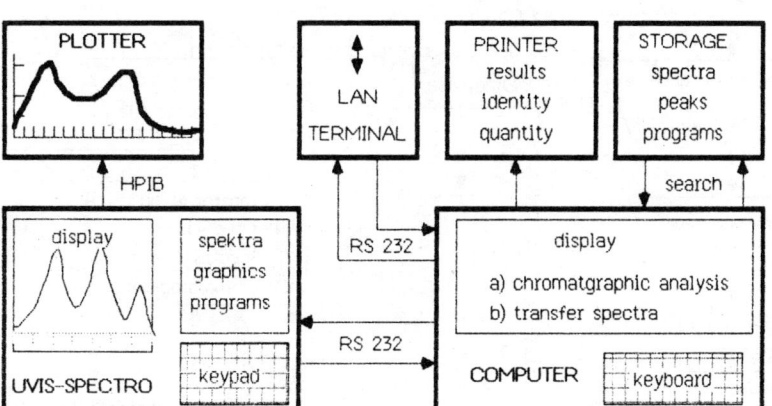

Fig 9   3-d Chromatography

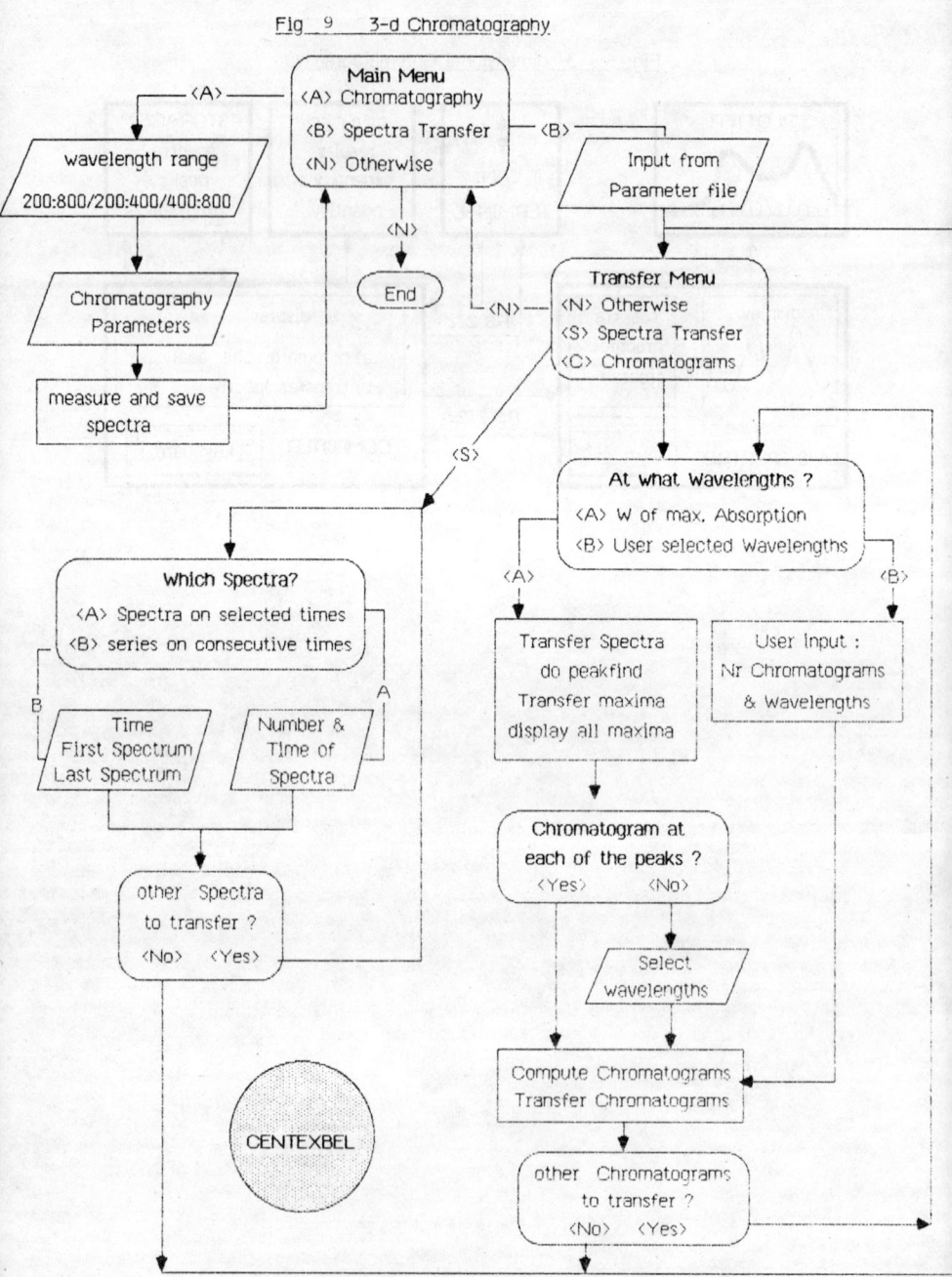

450

Figure 10 : 3-dimensional Chromatography - Chromatograms at 5 different pre-selected wavelengths.

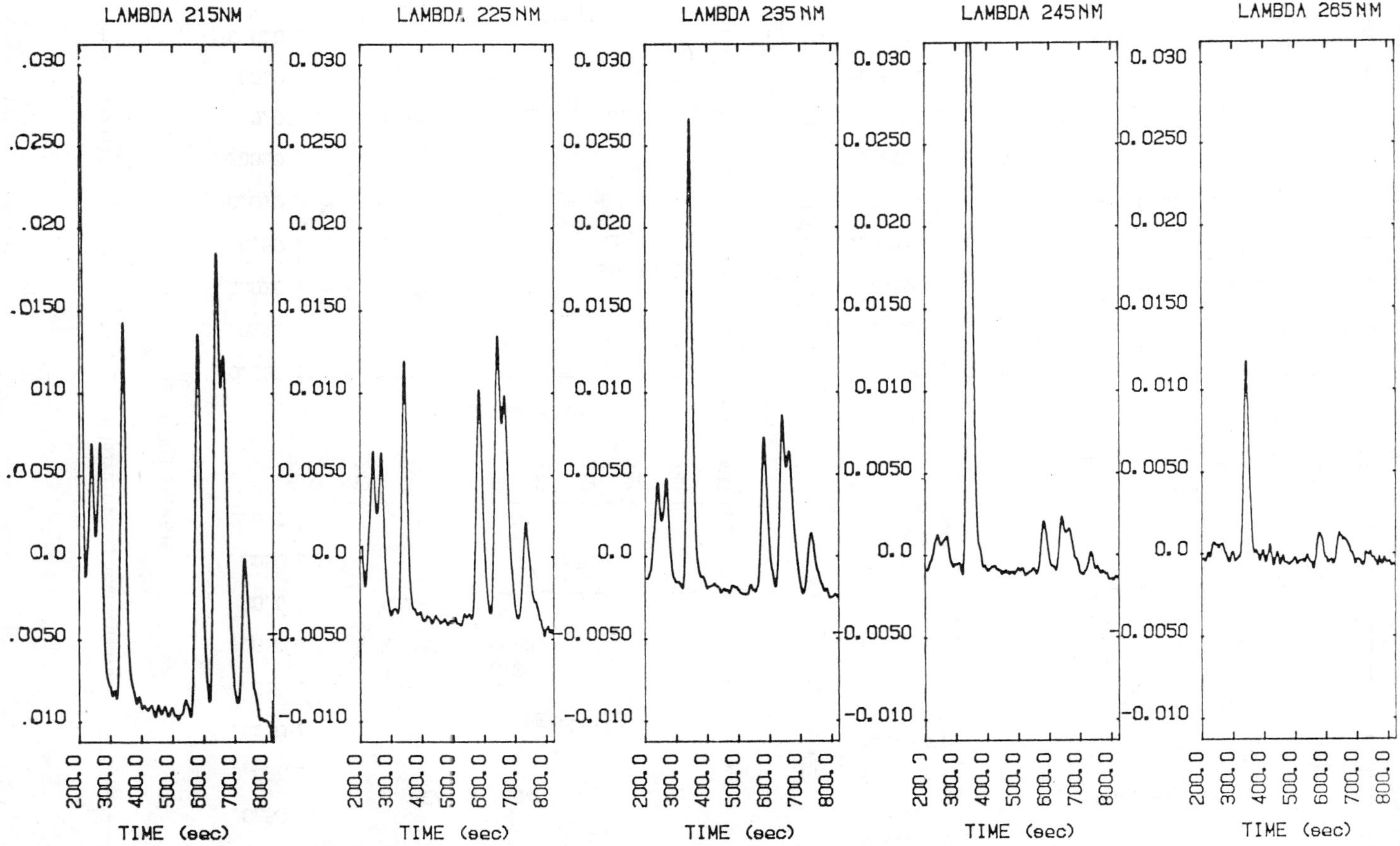

451

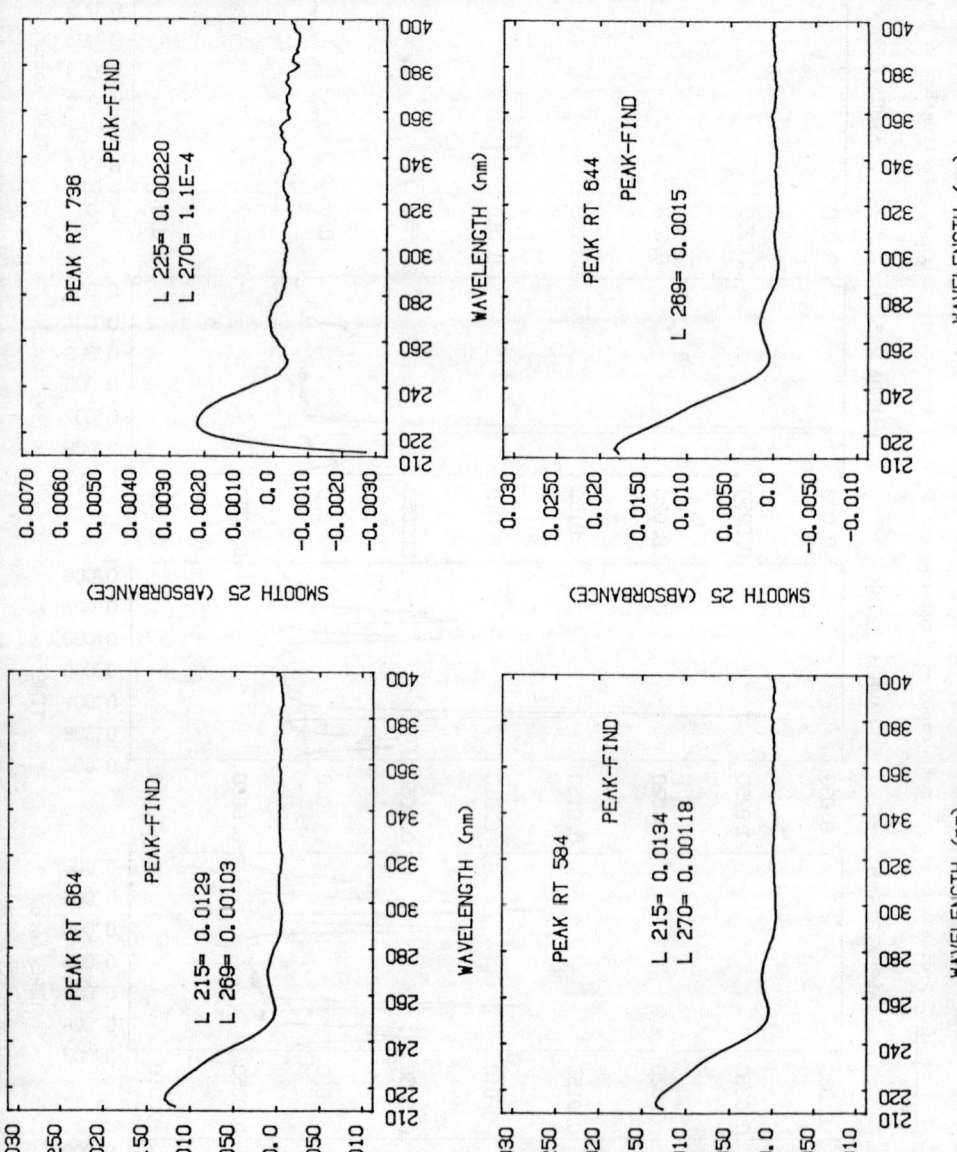

SPEKTRA EULAN SP

Figure 11 : 3-dimensional Chromatography - Selected spectra at different peak
retention times.

Figure 12 : 3-dimensional Chromatography - Chromatograms by several wavelengths.

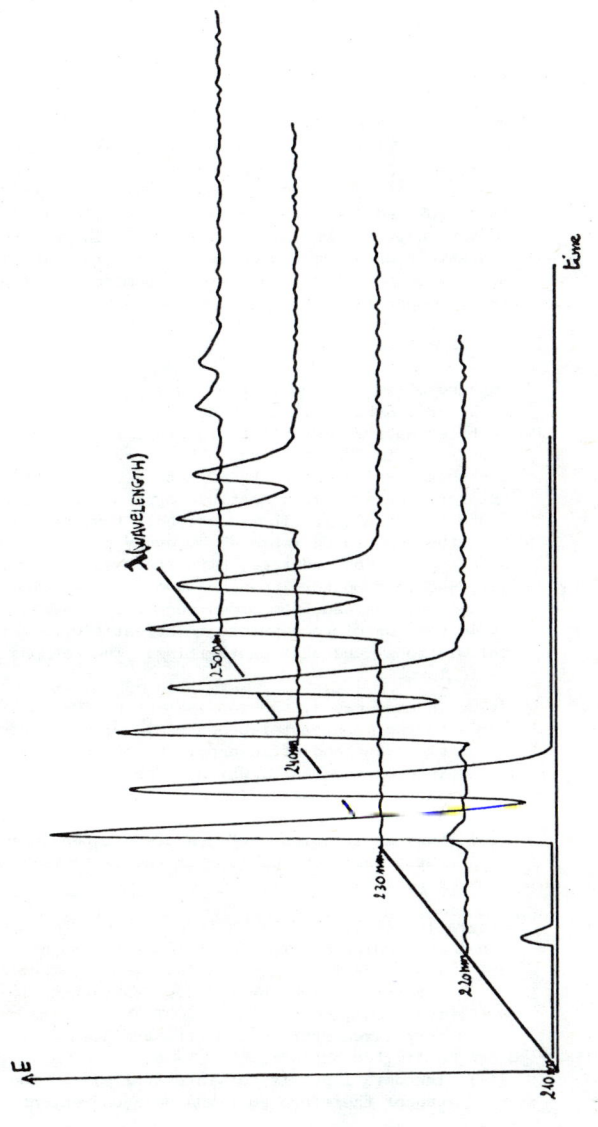

SOFTWARE FOR IMPROVING LOW-LEVEL MICROCOMPUTERS

X. Xiaojun

ABSTRACT

This paper is devoted to discussing the exertion of the efficiency of existing microcomputers of various types by using
software. It describes an assembly language program, which
enables Radio Shack TRS-80 Model I microcomputer to execute
large FORTRAN programs or assembly application programs
conveniently by overlaying, and a solution of the in-
convenient-data-input problem by software. The TRS-80
Model I is therefore made to have some of the functions of
large computers.

1. INTRODUCTION

Because of its low cost, the low-level microcomputer, such
as TRS-80, APPLE II, and others, has been widely used in the
textile industry as well as in other fields in the developing
countries, including China. It is reported that the mini -
disk-based Radio Shack TRS-80 Model I, with VDU and matrix
printer, and similar compatible systems have been widely
found in China (1). It is desirable that existing microcomputers should be improved by every possible means so that
some application programs, hitherto used only in mini and
large-scale computers, can be used by them. The present
author has learned from experience that FORTRAN is now
available on microcomputers in scientific research,
calculations, and other activities. The reasons for this are
as follows.

(i)   In most cases, the compiler-based FORTRAN is superior
        to the interpreter-based BASIC with regard to speed of
        execution and efficiency. On the other hand, the
        interpreted BASIC, which seems the simplest, but is,in
        fact, the slowest, is very unsuitable as a large-scale
        language.
(ii)   Many application packages are written in FORTRAN, and
        yet a tailored solution of the package will be very
        expensive.

Generally speaking, FORTRAN is unsuitable for use in low-
level microcomputers for the following reasons:
(i)   the FORTRAN used in low-level microcomputers lacks
        effective stage chains (i.e., an automatic overlay
        function), so the large FORTRAN programs requiring a
        very large storage capacity are used in the micro to
        a limited extent;
(ii)   the data input is not interactive, and the operator
        cannot therefore edit the data conveniently.

The disadvantages mentioned above could be offset to some
extent by using appropriate software. This paper is devoted
to means for improving the TRS-80 Model I FORTRAN in a large

program and making the data preparation conversational.

The characteristics of the TRS-80 Model I are well known,
but for the sake of completeness an outline description of
the basic facilities used by the author is given below:
- VDU and matrix printer;
- three 5¼ - in, mini-disk drives;
- 48 Kbytes store (32 Kbytes RAM only);
- Radio Shack FORTRAN package (version 1.0) supported by
  TRSDOS.

2.   THE ESTABLISHMENT OF THE AUTOMATIC OVERLAY FUNCTION IN
      FORTRAN PROGRAM

The objective codes compiled from the large FORTRAN program
are so numerous that there is not enough memory space in
the micro. This was known to be the greatest and most time-
consuming problem. However, the solution was rather simple.
The objective codes could not be loaded into the memory in
their entirety. One classical solution to this problem is to
split the program into a few parts and to execute them
sequentially.

2.1   The Principle of the Automatic Overlay System in a
       FORTRAN Program

The objective program established and stationed by the link
loader (L-80) in the FORTRAN package can be transformed into
a machine-language command file to be saved on the disk by
the -N command. When the file name is entered, TRSDOS will
load the objective program and attempt to execute it. Each
command file will be controlled by the program written in Z-80
assembly language, which is named LRP, so that it could be
loaded and executed in an automatic and orderly way.

2.2   The Loading of the Objective Program

The command-disk file created by the L-80 command -N contains
some packaging overhead and actual messages. Each data block
consists of a mark, a size, a starting point (lsb/msb), and
actual data. The mark of the last data block in the file is
02H 02H and the next is the transfer address (lsb/msb).
(Note: lsb = least significant byte; msb = most significant
 byte.)

With the meanings of these messages known, a program can be
written which loads the machine-language file   (see the part
with the LRP program list in Appendix 1). The LRP calls three
TRSDOS I/O system programs: OPEN, READ, and CLOSE.

2.3   The Change of the Objective Program Exit

Having been loaded, the objective program can begin its
execution at its entry point in the case where the exit instruction is JP 402DH, 402DH is the address of the normal

re-entry into TRSDOS, and 402DH contains JP 4400H. (Note: JP 402DH
means 'jump to address 402D Hex'.) In execution, LRP will
turn the transfer address of the instruction to an entry of
its own so that the system will be back under its control.
The system will not return to TRSDOS until the whole program
has been finished.

2.4 The Establishment of the Pointer of the File Name

Given a corresponding file name, the objective program may be
loaded and executed by LRP. In LRP, there is a pointer that
points to the existing file name in sequence. Here there is
a series of objective programs whose file names are FA/XX,
FB/XX, FC/XX, and FD/XX. The second byte of the file-name
area is defined as the pointer location (the label of which
is POINT:). The file-name locations should begin with FA/XX
(i.e., the first file name in the whole route). When the
first file has been executed, LRP will increase the pointer
location by 1, and the first name will change to FB/XX in
the locations ...... It is obvious that a one-byte pointer
location can control more than 36 different programs (ten
numerals + 26 letters).

2.5 The Introduction of LRP

The full list of the program is shown in Appendix 1. LRP is
loaded to a high-memory address, so the effect on memory is
minimized. It uses 384 bytes of RAM. The example given in
Appendix 1 is used to chain the four objective programs FA/XX,
FB/XX, FC/XX, and FD/XX. At the beginning, the file name of
the first program should be entered in order that LRP can
chain a series of new programs. Note that the location
labelled POINT: is the pointer. The value of the location
labelled COUNT: should be the number of programs minus 1.
LRP can chain not only large FORTRAN programs but also large
assembly programs, the sizes of which are limited by the disk
capacity. The capacity can also be increased by changing
disks. The machine-code instructions of LRP are entered by
using EDTASM (edit assembly program), and the machine-
language command file is saved to TRSDOS by the command
DUMP. After the file name has been entered, TRSDOS will load
the file and begin execution, and then the file will chain
the objective programs mentioned above.

3. DATA EDIT PROGRAM IN BASIC

Those who have used the Version 1.0 FORTRAN package know that,
FORTRAN not being interactive, the route, once initiated,
allows no programmer intervention (except perhaps to abort).
It is the same with the data input. After the data are entered,
nothing can be done but to stop the program if any adjustments
are needed.

The data set up by BASIC are saved on the disk so that, when
the FORTRAN program is executed, the data can be read from the
data file. It is therefore, by making full use of the
conversational BASIC that the data can be edited. The list
of a data-edit program in BASIC and part of the data-reading

in the FORTRAN program are given in Appendix 2. The simple command READ is used in the BASIC data-edit program. It is suggested that better input methods should be adopted (3).

RIN is a subroutine for reading-data. The main program and other subroutines, when requiring the data input, should call RIN.

4.   CONCLUSIONS

The techniques described in this paper are intended to illustrate the potential of using the low-level micro. With the above software, the author has succeeded in executing in the Radio Shack TRS-80 Model I long FORTRAN programs transferred from large-scale computers such as one for the analysis of frame structures of textile factory buildings, linear programming, PERT network, and so on. Here, even the smallest textile company can be provided with an opportunity of using existing mature software.

ACKNOWLEDGEMENT

I would like to thank Mr. Zhao Guoje, a teacher of Jiangxi University, for his support and encouragement. He also helped me to edit the draft of this paper into readable English.

REFERENCES

(1)   MICRO, China, 1984, No 1, P170

(2)   Radio Shack. 'TRSDOS & DISK BASIC Reference Manual' U.S.A.

(3)   Sinclair. 'Some Useful Subroutines', Ian R. Butterworth & Co., 1983

Jiangxi Textile Research Institute,
185 4th Jiaotonglu,
Nanchang, Jiangxi,
People's Republic of China.

```
00010              ORG OF600H
00020 STA:         LD D,06H          ;DCB<=THE FILESPEC OF THE FILE
00030              LD HL,(DCB)
00040              LD BC,NAME
00050 SUMD:        LD A,(BC)
00060              LD (HL),A
00070              INC BC
00080              INC HL
00090              DEC D
00100              JR NZ,SUMD
00110              LD HL,(BUFFER)    ;OPEN THE FILE
00120              LD DE,(DCB)
00130              LD B,0H
00140              CALL 4424H
00150              JR NZ,ER
00160              LD A,0FFH
00170 G01:         INC A             ;LOAD THE FILE
00180              JR NZ,G03
00190              CALL SUB
00200 G03:         LD B,(HL)
00210              DEC B
00220              JR NZ,ED
00230              INC HL
00240              INC A
00250              JR NZ,G04
00260              CALL SUB
00270 G04:         LD C,(HL)
00280              DEC C
00290              DEC C
00300              JR NZ,B1
00310              LD BC,100H
00320              JP B2
00330 B1:          INC C
00340              INC C
00370 B2:          INC HL
00380              INC A
00390              JR NZ,G05
00400              CALL SUB
00410 G05:         LD E,(HL)
00430              INC HL
00440              INC A
00450              JR NZ,G06
00460              CALL SUB
00470 G06:         LD D,(HL)
00480              INC HL
00500              INC A
00510              JR NZ,G02
00520              CALL SUB
00530 G02:         LDI
00540              JP PO,G01
00550              INC A
00560              JR NZ,G02
00570              CALL SUB
00580              JP G02
00600 ED:          LD DE,0E          ;PUT THE TRANSFER ADDRESS TO DE:
00605              LDI
00610              LDI
00630              LD DE,(DCB)
00640              CALL 4428H
00650 RT:          JP RUN
00660 ER:          JP ERR
00670 SUB:         LD (WORK),DE
```

458

```
00680              LD DE,(DCB)
00690              CALL 4436H
00700              LD A,OH
00710              LD HL,(BUFFER)
00720              LD DE,(WORK)
00730              RET
00740 RUN:         LD HL,ENTRY        ;CHANGE EXIT
00750              LD (402EH),HL
00760              DEFB OC3H          ;INSTRUCTION JP ...
00764 OE:          DEFW O             ;WILL CONTAIN THE TRANSFER ADDESS
00770 ENTRY:       LD HL,COUNT        ;OF OBJECTIVE
00780              XOR A
00790              CPI
00800              JR Z,HH
00810              DEC HL
00820              LD B,(HL)
00830              DEC B
00840              LD (HL),B
00850              LD HL,(POINT)
00860              INC HL
00870              LD (POINT),HL
00880              JP STA
00890 ERR:         OR 80H             ;DISPLAY ERROR MESSAGE
00900              CALL 4409H
00910 HH:          LD HL,4400H        ;RETURN TO TRSDOS
00920              LD (402EH),HL
00930              JP 402DH
00940 DCB:         DEFW OF6DOH        ;DCB ADDRESS
00950 BUFFER:      DEFW OF7OOH        ;BUFFER ADDRESS
00960 WORK:        DEFW O
00970 COUNT:       DEFW 3H            ;THE NUMBER OF ALL FROGRAMS - 1
00980 NAME:        DEFB 'F'           ;FIRST PROGRAM NAME
00990 POINT:       DEFB 'A'
01000              DEFB '/'
01010              DEFB 'X'
01020              DEFB 'X'
01030              DEFW ODH
01040              END
```

Appendix 2 BASIC data edit program and the part of the data-reading
in the FORTRAN

```
2 LPRINT CHR$(30)
3 CLS:INPUT"WHAT IS THE NAME OF THIS FRAM";N$:FORKI=0 TO 5:LPRINT" ":
TAB(20);"====== ";N$;" ====="
5 DIM M$(126)
10 OPEN"R",1,"FORT09/DAT"
20 FOR J=1 TO 32000
30 FOR I=0 TO 62
40 FIELD 1,(I*4) AS STARTHERE$,4 AS M$(I)
50 NEXT
60 FOR I=0 TO 62
65 READ A:IF A-INT(A)=0 THEN 75
70 PRINT USING "######.###"; A;:GOTO 77
75 IF A=-999999 THEN 332 ELSE PRINT USING "######";A;
77 A$=MKS$(A)
80 LSET M$(I)=A$
330 NEXT
331 GOTO340
332 FORI1=ITO62:LSETM$(I1)=MKS$(0.0):NEXT:PUT 1,J:GOTO360
340 PUT 1,J
350 NEXT
360 CLOSE
363 LPRINT CHR$(29):CLS
364 CMD"S"
365 END
```

BASIC data edit program

```
                    .
                    .
                    .
Page 1
01330               IF(NLJ)403,403,125
01340       125     DO 126 J=1,NLJ
01350               CALL RIN
01352               NO=IFIX(SD)
01354               CALL RIN
01356               KJ=IFIX(SD)
01360               CALL RIN
01362               Q=SD
01420               N1=3*NO-KJ
01422               WRITE(2,5001)NO,KJ,Q
01424       5001    FORMAT(1X,'NO=',I5,2X,'KJ=',I5,2X,'Q=',F10.4)
                    .
                    .
                    .
```

The part of the data-reading

```
Page 1
00100          SUBROUTINE RIN
00200          COMMON /RIN/DRIN(32),IRIN,IJL,SD,IG
00300          IF(IRIN-33)1,2,2
00400    2     IJL=IJL+1
00500          IRIN=1
00505          IG=IG+1
00600          READ(9,REC=IJL,ERR=333,END=444)DRIN
00700    1     SD=DRIN(IRIN)
00710          IF(IG-2)9,8,9
00712    8     IF(IRIN-31)9,7,9
00715    7·    IRIN=IRIN+1
00717          IG=IG-2
00800    9     IRIN=IRIN+1
00900          RETURN
01000    333   STOP ERR
01100    444   STOP END
01200          END
```

RIN subroutine

MICROS IN THE CONTROL OF RESOURCES FOR TEXTILE PROCESSING

D.J. Pearson

ABSTRACT

This paper is a practical review of the areas in which micro processors can be used within the textile processing field.

It is written from the viewpoint of a processor rather than a computer specialist and as such makes no reference whatsoever to the types of computers which can be used.

All systems described have been used and proven in production situations and are commercially available.

1. INTRODUCTION

As the title implies we are describing micro computers when used for controlling, regulating or monitoring the resources or available assets that are used in the textile preparation, bleaching, printing, finishing and examination industries.

We therefore need to list the resources available and in use within the various categories:

WATER	:	All wet processing areas		
ENERGY	:	All areas		
DYES	:	Continuous dyeing Batch dyeing Tinting Printing		
CHEMICALS	:	Preparation	-	Desize
			-	Mercerise
			-	Scour
			-	Bleach
			-	etc.
	:	Dyeing	-	Auxilliaries
			-	Fixation
	:	Printing	-	Thickeners
			-	Stabilisers
			-	Fixation
	:	After Print	-	Scouring
			-	Clearing
	:	Finishing	-	Resination
			-	Softening
			-	Water-repellent
			-	Other finishes
PEOPLE	:	All areas		
MACHINERY	:	Throughout		
FIBRE OR FABRIC	:	Any type		

As you will see we have a comprehensive list of resources
on which the micro processor can be used.

More specifically we itemise the areas which are benefiting
from the use of micro processors.

PROCESS CONTROL	:	Water and Steam Monitoring
		Liquor to Goods Ratio
		pH
		Temperature
		Chemical Feed
ENERGY MONITORING AND CONTROL	:	Humidity
		Moisture
		Temperature
		Total Energy Usage
CONTROLLED WEIGHING	:	Powders
	:	Liquids
COLOUR PHYSICS	:	Colour Match Prediction
		Pass / Fail
		Colour Sorting
CLERICAL USE	:	Storage of Recipes
		Calculations
		Costing
		Stock
		Management Information
		Production of Operators
		Tickets
		Budget Comparisons
DYEING MACHINE	:	Time / Temperature
		Control of Full sequence
		Control of Dyehouse
EXAMINATION MACHINES	:	Recording of Faults
		Analysis of Fault Rate

2. WATER

2.1 If we answer a few simple questions:

How is water used ? - Liberally

How accurately is it controlled ? - Poorly

Will it effect labour utilisation if improved ? - Doubtful

Will it effect machine utilisation if improved ? - Doubtful

Will it reduce wastage if improved ? - Certainly

Will it reduce energy consumption if improved ? - Certainly

we can see that if we concentrate on reducing wastage we will
in turn both save water and reduce energy consumption.

2,2 How do we reduce water consumption

Batchwise   :   Control processes with water metering devices
                to ensure constant liquor to goods ratio from
                batch to batch. (Dyeing Machine Control)

            :   Wash off reduced - do not overflow. (Dyeing
                Machine Control)

Continuous :   Control liquor to goods ratio.

            :   Ensure water only runs when cloth passing
                through machine.

It is perfectly possible to ascertain experimentally the liquor
to goods ratio required for any process and to then control the
quantity of water in proportion to the throughput of fabric.

In simple terms:

WE MUST   :   Measure the amount of water
            :   Measure the length of substrate

and from these two changing quantities along with:

            :   The specified liquor to goods ratio for that
                particular process and quality,

            :   the weight per linear metre for that quality;

the micro processor will calculate the flow of water required at
any particular moment and control a valve to ensure the actual
flow of water is the same as the calculated quantity.

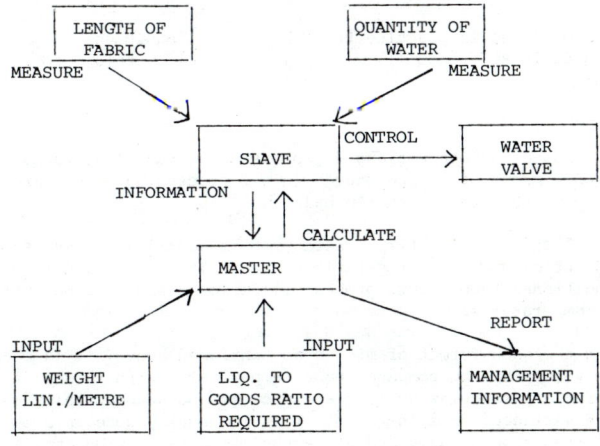

465

This apparently simple procedure will have various important effects on differing resources.

2.3 Savings

It will save water in two ways:

In most conditions far too much water is in use with water often being allowed to run when the machine stops.

Without specific control whilst running, a safety first policy has to be adopted which means that an excess of water flows so as to avoid problems caused by varying water pressure and increase of machine speed etc.

It will save energy in all processes involving hot water. This is because by saving water it is clear that the energy used in heating that excess water to the processing temperature will have been wasted when it is thrown away.

Chemicals will be saved if the process is one calling for a constant concentration. The more water passing, the more chemicals used. If water is wasted then so are chemicals.

The substrate will have a much better chance of consistent quality if the water flow is constant.

Washing out of impurities in preparation has to be correct to enable dyeing and printing to be completed satisfactorily. A poorly scoured batch could lead to reprocessing or at worst scrap.

The cost of this type of equipment is small in proportion to the price of either a 6 beck wash range or the cost of water and energy used in a year.

It has been found in practice that the control equipment referred to in Reference (1) will pay for itself within 3 to 9 months.

3. ENERGY

Energy is used in both wet and dry processing and whilst we have discussed a means of saving energy in wet processing, there are further ways that the micro can help.

The actual control of water temperatures in scouring ranges is carried out by use of thermostatic valves. It is our experience that additional temperature probes will allow a micro to monitor actual temperatures.

By using the same format of micros as mentioned above, it is perfectly possible to compare these temperatures with those needed for a particular quality and process and automatically indicate variances from the norm. This is usually done on a split screen showing demanded and actual temperatures pH etc.

With "dry" heat (as with wet) finite comparisons can be made, it is first necessary to measure accurately the amount of energy being used for a particular process. In other words we must know what we are using both before and after attempting to save it. It can then be monitored, recorded and compared with the theoretical or budget amount for management reporting purposes.

The energy used in dry processing can be monitored by using sensing heads for temperature, moisture control of substrate and humidity content of exhaust air, all linked to a micro computer. These parameters can be compared by the micro with standards for that process and then via a VDU/CRT reported to the operator for action if variations occur.

All variables i.e. temperature, moisture content and humidity should be controlled independently and we are therefore setting up a monitoring system to ensure process conditions are achieved.

The 'Stenter Monitor' so produced will also give management information on efficiencies of production and machines etc. per shift day or week and can therefore be a useful tool to the Finishing Manager or Works Manager.

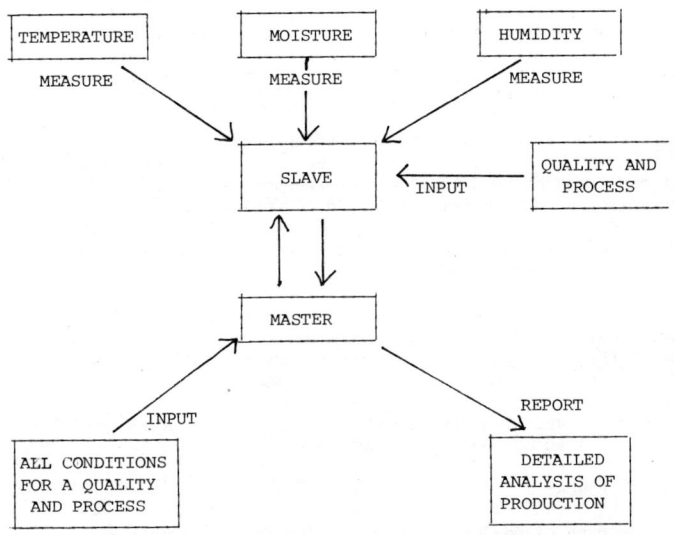

The Stenter Monitor which is more fully described in the data sheets as in Reference (2) will improve the quality of the substrate by ensuring management is kept informed of any variations from desired conditions, thus allowing them to take corrective action quickly if required.

The micro computer is also used in measuring the efficient
conversion of energy in the boiler house but we feel that this
subject, although of vital importance, is outside the scope of
this paper.

4. DYES AND CHEMICALS

Dyes and Chemicals are used in most wet processing areas and
can be controlled in many different ways by the micro computer.

Dyes and Chemicals are either weighed or measured in some manner
before use so that a regular scientifically applied quantity can
be used in proportion to eitherthe substrate or processing media
(i.e. water), such that this can be repeated on the next
occasion.

4.1 Dyes

Let us ask a few questions again:

How do we use our dyes ?

Are we confident that all our weighings are accurate ?

How do we select our recipes - are we satisfied with the
method ?

How do we calculate the batch quantities - can errors be made ?

We often find that the colour store and weighing area are the
'poor mans corner' of the finishing works.

How can we put the micro to work to help us ?

It can first be used to store the recipes and then to calculate
specific batch quantities required and produce hard copy.

This rather mundane use of the micro nevertheless takes out any
possible sources of human error such as:

Use of wrong recipe,
Wrong calculation of batch quantities,
Wrong transmission of recipe from supervisor/clerk to
dispensing department.

The actual weighing/dispensing of the dye or chemical can then
be controlled by the micro computer system.

4.1.1 Powder

In the case of powders it is usual for the electronic weigh
scales to be connected to a micro which has been supplied with
information either in a batchwise manner or continuously,
Reference (3).

There are three types of installation:

Simple check weigh systems where the operator either dials in
information of dyestuff and quantity.

"Instructa" weigh systems where the micro screen will inform
the operator of the dye/chemical to weigh and how much is
required. It will then take him through the weighing sequence
until the weight obtained is within the tolerance set in the
computer. The computer will only then indicate the next
constituent and so on.

A micro is used in the dyers office to produce a tape which
contains all instructions necessary for a batch.

Intelligent terminal. The micro processor can be used as a
terminal so that the operator need only feed in a batch number
or a continuity number into a keyboard and the instruction for
that batch will appear on a VDU. This option, of course,
necessitates the use of a computer elsewhere - powerful enough
to operate the terminal.

The same micro will control either lockable bins, paternoster
storage systems or light pens so that only the correct dye or
chemical is selected and used.

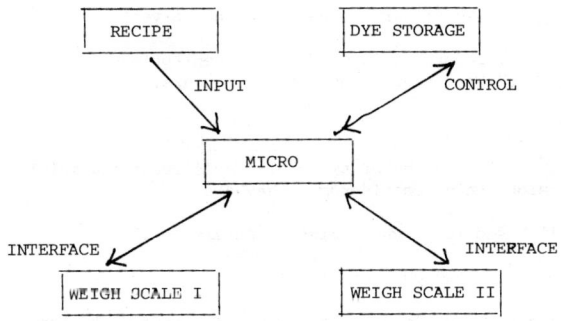

Automatic weighing of powders to the accuracy demanded by
Dyers and Printers is possible providing that the powders are
presented in a non-hygroscopic, non-dusting, free flowing
form with the largest particle being 1/20th of the smallest
weight required.

Samples from dyestuff makers of such powders are now
available but as yet the bulk supply of these products and
the automated operation has to be proven - but looks possible.

4.1.2 Liquid

In the case of liquids/dyes the use of micros enables a very
sophisticated weighing system to be developed which has four
vital components:

A valve to dispense each liquid
Accurate electronic weighing scales
Movement
Software

Valves:

The valve has of necessity to cope with both high and low flow
rates and large and small quantities.

It must be able to close instantly upon instruction from the
computer.

It must not drip.

The different flow rates must be fairly consistent from time
to time, but the actuation of the measurement to determine each
flow rate must give that consistent result even when subjected
to slightly different actuating pressures.

It must be reliable.

Virtually maintenance free.

Able to cope with different viscosities.

Able to cope with different chemicals and solvents.

Reference (4) refers to more detailed descriptions of such
valves, which have been in use for many years.

Weigh Scales:

The weigh scales can be of two basic types depending mainly
on the weight being considered. They are:

Load cell based for higher weights, Reference (5)

Force cell compensated based for lower weights, Reference (6).

The scales based on load cells are usually made up by the
manufacturer of dispensing systems from load cells of the
particular size and specification for each application.

4 load cells are used at the corners of a square and the
bending stresses obtained converted electronically into
weight readings.

With the best available electronics the scales can operate
typically up to 240 Kg with a readibility of 1 gm. or 16 Kg
with a readibility of 0.01 gm.

Movement:

In order to bring the receiving container and liquid together
it is necessary to either move the container or move the valve.

When the container is moved the weigh scale is controlled by the micro computer and moves along a track above which are mounted one or two lines of valves. The micro computer stops the scale at the correct position and only then will it allow the weighing to commence.

An unlimited number of valves can be used to dispense to one weigh scale in this format.

In the case of moving valves they are usually mounted in a circle above the container and on request the micro causes the valve to move to the centre of the circle directly above the container. At this point weighing will commence.

The moving valve or cluster technique is usually limited to around twenty valves per weigh scale.

Software:

The software is extremely critical to the accuracy of weighing. It is written in machine code for speed of operation and will continually update the micro with the following:

Rate of change of weight
Signal from load cells
The kinetic energy acting on the cell (relative to the in flight compensation)
Target weight
Quantity away from target
Flow rate necessary (in several bands)

The micro will decide when to change from one flow band to another and when continuous or 'pulsed' flow is required.

The software will decide when the valve should close so that after the column of liquid in flight enters the container, the weight is as required. This is termed 'in flight compensation'.

The equipment described is detailed in Reference (7) and other supplies in Reference (8).

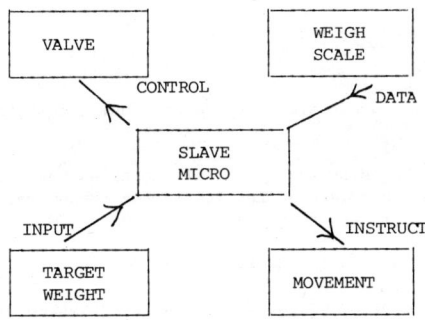

471

In the case of both solid and liquid dispensing systems
the central micro will carry out a number of clerical
functions as follows:

Stock control
Production control
Costing
Budget variance

The savings coming from accurate weighing cover the areas of:

Dyeing time
Wastage of colour
Down time on print machines
Reproducibility of shade
Reduction in reprocess
Reduction in down graded fabric or yarn

To quantify these savings for an international audience is
best done in percentage terms rather than in actual currencies.

Proven savings have been shown as follows:

Dyehouse:

Reduction in dyeing time by the equivalent of 2 additions i.e.
1 hour.

Reduction in reprocessing of 2%.

Total elimination of miss-weighs.

Printworks:

Total elimination in machine down time caused by shading
addition - usually half of down time.

Total elimination of gross errors leading to discarded colour.

A reduction in staffing of at least 1 operative per shift on
most installations.

Less down graded fabrics.

4.2 Chemicals

Most processing areas are dependent on chemicals to promote
reactions.

Our training tells us that chemical reactions have different
rates and possibly varying results if the concentrations of
chemicals are allowed to differ from time to time.

Do we use our chemicals carefully ? - NO

Liquids - we often use half full buckets instead of weighing
            or measuring them.

472

Solids - weighing (discussed earlier).

Are we confident that we put the same amount in each time

With a wet on wet application the problem is more critical as we could have a varying quantity of water diluting a batch. Even a steady flow of a constant liquor will not provide regular conditions as the speed of fabric may vary.

We have discussed most of the applications of micros to chemical additions by weight earlier but the same principles are applied to volume dispensing whether it be linked to a continuous bleaching line or simply the supply of a 'standard' bucket of liquid chemical on demand.

5. COLOUR PHYSICS

5.1 Recipe Match Prediction

The theory of recipe match prediction is not new and well documented but it is only with the advent of the mini computer and now the micro computer that the calculations can be done quickly anough to make the theory of real use to the dyer/printer.

There has been a gradual increase in the use of colour physics systems over the last 10 years with the biggest savings coming in the selection of recipes suitable for certain end uses at cheapest cost.

This often means that there is a marked reduction in the number of dyes in stock as well as a very substantial reduction in the average cost of a recipe.

5.2 Pass / Fail

The Pass/Fail equations help the dyer/printer to numerically assess the colour difference between pattern and production, and so be of use in determining numerical colour difference acceptable to various customers

It is a well known fact that in a lot of dyehouses relying on manual shade acceptance alone, the 4th sample when passed is no nearer than the 2nd, which had been previously rejected.

5.3 Colour Sorting

Colour sorting is of use both to the continuous dyer for him to assess the number and types of grade required, and for the garment maker to ensure that he maximises his cutting lay. Reference (9) gives more detailed information.

6. PEOPLE

We do not propose to detail the uses that micros can be put to for robotic control because although there are certain areas where this could be achieved, it is our experience in textile processing that there is little or no advantage.

We do however wish to point out that nearly all the uses of micros detailed in this paper help the individual to perform a better function. Their use may reduce numbers in certain areas but they usually enrich the jobs remaining.

We have detailed many clerical functions which follow as an automatic consequence of using micros in textile processing and all of these are a help for the individual.

7. MACHINERY

7.1 Control of Dyeing Machines

The advent of the micro made the control of time/temperature gradients, dwell time and chemical/dyestuff additions easier than had hitherto been the case.

The degree of sophistication however can vary enormously as follows:

7.1.1 Time Temperature Control

A simple control of time/temperature relationship with the temperature being controlled by the micro processor, linked to the steam valve and cooling valve.

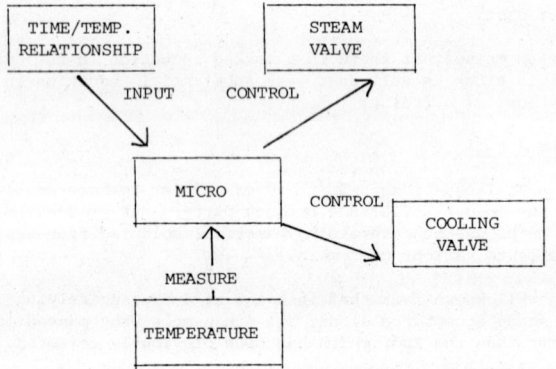

As can be seen the only information required by the micro is the time/temperature relationship and this can be fed in by punch card, keyboard, patterned disc etc:

7.1.2 Individual dye machine controller

Dye machine controllers specific to a machine where a micro is programmed with all the relevant information for a dyeing, from the minute the cloth is loaded until either a sample is required or the cloth is to be unloaded,

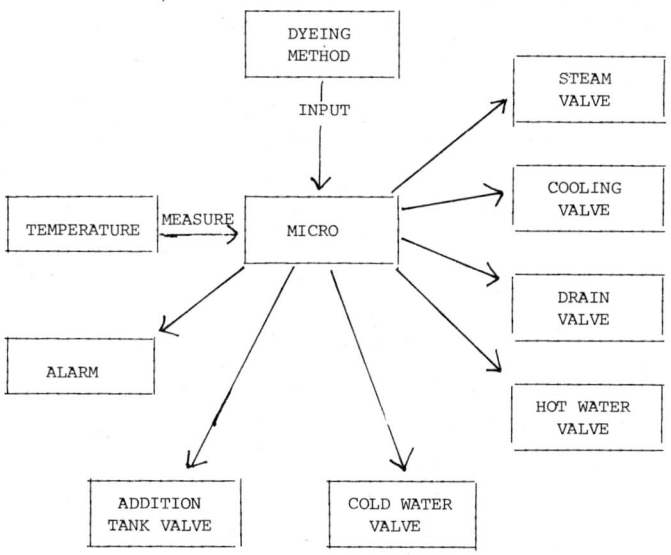

The full dyeing method is fed into the micro which then
controls all the functions relevant to a dye cycle with appropriate alarms for operator attention:

7.1.3 Dyehouse control

Full computerised control of a whole dyehouse from the dyers
office.

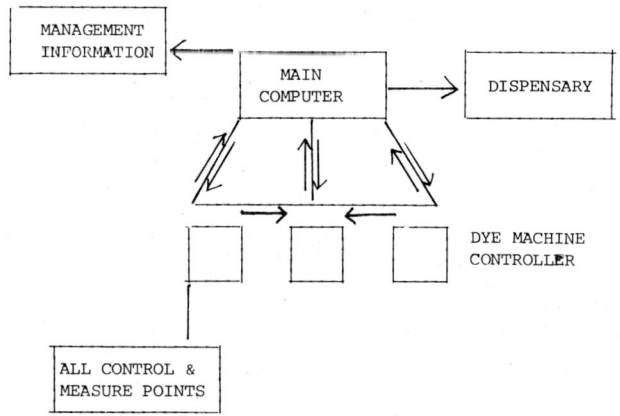

The main computer will contain all dyeing methods and request a dye machine controller to carry out the dyeing to a certain cycle.

It will continually monitor each controller to ensure that the desired conditions are being achieved and issue warnings if this is not the case.

It will produce management information on all dyeings and per shift or week and can be interlinked with the dispensary if required.

In all cases the control of conditions leads to a better level of reproducibility and reduced dyeing time.

The more sophisticated the product the greater the chance of labour saving. Reference (10) gives more detail.

7,2 Control of Examination Machines

Many companies are now offering logging facilities for faults on examination machines. The principle being that the operator holds a small keyboard and indicates the type of fault by depressing a different key.

The computer records the fault, its type, valve and position and summarises these at the end of the batch or roll.

The computer will then print out either piece tickets or a full table of faults and position, so that the manager can determine the most economical cutting pattern.

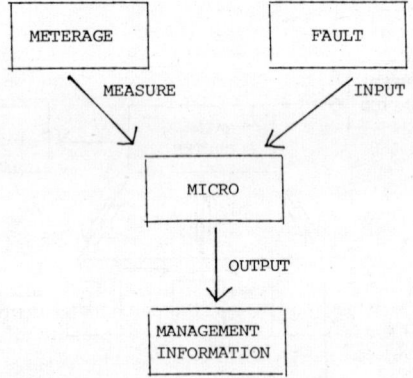

The more complicated computer systems in an examination department will take the information given by the computer at the examination machine and calculate from pre-fed

information the best and most economical way of cutting
faults to give maximum high grade fabric.

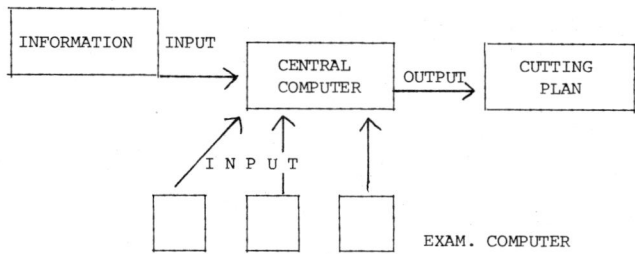

8.   CONCLUSION

We have tried to show the many and varied functions that are
now being carried out by micro computers within the field of
textile processing.

It is quite apparent that no company which is to survive long
term can ignore their existence.

It is also clear that any company can start in a simple way
and build more complicated systems as they progress.

There are many specialists each with his own view of the 'best'
way of computerising a process - it is for you to choose.

Make sure the systems are reliable and if your company is just
entering the micro field keep it simple.

REFERENCES

(1) Texicon   Literature   Aquasave

(2) Texicon   Literature   Stenter Monitor

(3) Texicon   Literature   Computaweigh
     I.C.S.   Literature   Controlled Weighing
                                          Systems

(4) Texicon   G.B. Patent No. 1338143

(5) Bofors   Literature
     Defiant   Literature

(6) Mettler   Literature
     Surtorius   Literature
     Sauter   Literature
     Berkel   Literature
     Thor   Literature
     Toledo   Literature

(7) Texicon   Literature   Autoweigh
                          U.S.A. Patent No. 40496

(8) Van Wyk   Literature
     C.I.R.   Literature
     Stork   Literature

(9) I.C.S.   Literature
     A.C.S.   Literature
     Pretema   Literature
     Datacolor   Literature

(10) Arel   Literature
     Textile Processing   Literature
     Beacon   Literature
     Zellor   Literature
     Gaston County   Literature
     Thies   Literature

(11) Texicon   Literature
     Trumeter   Literature
     Calator   Literature
     Campen   Literature
     Bastian   Literature

TEXICON
DINTING VALE
DINTING
GLOSSOP
DERBYSHIRE
SK13 9JD
U.K.

THE USE OF A PERSONAL COMPUTER IN THE SPECIALIZED TESTING OF TEXTILES

N. J. Abbott, F. S. Campbell and M. M. Schoppee

ABSTRACT

An IBM-PC computer has been used to great advantage in controlling the operation of an Instron testing machine, in reading and
analyzing the data, and in printing the desired measurements in
tabular or graphical form. This has been particularly valuable
in the case of two complex test procedures used on needled felt
material. The first of these was required in acceptance testing
of a Nomex felt used on the Space Shuttle. The second was part
of a detailed study of the structural mechanics of the Space
Shuttle felt in order to obtain a better understanding of the
mechanics of needling.

In both cases, the computer has provided improved control over
the test procedure, order-of-magnitude increases in the precision of the measurements, and elimination of the risk of the
effect of operator fatigue on the validity of the results obtained in repetitive but sensitive test procedures.

Both tests, and the means by which computer control is achieved,
are described, and the way in which the use of a computer has
influenced both the method of testing and the results obtained
are discussed.

1. INTRODUCTION

In a testing laboratory one is frequently confronted with the
need to repeat the same procedure many times, perhaps even for
days or weeks at a time. This carries the risk that operator
fatigue or, even worse, boredom may result in inattention to
detail and consequent inaccuracies in the test results. When
the testing is being done for quality control purposes such
lapses on the part of the operator may be identifiable and distinguishable from material variability when the series of test
results is examined, for in such cases one knows the result to
be expected and the limits within which the test results will
normally vary. If the testing is part of a study to determine
the interdependence of a measured characteristic with, say,
fabric structure, no such expected value is available, and operator errors can remain undetected and, therefore, result in
misleading conclusions about the relationship being studied.

The computer provides a solution to the problems posed by operator fatigue in repetitive testing, for it can be programmed to
control the testing machine in a totally reproducible manner,
and to read the output values, perform the necessary calculations
and display the desired test results in any desired form quickly
and reliably. It may also improve the precision with which test
results can be determined. The value of computer control of
testing for quality control purposes is well recognized, but the
opportunities which this technique presents in the evaluation of
specialized material properties is only beginning to be appreciated. An example of these two types of computer application
will be described herein.

2. USE OF A COMPUTER AS A CONTROL DEVICE

Most of the testing to be described has involved the use of an Instron test machine, which happens to be well suited for computer control. The specimen is held between a fixed and a moving jaw or platform, depending upon whether it is a tensile or compression test. The moving jaw or platform is mounted on a screw-driven crosshead. Load is measured by a load cell to which either jaw or platform is attached, and deformation is measured by monitoring the position of the crosshead, or by attaching an extensometer directly to the specimen.

The design of the Instron is such as to provide easy access to the circuits which control the operating parameters, or to those which read out the test results. Appropriate inputs from an external source such as a computer can be used to stop, start, and control the direction of motion and the speed of the crosshead. Outputs from the Instron can be used to provide a computer with readings of load and crosshead position at any time during the test. In fact, these output signals provide the opportunity for more significant figures for these measured variables than is provided in the readout devices on the Instron itself. A direct measure of extension can also be obtained when an extensometer is attached to the specimen. The nature of these output signals is summarized in Table I.

In order to connect a computer to the Instron, an interface unit is required which can receive signals from and communicate to the Instron on the one hand, and the computer on the other. The unit which we use* consists of two basic parts:

(1) Intelligent Machine Controller (IMC) hardware and software which acquires data from and controls the test machine. The IMC controls the crosshead UP/DOWN/STOP/RETURN motion and speed, and reads data from the load and strain channels every 40 msec. It also monitors machine status and converts raw data into physical units.

(2) Machine Drive (MD) software package with special function calls which permit a program written in enhanced BASIC to access the IMC. This permits the generation of programs to control and acquire data from test machines in a manner appropriate to any specific testing needs.

These special components are used in conjunction with a standard IBM-PC computer with 128 K bytes of RAM, 2 disk drives with a total capacity of 640 K bytes for program and data storage, a monochrome monitor, and a printer.

The associated software reads the load and crosshead position every 40 msec, or 15,000 times per minute. Load is read to an accuracy of 1 part in 2048, or 0.05%. The position of the crosshead at any instant is known to an accuracy of ± 0.000050 in. (approximately ± 1 µm). This is a precision which far exceeds

---

*Manufactured by Systems Integration Technology, Inc. (SINTECH), Norwood, MA, USA.

the mechanical rigidity of the test instrument. Indeed, to take advantage of this potential for accurate strain measurement, care must be taken to correct each reading for the compliance of the test fixture/machine combination being used. Extension of the specimen may also be read directly from an extensometer connected to the specimen itself, when this is feasible, which obviates the need for a machine compliance correction. It is clear that the precision of such measurements of load and strain is one to two orders of magnitude higher than is possible with normal manual operation of an Instron testing machine. This is one of the major advantages of computer control of tests done on an Instron.

A further advantage is the precision with which one can stop or reverse the direction of motion of the crosshead at a specific load or strain level. This precision will be influenced by the slope of the material stress-strain curve at the time of the event. In any case, machine control will be effected significantly more precisely than is possible using the microswitches which are built into the Instron mechanical drive controls.

In one of the applications to be described (uniformity mapping) tests are conducted over a 5 x 5 cm area of the specimen in a square matrix of test positions. In order to maintain close reproducible control over the geometry of the matrix, the specimen was mounted on a test table which could be moved in two orthogonal directions by stepping motors. Again, this was ideally suited for computer control.

Precise positioning of the test table was accomplished by supplying voltage pulses to each of the stepping motors. Each pulsed motor moved the table a distance of 0.001 in/step or pulse (0.0025 μm/step), with an accuracy of 0.0005 in. (0.00127 mm) per inch of travel. The reproducibility with which the table could be repositioned in the same location was +0.001 inch.

Because of the simplicity of the control signal which was required, namely the appropriate number of voltage pulses for any desired displacement, the computer was easily programmed to produce a matrix of test positions. This matrix was reproducible within 0.001 inch relative to an arbitrary reference point, which was taken to be the center of the table. The matrix which was most commonly used consisted of a square array of 16 x 16 test positions, giving a total of 256 test locations. Provision was made to expand this to a 100 x 100 square array if desired.

The reliability and reproducibility of such control is dependent only upon the stability of the electronic circuitry of the test and the control instrumentation. Modern solid state circuitry is notable for its stability, so that the zero drift or other instabilities which, in the past, were typical of vacuum tube-based circuitry are greatly reduced, to the point where a calibration check every few hours of operation is all that is needed to ensure reliable operation. Moreover, there is no concern that developing operator fatigue will jeopardize the validity of the test results, no matter how protracted the testing may be.

3. MATERIAL UNDERGOING TEST

Our laboratory is responsible for the manufacture of fibrous materials for insulation and structural purposes in the thermal protective system in the Space Shuttle. This needled Nomex felt material covers almost all the external surface of the ship, in one of three functional forms and a variety of thicknesses (see Figure 1):

(1) The Strain Isolation Pad (SIP) forms a deformable connection between the aluminum skin of the ship and the ceramic tiles (LRSI and HRSI) which cover the whole of the lower surface, the front and most of the sides of the fuselage, the lower surfaces and part of the top surfaces of the wings, and the whole of the tail fin.

(2) The Filler Bar is a heat-treated, thermally stable, silicone coated strip lying beneath the cracks between adjacent ceramic tiles.

(3) The Felt Reusable Surface Insulation (FRSI) is a heat-treated thermally stable, silicone coated needled Nomex felt material covering the remaining external surfaces on top of the fuselage and wings, the rear engine pads, and the rear control surfaces, except for their leading edges.

In all, more than 1000 square meters of surface in each ship are covered with needled Nomex felt. Approximately one-half of this area is covered with SIP which, because it forms the connection between the skin of the ship and the protective ceramic tiles, has a crucial mechanical requirement to meet. Because failure of this material in flight could have fatal consequences, every piece that is used must be carefully tested to be sure that it conforms to the stringent requirements of the material specification governing its manufacture. This is an extreme example of quality assurance testing in which no possibility of error can be tolerated. Thus, it is an ideal candidate for the application of computer control.

We shall be using SIP as the material to illustrate two applications of a personal computer in material testing. In one example, an actual quality assurance test will be described. The other example involves a test developed for use in a broader program in which we are studying through-the-thickness structural variations in textile structures. We have used this test to examine the effect of manufacturing variables on the mechanical properties of SIP.

4. STRAIN ISOLATION PAD TESTING

SIP is perhaps unique among needled felt materials in that its stress-strain behavior in a direction normal to the plane of its surface is its most important mechanical characteristic. Consequently, SIP manufacture involves multiple needling operations to obtain a high level of Z-direction fiber orientation. The SIP is attached to the aluminum skin of the Space Shuttle by using a silicone elastomer as an adhesive. The same silicone adhesive is used to adhere the bottom surface of a ceramic tile to the top surface of the SIP.

The function of the Strain Isolation Pad is two-fold: (a) to attach the ceramic tile to the ship, and (b) to prevent the ceramic tile from being cracked by the changes in shape of the ship caused by the temperature changes and external stresses encountered during a mission. Thus, its thickness, its ultimate "through-the-thickness" strength and its modulus at low levels of deformation are all important characteristics. These are the quantities defined by the specification, which must be measured to be within acceptable limits for every square foot of SIP that is shipped. This involves some 20,000 to 30,000 tests per year.

The material specification which pertains to through-the-thickness properties of the thickest (0.160 in.) silicone-coated SIP contains the following requirements for room temperature properties:

Thickness: 0.152 $\pm$ 0.016 in. (3.86 $\pm$ 0.41 mm)

Ultimate strength: Grade B material, not less than 35 psi
                    (2.5 kg/cm^2)
                    Grade A material, 25-35 psi
                    (1.8-2.5 kg/cm^2)

Secant modulus, 0-5.33 psi: Between 12 and 34 psi
                    (0.84-2.8 kg/cm^2).

The thickness is measured in three locations over each 10 x 10 or 12 x 12 inch piece under a pressure of 0.625 psi (45 g/cm^2). The test method which is specified for measuring ultimate strength and secant modulus uses a 2.25 in. (57 mm) diameter circular test specimen which is bonded by a prescribed procedure to two carefully cleaned aluminum blocks of the same diameter. These blocks are mounted in a special fixture in an Instron tester and a tensile test is performed.

Because the most important information is to be obtained from the early part of the stress-strain curve, the initial crosshead speed is only 0.05 in./min (1.27 mm/min). After the critical load of 5.33 psi (corresponding to 21.2 lb) is passed, the crosshead speed is increased to 0.1 in./min to obtain the ultimate strength. Similarly, the full scale load is set initially at 50 lb and changed to 200 lb when the crosshead speed is changed.

Two critical values must be read from the curve: the elongation corresponding to a load of 5.33 psi, and the rupture load. Finally, in order to obtain the required secant modulus, the starting point of the curve must be accurately located. Because of frictional restraints within the felt structure, the stress-strain curve may not rise smoothly from the zero-load axis, but may suddenly jump to a low load (see Figure 2). Determination of the best approximation to a true zero-load point involves the extrapolation of the initial part of the curve back to the zero-load axis. This intercept, and the chart travel to the point corresponding to 5.33 psi, are then used in the determination of the secant modulus.

Before a computer was used to control this complex tensile test, the values were obtained manually from the curve plotted on the Instron chart. This was a tedious, time-consuming task which

took more time and considerably more attention to detail than
did the actual determination of the stress-strain curve. Even
the latter was more complicated than simple tensile testing
because of the crosshead speed and full-scale load changes which
had to be made during the course of the test. Clearly, this
complexity, coupled with the fact that more than 100 tests were
often needed in a single day, made the procedure particularly
well suited to computer control.

The computer was programmed to operate the test, read the required measured values, perform the computations, and print the
results in the form of a tabulated report. In order to conduct
a test, the operator entered into the computer the test specimen
identification, its measured thickness, and the actual diameter
of the mounting block. Then a start key was pressed, and the
computer controlled all aspects of the test except the change in
full scale load in the middle of the test, which could not easily be done automatically in the Instron tester being used. The
crosshead speed was changed automatically when a load was
reached which was 10% higher than that corresponding to 5.33
psi. The assumed zero point was obtained by having the computer
read 10 points from the initial part of the stress-strain curve
and perform a linear extrapolation to the zero-load axis. The
maximum load recorded during the test was taken to be the rupture load, and the chart travel to the point where the load
corresponded to 5.33 psi was recorded. This was all of the
input needed for the computation of the two required parameters,
namely, ultimate strength and secant modulus to 5.33 psi, which
were then printed out in tabular form, along with the other
pertinent test specimen data (see Tables II and III).

Table II shows the information which must be entered into the
computer before each specimen is tested. This includes:

(a) a number identifying the test specimen
(b) the measured diameter of the blocks to which the specimen
     is attached
(c) the height of the two stacked blocks before the specimen
     is attached
(d) the height of the blocks after the specimen has been at-
     tached.

The last three columns of the table are computed from these data
and from the test results. The "ultimate load" is the maximum
load reached during the test, which will be converted by the
computer to a pounds per square inch value, using the block
diameter value to calculate test area. The column headed "chart
travel" is the inches of chart between the extrapolated zero-
load point (mentioned previously) and the point on the stress-
strain curve corresponding to 5.33 psi. This will be converted
by the computer to specimen elongation by using a chart:jaw
speed ratio, previously supplied as a test condition applying to
all tests. This number will then be used by the computer in the
calculation of secant modulus.

Table III gives the results of all of these calculations, along
with the three measurements of coated felt thickness which were
also entered into the computer before the test. The computer

then compares the three critical parameters, thickness, FWT
(flatwise tension) strength and secant modulus with the specified limits which are shown at the top of each column, and
classifies the piece from which the specimen was taken as Grade
A, Grade B or reject. If any measured value lies outside the
specified limits the piece is identified as "scrap," and the
off-spec characteristic is identified. In the heading of the
table pertinent manufacturing details are given, and the total
number of pieces tested, as well as the number and total area of
Grade A and Grade B pieces.

Experience with this method of running the test has shown that
the results are more precise by an order of magnitude than those
which had been obtained manually, and that they are obtained in
a fraction of the time and cost. Furthermore, no additional
report preparation time is needed, for the computer printout has
been accepted by our client, Rockwell International Space Division, who are responsible for manufacturing the Space Shuttle,
as certification that the square foot of felt from which the
test specimen was cut has or has not met the test requirements
of the specification. Such tests are carried out at room temperature and in a chamber heated to 400°F (205°C).

5. UNIFORMITY MAPPING

The structure of needled nonwoven fabrics is different from that
of other types of textile materials in that the fabric is made
directly from fiber without the intermediate step of making
yarn. The needled structure may, of course, be formed around a
woven base fabric which serves as a reinforcement. We are concerned here, however, with SIP, which is a baseless needled
felt. Consequently, the uniformity of the final structure depends directly upon the uniformity of the fiber batt from which
it is made, how multiple batts are assembled, and how the needling is done. In general, batt combination will have a uni-
formizing influence, while needling will tend to decrease small-
scale uniformity*.

Because of the absence of intermediate fibrous assemblies such
as yarns, such nonuniformity as exists before and after needling
will be principally on the scale of the fiber or needle dimensions. A study of needled felt structural uniformity, there
fore, will be most informative if it is done on the scale of
square millimeters or less, not on the scale of square meters or
even square centimeters. This eliminates conventional cutting
and weighing techniques as a basic measurement procedure and,
moreover, implies that the characterization of even a small area
will require a large number of tests.

A measure of uniformity was obtained by determining compressibility at pressures as high as 300 kPa (2000 psi), using pene-
trating probes having diameters as small as 0.28 mm. At these
pressures, the density of the structure is as high as 75-80% of
the fiber density, and the measured compressibility is dependent
primarily upon the mass of material being compressed, its elas-
tic characteristics and, to a lesser degree, the size, shape and

---

*In this context "uniformity" is taken to mean mass uniformity.

orientation of the fibers which comprise the structure. In order to characterize nonuniformity on this scale, multiple measurements must be done, preferably in a precisely defined matrix of points, which can then be analyzed for periodic variations, overall variability, and other indicators of uniformity.

We were confronted with the need to carry out a large number of repetitive measurements requiring meticulous attention to fine detail, characteristics which pointed clearly to the potential advantages of computer control. In this case the measurement parameters for each individual test must be controlled, and the test position must be moved over the surface of the test specimen to provide a precisely controlled matrix of test values. Finally, appropriate calculations or other manipulations of the test matrix of values must be made in order to provide meaningful measures of the variability of the specimen.

For the compression mapping test, the following parameters were selected:

test probe diameters	0.28, 0.40, 0.81, 3.18 mm
pressures	up to 300 kPa (2000 psi)
matrix size	up to 100 x 100 points, routinely 16 x 16
area covered	up to 46 x 46 mm.

The results which are used to illustrate this procedure came from a 16 x 16 matrix of 256 numbers, each of which represented the measured value at a known location in the specimen. These were stored on a floppy disk in the IBM-PC as they were obtained. Rather than operating on this matrix with the PC to obtain some measures of nonuniformity, the whole test matrix of numbers was transferred to the memory of an HP-1000 minicomputer in an adjacent room, so as to make use of its significantly greater computational capabilities. This was done through an RS-232 cable by writing software for both the IBM-PC and the HP-1000 which permitted the PC to act as a dumb terminal for the HP.

In the HP-1000 the data were reduced in a variety of ways:

1. Column and row overall means and standard deviations were obtained.

2. A two-dimensional analysis of variance was done to identify any major directional effects.

3. A histogram and frequency distribution curve of values was constructed.

4. A three-dimensional plot of values was made using dark, bold-line fields to represent values above the overall mean; light, fine-line fields for areas below the mean; and dotted line fields to represent areas lying between $\pm a$ of the mean, where "a" could be any arbitrary amount such as 1 standard deviation, 5%, or any absolute value.

486

A sample matrix of test results is given in Table IV. This represents a test done on a 1.8 x 1.8 in. (46 x 46 mm) square of SIP felt, using a 0.0316 in. (0.80 mm) diameter probe and a 16 x 16 array of test positions (center-to-center distance of adjacent test positions was 0.12 in. or 3.0 mm). Each number in the matrix of test results represents the load in pounds needed to compress the felt under the test probe to a thickness of 0.20 inch (5.2 mm). A histogram showing the frequency distribution of these loads is shown in Figure 3.

Means and coefficients of variation for each row, corresponding to the machine direction in the fabric, and each column, corresponding to the cross-machine direction, are also given in the printout of the text matrix, as well as corresponding values of the overall mean and coefficient of variation.

A two-dimensional analysis of variance, shown in Table V, showed that the variances in both directions give highly significant F-ratios, indicating a high probability that assignable sources of this non-uniformity exist somewhere in the design of the structure or in the manufacturing procedures. Our work has not yet progressed to the point where we can identify the sources of this variability, though this is an objective of the study.

Finally, the variability is made more visually comprehensible by plotting a contour map of the 1.8 x 1.8 inch specimen. In order to smooth this plot, a cubic spline interpolation is used to fit a curve between the measured points. A 3-D map is then constructed using bold lines for regions which lie above the mean value and light lines for regions below the mean. Such a map is shown in Figure 4. The map can be further refined by adding a "screen" which defines areas lying between specified limits on either side of the mean. These regions are plotted using dotted lines and can be, for example, ± 5% of the mean (Figure 5), ±10% of the mean (Figure 6) or any other desired limits.

As was mentioned before, these are not critical measurements for SIP, for which the important test direction is normal to the plane of the fabric surface, and the uniformity of tensile properties in this direction, as defined by the product specification, relates to 4 square inch areas. There is no obvious reason why this "large scale" uniformity should be related to uniformity on the scale which is being studied in the mapping test described above. However, it is an interesting observation that SIP does not have particularly good small scale mass uniformity in relation to many other needled structures which have been examined. This evidently is not needed for the high degree of uniformity of thickness and through-the-thickness tensile properties required by the specification. Indeed, only two batts were combined in its manufacture, which accounts for the non-uniformity of mass. The high degree of through-the-thickness large-scale uniformity is achieved by an unusually high level of needling through multiple passes, in order to achieve a high degree of fiber orientation normal to the fabric surface. This has not resulted in a high degree of small-scale uniformity.

It is apparent that this small-scale compression mapping provides a wealth of information about the uniformity of a needled felt structure which could be analyzed in many ways. This is a task which we have only begun, but we expect to employ two-dimensional frequency analysis and other statistical measures of variability characteristics in order to attempt to relate measured parameters to possible sources of the variation contained within the structural geometry or assignable to manufacturing processes.

6. SUMMARY

These two test procedures illustrate many of the advantages to be gained by using a personal computer to control the operation of the testing machine as well as to read out and analyze the test results. These can be summarized as follows:

1.   Precise, reproducible operation, often exceeding that which is possible in manual operation, is achieved. This is particularly important when a test is to be done repeatedly over long periods of time, or when the complexity and required precision of the operation is difficult to achieve through manual operation.

  2. Readout of measured parameters such as loads or extensions can often be made with greater precision than is provided by standard machine readouts. Moreover, values can be obtained reliably during the course of the test at predetermined points between the starting point and the end point.

3.   Other derived parameters such as initial slope, load at 5% extension, yield point, post-yield slope etc. can be computed and displayed immediately on completion of the test.

4.   The results can be tabulated in any prescribed form suitable for presentation in a report, and printed out as soon as the test series is completed.

5.   Statistical analysis of the results can be done by providing appropriate software.

6.   Graphical presentation of the results in a variety of ways is available from standard, inexpensive software.

For quality control or quality assurance tests, relatively simple computerized control provides the means for improving reliability at reduced testing cost. For analytical purposes, computerized control makes it feasible to design test procedures which, because of their complexity, may be impractical for manual operation. In either case, the availability of relatively inexpensive, yet remarkably powerful, computers and software provides both the test technician and the textile researcher with an important new tool. The intelligent use of computers in the textile laboratory can contribute substantially to the development of higher quality, better performing textiles for the consumer.

Table I: Instron Output Signals

Function	Signal	Source
load	0-10V	load cell amplifier
crosshead position	pulsed signal	tachometer attached to drive screw gives 1 pulse per 50µ in. (0.0013 mm) cross-head travel
extension	0-10 V	extensometer (LVDT) attached to specimen

Table II: Computer Input and Primary Output Data

Serial Number	Diameter	Total Block Height	Final Height	Ultimate Load	Chart Travel	Gauge Length
128299	2.240	2.194	2.332	211.12	5.04	0.138
128300	2.244	2.270	2.400	219.26	4.83	0.130
128301	2.245	2.175	2.329	210.28	4.39	0.154
128302	2.243	2.174	2.320	191.92	5.36	0.146
128303	2.242	2.203	2.345	210.92	5.26	0.142
128304	2.246	2.275	2.435	208.74	4.37	0.160
128305	2.245	2.263	2.393	248.64	4.10	0.130
128306	2.250	2.285	2.415	211.52	4.40	0.130
128307	2.244	2.247	2.388	242.39	3.72	0.141
128308	2.247	2.200	2.364	215.54	4.13	0.164
128309	2.246	2.187	2.340	235.34	3.70	0.153
128310	2.247	2.170	2.317	221.74	4.91	0.147
128311	2.242	2.201	2.351	229.44	4.97	0.150
128312	2.244	2.218	2.368	216.28	4.51	0.150
128313	2.245	2.216	2.370	225.91	4.08	0.154
128314	2.242	2.198	2.344	221.59	3.97	0.146
128315	2.246	2.360	2.508	231.92	4.78	0.148

Table III: Computer Output

MBO135-092 Type I   Silicone Coating: MBO130-119   Total No. of Pieces: 41
MBO135-051 Type III Class 3   Manufacturing Coating Date: 03/06/84   Grade 'A' Pieces: 0   Soft 'A': 0.00
RTV Lot Number: BK-838   Manufacturing Designation: S2544TC1   Grade 'B' Pieces: 32   Soft 'B': 22.22
Felt Lot Number: 5606-1519   Coating Manufacturing Run: 779A   Off-Spec Pieces: 9

All shipped pieces pass appearance examination per Par 3.3, SIP appearance in accordance with MBO135-092.

Individual Serial No.	Size 10 or 12 Inches Square	Thickness Reading[1] (mils) 136 to 168 mils[2]			Secant Modulus 12-34[2] psi	FWT Strength >=25 psi[2]	Grade A 25-35 psi[2]	Grade B >=35 psi[2]	Off Spec Strength Modulus Thickness Appearance	Notations
		Point One	Point Two	Point Three						
128299	10	151	151	155	24.33	54.63		55		
128300	10	150	145	139	23.90	56.53		57		
128301	10	152	151	162	31.14	54.16		54		
128302	10	145	147	148	24.21	49.52		50		
128303	10	159	154	153	23.97	54.48		54		
128304	10	168	170	166	32.56	53.72			Thickness	Scrap
128305	10	154	144	148	28.16	64.04		64		
128306	10	158	148	150	26.27	54.24		54		
128307	10	146	150	155	33.66	62.49		62		
128308	10	160	156	162	35.30	55.42			Modulus	Scrap
128309	10	154	166	167	36.78	60.56			Modulus	Scrap
128310	10	155	158	156	26.60	57.01		57		
128311	10	147	146	151	26.79	59.26		59		
128312	10	150	168	161	29.53	55.76		56		
128313	10	156	153	160	33.56	58.19		58		
128314	10	152	148	156	32.56	57.23		57		
128315	10	162	159	154	27.52	59.68		60		

[1] determined in a separate test
[2] specified limits of acceptability

Table IV: Test Matrix for Compression Tests of SIP

A83080 MF File	MPA106	X Spacing 0.12000 in
Weight Per Area	0.0342 g/sq cm	Y Spacing 0.12000 in
Avg. Thickness	0.0000 in	Crosshead Speed 0.5 in/min
Test Type	Const. Ext. = .020 in	Return Speed 2.0 in/min
Date	01-11-84	Full Scale Load 20 lbs
Operator	MK	Probe Diameter 0.03160 in
No. of X Points	16	Max. Ext. 0.02023 in
No. of Y Points	16	Min. Ext. 0.01977 in
Total Points	256	Avg. Ext. 0.01998 in

SIP, 500 cycles, CE=.020, repeat

	A	B	C	D	E	F	G	H	I	J	K	L
1	1.810	1.840	1.450	1.740	1.590	1.530	1.740	1.270	1.320	1.500	1.900	1.190
2	1.810	1.400	1.100	1.820	1.450	1.530	1.530	1.410	1.110	1.560	2.760	1.490
3	2.120	1.730	1.800	1.450	1.940	1.820	1.630	1.230	2.210	2.200	2.790	1.730
4	1.210	1.250	1.900	1.470	1.220	1.420	1.630	1.620	1.970	1.900	1.820	2.030
5	1.970	1.310	2.170	2.350	1.350	1.350	1.370	1.320	2.140	2.460	1.600	1.570
6	.980	1.420	1.770	1.720	1.160	1.380	1.200	1.540	1.300	1.670	1.620	1.260
7	1.300	1.700	1.430	1.540	1.210	1.220	1.970	1.320	1.070	1.700	1.690	1.380
8	1.750	1.980	1.320	1.140	1.820	2.010	1.540	1.640	1.270	1.360	1.520	2.030
9	2.120	1.610	1.740	1.330	1.270	2.010	2.360	1.810	1.560	2.030	1.970	1.930
10	1.290	1.590	1.230	1.150	1.410	1.260	1.410	1.720	1.620	1.670	1.550	1.280
11	1.320	1.390	1.820	1.770	1.240	1.200	1.690	1.830	1.750	2.060	1.750	1.840
12	1.390	2.110	1.630	1.350	2.190	1.160	1.580	1.740	1.730	1.710	1.490	1.120
13	1.920	1.280	2.660	1.440	1.470	1.740	1.420	1.280	2.100	2.130	2.080	1.510
14	2.210	1.710	1.990	2.800	1.610	1.910	1.930	1.280	2.300	2.890	1.440	1.570
15	1.970	2.790	3.070	2.350	2.500	2.340	2.290	2.310	2.300	2.110	2.310	1.810
16	3.130	1.730	3.690	2.450	2.250	2.250	1.440	2.110	2.500	2.040	2.290	1.500
min	.980	1.250	1.100	1.140	1.160	1.160	1.200	1.230	1.070	1.360	1.440	1.120
max	3.130	2.790	3.690	2.800	2.500	2.340	2.360	2.310	2.500	2.890	2.790	2.030
mean	1.769	1.678	1.923	1.742	1.605	1.633	1.671	1.589	1.766	1.937	1.911	1.578
C.V.	29.67	23.16	36.03	28.49	25.99	23.55	19.34	20.18	26.33	20.09	22.51	18.56

	M	N	O	P	min	max	mean	C.V.
1	1.500	1.800	1.690	1.790	1.190	1.900	1.604	13.64
2	1.640	2.090	2.440	1.850	1.100	2.760	1.687	26.24
3	1.890	1.510	1.270	2.040	1.230	2.790	1.835	21.47
4	1.140	1.380	1.680	1.880	1.140	2.030	1.595	18.91
5	1.190	1.690	1.430	1.250	1.190	2.460	1.657	25.46
6	1.110	1.520	1.470	1.390	.980	1.770	1.407	16.28
7	2.030	1.790	1.570	2.070	1.070	2.070	1.562	19.64
8	2.350	2.520	2.130	1.520	1.140	2.520	1.744	22.95
9	1.930	1.730	1.690	2.500	1.270	2.500	1.849	17.90
10	1.930	1.610	1.960	1.900	1.150	1.960	1.536	16.90
11	2.030	2.080	1.900	1.740	1.200	2.080	1.713	16.41
12	1.590	1.750	2.660	1.950	1.120	2.660	1.697	23.17
13	1.580	1.720	2.300	2.160	1.280	2.660	1.799	22.58
14	1.600	1.300	2.510	1.770	1.280	2.890	1.926	25.81
15	1.760	2.140	2.160	2.680	1.760	3.070	2.306	14.79
16	1.580	2.150	1.900	2.460	1.440	3.690	2.217	26.34
min	1.110	1.300	1.270	1.250	.980			
max	2.350	2.520	2.660	2.680		3.690		
mean	1.678	1.799	1.923	1.934			1.758	
C.V.	20.61	17.99	21.51	20.09				24.47

491

Table V: Two-Way Analysis of Variance of Compression Test Matrix

Source of Variance	Degrees of Freedom	Sum of Squares	Mean Square	F-ratio	Significance Level
Along machine direction	15	4.21632	0.281088	2.13630	0.990684
Across cross-machine direction	15	13.3945	0.892967	6.78665	>0.99999
Error	225	29.6048	0.131577	--	
Total	255	47.2156	--	--	

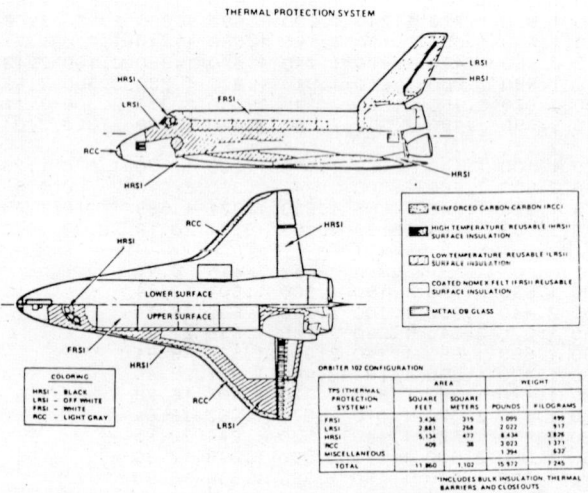

This diagram illustrates the various materials comprising the Space Shuttle's Thermal Protection System. The white areas indicate the location of white-coated surface insulation (FRSI). The striped and gray areas indicate the rigid silica tiles under which additional felt insulation is used. More than one ton of Albany's insulating materials is used on the Shuttle.

Figure 1:   Thermal Protective System of the Space Shuttle

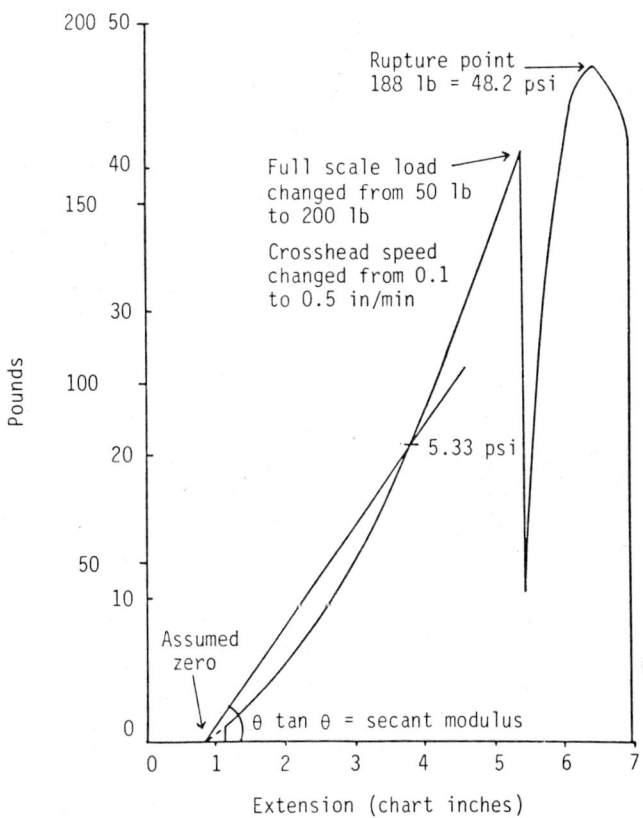

Figure 2:   Typical SIP Through-the-Thickness
Stress-Strain Curve

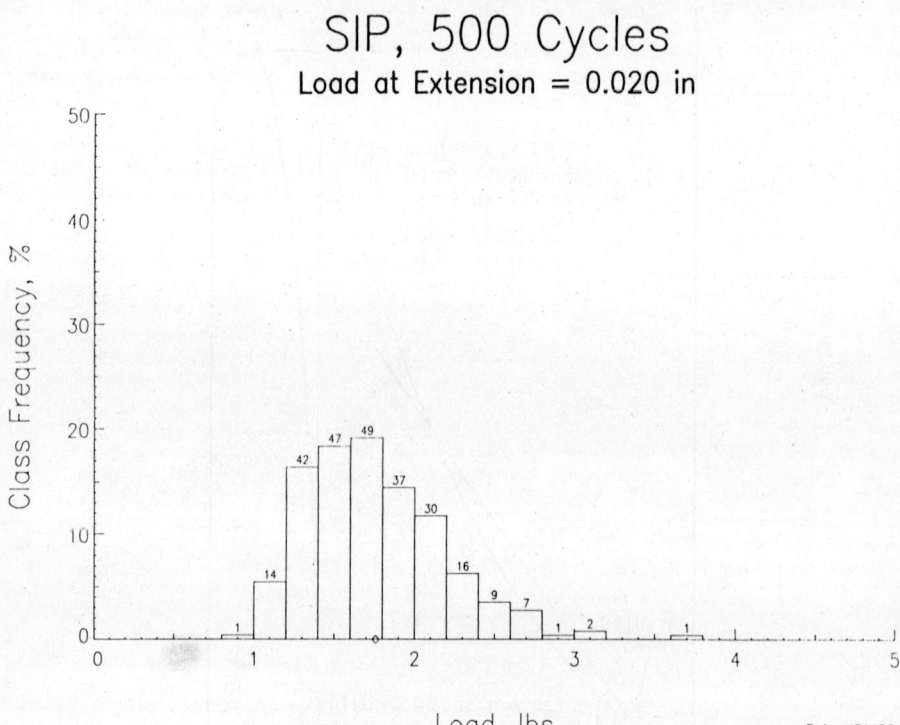

SIP, 500 Cycles
Load at Extension = 0.020 in

Figure 3: Histogram of Compressed Thicknesses of SIP

Ref: MPA106

SIP, 500 Cycles
Load at Extension = 0.020 in
Mean = 1.7584 lb, C.V. = 24.47 %

⊞ above mean

▦ below mean

Figure 4: Compression
Uniformity Map

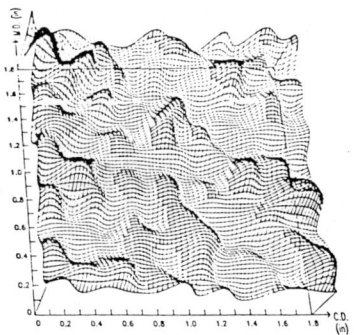

SIP, 500 Cycles
Load at Extension = 0.020 in
Mean = 1.7584 lb, C.V. = 24.47 %

⊞ more than 5 % above mean
   within 5 % of mean
⊞ more than 5 % below mean

Figure 5: Compression
Uniformity Map with +5%
Screen

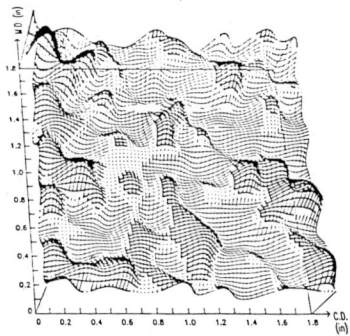

SIP, 500 Cycles
Load at Extension = 0.020 in
Mean = 1.7584 lb, C.V. = 24.47 %

⊞ more than 10 % above mean
    within 10 % of mean
⊞ more than 10 % below mean

Figure 6: Compression
Uniformity Map with ±10%
Screen

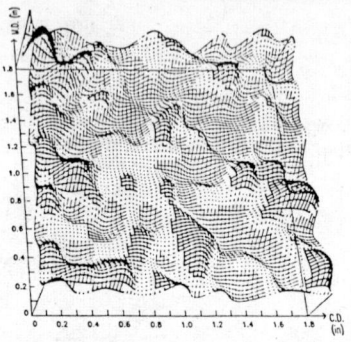

ACKNOWLEDGEMENTS

The authors gratefully acknowledge the contributions of the many
members of the staff of Albany International Research Co. who
have contributed to this work. Special mention should be made
of the support and technical contributions of Dr. John Skelton;
Dr. Maryann C. Kenney, who has had prime responsibility for the
development of the mapping techniques; Mrs. Mary M. Toney, whose
talents for careful experimentation were invaluable in the early
stages of the work; Dr. John R. Dent who developed many of the
computer data-handling procedures; and Mr. Rashid Nishar of
Sintech, Inc., who developed the specialized software used to
control the tests.

N. J. Abbott, F. S. Campbell, & M. M. Schoppee
Albany International Research Co
Dedham
Massachusetts 02026
U.S.A.

497

DATA ACQUISITION AND ANALYSIS FOR A SYSTEM OF FABRIC OBJECTIVE EVALUATION.

O. Zubzanda, J.I. Curiskis, T.J. Mahar and R. Postle

ABSTRACT

Fundamental fabric mechanical and surface properties are vitally important in the determination of the quality features and performance characteristics of fabrics and garments. Fabric object-ive evaluation systems based on the measurement of such fabric mechanical and surface properties are now being used for quality and process control in industry. The design and construction of a computer based data acquisition and analysis system are presented for the K.E.S.F. set of instruments measuring fabric tensile, shear, bending, lateral compression and surface roughness and surface friction. The most important hardware and software features of the computer based system are highlighted. The cur-rent applications of fabric objective evaluation in such fields as fabric finishing, fabric handle specification and garment manufacture are described. The potential uses of the system are discussed for engineering design of textile materials to meet specified levels of quality, mechanical and physical performance. Optimum search methods used in conjunction with dynamic data based systems represent very powerful short term methods by which the system can be applied in the fibre, textile and clothing industries.

1. INTRODUCTION

Microprocessors and microcomputers are rapidly developing into most important laboratory tools for data acquisition and analysis. The cost of microcomputer hardware and software is steadily dropping while their power is increasing. Much of the newest scientific instrumentation currently entering the market is micro-processor-controlled or includes a computerized system for data acquisition, processing and analysis. The rate limiting opera-tions in the laboratory will no longer be the slow and tedious tasks of measuring, recording, manually entering and analysing experimental data, but rather preparing and performing the actual experiments.

The aim of this project is to assemble and interface a modular microcomputer based data acquisition hardware and software system to be used, in the first instance for fabric objective evaluation. This system will increase significantly the performance power and versatility of fabric testing instruments already on hand while allowing routine experimental tests to be carried out more easily, quickly, accurately and reliably. The self-prompting control program should lead the operator, step by step, through complic-ated routines required by many instruments and experiments.

2. FABRIC OBJECTIVE EVALUATION

In recent years, interest has grown in the relationships between basic fabric mechanical and surface properties (FMSPs) on the one hand and, on the other hand, fabric quality and performance characteristics, e.g., fabric handle, tailorability or making-up properties, and garment appearance.

FMSPs are of critical importance in the determination of the
quality, appearance, and performance of fabrics and garments.
In Table I, the basic FMSPs are listed on the left while the
related fabric and garment quality and mechanical performance
characteristics of practical importance are listed on the right.
Much progress has been made in the accurate and reproducible
measurement in the laboratory of the basic fabric properties because of their essentially objective nature. However, the quality
and performance characteristics are largely subjective in nature,
so their assessment depends at least partly on our sensory percep-
tions. Most of them are notoriously difficult to test directly
in the laboratory despite repeated efforts to devise meaningful
testing procedures.

TABLE I

BASIC FABRIC MECHANICAL PROPERTIES AND RELATED QUALITY
AND PERFORMANCE CHARACTERISTICS OF FABRICS AND GARMENTS

FABRIC MECHANICAL PROPERTIES	*QUALITY AND MECHANICAL PERFORMANCE*
Uniaxial and biaxial tension	Fabric handle and drape
	Fabric formability and tailoring properties.
Fabric shear under tension	Garment appearance and seam pucker.
Pure bending	Mechanical stability and shape retention.
Lateral compression	Relaxation shrinkage, dimensional stability, and hygral expansion.
Longitudinal compression and buckling	Wrinkle recovery and crease retention.
Surface roughness and friction.	Abrasion and pilling resistance.
	Mechanical and physiological comfort.

Our basic aim in this work is to measure the mechanical properties
accurately and reproducibly and to relate these objective measurements to the quality and performance characteristics of practical
importance. Objective evaluation systems based on such measurements and scientific and engineering relationships are being used
for quality and production control, and product and process development in industry. This trend is inevitable because of the
gradual disappearance of personnel with traditional textile knowledge based on many years of experience and the simultaneous
emergence within industry of conventionally trained engineers to
carry out the production, research and development, and quality
control functions. This trend also satisfies the critical need
for an objective basis of communication between the fibre, textile,
apparel, and retailing sectors of industry, exporters and import-
ers, manufacturers, and research and development laboratories, and
between market research groups and the manufacturers they service.

2.1 Measurement of Fabric Mechanical Properties

The principles used to measure some FMSPs by the KES-F instrument (1) are shown in Figure 1, namely fabric tension, shear,
bending, lateral compression, and surface friction and roughness.

Figure 2 shows typical examples of the graphical output (1) from
the FMSP tests outlined in Figure 1. The characteristic shape of
deformation-recovery curves for a fabric subjected to extension
and lateral compression is presented in Figures 2(a) and 2(b) respectively. The different shape of the deformation-recovery
curves for a fabric subjected to bending, Figure 2(c), and shear,
Figure 2(d), and traces of the surface friction, Figure 2(e),
and surface roughness, Figure 2(f), tests are also given in
Figure 2. Digital measures characterising the response of a
fabric to a given deformation recovery cycle which can be extracted from these curves are the average slope or linearity of
the curves, the maximum deformation or strain, the energy loss or
hysteresis, and the residual strain or coercive stress. The KES-F
instruments, for example, provide both graphical output of the
type shown in Figure 2 and digital outputs in the form of the 16
parameters listed in Table II.

TABLE II

PARAMETERS DESCRIBING FABRIC MECHANICAL PROPERTIES

Tensile	LT	Linearity of Load Extension Curve
	WT	Tensile Energy
	RT	Tensile Resilience
Shear	G	Shear Rigidity
	2HG	Hysteresis of Shear Force at 0.5 Degrees (Shear Angle)
	2HG5	Hysteresis of Shear Force at 5 Degrees
Bending	B	Bending Rigidity
	2HB	Hysteresis of Bending Moment
Lateral Compression	LC	Linearity of Compression-Thickness Curve
	WC	Compressional Energy
	RC	Compressional Resilience
Surface Characteristics	MIU	Coefficient of Friction
	MMD	Mean Deviation of MIU
	SMD	Geometrical Roughness
Fabric Construction	W	Fabric Weight per Unit Area
	T_o	Fabric Thickness

The advent of modern instrumentation and control systems for the
objective measurement of FMSPs readily allows comparison of data
between laboratories and the development of fabric and garment
objective specifications, standards, and associated tolerance
levels. These objective data are now being used for the development of new products and processes, and quality and production
control in both the textile and clothing industries. In particular, the successful design and implementation of microprocessor
based data acquisition and analysis systems for the measurement of
FMSPs have accelerated the application of these measurements.
Later sections of this paper will describe one such system in
some detail.

2.2 Advantages of Microcomputer Based Design

The advantages of microcomputer based design are its:

- cost effectiveness;
- great power for data acquisition, processing and analysis;
- flexibility - many input/output configurations;
- many programs;
- software/hardware extensibility;
- multiple sources (in hundreds) of hardware and software (2,3).

The microcomputer-based design will facilitate the use and increase the flexibility of the KES-F system and other instrumentation. The experimental set up times will be more rapid and accurate and repetitive tests can be carried out more reliably through the reduction of human errors.

Microcomputers can be used to advantage in replacing or enhancing conventional 'hard-wired' instrument circuits. The function of traditional dedicated circuits is fixed and equipment is designed solely for each task. If any changes are required after the equipment is built, the process involved can be very costly and time consuming.

With microcomputers, one basic hardware/software design can be used with most of the different instruments, experiments or tests in any laboratory. Main control programs can be written after the design of the experiment or test has been truly finalised and changes can be easily made during or after testing. The flexibility of the microcomputer based design is demonstrated by the fact that it can be programmed or reprogrammed to suit the requirements of different instruments.

Because of Large Scale Integration (LSI), fewer components are needed with fewer interconnections. This reduces both physical size and power requirements. All these factors lead to improved reliability and lower cost.

3. DATA ACQUISITION AND ANALYSIS SYSTEM

3.1 Hardware Features

An important aspect of the microcomputer used in this project is its architecture. The microcomputer consists of a back-plane (mother board) into which various microcomputer boards (cards) are plugged. This system uses the S-100 standard bus. A bus is a group of conductors, along with assigned and defined signals, interconnecting all pins on the back-plane sockets. A computer can be made by plugging the required set of boards in to the back-plane. There are over 600 S-100 boards available from more than 200 companies (3). This plug-in approach can produce a custom built system having just the required specifications. There are advantages to this approach. As technology advances or requirements are changing, old boards may be replaced or appended by newer ones, increasing the usefulness, flexibility and life span. Another advantage is that trouble-shooting can be simpler and cheaper with a modular system since problems can be easier to locate by substitution with known working boards. The boards and peripherals that comprise our microcomputer are seen in Fig. 3.:

501

- CPU - Central Processing Unit which includes basic I/O -
     Input/Output parts
- RAM - Random Access Memory board
- FDC - Floppy Disk Controller
- ADC - Analog to Digital Converter
- GDC - Graphics Display Card
- Solid State Disk Emulator or RAM Disk
- Terminal
- Floppy Disk Drives

This hardware with appropriate software comprises a very flexible
and a powerful Data Acquisition system. The most important
features of the system are discussed in the following sections.

3.1.1 Analog to Digital Converter (ADC)

Interfacing a microcomputer with external instrumentation requires
skill in analog and digital electronics, knowledge of programming
in both high levels and assembly language and plenty of time to
spare. The most sophisticated and versatile types of Analog to
Digital Converters eliminate the need for most of the above-
mentioned requirements. The analog peripherals are interfaced by
simply running two wires to each analog signal output to be
connected to the computer. The available Software Support Package
is designed to help the user to perform complex analog data
acquisition tasks with the S-100 microcomputer operating under
CP/M Operating System using a high level language such as Fortran.
Thus it is now possible, with only a basic knowledge of computer
usage and little hardware experience, to do analog interfacing
and sophisticated data acquisition, using such a powerful board.

The Tecmar AD-212 board (4) is designed for sophisticated industrial, scientific, commercial, laboratory and educational applications requiring high-speed, accurate analog to digital conversion,
including real time applications. This board is designed to meet
a wide range of complex data acquisition needs with high reliability and minimum set-up time. The board contains an amplifier with
optional software-controlled programmable gains.

The standard Tecmar board has the following features:

- a selectable jumper for 16 single ended or 8 true differential
  analog inputs
- 12 bit resolution
- ± 0.025% accuracy
- a conversion rate of 30 kHz (with gain programmable option,
  the conversion rate is 40 kHz)
- an analog input with full scale ranges of ± 5V, ± 10V, 0 to 5V
  and 0 to 10V
- an analog input impedence of greater than 100 MΩ.

Using this board, up to 16 single ended analog channels can be
connected to the microcomputer. Under software control the
operator determines from which channels to obtain data and to
define the gain, sampling rate, number of points etc. Details of
software control are discussed later in this paper.

3.1.2 Graphics Display Card

It is necessary to have a good computer graphics system,
integrated within a laboratory microcomputer, to display experimental results and parameters as well as the results of an
analysis. Although data can be collected by the computer without
the graphics, in this case the user has no way of knowing whether
or not the data is valid. The graphical representation allows
the user to evaluate the measurements as they progress and to
correct experimental errors before the data is saved or analysed.
The computer graphics can be used as a very powerful, flexible
and cheap alternative to multipen fast recorders.

Besides replacing a chart recorder (or even an oscilloscope) the
system provides for permanent storage of the experimental results
that can later be redisplayed on a monitor or further analysed.

The modular microcomputer graphics system consist of standard
high resolution video monitor, high resolution monochrome graphics
board and graphics software. These components are appended to an
otherwise standard modular computer.

SME Systems GDC-512 graphics board (5) is an intelligent, high
resolution (512 x 490 points) single board capable of drawing
crisp graphics images, at high speed, on a standard video monitor.
It is actually a single board computer, completely independent,
supporting its own 64 k bytes of memory, input/output ports,
light pen interface and resident software. Because of its self-
reliant architecture, this board places no load on the host computer, allowing the system to work in parallel with this powerful
intelligent graphics.

The software supplied with the graphics board simplifies the work
of designing applications programs. Internal diagnostics exercise
the on board memory and provide a test program for video monitor
evaluation. The most valuable feature for this application is its
ability to run software written for SCION's Microangelo MA512
graphics board (6). This compatibility allows us to use a Software Support Package for analog to digital converter and Grafpak
3.0 (7) for graphics board.

3.1.3 Mass Storage

For storage of programs, data files and extensive instrument set-
up information, some form of nonvolatile mass storage is required.
The preferred medium for mass storage memory has changed over the
years from paper tape to magnetic tape, then to floppy and hard
disks. The rate of transfer, the total storage capacity and the
total cost has increased, but the cost per byte has decreased.
An interesting evolutionary step in memory storage technology is
the RAM-disk and the electrically alterable read only memory (8).

A storage medium which combines mass storage, reasonably fast
access, nonvolatility and low cost is the floppy disk. The floppy
disks themselves are both removable and very low in cost. They
are the most widely used form of mass storage for microcomputers
with 8 inch Single Sided Single Density (SSSD) format being the
industry standard. Every 8 inch Floppy Disk Controller (FDC)
supports this format. Noncompatibility of format is the main

problem of 5 inch FDCs.   It is claimed that there are over 200
different 5 inch formats.   It is possible that the IBM-PC
(Personnel Computer) will help to overcome the lack of 5 inch
standards.   Many 16 bit microcomputers claim IBM-PC compatibility
which must firstly include compatible FDC format.

The latest arrival, the 3 inch floppy, has very attractive features.   It is very small, compact and has low power consumption.
Some models have a very strong plastic case for the floppy disk
medium and automatic cover for the head access area.   The disk
is thus very rugged, insensitive to adverse handling and storing
conditions, including dust.

Execution times of some disk intensive tasks such as compiling,
assembling, text formatting etc., tend to be too long when
floppies are used.   The speed and reliability may be dramatically
improved when a hard disk is used because of its greater data
transfer rate and completely sealed construction.

A disadvantage of both floppy and hard disk drives is that they
are complex, precision mechanical devices not generally suitable
for harsh industrial environments.   For reliability in critical
storage applications requiring low power consumption, high speed
and excellent resistance to harsh environments, a Random Access
Memory-disk (RAM-disk) is recommended.   RAM-disk can run disk
intensive programs 5 to 30 times faster than with a floppy and
2-5 times faster than with hard disk drives.   8 bit microcomputers
can have 16-bit speed, in disk intensive applications, without
requiring a lot of new hardware and software.

We are using 128 k byte RAM-disk from SME System (type CRC-128)
with battery back up (5).   This very low power static memory
board requires only 0.4 m A in back up mode and allows the computer to be turned off without the loss of any data.   The RAM-disk
has no moving parts and it does not suffer from the mechanical
problems which are the main cause of computer failure.   It is now
possible to run a data acquisition and control system that would
not require maintenance even in the harshest environment where
tape or disk storage systems will become unreliable.

As semiconductor memory (RAM chips) prices will continue to drop,
large (1 M byte) RAM-disks will achieve effective cost-speed
ratios and will become a part of many microcomputer systems.   The
days of the two floppy drive system are numbered in proportion to
the price of memory chips as well as hard disk drives with removable cartridge media.

Putting a CP/M operating system and other commonly used utility
programs into electrically alterable read only memories would
eliminate the need to read a floppy during system initialisation.
The floppy could then be turned off except to load a RAM-disk or
to copy the data for back up purposes.   The SME systems 'Aries'
microcomputer with floppy option comes very close to such a system.   Aries forms the basis of this data acquisition design.

The monitor software in Read Only Memory (ROM) has required dual
ability to load the CP/M operating system from the ROM and also
from the floppy disk.   A floppy disk thus can be used to load or
unload the RAM-disk.   The only disadvantage is that when the CP/M

operating system from read only memory is loaded and run, the RAM-disk is accessed as the only drive and no provision is made for available floppy drive(s). The system is suitable for industrial control, data acquisition, communication and dedicated processing applications.

3.2 Software

3.2.1 Acquisition Software

In order to execute user commands and to facilitate the use of the hardware resources provided the microcomputer operating system is required. The hardware system uses a CP/M (Control Program for Microprocessor) operating system, which has become a widely used standard operating system. There are currently available on the market close to 1,700 CP/M compatible software items from more than 350 vendors (2). Industrial applications software is the largest general class.

Once installed in the microcomputer memory, CP/M becomes an integral part of the complete system. The user is then able to activate the desired application programs. Once an application program terminates, CP/M takes over again and awaits the next command.

Tecmar provides a very flexible Software Support Package for their analog to digital and digital to analog converters and the Scion Microangelo MA-512 graphics board. This software enables the collection and storage of analog data with or without simultaneous video display. A set of previously collected data can be taken and displayed on a monitor or set up to draw x-y plots.

With the hardware and software systems provided, the user can:

- take data from several channels;
- specify the channel numbers, or the beginning and ending numbers of a sequence of channels;
- specify the number of data points to be taken and the delay time between the points;
- set the gain of the input amplifier;
- specify that data collection only starts in response to an external trigger, the feature necessary for synchronizing computer and the test instruments.
- on the monitor, axes, ticks, scales and titles can be drawn along with the data.

Several other useful functions are supported:

- setting and reading the real time clock;
- setting and waiting for a 24 hour alarm;
- creating and reading graph set up parameters from disk files;
- reading and writing data to and from disk files.

This software is written for the nonprogrammer and allows us to enter a few parameters and to begin to take data immediately. The software support package graphics routines are limited to the ascending cartesian coordinates and the graphics monitor. The industry standard Grafpak (7) software graphics package will allow for more flexibility.

The Grafpak is a very powerful set of Fortran plotting subroutines which plot linear, semi-log and log-log plots, with labelled axes. Automatic scaling of the data is implemented as well as scaling of the overall size of the plots. A generalized grid drawing routine is also included. An interactive utility allows rapid creation of cartesian plots from user data values entered from the keyboard or read from a data file. With this utility, the nonprogrammer can quickly create high quality plots suitable for publication. The fact that these routines are largely device independent makes it easy to create a version that will drive both a graphics monitor and a pen plotter.

A friendly interface, between user and the CP/M operating system, can be easily created using a specialized high level language such as Stok Pilot (9). Using such a language a software designer can easily produce a friendly self-prompting supervisor to help guide the end-user through any complex application. It can pass control to a program written in another language such as Fortran or Basic. It can also call assembler subroutines. Another advantage of Stok Pilot is that it can provide an effective on-line user manual for inquiry into the usage of application programs.

3.2.2 Numerical Methods

The series of measurements listed in Table III are taken from the graphical output of the KES-F instruments. These measurements must be made in order to obtain the parameters listed in Table II from the series of digital values collected by the data acquisition system. Details of the measurements are provided in Fig. 2.

Three different numerical techniques are used to obtain these measurements from the raw data collected by the data acquisition system. These techniques, which are also included in Table III are:- Least Square Polynomial Regression (LSPR) using Gaussian elimination and back-substitution, Interval Halving and numerical integration using the Trapezoidal Rule. These well selected numerical methods enable the achievement of accuracy and consistency in graph evaluation for superior to normal manual processing by the operator.

3.2.2.1 Least-Square Polynomial Regression

Because the acquired data is a result of a physical experiment, the file entries contain inherent errors. These inherent errors are distributed according to some statistical pattern, and there is a reasonable probability that some of the errors are quite large. Before it can be used the data must be smoothed to eliminate the statistical errors as much as possible.

The theory of Numerical Analysis suggests that for statistical reasons the Least-Square Polynomial Regression (LSPR) of the appropriate degree should be used. If the statistical errors of the acquired data follow any distribution with constant variance, then the LSPR produces the most probable solution.

Any experimental curve can be approximated and smoothed by the LSPR at least in the narrow interval of interest. The regression coefficient can be used not only as a measure of the curve fit, but also as a measure of the smoothness of a curve as well.

TABLE III

Fabric Test	Measurements taken from graphical output	Numerical Methods Used		
		Least Squares Polynomial Regression (LSPR)	Interval Halving	Numerical Integration Trapezoidal Rule
Tension (a)	.INT	–	–	Yes
	.B-INT	–	–	Yes
	$.E_m$	Yes	Yes	–
Compression (b)	.To	Yes	Yes	–
	.Tm	Yes	Yes	–
	.INT	–	–	Yes
	.B-INT	–	–	Yes
Bending (c)	.M1 to M6	Yes	Yes	–
	.Km +	Yes	Yes	–
	.Km –	Yes	Yes	–
Shear (d)	.F1 to F10	Yes	Yes	–
	$.\phi m$ +	Yes	Yes	–
	$.\phi m$ –	Yes	Yes	–
Surface Friction (e)	INT,X	–	–	Yes
	INT,X	–	–	Yes
Surface Roughness (f)	INT,X	–	–	Yes
	INT,X	–	–	Yes

For the data acquisition and analysis system under discussion a program is used to load a specified range of discrete digital data points about the required load or stress (e.g. a compressive pressure equal to 0.5 gm cm^{-2}). This range of data points is loaded into a routine that will determine the coefficients of the required number of simultaneous equations for the solution of a given degree of the Least Squares Polynomial Regression equation. In this case, a smoothing polynomial equation of the 3rd order is considered sufficient for the accuracy required. A Gaussian elimination and back-substitution method are then used to determine the coefficients of the smoothing polynomial.

An extension of this technique is used to determine the point where a curve changes direction. A routine is used to search for the tabulated points which represent an estimate of the turn around point of the curve e.g. E_m for the tensile curve. Two LSPR equations are then obtained using the methods described above, one to cover a specified range of data points before this estimated turn around point and the second equation to cover a specified range of points after this estimate.

3.2.2.2 Interval Halving

Interval Halving is one of the simplest and most effective methods for obtaining solutions for the equation $f(x) = 0$ and is based on

507

finding an interval over which f(x) changes sign by using a search procedure. The main advantage of this method over other similar methods is that, provided the starting values are on either side of the solution, it is guaranteed to converge to a solution.

This technique is used to evaluate the strain or displacement during a fabric tensile or compression test (e.g. T_O, fabric thickness at 0.5 gm.cm^{-2} pressure) for a nominated value of stress or load using the smoothed polynomial calculated by the LSPR routine previously discussed.

The Interval Halving method is also used to search for the point of intersection between deformation and recovery curves in fabric tension (εm), compression (Tm), bending (Km$^+$, Km$^-$) and shear (ϕm$^+$, ϕm$^-$) tests. These intersection points represent the most reliable estimate of the actual turn around point for each of these curves.

3.2.2.3 Trapezoidal Rule

A relatively simple Trapezoidal Rule numerical integration technique is used to determine the areas under the deformation, INT, and recovery, B-INT, curves for fabric tensile and compression tests, and the total area under the surface friction and surface roughness traces and their mean deviation. The Trapezoidal Rule is preferred to the more complex and theoretically more accurate Simpson's Rule because of the high rate of sampling data points and therefore the very small interval between sampled data points.

4. APPLICATION OF FABRIC OBJECTIVE MEASUREMENT

The manner in which fabric objective measurement is used by individual researchers and companies will clearly depend upon the nature, priorities and particular aims of the relevant organisation. In the case of wool fabrics, the use of fabric objective measurement techniques should have five broad aims: 1) to maintain and upgrade the quality of all existing wool products; 2) to optimize the use of different qualities and varieties of raw wool fibres; 3) to provide a scientific basis for the control of wool fabric quality and performance as a result of new process and product developments; 4) to specify quantitatively and control the performance characteristics of wool and wool blend fabrics and garments; 5) to establish an objective basis for communication between different companies, industry sectors and traders in wool products.

In the two Australia-Japan symposia in 1982 and 1983 on Objective Evaluation of Apparel Fabrics (10,11), the initial implementation stages of fabric objective evaluation through the measurement of basic fabric mechanical properties were reviewed. Four examples of these applications in quality and production control are briefly discussed below.

4.1 Objective Evaluation of Fabric Finishing

In Figure 4, two bending hysteresis curves are shown - one for an unfinished wool worsted suiting material (the broken curve) and the other for the same fabric in the finished state (the full curve). The curves given in Figure 4 clearly show that the remarkable effect of finishing on fabric mechanical properties can

be expressed quantitatively by carrying out, for example, a
bending deformation-recovery cycle and by measuring the fabric
bending rigidity and more importantly, the bending hysteresis or
energy loss. These parameters are greatly reduced by finishing
and therefore may be used directly for production and quality
control purposes.

Very similar effects to those shown in Figure 4 are also apparent
in fabric shear deformation-recovery hysteresis curves showing the
effects of fabric finishing. Furthermore, fabric tensile, lateral
compression and particularly fabric surface measurements may also
be used to study quantitatively the effects of specific fabric
finishing processes and finishing routines.

4.2   Fabric Handle

Results of an extensive international fabric handle survey carried
out on a large number of men's worsted-type suiting materials
have been presented elsewhere (12). From these results, it is
clearly evident that both expert and consumer judges of fabric
handle from within any one country consistently place similar
emphasis on the various fabric characteristics which have been
identified (1) as the primary mechanical components of fabric
handle, e.g. fabric smoothness, stiffness, crispness, softness and
fullness. These primary components of fabric handle have been
related to objective measurements of the basic fabric mechanical
and surface properties.

It is difficult to overestimate the importance of fabric handle
as the traditional subjective measure of finished fabric quality.
Subjective expressions of fabric handle have invariably been used
as the basis of communication for development, production, quality
control, specification and marketing of textile materials and garments. The successful development of objective specification,
widely accepted standards, and quantitative tolerances for fabric
handle would greatly facilitate communication between all sectors
of the fibre, textile, clothing and marketing industries and
would also provide objective guidelines for research and development.

4.3   Fabric Tailorability and Making-up Properties

Although the textile material is regarded as the finished product
of the textile industry, it is at the same time regarded as the
raw material for the garment manufacturing or tailoring industry.
Garment manufacturers require a reliable objective method for
selecting suitable fabric to tailor into particular end products.
Furthermore, the tailoring industry also requires an objective
method for production and process control based on the quantitative specification of fabric mechanical properties required for
each particular operation in the tailoring or cutting and sewing
sequence. This latter requirement is becoming more urgent as
various forms of computer control, automation and robotics are
being introduced into the garment manufacturing industry.

Figure 5 shows the fabric extensibility in the warp and weft
directions measured on the KES-F for a range of men's suiting
materials provided by a large Japanese tailoring company. It is
evident from Figure 5(a) that those fabrics which were nominated

by the tailoring company as producing men's suits of good appearance generally have both warp and weft extensibilities greater
than 4%. On the other hand, those fabrics which produce suits of
poor appearance have an extensibility in either warp or weft
direction of less than 4%. Furthermore, it appears that the fabric extensibility in the weft direction is the more critical measure of tailorability in this particular context. Figure 5(b) also
shows a clear separation of the good and poor fabrics according to
the appearance of the tailored suit, by plotting the fabric
"formability" in the weft direction against the "formability" in
the warp direction. The measure of fabric formability was first
introduced by Lindberg et al (13) at TEFO in Sweden to define the
tailoring performance of fabrics and is equal to the product of
fabric bending rigidity and longitudinal fabric compressibility or
extensibility.

Although Figure 5 shows that the good and the poor fabrics
(according to their appearance in a made up suit) can be clearly
separated on simple fabric mechanical property charts, most of
the average fabrics which make up into suits of "normal" appearance (which are not shown in Figure 5 would appear on the charts
very close to the demarcation line between the good and poor
fabrics, i.e. 4% extensibility in Figure 5(a) and 25×10^{-4} mm^2
formability in the case of Figure 5(b). Further work needs to be
done in conjunction with tailoring companies in order to provide a
more precise and critical method of objective specification and
associated tolerances for these fabrics.

4.4 Analytical Fabric Engineering

The ultimate goal of theoretical and experimental studies of
fibres, yarns and fabrics is the engineering design of these
textile materials to meet specified levels of mechanical and
physical performance in terms of standard and reproducible
laboratory tests as required for further processing (e.g. tailoring) and in application. Since the objective measurement programmes are, in fact, defining such standard laboratory tests, it
is perhaps time to consider the development of integrated software
packages for the engineering design of fibrous textile assemblies.
Ideally, such an engineering design approach would negate or
reduce the need for expensive trial-and-error product development
programmes for new textile materials and applications.

Over the years, analytic and computational models of yarns and
fabrics have been devised primarily to explain various features
of their mechanical behaviour. Due to the complexities of structure and of deformation modes inherent in fibrous textile
assemblies (14,15) an analytical approach to the engineering
design of these materials requires a hierarchical framework with
clearly defined goals at each level of analysis. Such a scheme of
mechanical analysis and prediction is most conveniently devised
using the concepts of micromechanics and macromechanics (16) whereby the important fibre, yarn and fabric mechanical properties are
expressed in terms of one another - it is to be noted that this
approach represents the basic link between objective mechanical
measurements of fibres, yarns and fabrics. Applicable mechanical
models and analysis methods for this analytical scheme can then be
selected and a review of recent developments to this end are given
in reference (16).

4.5 Dynamic Empirical Database Systems

The above analytical approach represents a long term objective in
textile physics. Of immediate importance is the question of how
the vast quantities of data generated from objective measurement
programmes can be utilized in an empirical or semi-empirical
approach for the engineering design of fibrous textile assemblies.
This necessitates the development of dynamic database structures
which can be updated and expanded as further data are collected
and new objective test methods devised. Use of statistical and
other search methods can then be made in order to ascertain those
mechanical and other properties of the textile assembly of most
relevance to particular end-use applications. Examples of this
are discussed above with regard to fabric handle and tailorability.
Indeed, Postle et al (17) suggest the use of fabric maps to
engineer fabrics with different combinations of basic mechanical
properties to yield particular handle characteristics and tailored
garments of superior appearance. Since the achievement of a particular product specification represents the optimization of various parameters subject to certain constraints, use of optimum-
search methods (e.g. via mathematical programming models) may
provide a significant semi-empirical approach for the engineering
of textile assemblies; see, for example, the application of linear
programming methods to the specification of wool blends (18).
Inclusion of the effects of processing variables, as determined by
objective measurement data, into the database structure and subsequent analysis methods further extends the scope for engineering
design and may be considered the objective quantification of the
textile craftsman's experience; an example of this can be cited
with regard to fabric finishing (19).

A logical extension of such work is the application of a systems
approach to the processing of fibre masses to the final textile
product. In this approach (20), the contributions of various
investigations (experimental and theoretical) into different
aspects of the processing systems are welded together into
computer-based simulation models. This is done in such a manner
so as to mimic the behaviour of the whole system in terms of various material and processing parameters (including machine variables) thus changes in material and processing variables of economic significance may be ascertained from the model and so provide
decision support for management. With clearly-defined intermediate as well as initial and final stages where objective measurements can be made to ascertain processing and product performance, the systems approach can extend the goals of yarn and fabric
engineering to include process engineering and control.

5. CONCLUSION

The principal aim of the work reported in this paper is to measure
accurately and reproducibly FMSPs and to store and analyse the
resultant data using microprocessors to form the basis of a system
for the objective evaluation of fabric and garment quality, tailorability and performance.

The design and construction of a computer based data acquisition
and analysis system have been presented for the K.E.S.F. set of
instruments measuring fabric tensile, shear, bending, lateral compression and surface roughness and surface friction. The most

important hardware and software features of the computer based system have been highlighted. The objective measurements of FMSPs are related to fabric handle and drape, and the influence of finishing treatments, fabric formability and tailoring properties, garment appearance and seam pucker, mechanical stability and shape retention, dimensional stability, wrinkle recovery and crease retention, and mechanical and physiological comfort. Fabric objective evaluation systems based on the KES-F instruments, are now being used for quality and process control and product development in industry. This trend towards fabric objective specification is facilitating communication between research workers and industry and also between the various sectors of the fibre, textile, clothing, textile machinery and related industries.

The manner in which fabric objective measurement is used by individual researchers and companies clearly depends upon the nature, priorities and particular aims of the relevant organisation. In the two Australia-Japan Symposia held in 1982 and 1983 (10,11) four general lines of development of fabric objective specification were discernible, viz. engineering fabrics from a data base containing objective mechanical data, objective assessment of fabric handle, objective evaluation of fabric tailorability, and improvement of the performance characteristics of fabrics and garments. A feature of this work is the establishment of fabric objective specifications and tolerances by apparel company engineers in Japan and the consequent design and method of production control employed by textile technologists to meet these apparel fabric specifications.

Although the textile material is regarded as the finished product of the textile industry, it is at the same time the raw material for the garment manufacturing or tailoring industry. The fabric mechanical properties of extension, shear, longitudinal compression and bending are of critical importance in the shape formation obtained by design, cutting, sewing and fusing of flat pieces of fabric into three-dimensional garments. These fabric mechanical property data are now being used for fabric selection and buying control and also for process and quality control by large tailoring companies. It is anticipated that these developments occurring at the interface between the textile and clothing industries will become more crucial as the level of automation increases in clothing manufacture.

A microprocessor based fabric and garment objective evaluation system has the potential of providing an extensive data base to engineer fabrics and garments to meet specified quality and performance standards. Although the long-term aim of this research is to develop analytical methods for engineering textiles and clothing to predetermined quality and performance levels, the microprocessor based system described in this paper now enables these objectives to be achieved by numerical methods.

6. ACKNOWLEDGEMENTS

The authors are indebted to Mr. J. Galea for his technical assistance in the construction of the data acquisition system described in this paper. The financial support of the Wool Research Trust Fund of the Australian Wool Corporation is also gratefully acknowledged.

7. REFERENCES

(1) S. Kawabata. 'The Standardisation and Analysis of Hand Evaluation' Text. Mach. Soc., Japan, Osaka, 1980.

(2) S. Libes, J. Manno, C. Terry. Microsystems, 4, 1983, 12, 59.

(3) S. Libes. Ibid., 4, 1983, 5, 44.

(4) R. Newrock and W. Knesel. Ibid., 4, 1983, 7, 94.

(5) SME Systems, 22 Queen Street, Mitcham, Victoria, 3132, Australia.

(6) Scion Corporation, 12310 Pinecrest Road, Reston, VA22091, U.S.A.

(7) J.W. Long and J. Simon. Ibid., 3, 1982, 4, 84.

(8) B. Weidemann. Ibid., 4, 1983, 5, 64.

(9) Stok Software Inc., 17 West 17th Street, New York, NY 10011, U.S.A., (1981, 1982).

(10) S. Kawabata, R. Postle and M. Niwa (eds.), "Objective Specification of Fabric Quality, Mechanical Properties and Performance", The Textile Machinery Society of Japan, 1982.

(11) S. Kawabata, R. Postle and M. Niwa (eds.), "Objective Evaluation of Apparel Fabrics", The Textile Machinery Society of Japan, in publication.

(12) R.C. Dhingra, T.J. Mahar, R. Postle, V.B. Gupta, S. Kawabata, M. Niwa and G.A. Carnaby. Indian J. of Tex. Res., 8, 1983, pp 9-15.

(13) J. Lindberg, L. Waesterberg and R. Svenson. J. Text. Inst., 1960, 51, T1475.

(14) J.W.S. Hearle, M. Konapasek and A. Newton. Text. R. J. Vol. 42, 1972, 613-626.

(15) J.W.S. Hearle, J.J. Thwaites and J. Amirbayat. (eds.), "Mechanics of Flexible Fibre Assemblies", Sijthoff and Nordhoff, Netherlands, 1980, pp 1-33.

(16) J.I. Curiskis, R. Postle and A.H. Norton. in op. cit. (Ref. 11).

(17) R. Postle, S. Kawabata, M. Niwa, T.J. Mahar, R.C. Dhingra, M. Matsudaira and S. de Jong. in "Textile Machinery: Investing for the Future", Textile Institute, Manchester, 1982, paper 16.

(18) G.A. Carnaby, WRONZ Communication No. C81 (1983).

(19) M. Mori, in op cit. (Ref. 11).

(20) K.H. Elliott, J.B. Dent, G.A. Carnaby and A.C. Beck,
      Proc. 10th Annual Conf. Text. Inst. (N.Z. Section),
      Auckland, 1982, pp 105-116.

O. Zubzanda, J. I. Curiskis,
T. J. Mahar and R. Postle,
The University of N.S.W.
Kensington
New South Wales
AUSTRALIA.

FIGURE LEGENDS

Fig. 1   Principles used in the KES-F instruments for the objective measurement of fabric mechanical and surface properties.

Fig. 2   Typical graphical output from each of the fabric mechanical and surface measurements shown in Fig. 1. Note the
definitions included in these curves of the following
measures which are calculated from the digital output of
these tests and used in subsequent analysis:

(a) tension; εm;

$$INT \propto \int_0^{\varepsilon m} F d\varepsilon \text{ - deformation curve;}$$

$$B\text{-}INT \propto \int_0^{\varepsilon m} F' d\varepsilon \text{ - recovery curve;}$$

(b) compression; To; Tm;

$$INT \propto \int_{Tm}^{To} P \, dT \text{ - deformation curve;}$$

$$B\text{-}INT \propto \int_{Tm}^{To} P' dT \text{ - recovery curve;}$$

(c) bending; m_1 to m_6 (incl.); Km^+, Km^-; B^+, B^-;

(d) shear; F_1 to F_{10} (incl.); m^+, m^-; G^+, G^-;

(e) surface friction; MIU; MMD;

(f) surface roughness; $\bar{T}$; SMD.

Fig. 3   Block diagram of a microcomputer based data acquisition
system

Fig. 4   Bending hysteresis curves for a finished (full curve)
and unfinished (broken curve) wool worsted suiting
material.

Fig. 5   Mechanical property charts for fabrics classified
according to their appearance in tailored suits showing
a) warp and weft extension measurements; and b) warp
and weft formability measurements.

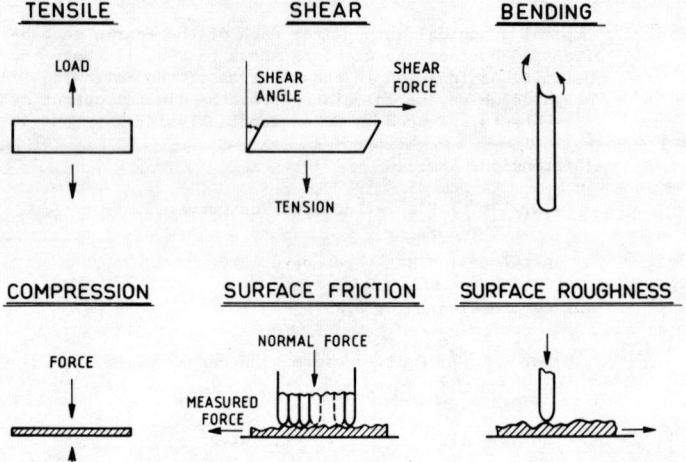

Fig. 1

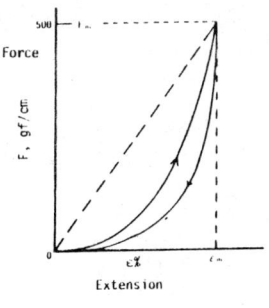

Force

TENSION
(a)

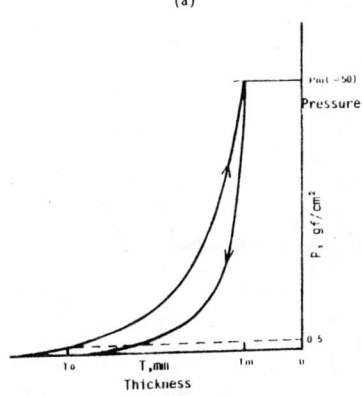

Pressure

COMPRESSION
(b)

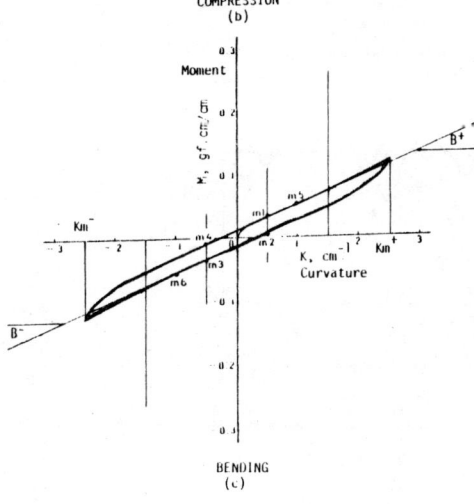

Moment

BENDING
(c)

Fig. 2

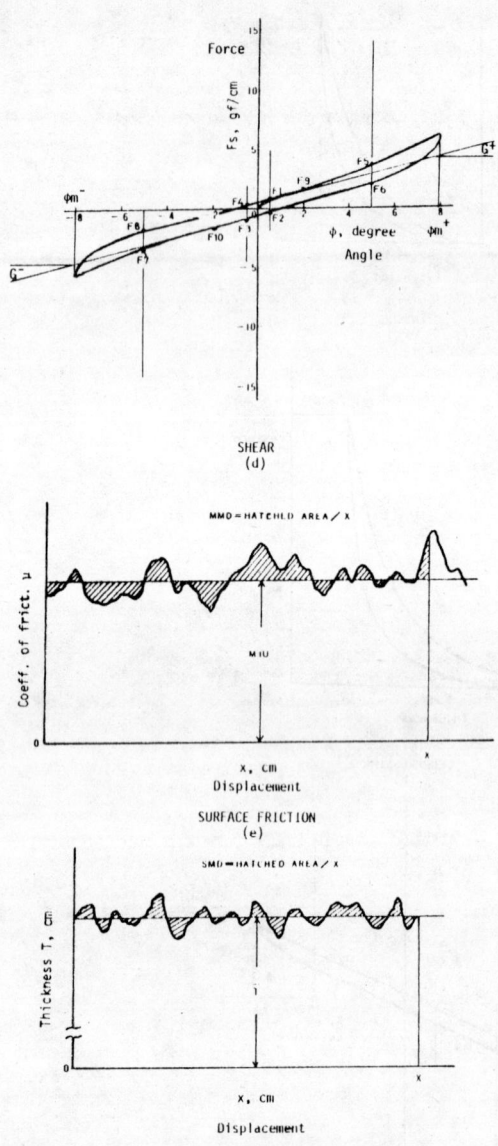

SHEAR
(d)

SURFACE FRICTION
(e)

SURFACE ROUGHNESS
(f)

Fig. 2 (Cont..)

Input and Output Peripherals

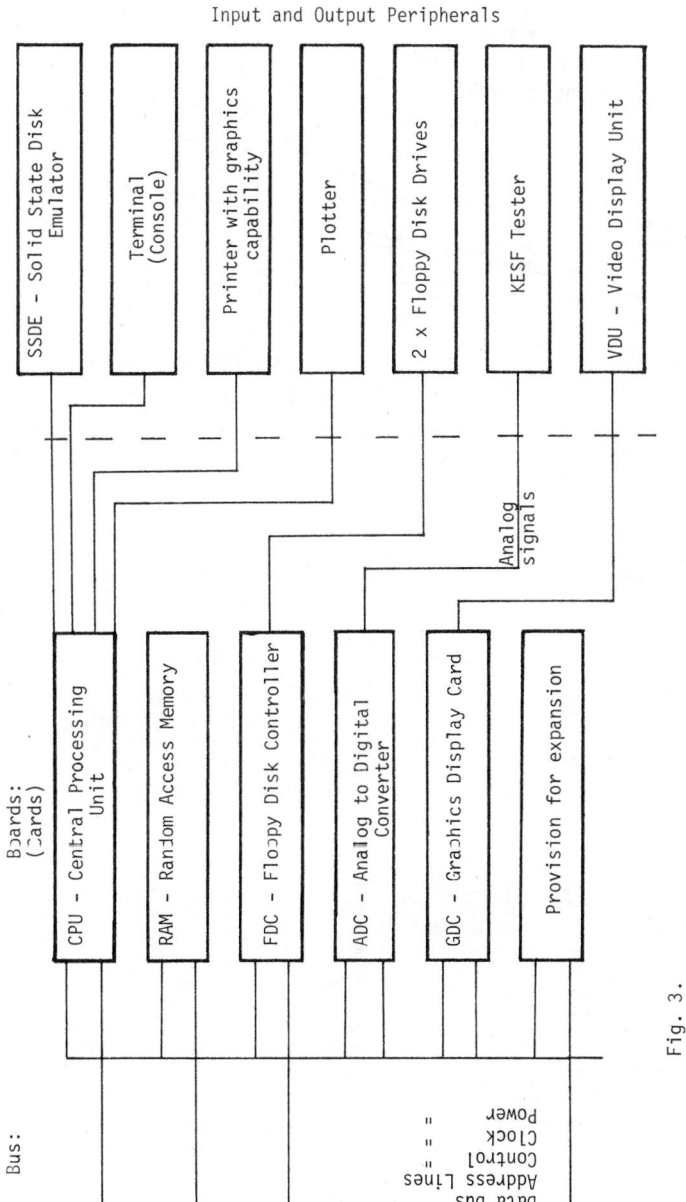

Fig. 3.

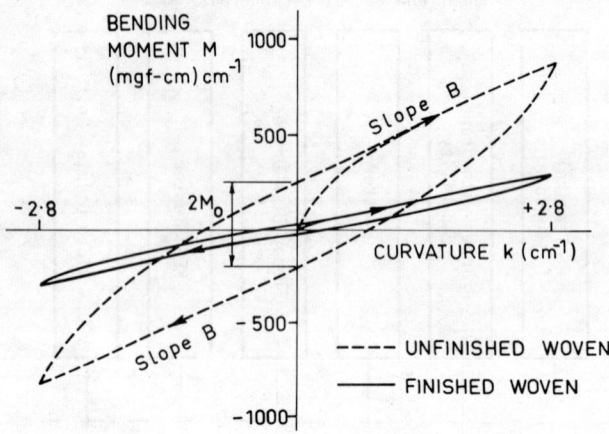

Fig. 4

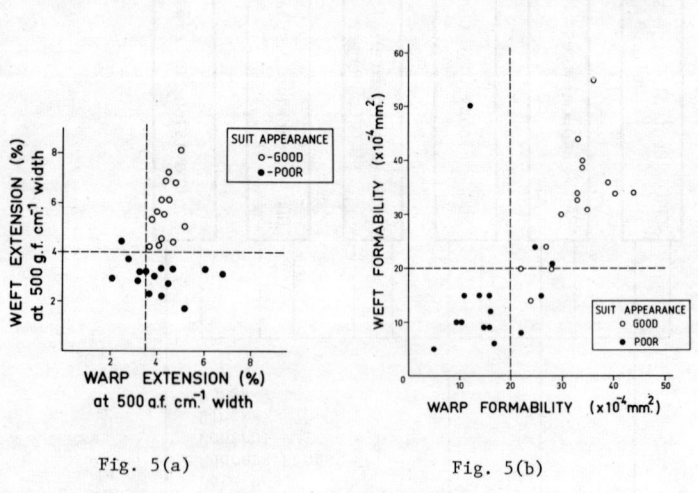

Fig. 5(a)   Fig. 5(b)

FROM CORE TO HEX
COMPUTERS IN A TEST HOUSE SITUATION

W.B.Sykes

ABSTRACT

The New Zealand Wool Testing Authority operates
eight objective measurement laboratories situated
in each of New Zealand's wool selling centres.
A network of WANG 2200MVP computers links the
various laboratories and provides test result
input, communications and printing facilities in
the centre closest to where each client resides.
The computer is also used for calculation,
analytical, costing and on line automatic
accounting purposes. Since its implementation in
1980 the current system has become an essential
part of the Authorities operation and has
resulted in a significant increase in accuracy,
efficiency and particularly speed of
documentation and delivery. The paper describes
the hardware configuration, reasons for its
selection, the relative merits of the approach
taken, the software and personnel requirements
and comments on future upgrading and expansion.
An exciting project involving direct input from
laboratory balances with automatic test number
identification is also covered in some detail.

Finally a look into the short, medium and long
term future includes a view of what might be in
2, 5 or even 10 yrs hence.

1. INTRODUCTION

New Zealand is a relatively small agricultural
country with a population of 3.3 million people
and some 70 million sheep. Each year we export
approx 300,000 tonnes of wool some greasy some
scoured. Export earnings total approx $1000
million and account for a significant percentage
of our total export earnings. It follows that the
wool industry is therefore a most important part
of the New Zealand economy.

2. ABOUT NEW ZEALAND WOOL TESTING AUTHORITY

New Zealand Wool Testing Authority (hereafter referred to as NZWTA) was set up under act of Parliament in 1964 to provide independent objective measurement of wool as a service to both Brokers selling on behalf of the Growers (or Farmers) & Buyers.(Actually the term Buyer is now something of a misnomer, since Wool buyers originally were merely agents for overseas principals and acted on their instructions. Todays approach is that they buy mainly on their own account and 'blend' and 'allocate' to meet overseas orders. Thus their function has altered and they are now known more correctly as 'Wool Exporters'.)

NZWTA is funded entirely from fees paid for services rendered and is not subsidised by Government or any other body.

Originally yield and mean fibre diameter (fineness) testing was carried out 'postsale' (i.e. on behalf of the Buyer, after he had bought the wool).Samples were drawn according to IWTO regulations from each bale in a parcel purchased then blended and tested in one of the NZWTA testing laboratories. The advent of Presale Testing, where each lot is tested prior to being offered for sale, has put a whole new complexion on the situation. In fact the South Island Laboratory situated in Christchurch was built especially to handle high volume Presale testing. For those unsure of what Yield Testing is all about may I refer you to the extract of the publication 'Why Test Wool' included as appendix 1.

Wool Sales are held and brokers reside at eight different centres spread through out the length and breadth of New Zealand. In addition, NZWTA offers Condition Testing facilities at each of its laboratories, thus providing accurate moisture content measurement of mainly scoured wool.
From reference to the Map of New Zealand (see over page) it will be apparent that yield testing will be carried out in either Wellington or Christchurch for clients residing in any of the eight centres and that condition testing will be carried out in any centre for clients who may reside in that or any other of the eight centres. This means that good communications are an absolutely vital part of our entire operation.

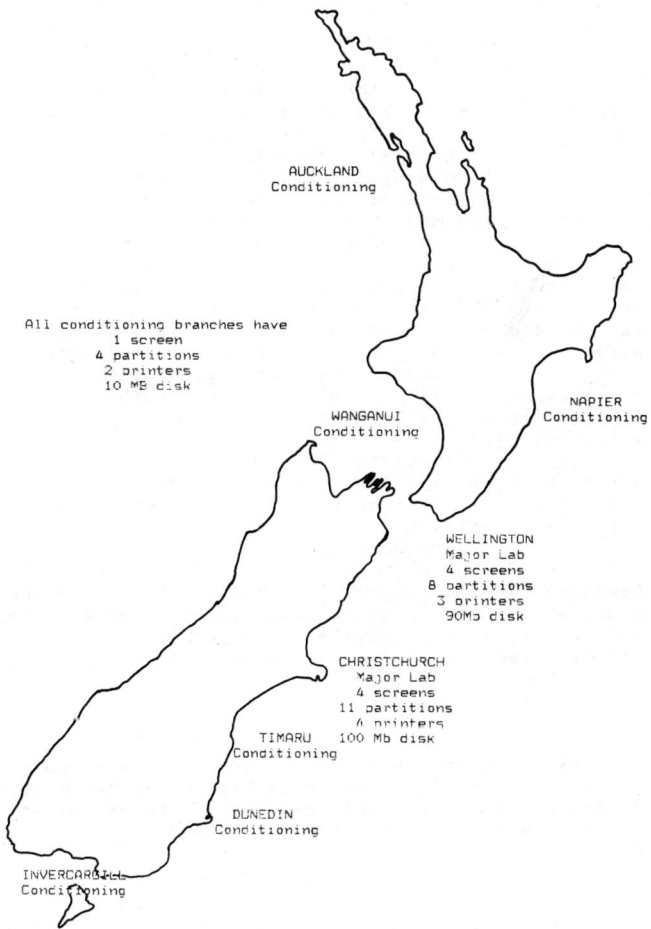

AUCKLAND
Conditioning

All conditioning branches have
1 screen
4 partitions
2 printers
10 MB disk

WANGANUI
Conditioning

NAPIER
Conditioning

WELLINGTON
Major Lab
4 screens
8 partitions
3 printers
90Mb disk

CHRISTCHURCH
Major Lab
4 screens
11 partitions
6 printers
100 Mb disk

TIMARU
Conditioning

DUNEDIN
Conditioning

INVERCARGILL
Conditioning

3. HARDWARE

At the time of establishing the South Island
Laboratory in 1980 NZWTA decided after in depth
consideration to upgrade its existing Burroughs
computer facilities by purchasing seven almost
identical WANG 2200 MVP computers — identical
that is except in number of terminals hence
supporting memory. The smallest centre Wanganui
(see map) was not included at that stage but was
added to the network last year. Each centre has

>1 Central Processing unit
>1 to 4 Visual Display units
>2 to 4 Printers
>10 to 100 Mbytes of on line disk storage
>communication driver

Each computer runs identical software, all
written in house by our E.D.P. section situated
in Christchurch, and operates in a stand alone
mode. Twice a day (but more often if necessary)
each centre communicates with each other centre
and transfers files between one another — at
other times each computer works entirely
independently

>—inputing basic data and results
for printing at its own centre or elsewhere.
>—printing certificates for presale,
postsale, condition or other testing
>—various other tasks.

Because of the quite remarkable ability of the
WANG 2200 MVP it is quite practical for more data
to be input or received via communications (
'comms' for short) even whilst printing is going
on. This 'distributed processing' approach is
relatively unusual. It is exceptionally
efficient, gives a good measure of equipment
backup & redundancy and does not rely on
permanent leased lines nor a true host computer
as such. It is also possible for either major
laboratory to access the other's computer direct
in the event of major hardware failure.

4. PERSONNEL REQUIREMENTS

At present approximately 12 people are directly involved in data processing and the 'output' of the system, our Certificates printed, would total some 160,000 per annum. Each certificate takes some 36 secs to print its 1500 or so characters.
If Certificates were typed (and as legal documents they must be typed error free) it has been estimated that 10 times as many people would be required and the task would be boring and stressfull to say the least.

Even more people would be required to carry out the calculations which would then need to be rechecked. Even checking the typed certificates would be much more time consuming than the cursory glance and quick scan necessary with the computer prepared copy. The system has the ability to produce actual Brokers Wool Sale Catalogues and where Brokers use these, their work involved in checking of Catalogues against Certificates received is very much reduced.

5. HOW IT WORKS

The system carries out a number of tasks as follows

      1.   Wool Test Work
      2.   Analysis - Technical and Calibration
      3.   Real   Time   Online   Automatic
Accounting
      4.   Miscellaneous Tasks

1.Wool Test Work.

Reference to 'Why Test Wool' will indicate that in yield testing the following is a brief description of what occurs -

    Weigh Sample
    Blend Sample
    Weigh Sample
    Subsample
    Weigh both Subsamples
    Scour (i.e. wash) subsamples
    Dry each subsample
    Weigh each subsample
    Subsample further
    Weigh it 3 times
    Soxhlet Extraction
    Weigh Extractables
    Combustion
    Weigh Ash
    Treat for alkali insolubles
    Weigh alkali insolubles
    Analyser processing
    Weigh micron subsamples
    Measure   mean   fibre   diameter   (airflow
technique)

526

As the sample proceeds through the laboratory various weighing tasks are carried out and the results are written by lab staff on to test cards (in some cases to a readability of 1 milligram). Meanwhile the basic data has been entered into the computer with information as regards Broker, Sale date, Lot number, no of bales, bale weights issue centre etc. The test data 'batch by batch' not test by test is handed into the office where it is keyed into the computer by the operators.

As all test data is received it is subject to checks for scale, value and variation so that a continuing check on the data generated by the laboratory is maintained. Suspicious data is immediately signalled to the attention of the production team for investigation.

Once all test data for a particular test is present the computer calculates wool base, V.M. base etc and if within specified tolerances passes to the printfile if it is to be issued locally or on to comms if(as is usual) the certificate is to be remotely printed. If subsample variation is too great or range limits are exceeded the complete test is repeated using some of the wool sample originally kept i.e. the keeper. Next comms will send the calculated data to the printing centre, shortly afterwards the certificate will be printed and delivered direct to the client. Some days could see upwards of 300 certificates printed in a branch manned by as few as two people. Generally a highly efficient, fast and error free system of which we are all quite proud.

5.1.1 Printing

Each branch has at least 2 dot matrix printers, 120 cps or 220 cps. A background partition i.e. part of memory without a terminal permanently attached controls the printing of Red or Green Certificates or Reports. Plain paper as also used for some tasks.
The file is scanned for all suitable certificates and reports to be printed, then after printing each out the various files are updated. The test data is then either filed locally if appropriate, or else it is put back on to the Comms file to 'go back home',and deleted from the print file. In this way the test data always comes back home and resides in the branch where the test was carried out , but a record of where and when it has been printed is also kept.. As mentioned elsewhere, printing 300 certificates per day would often be achieved in a single branch.

5.1.2 Communications

At first glance our communications setup is
unimpressive. A standard dial type telephone and
a 1200 bps half duplex modem are the only outward
sign of a quite clever system. The speed chosen
is quite deliberately "slow but reliable". We
have avoided the temptation to go to the "state
of the art" when it seems to us that there would
be little cost advantage and quite probably a
number of 'teething troubles' to contend with.
Remembering that our branch laboratories are
spread far and wide, we have opted for the tried
and true datel. Perhaps the devil you know
instead of the devil you don't would be more a
appropriate description.

In operation the comms file is scanned to pickup
any tests for a nominated centre, then the
operator dials an ordinary STD toll call, once
answered and pleasantries exchanged between
operators both modems are manually switched over.
The first record transmitted each way confirms
that the centres are correct i.e. that both
confirm who is sending to whom. The data
transmission then proceeds with any parity,
framing or other errors creating an error signal
at the receiving end. At the end of transmission
the error array is returned to the sending centre
and then only those tests not appearing in the
error array are then deleted from the comms file.
Any others are left to be sent again next contact.

5.2.   Technical Analysis and Calibration

The computers ability at number crunching, file
scanning, etc makes it an ideal tool for
analytical, calibration and similar mathematical
and statistical tasks. It is also used for
interlaboratory trials, productivity analysis &
similar work.

5.3.   Automatic Accounting

A major advantage of a distributed processing
approach is our Automatic Accounting System. As
each certificate is printed an invoice is raised,
a statement entry created and a detailed analysis
of the test i.e. Format,No of bales, Weight etc
is captured at the printing centre.

In addition sampling charges to be passed on to
the client are also included. Next morning these
detailed statistics based on certificates printed
are sent on comms to Christchurch where all are
married to give management an overall view of day
to day operation. Meanwhile each Branch is
building up its 'Local Statement File' with
charges for all Certificates printed during the
month.   On the evening of the last working day of
each month the contents of each branches Local
Statement File is sent to Christchurch and for
safety to Wellington,(after taking a local hard
copy printout in case of disaster).This is akin
to wearing a belt and braces and keeping one hand
in your pocket as a final safety precaution. Each
Local Statement File, month to date autostats
file etc is then cleaned out ready to start the
new month next day.
Meanwhile in Christchurch a merged statement
file is prepared overnight — statements are
printed and agents charges are determined and
printed out. I should like to be able to say that
these statements are then simply mailed out to
clients.   Unfortunately this is only almost true.
Garbage in — garbage out means that a Duplicate
charge check is necessary. i.e. each entry from
all around the country (& there could be 5000
individual records) must be compared with each
other entry to catch any duplicated charges
(caused by certificates being printed more than
once for whatever reason).This also checks
opening balances, monthly receipts etc. These
totals are all checked BEFORE statements are
mailed. In practice we usually manage to mail
statements on the 2nd or 3rd working day of each
month with payment due on 20th of month. A
schedule of agents charges 'passed on' is
produced at the same time — it is intended that a
more general use will be made of this schedule
but at the moment this is used to merely check
off agents charges to us. A neat trick though is
that fully half our agents wait for our schedule
to be made available to our branches on or about
the 1st of each month, then use it to create
their invoices .

The computer held merged statement file contains
a wealth of information from which is extracted
Statement Based Statistics (which are compared
with the daily autostats) and various management
reports - Credits, Debits, Deletions. Because
the computer charges every certificate printed
regardless, it was necessary to provide a
mechanism whereby charges could be deleted. This
can be done at the printing centre whereupon the
computer keeps on the record who deleted the
charge and why - this record is carried right
through the system and the Deletion report gives
the information back to management. Various
balancing techniques are used to ensure that
every test processed is accounted for in some
way. The ability also exists to reinstate a
previously deleted charge either in the branch or
later on - administratively.

Normal Trade Creditors invoices are entered into
the computer as they are received (not batched at
month end) then on the 20th of each month the
computerised cheques are written,Purchase
register, Payment listings,Cheque Register and
code analysis are all produced. Note that we pay
on invoice, invoice by invoice, not on the
creditors statements. Expenses are also analysed
branch by branch and compared with budgets month
by month and year to date.
By using an 'engineering' real time approach
rather that an 'accounting' batch type, the
database built up has many uses not to say
significant advantages. As the raw information
itself is kept in the computer for the whole
financial year reprocessing is in fact quite
simple.

5.4 Miscellaneous Tasks

A number of miscellaneous tasks are also carried
out. For example close track is kept of all tests
as they proceed through the laboratory. A daily
report is produced ,on demand, which shows
exactly how far through the process all current
tests have progressed,and a status of each
relevant test in the laboratory is reported back
to the branch each morning.
Messages can be sent to any other branch by means
of our Postbag system. We also have an Electronic
Diary into which reminders can be entered years
ahead if necessary. These reminders are then
printed out over night and are on the recipients
desk next morning.

5.4.1   Overnight Tasks

In each of the branches the computer cpu is left
running all the time, but screens,disk drives etc
are all run down and turned off each night.
However in Wellington and Christchurch this is
not possible because the computer works all
night. As previously mentioned it prints out
Datex messages, Scour Advices, Certificates to
print,and Daily reports etc — all unattended.

In both these major labs the disk drive and cpu
are housed in an air conditioned room, but in the
branches the ordinary office environment has
proved acceptable.

In Christchurch our computer room is monitored
for flame directly to the local fire brigade and
for power fail,smoke or over temperature by
Seekers Answering Service. Should any of these
last three occur Seekers will find myself, my
staff or someone in authority to advise of the
mishap if necessary by means of calling the
pocket beeper I always carry.

6. COMBINATIONS

The rapid increase in presale testing has meant
that on saleday, yield and micron information is
already held on either Christchurch or Wellington
computer for the majority of wool sold. Buyers
(or Exporters) can then request a 'combination'
of any number of lots. The computer accesses the
'component parts'(if not available locally it
obtains them from the other centre — any one of
the 100,000 tests live at any one time in each
centre can be found and accessed in just over 1
second) then mathematically combines the results
showing the range of input values as well as the
mean value. It passes the results to the
appropriate printing centre as previously
described. This service can be as fast as 10 mins
from request to certificate printed — actual
delivery could well be the longest delay in the
whole process.

Perhaps this might be an appropriate time to
introduce *KATIE* (Keyfile Access Technique
Including Extras).

This file handing procedure is quite remarkable.
It works on the basis that each test is unique
and there can be only one set of records for any
one test i.e. there can be no duplicates. There
is a keyfile associated with each data file and a
specific algorithm associated with each keyfile.
When writing a new record the file is checked
first to see that it does not yet contain a test
of the same number. If it does the incoming
overwrites the old — if not, a new spot is
allocated. What is so remarkable is that for any
given Test No and algorithm there can be one and
only one 'bucket' in which that key can be found
(or put)!. There is no point in searching more
of the file — it won't be there! To search up to
200,000 individual random records, find the
correct one or report that it is not there takes
about a second. This highly efficient file
handler was especially written for NZWTA and is
the basis of all our file operation.

7. DATEX

The N.Z. Post Office which provides all
telephone, telegraph and data communication
within New Zealand offer as one of their services
a 300 b.p.s. full duplex datex system which
allows computer to computer two way communication
in much the same way as the conventional telex
operates, but at the same charge i.e. 6 times
faster for the same fee. What is more, they
provide an automatic Datex/Telex interworking
buffer enabling any telex in the world to be
accessed by our computer network.

This has many advantages.

(a). Instead of one telex machine we can
input messages from any of our 17 terminals, yet
the actual rental is based on only one line.

(b). Information on computer calculated
results can be sent directly without operator
intervention thus reducing errors caused by
keying in.

(c). The actual sending does not require an
operator (although urgent Datexes can be 'forced'
by operator action), so that if the called number
is ABS or OCC etc then the computer 'tries again'
later.

(d). As the time of entering and the time of
sending are logged within the computer, cost
analysis is easily achieved.

What happens in essence, is that messages entered
from the key board or automatically within the
machine, are kept on a Datex file. Every half hour
- day and night -this file is automatically
scanned and any datexes 'not yet sent' are tried
(again). At midnight each night a printout of all
datexes sent that day is produced together with
the time of entry and the time of actual sending.

8. DATA LOGGING

A most exciting step forward is the introduction into our South Island Laboratory of Direct Balance Input to the Computer, known to us as data logging. It is expected that it should be operational towards the end of September and at the time of writing this report there seems to be no reason why this deadline should not be met.

From earlier information given, it will be clear that virtually all our input is "weight" (or mass for the purist) formerly read off balances, written down on to a card with Test No preprinted, then keyed into a computer terminal. Obviously having high quality milligram balances with a computer compatible output is half the battle but unless Test No, subsample and test type are known, having the weight available is really of little use.

Considerable experimental effort resulted in a decision to opt for a system based on Optical Character Recognition with a set of human and computer plainly recognisable figures on each test card.

The laboratory technician weighs the sample or residual as before but instead of writing the figure down merely inserts the preprinted cards into a slot adjacent to the balance. This action reads the Test No.,Subsample No. and test type, sends this information to the computer and triggers the adjacent balance which sends the weight (i.e. its reading). As far as the computer itself is concerned there is little difference between figures received this way and those entered via the keyboard.

One area of concern by our operations people is that with Data Logging nothing is written down and thus readings could perhaps become 'lost somewhere in the innards of the beast'. We have therefore arranged that the first thing the incoming data does is to get printed out on a simple OKI printer in the Computer Room. It is our fervent hope and desire that this printout will never be needed but it is there just in case. In similar vein our WANG 2200 MVP computer has proved to be an exceptionally reliable unit and there have been something like only 2 cpu failures in the last 3 years. However years of experience have taught me to expect that approx 1 week after we become utterly reliant on the machine to read incoming data it will fail probably drastically and certainly at the most embarrassing time.

if, however, a separate independent computer has been made available to cope with this eventuality it will never be needed. Of these options, I for one much prefer the latter and for this reason a small WANG Professional Computer (P.C. for short) has been installed in what might be called backup mode. That is, it is not normally connected to the logging system in any way, but if for any reason (including Preventative Maintenance) the 2200 is 'down' a simple 1 plug changeover would keep the lab working until the 2200 is up and running again. Hopefully this will never be needed either.

9. THE ELECTRIC TYPEWRITER SYNDROME

Since upgrading to our current system NZWTA has become very dependent on computerisation,and the hardware chosen has proved to be a wise choice, if somewhat expensive. The policy of in house software and innovative development has been highly sucessful . However, old habits die hard and the conservatives find new ways hard to swallow. Even now I sometimes accuse my colleagues of 'using the computer as a typewriter' i.e. do all the work by hand & pocket calculator then feeding the result into the computer to have it printed out wherever required. Perhaps this conservatism is industry wide.e.g This paper was, as you would expect, prepared on our WANG Word processor with drafts corrected many times — but, word processed documents were not really acceptable for this conference so after final copy was printed it should have been retyped. There was however simply no time to comply so here you are, a paper printed on a word processor!- there must be a moral in this story somewhere.

10. A PEEK INTO THE FUTURE

Crystal ball gazing is a pastime fraught with
danger but I would expect that within two years
a general increase in operating speeds assisted
by Data Logging techniques to allow even better
service to clients at probably very little
increase in costs in real terms. Within this
time it is likely that results will be able to
be sent directly to clients computers anywhere
in the world.

Within 5 years there may be a clearing house
type operation where Buyers, Brokers, Test
House, Wool Board etc would all pass information
computer to computer and our prime document of
today our Certificate may no longer even be
required.
Certainly it would be expected that increasing
use of automation within the laboratories will
lead to further use of the computers in
production control.

A ten year view is much more difficult to
predict. A whole new generation of computers may
be available. The Textile Industry itself may
well be completely different, wool testing may
be only a part of a much wider range of textile
testing work for us — who knows?
However, it is completely predictable that
computers in a test house will not only be, as
today, a fundamental link in the testing process
but the focus of all data collection and
transmission

Sykes

ACKNOWLEDGEMENTS

The author wishes to thank the board & General Manager of NZWTA for the permission to present this paper and all those who have contributed to making the presentation possible.

Excerpts from
WHY TEST WOOL
PUBLISHED BY NEW ZEALAND WOOL TESTING AUTHORITY

Because in a package of unprocessed wool (called a bale), there is wool plus moisture plus grease, suint and sweat, dirt and burr (called vegetable matter).

This varies according to how clean the pastures are, the amount of feed, variation in climate and the breed of sheep.

In the old days Wool Buyers had to guess the amount of pure wool in a bale. By:

Eye
Feel
Smell
Experience

Obviously, it is very difficult to guess, so for accurate assessment we measure the Wool Content.

METHOD

1. Sample the Greasy Wool with a core tube.

2. Blend the wool to ensure a representative sample.

3. Weigh out two sub-samples each of 150 grams. Keep 600 grams in case of retest required later.

4. Wash the wool to remove as much grease, suint/sweat and dirt as possible.

5. Then dry to a constant weight so we then have a greasy weight of 150 grams less impurities lost in washing, say 50 grams, i.e.. 67% of wool oven dry plus vegetable matter plus some residual grease/dirt etc.

6. Then we divide the oven dry sample into parts for further testing.

538

PART 1. We burn the wool away to get dirt
content.

PART 2a. We dissolve the wool in caustic soda to
isolate the burrs.

PART 2b. After we isolate the burrs we dry them
and weigh them.

PART 3. We treat the wool with alcohol to
extract the grease remaining after washing.

So we had original unprocessed wool (called
greasy wool)
LESS   Grease, suint, sweat and dirt
removed by
    washing (called scouring).

LESS   moisture when we dried the washed
wool.

LESS   remaining dirt when we burnt the
wool
              away (called ashing).

LESS   vegetable matter (burr) when we
              dissolved the wool.

LESS   remaining grease when we treated
the
wool with alcohol.

We are left with pure wool content (called Wool
Base).

We also test wool for Micron. This is the thickness of the fibre. The thickness is related to softness and end use, i.e.. a thin wool can be made into a fine yarn and then into tight woven cloth. A thick wool can be used for knitting and carpet yarns.

WHAT MAKES WOOL THICK OR THIN?

Some breeds of sheep produce thick fibres (called coarse).
BREEDING
Some breeds produce thin fibres (called fine).

If sheep are well fed then fibres tend to be
coarser.
CLIMATIC CONDITIONS
If sheep are not well fed then fibres tend to be finer.

In the old days buyers used to look at how curly the wool was.
The Buyer would look at the wool and guess the degree of fineness or coarseness. Fine wool is worth more money than coarse wool.

We do an accurate test by measuring the average fibre thickness (called diameter). This is done by use of a machine known as an Airflow. It measures accurately the thickness of the fibres by air resistance on a specially prepared 2.5 gram sample.

EXAMPLE: If you have a given weight of fly wire and the same weight of thick wire mesh.The fly wire will have much more resistance to the flow of air than the thick wire mesh will.
We call our measurement Micron. One micron is a millionth of a metre.

W. B. Sykes
New Zealand Wool Testing Authority
Wellington 1
NEW ZEALAND

ADAPTATION OF A STANDARD MANUFACTURING DATA BASE
A.T. Teller

ABSTRACT

This paper is addressed mainly to those textile companies who
are considering the acquisition of a general purpose manufacturing package but fear that some of their special requirements could not be properly handled by it. Two textile
related requirements for adapting a standard production
package are described. They involve the addition of data to
the files managed by the package and of new functions to be
performed on the new and original data. These examples are
used as a starting basis to treat the problem in general
terms: a checklist aimed at assessing the constraints
involved is presented and used to suggest customization
methods.

1. INTRODUCTION

Industex (Pty) Ltd is a South African company with a long
track record in the manufacturing of industrial fabrics and
yarns. The range of its products encompasses tyre cord, belt
duck fabrics, solid woven fabrics, filter fabrics, hose duck,
as well as consumer and industrial yarns.

In 1983, the company decided to computerize its production
processes in order to provide its managers with better
management information. The fastest way of achieving this
objective is to go the package way. However, production
packages tailored to the needs of a textile environment are
far from being numerous. This is why it was decided to select
a general purpose production package, namely PACS, that would
be at the same time reliable and sophisticated so as to cater
for a vast range of requirements. The selected software
proved moreover to be flexible enough to allow customization
in those areas where the standard features are not suitable.
Industex is currently taking advantage of this facility.
However, this paper aims at more generality and will attempt
to show how one can adapt a standard production control
package to specific manufacturing requirements by adding files
and programs on to it.

Although the following example is based on PACS and on the
manufacture of industrial fabrics, it is hoped that the
underlying principles will prove of a more general value, and
suggest a method of assessing the suitability of a production
package to their needs.

2. THE STANDARD FEATURES OF A PRODUCTION CONTROL PACKAGE

It is assumed here that the basic concepts of production
control are known. There are many textbooks on the subject.
Reference (1) is quoted as an example.

All production packages maintain, under one name or another, a

"manufacturing data base", i.e. a set of related files
describing the goods manufactured and the processes through
which raw materials and/or purchased parts are transformed
into finished goods.

This manufacturing data base will be the source of all
information processing carried out by the package, e.g.
Inventory Control, Standard Costing, Material Requirements
Planning (MRP), Capacity Planning. The forementioned data
base will classically include files such as: Production
Master file, Bills of Material (BOM), Work centre description,
Routings, etc.

Fig.1 represents some of the files making up the PACS
Manufacturing Data Base and their relationships.

3. REQUIREMENTS FOR CUSTOMIZATION

There are several areas where customized features are
desirable, but, at an early stage of implementation, two only
are considered: the first one is related to weaving only,
whereas the second one is of interest to both spinning and
weaving.

3.1 Management of product related data

The package being a general purpose one, it would not include
fields specific to managing the production of particular types
of goods. Industrial fabrics are however characterized by
product specifications and technical data having a direct
bearing on the manufacturing process (See Fig.2). It would
therefore be useful to push the computerization process one
step further by also storing the specification data in
computer file(s) in a structured way.

The advantages of this are easy to understand:

- Each fabric specification is stored and maintained
  centrally while being accessible to Sales, Production,
  Quality Control, Research and Development and Marketing

- Storage in a structured field format rather than in a free
  format allows comparisons between different fabrics. It
  also allows "specification matching", i.e. search for the
  manufactured item(s) which are closest to a new
  specification.

- The inclusion in the system of such specific data as number
  of picks per unit length, yarn weight, etc. allows a
  computation by programs of the raw material contents of the
  fabric, which is required anyway by the Product Structure
  file describing the Bill of Material. The use of the
  computer to generate this information ensures consistency
  between the various fields describing the item.

- The specification data and technical data can be used to
  generate the "production charts" used by the production
  managers to summarize the technical aspects of

manufacturing. It can also be used to generate the shop
paperwork accompanying each order for a given fabric: the
standard Bill of Material would give information on the
material contents of the fabric expressed in kg, which is a
useful unit accounting-wise, but on the shop floor, the
number of bobbins, together with the beam width, RP, etc.
are more meaningful.

When looking at the information recorded on specification
sheets (Fig.2), one realizes that it can be broken down into
sets relating to the various levels of the bill of material of
a fabric as shown on Fig.3.

Not surprisingly, most of the information will be stored in
the bespoke files. Information on the standard package files
would include:-
- part number and description, minimum process quantity,
  specification issue number and date of issue in Part Master
  file
- product structure and quantity of each component used in
  parent part in Product Structure file (Bill of Material)
- reed and beam characteristicsin Tooling Master and Tooling
  Bill files
- type of weave in Drawing Master and Drawing Bill files

The other data, broken down at Fabric, Warp, Weft and Yarn
level are summarized in Table I.

Fabric data
Type of materials used in Warp(s) and Weft
Material contents used in Warp(s) and Weft
Global characteristics and tolerances: Weight
                                         Gauge
                                         Tensile
                                         Elongation @ break
                                         Fabric width
Weaving data: Selvedges
               Fabric identification

Warp data: Threads /10cm and tolerance
            Crimp
            Number of layers
            Number of bobbins
            Roll length
Weft data: Picks /10cm and tolerance
            Crimp
            RP

Plied Yarn data
Characteristics (1 to 3 different sets of records)
                Yarn code (pointing to BOM)
                Number of plies
                Twist per metre and tolerance
                S/Z (twist)
Yarn data: Tex
            Material
            Single yarn twist

Table I

One can see that there is a strong link between the additional data listed in Table I and the PACS files because the way this additional data is structured hinges on the fabric bill of material stored in the PACS Product Structure File.

3.2 Management of Cost Related Data

Most manufacturing packages have a costing module allowing the computation of the cost of the parts present on the Part Master File. One of the main components of the cost of a part is the cost of labour, i.e. the machine run time per manufactured unit multiplied by the machine cost per unit of time. In the case of both Spinning and Weaving, the machine run time per manufactured unit is determined by fairly complex formulas involving both the part under consideration and the type of machine used to manufacture it. When the variety of manufactured parts and of textile machines is large, it can be useful to have a program to compute this machine run time for each combination of product and machine described in the Routing File. Such a program would ensure that this element of the product cost is computed without errors and is consistent with the part (described in the Part Master File) and the machine(s) (described in the Work Centre File) used to produce it.

4. ANALYSIS OF THE SITUATION

The two requirements described above are typical of two types of problems one might encounter when trying the customize a package:-

- in the first case (3.1), there is a need for adding new fields to the existing files supplementing the information already provided by the package and for new or enhanced programs handling the new fields.

- in the second case (3.2), there is a need for one or several new programs to carry out additional processing on data already stored by the package, more specifically to ensure that various fields are consistent with one another, according to rules not taken into consideration by the initial programs.

The way one goes about solving these two problems is deeply influenced by the answers to the following questions:-

4.1 Are the files of the package under the control of a Data Base Management System (DBMS)?

If a DBMS is used, new fields can be added to the existing Data Base without affecting the existing programs. If no DBMS is used, then it may be necessary to modify the programs or to create additional files linked to the existing ones through the relevant keys, which involves obviously more work than in the previous case.

The options related to this question are straightforward and will not be treated any further here.

4.2 Is the user of the package authorized to modify it?

Even if the package may be customized, we shall assume that the user wants to modify his package as little as possible, because a package is always better left untouched for maintenance purposes and it is more practical to write new programs when most of the fields to be processed are not stored in the original files, or not part of the original data base. If the package cannot be modified, there is no other solution than to create new programs generating results which are completely separate although they may partly rely upon information managed by the package.

4.3 What are the response time requirements when it comes to updating information managed by the package with new transactions?

The situation may require on-line updating or be adequately handled with a daily batch job.

4.4 Does the package provide a standard interface aimed at allowing communications with other systems?

By standard interface, we mean a file of a given format that can be read by programs of the package and written by external programs.

Most of the time, this facility applies only to transfers of data in batch mode. The architecture of PACS however allows on-line communication with its standard interface file. The exact nature of the interface must obviously be ascertained in each case.

4.5 Is the user willing to have package data directly updated by bespoke programs, either on-line or in batch mode?

We assume that the user will be most reluctant to answer this question positively in an on-line environment because of the danger this represents to data integrity, and will also avoid it in batch mode, except in the cases where the validity of the operation can easily be ascertained.

4.6 What are the features of the package that can be used to facilitate communications with other systems?

For instance, if the package logs all the transactions of the day on a file accessible to the user, this transaction file can be read by bespoke programs to propagate events in the package to other systems.

5. CHOICE OF A CUSTOMIZATION METHOD

When combining the situations corresponding to the answers to
the previous questions, one obtains relatively few cases: as
said above, the DBMS question is left out, we have made an
assumption regarding the answer to question 4.5, and some
combinations are redundant or not relevant.

Table II summarizes the cases to be considered.

| | Answers to Questions | | | Solution | Fig. |
Case	4.2	4.3	4.4	4.5		No.
1	-	daily batch	YES	-	standard interface	4a
2	NO	daily batch	NO	NO	manual transfer	4b
3	-	on-line	YES	NO	(standard interface)	(4a)
4	YES	daily batch	NO	-	?	
5	YES	on-line	-	YES	interface file	4c

Table II

5.1 Case 1

Case 1 is very simple and actually applies to the problems
described in paragraph 3: a daily batch job is sufficient,
PACS can be freely modified by its users, and it provides an
interface under the form of a transaction file collecting all
the update requests for processing either in interactive or
batch mode.

Requirement 3.1 can be met by adding files storing the new
data and by writing new programs reading some PACS files
(Part Master, Product Structure, etc.) and the new files.

Requirement 3.2 is met by generating transactions having the
required layout and by adding them to the transaction file
for further processing by the package itself.

Fig.4a summarizes the methods used in this case.

5.2 Case 2

Case 2 represents an unpleasant situation if one is to avoid
direct updating. The following measures have to be taken to
ensure that updates to the two sets of datas are carried out
in a consistent way:

- Fields that should be updated on the package files are
  simply listed in special reports; the printed information
  is then to be transferred manually through the data entry
  programs of the package.

  It must be noted that this solution is acceptable only
  when the volume of data involved is not too large.

- The method of manual transfer described above not being
  foolproof, it is useful to have one or several additional
  programs to check the consistency of the two sets of
  files, i.e. to check that related records are added and
  deleted together, and that fields related to one another
  by formulas have compatible values. The output is again
  only in printed form and requests a human intervention.
  Such programs are always useful in complex systems as a
  means of double-checking the validity of the data they
  maintain.

This method has a weakness as far as data integrity is
concerned: this is the price to be paid for not altering the
package. However, in the fluctuating environment of
business, the maintenance of a Manufacturing Data Base will
almost always require a Data Administrator who can take in
his stride the transfer of results to the package files and
the correction of erroneous data detected by the validity
checks.

If batch updating by bespoke programs is considered
acceptable, then a less tedious solution is at hand.

5.3 Case 3

If the standard interface caters for on-line communication,
then the situation is very close to case 1. Otherwise, there
is no solution, unless one can carry out on-line updating of
the package data in an orderly way, i.e. updating based on
recovery procedures integrated with those of the package.

5.4 Case 4

Case 4 does not lead to any definite solution: according to
circumstances it might be preferable either to modify the
package programs or to accept batch updating by bespoke
programs or to decide for a manual transfer. The factors
influencing the choice will be the difficulty of adapting the
package programs, the complexity of batch update, the volume
of data involved.

5.5 Case 5

Case 5 has been added despite the fact that some form of
direct updating is accepted. This is because it illustrates
an interesting feature: if the package can be modified, then
on-line updating of some of the package data can be simulated
without actually entailing on-line modification of the
package data by the foreign programs. This can be useful
especially when an on-line standard interface is not
available.

For instance, let us take the case where inventory levels can
be updated along two paths: one inside the package (e.g.
production of finished goods) and one outside it (sales of
the same finished goods through Order Entry).

The solution consists in creating an interface file where all
Order Entry generated movements are accumulated for all the
finished goods. The interface file, as opposed to the
standard interface, is a bespoke file with which the package
programs do not communicate before tailoring.

The relevant package programs must be made to read the
interface file as well as the package files so as to take the
update into consideration when displaying information on a
screen (in the example above, the amounts present in the
interface file must be added algebraically to the amounts in
the package file). Conversely, the relevant bespoke programs
also handling on-line the inventory levels must read the
package files concurrently with the transaction file in order
to yield the last value of the information.

The symmetry of the relationship between package and bespoke
interface file and programs can be seen on Fig.4c: each
category of program updates its own data and only reads the
other category of data.

At the end of each day, a program updates the package data,
using the contents of the interface file, and clears this
interface file for the next session.

6. CONCLUSION

This paper was aimed at showing that adapting a standard
manufacturing data base can represent a viable option in a
textile environment. If the package has a standard interface
and can be modified by its purchaser, the range of
customization strategies is very large indeed, depending on
the customer's appraisal of the various factors discussed in
section 4. If the package is non modifiable, or if the user
takes the cautious approach of not allowing bespoke programs
to update package files, there is still room for enhancements
in many instances through the implementation of manual
transfers of data and validity check programs.

ACKNOWLEDGEMENTS

The author thanks Mr R.W. Partridge, Senior Consultant, PA
computers and Telecommunications (PACTEL), for several
helpful discussions regarding the use of PACS. He also
thanks Mr R. ter Beek, Quality Control Consultant, Industex,
for many explanations concerning the technicalities of
weaving.

REFERENCES

(1) J.O. Mc Clain and L.J. Thomas. 'Operations Management',
    Prentice-Hall, Englewood Cliffs, N.J., 1980

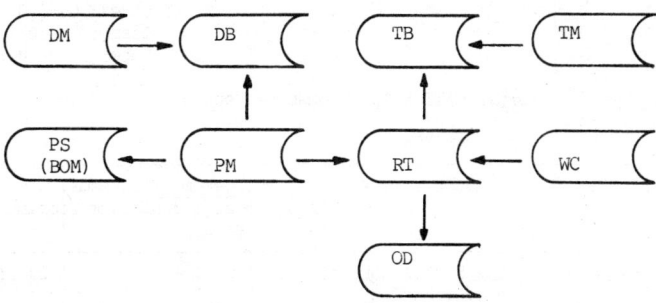

Legend: DB = Drawing Master
         DB = Drawing Bill
         TB = Tool Bill
         TM = Tool Master
         PS = Product Structure (BOM)
         PM = Part Master
         RT = Routings
         WC = Work Centre Master
         OD = Operation Description

Industex (PTY) Ltd.,
Neave township,
Port Elizabeth 6001
South Africa.

Fig.1

INDUSTEX (PTY) Ltd
PORT ELIZABETH

SABS-495-1975

Code: CC 340
Issue: No.2
Date: 11 04 84

SPECIFICATION FOR Loomstate Cotton Duck

STYLE: ....

	Material/Tex	Twist per m.			Threads! 10cm	% crimp
		Single	1st Fold	2nd Fold		
WARP	2 x 50 Tex cotton + S.A. Mix +	538Z	385S	--	182	23
WEFT	+ as warp +	--	--		140	5
WEAVE	Plain 1/1				Warp Beams	

CONTENT					
WARP	60%	Cotton: 100%	P.V.A.: ...%		
		Nylon: ...%	Polyester: ...%		
WEFT	40%	Cotton: 100%	P.V.A.: ...%		
		Nylon: ...%	Polyester: ...%		

PROPERTIES

Weight g/m2	340 + min	Fabric width mm: as ordered	
Gauge mm	+	Roll length m: 15m mim	
		130m min	
Tensile kg/cm			
WARP	18.0 + min		
WEFT	16.5 + min		
Elong/ WARP	+		
WEFT	+		

NOTE: This specification replaces issue no.1.
Reason: same yarn used for warp and weft.

Fig.2

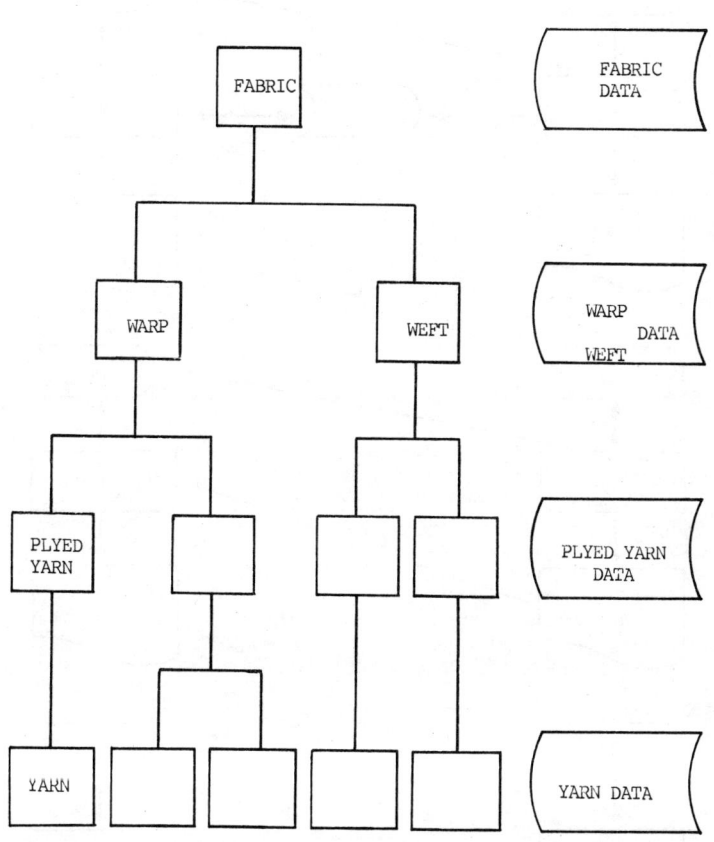

Fig.3

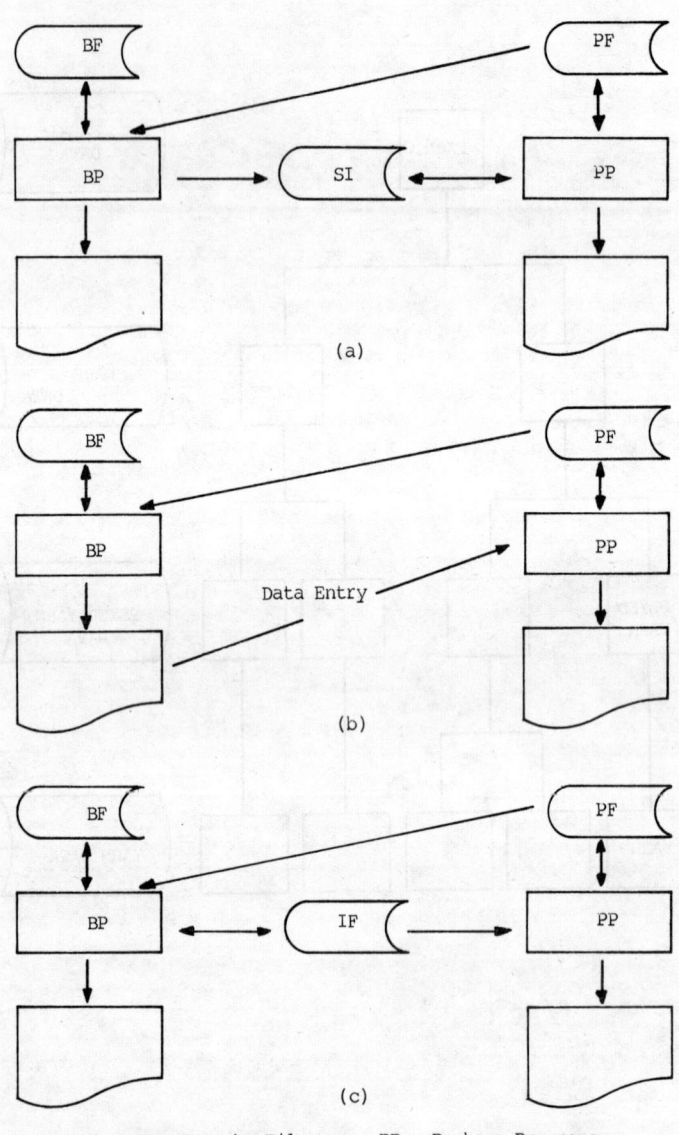

(a)

(b)

Data Entry

(c)

Legend: BF = Bespoke Files   PP = Package Programs
        PF = Package Files   SI = Standard Interface
        BP = Bespoke Programs   IF = Interface File (bespoke)

Fig.4

A STUDY OF A DISTRIBUTED MICROCOMPUTER MONITORING SYSTEM OF A WEAVING LOOM

Qian Lin Li Yu-Lai

ABSTRACT

This paper describes a two-level master/slave-distributed microcomputer monitoring system for a weaving loom, which mainly contains the following items: the fundamental function of the system, its technical and economic effects, the hardware composition of the system and its principle, and the construction of data and software. The system can easily perform real-time monitoring and data processing for 200-2000 looms by using a modular construction, which involves modular hardware consisting of the single-board microcomputer and the information station. The information station has a special method of respective multi-driving and respective multi-receiving and co-operates with the matrix-wiring mode in situ, so that this system pocessess a lot of advantages, such as savings in investment, a perfect function, high reliability, good flexibility, a remarkably economical effect, etc.

1. INTRODUCTION

In 1946, the first stored-program computer came into being. The middle 1950's saw the application of computers for scientific calculation in the textile industry. By 1965, the minicomputer was introduced, so the range of uses was expanded to business management, monitoring and controlling production step by step, in which the monitoring system for the weaving room was an early development. In the early 1970's, the microcomputer using large-scale integration (LSI) was produced. Microcomputers, characterized by smaller size, lower cost, and high reliability, have consequently been widely used in business, as well as in industry and science. The growing usage of microcomputers in the textile mill means that monitoring systems are seen in significant numbers in weaving rooms. As a management aid, this system is capable of monitoring the critical operating parameters, including running time, and recording down-time in relation to the number and reason for stops. Over the last few years, a large market for ends-down monitoring systems for winding, spinning, and open-end-spinning machines has been developed. In the past, production data in weaving room were not often in time, accurate, systematic, or complete, so that they led to some difficulty in relation to modernization of production management. This paper describes a low-level master/slave-distributed microcomputer monitoring system for a weaving loom, which may automatically acquire many kinds of data and process the data to display and print out the report. Thus the system can provide in-time, accurate, systematic, and complete data for the production management as a effective tool for modernization.

2. SYSTEM FUNCTION, TECHNICAL AND ECONOMIC EFFECTS

In general, a larger mill often possesses several hundred or even several thousand looms, so the monitoring system adopted must be a two-level master/slave-distributed microcomputer system suitable for a universal and general purpose. The master computer is an 8-bit microcomputer system, and the distributed system is composed of several hardware modules, which have the same configuration and are independent of each other. Each hardware module, consisting of a single-board microcomputer and an information station, takes on monitoring for 256-512 looms. The system may include six modules at most, which increase with the number of looms in the weaving room. Each subsystem is independent of the other, so that its reliability is greatly increased.

2.1 System Function

The computer monitoring system for a weaving loom is a real-time system of automatic acquisition of data for several thousand signal points and the automatic processing of data. Its main function is as follows.

2.1.1 Automatic Acquisition of Data

Any weaving loom may be fitted with six sensors, which are used for warp-stop, weft-stop, run/other-stop, output of product, plan-stop, and picking out. These sensors can automatically transmit various messages via the microswitches, non-contact switches, mechanical linkages, etc. A single-board microcomputer automatically acquires the status information of all looms every 5 seconds through the information station, and the acquired information is then automatically stored in the random-access memory, RAM.

2.1.2 Automatic Processing of Data

(1) When the system is running in the monitoring period, the single-board microcomputer pre-processes the acquired source data, such as production, number and time of stops for various reasons, various items of fault informating, etc.

(2) The single-board microcomputer automatically transfers the data into a master computer at the end of one shift. After pre-processing various source data, the master computer stores them onto exterior storage-a floppy disc. When printing-out is required or a large quantity of information is to be read out, the master computer can post-process various data stored on disc.

(3) According to the requirements for practical use, the trouble point and the type of error found by automatic diagnosis can be corrected or compensated by a program so that the relative exactness might be improved.

2.1.3 Automatic Output of Data

(1) Output and digital display: Each weaver can look at the total production at any time in the weaving room because the production data are read out by the single-board computer and displayed once every sixty seconds. The operator in the computer room may at any time inquire about the message concerning each running loom and weaver by CRT display/keyboard. Various fault signals may be displayed on the panel of the single-board computer box.

(2) Output and print-out of reports: At the end of one shift, the source-data of this shift are transferred from the single-board computer to the master computer. The master computer

stores them onto disc and prints out twelve reports, covering over 100 kinds of production data, indicating loom, weaver, group, workshop, fault diagnosis, auxiliary worker, maintenace worker, picking-out worker, loom number of various over-standard times of stoppage in one shift and in three shifts, forecast of changing warp beam, taking inventory of warp report, etc.

2.1.4 Automatic Storage of Data

(1) Memory stores data: The RAM (random-access memory) in the single-board computer stores the acquired source information on various numbers and times of stoppage, production in one shift.

(2) External storage: The floppy disc is mainly used to store source data of every shift so that the data can be preserved for a long time, and a 16-bit microcomputer or minicomputer may also batch-process these data and print out a report weekly, every ten days, or monthly for statistical analysis.

2.1.5 Automatic Diagnosis of Faults

(1) Diagnosis of microcomputer faults: Faults in single-board microcomputers and the master microcomputer are found by means of an automatic diagnostic program so that they can be quickly corrected.

(2) Diagnosis of hardware faults at information station: Through software and a verifying circuit, the hardware circuit can be checked for faults at the information station in order to deal with them quickly.

(3) Examination of signaller (sensor) in situ: The single-board microcomputer controls the monitoring device, thus verifying and finding the trouble points, which are displayed on the console and warn the maintenance engineer to repair it quickly.

(4) Power-failure check and data protection: The system may protect the data from power failure. If this occurs, a (back-up) stand-by battery is switched on, which can protect the source data in computer from being lost. After that, data are stored on the floppy disc immediately.

2.2 Technical and Economical Effects

A remarkably economical effect can be achieved by textile mills by adopting the microcomputer monitoring system for a weaving loom. The administrative personnel dealing with production apply the accurate data that the monitoring system has acquired over a period of time, and this strengthens the management of production, technology, equipment, and planning, etc. The production level can thus rise markedly. For an ordinary weaving room, the range of increased productive efficiency is from 2% to 8% in general.

Adopting the microcomputer monitoring system for a weaving loom can achieve marked technical and economic benefits from several aspects as follows.

(1) To raise the efficiency and output of a weaving loom. According to the data provided by the monitoring system, the machines with a high number of stops and low efficiency can be analysed before they are maintained and adjusted for speed and so on, and thus the efficiency and output of looms can be raised.

555

(2)   It can check the work of weavers, loom tuners, etc. by applying the data that represent the actual operating level and production level of various types of work in production, which will greatly increase the job responsibility and production.

(3)   The computer monitoring system is a useful tool for a technology test. For example, by making use of various primary data acquired by the monitoring system, one can select the appropriate sizing technology and sizing instructions, and optimize the temperature and humidity in the workroom.

(4)   To find the weak link in production rapidly and to reduce the number of warp stops and weft stops for looms will improve the quality of products and raise the efficiency in time.

3.   COMPOSITION OF SYSTME HARDWARE AND PRINCIPLE OF OPERATION

The monitoring system adopts a two-level master/slave-distributed structure, in which the subsystem consists of a hardware module including a single-board microcomputer and a monitoring device. Each module has individually the function of data acquisition and pre-processing, and acquires data for a block of a weaving room (200-512 looms).

Monitoring more than 1000 looms needs four modules. The master computer adopts an 8-bit microcomputer system, which post-processes various data and reads out and prints out many reports.

3.1   Composition of System Hardware

Composition of the entire system hardware is shown in Figure 1.

(1)   Master computer: The master computer is the BCM-II microcomputer system combined with the CPU "Z-80" chip. It includes 64k bytes RAM. The clock frequency of the CPU is 2 MHz. The master computer uses the CP/M operating system and has an expanded interface.

(2)   CRT display: The CRT display an ordinary 12-in. television, which can display 24 rows and 80 Chinese characters in each row.

(3)   Keyboard: The keyboard is the standard ASCII keyboard.

(4)   Floppy disc and driver: The driver an 8-in. double-sided single-density driver recording 500K bytes of data in each disc.

(5)   Printer: The printer is a Matrix printer with 24 pins, 132 characters per line. It can print out Chinese and ASCII characters.

(6)   Expanded interface: It includes four di-direction parallel input/output interfaces, which are used for transmitting data between the master computer and single-board computers.

(7)   Single-board microcomputer: It uses anexpanded single-board microcomputer CPU:Z-80 chip, 8-bits per byte, clock frequency is 2 MHz,
RAM: 10K bytes random-access memory is used for storing data and constant. Parallel interface: two Z80-PIO chips are used for transferring the message between the master computer and the single-board computers or between the single-board computer and the information station.

556

(8)   Controller of monitoring and display information station:
The controller can monitor 256-512 looms and control the
production display device of 12-64 weavers. Under the control
of the program in a single-board computer, the controller
monitors the switch quantity, such as warp-stop, other stop,
production, picking-out signal, etc.

(9)   Production display:Each weaver has a production display,
which outputs displays and the production once every minute
under the control of the single-board computer.

(10)   Signaller (sensor): The signallers are the foundation of
the monitoring system. Each loom is fixed with six signallers,
which are used for warp-stop, weft-stop, other stop, plan stop,
production, and picking out.

3.2   Controller of Monitoring and Display (Information Station)

Figure 2 shows the block diagram of the monitoring controller.
The controller can easily perform monitoring for 200-512 looms by
using the modular construction, which adopts four different
modular boards. Each loom might have installed on it from four
to eight sensors (signallers). The systme can monitor 200-2000
looms by using 1-6 modules which consist of the single-board
microcomputer and the monitoring controller.

Distinguishing from the general monitoring method of selecting
the address in multi-parallel, the controller of monitoring and
the display have a special method of multi-driving and multi-
receiving.

A controller can monitor 4000 signal points in using only 8-32
drivers and 8-16 receivers, co-operating with a signaller and
matrix-wiring mode on site.

3.2.1   Driving, Receiving, and Displaying

The single-board microcomputer sends the address data via the
input/output interface into the selection decoder, which converts
from it to control signals of X-driving, Y-receiving, and Z-
displaying. Under the control of these signals, the monitoring
controller acquires the data.

3.2.2   Matrix Wiring

Wiring at the working site can be greatly reduced by using this
method and the layout of the weaving room can be varied by close
co-operation with the circuit of the monitoring controller.

3.2.3   Diagnosis

The monitoring controller includes various diagnosis circuits,
which can diagnose the multi-receiver, signaller (sensor) in situ,
diode matrix etc. When the single-board microcomputer sends out
various address codes, the different diagnosis functions are
performed.

3.2.4   Isolating with Photoactor

By using the photoactor (coupler to isolate multi-driver, multi-
receiver, reverted-check and check receiver from the site, it
can protect the system from various distrubances at an industrial
site and improve the system reliability. The photoactor "GB-312"
is used as coupler because the practical work frequency is not
very high.

3.3   Work Principle

3.3.1   Starting the System

The system consists of several independent subsystems of
monitoring. Under normal conditions, the master microcomputer
starts every subsystem simultaneously and sends the initial
information into every single-board microcomputer, which starts
to acquire data in a shift.

3.3.2   Monitoring and Display

The clock signal of the system is the master signal of the single-
board microcomputer, which monitors in a fixed period (for
instance, 5 seconds). In a period, the single-board microcomputer
controls the controller of monitoring to send multi-driving
signals which drive the parellel signal point for 8-16 looms.
Then status message of the looms is then sent into controller
of monitoring by means of a group of returned signal wires for
each 8-16 looms. Finally, this message is sent into the single-
board microcomputer to be analysed and dealt with. After
dealing with the total production of every weaver, the single-
board microcomputer sends it into display, which changes every
minute.

3.3.3.   Data-processing and Print-out Reports

When the shift is changing, the master microcomputer requests an
interruption in the transfer from the single-board microcomputer,
which will accept and respond to the "interrupt" signal. It
then transfers data to the master computer, and the master
computer stores data onto the disk. Finally, it performs data-
processing and prints out various reports.

4.   DATA STRUCTURE AND SOFTWARE

The system consists of two main parts: Hardware and software,
which connect closely with each other. The hardware offers a
simple practical multiplexer and the software operationg in
conjunction with the hardware provides various functions. It
is certain that the monitoring controller acquires various items
of data on looms on site under the control of the program in
the single-board microcomputer.

Generally speaking, the software includes two parts, data structure
and program processing. According to the function and demand
of different systems, it is necessary to define different data
structures. However, the program will meet the system demand
by means of various types of processing on this condition.

4.1   Data-structure Form

The monitoring system acquires source data from signal points of
warp-stop, weft-stop, other-stop, plan-stop, production and
picking out. In addition, it gathers some messages of faults
from diagnosis circuits of the moinitoring controller.
The data of the monitoring system consist of several parts as
follows.

4.1.1.   Source Data of Each Loom

These are many data acquired by the monitoring system, which consist of source data of warp-stop number, warp-stop time, weft-stop number, weft-stop time, other-stop number, other-stop time, plan-stop time, total stop time, variety, rated production, non-rated production, and machine number. The structure of these parts of data is specially designed. The source data of each loom mentioned above make up a record section, and several records sections make up a record, which is stored into the data area of the memory in the single-board microcomputer in its proper order.

4.1.2   Up-dated Data of Some Looms

In weaving production, there are some messages on changing the variety in the production of any shift, and although it is not necessary for each loom to be involved in this, some looms will be needed to do it. Thus, in the data area of the single-board microcomputer, there is a special store area used for storing the messages relating to data of variety, rated production, and non-rated production. When indexes and sorting are used, the machine number is still the key word.

4.1.3.   Fault Message of Self-diagnosis

Besides the function of acquiring data, the monitoring system still has the important function of self-diagnosis. The system can perform various tests at any time and store the fault message obtained by diagnosis into the data area of faults in the single-board microcomputer according to the type of fault. The message can be displayed or warning given under the control of the program so that the operative and tuner may deal with it in time. At the end of a shift, three of the sources mentioned above are transferred to the master computer, sorted, and stored onto the disc according to the records so as to be printed out.

4.2   Program Construction

On the basis of the above-mentioned type of data structure and the demands of the system function, we can write the program and combine with it the features of the system hardware.

The software system is composed of two main parts: the program for monitoring and displaying and the program for data-processing and printing out.

Combined with the microcomputer features, the programming adopts the modular structure so that it will be convenient to write, modify, maintain, and operate the program.

4.2.1   Program for Monitoring and Displaying

Because it is a real-time system, the program for monitoring and displaying is written in assembly language and located in EPROM (shown in Fig.3), the function being as follows:

(1)   The function is to monitor automatically the status of the signaller for 200-512 looms, to pre-process the primary acquired data, and to store it in the data area in the single-board microcomputer once every 5 seconds.

(2)   The function is to control the display of production for 12-64 weavers and to change it once a minute.

(3)   The function is to diagnose and to self-verify. It can diagnose and self-verify faults in the driving circuit, in the

monitoring circuit, diode breakdown, grouding, the hardware
in the monitoring controler, and the signaller by means of fault
location.

(4)   The function is to warn and to display. It can display
and give warning of faults in the drive circuit mentioned, diode
breakdown, groundings, faults in the monitoring controller,
signaller, etc.

(5)   The function is to adapt to changing the variety.

(6)   It is not necessary to change the hardware system, since
the program for monitoring can adapt to various changes in labour
organization because of sharing the block with software, so that
it can improve the system flexibility.

The program for mointoring is divided into several separable
modules as functions in order to debug, link, call, and maintain
it easily.

4.2.2   Program for Data-processing and Printing Out

When the single module composed of the single-board microcomputer
and monitoring controller acquires the source data of a shift of
200-512 looms, the data are transferred into the memory of the
master computer under the control of the transferring program.

Then data are then stored onto the floppy disc in the form of a
data file. If there are over 1000 looms, each single-board
microcomputer of system stores all data onto the disc in the
same way.

According to the demands of production and maintenance in the
weaving room and the administrative department in the textile
mill, the software for data-processing deals with the relevant
data and prints out various reports.

The block diagram of the function of the program is shown in
Fig. 4,

(1)   Report on each Loom

According to the loom number, the system deals with and prints
out the data, such as warp-stop number, plan-stop time, total
stop time, speed, type of fabric, rated production, non-rated
production, operation rate, efficiency, and forecast of changing
the warp beam and marks them when the data are over the limit of
the various stop numbers, speed and efficiency separately.

(2)   Report on Weaver

As for each loom, it deals with and prints out the following data:
total number of stops, total time, plan-stop time, average speed,
average efficiency, operation rate, each stop number/machine/hour,
each stop time/stop number, rated production, and non-rated
production of each type of fabric.

In addition, there are other reports as follows: reports on auxiliary
worker, tuner, picking-out worker, working group, work room,
various faults of diagnosis, number of machines over the limit
of each number of stops, number of machines over the limit of the
stops in three continuous shifts, forecast of changing the warp
beam, taking inventory of warp, etc.

In executing the program, it prints out the separable reports according to the keying of different commands. On each report, there is the basic information of date, number of shift, time of shift, and so on.

5. CONCLUSION

The distributed microcomputer monitoring system of the weaving loom is developing continuously. To evaluate a system, one should actually analyse its availability, reliability, stability, flexibility, universality, and economics (performance/price). The idea described in this paper is just based on this requirement and has proved to be suitable for other processes of multi-machine and multi-monitoring points in the textile industry, such as winding, spinning, sizing and knitting.

Beijing Textile Research Institute,
Beijing,
People's Republic of China.

COMPUTER TECHNOLOGY AND APPLICATION

N. Akikusa

ABSTRACT

Computer technology being much more advanced in the 1980's than the 1970's, computers are now in use in almost all industries. A brief discussion is given on the computerization of manufacturing industries, in particular;

(1) Automatic data processing systems from product design to delivery

(2) Staff support systems

(3) Computer and telecommunication systems

Described here are the various information processing techniques such as (1) CAD/CAM systems, (2) robotics, (3) pattern recognition, (4) data base, (5) artificial intelligence (AI), (6) digital communication, (7) optical data communication, (8) local area network (LAN), and (9) integrated service digital network (ISDN).

1. INTRODUCTION

Computers have been rapidly making their way into all fields of home and industry. Japan alone produced 7.5 billion U.S. dollars worth of hardware and 4 billion U.S. dollars worth of software in 1982. This represents a three-fold increase in hardware and a four-fold increase in software compared with just eight years ago.

Japan only accounts for a portion of the world's computers. Of the total number of computers now installed, the U.S. accounts for 34.3 percent, Japan for 14.7 percent, western Europe as a whole for 27.9 percent, eastern Europe as a whole for 13.1 percent, and Canada for about 2.4 percent. This is roughly equal to the shares these countries and regions hold in the world's total gross national product. This reflects the extent to which computers have become the driving force behind the world's indusrty.

According to a 1983 survey by our Ministry of International Trade and Industry, Japan's textile industry is using a total of 2,205 computers, or 2 percent of all computers in Japanese industry. The ratio of electronic data processing costs as against total sales is 0.37 percent - about equal to the average in the secondary industries. By way of reference, the ratio of EDP costs to total sales in the steelmaking industry, which has made the greatest investment in computerization, is 0.66 percent - about twice that of the textile industry.

The scope of application of computers is increasingly expanding. The textile industry is traditionally labor-intensive, but we have great expectations for more aggressive use of computers there too.

2. TRENDS IN COMPUTER APPLICATION

Now, the start of the 1980's saw the end of the era of mass production and mass consumption and the start of an increasing diversification and personalization in consumer tastes and values. The implication for industry, of course, was increasingly shorter product life cycles. How to supply merchandise accurately reflecting consumer needs thereupon became one of the major facets of corporate strategy. Increased competition has further led to the need to promise faster deliveries, reduce inventories, and reduce the rate of defects.

On the other hand, there have been rapid advances in microelectronics - the backbone of computers. A look at the advances made in LSI's and other computer elements shows that in the past 10 years we have been able to increase densities up to a hundred-fold and speeds up to ten-fold. At the same time, we have cut prices to one-thirtieth what they were just two years ago. As a result, we are able to offer high performance, less expensive computers for application in fields never before dreamed of.

2.1 Automation From Product Design to Delivery

There are three main trends in the use of computers in the manufacturing industry.

First, the basic industries which have already been using computers are raising the level of their usage to automate everything which used to be done by manpower from product design to delivery. Through this, they are able to maintain continuity in the entire process from design to manufacturing and to delivery, can speed delivery times, stabilize quality, and reduce costs. Important facets of such systems are CAD/CAM systems, in other words, computer aided design and computer aided manufacturing systems, robot control technology, and pattern recognition technology.

2.1.1 CAD/CAM System

The CAD system was originally developed simply to aid draftsmen, but has now been upgraded to a powerful man-machine interface for designing semiconductor circuits, buildings, cars, airplanes, industrial equipment, and, for the textile industry, sewing patterns. The final image on the display screen can be immediately output as drawings or other documents for use as basic data in the production technology and manufacturing stages.

Use of the CAD system significantly boosts design productivity. For example, designers are able to

o display and modify detailed images of the product under design on the screen;

o   quickly compare and examine several draft designs;

o   facilitate design of part groups to enable interchange
    and compatibility of components in the final product;

o   simulate the various stages of production of the designed
    components of the product; and

o   obtain results of calculations necessary for the design
    in real time.

CAM, on the other hand, takes the data from the CAD drawings
and prepares the numerical control tapes for the control of
machine tools. In the broader sense, CAM enables efficient
use of computer technology for management and control of
manufacturing operations.

Together, CAD and CAM enable enhanced product design and
manufacturing. In the future, we will be further upgrading
their performance by enabling reading of hand drawings and
making use of a so-called "artificial intelligence." We
will also be enabling attachment of personal computers to
bring the price of such systems down further.

2.1.2   Robot Control Technology

Now, regarding robot control technology, Japanese factories
are rapidly introducing industrial robots under the so-called
FMS system, or "flexible manufacturing system." There are,
as you know, four main types of robots available:

o   sequential robots which operate by a predetermined
    operational sequence;

o   playback robots which repeat operations previously done
    by an operator;

o   NC robots which operate according to specified NC tape
    programs; and

o   intelligent robots which read data through sensors and
    operate according to specified programs.

Of these, the most flexible and powerful are the intelligent
robots and it is the intelligent robots that should become
the mainstream in the future due to their sensor and pattern
recognition capabilities. As for the other types of robots,
we should see continuing advances in the keypoint areas of
positioning accuracy and servo mechanisms.

2.1.3   Pattern Recognition Technology

Regarding pattern recognition, just as you and I perceive
the outside world by our five senses, an intelligent robot
must be able to sense and execute its task by recognizing
patterns, color, depth, sound, and other information.
Pattern recognition systems consist of sensors for input of
data, memories for classifying and storing various patterns,

a judgement mechanism for comparing the stored patterns with
input data and determining similarity or nonsimilarity and
an output device for displaying or printing out the results
of the judgement.

Recent developments in sensor technology and microelectronics have led to rapid commercialization of such
pattern recognition devices. They are now used for the eyes
and ears of many industrial robots. Under certain circumstances, such pattern recognition devices are more
accurate and reliable than human senses, but overall many
hurdles remain before they can recognize patterns on a par
with humans. Once the technology is developed, however,
robots will be able to take over even inspection work - for
which the human eye is now still essential.

2.2 Staff and Researcher Support Systems

A second trend is the use of computers by so-called white
collar workers. Many Japanese companies are installing
computers in their offices and laboratories in an effort to
cut down on routine work and leave more time for creative
work, thus boosting what we may call "intelligent productivity." At issue here is how fast to analyze large amounts
of data. We are pursuing this through the development of
data base technology and artificial intelligence technology.

2.2.1 Data Base Technology

A data base is a set of data previously collected and stored
in certain formats for quick, easy access. There are three
types of data bases: tree, network, and relational. Of
these, the tree and network types are strong for retrieving
data in a routine manner, but are not suited for retrieving
nonroutine data. The relational type, on the other hand, is
suited for nonroutine data retrieval in processing data in a
table format and in calculating group data. The relational
type takes up a large portion of the computer capacity, but
we are eliminating this problem through hardware of increased
memories.

Much of office and laboratory work consists of nonroutine
data retrieval and comparisons of relationships between data
and, therefore, relational type data bases are becoming the
mainstream. Recently, we have enabled use of relational
data bases on personal computers as well as large business
computers, thus further facilitating nonroutine processing.
To promote future use of data bases, we are now working on
"user-friendly" methods of computer operation and interfaces
between mainframes and personal computers.

2.2.2 Artificial Intelligence

Turning to artificial intelligence, what we are talking
about is providing computers with an ability to duplicate
human thinking. A computer with artificial intelligence
will be able to understand human speech, draw inferences
based on background information, and draw its own

conclusions therefrom. The U.S. and other countries have been studying the subject now for more than 20 years and returns are now beginning to come in. One system, known as the "Expert System," is already in operation and can provide medical advice, diagnose computer faults, and provide answers to a variety of other inquiries.

Once artificial intelligence is applied, unskilled workers will be able to handle tasks previously requiring the experienced judgement of skilled personnel. For example, artificial intelligence will enable analysis and decisions on petroleum mining blocks, troubleshooting for complex machinery and industrial plants, and the like.

In Japan, we have organized a research project for the development of fifth-generation artificial intelligence computers and are now studying new possibilities for artificial intelligence. We are aiming at the development of an intellectual information processing system based on a completely new concept within the next ten years.

2.3 Computer and Telecommunication Systems

The third trend is the merging of computers and sophisticated telecommunication systems for more advanced applications.

As computers come to handle an increasingly wide spectrum of information, the amount of information they handle increases and becomes more diverse in nature. By way of reference, you should note that it takes what we call an 8-bit code to represent a single letter of the alphabet in a computer. To display just this one letter as an image using a 32-by-32 dot matrix, the computer must therefore process 1024 bits of data. This increase in the amount of data necessitates a corresponding increase in the speed of transmission.

The greater range and higher quality of information makes good data communication systems crucial. Thus, we have had to develop data transmission technology enabling handling of large volumes of information at a high speed and network communication technology enabling simultaneous communication with two or more remote stations. Prime examples of these are digital data communications, optical data communications, local area networks (LAN), and integrated service digital networks (ISDN).

2.3.1 Digital Data Communication

In digital data communication, we convert character data, image data, which includes facsimile and display screen data, and sound data into digital codes for transmission. For example, we divide a voice signal into 1/8000 of a second subsections and change its waveform into 64,000 bits of high and low digital information. On the receiver end, we restore this information to a voice signal by an inverse process. Digitalization enables various information to be concurrently transferred through the same exchanger.

An especially efficient method of transmitting digital
information is the packet system. Here, a sequence of
information is formed into a so-called "packet" for trans-
missions. For example, we divide 1000 characters of data
into ten packets each consisting of 100 characters and
transfer the addressed packets in tens, enabling multiple
users to share a single communication line.

2.3.2 Optical Data Communications

In optical data communication, we transmit information by
laser beam in the dark sky or through optical fibers of a
diameter no greater than a human hair. Light and radio
waves are both electromagnetic waves, but the frequency of
light is much higher than that of a radio wave. Light also
has a wider frequency bandwidth. Thus, we can send much
more data with a single fiber cable as compared with
conventional coaxial cables. Specifically, we can transmit
data equal to more than that carried by 5000 coaxial
telephone cables or one optical cable. And we can transmit
both voice and image data through a single optical cable.
Other advantages are resistance to noise due to low energy
loss, flexibility and thinness, and low cost.

2.3.3 Local Area Network (LAN)

To facilitate more efficient data communication between your
computers, facsimiles, and other audio and video equipment,
we can set up what we call a local area network (LAN) - a
private information processing and communication system. We
can also attach personal computers and workstations to the
network. For large numbers of information processing
devices or the large amounts of transmission information, we
can use a loop optical fiber LAN or digital exchange LAN.

2.3.4 Integrated Service Digital Network (ISDN)

For integration with public telephone, telex, facsimile, and
other data communication lines to transmit high-speed,
large-capacity data, there is the integrated service digital
network (ISDN). Here, we transmit information in a digital
format through optical fiber lines. Besides conventional
telephone,
data communication, and facsimile lines, we can connect
Videotex, TV conference system lines, and communication
satellites to the ISDN. Partial service is already underway
in parts of Japan under the so-called "INS" information
network system.

3. CONCLUSION

In conclusion, let me say that the support technologies for
application of computer systems are very diverse.
Semiconductors and other advances in microelectronics have,
indeed, made all this possible, but we must not forget the
software which makes the hardware move. The easier and more
advanced a system you want, the more complex the software
required.

One of our highest priorities is therefore to boost
productivity in software development. We are, for example,
testing a CAD system for producing software similar as with
industrial products. We are also working on easy-to-use
programming languages but frankly we still have somewhat to
go in this area. For those of you who already have existing
systems, please rest at ease that we are not disregarding
old software and developing incompatible completely new
ones. Rather, we are using existing programs in combined
programs for improved productivity and more flexible
software products.

Just as important as efficient software development is
integrated system development. When putting together a
system for your applications, consider tieups with communication systems, use of data bases, and man-machine
interfacing in addition to the mainframe.

In any case, we promise to produce more and more powerful
hardware and software to support you in computer application.

Fujitsu KK
Tokyo
Japan

COMPUTERIZED GARMENT DIAGNOSIS

A.Mª Manich, R.Mª Saurí, J. Llória and A. Barella

ABSTRACT

On the basis that Reliability techniques conform to theories on
the statistical distribution of failures during the garments
life (Weibull's Law) in practice, the authors have developed a
systematic analysis that, through study of distribution parameters
and failure rate curve, allows diagnosis to be established on
design and fabrication quality, components adequacy, and wear
performance of garments, in connection with market requirements.
The development of complementary devices which simulate garment
wear, allows quick establishment of a diagnosis that agrees with
wearer appreciation. This diagnosis, can, in some instances,
lead to technical decisions affording to cut costs without loss
of garment quality.

The last steps of this process have been: optimization of the
test, and development of the suitable "software" for diagnosis
computerization.

In the present paper, after a summary on the diagnosis technique
developed earlier, the general scheme of the computer program
is detailed and the software explained. A practical exemple
allows identification of all the elements in garment diagnosis.

1. INTRODUCTION

Reliability techniques and theories on the failure distribution
during the useful life of garments are accomplished in practice
(1 to 5). The application of such techniques allows, through
analysis of distribution parameters and the failure rate curve,
to obtain inferences that, when systematically treated, permit
the establishment of a diagnosis related to the design and
fabrication quality, components adequacy and wear performance
of garments (6 to 10) in connection with market requirements.
The development of two prototypes simulating garment wear (7 to
12) improved the test and allowed test optimization (11, 12)
At present, it is possible, in a few days a diagnosis to be
obtained which is well correlated with wearer appreciation, and
allows technical decisions to be taken that will permit garment
costs to be decreased (9) without loss of quality.

2. FUNDAMENTALS AND DIAGNOSIS ESTABLISHMENT

2.1. Fundamentals

Diagnosis is based on a duly interpreted suitable testing system.
Tests can be functional; accelerated; with washings intercalated;
simulating wear and functional abbreviated. The mathematical
basis of the method is the well known Weibull's law (13). The
graphical representation of the rate of failure $z(t)$ is generally
the so called "bathtub curve" because of its shape (Figure 1),
which means that the function shows three stages with decreasing
failure rate (phase I), constant failure rate (phase II) and
increasing failure rate (phase III) respectively. The curve cannot

be represented by means a single mathematic model; but if Weibull's law is taken as a basis, the three phases are caracterized by $\beta < 1$, $\beta = 1$ and $\beta > 1$ respectively.

These periods successively represent premature failures (foreseeable), random failures during useful life (unforeseeable), and wear failures (foreseeable).

But in the garment industry not always the first phase shows a decreasing trend. On the contrary, in some instances it can be either flat or increasing. The trend of this first phase and the value of the failure rate for the second phase allow inferences to be made on the garment design and fabrication quality.

2.2. Diagnosis Establishment

The analytical sequence of a diagnosis includes the following stages:

a) Failures definition and listing;

b) Testing, generally alternate wear (or wear simulation) and wash;

c) Detection of failure during testing (Figure 2);

d) Calculation of V.a.a. values of failure distribution according to Nelson's technique (14), and plot on probability paper (Figures 3 and 4A);

e) Drawing of the failure rate curve (Figure 4B);

f) Determination of points for phase change (I to II and II to III);

g) Study of the failure nature during the three phases of garment life and establishment, for each phase, of the failures/washes ratio (or failures/elapsed time; washes are here equivalent to elapsed time), for the most frequents failure types (Figure 5). Drawing of Pareto's failure frequency distribution graph (Figures 4C and 5);

h) Compilation of the main six parameters for the formulation of diagnosis. This six parameters are: Weibull distribution slope β_I during the first phase, related to garment design and fabrication quality; number of washing cycles L_I (or time elapsed) corresponding to passage from phase I to phase II (duration of phase I); probability of failure F_I corresponding to this passage (preferential duration); failure ratio λ_{II} corresponding to phase II (garment failure rate), related to the adequacy of design to garment requirements; number of washing cycles (or time elapsed) L_{II} corresponding to the passage from phase II to phase III (duration of phase II) and probability of failure corresponding to this passage F_{II} (utilitarian life of garment). These six parameters can be graphically plotted in a multiparametric diagram (optional);

i) Garment diagnosis based on previous data. Such a diagnosis includes information and conclusions about both design and

fabrication quality; components adequacy; design to wear
adequacy, duration of phases I (preferential), II and III
(utilitarian) and recommendations on actions to be taken for
garment improvement.

The diagnosis calculation by means of conventional systems is
long, tedious and not free from possible mistakes. Thus, a
diagnosis concerning a sample of 20 garments and 150 failure
types can require 4 to 5 hours of calculation by a qualified
operator.

3. COMPUTERIZED GARMENT DIAGNOSIS: ITS REALIZATION

3.1. Used computer

Computerisation of data allows to drastically reduce calculation
time which is now about 45 minutes. The probability of mistake
is minimized and reduced to data input, that can be checked and
corrected if necessary. In addition, a qualified operator is
not required.

A mini-computer of 32 Kbytes RAM with a 256 x 192 useful points
RCT screen, thermical printer and a matrix ROM memory was used.
Peripheral devices were a 80 columns printer and a disk unit, which
can work with two 280 Kbytes and 130 mm discs.

The equipment works with BASIC language. Its flowchart is given
in Figure 7.

3.2. Software

3.2.1. General

The application of so called "GARMENT DIAGNOSIS" is formed by
three link programs: "DIAGNO", "CAL/DG" and "VAL/DG" which work
interactively. Such programs cover, respectively, 10 Kbytes,
10 Kbytes and 4 Kbytes, but because of the assignation of memory
fields and input/output channels, its operation requires a
minimum, of 11 Kbytes, 29 Kbytes and 5 Kbytes, respectively. The
general flowchart of the process is represented in Figure 8.

3.2.2. "DIAGNO" program

In the first part of data treatment, the "DIAGNO" program
(Figure 9) is applied. The actions carried out by means of this
program are as follows:

a) Help to operator: the necessary explanations to guide the
   operator in the program development are displayed on the
   screen;

b) Print the failures explanatory test. Because of the failure
   treatment characteristics of the mini-computer operating
   system, it has been considered that the optimal solution was
   the assignment of a growing numerical code from 1 to each
   failure. This print of the failures explanatory text, allows
   failures assigned to the aforementioned code to be identified.

c) Obtention of the failures explanatory list. This allows either
the complete failures list for correcting mistakes to be
obtained or only the list of major failures affecting
diagnosis;

d) Record on disc of data obtained from tests, named "Failure
Table". The columns of this table are headed by number of the
test garment, and each row by the failures code (1 to 150 as
maximum). The last row corresponds to the garments eliminated
during the test if any. In the corresponding intersection the
figure indicating the number of elapsed washes up to the
failure apparition (Figure 2) appears. This matrix is a basic
one for the further development;

e) Print the failures (from the disc as indicated in d). The
obtained list allows to check the existence of possible
mistakes due to data input;

f) Modification of the failure table or failures elimination.
This action permits to correct possible input mistakes, and
to entirely suppress any failure that, after obtention of
the first garment diagnosis it is shown that does not affect
final garment evaluation by the wearer. It is, then possible
to remake the diagnosis.

3.2.3. "CAL/DG" program

When a guarantee exists that the failure table has been correctly
recorded, the "CAL/DG" program is introduced. This program (Figure
10) acts as follows:

a) Charge the failures table to the computer memory;

b) Calculation of the failure rate and the failure distribution;

c) Graphical plot of the failure rate curve;

d) Obtention of failure distribution parameters and values for
phases I and II;

e) Calculation of failure frequency distribution (Pareto's curve);

f) Indication of the most frequent failures that must be analysed;

g) Calculation of the failures/washes ratio according to the
garment life phase;

h) To link with the "DIAGNO" program if it is considered to be
suitable to eliminate entirely any failure and to repeat
the diagnosis calculation;

i) To link the "VAL/DG" program for diagnosis evaluation.

3.2.4. "VAL/DG" program

The "VAL/DG" program (Figure 11) carries out the following
actions:

a) Evaluation of the garment performance data in connection with the design and fabrication quality;

b) Garment evaluation in relation with its ulterior use;

c) Garment evaluation on the good or bad adequacy of the components to use by indicating failures code, failures type, and recommendations for correction of eventual disfunctions;

d) Remarks about garment duration;

e) To link the "DIAGNO" program for printing the page foot and to finish the study.

The program development has been based on subroutines of independent calculation (structural programming). The complete scheme is not presented here because of its extension.

4. PRACTICAL EXAMPLE

A practical example of results presentation is added to the present paper (Figure 12).

5. CONCLUSIONS

The computerization of data treatment from the analytical sequence for the obtention of a garment diagnosis, decreases to 45 minutes only the time necessary for calculation, whereas the conventional systems would take as much as 4 or 5 hours. Mistakes are eliminated and qualified personel is not necessary.

A program of this type can be carried out by means of a relatively simple, i.e. a so called "personal", mini-computer.

6. REFERENCES

(1) A. Barella, R.Mª Saurí, C. Polo, J.Mª Etayo, J.Mª Arús and L. Viertel. Clothing Res. J., 1974, 2, 87-95.

(2) A. Barella, R.Mª Saurí, C. Polo, J.Mª Etayo, J.Mª Arús and L. Viertel. Clothing Res. J., 1974, 2, 97-100.

(3) A. Barella, R.Mª Saurí, C. Polo, J.Mª Etayo, J.Mª Arús and L. Viertel. Clothing Res. J., 1975, 3, 41-50.

(4) A. Barella, R.Mª Saurí, C. Polo, J.Mª Etayo, J.Mª Arús and L. Viertel. Clothing Res. J., 1975, 3, 50-55.

(5) A. Barella, R.Mª Saurí, C. Polo, L. Viertel and J.Mª Etayo. Clothing Res. J., 1975, 3, 111-134.

(6) A. Barella, R.Mª Saurí, C. Polo, J.Mª Etayo, J.A. Salmurri and L. Viertel. Clothing Res. J., 1976, 4, 59-73.

(7) A. Barella, R.Mª Saurí, C. Polo, J.Mª Etayo, J.A. Salmurri and L. Viertel. Clothing Res. J., 1977, 5, 103-105.

(8) A. Barella, R.Mª Saurí, C. Polo, J.Mª Etayo, J.A. Salmurri and L. Viertel. Clothing Res. J., 1978, 6, 60-80.

(9) A. Barella, R.Mª Saurí, C. Polo, J.Mª Etayo and L. Viertel. Clothing Res. J., 1979, 7, 22-38.

(10) A. Barella and R.Mª Saurí. 6th International Wool Textile Research Conference, Pretoria, 1980.

(11) A. Barella, R.Mª Saurí and A.Mª Manich. To be published.

(12) A. Barella, R.Mª Saurí, J. Llória and A.Mª Manich. To be published.

(13) W. Weibull. 'Fatigue Testing and Analysis of Results' Pergamon, Oxford, 1961.

(14) W. Nelson. J. of Quality Tech., 1969, 1, 1, 27; 1970, 2, 3, 126.

Instituto de Tecnología Química y Textil
C.S.I.C.
c/ Jorge Girona Salgado, 18-26
Barcelona (34)
Spain

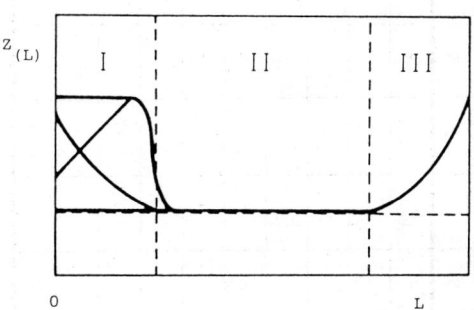

FIGURE 1 - THE SO CALLED "BATHTUB" CURVE

Manich

FIGURE 2 – DETECTION OF FAILURES PRODUCED DURING THE TEST. FIGURES SHOW THE NUMBER OF WASHES ELAPSED UP TO THE FAILURE APPARITIONS IN THE CORRESPONDING GARMENT

| GARMENT NUMBER | \multicolumn{10}{c}{FAILURES CODE} |
	1	2	3	4	5	6	7	8	9	10
1	-	-	-	-	-	1	0	-	7	-
2	-	4	-	-	-	-	1	-	7	-
3	-	-	0	-	5	-	0	-	7	6
4	-	6	-	-	5	-	-	-	-	-
5	-	-	-	-	-	-	-	0	7	-
6	-	-	-	2	-	0	-	-	7	-
7	-	-	-	-	-	2	-	-	-	-
8	-	-	-	-	-	-	-	-	7	-
9	1	-	-	-	-	-	-	-	7	-
10	0	-	-	-	4	-	-	-	7	-

576

WASHES	FAILURES CODE F	NUMBER OF FAILURES n.F	NUMBER OF GARMENTS P	GARMENTS WITHOUT FAILURE P.s.f.	FAILURE RATE		FAILURE DISTRIBUTION
					V.a.	V.a.t.	V.a.a.
0	1	1	10	10	10.0		
	3	1	10	10	10.0		
	6	1	10	10	10.0		
	7	2	10	10	20.0		
	8	1	10	10	10.0	60.0	60.0
1	1	1	10	9	11.1		
	6	1	10	9	11.1	22.2	82.2
2	4	1	10	10	10.0		
	6	1	10	8	12.5	22.5	104.7
4	2	1	10	10	10.0		
	5	1	10	10	10.0	20.0	124.7
5	5	2	10	9	22.2	22.2	146.9
6	2	1	10	9	11.1		
	10	1	10	10	10.0	21.1	168.1
7	9	8	10	10	80.0	80.0	248.1

FIGURE 3 – FAILURE DISTRIBUTION CALCULATION TABLE ACCORDING TO THE NELSON TECHNIQUE

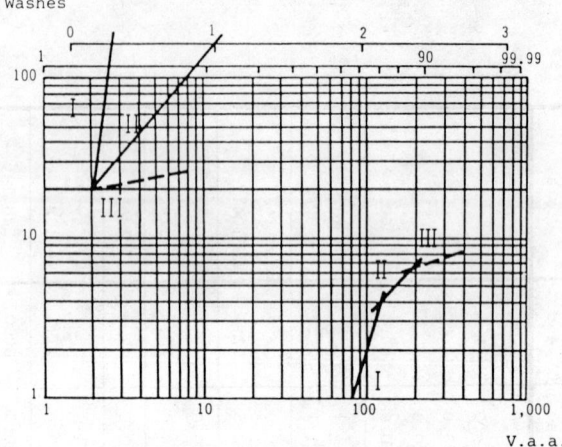

FIGURE 4A - FAILURE DISTRIBUTION ON NELSON PROBABILISTIC PAPER

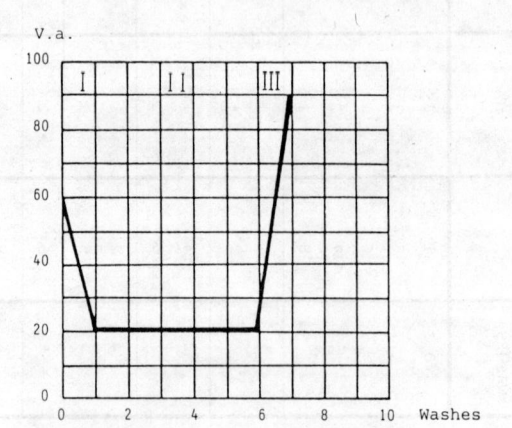

FIGURE 4B - FAILURE RATE CURVE

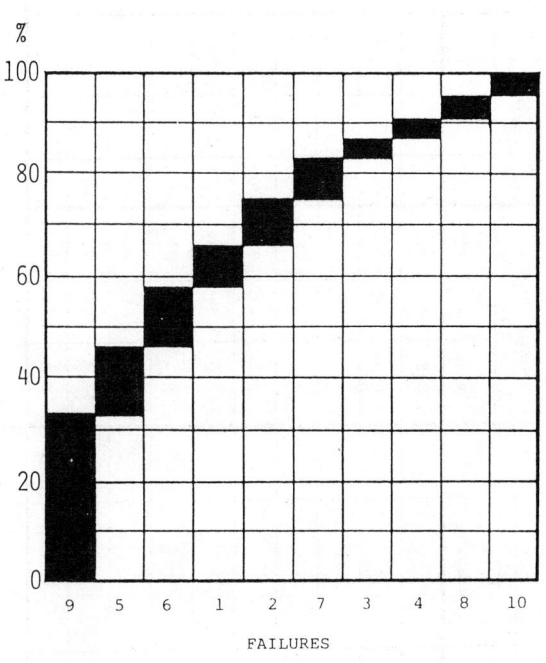

%

FIGURE 4C - PARETO'S FAILURE FREQUENCY DISTRIBUTION
GRAPH

DIAGNOSIS SCHEME

FAILURES	PHASES				PARETO GRAPH			FAILURES/WASHES RATIO			REMARKS
	I (1 washing)	II (5 washing)	III (1 washing)	Σ	%	Nº	Δ %	I	II	III	
1	2	–	–	2	8.3	4º	66.7				
2	–	2	–	2	8.3	5º	75.0				
3	1	–	–	1	4.2	7º	87.5				
4	–	1	–	1	4.2	8º	91.7				
5	–	3	–	3	12.5	2º	45.8	0	0.6	0	ACCIDENTAL
6	2	1	–	3	12.5	3º	58.3	2º	0.2	0	PREMATURE
7	2	–	–	2	8.3	6º	83.3				
8	1	–	–	1	4.2	9º	95.8				
9	–	–	8	8	33.3	1º	33.3	0	0	8º	WEAR
10	–	1	–	1	4.2	10º	100.0				
				Σ 24	100.0						

FIGURE 5 – FAILURES TYPE ACCORDING TO THE PHASES AND CALCULATION OF PARETO'S GRAPH AND FAILURES/WASHES RATIO

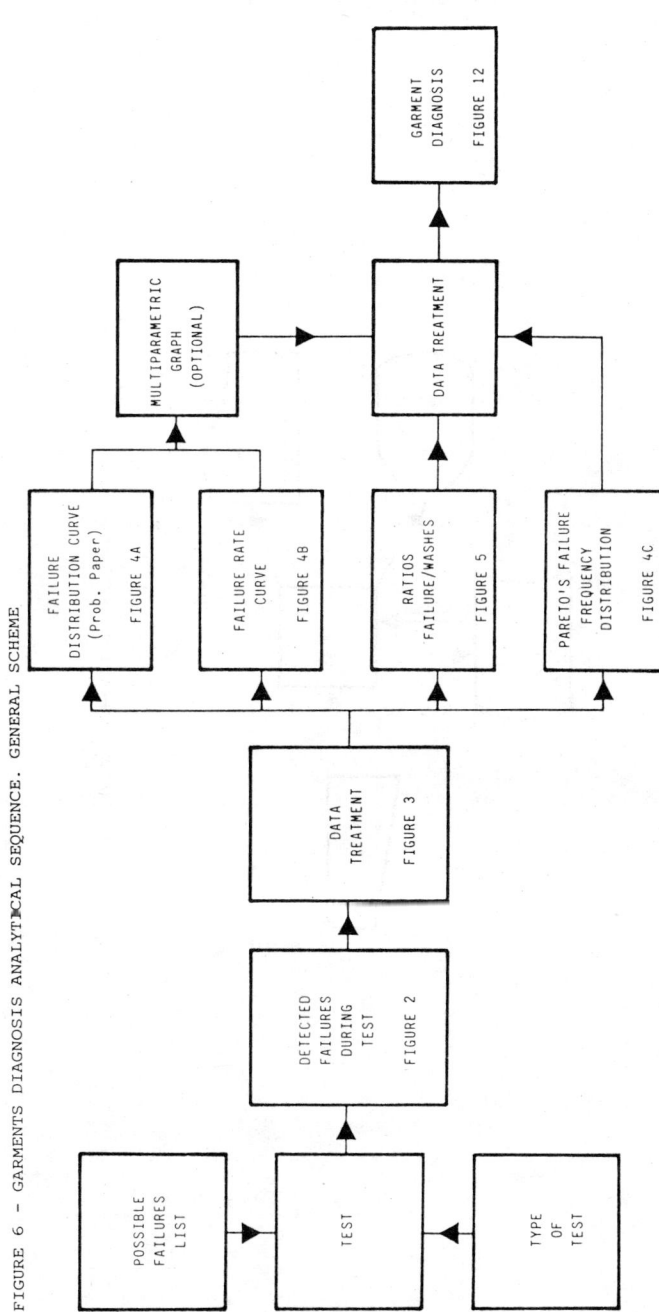

FIGURE 6 - GARMENTS DIAGNOSIS ANALYTICAL SEQUENCE. GENERAL SCHEME

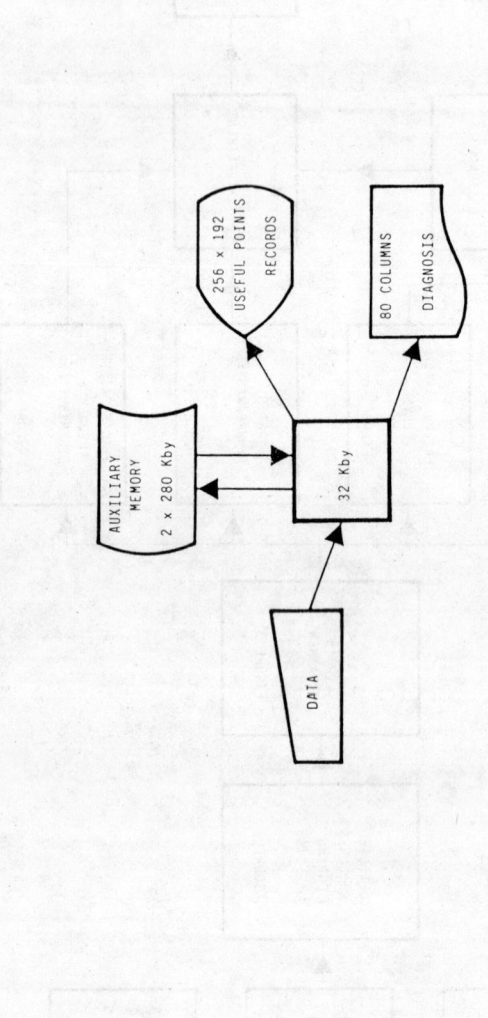

FIGURE 7 - USED MINI-COMPUTER FLOWCHART

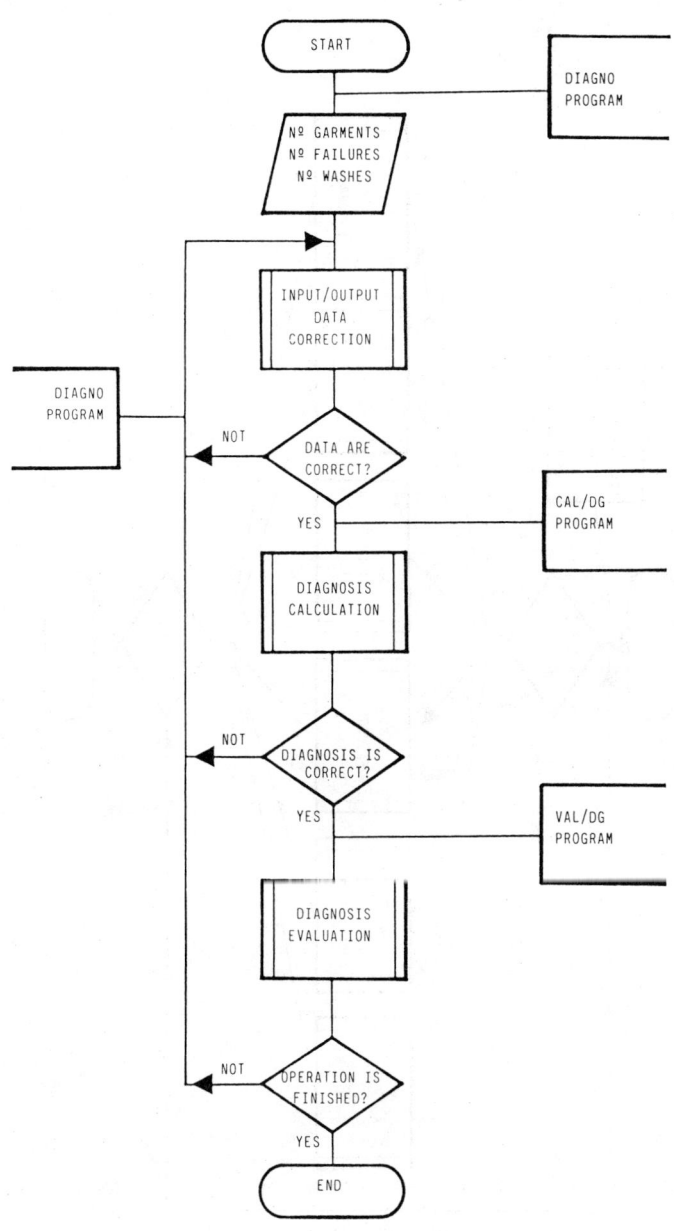

FIGURE 8 - PROCESS FLOWCHART. GENERAL SCHEME

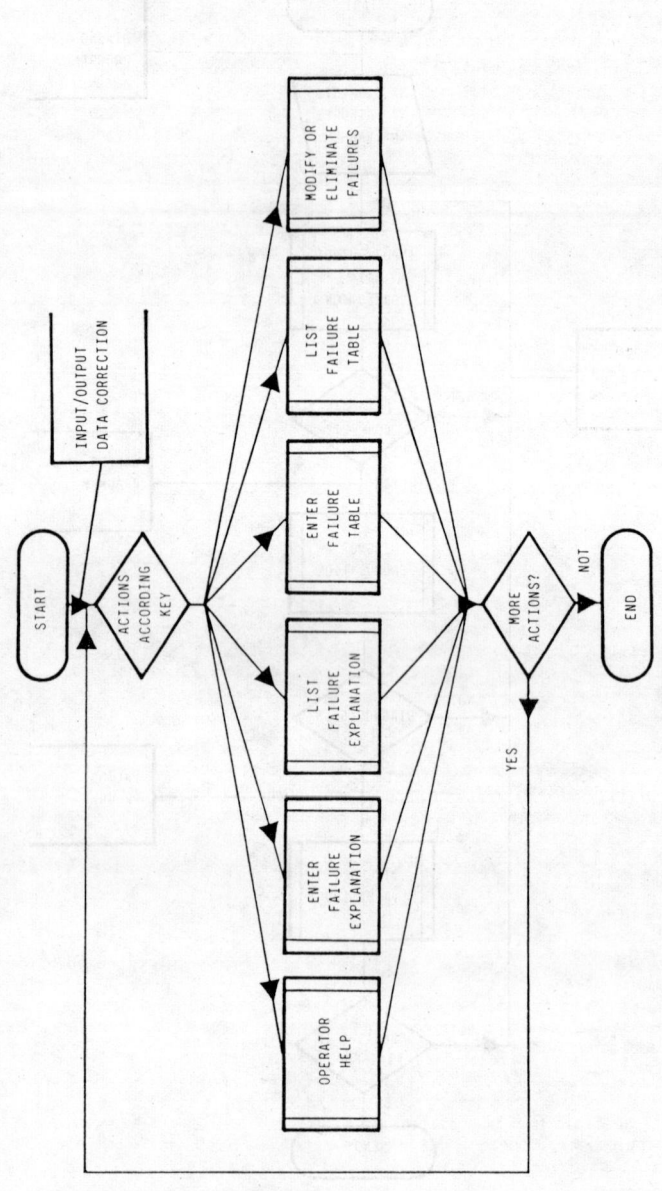

FIGURE 9 -- "DIAGNO" PHASE FLOWCHART

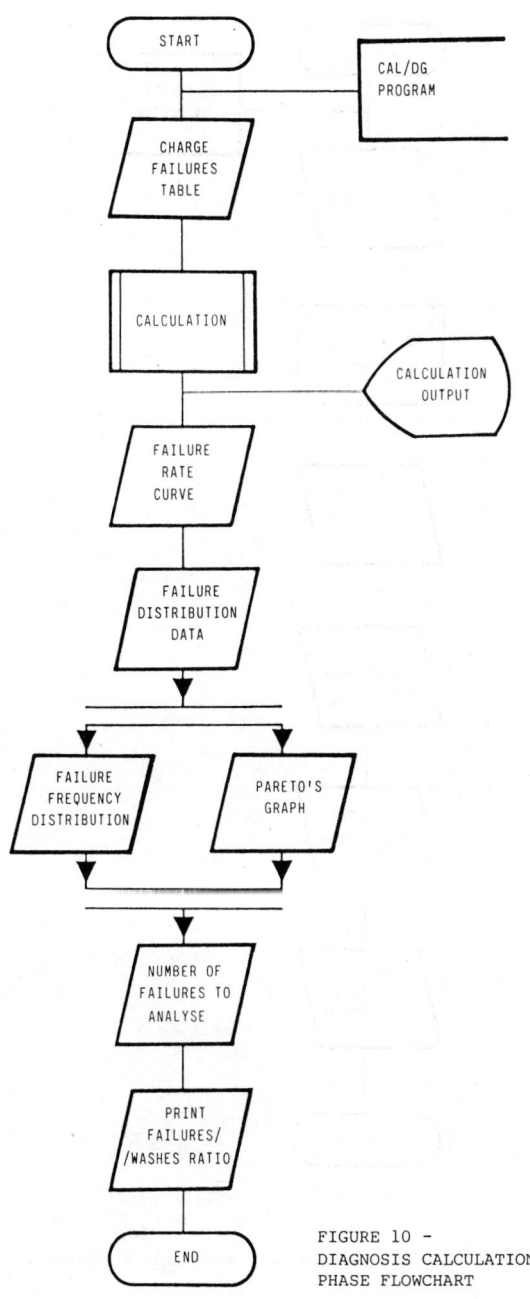

FIGURE 10 -
DIAGNOSIS CALCULATION
PHASE FLOWCHART

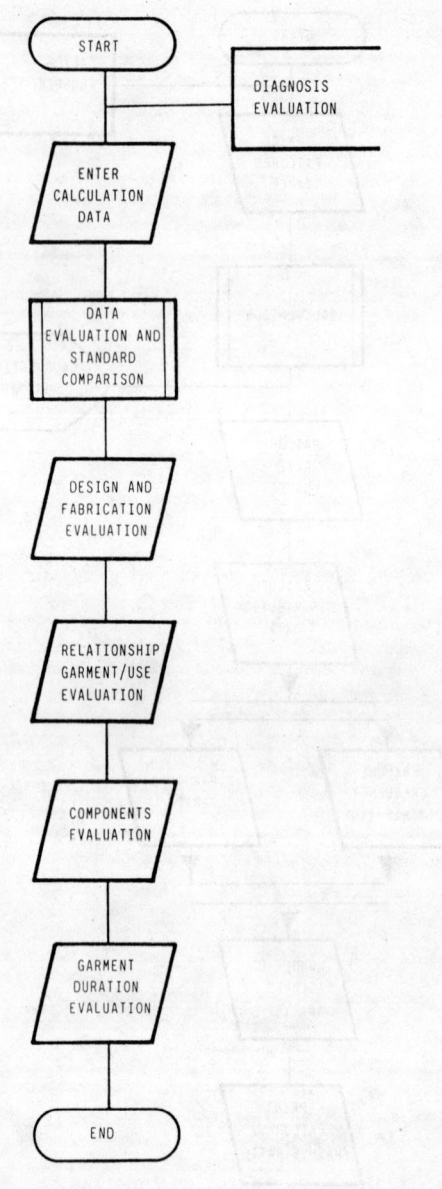

FIGURE 11 - DIAGNOSIS EVALUATION FLOWCHART

FIGURE 12 - PRACTICAL EXAMPLE

DIAGNOSTICO DE PRENDAS DE VESTIR

REFERENCIA: PRENDA 733 - MODELO 1539 - COLOR 25 - TALLA M

TASA DE FALLOS

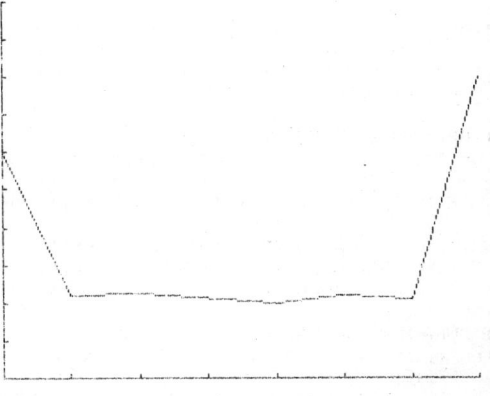

)-LAVADOS.Cada division 1 lav.
OTAL LAVADOS=7
)-Vát.=TASA DE FALLO. Intervalo 10
SCALA 0 a 100

    * * * * * * * * * * * * * * * *

o - %F= 50
etaI=DECRECIENTE
ASO I A II fase:
I=   1 -%F= 60
amda II= 17.167
ASO II a III fase:
II= 6 -%F= 80

**** ESTUDIO DE LOS FALLOS ***

RAFICO DE PARETO
SPECIFICACIONES:
RDEN COD.FALLO   %   %ACUM.

        9   33,3   33,3
        5   12,5   45,8
        6   12,5   58,3
        1   8,3   66,7
        2   8,3   75,0
        7   8,3   83,3
        3   4,2   87,5
        4   4,2   91,7
        8   4,2   95,8
       10   4,2   100,0

)-TIPO DE FALLOS.
ada division un fallo.
)-%. Intervalo =10.

    * * * * * * * * * * * * * * * *

                RATIO F/L
                  Fase
  FALLO   I   II   III   TIPO DE FALLO
     9   0.0   0.0   8.0   FALLO DESGASTE
     5   0.0   .6   0.0   FALLO ACCIDENTAL
     6   2.0   .2   0.0   FALLO INFANTIL

587

***** DIAGNOSTICO DE LA PRENDA **

VALORACION DE LOS DATOS DEL COMPORTAMIENTO DE LA PRENDA.-

* ESTUDIO DEL MODELO Y SU FABRICACION:
Los primeros dias de uso, la prenda presenta
FALLOS EN EL CONTROL -materia prima/fabricacion>>>*

* RELACION DEL ESTUDIO DE LA PRENDA Y SU USO POSTERIOR: (Obs.)
La cantidad de fallos que se producen
-pasados los primeros dias de uso y hasta que la prenda se empieza hacer vieja
RESULTAN ALGO EXCESIVOS

* RELACION ENTRE COMPONENTES DE LA PRENDA
Con las especificaciones anteriores - >>>* -,hay que considerar especialmente

FALLO	TIPO DE FALLO	PREVISION DE CORRECCIONES
9	FALLO DESGASTE	PREVISIBLE EN EL ESTUDIO DE LA PRENDA
5	FALLO ACCIDENTAL	IMPREVISIBLE SALVO F/L ELEVADO: USO NO PREVIST
6	FALLO INFANTIL	PREVISIBLE EN EL ESTUDIO DE LA PRENDA

* DURACION DE LA PRENDA: (Obs.)
Teniendo en cuenta las consideraciones anteriores
LA PRENDA ANTES DEL USO -control de fabricacion- DEBE PULIRSE MAS
LA DURACION-COMO PRENDA NUEVA-PUEDE ACEPTARSE COMO CORRECTA
LA DURACION-HASTA QUE LA PRENDA SE EMPIEZA HACER VIEJA-VER Obs.

* Obs.:en todos los casos hay que matizar segun modelo prenda y necesidades us

* VALORACION GLOBAL DE LA PRENDA:

TECNICO EJECUTIVO   Vo. Bo.

Fdo: R.M.SAURI/J.LLORIA   Fdo: A.BARELLA/A.MANICH

INSTITUTO de TECNOLOGIA
QUIMICA y TEXTIL
C.S.I.C.

Barcelona, 10 ,ABRIL, 1984 .

588

HOW SMALL CAN BE EFFECTIVE AS WELL AS BEAUTIFUL

D. F. Taylor

ABSTRACT

The development of the garment and textile industry during the past thirty years is explained and contrasted in various simple quantitative ways. The continuing growth of the garment industry during the past ten years is demonstrated and the strong and steady emergence of the small company is illustrated and explained. Certain limitations in the continued economic development of small companies are anticipated in the absence of technological change.

The prospects for technological and managerial improvement are forecast through the use of small computers. Two specific computer related projects are described, one to enhance managerial efficiency the other to enhance efficiency in grading and markers making. Finally it is suggested that the prospect for small companies in many sectors of industry will be enhanced because of the use of small computers.

1. EARLY HISTORY

In common with many newly industrialising countries the textile and garment industries are amongst H.K.'s oldest industries. The first weaving factory was established in 1922 and the first garment factory in 1934.

The eventual control of China by the Communists in 1949 and the Korean war in 1950 brought enormous change to H.K. and our industry. Capitalist Chinese mainly from the North fled here bringing capital, entrepreneurship and experience in textile manufacture, while over a million poorer immigrants mainly from Southern China provided a work force willing initially to work hard for low pay.

These beginnings established a textile and garment industry in H.K. that has been until now the mainspring of our industrial economy. It is however a mainspring that has undergone tremendous growth and change in a mere thirty years. A process of change that I will attempt to describe briefly through a few significant figures and ratios.

2. INDUSTRY TRENDS

The garment industry in 1983 directly employed 254 000 persons or about 30% of all our industrial work force. In 1959, the number employed was only 37 000 so you see a sevenfold increase in garment industry employment in 24 years.

In contrast the textile industry employed 43 000 persons in 1959 and grew to only 114 000 persons in 1983. It seems that the textile industry peaked in about 1976 and is now in slow decline. This decline results from a combination of two sets of factors. Firstly the industry today in H.K. enjoys no comparative advantage in terms of production inputs, land, utilities and labour costs are all relatively

high. Secondly the industry needs a substantial domestic
market to be viable and the changes that have overtaken our
garment industry majority of them in the past ten years are
increasingly denying our textile industry a share of this
domestic market.

Let me return to my central topic the garment industry. The
feature of sevenfold growth in employment has been accompanied
by major growth in the number of small and medium sized
enterprises and virtually no growth in the number of large
enterprises. This trend can be demonstrated through a
variety of figures such as ....

The average employment in H.K. garment factories has reduced
from 54 persons in 1959 to 28 persons in 1983 i.e. has halved
in 24 years. The gross output of factories employing less
than 200 persons has increased from 3 Billion H.K. dollars
in 1973 to 16 Billion in 1981 a fivefold increase in 8 years.
Factories employing over 200 persons only increased their
output from 16 Billion to 27 Billion over the same period.

Of course the backbone of the industry really comprises enterprises with employment in the range 100-500 persons such
enterprises employ today about one third of the workforce
and produce 40% of the industries' output. Larger factories
are not growing, with some 8 000 garment factories operating
in H.K. only 37 factories employ over 500 persons.

All these figures indicate that there is obviously substantial
comparative advantage in being small. The smaller enterprises
are winning, they are getting the growth share in output and
they are clearly preferred by the average employee.

3. WHY SMALL

The comparative advantage of small is derived from three sets
of inputs. Small fits better with the physical constraints
of the environment. Because of land shortage we build our
factories up in the air. A ten storey factory with 600 square
meters per floor is typical of the buildings we were creating
in the sixties. That sort of building encourages ten separate
factories, one per floor, rather than one factory. Stacked
living and stacked working promotes separateness.

Small fits better with the cultural expectations of the people.
The predominant workforce is of Cantonese extraction and so now
are most of the entrepreneurs running the industry in contrast
with the situation 20 or more years ago when Northern Chinese
would have been the dominant entrepreneurs. The Cantonese are a
clanish people, they lived in their walled villages for hundreds
of years and rarely mixed with persons from neighbouring villages
except for intermarriage. Big city living does little to promote
informal relationships at a distance, hence a built in preference
to work and communicate within small groups. Something in truth,
people in many other societies also prefer.

Small fits better with the overseas buyers'
needs and interests. Buyers are increasingly seeking

variety coupled with decreasing volume per order. They also
want to be certain that they are getting thoroughly
competitive quotes while still commanding substantial attention
from the managing entrepreneur.

Given that a society is capable of generating a sizeable
percentage of entrepreneurs, and this is certainly a strong
characteristic of the Chinese, and that those entrepreneurs
can afford to start up businesses, the ingredients promoting
smallness are all there.

4. THE PENALTIES

But the trend to reduction in size cannot continue indefinitely
without some adverse economic effects. Already we have probably
seen some loss of productivity as a result. Economically we
have probably compensated for this by doing more valuable
work and making more fashion oriented products. However the
warning signals are all clearly there and we must somehow try
to improve the capability and productivity of small enterprises
and maintain a momentum of improvement if the industry is to
prosper well into the future.

5. THE GOAL AND THE PROSPECTS

The prospects for making these improvements in the garment
industry are now very good thanks largely to the advent of the
inexpensive small computer and the microprocessor. Let me
try to explain why this is so.

Firstly much of the labour in a garment factory is employed
in a one to one relationship with only moderately expensive
equipment. Female workers sewing and male workers pressing
comprise majority of the workforce. Because the customer
wants it, and because technologically it will be difficult to
do the equivalent work in a more productive way, these jobs
will stay for some time much as they are. What we have to do
is to find ways and means to pay the essential labour as much
as we can while making the overall product as inexpensive as
possible. The garment industry must stay top payer to its
workers in the spectrum of H.K. industry if it is to continue
to succeed. If it fails to stay top payer then it will fail
to recruit its new essential workers and the whole industry
will start to slide.

So we have to attack and enhance productivity and capability
of the industry in all other respects, whenever and wherever
possible. We must do this both external to the enterprises
by continually improving the infrastructure and internal to
the enterprises by improving management and various supportive
work activities.

6. HOW CAN WE DO IT

I want now to illustrate this general concept by briefly
telling you about two programmes of work we are engaged in.
They are both highly reliant on the use of small computers
and are indicative of ways we believe the industry can be
improved.

6.1 Computers and Management

Effective management of enterprises is clearly of great
importance. There is a clear trend for the fashion oriented
work to be done in the smaller enterprises. Fashion work
requires production of a wide variety of small batch products,
this is especially demanding on management and in an entre-
preneurial situation one will compensate for increasing demands
by reducing total scale. I assume that the typical entrepreneur objects to expanding his management team.

We are aiming to compensate for this tendency to reduce scale
by helping entrepreneurs to use computers to carry out many
repetitive tasks that would otherwise take their valuable time.
The hardware needed to do this is clearly available today at
acceptable cost but the software is not. Consequently we are
engaged in developing a comprehensive suite of some sixteen
integrated programmes that will allow the small manufacturer
to increase the scale of his work in a fashion oriented
industry without increasing his managerial workforce. Virtually
everybody in the past in the Western world has developed computer
software for industry to allow big companies to do the same
amount of work with less people. We are developing ours to
allow small companies to effectively employ more workers. This
is I think an interestingly different way of looking at
employment.

6.2 CAD/CAM

Another way in which computers can be used in organisations is
to try and reduce the capital cost of carrying out certain
activities in a process centre. Computer aided design is an
area that is particularly vulnerable to capital cost reduction
as a result of the fairly recent introduction of powerful low
cost computers. Consequently about two years ago H.K.P.C.
began researching the local implications of CAD/CAM in pattern
grading and markers making. Of course computer based systems
facilitating these activities have been available in the U.S.A.
since the late sixties. But such systems were designed for
large scale operations they were oriented to high volume
outputs and high capital expense was consequently acceptable.

There has been some purchase and use of these systems in H.K.
but their penetration is not significant.

Our approach was to consider whether inexpensive systems could
be produced that would facilitate variety of output rather
than volume of output, the principal objective was not so much
to reduce cost of production but enhance opportunity for
production at affordable capital investment.

Markers making appeared to us to be a relative costly investment
prospect so we decided to develop a two pronged complementary
approach. On one hand we envisaged markers making bureau
services being established with the factories feeding already
designed patterns into these markers making bureaus. We therefore devoted our development effort to producing a lower cost

pattern grading facility. This has now been done and our
product is commercially available. Our CAD system consists
of a minicomputer and a 2 in 1 digitiser plotter. The application
software is user-friendly and Chinese character display is
available as an option.

The computer aspects of this work were not particularly
demanding as those of you who know something about grading
and computers will surmise. The digitiser-plotter development
was however quite a challenge because we wanted to make an
acceptable performance plotter available at a mere fraction of
the cost of normally commercially available equipment. The key
to this was recognising the limited accuracy that was the real
need for garment manufacturing since garments are not engineered
products. Once we accepted relevant accuracy requirements we
could employ drivers and slide mechanisms that were much less
expensive than those used on other digital plotters.

After direct manual input of the original pattern on the
digitiser plotter the user is able to use our CAD systems to
quickly grade and plot his own patterns. These patterns can
subsequently be laid up by hand in his own factory in a
conventional way to make markers, or an optional facility will
be available to transmit the graded pattern information and
markers requirement over the telecomms network to our markers
bureau. We then plan to give a 24 hours turn around in the
production and courier delivery of paper markers. This markers
making bureau service will enable the typical small factory to
dispense with the space required for a markers lay up table
and will avoid the necessity to keep a skilled markers maker
on the pay roll a potentially expensive and sometimes delicately
temperamental experience for small factories.

7. CONCLUSIONS

What I have tried to do is specifically illustrate in two ways
the impact of small computers on the ability of small enterprises
in the garment industry to enhance their technological and
managerial capability. HKPC's interests as an organisation
are not limited to the garment industry, in fact we devote only
a quite small fraction of our efforts to this industry.
Generally our work in other industry areas is also supportive
of the contention that inexpensive computers are destined to
have a major beneficial input on small industry and make small
become effective as well as beautiful. However societies will
have to be innovative if they are to realise the full benefits
of small computers. Such innovation is required throughout
their industrial community and its infrastructure and an
inability or unwillingness to innovate or accept the results
of innovation may prevent full realisation of these benefits
in some industrialised societies. Larger enterprises need to
continuously evaluate their comparative advantage in any field
of activity.The closer we already see and accept a one to one
relationship of workforce with a productive piece of equipment
the more likely it is that the progressive development in the
use of inexpensive computers will promote the growth of smaller
enterprises.

Seen from the viewpoint of the ordinary person the scenario
must be considered optimistic. Small employers have always
proven to be more reliable providers of livelihood than
the large. Now it seems they can hope to improve the
reward that goes with that livelihood.

Hong Kong Productivity Centre
World Commerce Centre
Harbour City
Kowloon
HONG KONG

MECHA-ELECTRONICS OF GARMENT SEWING SYSTEM

Y. Kawauchi

ABSTRACT

The wave of computerization in the industry today has at last
come to the garment manufacturing industry. The industrial
sewing machine, as the major equipment for manufacturing garments, is one of the typical machinery, and has been studied
purely as an object of mechanical engineering. However, we can
hardly find any mechanical engineering curriculums for sewing
machines. Recently, both the industrial and home sewing machines
are being included in the field of mecha-electronics engineering.
Mecha-electronics introduced in the garment sewing system will
lead to higher flexibility in the garment manufacture as well
as automatized garment sewing. This paper is primarily con·
cerned with the following subjects which may typically represent the results of mecha-electronics introduced in the garment
manufacturing system.
1. Numerically controlled sewing machine
2. Edge control seamer
3. Microcomputer-controlled sewing machine
4. Microcomputer-controlled garment press
5. Development of mecha-electronics in the future garment manufacturing system

In giving considerations to these subjects, I hope that the
mecha-electronic technologies will provide a breakthrough in
the garment industry faced with crisis in advanced countries.

INTRODUCTION

It was about 1970 that electronic technology was introduced in
the sewing machine which was, of course, one of the typical
machinery. At that time in Japan, "fusion of mechanics with
electronics" plan was framed in the industry, and this started
the introduction of mecha-electronics into sewing machines.
After that, development of industrial sewing machines and
household sewing machines based on mecha-electronic technologies progressed along with the growing computerization. In
the garment manufacturing, the operation processes up to cutting
are mainly controlled by computers, the sewing process, by
electronics and micro computers, and the finishing process, by
microcomputers as shown in Table 1.

This paper presents technical discussion about the mecha-
electronics applied to the sewing and finishing processes shown
in Table 1, then refers to the development of mecha-electronics
in the future garment manufacturing.

1. NUMERICALLY CONTROLLED SEWING MACHINE

In the conventional mechanical automatic control system, pattern
seaming is controlled mainly by templates and cam mechanism.
In numerical control, pattern automatization is achieved by
giving numerals for positional information. A numerically
controlled sewing machine has an "X-Y" table which is designed
to feed works along the path of a predetermined pattern.
Numerical information is given to the X and Y of the table in

order to drive the feed mechanism by means of a servo motor, thus achieving automatic control. The numerically controlled sewing machines may be classified according to the following methods:
(1) Numerical denotation method
(2) Numerical input method
(3) Numerical control method
The following discusses each of the above three methods.

1.1 Numerical denotation method

Coordinates are used to express patterns drawn on a plane in terms of numerical values. Coordinates come in Cartesian coordinates and polar coordinates. In the absolute dimensioning, the position of a certain point on coordinates is given in relation to the reference point of the coordinates. In the incremental dimensioning, the position of a certain point on coordinates is indicated in relation to the position of the preceding point. Fig. 1 shows the absolute dimensioning applied to the Cartesian coordinates, Fig. 2 shows the incremental dimensioning applied to the Cartesian coordinates, Fig. 3, the absolute dimensioning used for the polar coordinates, and Fig. 4, the incremental dimensioning used for the polar coordinates. The difference between these denotation methods is the difference in the input method of numerical values.

In numerical control, numerical information is entered by punching the tape. There are several input methods of numerical values in numerical control, and these methods differ in how the numerical values are coded and perforated into tape, i.e., what tape formats are used to program and enter numerical values. Each of the methods is discussed with the aid of illustrations. Fig. 5 shows an example of tape format based on the Cartesian coordinate absolute dimensioning method for denotation of numerical information. This tape format provides the seam line program for one-piece collar of a shirt and the like. In the coordinates, the actual dimensions are measured on a 0.1mm basis. For instance, "X + 130" means that the point is 13 millimeters away in the plus direction of X-axis. Fig. 6 gives an example of tape format based on the Cartesian coordinate incremental dimensioning method for denotating numerical information. This tape format contains the seam line program for two-piece collar of a shirt and the like. In the coordinates shown in Fig. 6, the dimensions are measured on a 0.2mm basis, and the incremental numerical values are represented in terms of the dimensions divided by 0.2. In the example of the polar coordinate incremental dimensioning method shown in Fig. 7, the programming is executed by simply specifying the directions. More specifically, each quadrant is divided into twenty-one directions, totaling eighty-four directions, and the eighty-four directions correspond to the eighty-four keys on the keyboard. This makes it possible to denote the numerical value of one stitch by one character.

The method in which numerical information is written into the PROM (Programmable Read Only Memory) of a computer has been replacing the conventional method in which numerical information is programmed into tape. For a 8-bit PROM, numerical information can be stored in the PROM through a tape format. Table 1 shows an example of format used to write numerical information into a 16-bit PROM which consists of two 8-bit PROMs (INTEL C1702).

1.3 Numerical Control Method

Numerical control comes in the closed loop method and the open loop method. In the closed loop method, the information contained in the tape is processed through the electronic information processor and sent to the direct current servo motor. The sensor feeds the outputs of the servo motor back for comparison with the command numerical information to maintain accurate control. On the other hand, in the open loop method, outputs are given directly to a pulse motor, eliminating the need for feedback of output results. In Japan, the open loop numerical control method based on pulse motor has been prevailing in the field of machine tools, therefore, the open loop method has been employed in most numerically controlled sewing machines. Recently, however, the closed loop method also started to prevail. Photo 1 shows Juki APS-175 as an example of N.C. sewing machine.

2. EDGE CONTROL SEAMER (5)

An operation like runstitching in which the edges of two cloths are trued up and seamed is called edge seaming. In this case, the inside line of the margin will be the line of stitch. The edges of the cloths will be shaped by cutting. Accordingly, a desired line of stitch can be obtained, in most cases, by simply sewing along the cloth edges without programming the desired line of stitch. According to this theory, it should be possible to automatically sew cloths by using an edge sensing means through which the cloth edges are controlled so that the distance between the needle entry point and the edges is kept constant.

Here, two sets of photoelectric sensors as the cloth edge detecting means are provided at a right angle to the advancing direction of the cloth edges. The photoelectric sensors will go OFF or ON as the cloth edges pass or fail to pass through the sensors, thus making it possible to reposition the cloth edges properly. To reposition the cloth edges, the roller of a manipulator is used. Fig. 8 illustrates this theory, and Photo 2 shows the edge control seamer.

3. MICROCOMPUTER-CONTROLLED SEWING MACHINE

Today, the use of micro computers is so popular that they are employed not only in industrial sewing machines but also in household sewing machines. This section describes Juki DDL-555-5/300 series (Photo 3) which is one of the typical examples of microcomputer-controlled industrial plain lockstitchers. For a plain lockstitcher, a series of repeated action to be automatized include counting of stitches, interrupting the machine according to the result of stitch count, stopping the needle at the highest or lowest point, and producing reverse stitches in a specified number at the start or end of a seam.

The revolution of the main shaft of the sewing machine is
detected by a noncontact sensor such as a Hall element, and
the detected revolution is sent to the micro processor to count
the stitches. The result of the stitch count is compared with
the preset number of stitches. When the number of counted
stitches coincides with the preset number of stitches, a
command is issued to stop the electronic-stop motor or to begin
automatic reverse stitching. Thus, automation of the plain
lockstitcher is achieved (6). Table 2 shows the specifications
of the Juki DDL-555-5/300 series.

4. MICROCOMPUTER-CONTROLLED GARMENT PRESS

The preceding sections all refer to the typical examples of
mecha-electronics applied to industrial sewing machines. This
section explains an example of mecha-electronics applied to
garment presses. Photo 4 shows Juki JRG-MOO & JVG-MOO series
presses which are controlled by microcomputers. The CRT has a
keyboard through which press conditions can be easily programmed by simple key operation. The 10-pattern memory feature
allows quick response to material changes. In addition to the
batting function, the pressure can be adjusted to three different levels. The pressure is applied vertically to minimize
stretch or slippage of materials pressed. Further, the presses
are provided with head safety guards are release pushbutton
switches for assured safety. The series of pressing operations,
including opening/closing of the head, lifting/lowering of the
buck, and application of pressure in three different levels (in
case of the JRG-MOO series, the 3-level control of the steam
and vacuum is added) are carried out in accordance with the
programs. The microcomputers issue sequential commands to
open or close the solenoid valves, or to coordinate timings,
thereby permitting high-level automation of the presses (7).

5. DEVELOPMENT OF MECHA-ELECTRONICS IN THE FUTURE GARMENT
   MANUFACTURING SYSTEM

Since the garment industry is supported by labor intensive
work, increases in wages add to managerial difficulty in every
advanced country. It has generally been considered that good
business results of a garment factory are contingent on good
production volume, high proficiency of operators, and streamlined production control. However, the recent trend in garment
factories towards manufacturing many types of products in small
quantity requires more frequent lot change, resulting in loss
in the learning of operators with consequent worse business
results in garment factories. To solve this problem, it is
necessary to achieve less dependence on the labor intensive
work in garment factories. From this point of view, labor
savings as well as automatization that would successfully meet
the requirements of diversified small-quantity production are
major subjects in the management of the future garment factories.

As understood from the examples described so far, the mecha-
electronic technology has enabled equipment to have higher
versatility and to allow quick changes. There is no doubt
that the mecha-electronic technology will be the key technology
also in the future garment manufacturing system. Automatization
to eliminate the need for sewing programs is especially useful

for permitting quick changes. For this purpose, an automatic
sewing method is suggested, in which a work is automatically
sewn along its contour by photoelectrically scanning the contour of the work (see Figs. 9 and 10). This method, which
belongs to a control method known as the adaptive control,
should prevail in the future in this industry.

As more mecha-electronic technologies are introduced in this
industry, more improvements are expected to be made. For
instance, work arrangements and procedures are expected to be
planned more efficiently by the use of still upgraded micro
computers which are sure to come out in the near future. Also,
the growth of LAN (Local Area Network) would enhance the intellectual part of sewing work. It is anticipated that the present
manual labor in sewing work or in the operation of equipment
will be increasingly replaced by automatic equipment and sewing
robots. All of these are expected to be realized in the 21st
century.

6. CONCLUSION

Successful solution of the problems which the garment industry
is facing now depends on achievement of less reliance on labor
intensive work. Automatization of sewing work, therefore, is
greatly expected to give a breakthrough to the industry.

In the 1960's, fashion itself was enough to give us a dream as
it was considered to produce high values in the garment manufacturing. Today, high sewing technology, instead of the
fashion, is accepted as an element to give us a dream.

We, a manufacturer of sewing machines are willing to further
proceed with our research and development through full utilization of mecha-electronics in order to realize the dream in
the garment industry.

7. ACKNOWLEDGEMENT

The author wishes to express his thanks to Dr. J. Shimizu of
Tokyo Institute of Technology, who gave the author the chance
to present this paper. The author also thanks Mr. Shiba of
Zellweger Uster Company for his help in presenting this work.
The assistance and cooperation of the following people of Tokyo
Juki Co., Ltd. are gratefully acknowledged.
Mr. M. Tomizawa and Mr. Y. Uchiyama (assisted in gathering
patent information)
Mr. Y. Kokubu (assisted in gathering the technical data)
Mr. S. Kondo and Mr. T. Oda (assisted in general arrangement)

REFERENCES

(1) Y. Kawauchi. J. Text. Mach. Soc. Japan, 1974, 9, 1.

(2) Y. Kawauchi. J. Text. Mach. Soc. Japan, 1978, 4, 158.

(3) USP. No.3, 752, 098.

(4) Japan Patent Appl. No. 52-59, 625, 50-125, 671.

(5) Y. Kawauchi. J. Text. Mach. Soc. Japan, 1978, 4, 162.

(6) Japan Patent Appl. No. 56-20, 497.

(7) Japan Patent Appl. No. 56-120, 874.

Apparel Manufacturing Research Laboratory
Tokyo Juki Industrial Co., Ltd.
2-1, 8-chome, Kokuryo-cho,
Chofu-Shi, Tokyo, Japan.

Fig. 1 Absolute dimensioning on Cartesian coordinates

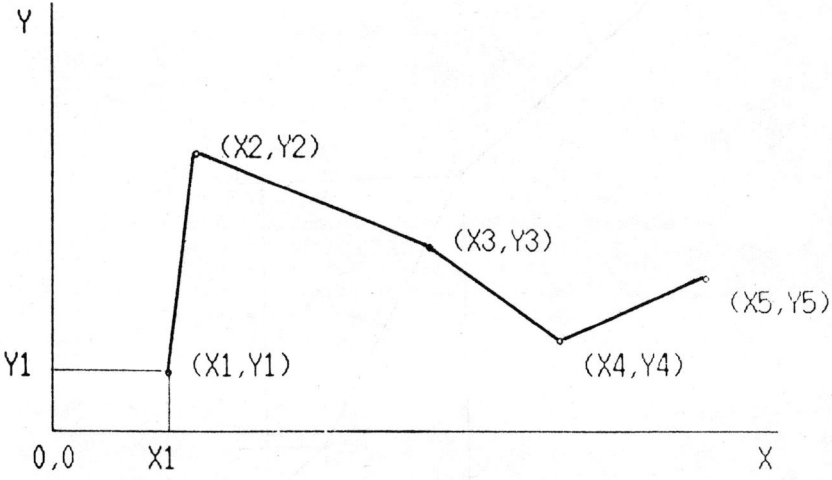

Fig. 2 Incremental dimensioning on Cartesian coordinates

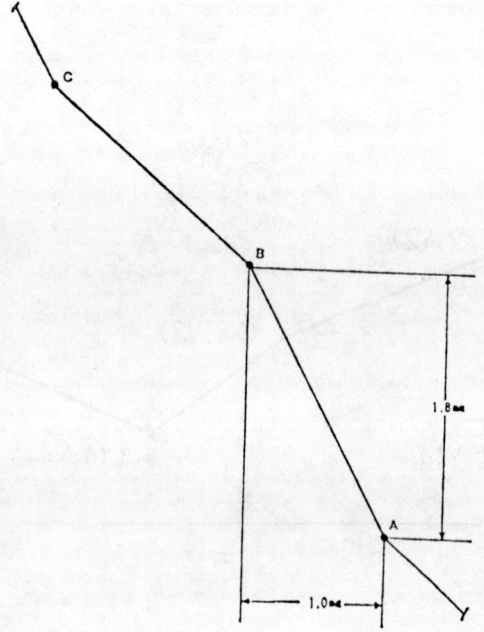

Fig. 3   Absolute dimensioning on polar coordinates

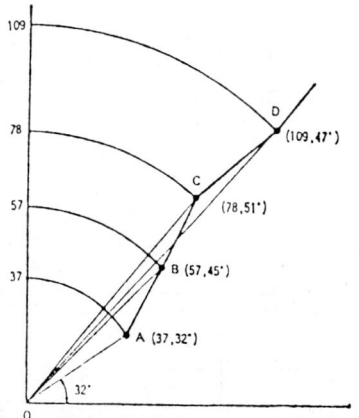

Fig. 4   Incremental dimensioning on polar coordinates

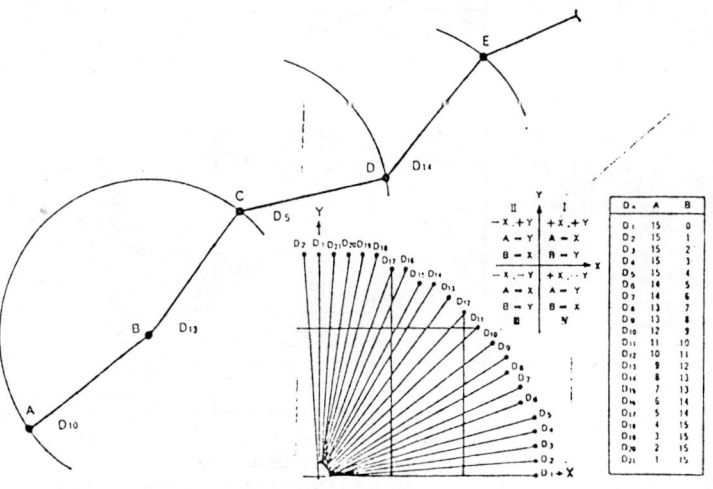

Fig. 5 Tape format of Necchi NC sewing machine   Kawauchi

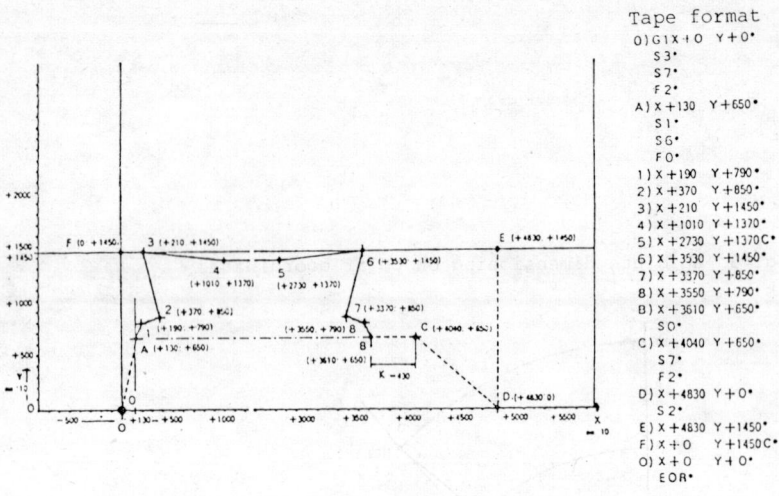

```
Tape format
0) G1X+0  Y+0*
   S3*
   S7*
   F2*
A) X+130  Y+650*
   S1*
   S6*
   F0*
1) X+190  Y+790*
2) X+370  Y+850*
3) X+210  Y+1450*
4) X+1010 Y+1370*
5) X+2730 Y+1370C*
6) X+3530 Y+1450*
7) X+3370 Y+850*
8) X+3550 Y+790*
B) X+3610 Y+650*
   S0*
C) X+4040 Y+650*
   S7*
   F2*
D) X+4830 Y+0*
   S2*
E) X+4830 Y+1450*
F) X+0    Y+1450C*
O) X+0    Y+0*
   EOR*
```

Fig. 6 Tape format of Juki NC sewing machine

Illustration	No. of stitches	Tape format	Description
	1	S*	S:START (SLOW) SEW COMMAND
	2	U8Y2*	
	3	U8Y2*	
	4	U8Y2*	
	5	U6Y5*	
	6	X2V8Q*	Q:FAST SEW COMMAND
	⋮	⋮	The part drawn on the right side to the center line is mirror image.
	96	X8V2S*	SLOW SEW COMMAND
	97	X8V2*	
	98	X8V2T	T:STOP SEW AND CUT THREAD COMMAND
	Remarks	The asterisked codes are classifying codes (LF) of one-stitch information. The displacement information figures, which are expressed in terms of the amounts (in mm) of displacements in X or Y direction divided by 0.2, can be entered up to 15.	
	604		

Fig. 7 Tape format of Gerber NC sewing machine (3)

Illustration	No. of stitches	Tape format	Description
		$\emptyset$	INITIAL VECTOR COMMAND
		S_0	SLOW SEW COMMAND
		S_1	FAST SEW COMMAND
	1	I	STITCHER VECTOR COMMAND
	2	I	"
	3	I	"
	4	J	
	⋮	⋮	⋮
	8	←	"
	⋮	⋮	⋮
	98	A	"
		S_2	STOP SEW COMMAND
		Blank	DELAY
		S_3	CUT THREAD COMMAND
		$\emptyset$	TO UNLOAD POSITION
		S_4	CLAMP UNLOAD COMMAND
		8	DISENGAGE COMMAND
		S_5	RETURN COMMAND
		S_6	STOP READER COMMAND
	Remarks		The maximum unit displacement of vector component is 15.

605

Table 2. Example of writing into PROM

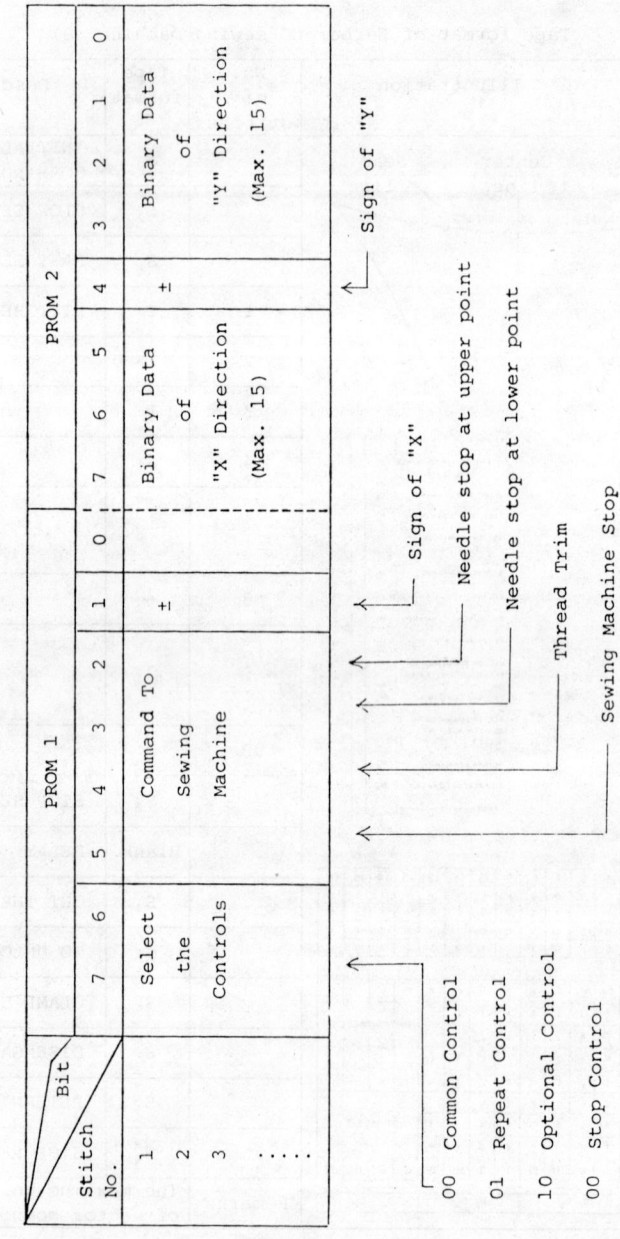

Bit \ Stitch No.	PROM 1								PROM 2							
	7	6	5	4	3	2	1	0	7	6	5	4	3	2	1	0
1	Select the Controls		Command To Sewing Machine				±		Binary Data of "X" Direction (Max. 15)			±	Binary Data of "Y" Direction (Max. 15)			
2																
3																
.....																

Sign of "Y"

Sign of "X"

Needle stop at upper point

Needle stop at lower point

Thread Trim

Sewing Machine Stop

00 Common Control
01 Repeat Control
10 Optional Control
00 Stop Control

606

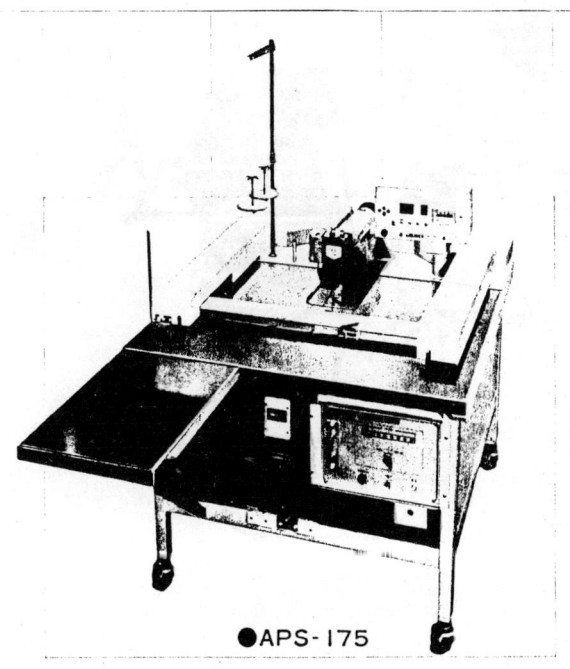

Photo. 1.   Juki N.C. Sewing Machine

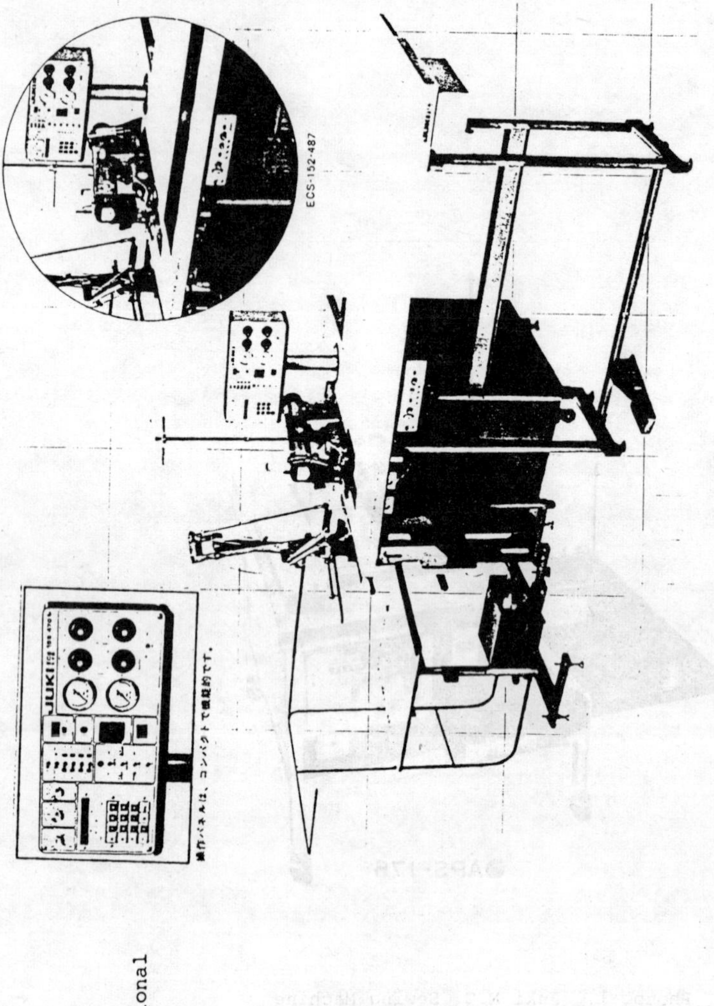

ECS-152-487

Compact, functional
control panel

Photo. 2   Edge Control Seamer

Photo. 3 JUKI DDL-555-5/300

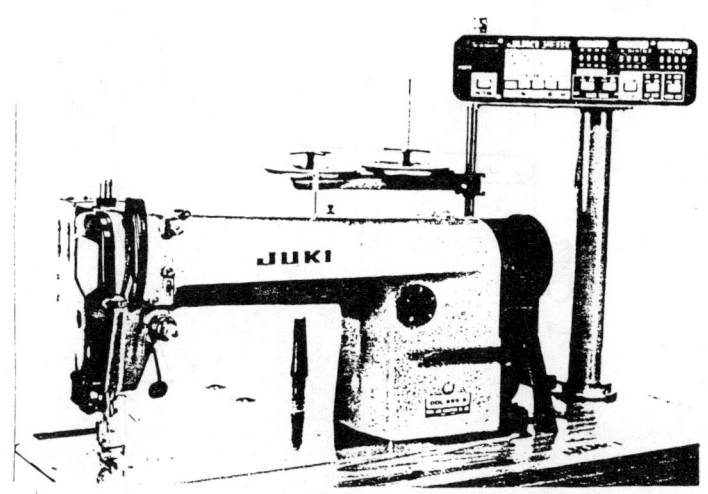

Table 3. Specification of Juki DDL-555-5/300 series

Model	DDL-555-5-2B/300	DDL-555-5-4B/300	DDL-555A-5-4B/300	DDL-555A-5-2B/300	DDL-555H-5-2B/300	DDL-555H-5-4B/300
Sewing speed	Max. 5,000 s.p.m. (for medium-weight materials)		Max. 4,000 s.p.m. (for light-weight materials)		Max. 3,500 s.p.m. (for heavy-weight materials)	
Stitch length	4.0 mm				Max. 4.5 mm	
Needle bar stroke	30.5 mm		29.0 mm		35 mm	
Presser foot lift (by knee lifter) (by hand lifter)	10 mm 5.5 mm (Finely adjustable)				12 mm 5.5 mm (Finely adjustable)	
Feed dog teeth	3 rows (feed dog teeth tilt adjustable)		4 rows (feed dog teeth tilt adjustable)		3 rows (feed dog teeth tilt adjustable)	
Presser foot	Special hinging presser					
Needle (standard)	DB x 1 #14 (Standard) #11 ~ #18		DA x 1 #9 (Standard) #9 ~ #11		DB x 1 #21 (Standard) #19 ~ #25	
Lubrication	Fully automatic					
Automatic reverse feed switch lever (one touch type) (number of stitch control type)	Equipped Variable from 0 to 9 stitches for both forward and reverse feed					
Pattern sewing (Z pattern) (Fixed pattern sewing)	6 steps variable from 0 to 99 stitches 3 patterns					
Wiper	None	Equipped	Equipped	None	None	Equipped
Speed control	From 500 s.p.m. to max. speed of pulley used (adjustable from outside)					
Power supply	3 φ 220 ~ 440 or 1 φ 110 ~ 250 V					
Motor	550 W (3/4 HP) & 400 W (1/2 HP) Electronic-stop motor					

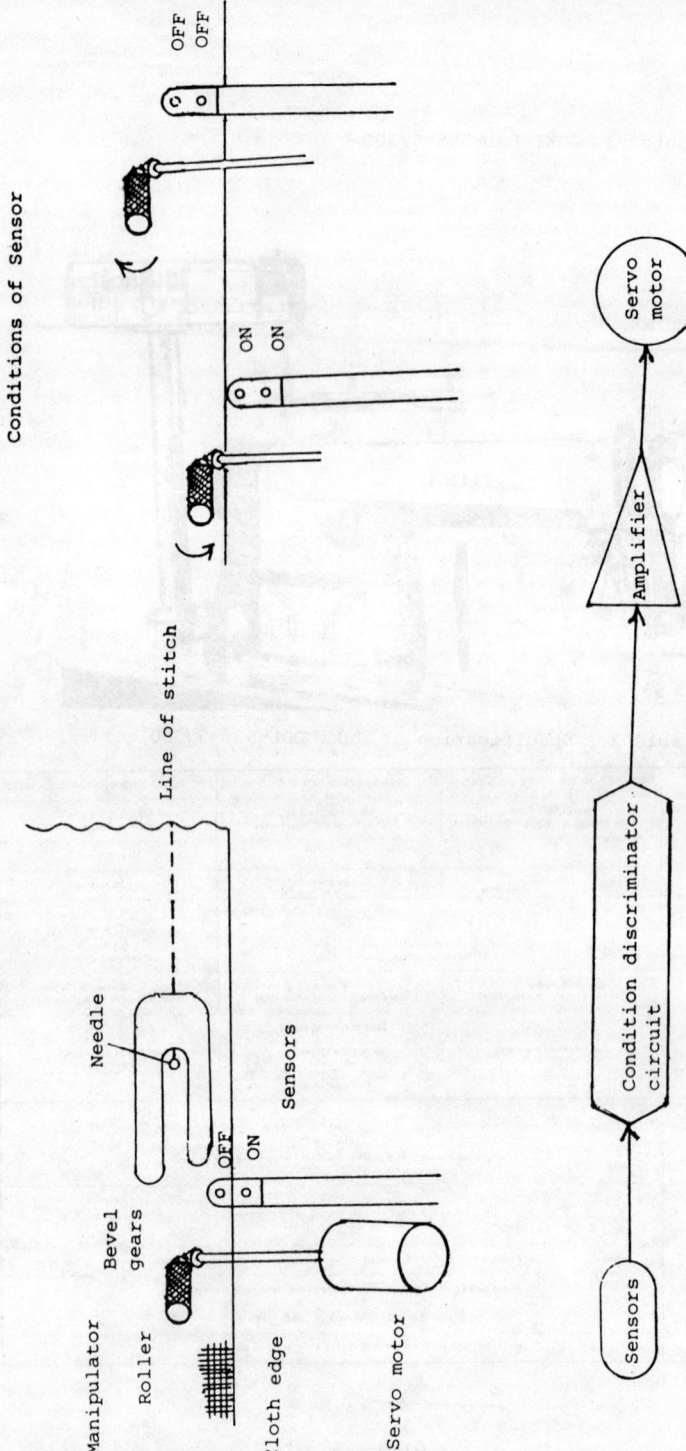

Fig. 8 Conditions of Sensor and Control of Manipulator

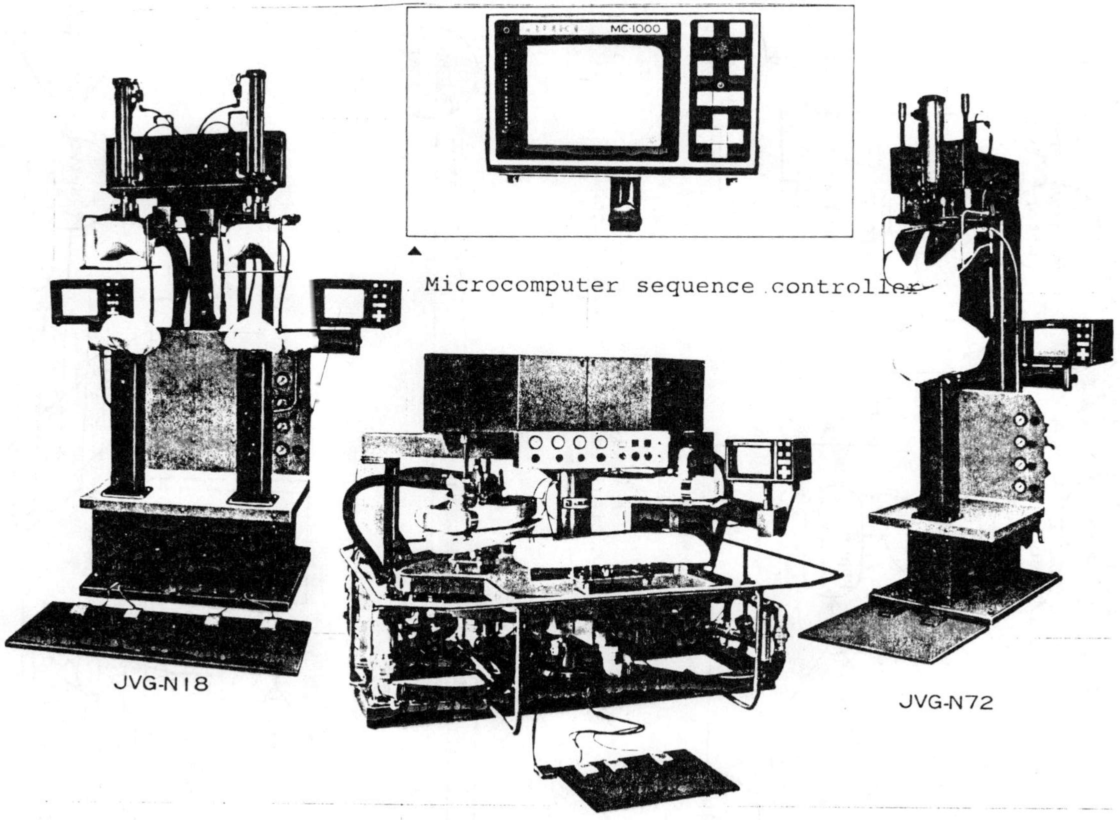
MC-1000
Microcomputer sequence controller
JVG-N18
JVG-N72
JRG-M07

Photo. 4 Juki JRG-MOO and JVG-MOO Series

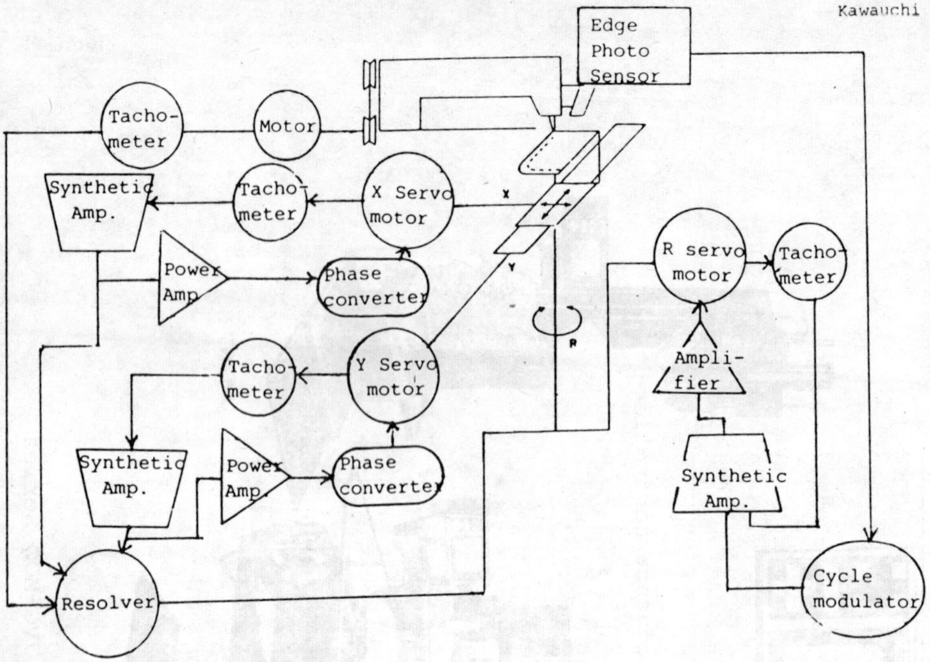

Fig. 9   Block Diagram of Work Silhouette
Optical Scanning Profile Stitching

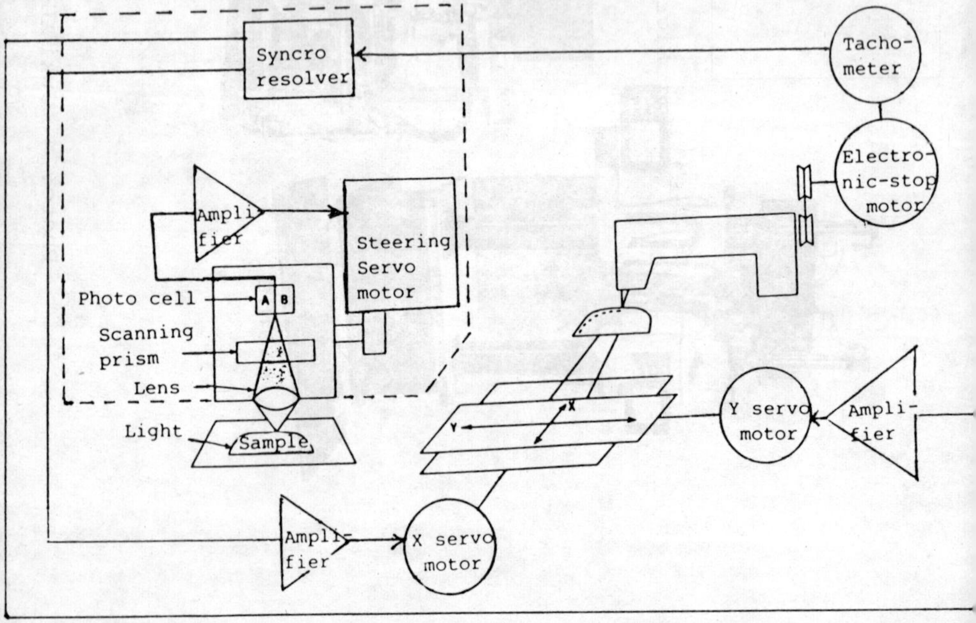

Fig. 10   Block Diagram of Optical Scanning Profile Stitching

COMPUTER AIDED TEXTILE DESIGN AND ELECTRONIC DOBBY MOTION CONTROL

Th. Baechinger and H.W. Krause

ABSTRACT

The features of various electronic hardware and software configurations with respect to their applicability for weave pattern
designing systems are described and the requirements and possible applications for electronically controlled dobbies are discussed.

A prototype of an electronic weave pattern programming system
is presented, characterised by efficient possibilities for designing fancy weaves on-line at the dobby-loom. A relatively
simple modul for the electromagnetic activation of selector
needles has been developed to replace the punched card input
of a standard dobby. A detailed description of the hardware
and programming procedure is given to demonstrate the versa-
lity of the system.

1 INTRODUCTION

The development of highly integrated circuits permits the replacement of conventional mechanical control techniques by digital electronics and electromagnetic components. In parallel
with their increasing sophistication, these integrated circuits
will become five to ten times cheaper with the result that an
increasing number of control functions are becoming attractive
for microprocessor application [1].

In weaving, classical mechanical control devices are the dobby
and the Jacquard. Up to now it has not been possible to replace
them by shedforming devices controlled by other means, mainly
for reasons of cost and reliability. Nevertheless, for many
decades attempts have been made to find a substitute for the traditional punched card. A patent granted in 1896 [2] proposes a
system using electromagnets for controlling the Jacquard mechanism. In this, the pattern card is the memory for the control
information. Later patents have concerned themselves with
whether and by what means it is possible to produce an interface between the mechanical movement and the electromagnetic
power source within the dobby or Jacquard. It proved that only
low forces and small amounts of travel can be used with electromagnets, and therefore a control mechanism needs to be amplified by a mechanical system.

When data processing began to expand at the start of 1960's,
work was done on how design information could be prepared in the
most rational way. An optical-electronic system was used for
Name-Jacquards [3], reading the pattern information directly
from a printed design. A prototype by IBM [4] enables Jacquard
patterns to be plotted on the screen and weaving them on a pattern machine with electromagnetic control. The cost of this
system was too high and its space requirements too great to permit its rational use in industry. In the 1970's various machine
makers began to offer specialised systems for Jacquard weaving
preparation [5, 6, 7]. These systems have the principal advantage of reading the pattern directly from drafts or sketches
with the possibility of then correcting or modifying on the

screen. The pattern information is then transferred to a
system for the cutting of the pattern card.

In parallel with this development, systems were introduced
for knitting, allowing the design of Jacquard patterned knitted fabrics on the screen [8, 9]. These have already become
widely accepted. No systems, however, have yet been proposed
for dobby weaving which are capable of use for both designing
and weaving. Certainly there are opportunities here for the
future, especially when it is considered that an increasing
number of electronically controlled dobbies will be coming
onto the market. The system described later in this paper was
developed as a prototype at the Swiss Federal Institute of
Technology in Zürich, Switzerland. The purpose of this work
is to demonstrate that it is now possible to develop a versatile compact system with low expenditure on hardware, meeting
the requirements of dobby weaving. The project also enables
microprocessor technology to be tested with a practical example,
thus showing the scope available for the application of microprocessors in textile machinery construction.

2 HARDWARE AND SOFTWARE SUITABLE FOR TEXTILE DESIGNING SYSTEMS

Depending upon the needs of the user, designing systems can
incorporate a wide variety of computer components. Below, a
number of criteria are evaluated in order to facilitate the
evaluation of designing system.

2.1 Computer

Size and configuration of the computer to be used are of vital
importance. A large number of systems are on the market, which
can be roughly divided into the following categories:

Microprocessor systems: - developed or adapted for a specific
                           application.
                         - only a few input and output units
                           (buttons, display)
                         - programming in machine language
                         - hardware configuration:
                             Microprocessor (4/8/16 bit)
                             RAM
                             EPROM
                             I/O components

Microcomputer systems: - programmable system for general
                         data processing
                       - microprocessor as central unit
                       - keyboard, display, floppy disc
                         drive integrated
                       - programming in higher languages

Minicomputer: - processor specially adapted to the
                needs of the computer (16-32 bit)
              - several terminals
              - various peripheral units
              - various higher programming language
              - faster processing (especially
                arithmetic)

As a rule, simple microcomputer and microprocessor systems
are not adequate for a sophisticated textile designing system.
Particularly when large repeats have to be designed, or if
manipulations of the pattern have to be carried out directly
at the terminal, the operations involved cannot be completed
quickly enough. This will be made clear in the following example:

A weave with 300 ends warp repeat and 500 picks weft repeat
contains 150'000 interlacing points. To store this weave repeat, approx. 20.000 bytes of memory capacity are needed. If
one desires to mirror half the design at an axis, a displacement of 75.000 interlacing points is required. In order to complete this operation within, say 3 seconds, only 40 microse-
conds are available for displaying each point. During this
time, however, a simple microprocessor can only carry out 6-8
machine commands, and since 30-60 commands are needed, to produce the entire display, at least 15 seconds would elapse for
the mirroring procedure. If during these operation sections,
pattern parts are to be read from an external memory, even
more time will be needed.

A designing system should therefore be capable of storing normal size patterns (differing in size depending on the user) in
the internal memory and its computer should be able to make
alterations in the pattern within a few seconds. Apart from
the cycle time of the processor, the following aspects have
to be considered:

- Configuration of hardware (are subprocessors
  used for keyboards, terminal etc.?)
- Command range of the microprocessor
- Programming (machine language is faster
  than higher programming language).

If sub-processors are used for individual input and output
units, the basic capacity of the microprocessor can be kept
low. Advanced microcomputer systems incorporate a number of
special components, which control communication between keyboard, terminals and external memories. The capacity of a computer can therefore only be determined in practice by means of
tests with software for a similar application.

2.2. Input equipment (table I)

Special input equipment is available to facilitate entering of
the pattern.
The input data should be sub-divided into alpha-numerical,
graphic and auxiliary data. Numerical and text data are best
entered via the keyboard. Programming function buttons are
available for frequently occuring length data. Graphic data
describe areas, lines, interlacing points etc. which can be
entered with the aid of drafting stylus. To control the program selection from menus ,(moving the cursor etc.),auxi-
liary data are needed, which are entered via keyboard or special equipment (mouse, joystick, lightpen etc.).

Patterns can be built up either from sketches directly at the
terminal or with the aid of a scanner or a camera from a
prepared drawing.

In order to enter designs which are not already in pattern form, drafting machines with trolley unit are quite suitable. The trolley always stops at the last point entered and horizontally and vertically running interlacing points are easily entered with the aid of the trolley unit. Less expensive however and easy to operate is the digitizer (graphic tablet) with freely movable pencil. Joystick, lightpen or mouse can also be used, but they are mainly suited only for positioning the cursor on the screen.

2.3. Output equipment (table II)

The most important output unit is the terminal. The alphanumerical screen usually has a capacity of 25 lines of 80 characters. It can only be addressed character by character, but is adequate for simple designing systems with small repeat sizes. On graphic screen on the other hand each point can be addressed separately and the resolution is somewhere between 400x400 and 4000x4000 points.

The terminal incorporates, in addition to the screen, an internal memory of a suitable size, as well as software and hardware to support the graphic display functions (enlarging, reducing) etc. On black and white screens one bit is needed to store each point. Coloured designs are stored with two bits (4 colours) to 10 bits (4096 colours) for each interlacing point. The colour shades of a picture can be varied on some models. For patterning with colours, the screen should be capable of displaying at least 1000x1000 points and 15 colours from a range of 10.000 colour shades. The appropriate display memory needs a capacity of 512 bytes. Versatile designing system should be equipped with a colour graphic terminal for the pattern display and an alphanumerical terminal for the dialog with the system.

A further important requirement is the possibility of obtaining a hard copy (printout) of the pattern. The low price matrix printers are fast enough for areal patterns. The latest ink-jet printers with the facility of blending the three primary colours are ideal for coloured hard copies. Pen plotters are rather slow and therefore less suitable for this purpose. Electrostatic plotters can also produce coloured designs, but they are very expensive, much like laser printers. Yet, in the future, laser printers will no doubt be the fastest printers for mixed graphic and text output.

2.4. Data storage

For storing the information of large patterns, a considerably high memory capacity is needed. The internal memory (RAM = Random Access Memory) must correspond to the desired maximum repeat size. In simpler systems the lifting plan, instead of the weave pattern, is stored, which requires less memory space, because only one piece of information has to be stored for each heald frame (harness up/harness down). The external memory (floppy, hard disc) is used for permanent storage of the pattern. To ensure optimum utilization and rapid retrieval, the memory capacity for the design should be proportional to the number of interlacing points. Furthermore, the memory capacity should not be limited in warp and weft direction, but

rather by the total number of interlacing points. If
100.000 interlacing points can be stored, then it is possible to display a repeat of 50 warp ends by 2000 picks or
a repeat of 200 warp ends by 500 picks. For smaller systems
floppy discs are ideal. With memory capacities of 0.5 - 2.0
megabytes, several hundred small-scale patterns can be stored
on such a disc. For storing additional information in a data
bank, hard discs with 20-50 megabytes capacity are best suited.
For minor applications, audio cassettes are still being used
as data carrier in existing systems. However, due to their
slow data transmission and limited memory capacity, they
cannot be recommended, despite the low price.

In order to transfer the data produced on the design terminal
to the electronically controlled dobby, an additional small
data carrier is also needed. So far, the following techniques
are being used:

- UV EPROM   (erasable with UV light)
- E-EPROM   (erasable with overvoltage)
- CMOS-RAM   (with battery).

The memory capacity needed for a picking pattern with max.
32 pieces of information per pick (harness position, weft
colour selection and special functions) is 4 bytes per pick,
and thus 4 kilobytes for 1000 picks. It is possible to store
this information with one chip in any of the above-mentioned
memories. The CMOS RAM needs, in addition, a small battery to
buffer the information, but is has the advantage that it can be
re-programmed at the machine or it can register data from the
loom.

2.5. Software

The various functions of a designing system are controlled
by software. To enter and manipulate a weave pattern, the
following functions are important:

- entering or changing an individual interlacing point
- shifting of patterns or sections of it
- formation of symmetric weaves by means
  of geometric projection
- obtaining new patterns by combining stored
  pattern sections
- parametric input of weaves (by commands
  such as for instance "TWILL 3:2")

The software should meet the following requirements:

- dialogue technique
  (user-oriented, easy to learn)
- short response times of the system
- weave pattern creation synchronously displayed
  on the screen
- possibility of extending the system and/or
  changing the computer without too much software updating.

The software package should be produced by means of a
higher programming language and standard software tools.
To store the graphic, text and numerical data, a memory
concept is to be prepared, if necessary in combination with
a special data bank software. The programmes should be modular in design, enabling the system to be extended step by
step.

3. DISCUSSION OF DESIGN SYSTEM CONFIGURATIONS

Depending upon the requirements of the user, the ideal design
system may be quite different. Three possible solutions shall
be discussed, namely the "designer system", the system for
mills with "frequent pattern change" and a system for "mass
production" mills.

3.1. The "designer system" (fig. 1)

It is meant for the free-lance designer who sells varying
fabric styles. Here, the emphasis must be put on quick changes of colour and weave pattern and the final results must
enable the production of the pattern draft. To fulfill this
task, the highest degree of sophistication of hardware and
software is required. The system must allow to compose and
alter the pattern with respect to colour and weave construction directly on the screen. The display should represent
the cloth to be woven as closely as possible, and the system
should be capable to transfer the pattern information directly onto the punched cards or other data carriers which are
used to control the dobby or jacquard device on the loom.

While methods of this kind are already in operation in the
Jacquard weaving sector, a sufficiently natural simulation
of the fabric structure has not yet been achieved. Systems of
this kind are, no doubt, very expensive.

3.2. "Frequent pattern change" (fig. 2)

In a weaving mill with frequent pattern changes and producing
fashion goods a similiar system is required, however it must
fulfill less stringent requirements with respect to simulating fabric structures. Instead, the emphasis here is on the
machine setting parameters necessary to produce a particular
fabric. For this purpose the system should be connected to
the production control system, containing previous production data. Thus it becomes possible, to make use of the practical production information already available from earlier
runs in order to arrive quickly at the setting parameters for
the new fabric. The data carrier should contain the weave
data as well as the other pertinent machine data. On the
weaving machine, the overseer can call up the manual setting
data via a terminal.

3.3. "Mass production" (fig. 3)

Finally, a weaving mill with infrequent changes of article
needs only a simple portable system with keyboard and LCD
display as well as 2 microfloppies. Techniques of this kind
may also be used directly at the weaving machine. The input
unit is equipped with a special keyboard, enabling the selection of simple weaves and settings in a relatively simple

manner. It is feasible to install a data carrier also on the machine. Direct connection to the production control system would permit the setting data to be transferred directly to the weaving machine and vice versa.

4. THE ELECTRONICALLY CONTROLLED DOBBY

In order to be able to weave the patterns produced on desig-ning system on the weaving machine, either the pattern has to be punched by means of a card puncher into a conventional dobby card, or processed straight from an electronic data carrier in combination with an electronically controlled dobby. Sulzer in-troduced a prototype version of an electronically controlled dobby at the ATME in Greenville in 1981; other systems followed in 1983 by leading dobby manufacturers (Stäubli, Müller, Yamada etc.).

What are the requirements of electronic dobbies?

Mechanically and electronically, their reliability should equal or even exeed that of conventional dobbies. The most cri-tical area is most likely the interface between the electro-nic components and the mechanical system. Electromagnets must have a life expectancy of at least 100 million cycles, a number which is easily reached on a modern weaving machine within two years. In the narrow fabric weaving sector, electromagnets have been used to control the harness motion since about 1972. If feasible, the magnets should have a holding function only. On narrow fabric looms, running at speeds of more than 1000 r.p.m., adequate reliability has been obtained by careful design of the mechanical construction. Therefore, it is to be expected that viable electronic dobbies for broad looms may be built as well.

An electronic dobby will no doubt enable higher weaving speeds by eliminating the dynamic problems associated with the spring loaded reading-in needles.

An electronic dobby is more compact in design, and-as cards are no longer needed - it can also be mounted on the weaving machine in a less accessible position.

In combination with their electronic dobby, Stäubli (Horgen, Switzerland) and Müller (Frick, Switzerland) are offering very practical programming systems. In the Stäubli version (fig 4), a programmer connects to a video screen, a combined plotter/reader, a floppy disc and a UV-EPROM. The latter is to be used for the control of the dobby motions or the dobby card punching unit. The simplest configuration of the Müller System (fig 5) includes a portable programmer, a cassette recorder and an EEPROM (as input for the electronic dobby). The system also has the capability for direct pattern input on the loom. A somewhat more sophisticated configuration uses a microcom-puter ("APPLE"), floppy disc, printer and mouse.

5. PROTOTYPE OF AN ELECTRONIC PATTERNING SYSTEM IN COMBINATION WITH ELECTRONIC HARNESS CONTROL.

At the Institute for Textile Machinery at the Federal Institute of Technology (ETH) in Zürich, a prototype of a simple program-ming and control system for dobby weaving has been developed with the following objectives:

- application of modern technology
  (microcomputer/microprocessors)
- design and construction of an experimental
  system on-line with a rapier loom
- capable for programming simple as well as
  complicated patterns at low cost
- microcomputer as hardware
- conversion of "Stäubli" dobby, by replacing
  the dobby card by an electronic read-in modul.

5.1. The electronic read-in attachement

The standard card cylinder was replaced by a brass beam containing vertical and horizontal bores in the pitch of the
reading-in needles (fig. 6). The reading-in needles of the
dobby protrude into the vertical holes. The transverse needles
which are activated by magnets run horizontally. These needles
simulate the positions "hole" or "no hole" of the dobby card.
Each heald frame requires four magnets (2 for double-acting
dobby and 2 for reverse motion in weft searching). The prototype machine operating with 18 heald frames, is equipped with
a six colour-weft changer and has a dobby control for the cloth
beam drive release. For this purpose a total of 88 magnets
were needed.

5.2. Hardware configuration

A schematic layout of the hardware configuration is shown on
fig. 7. It serves as pattern design system as well as actual
dobby control. The central unit is an 8 bit microcomputer
CBM 8032 type Commodore, including display and keyboard. The
graphic tablet (digitizer), a printer and double floppy drive
are connected via IEEE-bus (parallel bus). The computer incorporates a 32 Kbytes internal memory and 2 x 512 Kbytes on the
floppy disc.

The dobby interface is directly connected to the internal bus
of the computer. Data and control lines of the computer (fig.8)
are connected to the I/O components PIA 6520 each with 16
outputs. A semi-conductor relay is controlled by each output
via a buffer. These relays are switching the electromagnets,
whereby the circuits are galvanically separated from the computer. Sensors are located in the dobby, which inform the computer of the reading-in moment of the needles and indicate
whether the dobby is in forward or reverse mode. The functions,
such as stop, crawl-speed and normal operating speed of the
weaving machine are controlled from the computer via 3 output lines.

5.3. Software

The software is made up of a BASIC programme as well as several machine language programmes. To enter or alter the design,
a section of 20x74 interlacing points is displayed on the
screen. The warp and weft colours are indicated separately
by numbers along the border of the pattern display. The
pattern section shown can be shifted as required over the
entire repeat. Furthermore, a cursor may be moved by aid of
the digitizing pencil over the digitizing surface. Synchronously,

the cursor moves on the screen within a field of 20x74 points.
An interlacing point is set definitely by pressing the pencil.
Besides entering individual interlacing points, a number of
auxiliary functions are available and can be called via keyboard or digitizer tablet, namely:

- duplicating of weave sections of any size
- symmetrical mirror effects of weave sections
- inserting pattern sections from discette
- storing pattern sections on discette
- inserting or eliminating a single pick
- erasing entire sections of the pattern
- entering the drawing-in plan
- entering the warp and weft colours.

The pattern repeat may contain up to 64000 threads, however the
memory of the microcomputer permits, for the time being, only
a maximum repeat size of approx. 20000 interlacing points.
By entering the weave pattern and the drawing-in plan, each
warp end is allocated to the appropriate heald. As the entire
weave programme is stored on a discette, it can be called-up
and modified at any time. Weaves for approx. 120 000 picks
can be stored on one discette, which would require about 360 m
of standard punch card length.

The weaving programme is being called up directly by the input
programme and permits the following additional functions:

- weaving any section of the pattern
- stopping the machine after a pre-determined number
  of picks
- indication of the current pick number
- crawl speed and start/stop via computer keyboard
- interruption of weaving and return
  to the input programme

5.4. Possible applications

An on-line system of this kind is most likely to be used for
pattern creation on the loom. The designer can, at no time,
produce a wide variety of colour patterns and weave patterns,
without loosing time for the preparation of punched cards.
If the electronically controlled dobby becomes popular, there
will surely be a demand for existing dobbies to be converted
to electronic control. A system whereby only the card cylinder
has to be replaced by an electronic module would be advantageous, as it can be adapted to a wide range of dobby makes
without difficulties.

6. STANDARDISATION

The complexity of these integrated systems can no longer be
handled by one manufacturer. If each weaving machine manufacturer is going to develop his own concept for the microprocessor control, the systems are no longer compatible, and
servicing as well as the connection to central computers become nearly impossible. If the adaptation to existing systems
is too complicated, then for certain applications, the profit
threshold will not be reached. For this reason, it is of ut-
most importance to set-up standards with respect to the following view points:

- uniform interface between machine controls
  and computers for data transmission
- format of the data to be transmitted
- system bus for machine control
- uniform data carriers for machine data
  (inexpensive module which can be used on
  any machine).

At the start of a development, individual manufacturers usually are not interested in standards, as they want to protect
their product. It must be stated very clearly however, that
standards of the kind mentioned, should be set up as early as
possible, especially in communications technology, as otherwise many useful developments will never get off the ground.

7. OUTLOOK

In which direction will dobby controls and pattern design
systems develop?

Machine controls, no doubt, will become even more sophisticated, informing the operator of the machine status by means
of flexible LCD displays, and by enabling a self control of the
production process. The individual control units of a loom will
be integrated into a single control system, monitoring and regulating all functions of the machine. The single controls then
will be connected to a central computer via data lines.

Thus, the production supervising system will grow into actual
production control systems, which not only connect data, but
actively control individual machines and the entire production
process.

Comprehensive data bases will be available from current and
past production, informing about quality and productivity
data of earlier or current products. As the designing and
production control systems are interconnected, the know-how
of manufacturing data can be directly implemented into new
products.

REFERENCES

(1) K.P. Friebe. VDI-Berichte, 1979, 348, p. 5-12

(2) L. Kleinberg, J. Szerepanik. DP 14 127 (2. June 1896).

(3) H. Walter. Melliand Textilberichte, 1969, 50, No. 12,
     p. 1428-1432.

(4) K. Albrecht. Melliand Textilberichte, 1971, 52, No. 7,
     p. 782-788.

(5) R. Seidl. Textiltechnik, 1981, 31, No. 5, p. 298-303.

(6) K.P. Lepka. Melliand Textilberichte, 1977, 58, No. 7,
     p. 551-556.

(7) R. Kruse. Melliand Textilberichte, 1979, 60, No. 2,
     p. 123-124, No. 4, p. 310-311

(8) D. Tollkühn. Melliand Textilberichte, 1982, 63, No. 9,
     p. 501-507.

(9) H. Schlotterer. Melliand Textilberichte, 1982, 63, No. 10,
     p. 704-706, No. 11, p. 784-786.

Prof. Hans W. Krause
Thomas Bächinger
Swiss Federal Institute of
Technology

CH-8092 Zürich
Switzerland

INPUT EQUIPMENT			
UNIT	FEATURES	ADVANTAGES (USEABLE FOR)	DISADVANTAGES (NOT USABLE FOR)
KEYBOARD	– TYPEWRITER KB – NUMERICAL KB – FUNCTION KEYS – SPECIAL KB	– ALPHANUMERICAL INPUTS – ADVANCED USER	– GRAFIC INPUTS (LINES ETC.) – CURSOR CONTROL – SPORADIC USERS
DIGITIZER (GRAPHIC TABLET)	– PEN FOR DIRECT ON A SPECIAL BOARD – DIFFERENT SIZES OF BOARDS	– DIGITIZING OF DESIGNS / MAPS – HIGH RESOLUTION – MENUS ON THE BOARD POSSIBLE – FREE MOVABLE PEN	– ALPHANUM. DATA – LARGE SIZES EXPENSIVE
DRAFTING MACHINE	– COORDINATES OF THE POSITION OF A TROLLEY	– DIGITIZING OF DESIGNS ETC. – RESOLUTION – HORIZONTAL AND VERT. PATTERNS	– MENUS – NOT PORTABEL – EXPENSIVE
MOUSE	– MOVABLE BY HAND	– CURSOR CONTROL – MENUS – SPORADIC USERS – RESOLUTION – LOW COSTS	– CHANGE FROM KEYBOARD TO MOUSE – ADVANCED GRAPHIC SOFTWARE REQUIRED
LIGHTPEN TOUCH SCREEN	– POSITIONING DIRECT ON SCREEN WITH FINGER OR WITH PEN	– SPORADIC USERS – MENUS – INEXPENSIVE	– RESOLUTION BAD – GRAFICS
CAMERA	– RESOLUTION ABOUT 1000X1000 PIXELS	– FAST DIGITIZING OF PICTURES	– ACCURACY – FAST PROCESSOR REQUIRED – EXPENSIVE
SCANNER	– AUTOMATICALLY DIGITIZING POINT BY POINT	– DIGITIZING OF LARGE PATTERNS – ACCURACY	– PATTERN MUST BE ON A PAPER – VERY EXPENSIVE

Table I   Comparison of input equipment for electronic
pattern design

OUTPUT EQUIPMENT			
UNIT	FEATURES	ADVANTAGES (USEABLE FOR)	DISADVANTAGES (NOT USABLE FOR)
ALPHANUM. DISPLAY	– 25 LINES X 80 CHARACTERS DISPLAY AREA	– LOW COST – SIMPLE GRAFICS POSSIBLE – SIMPLE SOFTWARE TO CONTROL DISPLAY	– NO SOPHISTICATED GRAPHICS – NO COLOURS
GRAFIC DISPLAY	– PIXELS ADRESS-ABLE (=LIGHTPOINTS) – RESOLUTION 400 X 400 TO 4000X4000 PIXELS	– ALL KIND OF GRAFICS (LINES AND AREAS) – DIFFERENT CHARACTER SETS	– HIGH RESOLUTION VERY EXPENSIVE – NOT EFFECTIVE WHEN SOFTWARE SLOW
PRINTER	– MATRIX PRINTING – INK JET OR RIBBON – COLOURS WITH BLUE/RED/YELLOW RIBBON OR INK	– FAST IN FILLING AREAS – MIXING COLOURS – HARDCOPIES FROM DISPLAY	– LINES / CIRCLES – LESS SUPPORT FOR GRAFICS – QUALITY DEPENDS ON INK OR RIBBON
PLOTTER	– DRAWING WITH A PEN – COLOURS WITH DIFFERENT PENS	– LINES / CIRCLES – CHARACTER SETS – CHARACTER SIZES – HIGH RESOLUTION – GRAFICS SUPPORTED BY SOFTWARE	– NO HARDCOPIES – FILLING AERAS TOO SLOW

Table II   Comparison of output equipment

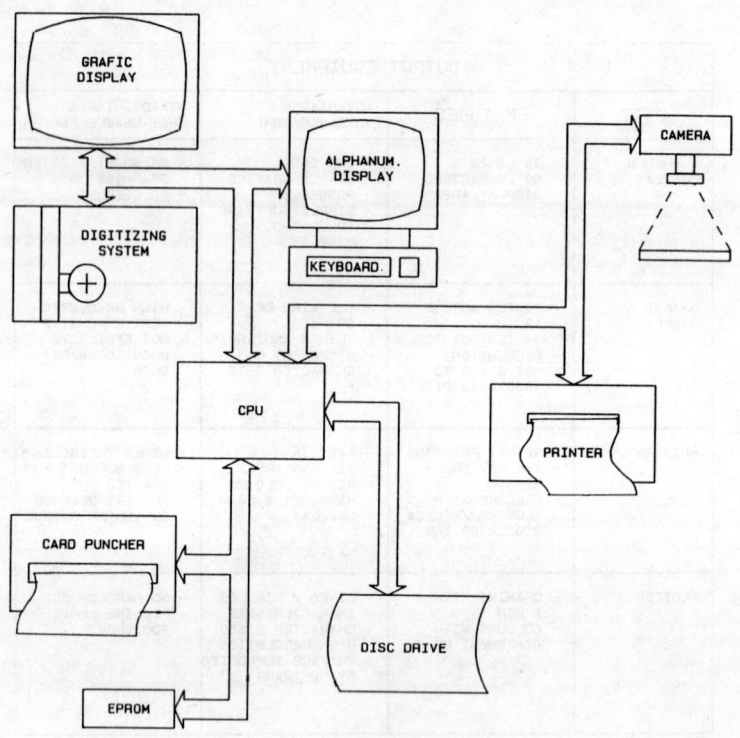

Fig. 1   Programming configuration "Designer System"

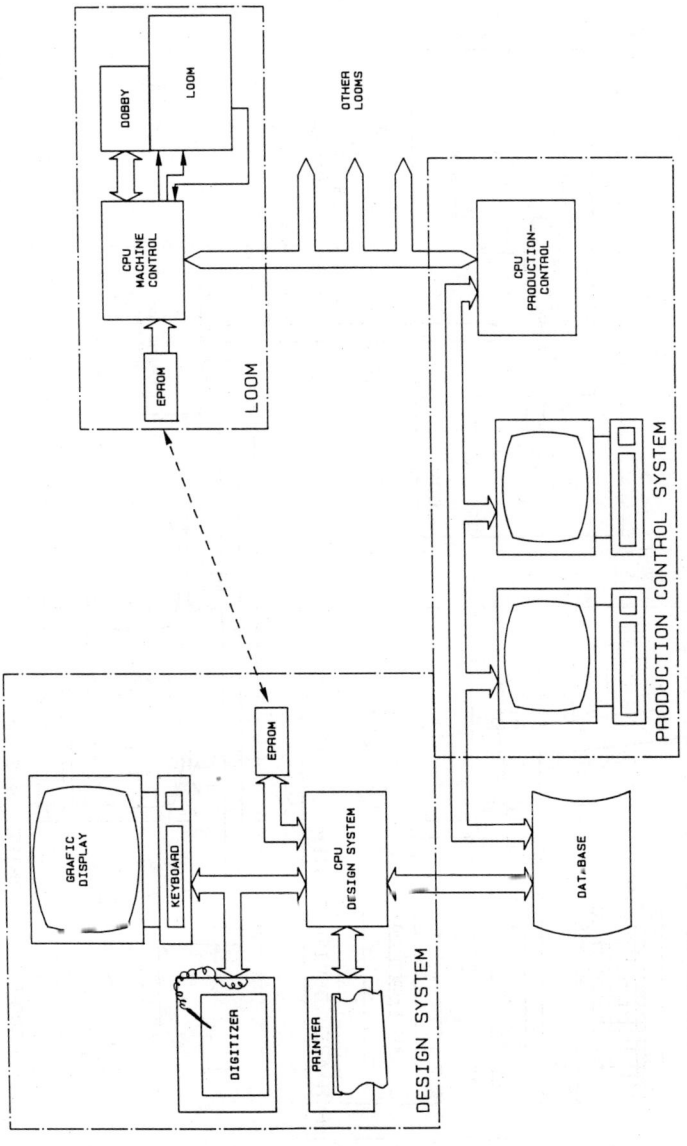

Fig. 2   Programming system "Frequent Pattern Change"
combined with production control

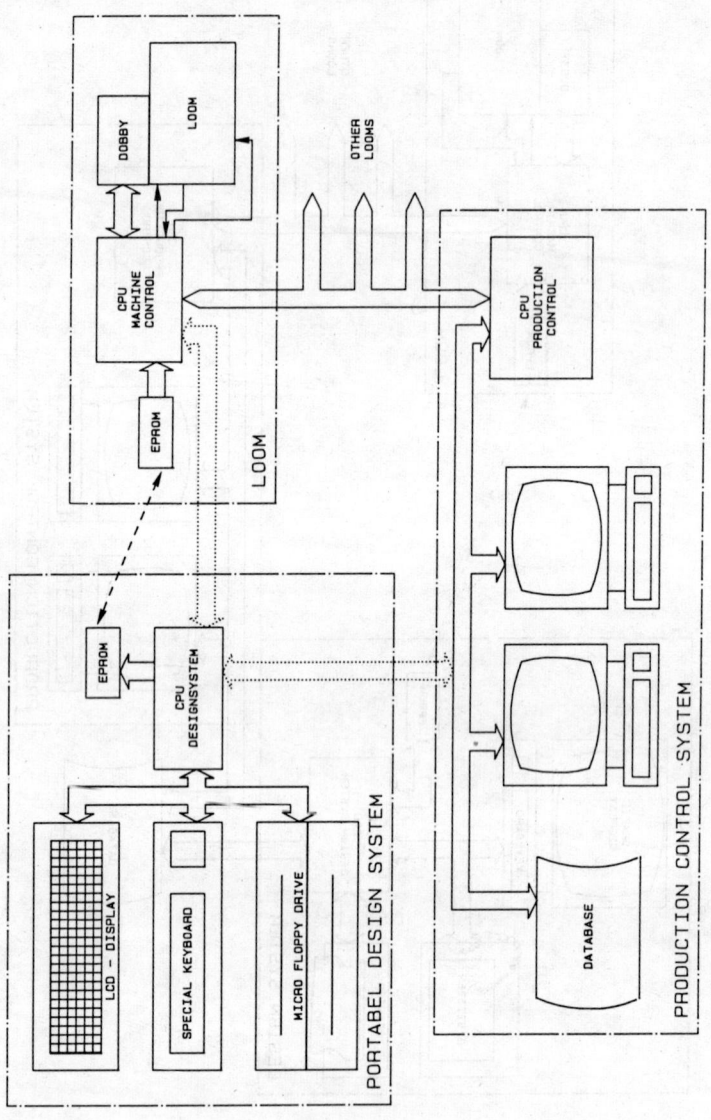

Fig. 3   Programming system "Mass Production" connectable
to production control

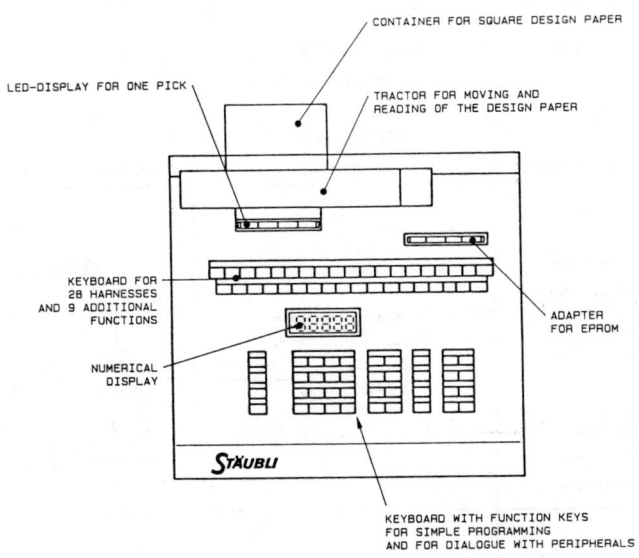

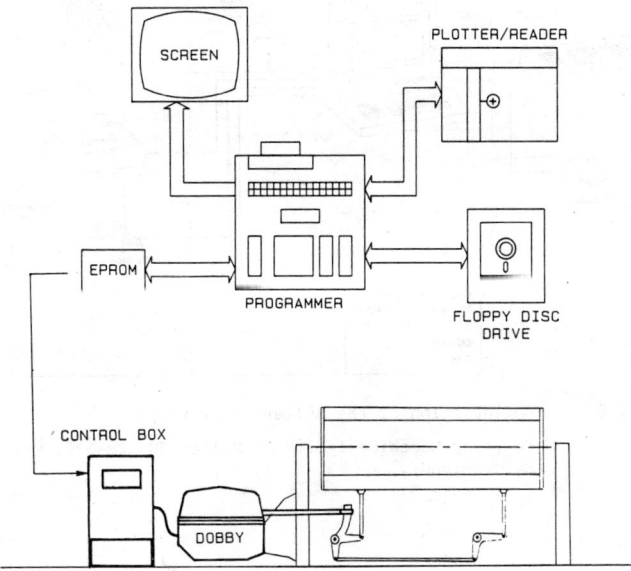

Fig. 4   STAEUBLI Programming System

programmer for entering pattern (above)
system configuration (below)
(Courtesy Stäubli AG, CH-8810 Horgen, Switzerland)

629

MÜPROG — SYSTEM

(Data processing procedure)

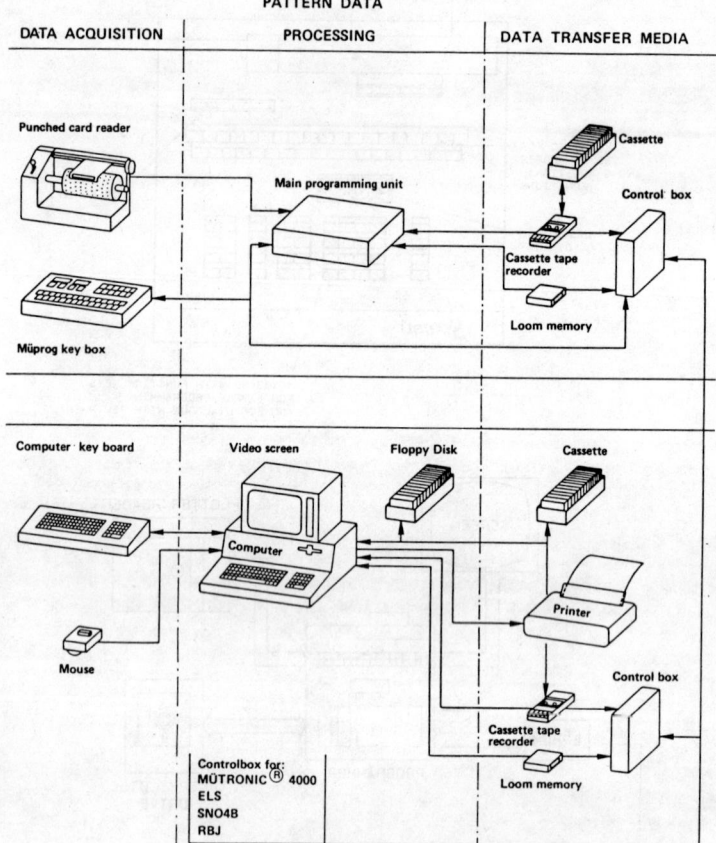

Fig. 5   configuration of the Müller "Müprog-System"

(Courtesy Maschinenfabrik J. Müller AG, CH-5262 Frick, Switzerland)

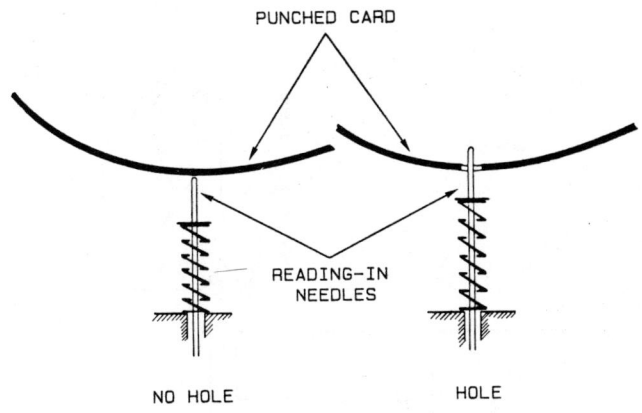

PUNCHED CARD

READING—IN
NEEDLES

NO HOLE   HOLE

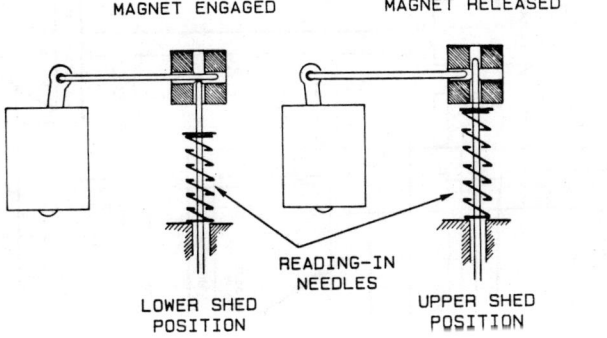

MAGNET ENGAGED   MAGNET RELEASED

READING—IN
NEEDLES

LOWER SHED   UPPER SHED
POSITION   POSITION

Fig. 6   replacement of the punched card by magnets
          and selector needles

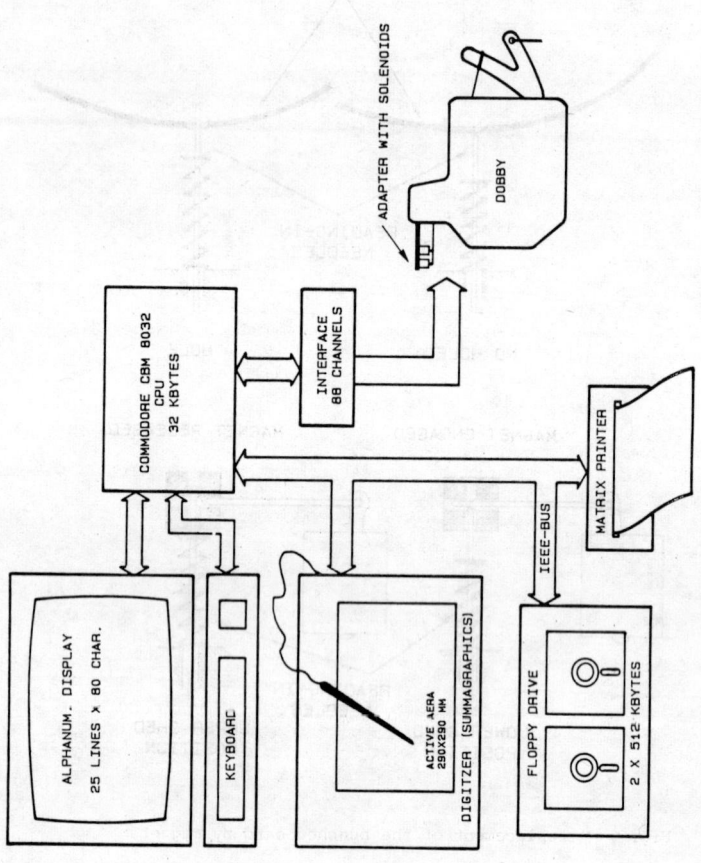

Fig. 7   configuration of the patterning system of the
Swiss Federal Institute of Technology, Zürich

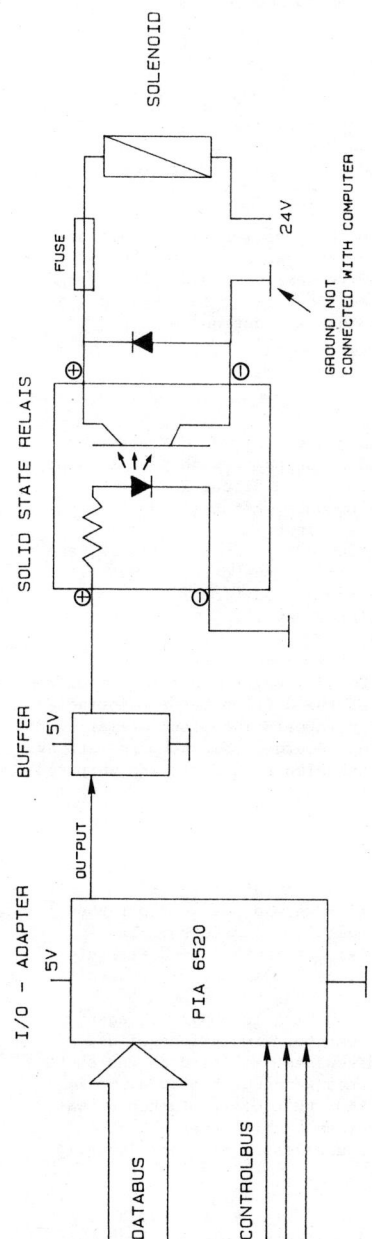

Fig. 8

Interface between Computer and Magnets

COMPUTER GRAPHICS AND THE WOVEN FABRIC DESIGNER

Leslie Miller

ABSTRACT

The simulation of woven fabrics by Computer Graphics, to give
a full-colour representation of the designer's ideas, with
acceptable accuracy, has been the subject of a research
project at the Scottish College of Textiles, Galashiels, over
the past three years.

With issue 1.0 of the software package commercially available
in summer '84, the paper looks at the background to the
development project, and deals with some of the problems
encountered, concluding with some thoughts on the implications
of this type of technology on tomorrow's designers.

1.   BACKGROUND

1.1   The Woven Fabric Designer

Woven fabric designers are, in a sense, unique.   Most other
designers can reproduce their ideas on paper with pen or paint,
permitting assessment of their ideas and discussion with
colleagues.   The architect can produce sketches and plans of
his buildings before any investment in bricks and mortar is
called for; the print designer can paint out his croquis, and
offer it for sale on that basis alone; the carpet designer
can paint out his interpretation of a traditional Persian
design, and discuss it with a likely buyer.

Woven fabric designers rarely use paintings or sketches of
their design ideas, not simply because buyers insist on seeing
it in cloth anyway, or because of the difficulty of painting
out all the intricacies of thread interlacings, but primarily
because so·many successful designs emerge from the permutations
of "crossings" obtained by weaving blankets of varying warp and
weft patterns.

1.2   Why Computer Graphics?

At the Scottish College of Textiles we decided to investigate
the practical value of woven-fabric simulation by means of
computer graphics.   From the start we did not consider the
computer simulation as a replacement for fabric sampling.   It
might come to this . . eventually, but in the immediate future
we saw the simulation essentially as a design tool, enabling
the designer to try out his ideas on the screen before
committing them to fabric.   In addition the buyer or agent
could be shown a collection of computer simulations of new
design ideas; these could be discussed, modified on the spot,
and decisions made as to which ones were worth weaving up.
In this way the designer would know that every blanket he was
weaving already carried the interest of his buyer.
Theoretically there should be no unsaleable blankets actually
woven.

With patterning costs getting higher every year, even a
reduction of 20% or 30% of woven blankets would be a substantial
saving/

saving, and in most cases would justify the outlay involved in a computerised design system. Offshoot benefits would include automatic print-out of the weaver's ticket from the data put into the simulation by the designer, eliminating the need for laborious ticket-writing and checking. An increase in the designer's "sense of adventure" and a willingness to try out fresh ideas on the screen - after all, it doesn't cost anything - can only result in wider ranging designs, and increased competitiveness. The simulation also permits an easy way of checking out new colours, seeing how they "bed in" together, or how they blend with existing shades by examining them in fabric simulations, before a commitment to the expense of new dyeings.

Such a simulation system would only be of value if the screen rendering of the fabric bore an acceptably close resemblance to the actual fabric it represented. This meant it had to look right in terms of colour, scale, and woven appearance.

1.3   Setting and Yarn Thickness

A consideration of fabric setting will normally refer to both yarn thickness and thread spacing. For example, a yarn of 0.6mm diameter may be woven with a setting (or spacing) of 1.0mm, the difference being an allowance for thread interlacing (dependent on the weave intersections), plus an allowance for fabric handling (firm or soft setting). The desired setting is maintained by the reed in loom, regardless of yarn diameter(s). If this was represented literally on the screen (and resolution limitations make this difficult anyway) the effect would be that of an open fabric with spaces between the threads, an effect that is not frequently seen in actual fabrics. It was decided therefore that the simulation should initially be based on yarn setting only, disregarding the actual thread thickness. Later development might include an investigation into the representation of thick and thin yarns within the simulation.

1.4   Setting and Resolution

The smallest individual point or area that can be represented on a graphics monitor is known as a pixel (or picture element), and the resolution of any graphics system is an expression of the number of pixels, horizontally and vertically, that can be shown on the screen (or addressed in memory) - e.g. 640 x 400.

To simulate a woven fabric at its highest setting, each thread must be represented by a line ONE pixel wide. The equivalent setting in threads/cm is then governed by the resolution of the graphics system and the size of the monitor. With the system referred to above, having a resolution of 640 x 400, and using a monitor 320 x 200 mm, would give 2 threads per mm as the finest setting (20 threads/cm or 50 ends/inch).

Using 2 pixels for the width of each thread would halve the setting (10 threads/cm; 25 ends/inch); 3 pixels would give 6.7 threads/cm (16.7 end/inch). Without alteration to the system specification, it is not possible to strike values in between those given, as you cannot use fractions of a pixel. Setting in simulations is thus restricted to an arithmetical range/

range of values on a scale of 1.0, 0.5, 0.33, 0.25, 0.20, 0.167 etc. The specific range of actual setting values obtained with any given resolution is governed by the monitor size, so that a degree of adjustment is available by varying the monitor size. (Electronic compression of the monitor image, to give a stepless range of image settings, is an area for further investigation).

1.5   Early Development

At the College we had a Cromemco Z2d, 8-bit, Z80 based processor, and this was earmarked for initial trials. Cromemco's SDI Graphics were added, plus a high resolution monitor, and we set out to see if we could simulate woven fabric.

The Cromemco allowed a display of 16 colours on screen, each of these colours being selectable from a total palette of 4096 colours. This sounded like a lot of colours, and if looked on as a paintbox with 4096 options, then it is a lot. But if you approach it with a specific colour in your hand, in the form of a yarn sample which you wish to reproduce on screen, then 4096 colours proves utterly inadequate. If accuracy of colour is important, and we felt it was vital if the simulation was to have any industrial value, then a much larger palette would be necessary to ensure an acceptable level of colour matching.

We were also concerned about the resolution of the Cromemco. Using one pixel per thread gave a setting of 38 ends/inch (15 threads/cm), and would allow us to display a blanket of 378 threads wide by 241 threads high.

Within these limitations we created our first simulation program, able to represent only one pattern section (one warp pattern crossed by one weft) with any single-cloth weave. We added a tie-in facility, allowing replacement of individual threads, and a colour option to permit modification of any colour used in the simulation. Encouraged by the Scottish Development Agency, we carried out a feasibility study through-:out the Scottish Industry to get a measure of the commercial interest in the simulation, and from the questionnaires answered at each demonstration, we came to certain specific conclusions:

a)   The simulation generated considerable excitement, and there was almost universal enthusiasm for its value as a design tool.

b)   The 4096 colour palette was inadequate.

c)   The 16 colour display was barely enough.

d)   Greater resolution was needed to give finer settings and larger pattern displays.

The College's commitment to the development of the simulation package was reinforced by the purchase of a Chromatics CGC7900 Graphics Computer, which would eliminate the problems encountered on the Cromemco. The project was further supported financially by British Technology Group, in return for marketing rights of the software, and by the Illingworth Morris Group, a major U.K. textile manufacturing group.

2.   HARDWARE CHANGES.

2.1   Colour in Computer Graphics

Colour is created on a monitor by the additive mixing of dots
of Red, Green, and Blue light at any given point on the screen.
If each of these three primaries has two options - ON or OFF -
there are two to the power three (= 8) possible colours.

	PRIMARIES		
SCREEN			
COLOUR	Red	Green	Blue
Black	X	X	X
Red	O	X	X
Green	X	O	X
Yellow	O	O	X
Blue	X	X	O
Cyan	X	O	O
Magenta	O	X	O
White	O	O	O

X = off
O = on

This accounts for the eight basic colours available on many
micros.

If, however, instead of simply being ON or OFF, each of the
three primaries can be controlled over a range of intensities
between fully on and off, then the number of colours available
increases considerably.   In the Cromemco each of the RGB
primaries can be varied from O (or off) to 15 (or fully on) in
single steps, giving 16 steps per primary.   This permits 16
cubed possible colours = 4096.

The Chromatics on the other hand allows a range of O to 255 per
primary, giving 256 cubed possible colours in the palette, a
total of 16.7 million.

The number of colours displayed at any one time on the screen
is governed by the computer's colour look-up table, being a
table where the RGB values for the display colours are stored.
The size of this look-up table directly relates to the number
of colours that can be displayed, and this in turn is usually
governed by memory constraints in the computer.   The three
aspects of computer memory, screen resolution, and number of
displayable colours, are directly related, and the resultant
pay-off of one aspect against another is decided by the
architecture of the particular hardware system.

2.2   From Cromemco to Chromatics

The change from the 8-bit Cromemco to the 16-bit Chromatics
solved the main problems revealed and reinforced by the
feasibility study.

a)   The 4096 colour palette was now increased to 16.7 million
     - more than the human eye can distinguish.

b)   The 16-colour display could be enhanced on the Chromatics
     to 32, 64, 128 or 256.   We opted for 32 as being adequate
     and reasonable.

c)   Resolution was increased to 1024 x 768 viewable on the Chromatics
     which on the 340mm wide screen gave a highest setting of

637

30 threads/cm (or 76 ends/inch), plus the capability of larger pattern sizes.

The Z80 based Cromemco had also proved inhibiting in terms of memory constraints. With only 50k of Ram available (after the Operating System was booted), this rapidly diminished when the Graphics (14k) and the Graphics Library (5k) were loaded in. Adding a programming language could take up another 25k, leaving us with 6k to hold and run the program. Not a promis-
:ing route to follow.

The Chromatics, with 128k of RAM - upgrading to 512k - removed these memory constraints.

3.   OBJECTIVES OF THE SIMULATION PROGRAM

The prime objective was to develop a software package which would be of value to designers in the woven-fabric industry. Designers, of course, do not all work the same way, and there are also national differences in working practice.   In the U.S.A. the tendency is towards a stylist who generates the ideas, and a mill designer who executes them, whereas in the U.K. both jobs are probably done by the same person.   We decided to follow the pattern we were familiar with, and aim the package to suit the needs of the U.K. designer, in the hope that it would also prove of value to others.

Simulation of a woven fabric on a colour monitor is of little value to the industrial designer unless the colours shown on the screen are an acceptable representation of his actual yarn colours.   It was recognised that some form of colour-matching module would have to be incorporated, which would enable the designer to modify the screen colour until it was an acceptable match to his standard yarn shade.   Once matched it would then be filed under the yarn name, ready to be recalled on screen within the simulation program.

It was essential that the program should be - to resort to an over-used phrase - "user-friendly", calling for no computer skills on the part of the user, but relying on a straight-forward question/answer approach.   The designer must be able to feed in the data for his design in much the same way as he might write a weaver's ticket - selecting his yarns, entering the colour patterns for warp and weft, and indicating the thread interlacings of the weave.   Options should include adding further sections to warp or weft to build up a blanket of designs and crossings, with the opportunity to rewrite or alter any section at any time, and the ability to see the fabric simulation on screen at any time.   Some variation in the apparent setting of the cloth should also be available, and the practice of tie-ing out individual threads in a blanket (e.g. to create an overcheck) should also be included, along with the ability to exchange any colour of yarn for another one through-
:out the blanket (something not possible in loom).

A late option, developed from the raster processor facility on the Chromatics, was to allow a single section of a pattern blanket to be run out in repeat over the whole screen, to show a larger area of it, and still permitting return to the full blanket display on request.

With this specification it was felt that the program would
provide the designer with a useful tool, allowing him to
generate, view, and quickly alter his design with much greater
ease than could be done in the loom.

4.   THE DESIGNER INTERFACE

Planning the user interface (or how the designer and computer
inter-react) is a vital consideration in writing a program of
this nature.   At its simplest it might be a case of asking "Does
the user reply to this question by typing YES, Yes, yes, or Y
- or do we give him the option of all four"?   In its more
complex form it entails planning the route, or variety of
routes, that the user may take through the program.

In the early development of the program we followed what seemed
a natural route - taking the user sequentially through the
fundamental requirements of specifying the details of a fabric,
asking for a setting, for yarn colours, for a warp pattern and
weft pattern, and for a weave.   Having obtained this informat-
:ion from the designer he would then be shown the simulation
of the pattern.   From this point the sequential approach fell
apart.   A series of modification options had now to be offered,
covering the alternatives that the designer might (reasonably)
want, such as trying a different weave, or adding another
section, or tie-ing out some threads.   A menu selection was
developed, allowing the designer to pick his option, modify
his design, view it, and return to the menu for further
modifications.

Having developed such a menu system for the modifications, with
the freedom of movement from option to option, coupled with the
ability to see the design at any stage, it then seemed
desirable to have this freedom right from the start of the
program.   The main purpose of the linear opening sequence was
to ensure that all the data necessary to generate the fabric
simulation was present before offering the display facility.
If we started with a full menu of options, including the
display facility, it was more than likely someone would try to
view a simulation without giving a full specification.   A
default pattern provided the answer.

The data for a simple 4 white, 4 black colour pattern, in plain
weave/basket, sett at 10 ends/cm (25 epi) is fed in at the
start of the program, and then the user is taken straight into
the menu.   In putting in details of his own pattern, if he
omits to specify an essential piece of data (e.g. the weave)
and then asked to see the design, he would be shown the fabric
simulation with the default weave (plain/basket).   It is then
a simple matter to go back to the menu, select the "Change
Weave" option, and insert the desired weave and then view it.

In this way the designer now has complete freedom in the
sequence in which approaches his fabric design.   He can add
new sections or change existing ones, alter weaves or setts,
change colours, or tie-out individual threads.   On completion
of each task he is brought back to the main menu with the

option to view the simulation at any time.

5.   PATTERN STORAGE

Having created a fabric design, whether it is a single pattern
or a pattern blanket, the designer must be able to store this
and retrieve it at any time.   The most obvious approach was
to use a straight screen-dump of the image on to disc.   This,
however, has two major disadvantages.

1)   Storing the image of the fabric merely allows one to
      recreate the image.   The data that generated the image
      is not retained, only the image itself.   This means you
      cannot interact with the image and make further changes
      or modifications to it, other than changes of colour.
      It is equivalent to simply photographing the screen
      electronically.

      Obviously one of the main advantages offered by the
      simulation program is to permit the designer to present
      ideas to his agent or buyer prior to cloth sampling, but
      if he is unable to modify the design in front of the
      buyer, then this would seem an undesirable constraint.

2)   The amount of disc-space taken up by one pattern image
      of reasonable size is considerable, even with image
      compacting techniques, and the reality of the situation
      is that in most cases (if the screen is more than half
      full of fabric) you will only get one design on an 8"
      Floppy Disc.

The obvious answer was to store, not the image, but the data
that generates the image.   This data is filed away under the
name (or reference number) of the pattern, and by calling this
up from within the simulation program, the pattern is instantly
displayed with full control and modification capability.

6.   YARN COLOUR AND SCREEN COLOUR

6.1   The Colour-Match Module

One of the menu options in the program allows the designer to
select the yarns he will have at his disposal; in weaving terms
this is equivalent to selecting the yarn colours he might want
to use for his blanket.   Obviously if he selects Shocking Pink,
and this is displayed on the screen for use within the
simulation, then the screen version of Shocking Pink should
correspond visually with his yarn colour of Shocking Pink.

The Colour-Match Module is a separate program included in the
package which allows the designer to modify the screen colour
until he has an acceptable visual match for his yarn colour.
He can then file this away on disc, under the name of Shocking
Pink, ready to be recalled within the simulation program.

6.2   Making Colours Designer-Friendly

The colour on the screen is created additively;   it is
generated by the additive mixing of three primary light sources,
ultimately building towards white.   This is the opposite
approach to the subtractive mixing of colours found when using

paints, dyes, or pigments, where the addition of more colour
darkens the result, leading towards black.

It is unreasonable to expect a designer to have to adjust his
concepts of colour mixing to suit the computer's Red, Green,
Blue values.   For example, consider the problem of making a
Brown slightly less intense.   ·If the colour is represented as
150 Red, 100 Green, 50 Blue, then to make it less intense (or
less saturated) entails a proportional reduction of the three
elements - e.g. removing 15R, 10G, 5B, giving a resultant
colour of 135R, 90G, 45B.   This in turn results in a darkening
of the overall value of the colour by 30, and to counteract
this a neutral grey of 10R, 10G, 10B has to be added.   The
final colour becomes 145R, 100G, 55B - i.e. 5 off the red and
5 on the blue compared to the original colour.   This method of
adjusting colour was not likely to be of any practical value to
textile designers.

Most designers are familiar with the Munsel colour system, and
although the terminology may vary, the concepts are universally
understood.   Colour is measured or assessed in terms of three
parameters:

> Hue - changes solely in terms of colour
> Value (Lightness, or Tone) - changes solely in terms of
>   light to dark
> Saturation (Chroma, or Intensity) - changes solely in
>   terms of the intensity of greyness of the shade.

The Chromatics permits screen colour to be specified either in
terms of Red, Green, and Blue, or alternatively in Hue, Value,
and Saturdation.   In the latter case, colours specified in HVS
terms are converted within the computer to their equivalent RGB
values.   Using this facility allowed us to develop the Colour-
Match Module on the basis of adjustments to Hue, Value and
Saturation.

The program starts by offering a spectrum of colours from which
the designer selects the one nearest to his yarn sample.   He
then adjusts his colour (interactively) in terms of Hue (e.g.
"Let's make it redder"), Value (" - and a bit lighter, perhaps")
and Saturation ("- but now it's too bright") until he is
satisfied that the colour on screen is an acceptable match to
his yarn.   He then asks for the colour data to be filed,
quoting the name of his Yarn File and the name of the colour,
and is able to recall that colour by name from within the weave
simulation program.

6.3   Problems in Colour Matching

6.3.1 Reflected and Transmitted Light

The Colour-match module is essentially based on subjective
assessment of a satisfactory visual colour-match, and the
fundamental problem encountered is that of making a comparison
between two different light sources.   The yarn being matched
is seen by daylight reflected from the sample, and its colour
is created by the subtractive effect of the dyestuffs and the
reflections of any wavelengths not absorbed.   So the sample is
subtractive colour seen by reflected daylight.

The screen colour is generated by additive mixing of the Red, Green, and Blue spots of light created by the screen phosphors. The colour is transmitted directly from the screen and is not reflected. So the screen colour is additive colour mixing by transmitted light.

Subjective comparisons of two totally different forms of colour is not wholly satisfactory. To improve the situation we are currently looking at the idea of linking CIE colour co-ordinates with the RGB values of the monitor, so that an input of the CIE values will reproduce the colour on screen. The CIE values for a yarn sample can be found either with a Spectrophotometer, or by matching the yarn to standard colour samples whose CIE values are known. This at least provides a matching of two similar types of colour - both reflected.

6.3.2 Viewing Conditions

If consistency of screen colour is important, then equally important is consistency of viewing conditions. It is self defeating to colour-match yarns on the screen in a darkened room, and then view fabric simulations from these yarns in bright sunlight.

Colour-matching and simulation viewing should be done under similar conditions, ideally with the screen as dark as is practical. Even under low ambient light conditions, with any light falling on the screen you will find that the "black" screen is lighter than your darker yarns.

The screen should be hooded, and should face a black wall (to minimise reflections), with as low a level of general lighting as is acceptable for working. The yarn sample being matched should be closely wound on card to present a flat smooth surface for colour-matching, and then placed in a small box with a black interior containing a standard daylight light-source. An aperture in the front of the box permits the illuminated sample to be viewed for matching. This arrangement ensures constant viewing conditions for the sample, and the box prevents extra light falling on the screen.

6.3.3 HVS and HLS

The Chromatics ability to handle colour in terms of HVS was not the total panacea that it first appeared. The HVS colour model is based on a HEXCONE, in which full colour saturation is always specified at full <u>value</u> as well. This means that a full red, for example, (Hue-1) would be specified in HVS as 1,255,255. Reducing the Saturation only, progressively to zero, would eventually produce pure White (1,255,0), as any colour - regardless of the Hue value, with zero saturation, would be on the neutral grey-scale in the centre of the cone. As Value is 255, the colour is White.

This created the situation where a designer wishing to reduce the Saturation of a colour would get an accompanying increase in lightness, an undesirable result as any alteration of Hue, Value, or Saturation should affect that parameter only and have no influence on the other two. A compensating adjustment has been incorporated to counteract this, in effect converting the

HVS Hexcone to the more acceptable HLS double cone.

7.   THE LONGER VIEW

7.1 Ongoing Development

The Weave Simulation program will be the basis of ongoing
development.   In its current form it allows woven blankets to
be simulated in a fixed range of settings, using any single-
cloth weave, with full colour-pattern control, and using self-
coloured flat yarns.

Although the software is tailored to suit the Chromatics CGC7900
Graphics computer with Idris Operating system, alteration of
the graphics primitives to suit other graphics systems of similar
capability is a natural development, making the program - within
limits - machine independent.

On the software package itself specific areas of development now
being undertaken include:

a)   Colour-matching through CIE values
b)   Printout of a Weaver's ticket with drafting and pegging
     capability
c)   Standard weaves on file.

Other possible areas of development might include:

a)   Use of two-colour twist yarns, and blended mixture yarns
b)   Use of thick and thin yarns
c)   Use of extras for figuring, leading to double cloths
d)   Simulation of finishing effects - e.g. raising or milling
e)   Simulation of garments using the simulated fabric

7.2 Designers and Computers

It is a reality of life that to-day's school children are
considerably more familiar with computers than their parents -
even if only at Space Invaders' level.   Tomorrow's designers
will not have the inherent "fear of the unknown" which computers
present to many of to-day's designers.   Schools, colleges, and
universities are already introducing computers on an ever
increasing scale, and it is inevitable that tomorrow's designers
will wish to make full use of the available technology.

With this in mind, we have also developed at the Scottish
College of Textiles a simplified version of the simulation
package to run on a BBC Micro.   For teaching purposes colour
accuracy is not important, so the Micro's eight fixed colours
are quite acceptable.   The package is intended for use by the
Tutor, allowing him to show basic fabric simulations, plus
"exploded" views to show detail of interlacings.   But it also
introduces the student designer to to-day's technology, making
it easier for him to cope with tomorrow's technological
revolution.

It is, however, to-day's designers who feel threatened, although
largely without cause.   Computer experts will always remain a
minority.   We can all drive a car to-day without knowing - or
wishing to know - what goes on under the bonnet.   We can all
operate computers without knowing our RAM from our ROM.   And
if the package is properly designed, we will communicate with

the computer both on and in our terms.

The computer will not replace the designer any more than the screwdriver replaced the carpenter. It will simply provide him with another tool. He may decide not to use it. What's wrong with the way we've always done it? - after all, as they say in Scotland, "It's aye been".

That choice is his. But, like it or not, computer aided design is with us, and ignoring it will not make it go away. Certainly the next generation of designers will accept and use computers as naturally as to-day's designers use ready mixed pigments.

Improved communications technology will permit and encourage the rapid transfer of image data across the globe. When it becomes easy and cheap to transmit digitised images in this way, the concept of sending packages of fabric patterns by air-freight will become outmoded and redundant, and buyers will become conditioned to viewing and selecting designs from electronic images.

Not to-day, probably not tomorrow, but not long afterwards.

Scottish College of Textiles
Netherdale
Galashiels
SCOTLAND

COMPUTER-AIDED OPTIMUM PLANNING OF SPUN-YARN TEXTILE PLANT

J. Hasegawa, T. Sakai and C. Nozaki

ABSTRACT

For many hundred years, the technical know-how and/or intelligence in the textile technology has been stored up. If it is possible to systematize those total knowledge in some order from the old administrative and information method to the new computer based system, the activity in technical analysis may be carried out effectively. Also, more complicated or boundary problems between engineering subjects can be solved on the whole scale view point of textile technology as well as the routine work of the quick handling of quantitative intelligence.

As an approach to the systematization, the authors attempted the computer based software system aiding to design the optimized construction of the spun-yarn mill plant according to each purpose of the production as well as to optimize the manufacture planning in a manner of comprehensive evaluation on the productivity of a spinning mill, in addition to the complete automatic production control by means of computer on the spinning mill.

The backgrounds, concept, and structure of the systematization are described with several case studies.

1. INTRODUCTION

For more than 30 years, the authors have engaged in research and development works on spinning and weaving machines. Although the center piece of their research works is machine design technology, lots of experiences and perception on textile technology (textile engineering) were required in design and production of such textile machines. That is to say that the authors have chosen useful technical data for their research and development work out of enormous amount of knowledge and information on textile technologies that have been accumulated for many hundred years, and utilize them aggressively in designing highly productive textile machines quickly by collecting technical information, understanding the existing phenomena, and conducting simulations of them.

Meanwhile, computer systems have remarkably been developed for the last 20 and some years. With the fast development of integrated circuits such as LSI and VLSI one after another, computer and its system (hardware) are getting much faster computation speeds, much improved memory capacity, and much better interface between man and machine.

However, the textile industry widely extends, for example, polymers, fibres, spinning, weaving and knitting, dyeing, sewing, apparel and end-products. As technical data are stored in each of the speciality fields, it is desirable to have a system capable of providing totalized services covering all these fields. And yet we ourselves alone cannot afford to complete

645

such a system.

For the first step, however, we attempted to set up a system in the field of producing spun-yarns as an approach to systematization of textile technology as a theme for our research and development for the last several years. In so doing, we tried to establish software department vis-a-vis hardware deparment dealing with design and production of spinning machines.

In this paper, the authors will describe the backgrounds, concept, and structure of systematization and case studies which were made by utilizing the complete computerized system.

2. A COMPUTER-AIDED PLANNING OF SPUN-YARN MILL PLANT

Taking a look at the spun-yarn plant from a viewpoint of material flow in the entire mill, such a plant can be classified as an inverse pyramid type similar to an oil plant or chemical plant, which is different from a pyramid type plant represented by a machinery plant or an automobile assembly plant. In an inverse pyramid type plant, there are not so many kinds of inputs (materials and/or parts), but there are so many kinds of outputs (product, brand, model, etc.). In particular, there are difficulties in assessing the adaptability and diversity of the work processes in the spun-yarn mill, and the productivity or production cost.

For this reason, the authors will describe in this paragraph a case of working out a new working process plan for the purpose of newly producing yarns at the spun-yarn mill plant.

When working out a working process plan for a spun-yarn mill plant, we can think of millions of different combinations such as selection of the types of raw material fibres, choosing yarn specifications (yarn count, number of twists, direction of twists, yarn structure) as shown in Table 1, selection of combination of work processes to produce yarns, or selection of production capability for individual processes. That is to say that the production of certain yarn requires the selection of 1 combination out of these millions of different combinations of the possibilities.

Of course, it does not mean that all the combinations are feasible. In view of the currently available production technology and market needs, some of them may not be actually in existence. Take the working process plan of a spun-yarn mill, for example. The volumes of technologies and know-hows are enormous, and it is necessary to provide an ordered system for this complexity.

From such a view point, we worked on software development called "A computer-based software system on the design of spun-yarn textile plant".

2.1 System Configuration

As indicated in Fig.2, this system consists of 4 program groups, each of which is operating independently from others in terms of installing machines, power consumption, operators, and productive cost. For instance, the installing machines program group

comprises 25 subroutines, source cards numbering 4615, 882 basic
parameters, and 610 different equations. Additionally, 18,503
standard data on respective equipments required for selection of
spinning process combinations, or selection of production capacity of each process, and workability and efficiency for each
spinning technology level (including not only domestic plants but
those operating abroad) are available for use. These standard
data are coded information, namely various kinds of knowledge and
information accumulated for many years.

2.2 Systems Approach

As an example of systems approach the authors will describe the
one of cases related to the above said installing machines and
equipments. As shown in Fig. 3, the 1st step toward systems
approach is to analyze the functions of the spun-yarn mill plant
and to investigate operational conditions.

Of course, filing of a large amount of data accumulated so far is
included in the work required. As the next step toward systems
approach the quantification, systematization, and modelling work
were necessary to be put into practice at each process, and the
final computer program has also independently been prepared as
subprogram for each process of the mill. Table 2 shows the
details of the facilities program group for installing machines
and equipments.

In actual computation operation, what is required is to determine, in consideration of target yarn, the final production scale
and the quality of product, and then the combination of processes
at the spun-yarn mill plant currently under designing. In
correspondence, subprograms separately prepared by each process
will be necessarily and automatically put together likewise in
the computer, so that a series of spinning processes can be
organized also in the computer. In other system dealing with
power consumption, operators, and productive costs, the similar
type approach is made and the idea has been put into software.
As a result, as shown in Fig. 3, it has become possible for us to
forecast, predict, and estimate the number of machine units
required, power consumption, essential plant floor space, number
of necessary workers, and yarn production cost.

2.3 Example of designing a spun-yarn

In this section, the authors will describe the output we had out
of case studies which we made assuming an actual spun-yarn mill
plant operations. In the plant facilities system, for example, a
comprehensive chart indicating the optimum number of machine
units and output for each process of work in correspondence to
the prodution scale of the spun-yarn mill plant and performance
of individual machines used in each process of work, and a
detailed table for each work of process are printed out. Fig. 4
shows an example of a comprehensive chart printed out by a
computer. When the system is connected to a power consumption
system, it enables us to estimate not only the volume of electric
power required at each process of work for machine operation but
also power volume required for air-conditioning and lighting
equipment in correspondence to the size of the plant. Fig. 5
shows an example of such an output. Likewise, combining the

system with operators program enables us to estimate and
calculate the manpower number of direct workers in right
proportion to the size of the plant. Together with a comprehensive chart showing the optimum number of personnel for each
process of work, and a detailed table for each process of work
are to be printed out. Fig. 6 shows an example of a
comprehensive chart.

By combining these 3 different systems and yarn-productive cost
system, it has become possible for us estimate and calculate the
production cost of yarns which are the ultimate product in the
spun-yarn plant. Fig. 7 shows an example of the output.

Additionaly, examples of the outputs shown in Fig. 4 through Fig.
7 shows an actual case of 20400 spindles production scale of a
plant producing cotton yarn Ne-30. By the way, those data used
in the calculation were prepared by assuming a plant whose
technical standard were relatively high.

3. A COMPUTER-AIDED MANUFACTURE PLANNING OF SPUN-YARNS ON A SPINNING MILL

Compared with the number of various kinds of inputs (raw material
fibres) supplied to the mill, the number of the kinds of outputs
(yarn specification, brands, types) is much larger. If we
attempt to work out a producion plan by evaluating the productivity of a spinning mill with such characteristic features
comprehensively and speedily, it must be necessary for us to deal
with the mill in a manner of system engineering.

The authors have developed as software a "Total evaluation system
on the productivity of a spinning mill", from a viewpoint of a
systematic analysis of the manufacturing system called 'spinning
mill'.

As shown in Fig. 8 and Table 3, the software consists of
approximate 300 kinds of parameters, approximate 400 kinds of
stored data, approximate 1700 kinds of relational equations and
regressional equations. As a group of 89 different programs,
they are comprehensively organized as a total system.

By using the system, we are able to assess the productivities of
spinning processes, where raw materials, production scale,
production time and product specifications are different from one
another. In other words, it has become possible for us to find
out immediately the manufacturing cost by product type. Not only
that, we can utilize the system in order to make predictions
required for our production plan and production control where the
optimum control can be expected.

The following is an explanation on the input/output of respective
subsystems of this computerized total system (Refer to Table 3).

3.1 Spinning Grade System

This is a subsystem which evaluates the productivities of spinning process to spin a yarn which is the most main process in a
series of spinning processes. If the 13 to 19 different items
data such as yarn specifications, machine revolutions

648

maintenance, and so on are put in the system, the production
weight per spindle and others are then put out. As yarns are
twisted, twist shrinkage may occur, shortening the length of the
yarns. In this sub-system, the regression equations are also
stored to be able to assess quantitatively the accurate degree of
shringkage and the length shortened according to various yarn
specifications.

3.2 Facilities System

In correspondence to the combination of a number of working processes, a subsystem enabling us to predict the optimum number of
machine units for achieving a production goal will put out
together with the number of machine units required for each process of work, corresponding to the machine model used and the
target production output, together with a typical chart of a
series of processes of work (e.g. Fig. 9).

3.3 Manpower System

A subsystem capable of computing the number of workers required
for production activities at each process of work in right proportion to the scale of manufacturing facilities. Manpower
required per Bale is also computed out at the same time, so that,
for example, the labor productivity of each yarn brand can also
be checked out.

3.4 Electric Power System

A subsystem capable of computing the amount of power required
for each process of work in correspondence to the type of machine
used and the process pattern of combination. This subsystem
enables us to evaluate the productivity per power cost at a
spinning mill where electric power is the major source of energy
supply.

3.5 Equivalence Rate System

The above mentioned output from the 'manpower' and 'electric
power' subsystems, namely a manpower conversion rate and an
electric power conversion rate, and other data are then put in
this subsystem. Then, labor cost, power cost, processing work
cost required for each production are put out by each yarn brand.
As stated above, individual subsystems can be interrelated to
each other as shown in Fig. 8, forming a total system. Such a
total system enables us to predict the optimum number of machines
in operation, the number of workers required and the amount of
electric power used in working out a production plan. At the
same time a flexible use of the system enables us to make an
accurate estimate of a brand merchandise with high values produced at the spinning mill to satisfy the needs of the market
from cost calculation, labor productivity, and energy productivity.

4. AUTOMATIC PRODUCTION CONTROL ON A SPINNING MILL

At a certain series of spinning processes, a production control
capable of providing an automatic control of required production
quantity at the spinning process by each spun-yarn count may be

desirable at spinning mills for the future.

The production conditions for each process in a series of
spinning processes and for each unit of machine are already clear
from the plant planning and manufacture planning which were mentioned in the preceding paragraph. These parameters and relational expressions on production processes are stored in the
computer for control shown in Fig. 10.

On the other hand, the central main computer as shown in Fig. 10
is given a production plan stating the required production quantity in the spinning process by each spun-yarn specification. A
production program instructions for executing the production
control are then given to the computer for control as well as
each unit assigned to each process of production work, after
which production starts.

At that time, production quantity at each process in manufacturing, namely the output required, is compared automatically, if
necessary, with actual production quantity monitored by the monitoring device attached to each machine unit and total quantity of
surplus or shortage up to a certain point of time is calculated.

As long as the cumulative surpluses or shortages for each process
in manufacturing stay within the allowable limit, the user can
let the manufacturing work continue by executing the manufacturing program for respective processes of manufacturing.

Should cumulative surpluses or shortages stay beyond the afore-
mentioned allowable limit, modify the program automatically,
causing at least one of the variable parameters, out of those
parameters used in the process (or processes) of manufacturing
work, to be changed and adjusted so that cumulative surplus or
shortage will stay within the allowable limit (bringing the production quantity closer to the production quantity required), and
also change the parameters of each plant with the instructions
given by the computer for control through execution of the
modified program. Being available for use is such a concentrated
automatic control method of a production system in which the
results (achievements) and plans (requirements) are repeatedly
compared with each other and modified when necessary.

Fig. 11 shows one example. Please refer to it. Here, we have
shown only an example of production control. It is considered
that the same sort of a control system should be made available
for quality control and cost control.

ACKNOWLEDGEMENTS

The authors have prepared this manuscript by adding the contents
in the first issue of "Toyoda Technical Review" published first
in April, 1980 and also the points which were spoken several
times at the annual conferences of the Textile Machinery Society
of Japan.

Therefore, the authors would like to express their heart-felt
appreciation to Toyoda Automatic Loom Works, Ltd. and Toyoda
Spinning & Weaving Co., Ltd. as well as to those who are from the

Textile Machinery Society of Japan for their help.

REFERENCES

(1) T. Sakai. Proceeding of 32nd Annual Conference of The
    Textile Machinery Society of Japan (June, 1979).

(2) T. Sakai, W. Yamada and Y. Sato. Proceeding of 30th Annual
    Conference (June, 1977).

(3) T. Sakai, K. Motobayashi and M. Hayakawa. Toyoda Technical
    Review, No. 1, (April, 1980).

Toyota Central Research & Development Laboratories, Inc.
Nagakute, Aichi, 480-11,
Japan.

Fibre Types	Natural Fibres (Vegetable, Animal, Mineral) Man-made Fibres (Synthetic, Regenerated, Inorganic)
Fibre Parameters	Habitat and/or Maker, Range of Linear Density, Length, Shape of Cross-section, Other properties

Yarn Type	Spun
	    Process Designation : Carded, Combed, Condensed
	    Spinning System : Cotton, Woollen, Worsted
	    Manufacturing Process : Ring, OE, Bonded, Core-Spun
	Filament
	    Bulked, Crimped, Stretch, Interlaced, Bonded
	Homogeneous or Blended

Yarn Designing	Yarn counts, Direction of Twists, NO. of Twists, Structure

Table 1   Roughly Ranging of Fiber and Yarn Choices

Process		Name of Program	No. of Steps
	Main Program	MAIN	228
		BLOCK DATA	33
Sub-Routine		OVTP	141
		CLDAT 1	283
		CLDAT 2	257
Ring Spinning		SPIRIN	219
OE Spinning		SPIOE	216
Simplex		ROVE	180
Drawing (3rd passage)		DRAW T	174
DO. (2nd passage)		DRAW S	175
DO. (1st passage)		DRAW F	199
Combing		COMB	179
Cotton Side	Pre-combing (Ribbon)	RIBLAP	167
	DO. (Sliver)	SLVLAP	169
	Pre-drawing	PRDR 1	174
	Card (CK type)	CRD 1 K	175
	DO. (CE type)	CRD 1 E	172
	Blow room (chute)	BLW 1 C	142
	DO. (lap)	BLW 1 L	153
Man-made Side	Pre-drawing	PRDR 2	174
	Card (CK type)	CRD 2 K	174
	DO. (CE type)	CRD 2 E	173
	Blow room (chute)	BLW 2 C	140
	DO. (lap)	BLW 2 L	154
	Winder	WIND	157

Table 2   Datails of Subsystem for
Installing machines

Subsystem name	Input (The qty. of production goal or fig. collected from the plant)	Output (Prediction assessment on actual performances)
Spinning Grade	Yarn specifications, no. of machine revolutions, maintenance, lot change, etc. (13-19 items).	Production efficiency of spinning mill, production quantity, and production amount conversion rate, etc.
Facilities	Fixed quantities of lap sliver, roving, etc. spinning speed at each process, machine efficiency, percentage of flocks, machine specifications (30-96 items).	Necessary no. of machine units for each process of work and a forecast of production quantity, etc.
Man power	No. of work-in-process machine units, output of interim products, etc. (15-35 items).	No. of personnel required for each process of production, no. of workers per unit production weight (per package), manpower conversion rate, etc.
Electric power	No. of work-in-process machine units by process of manufacturing work, no. of machine revolutions, operating hours, efficiency, etc. (24-50 items).	Estimated amount of electric power consumption for operating air-conditioner, using lighting equipment and mechanical operation, power required for production qty., power conversion rate, etc.
Equivalence Rate	Total personnel cost such as salaries, bonuses, welfare expenses, total amount of power consumption expenses, packing expenses and actual no. of packages containing products, power conversion rate, personnel conversion rate, etc. (13 items).	Personnel cost per package of each yarn brand, power consumption for operating machines, total amount of process work expenses per package, equivalence rate, etc.

Table 3. Each subsystem's input/output

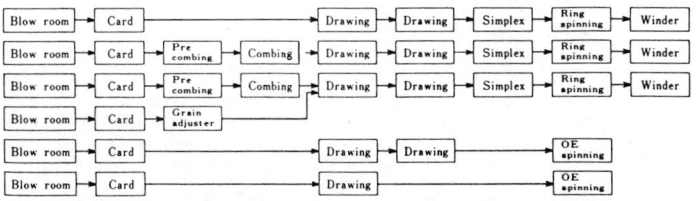

Fig. 1 Process Examples of Producing Spun-yarn

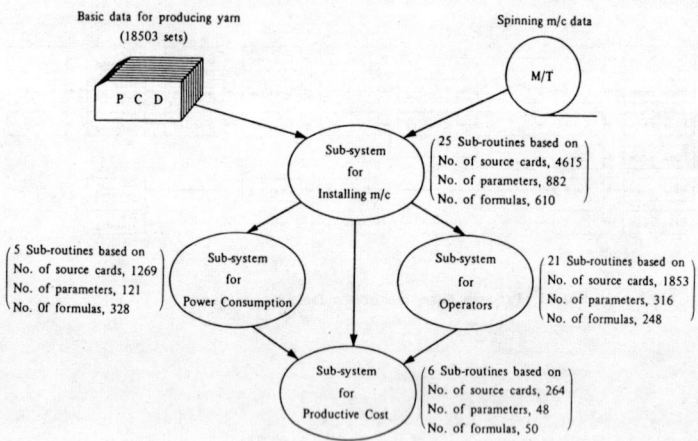

Fig. 2 Configuration of Total System

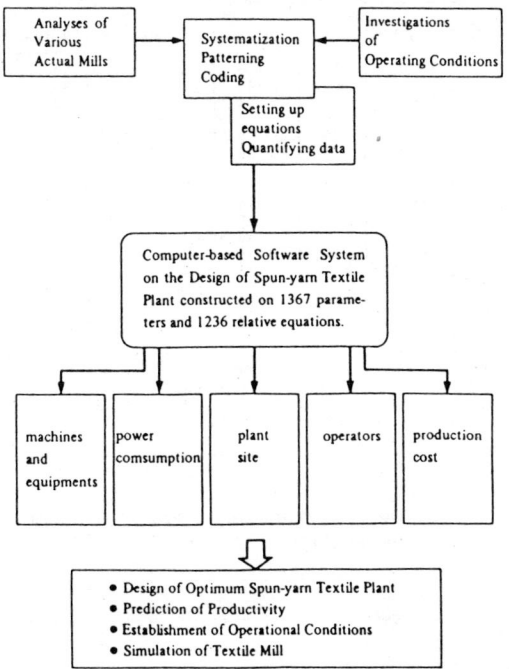

Fig. 3 Procedure to develop a Computer based Software on
Spun-yarn Textile Plant

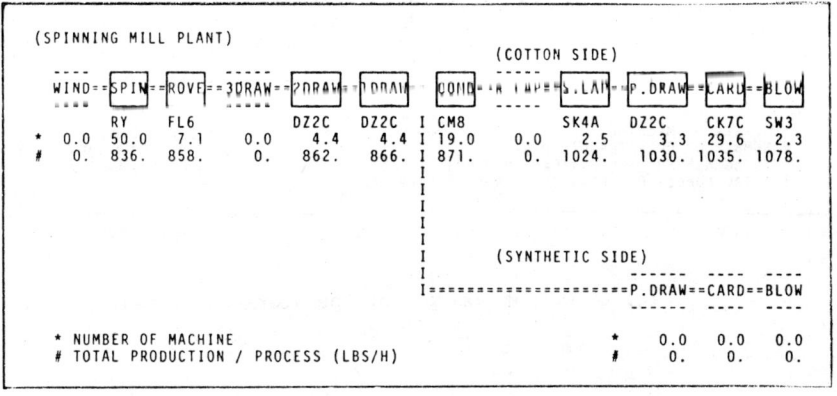

Fig. 4 Output example of Installing machines
Subsystem

```
PROCESS              I MODEL   I SETS I MOTOR (kw)I CONS. POWER (kw/H)
-----------------------------------------------------------------------
WINDING              I #550    I  7. I 116.55  I        80.50
SPINNING             I RY      I 50. I 845.00  I       566.95
ROVING               I FL6     I  8. I  90.40  I        69.82
3RD DRAWING          I         I  0. I   0.    I         0.
2ND DRAWING          I DZ2C    I  5. I  38.00  I        29.65
1ST DRAWING          I DZ2C    I  5. I  38.00  I        29.65
 (COTTON SIDE)       I
COMBING              I CM8     I 19. I  70.30  I        53.39
S.LAP FORMING        I SK4A    I  3. I  16.20  I        10.98
R.LAP FORMING        I         I  0. I   0.    I         0.
PRE.DRAWING          I DZ2C    I  4. I  30.40  I        23.72
CARD                 I CK7C    I 30. I 135.00  I       112.80
BLOW ROOM            IBM29BA03I 2-- 3I 127.87  I        91.26
 (SYNTHETIC SIDE)I
PRE.DRAWING          I         I  0. I   0.    I         0.
CARD                 I         I  0. I   0.    I         0.
BLOW ROOM            I         I 0-- 0I  0.    I         0.
-----------------------------------------------------------------------
AIR CONDITIONING               I 389.93  I       311.96
WASTE COLLECTING               I 111.96  I        89.57   TOTAL SPACE OF
LIGHTENING                     I         I        27.07   SPINNING MILL
                     (TOTAL) I 2009.60  I      1514.22        8130.3 M2
```

Fig. 5 Output example of Power Consumption
       Subsystem

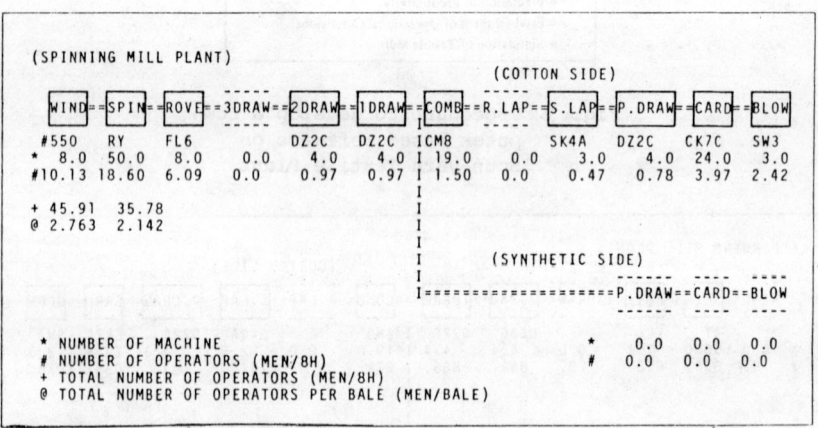

Fig. 6 Output example of Operators Subsystem

```
YARN PRODUCTION PER YEAR              I (BALES/YEAR) I CROPT I    17562.3
NO. OF OPERATORS                      I (OPRS)       I CTJ   I      160.7
     (INCL. MAINTENANCE)             I              I       I
POWER COMSUMPTION PER YEAR           I (KWH/YEAR)   I CTP   I 12577404.0
FLOOR SPACE OF MILL                  I (SO.METER)   I ARIAT I     8130.3
MACHINE PRICE                        I (x1000 YEN)  I YCTCM I   804000.0
BUILDING PRICE                       I (x1000 YEN)  I YCTMK I   813030.0
MACHINE WORKING HOURS PER DAY        I (MRS/DAY)    I CMWH  I       24.0
MACHINE WORKING DAYS PER YEAR        I (DAYS/YEAR)  I CMWD  I      350.0


    ==== YARN COST PER BALE  ( x1000 YEN/BALE) ====
-------------------------------------------------------------------------------
                                                                       (YEARS)
ITEM.          I   1     2     3     4     5     6     7     8     9    10
-------------------------------------------------------------------------------
LABOUR COST    I  18.3  19.6  21.0  22.4  24.0  25.7  27.5  29.4  31.4  33.6
POWER COST     I   7.2   7.7   8.2   8.8   9.4  10.0  10.7  11.5  12.3  13.2
MACHINE COST   I   9.4   7.5   5.9   4.7   3.7   3.0   2.4   1.9   1.5   1.2
BUILDING COST  I   9.5   7.6   6.0   4.8   3.8   3.0   2.4   1.9   1.5   1.2
INTEREST COST  I   3.7   2.9   2.3   1.8   1.5   1.2   0.9   0.7   0.6   0.5
SPARE PARTS COST I 0.4   0.5   0.5   0.6   0.6   0.7   0.8   0.8   0.9   1.0
-------------------------------------------------------------------------------
TOTAL          I  48.5  45.7  43.9  43.1  43.0  43.6  44.6  46.2  48.2  50.7
```

Fig. 7   Output example of Productive Cost
         Subsystem

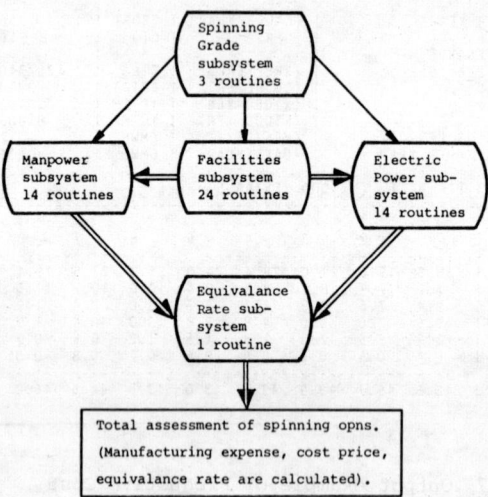

Fig. 8. Computation procedure flow for total assessment of spinning operations

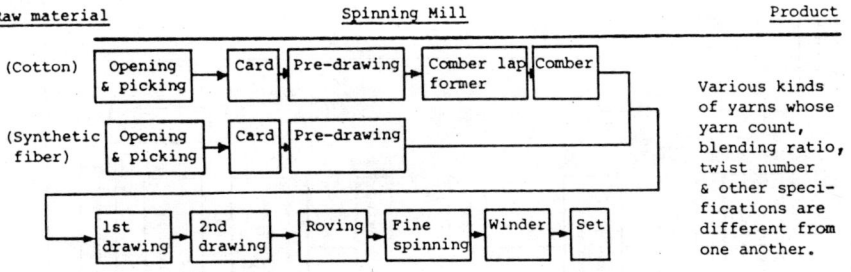

Fig. 9. An example of combined spinning processes
(Case of Pattern NO. 2).

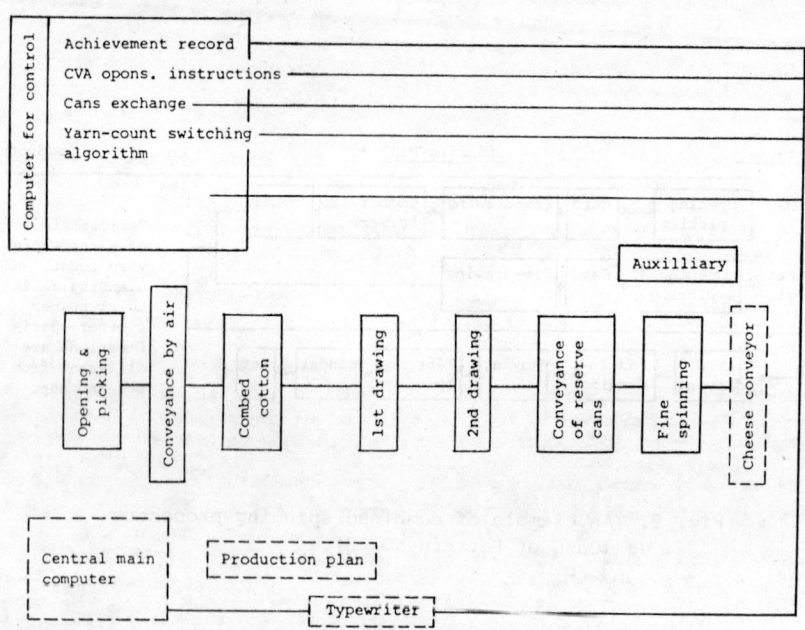

Fig. 10. Automatic production control of
Spinning mill (example)

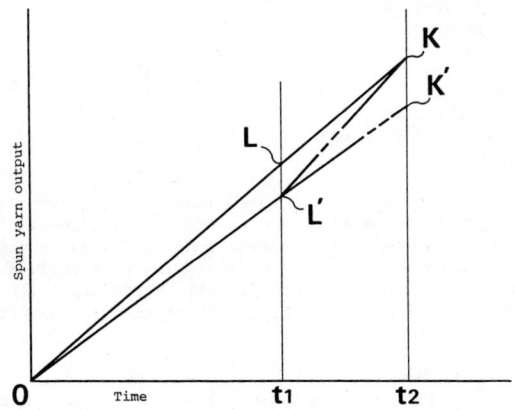

Fig. 11. Production control chart (example)

MEASURING THE CONTROL EFFECTIVENESS OF A COMPUTER-AIDED-MANUFACTURING SYSTEM

Neil Cahill

ABSTRACT

When designing a Computer-Aided-Manufacturing System, it is
essential to define how control effectiveness will be measured.
One key was uncovered in plant surveys aimed at determining how
much of performance losses in textile manufacturing could be
directly related to the occurrence of malfunction in the manufacturing process. The performance losses measured were such
things as spinning, ends-down, fabric defects or uneven yarn.
Of the total performance losses incurred in these textile plants,
only about 25 percent was in fact related to the actual occurrences of a process malfunction, while the remaining 75 percent
of the losses was due to delay in reacting to these problems.
This delay between when a process malfunction occurs and when
it is corrected is referred to as the control time of the manufacturing system.

By using delay time as a performance indicator, it is possible
to develop a model to measure the control effectiveness of a
manufacturing process. This control model is based on the fact
that there are three flow networks operating in textile manufacturing which determine control delay. These are: (1) Defect
Flow Network, (2) Information Flow Network, and (3) Decision
Flow Network.

Although textile manufacturing consist of a series of separate
processes such as carding, spinning, and weaving, they are
physically linked to each other by the flow of material. This
movement of material acts as a coupling between the processes
and, thereby, forms the material (Defect) Flow Network. The
second network is Information Flow. This determines how quickly
management is made aware that a malfunction even exist. And
finally, there is the Decision Flow Network which determines
how rapidly management can diagnose and take action. It is
these three networks which determines how much delay will occur
before a malfunction is brought under control.

It must be recognized that the real measure of delay is not time,
but rather the quantity of defects generated during that time.
Consequently, time by itself is not an adequate measure of control
effectiveness. However, by combining delay time with the rate
at which defects flow from the process, the total number of
defects generated after a malfunction can be known. This
measure of control effectiveness includes technical factors
such as machine output rate and frequency of defects, as well
as, managerial factors such as delay in exercising control.
This relationship can be expressed mathematically as follows:

$$N \simeq \frac{\text{Control Delay Defects}}{\left[(F)(D)\right]} + \frac{\text{Ineffective Control Defects}}{\left[(F)(1.0 - R)(P - D)\right]} + \frac{\text{Repeat Malfunction Defects}}{\left[(r)(d + L)\right]}$$

Where: N = Number of defects generated
        F = Defect flow rate (defects/hour)
        D = Control delay time (hours)
        R = Degree of recovery (%)
        P = Total run time (hours)
        r = Repeat malfunction (yes/no)
        d = Number of defects for control delay
        L = Number of defects for lack of recovery

Since all of these factors are measurable by a computerized
monitoring system, the means are then available for a Computer-
Aided-Manufacturing System to self-diagnose its own control
effectiveness.

1. INTRODUCTION

Textile manufacturing is rapidly moving away from a man-controlled
to a technology-controlled production system. Traditionally, our
plants have been manned by large numbers of people who were constantly attending and patrolling the production processes. Their
eyes and ears are the monitors used to detect process malfunctions
and product defects. But these people do a lot more than just
monitor. They also carry out the second part of a control system
which is analysis, because it is their skill and training that
determine what is wrong. These same people, because of their
experience and judgment, also make the decisions of what action
should be taken. Therefore, within each of these individuals
are all three elements of a control system: detection, analysis,
and decision. People are the control system of today's textile
manufacturing operations.

But the number of people needed to operate textile plants is
being significantly reduced. This means we are simultaneously
eliminating the traditional manufacturing control system. It
is, therefore, of necessity that we will move increasingly toward
Computer-Aided-Manufacturing as the new controller. These monitors
and computers will carry out the same basic control functions of
detection, analysis, and decision presently done by people. But
we must recognize that many of the traditional methods for measuring manufacturing effectiveness developed when people were the
controllers will not be appropriate for a technology based
control system.

For example, when asking a production manager what performance
measures indicate whether a manufacturing operation is "effectively"
controlled or not, the responses are usually such things as low
off-quality, high productivity or low cost. But consider this,
is low off-quality, high productivity and low cost the measures
of manufacturing effectiveness or are they the "rewards" for
having been effective? The fact is they are the rewards and not
the measures of manufacturing control effectiveness.

2. KEY MEASURE OF EFFECTIVENESS: CONTROL DELAY TIME

If we are to design a Computer-Aided-Manufacturing System, it
is essential we define how we will measure control effectiveness.
One key was uncovered recently in a plant survey aimed at determining just how much of the performance losses in textile manufacturing could be directly related to the occurrence of malfunction in the manufacturing process. The performance losses
measured were such things as spinning ends-down, fabric defects

or uneven yarn. The results were most surprising; of the total
performance losses incurred in these textile plants, only about
25 percent was in fact related to the actual occurrences of a
process malfunction, while the remaining 75 percent of the losses
was due to delay in reacting to these problems. It is control
delay which is a decisive key to improving manufacturing effectiveness. This delay between when a process malfunctions and
when it is finally corrected is referred to as the control time
of the manufacturing system.

2.1 Defining Control Delay

The impact of delay on performance losses in manufacturing can
be visualized graphically. As seen in Figure 1, the vertical
axis indicates the number of defects which are generated after
a malfunction of the process has occurred. The horizontal axis
represents increasing elapse time. Since no manufacturing process is capable of producing perfect material, there is a certain
level of normal or acceptable defectiveness as indicated by the
horizontal/dashed line. This is the standard. Let's assume
that this graph represents the evenness of sliver being produced
by a card. For example, the card may operate for weeks producing
sliver of acceptable evenness until a serious malfunction occurs,
such as a loose bracket or worn gear. From this point on
defective sliver is being produced. The accumulation of this
defective sliver is represented by the upward slope of the curve.
How rapidly this defective sliver accumulates in the plant will
be determined by the output rate of the machine and the frequency
of the defects, that is, does it repeat every 100 yards or every
inch. Both machine output rate and defect frequency are technical
factors determined by the process itself.

2.1.1. Reaction Threshold

However, we see there is a delay before management is even aware
that a malfunction has happened. This condition is not technical,
but managerial. That time when management is finally made aware
that a problem has occurred is called the Reaction Threshold of
the control system. In a traditional manual control system, the
Reaction Threshold may be measured in days or weeks. But even
after management is aware, there will be further delays as
management takes time to gather the needed information and then
diagnose what went wrong. During all this time, defects have
been flowing into the manufacturing operation. And finally,
there is one other delay we must consider which is related to
how effectiveness was the response taken to correct the problem.
If the corrective action taken fails to return the process to
its original level of performance, then defects will continue
to flow into the operation even after action is completed.

As seen here, it is not really surprising that delay is perhaps
the major contributor to textile performance losses. And by
using delay time as a performance indicator, it is possible to
develop a model to measure the control effectiveness of any
manufacturing process.

3. MANUFACTURING CONTROL MODEL
This manufacturing control model is based on the fact that there
are three flow networks operating in a textile plant which

influence control delay. These are: (1) Defect Flow Network, (2) Information Flow Network, and (3) Decision Flow Network.

Let's look at the Defect Flow Network first. Although textile manufacturing consist of a series of separate processes such as carding, spinning and weaving, they are in fact physically linked to each other by the flow of material. This movement of material acts as a coupling between the processes and, thereby, forms the Material Flow Network. But we must remember it is this material which carries defects from process to process and for this reason it is called the Defect Flow Network. The second network is Information Flow. This determines how quickly management is made aware that a malfunction even exist. And finally, there is the Decision Flow Network which determines how rapidly management can diagnose and take action.

Let's see how these three networks working together determines how much delay will occur before a malfunction is brought under control. We will analyze the control effectiveness of manually checking the weight variation of card sliver.

3.1 Manufacturing Control Loop

As seen by the arrow in Figure 2, sliver moves from the cards to drawing. This arrow represents the Material or Defect Flow Network. Since the sliver is only sampled once each day, the very earliest we could detect a problem is 24 hours. The sample is now brought to the lab, stored and then tested. This usually takes about three hours. There is a further delay of about two hours while the data are calculated and the report written. This is the Information Flow Time, since it is only now that we are able to actually notify production managers that a problem exist. In other words, it has taken 29 hours to reach the Reaction Threshold of this manual control system. Identifying the Reaction Threshold of a control system is most important since it tells us how long a problem can exist before management is even aware something is wrong. When we reach the Reaction Threshold, we now enter the Decision Flow Network.

As seen here, the time needed to diagnose the situation, to reach a decision, and transmit instruction to the maintenance personnel has added another four hours of delay. And finally, two more hours are needed to make the repairs and retest the sliver. In this example of a manual control loop, the total control time was 33 hours of which 29 hours were needed just to reach the Reaction Threshold to initiate management action.

4. CONTROL EFFECTIVENESS EQUATION
Although knowing the control delay time is necessary for design-ing a Computer-Aided-Manufacturing System, it must be recognized that the real measure of delay is not time, but rather the quantity of defects generated during that time. A process mal-function which generates one defect per hour is hardly the same situation as a malfunction generating 100 defects an hour. Consequently, time by itself is not an adequate measure of control effectiveness. However, as seen in Figure 3, by combin-ing delay time with the rate at which defects flow from the pro-cess, we now know the total number of defects generated after a malfunction has occurred. This measure of control effectiveness

includes the technical factors such as machine output rate and
frequency of defects, as well as, managerial factors such as
delay in exercising control. This relationship can be expressed
mathematically as follows:

$$N \simeq \frac{\text{Control Delay Defects}}{\left[(F)(D)\right]} + \frac{\text{Ineffective Control Defects}}{\left[(F)(1.0 - R)(P - D)\right]} + \frac{\text{Repeat Malfunction Defects}}{\left[(r)(d + L)\right]}$$

Where: N = Number of defects generated
        F = Defect flow rate (defects/hour)
        D = Control delay time (hours)
        R = Degree of recovery (%)
        P = Total run time (hours)
        r = Repeat malfunction (yes/no)
        d = Number of defects for control delay
        L = Number of defects for lack of recovery

Since all of these factors are measurable by a computerized
monitoring system, the means are then available for a Computer-
Aided-Manufacturing System to self-diagnose its own control
effectiveness.

In this approach, we are measuring control effectiveness in terms
of the number of defects generated after a malfunction has occurred.
But more importantly, this effectiveness is expressed in terms
of delay time, and delay is management controllable. It is
management decision which decides what will be the Reaction
Threshold of their control system. It is management decision
that decides how much delay there will be in the Information
and Diagnostic Networks. As has always been the case, management is responsible for manufacturing control effectiveness and
it does not really matter whether it is a man-controlled system
or technology-controlled system; the major difference is how you
measure effectiveness.

Institute of Textile Technology
P. O. Box 391
Charlottesville, Virginia 22902 (U.S.A.)

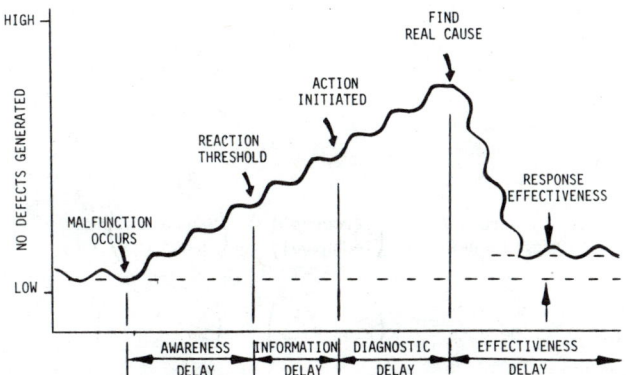

Figure 1. Schematic representation of Control Delay in
responding to manufacturing malfunctions.

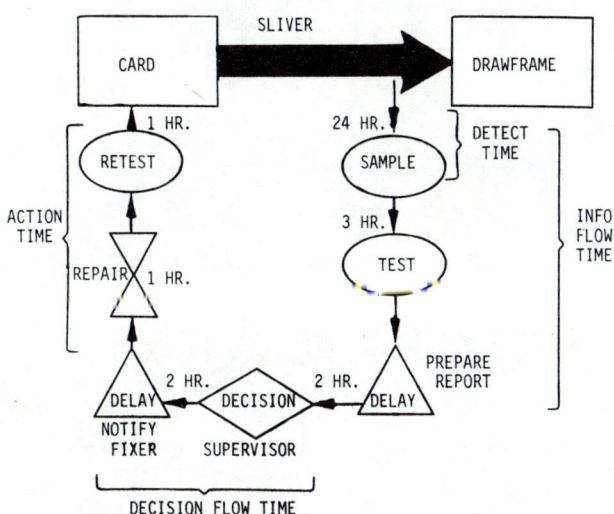

Figure 2. Control Delay caused by three flow networks
in manufacturing.

669

$$\begin{matrix} \text{Control} \\ \text{Effectiveness} \end{matrix} = \begin{pmatrix} \text{Process} \\ \text{Technical} \end{pmatrix} \begin{pmatrix} \text{Managerial} \\ \text{Reaction} \end{pmatrix}$$

$$\begin{matrix} \text{Number of} \\ \text{Defects} \end{matrix} = \begin{pmatrix} \text{Defect} \\ \text{Flow Rate} \end{pmatrix} \begin{pmatrix} \text{Control} \\ \text{Delay Time} \end{pmatrix}$$

Figure 3. Number of defects generated after a malfunction as a measure of manufacturing control effectiveness.

LEGAL PROTECTION FOR COMPUTER SOFTWARE APPLIED TO TEXTILE TECHNOLOGY

A. Aoki

ABSTRACT

Computer technology has perhaps the greatest potential for improving the textile industry. Along with our efforts to promote greater development in the industry through computer technology, however, we must consider the protection of the relevant software. The legal system for protection of computer software has still not been well established worldwide. Here, an introduction will be given on the state of software protection in the industrially developed countries and problems therein.

1. INTRODUCTION

The creation of computer software requires a certain level of technical knowledge and professional experience and knowledge in the field of engineering to which the computer software is related. It must be recognized that, to create useful and practical computer software, a proportionate time and expense must be spent. It is obvious that when computer software is copied or imitated, the costs and time of the copier or imitator are considerably reduced in comparison to those of the creator of the original software. It is also obvious that such copying places the creator of new computer software under a great disadvantage in terms of costs and time expended. When considered from such a viewpoint, it seems only common sense to protect the newly created software against any illegal illegal imitation or copying by a third party: to ensure that the creator is allowed to enjoy the profits which are any creator's due, and to promote the development of the industry to which this newly created software can be applied. Thus, there does exist significance in the present ongoing discussions of legal protection for computer software.

Since the subject matter of my talk is rather complicated, I think it best to first clarify definition of computer software. In one definition, computer software is referred to as "a concept consisting of a computer program, program-related documents for efficiently utilizing this computer program, and a machine or an apparatus wherein this computer program is built in". In another definition, a computer program is referred to as "a set of commands which operate a digital computer or a machine or an apparatus, wherein the digital computer is built in, to attain a specific result, that is, a set of procedures".

2. WORLD-WIDE TRENDS ON THE LEGAL PROTECTION OF COMPUTER SOFTWARE

(1) ACTIVITY OF WIPO (WORLD INTELLECTUAL PROPERTY ORGANIZATION) AND AIPPI (ASSOCIATION OF INTERNATIONAL PROTECTION OF INDUSTRIAL PROPERTY)

In 1978, WIPO proposed the "Model Clauses of National Laws for the Protection of Computer Software". In 1979, AIPPI recognized the problem of the protection of computer software and adopted discussion thereof as one of the important on the agenda of its executive committee. Since then, AIPPI has carried out in-depth studies, undertaken with the assistance of experts in the field, into ways in which computer software can be protected by existing Laws, such as the Patent Law, Contract Law, Unfair Competition Prevention Law, Trade Secrets Law, Copyright Law, and the like, and into exactly what problems are involved in such protection.

The second conference by experts on computer software was held by WIPO in Geneva in 1983, where the subject was debated on the basis of the previously-mentioned model clauses of 1978. These facts should be acknowledged with great care and without prejudice. It should be noted that it was revealed through the activities of WIPO and AIPPI that the world tendency concerning the legal protection of computer software is toward legal protection mainly by the Copyright Law, even though there remain a number of problems to be solved.

In Japan, a compromise has not yet been reached between the proposal by the Ministry of International Trade and Industry regarding legislation of the so-called Program Right Law, as a measure from the industrial policy viewpoint, and the proposal by the Ministry of Education regarding the partial revision of the Copyright Law. In connection with this, it should be noted, as background to the above-mentioned movements in WIPO and AIPPI, that the protection of computer software by the Patent Law has never been opposed or denied. Many computer software technologies are entitled to be designated as an invention and many microcomputer-application technologies have actually been patented in such industrially developed countries as the United States of America and Japan. In European countries such as Great Britain, West Germany, and France, even though their Patent Laws deny that computer software is a subject matter of their Patent Laws, it is possible that an invention which involves computer technology such as microcomputer technology can obtain a patent. Under these circumstances, wherein the actual manner of the protection of computer software to be provided by the Copyright Law has not been confirmed, enterprises should keep it in mind that new technology created by the application of computer software, at a considerable expenditure of time and money, has great possibilities of being allowed protection under Patent Law.

3.   PROTECTION OF COMPUTER PROGRAM BY COPYRIGHT LAW

3.1 As described above, in the industrially advanced countries, such as the United States and European countries, (excluding Japan), the situation seems to be approaching the establishment of a legal system whereby

the protection of a computer program will rely mainly on
the system of protection afforded by the Copyright Laws.

For example, in the industrially advanced countries
(including Japan), the attitudes of the courts toward
the protection of computer program have become clear
insofar as video game devices are concerned. However, it
is a fact that the attitudes of the courts toward the
protection of computer programs related to the application
of computers to industrial technologies (for example,
computer program related to the use of a personal computer,
a microcomputer, or a large scale computer) are still
unclear. Thus, it can be said that there are problems
remaining, which are unclear and should be solved, with
regard to the protection of computer programs by Copyright
Law.

Meanwhile, the contents of the protection of computer
programs by Copyright Law in the United States has become
considerably clearer, in view of the report from CONTU
(the National Commission on New Technological Uses of
Copyrighted Works) and the legal precedents set by the
courts in the United States.

In Japan, a certain number of court decisions on the
protection of computer programs concerning video game
devices have been actually issued, and in these court
decisions the court's judgement is that computer programs
concerning video game devices are within the category
of protection by Copyright Law. However, no lawsuit
concerning protection of a computer program related to the
application of a computer to industrial technologies seems
to have been raised, and accordingly no court decision for
such a lawsuit has been issued.

3.2 From the viewpoint of the protection of computer
programs by the Copyright Law in the United States, this
can be divided into two categories; that is, the protection of computer programs concerning video game devices,
and the protection of computer programs concerning personal
computers, microcomputers, and large scale computers.

Judging from the court decisions in the United States
given for the former case, the attitude of the court is
that the computer program can be protected by the Copyright
Law, while, in the latter case, the attitude of the court
is that an object code is a substantial translation of a
source code and, hence, can be covered by the copyright
on the source code (GCA Corp. v. Chance, F. Sup p. 217
USPQ 718). With regard to the problem of whether a copyright concerning a source code or an object code covers a
ROM (read only memory) on which the program is physically
fixed, the attitude of the court is that a computer program
fixed physically on a computer chip can be protected by
the Copyright Law, as indicated in a court decision
(Williams Electronics Inc. v. Artic International Inc. 215
USPQ 405).

Also, with regard to the problem of whether a copyright is applicable to an operating program, which is a program for managing the internal function of a computer, the attitude of the court is that such an operating program is entitled to be a subject matter of protection by copyright, as indicated in a court decision (Apple Computer Inc. v. Franklin Computer Corp. 219 USPQ 113).

Yet, there still remains a problem to be solved. The problem is how can a plaintiff verify the "substantial identity" of a computer program in a suit against infringement of a copyright on a computer program. The attitude of the court as to how such judgement should be conducted has not yet been revealed.

3.3 As I mentioned earlier, there remain problems to be solved in the protection system of computer programs by the Copyright Law in each country. From the viewpoint of the establishment of an internationally common protection system of computer programs, also many problems remain to be solved, as exemplified in the following.

That is, whether or not the content of right of a conventional copyright is suitable and sufficient to protect a computer program, in relation to the problem of the right of use, whether or not the practices in most countries, where a copyright is established simultaneously with the creation of a literal work by an author and the author has no obligation to publish his work, is suitable and satisfactory from the viewpoint of the state policy concerning industry; who should be treated as an author from the viewpoint of moral right (particularly, in relation to the creation of a computer program by a juridical person), whether or not the deposit or the registration should be required as the condition for protection; whether or not revisions of the present conventions concerning copyright, such as the Universal Copyright Convention or Bern Convention, are necessary from the viewpoint of the protection of computer programs; and the like.

3.4 In the application of computer technology to the textile industry, almost no application of computer technology in the manner of a video game device, on which the protection system by copyright law has been already established in many countries, can be found. Actually, in many cases, such application of computer technology to the textile industry constitutes a creation of technical ideas. Under the circumstance where many inventions concerning computer application technology have been actually patented in the United States of America, Japan, and according to my investigation, even in Great Britain, France, and Germany, it becomes clear that, if the invention created by the application of a computer program indicates a novel and useful technical advance as a whole, there is a possibility of such an invention obtaining a patent.

4. PROTECTION OF COMPUTER PROGRAM BY THE PATENT LAW

4.1 In order to protect a computer program under the Patent Law in a nation where the computer program is excluded as subject matter under that Patent Law, it must be first determined whether or not the computer program concerned can be regarded as an invention which qualifies as subject matter under the Patent Law, through the examination procedures. If this is so, then the patentability of the invention concerned is examined, and only an invention passing the examination procedures will be granted a patent in this nation.

When the patent laws of various nations are reviewed, it can be seen that, with the exception of Japan, the U.S.S.R., and the like which provide a definition of an invention, the Patent Law of nearly all nations do not define an invention in a concrete form. For instance, even if the Patent Law defines an invention in general, in actual practice any concrete interpretation is principally committed to juridical precedents and doctrines.

Thus, if a study is made of the present situation, that is, in Japan the Patent Law clarifies the definition of an invention, in the United States of America it is based on case law, and the various concepts of the European countries, it is possible to gain an understanding of the latest trend toward ways of protecting the computer program under Patent Law on a worldwide scale.

4.2 JAPAN

4.2.1 In Article 2 of the Japanese Patent Law, an invention is defined as follows;

"Invention means the highly advanced creation of technical idea by which a law of nature is utilized".

In Article 2, a Utility Model invention is defined as;

"Device means the creation of technical ideas by which a law of nature is utilized".

Both are dealt with as subject matter qualifying for protection. It must be understood that the definitions regarding the subject matter of Japanese Patent Law and Utility Model Law are responsive to the statutory subject matter as defined in the U.S. Code, Title 35, Patents, §101. The procedures carried out by the Japanese Patent Office to determine whether or not an invention qualifies as subject matter entitled to be examined for patent grant, are as follows.

4.2.2 In the examination standard, a computer program is defined as "a procedure for controlling the machine or apparatus and processing desired information, on the assumption that an electronic computer is utilized". That is, an electric computer is considered to operate in response to a programmed procedure wherein a formatted

program is input to the computer, and, consequently, it
may attain inevitably, for example, the processing of
information and the controlling of machines. It is also
considered that the procedure is interpreted as a set of
separate commands, and that the procedure is a creation of
a technical idea, in that a causal relationship between
these commands is utilized to attain a desired object of
this procedure.

However, in another consideration, it is regarded that, as
the data per se processed by a computer represents only a
social phenomena or natural phenomena as an assemblage of
numerals or symbols, such data is limited to the area of
abstract information, and as such is not considered to
form technical idea.

4.2.3 In the latest examination manual, a principle
utilized for creating a specific result is defined as
"causality of technique". When the causality of technique
follows a law of nature, the creation of this technical
idea is recognized as utilizing a law of nature. For
instance, from such a viewpoint concerning the causality
of technique, the afore-mentioned computational method
used to calculate the mathematical symbol π is only a
utilization of a principle in mathematics and is not
regarded as a utilization of a law of nature. For example,
if a program has been made for solving chess-problems, as
the causality of technique is based on the rules of chess,
it cannot be regarded as the utilization of a law of nature.
It is the same when the causality of technique is based
on a mental activity of a human being or solely on an
agreement; it cannot be said to be a utilization of a law
of nature.

[Note] Following three developments related textile
technology are examples which satisfy the requirement to
be patentable subject matter.

(1) Toyoda Jido-Shokki KK; Automatic production control
method for a spinning production system. Japanese Patent
No. 917,267

(2) Toyda Jido-Shokki KK; Automatic method for controlling
the quantitative balance between two adjacent processes in
a spinning mill. Japanese Patent No. 917,268.

(3) Kanebo Ltd; A pattern analyzing system. Japanse
Patent No. 1,147,734.

4.2.4 However, if an invention on a computer program
satisfies the requirements for being a subject matter and
the required patentability of the Patent Law, a patent
could be granted to this invention as a "process patent".

Regarding the application of a computer program to create
a new fabric structure, which structure did not previously
exist, it is my opinion that even if the computer program
concerned does not satisfy the requirements for being a
subject matter of the Patent Law, such a new creation in

676

textile technology can be protected by the Patent Law as
a product patent, and such a computer program could be
protected under the Patent Law as a process patent to
create such a new fabric structure. I am expecting the
result of an examination on an application involving
such an invention, which is now pending. By the way, a
patent application as an invention related to a designing
procedure of a fabric structure has been regarded as
an invention in a category of method by illustration,
therefore such an invention has not been recognized as the
required subject matter of the Patent Law, as it does not
utilize a law of nature.

4.2.5 Protection of Microcomputer-Application Technology

(a) There have been enormous developments in microcomputer-application technology recently, and it has
become popular in a wide range of technological fields.
The textile technology is no exception, and such development is actively implemented in our field. In order to be
the subject matter of the Patent Law it is necessary that,
first, the microcomputer-application technology should be
concluded as an invention and second, that it should
satisfy the patentable requirements of the Patent Law.
By the way, in spite of its wide-spread utilization, the
terms, for the microcomputer-application technology are
not as clearly recognized as is thought, thus it seems
to be better to clarify this subject. Microcomputer-
application technology is divided briefly into the
following two categories: (1) The application-technology
of a microcomputer to information processing and process
control; and (2) the microcomputer-application technology
of "microcomputer-byte-in apparatuses and devices". The
former is generally concluded to be a method invention and
the latter to be an apparatus invention, in order to be
the subject matter of the Patent Law. Since the former
has been already explained, I will now explain the latter.

(b) The Japanese Patent Office established the Examination
Application Standards in 1982, which indicate the criterion
for the examination of inventions related to microcomputer-
applied apparatus and devices, whereby the criterion for
judging patentability, for instance, identity rule or
inventivesteps are indicated. This criterion clarifies
the basis of judgement for solving these problems. The
basis for carrying out the information processing and
control operation, wherein a microcomputer is utilized, is
a program used to decide how to operate the microcomputer.
This program is deemed to form a part of the automatic
control and production working apparatus, and the information processing and the control operation is carried out
by the cobmination of software and hardware. Such a
combination of software and hardware is essential to
satisfy the requirements of subject matter of the Patent
Law as a new creation of a technical idea utilizing a law
of nature.

According to this examination application standard, first,
the functions of a microcomputer are recognized, then,

in response to its functions, implementing means of the
respective functions are deemed to exist and the invention
is regarded as an apparatus wherein a microcomputer is
utilized, and thus is regarded as an apparatus invention
which renders these means as a requisite for composing
elements.   This is clarified in the following example.

Speed control apparatus of electronically-controlled
sewing machines for a pattern stitch

This invention is recognized as an apparatus invention,
which is formed by such several elements as a pattern
stitching speed limiting device, a stitch pattern forming
device, memory means, a pattern selection switch, pattern
selecting means, a timing detector, addressing means,
etc.   The claim is drafted in the combination form of the
above-mentioned elements to clarify the causal relationship
therebetween.

4.3   UNITED STATES OF AMERICA

4.3.1   The United States Code, Title 35 Patents defines in
Chapter 10 (Patentability of Inventions) §101 that "whoever
invents or discovers any new and useful process, machine,
manufacture, or composition of matter, or any new and
useful improvement thereof, may obtain a patent therefor,
subject to the conditions and requirements of this title".
It is noticeable that there exist three separate requirements, that is to say, novelty, usefulness, and statutory
subject matter, and that, above all, novelty is subject to
Chapter 10, §102 (conditions for patentability; novelty
and loss of right to patent).   Whether or not a specified
invention may be novel and useful is quite different to
whether or not this invention is attributed to a statutory
subject matter.   Therefore, the question that one should
ask first of all when determining whether or not the
computer program is considered to be able to protected
by the U.S. Patent law, is whether or not the computer
program concerned is a statutory subject matter as defined
by the United States Code.   After a long and arduous
series of decisions from the Court of Customs and Patent
Appeals (C.C.P.A.), as well as the United States Supreme
Court, this question has been clarified.   The present
Manual of Patent Examining Procedure indicates the
criterion of examination in Section 2110, Patentable
Subject Matter-Mathematical Algorithms or Computer
Programs.

4.3.2   (a)   The question has been elucidated in several
court decisions; for instance, (1) Gottschalk v. Benson
decision (1972), (2) In re Freeman case decision (1978),
(3) In re Flook decision (1978), (4) In re Walter case
decision (1980), (5) Diamond v. Diehr decision (1981),
(6) Diamond v. Bradley et al decision (1981), and so on.
A study of these historical developments will enable you
to understand how a computer program may be considered a
statutory subject matter.

(b) The above-mentioned case (1) is connected with a
patentability of a method for converting signals from a
binary coded decimal form into a pure binary form. The
court affirms that, because phenomena of nature (a recent
discovery), mental processes, and abstract intellectual
concepts form a fundamental implement for a scientific and
technical work, these cannot be considered a statutory
subject matter, and this fundamental rule is also applicable to an invention concerning a product and a process.
In this decision, it is recognized that a procedure for
solving a given type of mathematical problem is known as
an "algorithm". From such a standpoint of view on the
above-mentioned definition, as an algorithm or the
mathematical expression of it is similar to a law of
nature, it cannot be considered a statutory subject
matter, so it is judged that the claim of the present
application does not fall under the statutory subject
matter.

Remarks: The scope of the above-mentioned definition of
"algorithm" is narrower 4223 than that of the definition
by the U.S. Government as "a fixed step by step procedure
for accomplishing a given result; usually a simplified
procedure for solving a complex problem, also a full
statement of a finite number of steps." (See 209 USPQ 8),
and, in the Random House Dictionary, "algorithm" is defined
as "any particular procedure for solving a certain type of
problem".

(c) The afore-mentioned case (2) is related to an example
which renders a system for typesetting alphanumeric information using a computer-based control system in conjunction
with a photo-typesetter of conventional design as a subject
matter of an invention. This example denotes that the
trial decision of the Board of Appeals recognizing that it
was not a statutory subject matter based on the Benson
case decision, was reversed by the CCPA. The decision
reveals a judgement criterion on how claims are to be
analyzed to determine whether or not the claim is recognized as pre-empting the mathematical formula. And,
referring to the Walter case decision (4), its essence is
applied to the judgement of claims as a whole as a two-step
analyzing method and is now a standard of a claim analysis
indicated in the Manual of Patent Examination Procedure
§2110, Patentable Subject Matter ---Mathematical Algorithms
or Computer Programs.

(d) The decision of the above-mentioned case (3) relates
to a Flook patent case in which, during such a chemical
process as Flook's catalytic conversion processes, when
any of the process variables, such as temperature, pressure
and flow rates, exceeds a predetermined alarm limit, a
revised alarm limit value is calculated and controls the
process. Moreover, the court recognized that, only owing
to the fact that a process claim involves description
regarding the Law of nature on a mathematical algorithm,
the patent application should not be judged as unpatentable.

(e) In the decision of CCPA In re Walter case (4), CCPA indicated that, where the mathematical algorithm is implemented in a specific manner to define structural relationships between the physical elements of the claim (in apparatus claims) or to restrict claim steps (in process claims), the claim satisfies the requirements for statutory subject matter under 35 USC 101.

(f) The afore-mentioned (5) In re Diehr case is related to a patent application for a method of operating a rubber molding press for producing rubber goods by means of a digital computer. In the procedure of examination and appeal, the Patent Office refused this application by stating that this invention cannot be deemed as statutory subject matter under §101, because the processing is carried out by a computer. On the contrary, CCPA indicated that "even if the invention contains a computer operation, the claims do not purport to improve only a mathematical algorithm or computating method, but purport to improve a method for solving problems originated from the mold step of a rubber goods, so the invention satisfies the requirements for statutory subject matter and the claims are patentable". The Supreme Court also supported the decision.

In the Supreme Court decision, it requires that the claims must be considered as a whole. Consistent with this requirement, the Supreme Court concluded that "a claim drawn to subject matter otherwise statutory does not become non-statutory simply because it uses a mathematical formula, a computer program, or digital computer. The Court also stated that, "while a scientific truth, or the mathematical expression of it, is not a patentable invention, a novel and useful structure created with the aid of knowledge of such scientific truth or the mathematical formula may be considered patentable."

The decision in 'In re Diehr' has been adopted by the Patent and Trademark Office of the United States as an examination standard, and the content is explained in detail in Section 2110 of the Manual of Patent Examining Procedure.

[Note 1]: Court Decision (1) 175 USPQ 673,
                          (2) 197 USPQ 197,
                          (3) 198 USPQ 193,
                          (4) 205 USPQ 397,
                          (5) 209 USPQ 208,
                          (6) 209 USPQ 1

[Note 2]: US patents related to inventions in the textile field.

(1) Richmond: PROCESSING OF MULTILAYER WEAVE DESIGN DATA. USP3634827 (1972)

(2) Dubner: METHOD AND APPARATUS FOR PRODUCING JAQUARD CARD. USP3671944 (1972)

(3) Geirhos: METHOD OF AND APPARATUS FOR
REPRESENTING A PROGRAM FOR A TEXTILE
MACHINE. USP3744035 (1973)

(4) Seitz: SYSTEM FOR THE ELECTRIC CONTROL OF TEXTILE
MACHINES OR FOR THE MANUFACTURE OF CONTROL
STRIPS FOR TEXTILE MACHINE. USP3924244
(1975)

(5) Kajiura: PATTERN GENERATING SYSTEM. USP4078253
(1978)

4.4 EUROPEAN COUNTRIES

4.4.1 In the European Patent Convention, computer programs
are excluded from the subject matter needed for a grant of
a European Patent. (Art 52, 2-C EPC).

The guidelines for examination in the European Patent
Office clarify just what is considered as a computer
program. However, according to my investigations, the
attitude of the European Patent Office seems to have
changed toward one like the recent attitude of CCPA in the
United States. It is said that the EPO intends to revise
their guidelines for examination.

Under the present patent laws in Great Britain, France,
and West Germany, the computer program is excluded from
the subject matter to be protected by the respective
patent laws. (British Patent Law, Art 1; French Patent
Law, Art 6; German Patent Law, Art. 1). However, according
to my investigations in those countries, it seems that,
where the invention is created by the application of a
computer program, the invention is examined as a whole,
and if it is clear that novel and useful technical advances
can be made by this invention, there is a possibility of
obtaining a patent. For example, in France, the Appeal
Court of Paris has recognized (with regards to the French
patent application 2481811) that a method cannot be held
unpatentable on the sole ground that one or more steps
thereof are carried out by means of a computer program,
and without determining whether an industrial result is
obtained. (Court decision given on June 15, 1981.)
In France, it is said that a combinations of computer
software with computer hardware is patentable. In Great
Britain, the British Patent Office is granting patents
under the 1977 Act for apparatus when programed to operate
in a particular manner (for example, B.P Nos. 2055270 and
2053536) or for methods of effecting operation under
program control (for example B.P Nos. 2053510, 2062896).
It is our understanding that if the claimed invention is
mainly characterized by a computer program, it is almost
impossible to obtain a British Patent for the invention.
In the West Germany, if we carefully review the Supreme
Court decisions related to the invention utilizing a
computer program (In re Schloemann AG, GRUR 1981, 39;
Teldix GmbH V. Ate Alfred Teves GmbH GRUR 1980, 849),
it can be said that, in West Germany, it seems rather
difficult to obtain a patent to an invention which involves

an application of a computer program, in comparison with other industrially developed countries. Therefore, if we want to obtain the patent protection of a computer program applied to the textile technology, we must be careful to draft the specification so as to overcome the reason for rejection based upon the German Patent Law, Art 1.

Note   The following patents related to the textile technology were granted before   the application of the present Patent Laws in Great Britain, France, and West Germany.

(1)   Franz Morat GMBH: CONTROLLING A MACHINE WITH SIGNALS DERIVED FROM A PATTTERN. British Patent 1379765 (1975)

(2)   Franz Morat GMBH: METHOD AND APPARATUS FOR TRANS- FERRING A PATTERN TO A PROGRAMME CARRIER.   British Patent 1382723 (1975)

(3)   Wildt Mellor Bromley Limited: IMPROVEMENTS IN OR RELATING TO THE CONTROL OF KNITTING MACHINE. British Patent 1398924 (1975)

(4)   Wildt Mellor Bromley LIMITED: IMPROVEMENTS IN OR RELATING TO PATTERN PREPARATION AND CONTROL OF KNITTING MACHINES.   British Patent 1399457 (1975)

(5)   Kanebo: A PATTERN ANALYZING SYSTEM.   British Patent 1508354 (1978)

(6)   Kanebo: A PATTERN ANALYZING SYSTEM.   French PATENT 7511105 (1979)

5.   CONCLUSION

In summary, computer programs can be protected by a variety of methods in each country. However, if we seek an effective method to protect the application of computer technology to our textile technology, it is clear that patent protection is probably the most effective method on a worldwide scale, at the present stage.

A. Aoki & Associates
Seiko Toranomon
Tokyo 105
JAPAN

COMPUTERS IN THE WORLD OF TEXTILES: THE ECONOMIC IMPACT

O.E. Thur

ABSTRACT

The microprocessor has automated production functions and
the silicon chip can thrust robots from fantasy to reality.
This new technology is being pursued with remarkable speed
and vigor in many quarters, one of these being the textile
equipment manufacturers.

The economic impact of the new technology is wide-ranging.
It substitutes capital for ever more expensive labour, thus
changing the cost structure of textile production by
significantly decreasing the share of labour costs in total
production costs and by increasing the proportion of fixed
costs. With this new cost structure the level of wages
becomes a competitive factor of lesser importance. The
investment requirements of the new technology are high and
will hamper its adoption. Through the Canadian experience
it is demonstrated that, because of the strong national and
international competitive pressure, consumers were the main
beneficiaries of total productivity growth and not capital
or labour. In these conditions, internal generation of
funds and return on capital were modest in the textile
activities.

The new technology also improves quality which, in turn,
becomes the new international standard for quality. Finally,
the new technology reduces or eliminates non-quality,
diminishes inventories and contributes to cost savings.

With all these economic changes, international competition
in the future will become less cost and price determined
and more quality, design, and creativity oriented.

1. INTRODUCTION

Technology and economics are, like Siamese twins, organically
interrelated. Science and technology, basic or applied,
create an endless flow of new knowledge. This new knowledge
opens the door to new products and new production technologies.
The role of economics is to select from this abundance of new
technological opportunities those which are actually feasible
from an economic point of view.

Looking at the evolution of the textile sector in the last
five or six years, an economist cannot but be impressed by
the receptivity of textiles to change. The most important
technological change occurred in an area far way from
textiles, in electronics. Nevertheless, textile equipment
manufacturers had already borrowed heavily from electronics
at the time of ITMA 79. As we have all seen at ITMA 83,
electronics ceased to be borrowed and were fully integrated
into the last generation of equipment. This is quite a

remarkable achievement and proves the vitality of textile
of textile equipment producers. Over a very short period
of time they were able to understand and develop the new
technology, adapting it to the specific needs of the textile
sector. At a time when there is such a wealth of knowledge
embodied in each and every technology, developing two very
different clusters of technology in parallel should be
considered a real challenge, and textile machinery producers
were able to defy it brilliantly.

When an economist looks at technological progress his main
interest is not in technology per se. He is much more
interested in the longer term economic consequences of this
progress, namely, does it affect costs, productivity,
competitive capacity, quality of products, manpower. Because
technology does not come free of charge he is also interested
in finding out how the textile industries will manage to
generate sufficient funds to pay for the progress.

2. THE NEW TECHNOLOGIES IN TEXTILES

The common denominator of recent new technologies is automation. However, perhaps the first problem one encounters
when addressing the question of automation is defining
exactly what automation is or, more importantly, what facet
of automation is most relevant to an industry's needs.
Looking through current literature, one is confronted with a
wealth of articles all purporting to deal with automation,
yet using an array of names such as automated manufacturing,
CAM, Robotics, Process control, Programmable instruments,
Factory Automation, Networking, and so on, ad infinitum.

This is to be expected. There are so many different
manufacturing activities that many different capabilities
are needed in order to offer automation solutions to the
complete range of these activities.

Most manufacturing/assembly sites abound with opportunities
to install automated systems. The challenge is to identify
those areas that will have the greatest economic impact on
the operations.

2.1 The Silicon Chip

Today, rather than anticipating incremental advances,
futurists are increasingly discussing the onset of a sweeping
technological revolution, one that would rival or surpass
the Industrial Revolution of the 19th century in importance.

At the center of the flurry of interest in technological
change is the microprocessor. While computer technology has
made widespread automation theoretically feasible for more
than a decade, barriers of size and cost have blocked the
economical application of computer capabilities in most work
settings. Large and expensive computer systems could produce
cost savings only in the most massive industrial settings, and
automated machinery could not be easily adapted to serve
various production functions. Yet, with the development of

684

the microprocessor, these obstacles have been overcome and
the potential uses of computerized machinery at the workplace have dramatically increased.

Microprocessor technology is best symbolized by the silicon
chip, a miniaturized system of integrated circuits that can
direct electrical current and thereby generate vast computational power. With current technology, a silicon chip the
size of one square centimeter can perform millions of
multiplications per second and enable the storage of volumes
of data. Technological advances are expected to result in
at least a tenfold expansion of these capabilities within a
decade, so that the microprocessors of the future will be
extremely powerful computers on a single silicon chip or
combination of chips. The reduction in size is astounding -
today's hand-held programmable calculators have more
computational power than the first full-scale computers
built during World War II, computers that could have been
"hand held" only by juggling 18,000 different vacuum tubes.

The miniaturization of computer technology is particularly
important because it has been accompanied by dramatic cost
reductions, making miniprocessors economically competitive
in a wide range of industrial applications. Once designed,
silicon chips can be mass produced at a very low cost, and
even further price declines are anticipated as volumes rise.
The combined reductions in size and cost of microprocessor
technology have triggered renewed interest in prospects for
automation and in the broader possibility of a wholesale
transformation of modern society driven by these new
technological capabilities.

The silicon chip is particularly important to economical
automation because it provides the basis for fully integrating
computer and machine. In industrial settings, the microprocessor makes possible the development of manufacturing
machinery with unique adaptability.

The great majority - at least 75 per cent of all
manufactured goods involve shorter, lower volume production
runs, with only the most basic industries, and textiles are
not one of them, continuing to fit the mass production
stereotype. Technological advances in microelectronics,
therefore, were an essential precondition to widespread
automation, and the expanding use of programmable machinery
has triggered today's intense debate regarding the future of
industrialized societies.

The potential impact of microprocessors is heightened by
their seemingly endless number of applications. This new
technology promises to alter not only the factory, but
warehousing and the office as well. Sophisticated word
processors and computerized information storage and retrieval
are becoming increasingly cost-effective. And because this
new technology does not require knowledge of specialized
computer languages, its growing use raises productivity
among office workers. As in the case of factory technologies,

these office innovations are seen by many as qualitatively
different from previous office equipment that merely
"mechanized" or "automated" routine tasks; emerging
computer technologies may change the means by which
information is transcribed and made available to others.
The "Integrated Information System for Textile Mills" is a
good example of such a development.

2.2 Robotics

A robot consists of a hand-like device (gripper) connected
to a mechanical arm, serviced by control and power sources.
The arm may have from 3 to 7 "joints" or "degrees of freedom".
A robot with seven degrees of freedom will have the capacity
for three primary arm movements, and three end-of-arm
movements. The seventh movement is the axis of motion of
the entire robot. All of these freedoms endow the robot
with its tasks in life: to manipulate tools or move materials.
It needs to be emphasized, however, that there are many
distinctions among the present generation of robots. Some
2,000 individual robots have been developed worldwide in
recent years, though not many have survived industrial
application. Among the survivors, one can discover three
levels of sophistication having to do with their control:
the simple pick-and-place robots, the servo-controlled, and
the computer controlled.

The present generation of robots of any of these three
families suffers from the limitation that they cannot "look"
for a part. They require that the pieces to be handled be
of an expected size and shape and precisely located. They
are very poor at adapting to the unexpected. The new
generation of "smarter" robots are being fitted with sensory
systems to locate and orient parts as required. By means of
a memory device linked to TV eyes, some are acquiring an
ability to select, sort and remove faulty or wrong parts:
yet others can "feel" the differences between various sizes
or orientations of parts.

The new generation of robots will be of two "sensory" types:
one fitted with a force and tactile system and the other with
sensory feedback control based on vision.

Both force and tactile sensing would enable the robot to
measure the size, shape, temperature, softness or vibration
of the object held by the "arm". Optical sensing or vision
through image processing is also aimed at building a robot's
capability for recognition of parts. In addition, it aims at
providing such abilities as orientation of parts on feeding
equipment, inspecting parts for defects, and monitoring the
assembly process. One vision system, already developed,
uses back lighting for recognition and inspection of parts.
Another system is attempting to solve the problem of visual
identification of parts in a "heap" and the acquisition of a
recognized part from the heap.

Beyond this new generation of "touch" and "see" robots, we

can foresee machines that will "hear" (understand spoken commands) or "read" (convert printed language into operating instructions).

The recent trend in size differentiation of robots away from larger than human size only to all sizes, including the man-size (PUMA), minirobots (Seiko or Mobots) and Microrobots (Texas Instruments) is likely to continue. As far as price is concerned, unit prices are expected to decrease from the current average of some $60,000 to $90,000 in 1980 to the $10,000 to $20,000 range by the end of the decade.

Such advances in specific areas of robotics could lead, in textiles as well as in clothing, to significant developments in incorporating robots into integrated manufacturing systems. There are some specific robots at work in textiles today but they are relatively sparse. New robotics were demonstrated at ITMA 83, particularly in spinning and knitting. Further developments will be introduced by textile equipment manu-facturers over the next several years. In clothing, a major break-through can be expected from the Automated Apparel Manufacturing System Research Project established in Japan in 1982. A pilot plant, integrating all development targets into a total automated apparel production system and reducing production time by 50 per cent, is planned to be built, operated and evaluated in 1988-1989.

2.3 A Global Perspective on Technology

Many manufacturers of textiles and clothing in the developed countries will equip many of their factories with an array of highly sophisticated and computerized new technologies in a powerful move to reassert their competitive position eroded by intense international competition.

Manufacturers in newly industrialized and developing countries will follow the move, for reasons of quality of production, whenever the economics of capital for labour substitution become profitable.

Today's industrial pioneers are looking for more and more complex, integrated automation systems. They are hooking new technologies into electronic networks, creating "spinal-cords" and "central nervous systems" for factories that can progressively streamline operations from control rooms to assembly lines, to shipping docks, to offices.

The microprocessor has automated production functions and the silicon chip can thrust robots from fantasy to reality. This new technology is being pursued with remarkable speed and vigor in many quarters. Most importantly, microprocessors seem to be in a prime position for the implementation of "learning curve pricing" strategies in which firms lower prices in anticipation of rising volumes and declining unit costs.

It is this overwhelming diversity of applications of

microprocessor technology that distinguishes it from less
significant incremental innovations. The microprocessor
represents the link that makes the considerable leap toward
the fully automated factory possible.

However, the new technology is still at its beginnings in
the textile, knitting and clothing sectors, and some
practical difficulties have to be overcome. These
difficulties will be ironed out in the next 10 to 15 years
and the plants of the future will probably look like the
automated spinning operations of ITMA 83.

3. THE ECONOMICS OF NEW TECHNOLOGY

Technical advance has been identified as a major souce of
economic growth in modern times. However, estimates of its
relative importance vary because of lack of statistical
methodology which could capture its contribution directly.

Technical advance can occur in each and every sector of
economic activity. Historically, however, manufacturing has
always been the leader in technological progress because
production of physical goods involves much repetitive
activity which can be mechanized first and automated later.
Despite spectacular advances of technology in other activities
like service activities, manufacturing still remains the main
area of technological progress and of growth in productivity.
In North America (United States and Canada), where employment
in manufacturing barely exceeds 20 per cent of total
employment, increased productivity in manufacturing accounts
for 50 per cent of total productivity growth. That is why
manufacturing plays such an important role: it is still the
main provider of increased productivity and, consequently,
of rising standards of living.

If we analyze the economic history of the last 150-200
years we will see that there is only one factor of production
whose relative price has been growing regularly and that is
labour. Thus, technological progress and labour saving have
become synonyms.

The only real substitute for labour is capital. At the same
time the only way of introducing technological progress into
the production process is through capital investment.
Without research there are no ideas to be implemented and
without capital there is no way of implementing them.

3.1 Substitution of Capital for Labour in New Technologies

Economically, automated equipment and robots are attractive
"workers". They can do work that humans would "rather not"
and they are well suited to short production runs which now
account for such a large proportion of manufacturing. They
can work three shifts a day without slowing down: their
"down time" on the job averages around 5 per cent compared to
25 per cent for the average industrial worker. They can be
employed for as little as $6.00 per hour and, with the
benefit of inexpensive microcomputers, easily retrained.

Socially, equipment and robots are utterly indifferent to
the monotony and possible discomfort of manufacturing.

As a consequence of this capital for labour substitution
process changes will occur at the workplace. The debate
goes in two directions: one over the impact of new
technologies on work quality and the potential for job
satisfaction and the other over the general impact of new
technologies on employment.

During the 1960s and 1970s the prophecies of "technological
optimists" abounded. Technology would have liberated
workers in fully automated plants from their former bondage
to machines. More responsible, highly trained individuals
would be employed at broader, more rewarding tasks, and
automation would make the factory cleaner, safer and more
challenging. Blue-collar work would tend to become "white-
coated" if not white collared, and implicitly more varied
and creative as well.

No doubt, part of this vision will indeed be realized. Yet
the promise of a new day for blue-collar work in terms of
skill, challenge and interest will only be realized for a
few. Whatever the variety of product lines, efficient
manufacturing of standardized products will still leave
routine jobs to be performed.

In the late 1970s and in the 1980s the issue of technologically induced unemployment increasingly is capturing the
attention. Perennial fears that machines will replace men
and women reappear with demands for shorter workweeks to
protect employment levels. In spite of the relatively
unique characteristics of microprocessor applications,
predictions of immediate and massive job losses tend to
ignore the market forces that slow the pace of technological
progress. The size of investment requirements, the
difficulty of increasing internally generated funds, the
presence of many small and medium size firms in the
industry structure, the cost of acquiring information,
present capacity utilization, access to financial markets
and high degree of unionization are all factors slowing the
diffusion of automated technologies. Furthermore, all
capital-intensive industries have a massive investment in
existing plant facilities, and they cannot afford to
squander these facilities through a wholesale replacement
of working machinery.

Nevertheless, adoption of the new technology will proceed
because the competitive pressure of the world textile
market render it mandatory.

3.2 Alteration of the Cost Structure

Any process changing the basic proportions of inputs modifies
the cost structure of production. Automation changes these
proportions significantly, increasing the share of capital
and decreasing the share of labour or, in economic terms,

increasing the proportion of fixed costs and diminishing the proportion of variable costs.

Decreasing labour costs as a proportion of total costs of production is the only feasible strategy for textile manufacturers in developed countries. Their fundamental disadvantage is in labour costs and their aim must be the reduction of labour inputs in order to stay competitive. Even if wage rates in a developed country are two or three times higher than the wage rates of a developing country, their cost disadvantage could be a minor competitive factor when labour costs do not exceed 8, 10 or 12 per cent of the total cost. The cost disadvantage will still exist but could be compensated by better styling, quality of service or better management practices or any combination of the three elements.

If, in the future, the industry becomes considerably more capital-intensive than it is today, another problem looms at the horizon and that is the necessity of a high degree of utilization of the production capacities in a market characterized by short-term, cyclical instability. Only a relatively high degree of capacity utilization can produce an adequate return on capital in capital-intensive industries, and a five or eight per cent decline in capacity utilization can make all the difference between black and red bottom lines. In order to reduce the impact of cyclical instability, more and more producers will feel compelled to opt for niche marketing which would probably prove itself a safe strategy because producers could acquire a more or less dominant position on niche markets and become less vulnerable to the overall textile business cycle.

Anyway, producers of developed countries cannot even afford the luxury of asking themselves if higher intensity is a good or bad thing for them. In the present conditions of cost competitiveness, they must opt for more capital and less labour, they must decrease the share of labour costs in their total costs.

3.3 Financing of the Required Investments

It is one thing to know what should be done, and it is a different thing to be able to do it. Introducing new technology is always an expensive proposal of which computers, microprocessors and possible robots represent altogether a relatively small part. The expensive part is acquiring updated, modern machinery which can justify all the electonic attachments. The basic question which arises here is to know whether the industry can afford to finance the investment requirements dictated by the new technology.

Unfortunately, the evidence I am using is very limited. It is based on Canadian data only, and the results should be handled with care. Developing even this limited information required more than a year, and it was not possible to develop relevant information for other countries.

The results are derived from an econometric analysis of
growth in total factor productivity, on the basis of gross
production, in Canadian manufacturing industries from 1967
to 1980. The purpose of the analysis was to estimate the
distribution of productivity gains between the various
economic partners involved (labour, capital, government and
consumers), and to emphasize the relationship between
productivity growth, intersectoral changes of relative
prices and primary income formation in manufacturing. Total
factor productivity growth is the increase in gross
production which can not be "explained" by an increase in
the total volume of factors (labour, capital, raw materials,
intermediary products, energy). On a simple accounting
basis, an increase in total factor productivity at a
sectoral level generates a surplus of wealth which will accrue
either to factors of production through a rise in their
relative prices (i.e. in the form of an increase in the
price of raw materials, intermediary products, supplies or
in real earnings of labour and capital), or to "consumers"
of the final products in the form of a decline of relative
selling prices. Government will also take a share of total
productivity gains through increased taxation which is not
compensated by rising prices.

Total productivity of textile activities grew significantly
between 1967 and 1980. Out of twenty individual manufacturing
sectors, the textile industry placed fourth in Canada,
knitting fifth and clothing sixth. The average annual rate
of growth of total productivity was 1.63 per cent in
textiles, 1.60 per cent in knitting and 1.39 in clothing,
but 0.88 per cent only in total manufacturing.

However, because of a decline in relative prices of materials
and supplies used in the textile activities, the surplus to
be distributed was higher than the growth of total
productivity. Ranking the twenty manufacturing sectors by
decreasing order of surplus to be distributed the knitting
industry ranked first (+4.66 per cent per annum), the
textile industry second (+4.01 per cent per annum) and the
clothing industry fourth (+2.48 per cent per annum). In
total manufacturing the surplus was 0.92 per cent per annum,
and the third position was taken by electrical and
electronic equipment with a surplus growing at a rate of
3.40 per cent per annum.

The most remarkable thing is to observe how the surplus was
actually distributed among the factors. In total manufacturing more than half of the surplus went to labour and one
third to consumers through relative price declines. In the
textile industry only 10 per cent of the surplus went to
labour and more than 80 per cent to consumers through
relative price declines. In knitting the share of labour in
the surplus was 10 per cent, and the share of consumers 87
per cent, and in clothing the shares were 27 and 50 per cent
respectively.

While an average 12 per cent of the surplus increased the

691

share of capital, this share was decreasing in the case of
textiles and knitting and increased by 4 per cent only in
clothing.

These numbers illustrate the fundamental dilemma of the three
textile activities. Because of the strong national and
international competitive pressure consumers of textiles
and textile products were the main beneficiaries of total
productivity growth and not capital or labour. With such a
distribution of the surplus, internal generation of funds
was relatively weak and return on capital very modest.
Financing new investment requirements in order to upgrade
plants to the level of the new technology which is becoming
available constitutes a major problem for Canadian
manufacturers of textiles, knitting and clothing.

The government recognized the problem in 1981 and put into
place the Canadian Industrial Renewal Board which earmarked
well beyond $100 million for investment subsidies in
textiles. This contribution was helpful in 1983 and is
helpful in 1984, and Canadian companies are making a major
investment effort. But they could do better if they had more
financial means.

3.4 New Technology, Product Quality and Product Inventories

Once the new technology is mastered satisfactorily it can
lead to general quality improvements. These improvements
are related less to actual improvement of quality and more to
reduction or elimination of non-quality in the form of
defects, off-specification or off-shade products, etc. With
the monitoring and control devices built into the new
generation of equipment constant auscultation of the
production flow is performed and problems can be detected
immediately. Continuous auscultation is a more economical
procedure than autopsy.

The costs of non-quality are often not negligible,
particularly if they are all added up: costs of mending or
discarding products, price concessions on seconds and for
defects, costs and time losses on shipping and litigation.
The possible decline or elimination of such costs could
contribute to a better overall performance.

However, the most important quality improvement will derive
from new equipment working at high speeds at all stages of
textile production, from yarn to finished garment. Each and
every step in the transformation process will become critical
for the overall performance of the system and precise quality
control at each stage will guarantee a better quality end
product. In this regard, better quality will be the direct
consequence of technological progress.

Another source of cost savings due to more flexible
manufacturing should appear in the financial costs of
inventory accumulation. The average volume of product
inventories carried, end-of-season inventory valuation

adjustments and outright write-offs could be minimized and recourse to bank loans checked. At present levels of interest rates such savings could be significant.

The move toward a more flexible manufacturing process is becoming of paramount importance for every producer because of fashion trends in clothing. Consumers do not dictate these trends. Rather, it is the retailers, and particularly the big chains of department stores and specialized stores, who dictate them. They are looking for a permanent flow of novelty items in their stores because they seem to be convinced that it will increase customer traffic and income flow correspondingly. This run for six or seven lines annually instead of three or four seasonal changes is now becoming technically possible. Moreover, it would make good economic sense because permanent creation would replace seasonal rush, and capacity utilization would be better balanced. However, it remains to be seen if the final consumer is really interested in such permanent creation, and if he will not oppose some resistance sooner or later. Thus, permanent change may well prove itself a temporary phenomenon because we can not be sure today that the consumer really wants such an approach.

4. CONCLUSION

High performance, high speed textile equipment is increasingly fitted out with microprocessors and hooked to computers in an effort to move to an ever higher degree of automation.

High speed automated equipment requires high quality inputs and yields high quality products. Quality standards in the market tend to be defined in relation to the quality obtained by the new equipment. These new quality standards are one of the driving forces of investments in textiles.

Automation represents a very powerful labour saving technique. Labour saving is of vital importance in high wage countries. Developing countries may or may not adopt all labour saving techniques in the medium-term, depending on pay-back conditions, but they will adopt the most efficient high speed equipment. In any case the new technology will significantly reduce the share of labour costs in total costs and will contribute to a reduction in the cost gap between developed and developing countries.

Investment requirements for the new technology are large and progress will be achieved over a relatively long period. How long will depend on financing opportunities. If the industry has to finance the whole adjustment, it will be long. If government contributions to the investment effort were forthcoming, the adjustment period could be shortened proportionately.

Once the new technology is in place, after a longer or shorter diffusion period, international competition in textiles will be as strong as it is today. But this new

competition will be different from today's competition:
costs and prices will play a less prominent role; quality,
design and creativity will become the main criteria.

Textile and Clothing Board
Federal Government of Canada
Ottawa
Ontario
CANADA

COMPUTER GROWTH AND THE TEXTILE INDUSTRY IN WORLD PERSPECTIVE

Raoul Verret

ABSTRACT

The introduction of computerized production processes will not be the "Kiss of Death" to the textile and apparel industries in developing countries, but rather will be the salvation of the industries in the industrialized nations. An analysis of the ways in which computerization will benefit the industrialized countries is presented as well as the necessity of inter-relating computer technology with all of the technologies available to the industry. However, the road will be diffiult. The role and responsibilities for each member of the workforce will change dramatically and more use of outside expertise in optimization of man and machine will occur.

1. INTRODUCTION

Given the title of this presentation, "Computer Growth and the Textile Industry in World Perspective," and given the nature of ongoing cost/quality competitiveness between nations, a number of thoughts related to the impact of the computer revolution on future competitiveness are brought to mind. We could well ask the question, "Will the development of computerized automation technologies be the 'KISS of DEATH' to developing countries' textile industry?"

This is a very dramatic question with which to lead off a speech! We wanted to be thought provoking, because the answer is just as dramatic.

The answer is, "NO, but computerization will be the SALVATION of the industrialized countries."

This presentation today discusses the state of the art of computer technology, past, present and future vis-a-vis the textile and apparel industries, with specific reference to the opportunities which will be made available through developments in computer application technology to all nations alike, from within and without the textile/apparel complex. Furthermore, we plan to discuss why the industrialized nations will have the most to gain - both near and far term - from state of the art computer application technology.

At the outset, it is important to make two points very clear:

> Firstly, WE CANNOT TALK ABOUT COMPUTER APPLICATION TECHNOLOGY IN A VACUUM. When we examine the state of the art, we cannot lose sight of (ILLUSTRATION 1).

> > .computer technology
> > .systems technology
> > .automation technology

.machine technology
.robotics technology
.communications technology, and
.the future, embodied in artificial intelligence

because, separately each is nice to have available to us,
and to use, but this represents, more importantly, the
exception to the rule, because in this case - THE SUM OF
THE PARTS IS SIGNIFICANTLY GREATER THAN THE WHOLE.

Secondly, this means that INTEGRATED TOGETHER, THIS STATE
OF THE ART TECHNOLOGY AS IT WILL EVOLVE WILL PROVIDE THE
MEANS FOR THE WESTERN NATIONS TO BE MASTERS OF THEIR OWN
TEXTILE AND APPAREL DESTINY.

Referring to a G.E. robotics expert, integrated automation will
not only determine the FACTORY OF THE FUTURE, it will define
the FACTORY WITH A FUTURE. IT IS THE INDUSTRIALIZED NATIONS
WHICH WILL MOST BENEFIT FROM THE INTEGRATED STATE OF THE ART
TECHNOLOGIES FROM COMPETITIVE COST AND ACCOUNT SERVICEABILITY
VIEWPOINTS.

The benefits will be twofold (ILLUSTRATION 2):

1.   UNIT COST reduction - not only for large volume but
      for high style short runs as well.

2.   Improved ACCOUNT SERVICEABILITY through:
              .improved quality
              .reduced leadtime
              .increased adaptability to change

2. NEW TECHNOLOGY COMPETITIVE IMPLICATIONS

The world is now experiencing the early impacts of "The
Information Age" which is a direct producer of computers and
the sophisticated systems and capablilities offered by these
technological advances. Its effect on industry will be
significant and expectedly traumatic in particular, on human
resources and business leadership.

Firstly, with the new high tech machinery and process
technology now available, which deskills operations as it moves
toward full automation and robotics, labor content and related
costs are significantly reduced in labor-intensive industries.
Such reduction will result in costs which may be equal to or
less than traditionally low-cost labor countries which will
tend to negate the competitive advantages enjoyed by such
countries to date.

Secondly, the information age will provide management with a
proliferation of instant data to enable sophisticated
monitoring of operations, variables, process standards,
specifications, etc. and the opportunity to control performance
immediately at preset parameters. This will require major
changes in managerial mentality and perspectives and also will
require retraining programs to learn and adopt the new systsms.

Illustration 3 and 4 depict as a generalization (obviously,
dependent on specific country, products, duties, exchange
rates, type/age of machines in place, etc.) the effect of state
of the art technology on competition between the industrialized
nations and the Far East in particular.

From the textile viewpoint (ILLUSTRATION 3), there is a current
Far East labor cost advantage (taking into account
productivity) of 21% which would potentially reduce to 10% with
state of the art investment. Translated to product costs, the
10% disadvantage can be eliminated, on the assumption that
state of the art technology will be run 7 days a week 24 hours
per day in order to minimize capital cost apportionment.

From the apparel viewpoint the labor cost disadvantage can be
reduced from 27% to 13% and product cost disadvantage from 20%
to 5% (Far East existing technology) or 3% (Far East state of
the art).

Coupled with the very significant advantages that state of the
art will bring in account serviceability, the pendulum will
swing in favor of those industrialized companies that make
timely investments in state of the art technology.

In simple terms, computers and their application relationships
to evolving state of the art technology in all business sectors
potentially represent the salvation of the textile and apparel
industries in the industrialized world. However, one note of
caution - for the apparel industry to adapt to the new role of
technology, will require a radical change in capital investment
mentality compared to what they have been accustomed to in the
past. To survive, however, they will have to adapt.

3. COMPUTER APPLIED "TECHNOLOGICAL TOOLS" FOR MANUFACTURING

A number of "technological tools" are available to the textile
and apparel manufacturer which can help in the effort to
automate his operation.

3.1 Computer Aided Design and Manufacturing Systems (CAD/CAM)

for example are being used in knitting to cut the time required
to go from design conception to sample producion from two weeks
to two hours. Machines such as Gerber/Camsco's AM-5
electronically nest and cut apparel fabric or draw paper
patterns, saving 3-4% of the firm's annual fabric consumption.
Current research and testing is aimed at allowing more garment
design to be performed on the computer's screen. Soon
designers will create apparel in three dimensional shapes and
the resulting two-dimensional patterns will automatically be
sized, graded and nested by computer. Furthermore, with the
database of designs and styles stored on the CAD/CAM computer
system, features such as job costing, scheduling and inventory
control can be added as peripherals.

3.2   Computer Assisted Manufacturing Planning and Control Systems

Complex manufacturing, scheduling and control systems are essential for the management of automated textile manufacturing plants. Systems such as MRP II keep track of inventory data, delivery and shipping schedules, and order entry information to create critical path method-type schedules. This method of scheduling, when coupled with plant information such as production flow, bills of materials, work-in-process inventory and queue times and product/process mix, can create schedules offering low inventories and storage, tracking and status of jobs at as fast as fifteen minute intervals, and implementation of just-in-time delivery systems.

Companies in other industries which currently use sophisticated planning and control systems often tailor-make the basic programs to their own in-house operations. Many firms offer MRP-type programs, some even available through on-line communications systems, that can perform a number of functions useful to textile and apparel manufacturers. The more of these off-the-shelf programs will be used as they are written as more technicians are trained in the method of operation of this type of control system.

3.3   Microprocessor Controlled Monitoring/Process Control Systems

Process controls are used to electronically "oversee" production operations and make adjustments to the process when measurements fall out of tolerance levels. For example, if the liquor ratio in one segment of a continuous finishing range is too low, a process control system monitoring device would detect the problem. The system would then open the flow of caustic, etc, into the bath until the liquor ratio returned inside the tolerance levels as prescribed by the specifications program. These systems can be found from the fiber opening room through finished fabric inspection.
   As an aside, the concept of integrated factory process control and computer interaction should quickly leap forward as a result of the formation of the American CAM/TEX group. This group is an association of process control suppliers, who this year established a precedent by setting mutual electronic specifications enabling total compatibility of all of the members' lines of process control equipment.

3.4   Host Computer-Controlled Manufacturing Work Cells

Work cells add flexibility to the manufacturing system through being able to operate automatically with other plant work cells, or independently. Cells normally consist of a number of machines which process a single part, or garment component, through a series of operations. The part or component is moved between these machines by a robotic device. Future apparel manufacturing will incorporate a number of work cells in the making of shirts, jeans and trousers. The components of manufacturing work cells include work cell controllers, the cell machinery involved, and robotics for material handling purposes.

3.5   Work Cell Controllers

Work cell controllers are defined as software systems which
enhance the capability to interface intelligent manufacturing
machines or manufacturing work cells to Computer Aided Design
(CAD), and manufacturing planning and control systems in a
controlled and flexible manner. In essence, these devices are
the link between the work cell machines and their controllers
away from the plant floor. Some of the functions work cell
controllers perform include:

> 1) The initiation of work cell activities through an
> interface with the operator and the dispatching of
> control to other processing routines.

> 2) Accommodation of scheduling information from data
> entry by an operator, magnetic tape or floppy disk, or
> down-loaded information from the host manufacturing
> control system. This ability is an example of the
> flexibility of the controller to run stand-alone or
> completely integrated with an overall plant system.

> 3) Downline loading of Computer Aided Design product
> information and manufacturing process data from which
> the machines in the work cell will be controlled.

> 4) Downloading of the CAD data received to the various
> machines used in the work cell (also called "work
> stations"). The controller also sends commands to
> begin and end operations, and controls the material
> handling flow between the workstations.

> 5) Collects monitoring/process control type data
> produced by the workstations and transmits it to the
> host computer for quality control analysis and storage.

> 6) Provides status informaton about the workstation
> and the controller to operators at the work cell or
> to the host system.

> 7) Deletes old production information.

> 8) Manages all of the data communications interfaces
> and maintains a database of information.

3.6   Progammable Manufacturing Machines

The Saurer 600 loom is one recent example of how the textile
industry is moving toward quick production specification and
style changeover. Electronic solenoids eliminate the need for
large inventories of gears. Furthermore, machine speeds and
timing can be set to provide the optimal running settings in
terms of production as well as energy consumption and
efficiency. As with electronic knitting machines, spinning
frames and looms are capable of style and/or count changes
within minutes rather than hours.

Future programmable machines will incorporate more diagnostic equipment to detect and display the location of mechanical and electrical problems. These machines will also be controlled from a central location with production data being transmitted to and from the loom at quicker speeds than ever before.

3.7   Hard Automation Machines

Machines such as Schlafhorst's Autocoro with automated features but with limited flexibility in style/count changes, etc. are machines in the hard automation area. These devices can process a set type of good in a work cell with little product change.

3.8   Semi/Non-Automated Machines

Machines with little or no capacity for electronic control of performance variables are listed in this category. Although these machines will have little use by themselves, they will play an important role in the work cell process.

3.9   Robotics Systems

Of all of the items mentioned here, robotics is probably the best known. They are less affected by inflation than labor costs, provide consistent production in areas where the available labor pool is decreasing or where labor training costs are high, and are superior to other automated production machines in terms of manufacturing flexibility. Robot systems employing today's
industrial engineering based technology are used in the areas of materials handling, inspection, process control, and process operations. Future applications of robotics will be based on artificial intelligence technology and will include applications like:

  1) random doffing of yarn, beams, etc.
  2) decisionmaking based on both plant and customer specifications
  3) machine fabric inspection and repair of broken ends

The importance of future developments in robotics will depend on how well the new robotics systems can be combined with hard automation and computer controlled design and information systems in flexible manufacturing operations

4.   THE GOAL: COMPUTER INTEGRATED MANUFACTURE

By combining the tools above with other machines, communications networks and control systems, wew arrive at the integrated combination of technologies we talked about at the first of our discussion. This combination of technologies is called "Computer Integrated Manufacture" or CIM (ILLUSTRATION 5). As you can see, Computer Aided Design systems, acting as a source database, becomes our computer technology. Systems technology incorporates the sophisticated scheduling and inventory programs (and in the future controlled by artificially intelligent machines).

Monitoring and process control systems, part of automation systems, are the center for reporting of statistical quality control information, and the issuance of commands for reaction to out of tolerance process units. Below that are the groups of manufacturing work cells which contain the work cell controller, variety of programmable and various non- to fully-automated hard automation machines, robots, and process control systems feeding data back to the three controlling operations above. The entire manufacturing process is a structured hierarchy. Built from a number of smaller technologies, this end combination is synergistic and efficient - and surpassed in competitiveness with similar labor-intensive operations.

5. COMPUTER CONTROLS FOR PROFITS

We have detailed the significance of the computer in the Computer Aided Manufacturing process. However, computer controlled manufacturing is only one step in assuring a profitable business. Illustration six (ILLUSTRATION 6) outlines the importance of interacting every business aspect from asset management to inventory control, from customer service to sales, etc. through computer systems. Computerized information/communications systems between all business segments in a proactive (as in the past reactive) mode will be just as essential to profits as CIM is.

Communication of information is the stumbling block for many companies that attempt to computerize their manufacturing operations. On many of our assignments, we found a lack of communication to be a major contributing factor to the problems faced by the client company. The automation implementation situation is no different.

Managers need to clearly know the objectives of the electronic equipment being installed, jointly develop with programmers the methods in which the equipment will be used, and seek feedback from the employees as to their ideas from experience with the machinery--and their problems, and fears.

In additon, managers have to realize the necessity of training and continuing education to both the short and long run health of their plant and it's modern machinery. In a number of operations, studies have shown a direct coorelation between the successful implementation of automation and the proper training of the plant's employees . Computers can also aid in this area by providing instructional programs whose structure is based on the concepts of Computer Aided Instruction (CAI). These systems allow the firm's personnel to learn at their own pace and quickly review areas of instruction at a future date. CAI will similarly work in the areas of sales, marketing, human resources, providing more tools for the company to take advantage of.

6. SUMMATION

The bottom line is "What do the strides in computer application technology mean in terms of our business future?" The advances have been significant. The ability to interrelate Management Information Systems and Computer Integrated Manufacturing via sophisticated computer controlled communications technology is an important advance. The role of CIM in controlling flexible work modules with a new market responsiveness is also of significance. However, the rate of future growth in computer application technology will be key as to who benefits by how much.

We can safely predict that if there is little or no major advance in technology in the future, the productivity gap between industrialized and developing nations would close considerably at the expense of the developed countries.

On the other hand, if there are significant gains in computerized and related technological (CAD/CAM/CAI/AI etc.) growth, the industrialized nations are the first to benefit in terms of:

1) Capital investment is most attainable - replacing high cost labor and increasing/maintaining high quality goods
2) Reducing cycle time for style fashion runs
3) Having quick response to the marketplace and therefore better service

Computerized technology in effect provides the means to be the salvation of the textile industry in industrialized nations because it provides manufacturers a tool to increase productivity, quality, turnaround time and service versus competition from developing countries. The quicker the growth rate of this technology, the more advantageous it will be.

However, this change will not be easy. Future factory workers will be decision oriented. Maintenence workers will be high technology trained. Management will be proactive and adaptable to change. The interaction of the computer, new technologies, and all levels of the workforce will require more sophistication than ever before. Outside expertise and specialists will be in more demand, because shareholders will demand optimum use and interface of high investment equipment with a highly responsible workforce.

Werner Management Consultants
111 West 40th Street, 14th Floor
New York, New York 10018 USA

STATE OF THE ART TECHNOLOGY

```
┌─ ─ ─ ─ ─ ─ ─ ─ ─ ─ ─ ┐
      FUTURE:
│ ARTIFICIAL INTELLIGENCE │
└─ ─ ─ ─ ─ ─ ─ ─ ─ ─ ─ ┘
```

COMPUTERS

SYSTEMS

AUTOMATION

MACHINERY

ROBOTICS

COMMUNICATIONS

SEPARATELY	EACH PART IS BOTH NECESSARY & USEFUL.

INTEGRATED	THE SUM OF THE INTEGRATED PARTS IS SUBSTANTIALLY GREATER THAN THE WHOLE.

ILLUSTRATION #1

**YOU CAN'T LOOK AT COMPUTER
TECHNOLOGY IN A VACUUM**

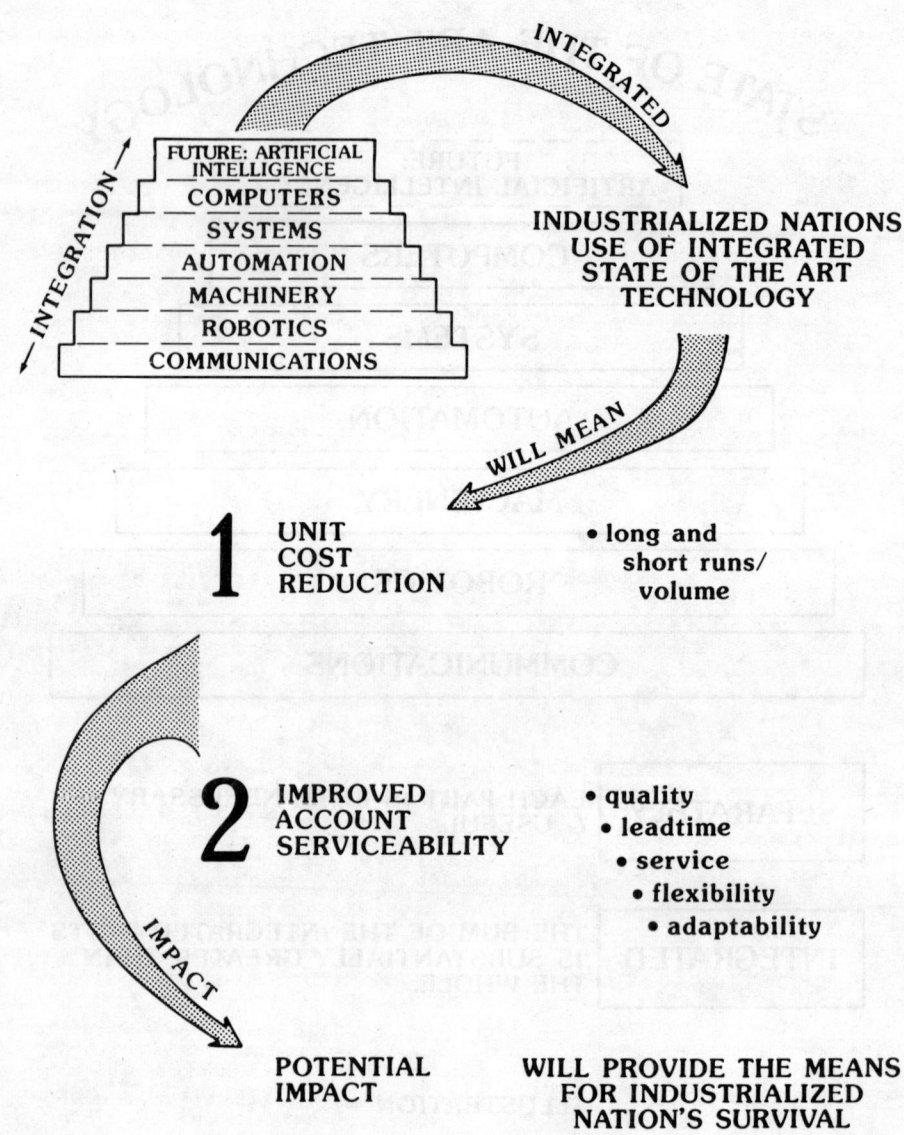

ILLUSTRATION #2

ILLUSTRATION #3

PRIMARY TEXTILES
(KEY POINT COST GENERALIZATION)

TYPICAL CURRENT SITUATION	LABOR COST AS % OF PRODUCT COST	PRODUCT COST (LANDED)
INDUSTRIALIZED NATIONS	30%	100% (base)
HONG KONG/ KOREA TAIWAN	9%	90%
FAR EAST ADVANTAGE	21%	10%

eliminates Far East advantage

STATE OF THE ART POTENTIAL	LABOR COST AS % OF PRODUCT COST	PRODUCT COST (LANDED)
INDUSTRIALIZED NATIONS	15%	90%
HONG KONG/ KOREA TAIWAN	5%	92%
FAR EAST ADVANTAGE (DISADVANTAGE)	10%	(2%)

ILLUSTRATION #4

APPAREL SECTOR
(KEY POINT COST GENERALIZATION)

TYPICAL CURRENT SITUATION	LABOR COST AS % OF PRODUCT COST	PRODUCT COST (LANDED)
INDUSTRIALIZED NATIONS	40%	100% (base)
FAR EAST	13%	80%
FAR EAST ADVANTAGE	27%	20%

5% advantage

STATE OF THE ART POTENTIAL	LABOR COST AS % OF PRODUCT COST	PRODUCT COST (LANDED)
INDUSTRIALIZED NATIONS	20%	85%
FAR EAST	7%	82%
FAR EAST ADVANTAGE	13%	3%

706

COMPUTER INTEGRATED
MANUFACTURING (C.I.M.)

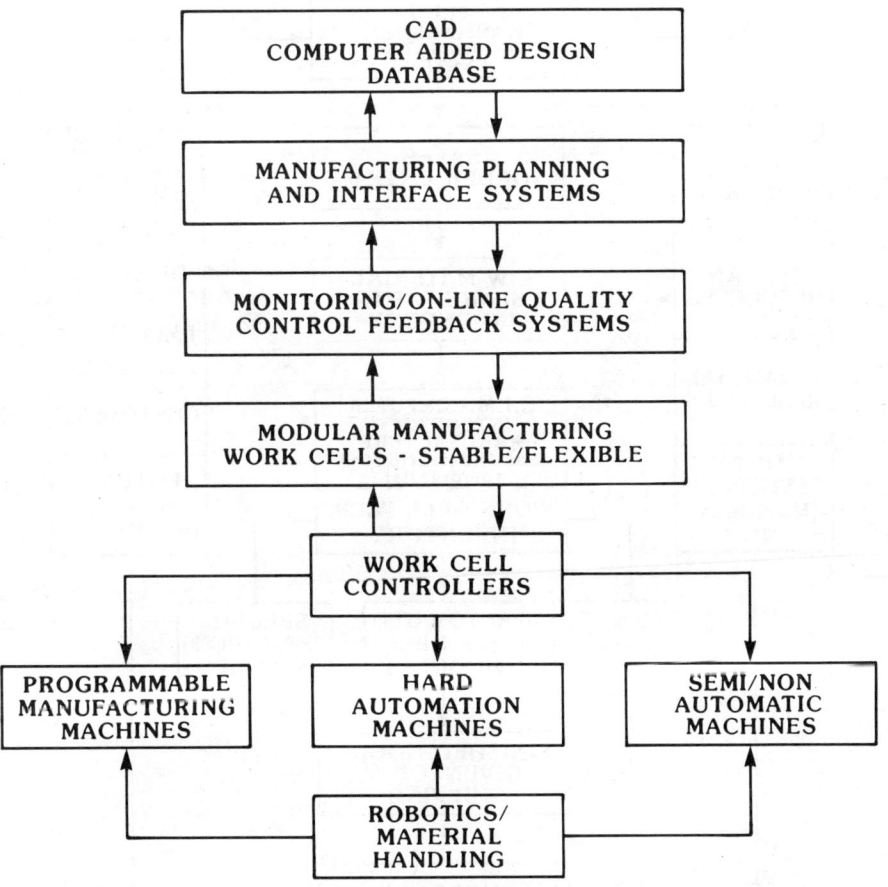

ILLUSTRATION #5
(Refer to Illustration #6 also)

C.I.M. WITHIN A
BROAD M.I.S. PERSPECTIVE

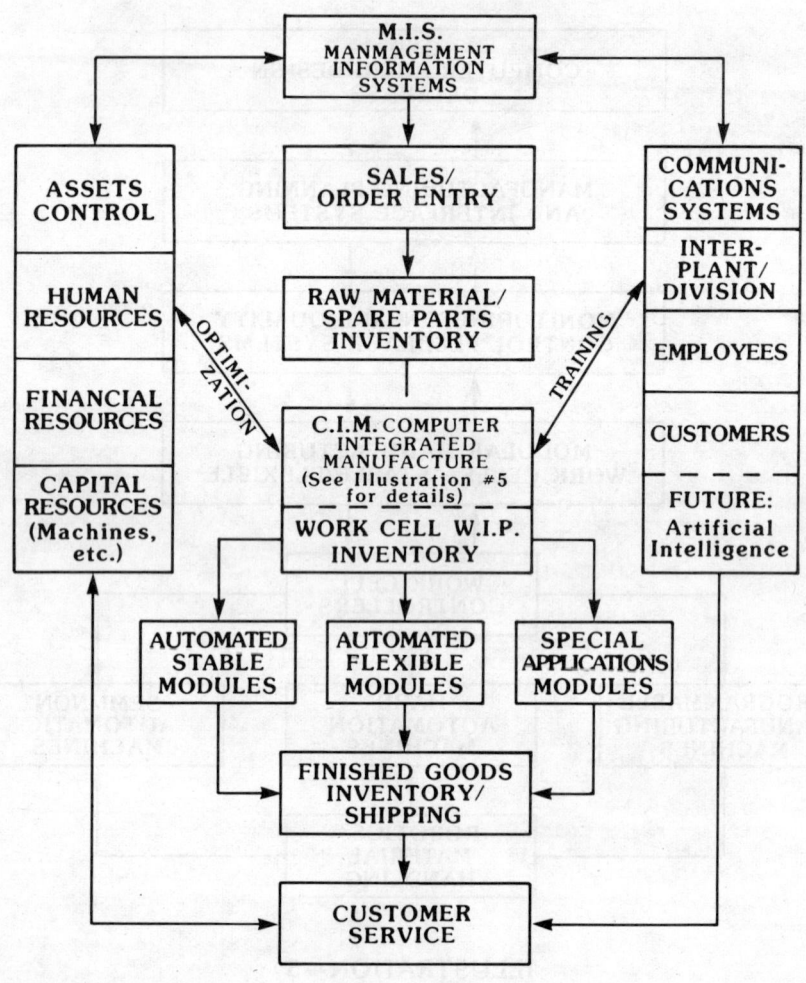

ILLUSTRATION #6

A STUDY OF THE PATTERN-PREPARATION UNIT OF KNITTED FABRICS: PATTERN DESIGN

Cao Shouzhen

ABSTRACT

This article arranges to apply the computers in complying the pattern programme of the pattern preparation unit. In applying calculating aid textile design(CAD), it aids the production pattern designers to create art works and becomes as the designers' intelligence instrument. Through practice, it proves that in applying CAD, it possesses many advantages. This method is up-to-date.

In order to aid majority designers can utilize the computer to create pattern works, this article applies BASIC Dialogue and micro computer with little-tape monitor and graph-platter as instrument.

The method of compiling pattern software arrangement are: 1. Printing Method 2. The Drawing Method

The period of production design is short, and lessens the designer's labor intensity. Play the strength of computer as the intelligence instrument, the design method is more active and efficient. In creating knitting fabric pattern with CAD, it will be applied widely in knitting industry.

1. INTRODUCTION

The application of a computer as a high-speed numerial calculating instrument, at the beginning, is of great value. People gather the scientific and technical problems, set up the mathmatical modules, then seek for the calculating method of the limited procedures for getting the mathmatical value result of efficient place to satisfy the practical needs. With its rapid development the computer has extensively been used in the national economy and in all areas of social life. It has become a helpful assistant or a valuable instrument of human beings. The pattern preparation unit is an example of the application of the computer to the knitting fabrics.

This article deals with the compilation of the pattern subprogram of the pattern preparation unit by the computer. With CAD the computer helps the pattern designers do some creative work of art easily. This makes the computer as an intelligent instrument of the designers. Through practice it seems that there are many obvious advantages in designing with CAD. In order to help the majority of the designers make use of the computer in designing patterns, this article takes Basic Dialogue and the microcomputer as the instrument with the printers, plotters, magnetic disc drivers, displays and some other installations attached. It is obvious that:

(1) It is easy to be popularized. Basic Dialogue is easy to be understood, convenient and reliable to be used by the designers.

(2) The consideration for the practical possibility is well taken into account. The price of a micro calculator with Basic Dialogue is quite cheap and it can be widely brought into use in the factories. All this feasibility is expected to be carried out smoothly.

The Basic Dialogue is the dialogue of man-machine interaction, it is conformed to the process of a creative work of art of the designers. Through man-machine interaction it enriches the conception of patterns. When the pattern information is stored in disc, it is convenient to be dispatched and increases the designing efficiency, shortens the period of the process. This auxilliary designing process, in fact, is the process of an interchange and a function of the conception of designing and drawing. It is a new recognition of the progressive objective law. Designing knitting patterns with CAD will enable man to gain a new recognition of it. It must be pointed out that the CAD pattern designing is now producing an important and profound influence on the development of knitting products.

2. THE METHOD OF PATTERN PROCEDURE--THE PRINTING METHOD

The knitting fabrics are composed of certain arrangements of different structure units. In order to analyze and design the fabric patterns and apply them to the machines a notation is often used. The designed pattern with the aid of Basic Dialogue makes good use of the punctuation drawing device (See Fig.1) -the keyboard of the teletype-writer with many letters and characters on it. The printing charts-symbol combination of certain arrangements will be shown on it by means of the printing output. It enables the computer to be directly used in the fabric pattern designing.

There are a veriety of pattern graphic programmes, i.e.:

(1) The Pattern of Basic Graphic Arrangement Composition.

(2) The Random Array of Basic Pattern.

(3) The Composition Pattern of Mathmatical Curve.

(4) The Mathmatical Module Substitute Method.

(5) The Composition of Geometric Pattern Skelton...etc.

(6) The Basic Changeable Subprogrammes.

A description of these patterns is given below:

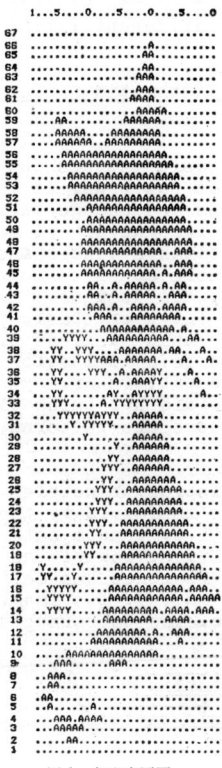

図1 打印意匠図

2.1 The Pattern of Basic Graphic Arrangement Composition

In programming the basic graphs should be stored in the computer, then arranged by changing their orders. According to man's imagination different patterns can be rapidly drawn up by changing the arrangement orders.

In designing programme the line variables (string variables) are mainly used. The basic patterns are stored in different line variables consisting in a certain number of sentences. The basic horizontal lines is formed by adding substrings. When the basic horizontal lines are arranged and printed in a certain sequence, the printing chart with the basic graphic arrangement pattern will be obtained.

When the form of arrangements is changed, a new total

pattern will appear. Similarly, the basic horizontal line can be connected with one or more basic patterns. The procedure of forming total patterns from basic graphic arrangements should be engaged in two steps. As a result of changing anyone of these two steps, even in any form, a set of different fabric patterns will be obtained.

2.2 The Basic Graphic Automatic Random Arrangement Composition

As stated above, the basic pattern can be arranged from different types of patterns. It is easy to design these types of patterns and change their arrangements with the mathmatical dialogue. These activities are conducted according to man's conciousness. Through the printer the designers compile and write the programmes required by the designs. There are quite a lot of arrangements for every basic pattern, some of them even have more than hundreds of thousands of them. After all, there is a limitation of man's imagination and these basic pattern arrangements of which some other people even did not think of will be certainly shown on it. These are patterns with a unique style.

According to the statistics principles of probability, if every total pattern is formed by the arranged basic graphic random array (i.e. random nature), thus it will represent the diffrent law of the different types of pattern. The Basic Dialogue has defined the internal random array function RND(X). Its imagination, of course, will come true. The pattern programme frame chart is as figure 2.

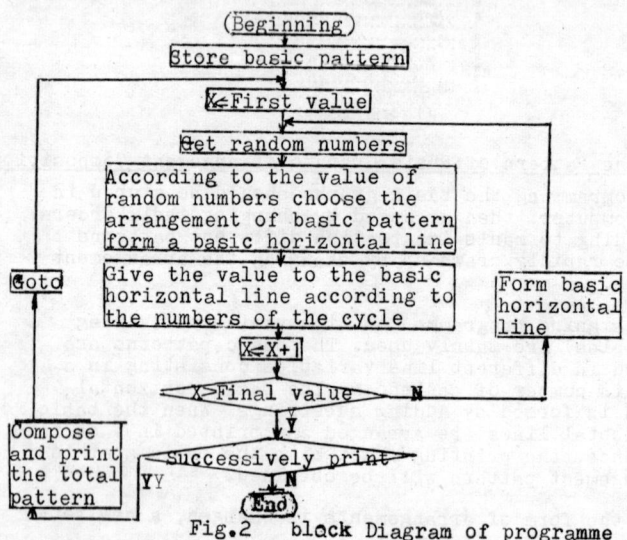

Fig.2   black Diagram of programme

It seems that there is a quite great difference
between these two charts of the graphic programme
composition in the "basic horizontal line composition"
after making a comparision between them. The former
gives the value of basic graphic line variable to the
basic horizontal line variable directly, thus forming
a definite pattern, the latter forms a horizontal
line by applying a big dialogue sentence cycle.

2.3 The Mathmatical Equation Composition Pattern

There are many equantions producing new rich, elegant
patterns in the mathmatical sphere. The pattern arts
in the countries over the world almost begin with
the geometric patterns and they have still been the
main subjects in the fabric designing so far. Because
it needs a great deal of repeated calculating the
patterns in the mathmatical sphere hinders man from
doing imaginative activities. With the aid of the
calculating function of the computer it is easy to
design mathmatical curve patterns and will offer man
a lot of materials of new style for choosing, modifying
and compiling. This is a reflection on the distinguishing features of the computer suitable for scientific calculating. By means of CAD many acceptable
patterns may be got from the various mathmatical
curve compositions.

According to one's conception these mathmatical
equations can be sought for in compiling these pattern
programmes, then the various mathmatical equations
chosen can be programmed. In the programming process
the parameter may be revised to get the satisfactory
equation curve patterns.

2.4 Mathmatical Module Substitution Method

The substring, the length of which is substituted
from the pattern mathmatical module characters, is
taken from a known string variable representative
of horizontal coil. The original characters will
be concelled and replaced by the characters representative of pattern module. The designing pattern can
be considered first, a corresponding mathmatical
module will be built up then, or otherwise it can be
drawn up directly according to the mathmatical module
known.

(Beginning)

Input parameter of the pattern mathmatical module

X←First value

Calculating the substring length
of the pattern mathmatical module

Replace
Print
X←X+1

N   X←Final value

(End)

2.5 The Composition Pattern of Geometric Pattern Skelton

The geometric pattern skelton is stored in "Data" sentences form, the corresponding design is carried out by matrix calaulating. A matrix calculation, such as replacement, multiplication is used here. These pattern designs are of great convenience. If there is one geometric pattern skelton--**basic** subpattern, while angles of various degrees, distances and directions prolonged and composed, a series of regular wonderful geometric patterns may be obtained. There are, on the whole, three types of arrangements:

1) The interweave arrangements at 45°, 60°, 90° among the horizontal, straight, oblique and broken lines.

2) The changes of fixed letters for arrangement of various pattern succession, e.g. rectangle, cross, L-shaped, T-shaped and convex shaped.

3) The interweave compositions of pattern and arc lines, and the other different angles--horizontal, straight and oblique lines interweave compositions, from which enormous different patterns can be formed.

2.6 The Basic Changeable subprogramme composition

The Designers have fundamentally to change the pattern subprogramme. The basic changeable subprogramme should satisfy the following functions:

1) The realization of the basic change of patterns, e.g. translation, revolving, alternation and perspective, etc.

2) The pattern composition, inlay and overlapping.

The patterns are stored in matrix or **array**, Taking the document form, they are stored inthe magnetic disc and dispatched at any time. There will be a data storage needed for large patterns. The simple data storage construction is compiled for them to be stored in and taken out. The data storage may be composed of a cyclic structure, a treeshaped structure, etc.

3. THE DRAWING METHOD

In the knitting fabric compositions some of certain compositions are not accustomed to be drawn out in sketch notations. As in warp plain fabrics, fabrics in double-combing effect, in short weft-inserting etc. The drawing method is used to design these fabric patterns.

In the knitting process the sequence of the lapping programme of the guide bar shogging defines the compositions of warp-knitted fabrics. In order to

explain how yarns are arranged in a complete pattern
design and how the guide bar shogging plate is laid
out on the machine the composition record method is
often used to show the structure of warp-knitted
fabrics.

There are two kinds of the record: the diagram record
method and the numeral record method. It is very
convenient for a computer to record the guide-lapping
motion in a drawing. In programming the even distributed circle group is drawn out on the notation paper.
The size of the circle group is defined by the number
of the vertical and horizontal lines in a warp-knitted
-fabric design pattern. The guide bar motion is then
recorded. If the yarns are guided by more than one
guide bar and owing to the different motion rate of
each guide bar, the locus of the guide needle's motion
of every bar must be drawn up in various colours.
Thus the diagram record of a warp-knitted-fabric can
be drawn up with the drawing instrument of a computer
for purposes.

The subprogramme for recording graphs and circle groups
is often mainly used in the designing programme.
During compiling records, with the input data the
graphic records of the fabric needed can be obtained
at once. Owing to the various colours recorded for
every guide bar, the locus of a guide needle motion
is recorded by a mathmatical module, the diagram
record is clear and attractive. Meanwhile, as the locus
of needle notion is recorded by the mathmatical
module, it is readily dispatched. The structures, as
a weft insertion and etc., can be described by the
different mathmatical modules.

This drawing method isn't only suited for recording
the warp knitted fabrics, but suited for recording
some special weft-knitted fabrics. As the graph is
drawn out in colours, the diagram record is quite
clear.

3.1 Notation Displaying Documents

A notation paper is constructed first with the specification and size needed. It is defined by a complete
composition, the warp gaiting rule, butt yarn form
and the number of repeated prolongation. There are two
forms:

1) The spacing size of the rank and file dots in a
notation depends on the customers' purposes.

2) The spacing size of the rank and file dots is
defined by the size of a printing paper.

3.2 The Geometric Module and Its Display

The characteristics of the record module of the warp
lapping movement define the special geometric form

of lapping movement. The modules describing open-loop, closed-loop, prolonged line and short weft-insertion can be defined in data constructions. The normal method puts all geometric relations into a data composition and takes one procedure to calculate the geometric shape and size.

The chosen method displaying the module of an object partly depends on its desplayed aim and on the hardware and software for displaying.

3.3 The Basic Graphic Function

The basic graphic function of a loop must be carefully chosed to provide the customers with the convenient method to draw graphs. At the same time it is fully used to show the ability of displaying the hardware.

In order to be put into use a set of functions will be chosen as a basic graphic one which contains point, circle, $\frac{1}{2}$arc curve, 3/4 arc curve, $\frac{1}{4}$arc curve and straight line, etc. But too many basic graphic functions will make the problem more complicated and expensive, so they are not used in warp fabrics.

3.4 The Medium of Numeral Record Input and Graph Record Output

The medium of numeral record input and graph record output is connected with and distinguished by mathmatical modules. These graphs, on the whole, are composed of circles, arc curves and straight lines. The following parameters should be defined.

Let an extended line defined by the end coordinates (Xo, Yo), (X1, Y1)

Circle radius R

Central angle φ

circle center (Xo, Yo)

For simplicity, suppose:

1) The circle center is on the circle coordinate in a notation.

2) The circle radius is $\frac{1}{2}$ of the unit length between the points in the notation or an appointed radius.

As the graphic record is defined by the parameter of the lapping number, input the lapping numerial record and a corresponding geometric graph will be got. So in the designning programme the parameters must be differentiated.

The graphic record programme frame graph is as follows:

(Take the double guide bar warp-knitted fabrics as an example.)

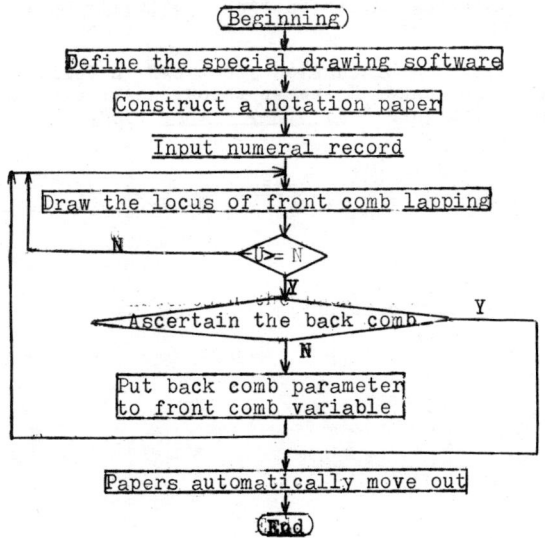

CONCLUSION

1. By means of man-machine interaction of Basic Dialogue to do the graph designing, the construction of the graph and the drawing can be conducted simultaneously. The designing efficiency is high, the modification and alteration can be rapidly performed.

2. The storage, duplication and dispatch of patterns are of great convenience and can be **permanently stored** as technical materials.

With the rapid development of the present computers, their processing ability are fully recognized. It **must** be pointed out that CAD is producing an important and profound influence on the development in science and technology. How to bring the computers as the potentialities of intelligent instruments into full play will be the subject to be studied and discussed of the warp-knitted fabric designing.

The design of knitting fabric patterns with CAD will find wide applications in the knitting industry.

REFERENCE

(1) Cao Shouzhen. " A Discussion on The Plan of
    Jacquard Knitting Fabric Design " J. ECITST.CChina,
    1982, 8, No. 3, 75.

(2) Cao Shouzhen. " A Discussion about CAD in Designing
    SSemi-Fashioned Fancy Knitwear through Narrowing and
    Widening Techniques " J. CTEA. China, 1984, 5,
    No. 3, 29.

(3) Cao Shouzhen. " Computer Aided Design of Knitting
    Fashioned outerwear " J. ECITST. China, 1984, 10,
    No. 2, 93.

East China Institute of
Textile Science and Technology,
1882 Yanan Road West,
Shanghai, China.